A TRAVEL GUIDE TO
JEWISH EUROPE

A TRAVEL GUIDE TO
JEWISH EUROPE
FOURTH EDITION
Ben G. Frank

PELICAN PUBLISHING COMPANY
Gretna 2018

*The word "Pelican" and the depiction of a pelican are
trademarks of Pelican Publishing Company, Inc., and are
registered in the U.S. Patent and Trademark Office.*

ISBN: 9781455623570
Ebook ISBN: 9781455623587

Maps by Joseph Honig

*Information in this guidebook is based on authoritative data available at
the time of printing. Prices and hours of operation of businesses are subject
to change without notice. Readers are asked to take this into account when
consulting this guide.*

Printed in the United States of America

Published by Pelican Publishing Company, Inc.
1000 Burmaster Street, Gretna, Louisiana 70053
www.pelicanpub.com

*To my lovely wife, Riva, and
to our children and grandchildren*

Contents

Foreword

"Jewish Europe" is not just a place, but an old and beautiful way of life—a blend of hope and despair, death and rebirth, endings and beginnings. So, as Jewish travelers walk the ancient cobblestone streets of any European city, the shadows of our ancestors walk by them, ushering travelers into eras past. Yet at the same time, a vivid Jewish community of here and now is thriving just nearby. One cannot understand the latter without knowing the former.

For the past 102 years, JDC has played a part in the unfolding story captured in this book, which is written with deep knowledge and love. The timing of publication is perfect, as the political and cultural kaleidoscope again turns around European Jewry. We need a "Guide for the Perplexed" to understand these evolving realities, and this book offers the perspective we need. It is more than a travel guide— it also encompasses current events, and outlines aspects of cultural, historical, and political life of each country in which Jews reside and how they are reacting to the volatile political and social movements that are sweeping that continent today.

Ben G. Frank, a veteran travel writer, has stamped his passport in more than 90 countries, written numerous Jewish Travel Guides, and set the gold standard for what a Jewish travel guide should be. A meticulous researcher, he often turned to JDC for facts and figures, leaving no stone unturned in an effort to offer a reliable and comprehensive account. For this updated edition, he interviewed numerous cultural, political, religious, and demographic experts—all contributing to this fresh look at the European-Jewish picture.

This Fourth Edition is a companion guide for the traveler, but also a source book for any reader interested in contemporary Jewish Europe. I hope that many American Jews will carry this guide with them as they visit Jewish Europe. For me, personally, being both a descendant of European Jews and an Executive of an American Jewish organization that has been inextricably entwined with Jewish Europe, this travel guide is a special gift.

David M. Schizer
Chief Executive Officer
The American Jewish Joint Distribution Committee (JDC)

Acknowledgments

It is one thing to write a first travel book; it is another to write a second and then a third one in order to bring the first and second ones up to date and to add new chapters. And then a fourth, a testimonial to needs and desires of travelers and armchair travelers to guide them on foreign travels, to broaden their horizons, and to learn about Europe, its culture and civilization and its vibrant and active Jewish community.

Patience and skill are not enough. And even though I have traveled to every one of these 24 European countries, some more than others, one needs the encouragement, advice, and help of friends, colleagues, and fellow writers, as well as many wonderful individuals and groups. It could not have been done without them. And yet, a core of individuals, in this case devoted professionals in helping and aiding the Jewish people worldwide, provided me with heartfelt advice, as well as contacts to bring this fourth edition of *A Travel Guide to Jewish Europe* together; namely, Amir Shaviv, assistant executive vice president for special operations of the American Jewish Joint Distribution Committee; Michael Geller, director of communications and media relations, American Jewish Joint Distribution Committee; and Rabbi Motti Seligson, director of communications of Chabad.

Among those who helped me through the entire project were Diego Ornique, JDC's Europe regional director; Rabbi Daniel Freelander, president of the World Union for Progressive Judaism; Avigayil Roth, project organization and administration of the World Union of Progressive Judaism; Tehila Reuben, director of missions and events; Masorti Olami and MERCAZ Olami; Joshua Spinner, executive vice president and chief executive officer of the Ronald S. Lauder Foundation; Nataly Fischmann of the Ronald S. Lauder Foundation; and Amikam Nachmani, professor emeritus, Bar-Ilan University, Tel Aviv, Israel.

I am indebted for inspiration and guidance to Robert Leiter, writer, editor; Ed Robin, Co-CEO Sustainability Analytics Corp.; Allan "Geli"

Gelfond, MSW, retired Jewish community executive and mission leader.

I am grateful to Max Rechtman for computer help; Jeanette Spitz for research and computer; and Larry Colby for photography, Arnold Sarasky, consultation. Ira M. Sheskin, PhD, professor and chair of Geography at the University of Miami and director of the Jewish Demography Project of the Sue and Leonard Miller Center for Contemporary Judaic Studies at the University of Miami, helped me analyze the population data in this volume. Dr. Sheskin is also editor (with Arnold Dashefsky of the University of Connecticut) of the *American Jewish Year Book 2016*, Volume 116 (Dordrecht: Springer). The year book features reliable population data gathered by Sergio DellaPergola of The Hebrew University in Jerusalem. In citing population data, I often refer to "core Jews." The "core Jewish population" includes people who consider themselves to be Jewish either by religion or in an ethnic or secular sense.

Of necessity, this travel guide with its detailed information could not have been written without the expertise and professionalism of tourist offices, information centers, and individuals engaged in travel, especially Marion Fourestier, director of communications, USA, ATOUT FRANCE-France Tourism Development Agency; Lisa Hubner, head of public relations of the German National Tourist Office; and Kirsten Schmidt, head of KMS Communications Inc.

Naturally, I want to thank the many who aided me in previous editions. Their knowledge and experience was retained in this fourth edition of *A Travel Guide to Jewish Europe*.

But, I must recognize those that offered their knowledge and analysis to me for this updated fourth edition. A special thanks to those contacts in each individual country.

France: Frederic Attali, director of the Consistoire Central, Union des Communautés Juives de France; Leon Masliah, honorary executive director, Consistoire Central, Union des Communautés Juives de France; William Labi, former deputy president of the Jewish community of Marseilles; Marion Fourestier, director of Communications, USA, ATOUT FRANCE-France Tourism Development Agency; Shimon Samuels, the director for international relations of the Wiesenthal Center, Europe, Latin America, Middle East, and Europe; Rabbi Sholom Pinson, Chabad, Nice; Rabbi Mendel Samama, Chabad, Strasbourg; Yonathan Arfi, vice president of CRIF, France; Rabbi Michael Rosenthal, Chabad, Marseilles; Maurice Niddam, president of the Jewish Community in Nice.

England: Avigayil Roth, project organization and administration of the World Union of Progressive Judaism; Rabbi Jeremy Conway, Kashrut Division, London Beth Din; David Frei of the London Beth Din, UK; Mark Fraser, office of the chief rabbi of the United Synagogue, UK; Rabbi Bentzi Sudak, Chabad Lubavitch, UK; Hanna Cabessa, Chabad Lubavitch, UK.

Ireland: Rabbi Zalman Lent, Irish Jewish Community; Nora Tillman, Irish Jewish Community, Irish Jewish Travel Guide.

Italy: Melina Rosenberg, JDC; Daniel Funaro, member of the board, Rome Jewish Community; Adam Smulevich, Union of Italian Jewish Communities, Rome; Guido Vitale of the Union of Italian Jewish Communities; Avigayil Roth, project organization and administration of the World Union of Progressive Judaism, Jerusalem, Israel; Micaela Pavonello, guide, Rome; Rabbi Shalom Hazan, Chabad of Rome; Chani Benjaminson, Chabad Lubavitch of Rome; Ursula Subatzus, Jewish Museum of Rome; Lenore Rosenberg Bahbout, Venice Jewish Community; Rabbi and Mrs. Ramy Banin, Chabad of Venice; Rabbi Levi Wolvovsky, Chabad of Tuscany; Francesca Rachel Valle, Florence guide; Giovanna Bossi Rosenfeld, guide, Florence; Rabbi Ariel Finzi; Enrico Fink, Jewish community leader and founder and artistic director of the Balagan Café, Florence; Rabbi Barbara Aiello of Calabria; Angela Yael Amato, Jewish Community of Naples.

Spain: Victor Sorensen, director of the Communidad Israelita de Barcelona; Assumpcio Hosta Rebes, Rabbi Yitzchok Goldstein, Chabad Madrid; Heritage Tours Private Travel, New York, NY, Chabad Lubavitch of Madrid; Rabbi and Mrs. Dovid M. M. Libersohn of Chabad Lubavitch of Barcelona; Ziva Freidkes Szeinuk, Sefarad Connection, Madrid; Assumpcio Hosta Rebes, Director of the Patronat Call de Girona.

Portugal: Michael Rothwell, member of the board of directors of the Jewish Community in Oporto; Rabbi Eli Rosenfeld, Chabad Lubavitch of Lisbon and Cascais.

Austria: Susanne Trauneck, director, Jewish Welcome Service, Vienna.

Switzerland: Rabbi Sholom Rosenfeld, Chabad Zurich; Rabbi Yaakov Kantor, Chabad Lugano.

Belgium: Yohan Benizri, president of the Coordinating Committee of Belgian Jewish Organizations, CCOB, Brussels; Yenty Lasker, Chabad Lubavitch of Brussels; Ms. Yardenah Presler, Synagogue Beth Hillel, Brussels.

Germany: Kirsten Schmidt, head of KMS Communications Inc.; Lisa Hubner, head of public relations of the German National Tourist Office; Hartmut Bomhoff, Abraham Geiger College, and the University of Potsdam; Professor Dr. Julius H. Schoeps managing director of the Moses Mendelssohn Center for European-Jewish

Studies; Deidre Berger, director of the American Jewish Committee Berlin Ramer Institute for German-Jewish Relations; Michael N. Szentel-Heise, Jewish Community of Dusseldorf, Chabad of Dresden; Rabbi Avraham Golovacheov, Chabad of Berlin; Ronnie Golz, guide, Berlin; Rabbi Daniel Freelander, president of the World Union of Progressive Judaism; Nirit Ben-Joseph, guide, Berlin; Susanne Reichelt, guide, Dresden; Jewish Community of Frankfurt; Jewish community of Munich; Chabad of Munich; Rabbi Nahum Presman of Chabad, Potsdam.

Greece: Victor Eliezer, second vice president of the Central Board of Jewish Communities of Greece; Amikam Nachmani, professor emeritus Bar-Ilan University, Ramat Gan, Israel; Effie Ezrati, Central Board of Jewish Communities in Greece; Elisa Solomon, communications officer, Jewish Museum of Greece; Micha Garyfallia of the Jewish Community of Greece; Zanet Battinou, director of the Jewish Museum of Greece, Rabbi Mendel Hendel, Chabad, Greece

Turkey: The Chief Rabbinate; the Jewish Community of Turkey; Amikam Nachmani, professor emeritus, Bar-Ilan University, Ramat Gan, Israel.

Scandinavia: Rabbi Ute Steyer, The Jewish community of Stockholm; John Gradowski, head of information of the Jewish Community of Stockholm; Avigayil Roth, Project Organization and Administration of the World Union of Progressive Judaism; Tehila Reuben, director of missions and events, Masorti Olami and MERCAZ Olami; Marianne Prager, guide, Stockholm; Rabbi Chaim Greisman, Chabad of Stockholm; Rabbi Alexander Namdar, Chabad, Gothenberg; Rabbi Yitzi Loewenthal, Chabad of Denmark; Rabbi Yair Melchior, chief rabbi of Denmark; Rabbi Joav Melchior, The Jewish Community of Norway; Catherine London Adler, Jewish community of Norway; Rabbi Shaul Wilhelm, Chabad of Norway; Rabbi Benjamin Wolff, Lubavitch of Finland.

Czech Republic: JDC Prague; Avigayil Roth, project organization and administration of the World Union of Progressive Judaism, Jerusalem, Israel; Tehila Reuben, director of missions and events, Masorti Olami and MERCAZ Olami, Jerusalem, Israel; Ronald S. Lauder Foundation.

Hungary: Guide Nandor Gerei, M.Sc, Budapest; Dr. Ivan Rona, managing director of the tourism department of MAZSIHISZ, Budapest; Avigayil Roth, Project Organization and Administration of the World Union of Progressive Judaism, Jerusalem, Israel; Ronald S. Lauder Foundation, Rabbi Shlomo Koves, Chabad, Budapest.

Slovakia: Rabbi Baruch Myers, Chabad of Slovakia, Bratislava; Ronald S. Lauder Foundation.

Poland: Chief Rabbi of Poland Michael Schudrich; JDC Poland; Konstanty Gebert, founder of *Gazeta Wyborcza*, Poland's biggest daily, non-tabloid newspaper; Ronald S. Lauder Foundation; Rabbi Anna Gorkiewicz-Sullivan, Chabad Lubavitch, Cracow; Rabbi Eliezer Guray, Chabad Lubavitch Cracow; Grzegorz Tomszewski, Museum of the History of Polish Jews, Warsaw; Rabbi Shalom Stambler, Chabad, Warsaw.

Romania: JDC Romania; Rabbi and Mrs. Ber Orgad, Chabad, Romania; Dr. Aurel Vainer, president of FEDROM, Bucharest.

Bulgaria: JDC Bulgaria; Rabbi Yosef Salamon, Chabad of Bulgaria; Alek Oscar and Tsvetina Vragova-Kane, of OJB, Shalom Bulgaria, Sofia.

I can only hope that I am not omitting any names. If I am, I apologize. I am especially indebted to the unnamed helpful residents of many countries who pointed me in the right direction.

I offer praise to the late Dr. Milburn Calhoun, publisher and president of Pelican Publishing Company, and to his successor, Kathleen Calhoun Nettleton, publisher and president. And of course, thank you to the entire staff at Pelican, who immediately saw the need for this travel book all the way to a fourth edition. I owe a special debt of gratitude to my editor at Pelican, Nina Kooij. This book would not be what it is without her. A thank you also goes out to Susanah Smith and Eugenie Brignac who helped edit this travel guide.

My deepest thanks, of course, go to my family: my late parents, Nathan M. Frank and Sonya Winerman Frank, and my wife's late parents, Rabbi Solomon Spitz and Jeanette Joskowitz Spitz. They inspired my wife, Riva, and me to learn more about and keep alive the traditions of the Jewish people, and this certainly encouraged us to seek out details of our roots and of the Jews of Europe.

Finally, any author knows how at times, especially as deadline approaches, pressure can become burdensome on one's wife— or husband. As for my wife, Riva, her love and devotion, her encouragement and steadfastness, not only kept my resolve moving on track, but also reinforced what we both knew: that this was a worthwhile project for this generation and future generations.

Introduction

There are no Jews in Tudela, Spain.

But I went there anyway.

You see, Tudela is the birthplace of my namesake Rabbi Benjamin of Tudela. In the 12th century he became the first Jewish travel writer, pioneering an entire branch of writing.

Like that travel writer, I chronicle the Jewish world of Europe; record the Jewish population and describe the people; relate their history; comment on their rulers and define the Jewish community.

I specifically went to Tudela in preparation for this book, the fourth edition of *A Travel Guide to Jewish Europe*. What I discovered there (as in many other cities of Europe—whether Jews live there or not) is a Jewish presence in the city square, on plaques on the walls of an old capital, in the air that hovers over lands where many of our ancestors lived for centuries.

I also came to Tudela for inspiration. This was the home of two other famous Jewish writers: Judah Halevi, born about 1075 and Abraham Ibn Ezra, born 1092.

Then, like Benjamin, I again set off to update this practical, anecdotal, unique travel guide to a fourth edition for you, the eager tourist or the knowledgeable armchair traveler. And, because of my sojourns throughout Europe, past and present, I am able to offer you the history of my brothers and sisters on that continent, as well as note the synagogues, monuments, museums, kosher restaurants, cafes, and cultural heritage sites. These listings are all inscribed here.

I danced at a bar mitzvah party in Marseilles, shared food at a *shalosh s'udot* (a gathering of the third meal of the Sabbath) in the *Altneuschul*, the Old New Synagogue in Prague. I spent hours at The Shoah Memorial and Holocaust Center in Paris. I people-watched on the Champs-Elysées and the Via Veneto and stared at stately statues in London.

Of course, there has been a major change in Europe since the previous edition of this guide.

Everywhere I went I felt the presence of tightened security: cameras, soldiers, police cars, guards who searched you: "Passport please!" Welcome to the world combatting terrorism in Europe, as well as in the U.S—lest we forget San Bernardino, New York City, London or Paris. As many in humankind say "Never again," many promise: "Never give in to terrorism." At least that is the declaration of thousands and thousands of tourists that will not be deterred from the joy and inspiration and knowledge gained though travel. So I obeyed the rules: Notified government buildings and institutional offices and security, as well as Jewish establishments, way in advance. I carried ID at all times. I discovered that European Jews who want to reside in Europe, who want to live safely, are above all, resilient. The visits of Americans and other nations' tourists fortify them.

Anti-Semitism is rising. Various political movements are spouting anti-democratic principles and prejudice. So, should Jews leave Europe? That is their choice. Most are remaining though many are on the move; some on *aliyah* to Israel; some from Turkey to Spain; some from Belgium to Canada, some from France to the UK, some from the UK to Portugal.

I pass on to you, the reader, what I learned and observed regarding the situation of Jews in the volatile political climate of Europe today. Besides being a travel guide, this volume explores the political and social condition of the Jewish communities in Europe.

I believe this new edition of *A Travel Guide to Jewish Europe* will help the reader understand the past history of Jews in Europe, as well as the present and future.

So, let's travel. As the Chinese say, the journey of a 1,000 *li* begins with the first step.

A TRAVEL GUIDE TO
JEWISH EUROPE

France

The Third Largest Jewish Community in the World

The noted Jewish writer Joseph Roth was correct when he noted that France possesses "mountains, sea, mystery, clarity, nature, art, science, revolution, religion, history, pleasure, grace and tragedy, beauty, wit, satire, enlightenment and reaction."

But for Jews it is all that and more.

France is the home of the largest Jewish community in Europe, the second largest in the Diaspora, and the third largest in the world.

France is home to about 460,000 Jews in about 230 Jewish communities, with more than 300 Jewish organizations and associations, about 500 synagogues, more than 100 day schools, 180 Talmud Torahs (Jewish schools), many kosher butcher shops, as well as B'nai B'rith lodges, a Jewish art museum, and a Jewish library of more than 160,000 volumes.

France is the home of several hundred thousand Jews from North Africa, who, in the 1960s, settled in towns and villages where at the time there were no Jews.

France, which has a diverse Jewish population, is one of the few countries outside of Israel where Sephardic Jews now outnumber the Ashkenazim. "Sepharad" is the Hebrew word for Spain. Sephardim are those Jews who trace their origins to Spain or Portugal before the 1492 expulsion, and include Jews from the Mediterranean basin who share a common cultural legacy, as well as those Jews who follow the traditions, customs, rituals, and culture of the Jews of Spain and Portugal.

Ashkenazic Jews are those whose religious rites and customs stem from Germany and Eastern Europe, and whose household language at home was Yiddish.

A Brief History

Jewish history in France probably begins with the Roman period after the conquest of Jerusalem, and certainly by the fourth century, when Jews pitched their tents along the great trade routes. Jews migrated to the French Mediterranean coast in and around Marseilles. Soon they settled in the south of Gaul, near Bordeaux and Avignon. By the fourth and fifth centuries, Jews lived in Metz, Poitiers, Avignon, Arles, Brittany, Clermont-Ferrand, and Narbonne. By 524, they settled in Valence. A synagogue was founded in Paris in 582. Jews served as merchants, physicians, and sailors. Although restricted by Christianity, they lived comfortably. They fared well under Charlemagne and his successors in the eighth and ninth centuries. The days of the intellectual glory of French Jewry did not occur until the eleventh and twelfth centuries. This Golden Age of French Jewry was sparked by such luminaries as Rabbenu Gershom, the Light of Exile (960-1030), and Rashi (1040-1105), the great commentator on the Bible who lit up the sky of Jewish religious thought. By the mid-eleventh century, Joseph B. Samuel Bonfils taught in Limoges, and Moses haDarshan in Narbonne.

The first significant act of anti-Semitism in the form of a blood libel charge occurred in 1171 in the Loire town of Blois. Thirty-two Jews were burned at the stake. A similar event had already taken place in Norwich, England, in 1144.

Many times since, the Jews of France and Europe were to suffer from the false charge of murdering Christians and draining their blood for Passover. Thus began a period of expulsions and murder. In 1182, King Philip Augustus expelled the Jews—only to recall them sixteen years later.

In the next century, severe anti-Jewish persecutions erupted. In 1242, at the instigation of the Catholic Church, copies of the Talmud were seized from French Jewish homes, libraries, and synagogues and hurled into town squares, where they were burned.

On July 22, 1306, Philip IV, known as the "Fair," seized Jewish property and banished the Jews from France. More than 100,000 Jews fled. They found refuge in Belgium, Italy, and Spain. Several decades later those Jews who had remained in France would again be victimized. Now they would be charged with poisoning the wells during the Black Plague.

The great creativity of medieval French Jewry soon ended, even though they were readmitted to France in 1315. We know that Jewish communities thrived in Bayonne, Bordeaux, Toulouse, Marseilles, Limoges, Poitiers, Nantes, Angers, Dijon, Le Havre, Rouen, Verdun, Valence, and, of course, in Alsace and Lorraine, in such cities as Mulhouse, Colmar, and Strasbourg. While some were purveyors to the Imperial Court, most were engaged in finance.

In 1394, Charles VI expelled the Jews once again. For two hundred years, only a handful of Jews remained on French soil—

in Alsace-Lorraine and Avignon, the latter called the "Pope's Jews" because they were protected by the pope. Much has been written about these Jews of Avignon who, with their brothers and sisters of Carpentras, Cavaillon, and L'lsle-sur-la-Sorges, comprised the four communities of the Comtat Venaissin (lands of the pope). Here Jews established centers and historical sites, one of which is the Synagogue in the Round in Avignon. Large concentrations of Jews had settled there in the fifth and sixth centuries. After 1394, Jews in France did not practice their religion openly. Yet, following the Spanish Inquisition and expulsion in 1492, Marranos (secret Jews) began to arrive in the southwest corner of the country. Called members of the "Portuguese Nation" or "Portuguese merchants," they crossed the border near the Pyrenees. It was safer to be Portuguese than to be known as a Jew. Starting in 1550, under the guise of being "New Christians," these Marranos were granted letters of protection by Henry II, who permitted them to live in France wherever they desired. Other Marranos and Jews settled in Bayonne and Bordeaux and in numerous small cities in this Atlantic-coast corner of France. Some went north to La Rochelle, Nantes, and Rouen.

The 1648 Chmielnicki massacres in the Ukraine caused Jews to flee to France from Poland and Russia and to settle in Alsace-Lorraine. By 1657, there were 96 Jewish families in Metz. After the Treaty of Westphalia in 1648, Jews were allowed to remain in Lorraine. For the first time since 1394, Jews were legally permitted to live in France.

Later Cardinal Richelieu invited Marranos to settle in French port cities for the purpose of expanding French overseas trade.

By the close of the seventeenth century, Jews were welcome in France because of the policies of Jean-Baptiste Colbert, finance minister to Louis XIV. Colbert believed in mercantilism, that the purpose of the state was to increase its wealth. Colbert figured Jews would bring business skills to France. This they certainly did, including chocolate-making in Bayonne. They enhanced shipping and trading in the port of Bordeaux.

By the beginning of the eighteenth century, Jews began to return to Paris. They were peddlers who sold secondhand clothes and rags. Because of occupational restrictions, Jews were forced to become moneylenders, military purveyors, and petty traders.

Two groups existed side by side in France: Sephardic Jews in Bordeaux, Avignon, and Comtat Venaissin, and Ashkenazim in Alsace-Lorraine and other provinces.

In 1732, Sephardic Jews were formally recognized by royal decrees and permitted to practice Judaism. In 1787, on the eve of the French

Revolution, 40,000 Jews lived in France, 20 times more than in the fledgling Jewish community in that new republic across the ocean, the United States. During those years, a part from a few wealthy capitalists, the great majority of French Jews were middle class—peddlers, merchants, craftsmen, painters.

By 1914, the Jewish population of France included 20,000 Eastern European Jews. Their brothers and sisters migrated to Paris during the upheaval caused by the Russian Revolution. In 1935, 260,000 Jews lived in France.

Between World War I and World War II, Eastern European Jews continued to flee to France, which had become a land of refuge. By 1939, there were about 300,000 Jews in France, half of whom were not French citizens.

In the late 1930s, as in all of Europe, a wave of anti-Semitism enveloped France. Following Franco's win in Spain, France found itself facing totalitarianism on three of its borders, Spain, Italy and Germany. "The Jews in France believed in the strength of the Third Republic, and the Jews of East Central Europe believed in France. Few imagined that Nazi Germany could become a real threat beyond its own borders," wrote Saul Friedlander in *Nazi Germany and the Jews*. France would surrender in 38 days and its capitulation would result in Vichy's hoisting the white flag as well as its subsequent collaboration with the Nazis. Despite the roundups and the terror, more than two-thirds of the estimated 350,000 Jews who were living in France in 1940 were saved.

After the war, Jews from Eastern Europe flocked to France, many on their way to the future Jewish state in Palestine. For a decade, the old-time French Jewish community was weak. On the one hand it tried to aid the Jewish displaced persons and on the other it sought to revitalize itself. Only the arrival of the Sephardim from North Africa rejuvenated the community, and in France today, Jews are vocal and visible.

The one "burning issue" uniting all French Jews is the survival of the State of Israel and the activism that is needed to ensure that ideal and goal. And the strength to archive that goal was enhanced by the influx of North African Jews.

In the 1970s, activism on behalf of Israel found its expression in *Renouveau Juif,* Jewish Renewal. This group galvanized the community and encouraged Jews to be more vociferous in espousing the cause of Israel and the Jewish people. They felt that, to reach French public opinion, they had to hold rallies and demonstrations against the policy of the French government toward Israel, a policy that from time to time has tilted towards the Arabs. The purpose of Jewish Renewal was "to create a sense of renewal in the Jewish community, to unify the community through political activism and to integrate French Jews into Jewish life."

As we have seen, observers of French foreign policy have noted that since 1967, France and Israel have been on a rocky road regarding their relationship. More often than not "tepid relations" have existed between France and Israel.

The Jews from Algeria, Morocco, and Tunisia who arrived in France after Israel's independence in 1948, were more observant than their Ashkenazic co-religionists. Major publishing houses began printing well-known Jewish authors, Hebrew classics, and contemporary books on French history, theology, Israel, and Jewish tradition.

Enrollment in Jewish schools in France today is higher than ever, consisting of 10 percent of school-age children. About 16,000 students are enrolled full-time in France's more than 100 Jewish schools. An equal number attend Sunday school. The new economic prosperity of the Sephardim fuels a revival of religious education. They realize that only Jewish education can save them from rampant assimilation.

Jews around France can tune in to any of 13 radio stations playing Hebrew and Yiddish songs and broadcasting cultural programs and news commentaries. The three Paris stations alone claim a daily audience of 37,000 Jews. Judeotel, a video magazine, has introduced programs that consist of Jewish news and culture and is accessible on the Internet.

Jewish publications have more readers than ever. Numerous weeklies are distributed free of charge in Jewish centers and shops. The monthly *L'Arche,* aimed at France's educated middle class, reaches about 1,000 subscribers. Every year, an international festival of Jewish films is held.

So what happened to this idyllic life for the French Jewish community? First, age-old anti-Semitism that has not been extirpated from the body politic including neo-Nazi ideology. Many believe "that most anti-Semitic attacks in France since 2000 have been committed by people with an immigrant background from Muslim countries who target Jews over Israel's actions."

This author shall discuss these factors and the rise of Islamic terrorist attacks on France itself in recent years as we visit various sites and institutions in Paris in in this chapter.

Notable French Jews

By the end of the nineteenth century, the Jewish population had increased to 90,000, of which 50,000 lived in Paris, the center of European capitalism. It was then that Jews achieved fame in France, which until World War I was certainly the cultural center of the world. Before World War I, Jewish painters and sculptors helped make the so-called "Paris School" famous: Pissarro, Soutine, Pascin, Modigliani, Chagall, Mane Katz, as well as Benn. (They also used Jewish subjects in their works.)

The names of Jacques Offenbach, Claude Kahn, Darius Milhaud, Paul Dukas—all of whom are Jews—are well known in French music; and Jews in French literature are legion, both past and contemporary. France boasts two Jewish Nobel laureates, Henri Bergson in literature and Rene Cassin, winner of the World Peace Prize in 1968. Writers include Marcel Proust, André Maurois, Edmond Fleg, Eugene Ionesco, Armand Lurel, Albert Memmi, Clara Malraux, and Joseph Kessel of the Académie Française. Goncourt Prize winners include Roger Ikor, Romain Gary, André Schwarz-Bart, and Anna Longfus. Philosophers and writers Bernard-Henri Levy, Alain Finkelkraut, Victor Malka, Roland Goetschel, and novelists André Schwarz-Bart and Marek Halter, have achieved world acclaim. The writer Elie Wiesel, who received the Nobel Peace Prize in 1986, is well known in France. He lived there after his release from the Nazi death camps and wrote distinguished literary works in French.

Jews in academic life include Raymond Aron, Robert Aron, George Steiner, Claude Levi-Strauss, Georges Friedman, and Bernhard Blumenkranz.

French Jews have starred in the theater, film, and television: Rachel, Sarah Bernhardt, Jules Dassin, Simone Signoret, Marcel Marceau, Anouk Aimee, Jean-Pierre Aumont, Claude Lelouch, Claude Berri, Regine, and Claude Lanzmann. The latter won a "Cesar," France's equivalent of the Oscar, for *Shoah,* his epic film on the Holocaust.

Some notable French Jews who excelled in science include Henri Moissan, Andre Lwoff, Gabriel Lippman, François Jacob (all Nobel Prize winners from France), Henri-Marc Baruk, Bernard Halpern, and Eugene Minkoski.

In industry, Max Hymans and Bernard Attali each served as the director general of Air France. Andre Citroën founded the famous French automobile company.

Finally, Jews played a role in government and politics. Leon Blum, Rene Mayer, and Pierre Mendes-France were prime ministers. Daniel Mayer, Jules Moch, Pierre Masse, Georges Mandel, Jean Pierre-Bloch, the late Simone Veil, Lionel Stoleru, and former Minister of Justice Robert Badinter. All achieved prominence in government. Isaac-Adolphe Cremieux was a foreign minister; he gave French citizenship to Algerian Jews. Nearly a hundred years later, his act enabled the Jews of Algeria to leave and resettle in France as full citizens of the Republic.

The Champs-Elysée near the Arc de Triomphe. (Photo credit Atout France-France Tourism Development Agency, Jacques Lebar photographer)

Jewish Paris

For nearly everyone, there is the Paris of art, culture, and romance; the banks of the River Seine; the galleries, museums, and cathedrals; the Champs-Elysées; the Eiffel Tower; the parks; the superb restaurants, as well as thousands of sidewalk cafés and bistros. To arrive in the "City of Light" for the first time or the tenth time is to be touched by beauty.

It has been said that one half of Paris makes love to the other half. Wherever you go, Paris boasts the best-dressed women, the best food, and the best wine. That's at least what the guidebooks say, especially since this wonderful city is known as the "City of Love."

This is the city of Hugo, Dumas, Flaubert and Balzac; Zola, Baudelaire, and other literary dreamers. This is a city mad on pleasure and passionate about food. Movies, and especially books, by Ernest Hemingway, William Carlos Williams, John Dos Passos, and other American writers who described the city on the Seine for two decades between the world wars helped enhance America's love for this city.

As author William L. Shirer said, Paris is "as near to paradise on this earth as any man could ever get." The writer John Galsworthy noted "Paris pets the senses."

Observe the cafés; sail on the river; walk along the boulevard St-Michel; inhale the "Paris of the common man, the Paris born of the French Revolution."

For Jews, there is another Paris. It can be found on the Left Bank and on the Right Bank, on the avenue de Wagram, in the student quarter on the boulevard St-Michel, in the rue Richer and the rue des Rosiers.

Before there was France, even before there were a people called the French, there was Paris. And Jews have lived in Paris since the year 582.

The capital of France is the center of French Jewish activities. Two-thirds of the approximate 500,000 French Jews live in and around Paris. You meet them everywhere: on the Champs-Elysées, in the fashionable Sixteenth Arrondissement, in the attractive suburb of Neuilly, in the elite shops of the exquisite rue Faubourg de St-Honoré, in the restaurants on the rue Richer, on the bateaux mouches that cruise up and down the Seine, and in the immaculate and superb gardens and parks of this beautiful metropolis. In the elegant Place des Vosges, one of the most beautiful squares in Europe, just outside the Temple des Vosges at No. 14, I saw a bride and groom leave the synagogue after a Jewish wedding where the *shamash* was dressed in the bicorne (cocked hat of the Napoleonic era), knee-length black coat, and silver chains of office.

JEWISH SITES IN PARIS

One subway stop most important to the Jewish traveler who wishes to connect with his brothers and sisters in Paris, is metro stop Saint-Paul on line one. This is the main station for the Le Marais district, also known as the *Pletzel* and still a viable center of Jewish life in Paris, though much less these days because of a wave of new, fabulous boutiques and town houses that have taken over.

When I walk through the Marais section of Paris, I'm reminded of the Lower East Side of Manhattan. Both areas once contained a large Jewish community. Still, they remain very tourist-attractive areas, each drawing thousands of travelers of all religions and ethnicities every day.

My advice to travelers interested in Jewish sites, visit the **Pletzel.**

Jewish tourists should know that the Marais is not just a "gentrified Jewish district where boutiques are overtaking Judaica shops and delis," but also historically the site of the 13th century ghetto of Paris known as the **Juiverie,** later known by the Yiddish word, "the Pletzel, little square."

The Marais—like the Lower East Side of Manhattan, which also once had a large Jewish immigrant population—remains; a fact that reminds all humankind that though a neighborhood changes, one must never forget the memories of a varied past.

For example, today in the Marais: The Shoah Memorial and Holocaust Center, rue Geoffroy l'Asnier; the Memorial to the Deported, located behind Notre Dame; the historic synagogue Agoudas Hakehilos, rue Pavee, which was designed by Hector Guimard, the famous art nouveau architect of the metro; the former Jo Goldenberg's restaurant, rue de Rosiers, the scene of a terrorist attack in 1982, but never closed a single day.

Like other ethnic groups, Jews remain part of the Marais mosaic: Synagogues, prayer halls, kosher falafel stands, book stores. Few in numbers and shops, yes; but their presence resounds in the sweep of history. Their sights, past and present, are part of any sentimental journey of a visitor to the area who wants to absorb the "unrelenting tide of history." That is the Marais.

When the Jewish people were permitted to return to the Kingdom of France in 1198, they settled on what is now the rue Ferdinand Duval, then called "street of the Jews." Once it was in the neighborhood of the rich, but after the storming of the Bastille on July 14, 1789, the poor moved in. When those first Jewish immigrants settled in this section in the twelfth century, they called it "little square," or in Yiddish, the "Pletzel."

Today, several thousand Jews, many of them religious, live in the Pletzel. On Friday afternoons, one can observe Chassidim dressed in long black coats with their round *shtreimels* (fur hats), scurrying home to prepare for the Sabbath Queen.

As you walk through the maze of those tight alleys and winding streets with walls of quaint old buildings forming odd angles at the narrow streets below, you quickly sense that you are taking a sentimental journey. Depending on the world situation, you can always spot the Jewish synagogue, community center, or museum from several blocks away, simply because there are armed security forces standing in front of these institutions.

Usually when I go to old neighborhoods such as the *Pletzel*, it is just as if I am meandering along the Lower East Side of New York. As I watch the bearded Orthodox men with long black coats and fur *shtreimels*, all engaged in deep conversation, I romanticize that this is the way it must have been years ago, when the Jews started settling here in large numbers. To this day in the *Pletzel*, on the rue des Rosiers, rue des Hospitalieres-St-Gervais, rue des Ecouffes (pawnbrokers), rue Ferdinand Duval, rue Geof-froy l'Asnier, and rue Vieille du Temple, you will find a Jewish atmosphere.

Yes, there is much to see!

To start, here are some art and book stores in the Pletzel:

Libraire du Progress, 26, rue des Rosiers, 75004, Paris. Tel: 1-40-09-97-13. libraire.progress@gmail.fr, www.libraire-du-progress.com.

Diasporama, 20, rue des Rosiers, 75004, Paris. Tel: 42-78-30-50. FAX: 42-74-38-76. www.disaporama.com. Open Sunday to Friday, 10:00 a.m.to 7:30 p.m., except Friday when it closes before the Sabbath. It stays closed on the Sabbath.

JEWISH RESTAURANTS IN PARIS

In Paris, one place to meet Jews is in restaurants and cafés. Meeting people in a café is typically French, for the Parisians include the surrounding eating establishments in their definition of home.

Most would agree that Paris is the gastronomic capital of the world. This city loves a carefully prepared meal that is appreciatively savored. According to Parisians, a meal is a very special experience, a pleasure of life. The French do not eat; they dine. The traveler seeking kosher cuisine does not have to be wary about finding it in Paris, where there may be more kosher facilities than in New York, Chicago, and Los Angeles combined. One can certainly enjoy a wide variety of French, Eastern European, and North African specialties here.

More than 100 kosher restaurants in Paris will certainly meet the traveler's needs. Most kosher restaurants carry the sign of the Beth Din of Paris, certifying "kosher here," but some also have the approval sign of Lubavitch.

Jewish restaurants are institutions where people are ready to extend a warm welcome to the visitor, though in recent years, security costs have caused a number to close.

Kosher Restaurants in Paris

L'As Du Fallafel, 34 rue des Rosiers, 75004, Paris. Tel: 01-48-87-63-60.
Les Salons Bench, 4 bis rue des Rosiers, 75004, Paris. Tel:01-42-77-32-45.
Rodchenko, 17 rue des Ecouffes, 75004 Paris. Tel: 01-75-50-77-95.
Tchik chak 44 rue des Rosiers, 75004, Paris. 01-42-74-44-44
Tutti Frutti, 38, rue des Rosiers, 75004, Paris. Tel: 42-76-04-75. This is a very popular takeout place with a small counter. It is especially known for grilled panini sandwiches of tuna and cheese. It also serves yogurt. English and Hebrew are spoken here. (Tutti Frutti is strictly kosher, "Halav Yisrael.")
Yahalom, 24, rue des Rosiers, 75004, Paris. Tel: 42-77-12-35. This place is strictly glatt kosher. They offer you falafel, humus, tahini, and eggplant. Full-course meals include Israeli dishes as well as meat dishes. You will find that snacks are also available.

Other Kosher Restaurants approved by the Beth Din de Paris.

Bistro 85, Ave. des Ternes, 75017, Paris. Tel: 01-45-74-01-02.
China Lee, 12 rue Armand Carrel, 75019, Paris. Tel: 01-42-02-18-00.
Centre Communautaire, 5 rue Rochechouard, 75009, Paris. Tel: 45-95-95-92.
Centre Communautaire, 119 rue La Fayette, 75010, Paris. Tel: 01-53-20-52-52.
Centre Edmond Fleg, (Resto Fleg) 8 bis, rue de l'Eperon, 750006, Paris. Tel: 09-50-75-96-75.
Douieb, 11 bis rue Geoffroy Marie, 75009, Paris. Tel: 01-47-70-60-31.
Heat, 35 Ave. Charles de Gaulle, 92200, Neuilly Sur Seine, Tel:01-47-38-33-33.
Gospard, 84 rue Lauriston, 75016, Paris.Tel: 01-45-05-31-89.
King David, 14 rue Paul Chatrousse, 92200, Neuilly Sur Seine, Tel: 01-47-36-33-33.
Il Conte, 47 Raymond Poincarre, 75016, Paris. Tel: 47-27-98-40.
Il Vantagio, 209 Ave. de Versailles, 75016, Paris. Tel: 09-82-49-06-00
Internet Café, 22 rue Cambaceres, 75008, Paris. Tel: 01-40-07-03-90.
Itsik, 78 Ave. Secretan, 75019 Paris. Tel: 06-11-08-93-41.
Kifoli, 122 Blvd. de Belleville, 75020, Paris. Tel: 01-47-97-53-13.
Chez Isaac, 52 rue Volta, 75003, Paris. Tel: 01-42-71-19-09.

Chez Papy, 33/35 passage du Ponceau, 75002, Paris. Tel: 01-42-33-80-95.

Chez René et Gabin, 92, Blvd. de Belleville, 75020, Paris. Tel: 01-43-58-78-14.

Chez Vicky, 13 rue Rennequin, 75017, Paris. Tel: 01-40-53-03-03.

La Citadelle, 21 rue Mederic, 75017, Paris. Tel: 01-56-79-77-15.

La Fille de Boucher, 20 rue Cardinet, 75017, Paris. Tel: 01-42-67-14-19.

La Marina, 159 rue Manin, 75019, Paris. Tel: 01-42-01-36-26.

Les Garcons Bouchers, 33 Ave. Phillipe Auguste, 75011, Paris. Tel: 01-43-67-01-23.

Les Jardins du Belvedere, 111, Ave. de Villiers, 75017, Paris. Tel: 01-42-27-16-91. Highly recommended. Excellent food.

Le Manahattan, 231, Blvd. Voltaire, 75011, Paris. Tel: 01-43-56-03-30.

Le Monde du Sandwich, 203 Ave. Charles de Gaulle, 92200, Neuilly Sur Seine, Tel: 01-46-24-60-01.

Mama-Mia, 157 Blvd. Serrurier, 75019, Paris. Tel: 01-42-81-07-00.

Matann, 10 Ave. de Villiers, 75917, Paris. Tel: 01-46-22-11-77.

Nini, 24, rue Saussier-Leroy, 75017, Paris. Tel: 01-46-22-28-93. Excellent food and highly recommended. Nini is very popular with American Jews. It has been called a "Tunisian-chic restaurant." Served here are steaks, veal, lamb chops, mixed grill, and couscous.

Nina Sushi, 86 Ave. de Villiers, 75017, Paris. Tel: 01-2-67-99-13.

Nin Sushi, 213 Blvd. Voltaire, 75011, Paris. Tel: 01-42-39-04-38.

Oz, 19 rue Beffoy, 92200, Neuilly Sur Seine, Tel: 01-47-47-53-10.

Pilpel, 28 rue Manin, 75019, Paris. Tel: 01-40-40-26-26.

Poulet Hoff, 78/80 rue Notre Dame de Nazareth, 75003, Paris. 01-42-76-03-02.

Yapany, 4 rue Armand Carrel, 75019, Paris. Tel: 01-45-00-66-66.

LODGING

Lebron Hotel, 4, rue Lamartine, 75009, Paris. Tel: 48-78-75-52. FAX: 49-95-94-64. Besides fine hotel rooms with TVs, this kosher facility maintains a glatt kosher restaurant, dining room, and conference room. One can order meals ahead of time for the Sabbath. The hotel is near numerous synagogues and not far from Temple Victoire, as well as the synagogue on rue Buffault. Chabad House is several doors down, at 8, rue Lamartine. Moreover, the hotel is near fine kosher restaurants in rue Richer and the surrounding area.

The quarter around rue Richer is another Parisian section where one can often meet Jews. Throughout the world, No. 32 rue Richer is known as the Folies Bergere. This is one of the most dynamic streets of Paris.

Walk along the rue Richer, between rue du Faubourg-Poissonniere and rue Faubourg-Montmartre. Explore the side streets. Lunch or dine in one of the kosher restaurants and snack bars.

SYNAGOGUES IN PARIS

The Jewish tourist in France has no difficulty finding a synagogue to visit, whether in Paris or the countryside. Several hundred exist in France. There are more than 50 Jewish houses of worship in Paris alone. And many of the Parisian suburbs contain synagogues. To check times of services, please contact the **Consistoire Central,** 19, rue St-Georges, 75009, Paris. Tel: 1-49-70-88-00, administration@consistoirecentral.fr, or the Consistoire de Paris, 17, rue St-Georges, 75009, Paris. Tel: 40-82-26-26. FAX: 01-42-81-92-46. contact@consistoire.org.

Temple Victoire, 44, rue de la Victoire, 75009, Paris. Tel: 45-26-95-36. infos@lavictoire.org.www.lavictoire.org. Metro: LePetetier or Notre-Dame-de-Lorette. A must for American visitors. This beautiful, austere building is frequently referred to as the Rothschild Synagogue because members of the renowned family attend services here. Built in 1874 in neo-Romanesque style, it is lavishly decorated with marble and stained glass, and is dominated by opulent candelabras. It is often called the "Cathedral Synagogue."

The synagogue is on a relatively narrow street. Jewish officials had hoped to have the façade on the somewhat more conspicuous rue St-Georges, from which one now enters the community offices, but the empress's confessor, reportedly a converted Jew, did not want the building to be visible on a heavily traversed thoroughfare. So the congregation had to put up with the resulting incorrect orientation of the Holy Ark, writes Carol Herselle Krinsky in Synagogues in Europe. The interior is impressive.

Because the Rothschilds pray here, let us reflect on this family of financiers and philanthropists, who have contributed greatly to Jewish causes. The head of the Rothschild family was Mayer Amschel Rothschild of Frankfurt (1744-1812), who had five sons. They were Amschel Mayer (1773-1836), who stayed in Frankfurt; Solomon Mayer (1774-1855), who went to Vienna; Nathan Mayer (1777-1855), to London; Karl Mayer (1788-1855), to Naples; and James Jacob (1792-1868), to Paris.

The French branch of the family was founded when James, the youngest of the sons, settled in Paris in 1812. As an agent of his brother Nathan, James established the firm of Rothschild Freres. Financially, he aided the Bourbon and Orleans families, the kings of France, and Napoleon III. From then on, apart from its banking activities, the Rothschild family was active in the French Jewish community. James de Rothschild built the Rothschild Hospital, which still stands today in Paris. An early railroad entrepreneur, James helped set up many government railroad lines. The Rothschilds financed the main rail networks in France, including the Chemin de Fer du Nord. The Rothschild family assumed positions of responsibility in the French Jewish leadership, holding respected posts. Synagogue services: Friday nights at 6:30, Saturday mornings at 9:30. (Metro: Le Peletier). There is also a Tunisian and an Egyptian congregation on the premises.

Agoudas Hakehilos, 10, rue Pavée, 75004, Paris. Tel: 48-87-21-54. A school is located here. Austere on the outside and beautiful inside, this Orthodox synagogue in the *Pletzel* was designed in 1913 by Hector Guimard, the famous art nouveau architect of the Metro, who fled to the United States in 1942 and whose wife was Jewish. The building itself is neo-Gothic in feeling. There are two lateral aisles, each having two rows of overhead galleries for the women's section, supported by four massive pillars, plus wooden benches. Orthodox Ashkenazic services are offered every day. Sabbath morning services at 9:20. (Metro: St-Paul).

A second synagogue, located at 23, rue Petion, 75011, Paris, opened in March 1991. Services are held Friday evenings at 6:30 and Saturday mornings at 10. (Metro: Voltaire-Leon Blum).

Ohel Avraham, 31, rue Montevideo, 75016, Paris. Tel: 45-04-66-73.

Oratoire, 223, rue Vercingetorix, 75014, Paris. Tel: 45-45-50-51. (Metro: Daumesnil).

Oratoire, 42, rue des Saules, 75018, Paris. Tel: 46-06-71-39. (Metro: Jules Joffrin).

Oratoire, 120, Blvd. de Belleville, 75020, Paris. Tel: 47-97-46-96.

Oratoire, 13, rue Fondary, 75015, Paris. Tel: 45-04-66-73. (Metro: Grenelle).

Synagogue, 15, rue Notre-Dame de Nazareth, 75003, Paris. Tel: 42-78-00-30. Fax: 01-42-78-05-18 (Metro: Republique). synagoguenazareth.@free.fr.

Synagogue, 21 bis, rue des Tournelles, 75004, Paris. Tel: 42-74-32-80. FAX: 01-48-04-93-74. contact@synatournelle.fr.

This is a Sephardic synagogue known for its wrought-ironwork interior. It is situated back-to-back with the Ashkenazic synagogue known as **Temple des Vosges,** which fronts on the Place des Vosges, 14, Place des Vosges, 75004, Paris. Tel: 1-48-87-79-45. FAX: 01-48-87-57-58. secretariatplacedesvosge@gmail.com. A must for the visitor, the Place des Vosges, located in the heart of the Marais, is probably one of the most beautiful squares in all of Paris. Victor Hugo lived at No. 6; the house is now a museum. (Metro: Bastille).

Synagogue, 9 rue Vauquelin, 75005 Paris. Tel: 01-48-35-67-66. FAX: 1-43-37-75-92.communautevauquelin.fr. www.synagoguevauquelin. com. (Rabbinical Seminary), 9, rue Vauquelin, 75005, Paris. Tel: 47-07-21-22. FAX: 43-37-75-92. (Metro: Monge).

Synagogue, 28, rue Buffault, 75009, Paris. Tel: 01-49-70-70-00. FAX: 01-48-78-44-02. communaute@buffauit.net.www.buffauit.net. (Metro: Cadet).

Synagogue Kahal Yreim, 10, rue Cadet, 75009, Paris. Tel: 42-46-36-47. (Metro: Cadet).

Synagogue Berith Shalom, 18, rue St-Lazare, 75009, Paris. Tel: 01-48-78-45-32. FAX: 01-48-74-65-29. berit.ch@orange.fr.

Synagogue Rachi, 6, rue Ambroise-Thomas, 75009, Paris. Tel: 48-24-86-94. This synagogue is named after Rashi, who is considered the leading commentator on the Bible and the Talmud. Born in Troyes in 1040, he learned a great deal about viticulture and husbandry. In Rashi's time, Jews lived in Champagne and other wine districts of northern France. He himself studied in Worms and Mainz. About 1070, he founded a school in Troyes that made French Judaism renowned for its scholarship. But not all was tranquil. During the First Crusade, Rashi had to flee anti-Jewish riots in and around Troyes. Once he established himself in Worms, Germany, he lived and studied there. Rashi died in 1105. His burial place is not known. (Metro: Cadet).

Synagogue, 130, rue du Faubourg-St Martin, 75010, Paris. (Metro: Gare de l'Est).

Synagogue Don Isaac Abravanel, 84-86, rue de la Roquette, 75011, Paris. Tel: 47-00-75-95. (Metro: Bastille).

Synagogue, 14, rue Chasseloup-Laubat, 75015, Paris. Tel: 42-73-36-29. (Metro: Segur).

Synagogue de Montmartre, 12, rue Ste-Isaure, 75018, Paris. Tel: 42-64-48-34. (Metro: Jules Joffrin).

Synagogue de Neuilly, 12, rue Ancelle, Neuilly Sur-Seine. (Metro: Las Sablons). Tel: 46-24-49-15.

Synagogue Or Torah, 15, rue Riquet, 75019, Paris.

Synagogue, "Marche Saint-Didier," 75016, Paris.

Liberal Synagogues in Paris

The Liberal Synagogue, 22-24, rue Copernic, 75116, Paris. Tel: 1-47-04-37-27. FAX: 01-47-27-81-02. communication@ulif.org. www. ulif.org. On Friday night and Saturday, many American visitors and residents pray at the Union Liberale Israelite de France (The Liberal

Synagogue). Services at 6:00 on Friday evenings and at 10:30 a.m. Saturdays. Holiday services at 10:00 a.m. On Passover, there is an attempt to have part of the traditional Seder in English. An English-speaking secretary is available all week long to aid travelers. (Metro: Victor Hugo. Bus: 22, 82, 30, 52). The wave of Islamic terrorism that swept Europe in the last decades probably began in France. The 1980 Paris synagogue bombing was a bombing directed against the synagogue of the French Israeli Liberal Union and was committed on 3 October 1980 on Friday night. It was the first deadly attack against Jewish people in France since the end of the Second World War. There were 4 dead and 46 injured. Many consider this attack the beginning of the wave of terrorism against Jews in France that has continued to plague the Jewish community in the last 35 years.

Terrorism and Anti-Semitic Violence in France

Commenting on the incident at rue Copernic, it is fitting that we discuss anti-Semitic violence and Islamic terrorism in France at this point in this chapter

The year 2015 was traumatic for France and its Jews, with two horrific terrorist attacks on the Republic. Note that between January 2015 and March 2017, according to the BBC of March 20, 2017, more than 230 people died in terror attacks.

On January 9, 2015, a "black time," descended on Paris. Hit by Islamic terrorists were the offices of Charlie Hebedo, satire magazine and the Hyper Cacher kosher supermarket. From January 7 to January 9, 2015, a total of 17 people were killed. Four were murdered at the supermarket. Three suspects were killed by police.

During those days, the world watched as dozens of world leaders, including Muslim and Jewish statesmen, linked arms leading more than a million French citizens in an unprecedented march under high security to pay tribute to victims of Islamist militant attacks.

Then came the attacks in Paris on the night of Friday, November 13, 2015 by Muslim gunmen and suicide bombers who hit a concert hall, a major stadium, restaurants, and bars, almost simultaneously, and left 130 people dead and hundreds wounded.

But despite it all, tourists have been coming back to Paris and its charming countryside. After all, France itself is the number one destination in the world, with 83 million visitors annually, and Paris welcomes 16 million visitors a year. As one travel writer put it after the attacks: "Paris is my favorite destination in the world. I was not going to have the life-long pleasure of being there taken from me now." He returned to Paris and so have more visitors since those horrible days. Indeed, "tourism in Paris, which plunged after the series of terrorist attacks in 2015, has recovered strongly," according to the *New York Times*. In fact, Atout France-France Tourism Development Agency, reported in the spring of 2017, that that year "seemed very promising concerning American travel to France. Bookings for the first three months of 2017, compared to the same period in 2016, were 20 percent higher. Good news!" After all, "we'll always have Paris," as noted in the famous film, *Casablanca*. But the "good news" often does not last long. Three days before the first round of elections in 2017, a terrorist shot and killed a policeman on the Champs-Elysées. And yet the resilience of the French people came to the foreground and the first round of the election was held and two candidates, Marine Le Pen and Emmanuel Macron would face off two weeks later. Macron won.

But to continue our review of Liberal synagogues in Paris:

Movement Juif Liberal de France, 11, rue Gaston de Cailavet, 75015, Paris. Tel 33-1-44-37-48-48 or FAX: 33-1- 44-37-48-50. secretariat@rnjlf. org. www.rnjlf.org. Spiritual leaders are Rabbi Daniel Farhi and Pauline Bebe. Services at 6:15 p.m. on Friday evenings and 10:30 a.m. Saturday mornings. Telephone first for directions. (Metro: Charles Michels).

Kehilat Gesher, The French-American Congregation in Paris. 7 rue Leon Cogniet. 75017, Paris. Tel: 01-39-21-97-19. FAX: 1-44-37-48-50. contact@kehilatgesher.org. www.kehilatgesher.org.

MJLF-East, 24 rue Surmelin.75020, Paris. Tel: 33-1-40-30-18-60. secretariat@mjlf.org.www.mjlf.org.

Alliance pour Judaïsme Traditional et Moderne, 45 rue Pelleport, 75020, Paris. Tel: 6-07-18-37-87. administrateur@ajtmonline.fr. www. ajtmonline.fr.

CJL-Communaute Juive Liberale Ile de France, 10-14 rue de Moufle, 75011, Paris. Tel: 1-42-93-03-44. Contact@cjl-paris.org. www. cjl-paris.org.

Assembly of Masorti Synagogues

Adath Shalom, 8 rue George Bernard Shaw, 75015 Paris. Tel.: 45-67-9796. FAX: 45-56-89-79. RUZIEDR@aol.com. Services are held here at 6:30 p.m. Friday nights and Saturday mornings at 10:00 a.m.

Dor Vadora. 10, rue du Cambodge 75020 Paris Tel: 33-1-73-71-34-18. massorti@wanaddo.fr. www.dorvador.org.

Masorti Olami, Mercaz France, 40 Ave. de Suffren, Paris 40 Ave. de Suffren, Paris.

OFFICIALS AND ORGANIZATIONS

Rabbi Haïm Korsia serves as chief rabbi of France. His office is at 19, rue St-Georges, 75009, Paris. Tel: 49-70-88-00. FAX: 42-81-03-66. **Rabbi Michel Gugenheim** is the grand rabbi of Paris. His office is located in Consistoire de Paris, 17, rue St-Georges, 75009, Paris. Tel: 33-1-40-82-26-26. FAX: 33-1-42-81-92-46. contact@consistoire.org.

Note: For American travelers, questions regarding synagogue services, religious matters, and tickets for high holidays should be directed to Consistoire Central, 19, rue St-Georges, 75009, Paris. Tel: 33-1- 49-70-88-00. FAX: 33-1- 42-81-03-66. administration@consistoirecentral.fr. Many officials here also speak English and Hebrew. Contact: Frederic Attali, executive director, Leon Masliah, honorary executive director.

Paris is the center of Jewish activities in France, as all major institutions have their headquarters there.

Conseil Representatif des Institutions Juives de France, (CRIF), 39, rue Broca, 75005, Paris. Tel: 33-1 42-17-11-11. FAX: 42-17-11-13. Info@crif.org. www.crif.org. CRIF, the representative council of Jewish organizations, was founded in 1944 to protect the rights of Jews in the Republic. Today, more than 35 groups belong to CRIF, which speaks and acts on behalf of the organized Jewish community in representations to the government.

The president of CRIF is Francis Kalifat who was elected to the post in 2016. Three vice-presidents are Yonathan Arfi, Gil Taleb, and Gerard Unger.

CRIF deals with the threats of radical Islamic terrorism, right-wing extremism, and anti-Israeli manifestations, as dangers to the Jews of France. The organization works closely with all French public authorities to share with them their concerns, feelings and analysis, according to Mr. Arfi.

One concern is the attitude of France toward Israel. CRIF faces a strong pro-Palestinian bias among the French diplomatic administration (Quai d'Orsay), which is often much tougher toward Israel than the French politicians.

"Over the last years, we had to deplore many French votes in the UN or UNESCO even if Nicolas Sarkozy and Francois Hollande . . . are good friends of Israel," added Mr. Arfi.

On the political front, Arfi believes that "we in France live in the most unstable political period France has experienced for decades." Many would agree.

Cnaan Lipshiz echoed Arfi when he wrote in a JTA dispatch:

In 2016, "French citizens have endured a dramatic campaign season amid growing nationalism, Islamist terrorism, financial stagnation, and deepening resentment of a political establishment that is widely perceived as corrupt or incompetent."

Right-wing parties are on the rise in Europe, especially in France. There, right-wing parties have traditionally been too toxic for a majority of the French to embrace. That is, until now. With Marine Le Pen heading the National Front, which has taken advantage of the political uncertainty that has swept Europe, such as the Brexit vote in the UK, the massive wave of immigration from the Middle East, as well as life-taking terrorist attacks, she was in a position to sway French voters in 2017.

Marine Le Pen remains a danger for Jews. CRIF and most Jews shun this leader of the far-right National Front. Le Pen was expected to do well in the April 2017 presidential election in France. She was sure to win a place in the first round, but again sure to lose in the run-off in May, 2017, said the pundits. She was defeated in the final May election. Emmanuel Macron became the new president of France.

In the second round French voters put aside their differences and voted in the "republican candidate." Her policy of trying to push through Brexit-style referendum on France's membership in the European Union, her demands to slash immigration and hand out jobs, welfare housing, and school provision to French nationals before foreigners, were all buried for now.

Her defeat, like that of a right-wing candidate in Holland in 2017, was a loss for the populist and extreme right movement that was spreading throughout Europe.

This woman who wanted to lead France also backed legislation that would ban religious clothing in public. That would include banning Jews from wearing a *kippa* (skull cap) in public. She was also opposed to ritual kosher slaughter.

Marine Le Pen is the daughter of Jean-Marie Le Pen, "a Holocaust revisionist and openly anti-Semitic nationalist," according to the *Times of Israel*, April 24, 2017.

However, it must be noted that Marine Le Pen kicked out her father from the party in 2015 following his conviction for inciting racial hatred against Jews. He suggested a Jewish singer critical of the party be "put in the oven," the *Times of Israel* added.

Just before the first round of elections, however, she said France was not responsible for its authorities' rounding up of Jews for the Nazis, the *Times of Israel* reported.

"Le Pen who has been leading a staunchly anti-Islamic line, has compared public Muslim prayers in France to the country's occupation by Nazi Germany during the Second World War," according to the *Times of Israel*, February 3, 2017.

"After the people of Friday, come the people of Saturday," warned Shimon Samuels, the director for international relations of the Wiesenthal Center, Europe, Latin America, Middle East, and Europe. Samuels is correct: For now, far-right groups appear to be focusing their attacks on migrants who have reached the continent in large numbers. **The Simon Wiesenthal Center Europe**, Paris, Tel: 33-1-47-23-76-37. csweurope@gmail.com. www.wiesenthal-europe.com. The European office of the Simon Wiesenthal Center is headquartered in Paris, France. Shimon Samuels serves as director. He and the center actively promote and support the Center's mission in Europe by combating anti-Semitism, Holocaust denial, extremism, and neo-Nazi activity. The European office brings these issues to the attention of government leaders, members of the media and communities throughout Europe.

"Today," says Samuels, "across the face of Europe, the Old World is revising the most ancient disease: anti-Semitism. Describing anti-Semitism on the continent, Samuels cites "the Islamization of Western Europe." "The danger for Jews is the growing polarization of the extreme right and the extreme left," he declares, a message that is heard from Jewish leaders throughout Europe.

Consistoire Central, Union des Communautés Juives de France, 19, rue St-Georges, 75009, Paris. Tel: 1-49-77-88-00. FAX: 1-42-81-03-66. The Consistoire is a major force in French Jewish organizational life. The building contains an assembly hall for lectures and ceremonies and special offices. **Frederic Attali** is director of the Consistoire. **Leon Masliah** is honorary executive director.

Fond Social Juif Unifie (FSJU), 39 rue Broca, 75005, Paris. Tel: 1-42-17-10-10. FAX: 1-42-17-10-45. contact.info@fsju.org www.fsju.org. The words on the banner at the entrance of this important institution tell the story of the goals of the revitalized Jewish community of France:

For a strong community

To help Israel.

For your active participation in Jewish life.

These words define the goals of the Fonds Social Juif Unifie, translated as the United Jewish Social Fund, similar to a federation and welfare fund in the United States.

The FSJU coordinates, supervises, and plans major social, educational, and cultural activities and enterprises of the French Jewish community. This building also houses the offices of L'Appel Unifie Juif de France (the French UJA) and the Conseil Representatif des Institutions Juives de France (CRIF), which is a council of Jewish organizations.

The "Appel" has introduced American fund-raising techniques in soliciting funds.

Chabad is very active and maintains numerous centers in France, as well as many synagogues. There are about 375 Chabad rabbis in France, of which 120 are in Paris. That translates to several rabbis in every major city of the Republic. The main **Synagogue and Center** is located at **Beth Loubavitch**, 8, rue Lamartine, 75009, Paris. Tel: 45-26-87-60. Orthodox Shabbat service is at 10:30 a.m. on Saturdays. Call for a list of group activities and services. You will be welcome. For security purposes, please contact Chabad well in advance of an upcoming visit.

In addition to the above organizations, there are hundreds of distinguished groups, international and local, which are active. A partial list includes the World Jewish Congress, ORT, B'nai B'rith, a number of Sephardic and Zionist groups, the American Jewish Joint Distribution Committee, the Jewish Agency for Israel, the Weizmann Institute, the France-Israel Alliance, and WIZO (Women's International Zionist Organization).

The American Jewish Joint Distribution Committee does not maintain an office in France. Its work in France today is by invitation of the community and is focused on building resilience and strengthening the Jewish community in the face of challenges today and tomorrow. That includes the establishment of a resilience center offering post trauma and psychosocial support; trainings on volunteerism, community development best practices, and fundraising; as well as the inclusion of young French Jews in JDC's pan-European leadership training and volunteer programs.

Maguen David Adom France, 40, rue de Liege, 75008, Paris. Tel: 01-43-87-49-02. FAX: 01-45-22-56-28. contact@101@mda-france.org. www.mda-france.org.

B'nai B'rith, France, 5, rue Moll, 75017, Paris. Tel: 01-55-07-85-45. FAX: 01-42-82-70-65. www.bbfrance.org

Embassy of Israel, 3, rue Rebelais, 75008 Paris. Tel:33-1-40-76-55-00. FAX: 33-1- 40-76-55-55. info@amb-Israel.fr. www.paris.mfa.gov.il

Hadassah France, 6 rue Legraverend, 75012 Paris. Tel: 1-53-42-67-06.

Jewish Agency, 140 Blvd. Malesherbes, 75017, Paris. Tel: 1-44-15-23-01,

O.R.T., 24 rue Erlanger, 75016, Paris. Tel: -1-44-17-30-80. FAX: 1-45-01-80-21. ortfrance@ort.asso.fr.

WIZO, 10 rue Saint –Augustin, Paris. Tel:1-48-01-97-70. FAX: 48-01-97-77

European Jewish Congress. wweurojewcong.org

Jewish Community Activity Centers

Centre Bernard Lazare, 10, rue Saint-Claude, 75003, Paris.

Centre Communautaire de Paris, 119, rue La Fayette, 75009, Paris. Tel: 53-20-52-52. FAX: 53-20-52-50. Located here are many activities, such as sports, lectures, theater programs, and an *ulpan* to study Hebrew. A kosher cafeteria serves lunch from noon to 2:00 p.m. and dinner from 6:00 to 8:00 p.m. There are services on Friday nights and at 8:45 a.m. on Saturdays.

Centre Edmond Fleg, 8 bis, rue de l'Eperon, 75006, Paris. Tel: 1-55-42-16-40. contact@flegparis.com. www.flegparis.com. This is a university student center, sponsored by the Consistoire de Paris and named after a French Jewish writer. Young visitors should inquire about activities. A cafeteria serves hot kosher lunches.

Centre Israel Jeffroykin, 68, rue de la Flie Maricourt, 75011, Paris. Located near the Bastille. (Metro: Oberkampf).

Centre Rachi, 39 rue Broca, 75005, Paris. Tel: 43-31-98-20 or 43-31-75-47. Open from 9:00 a.m. to 11:00 p.m. A good spot, especially for university students and adults interested in intellectual activities. Seminars, lectures, and films. A kosher cafeteria and circular coffee bar make it a fine gathering place. Services are at 8:00 p.m. Friday night and 8:00 a.m. Saturday morning in the summer; 4:30 p.m. Friday and 9:00 a.m. Saturday in the winter.

Centre Rambam, 19-21, rue Galvani, 75017, Paris. Tel: 45-74-52-80 or 45-74-51-81. Located in a growing Jewish neighborhood, this Sephardic center contains a beautiful Moroccan-style synagogue, library, meeting rooms, reception, and catering area. Sabbath services. Centre Rambam is a good site to reflect upon the impact of the arrival in the 1960s of Sephardim to France.

During the forty years since their departure from North Africa, Sephardic Jews from Morocco have established this Sephardic center in Paris. The center, which was named Rambam, hosts study groups devoted to Spanish Jewish traditions as well as organizes lectures. Rambam is the acronym of Rabbi Moses ben Maimon (1135-1204), or as he is more widely known, Maimonides, one of the most illustrious figures of the post-Talmudic era.

The massive flux in the 1950s and 1960s of Sephardic Jews from North Africa to France was one of the most exciting movements of immigration in contemporary European history. Nearly 300,000 Sephardic Jews came to France in the early 1960s. They revitalized and revolutionized French Jewry to such an extent that some have called the present community the Second French Jewry.

The Sephardim brought activity and momentum, an infusion of new blood. They set up community institutions, synagogues, and Talmud Torahs. They were proud of their Jewishness.

Although half settled in and around Paris, many moved into towns such as Avignon, Arles, Aix-en-Provence-towns that had heretofore contained few Jews. This was one of the few times in Jewish history when the Jewish community changed from Ashkenazic to Sephardic. Not only was their arrival welcome, their integration into Jewish and French society was also very successful. They launched themselves into key positions in French government, education, art, and science.

But after five several decades of first adjusting, striving and reaching the stage of enjoying living in France, came the scourge of Islamic terrorism and the rise of anti-Semitism. No wonder one easily calls to mind the increase of *aliyah* to Israel. Naturally, fear regarding anti-Semitism and terrorism are a motivating factor for immigrating to Israel. However, that might not be the whole story. There are those who believe that since the European economies are hurting, there is more opportunity in Israel, especially in high-tech industries. And rising immigration to Israel from Western Europe, especially France, Belgium, and Italy remains largely unaffected by the security situation in the Jewish state, according to the London-based Institute for Jewish Policy Research. *Aliyah* from France to Israel was approximately 2,000 newcomers annually until a few years after 2010. But then it increased dramatically during and after 2013 when more than 3,000 Jews arrived in Israel. The following year, 2014, 7,238 went to Israel and in 2015, 7,900 arrived in the Jewish state, followed by another 5,000 in 2016.

In an article for JTA, January 5, 2016, Cnaan Liphshiz writes that "while violence against Jews is often identified as the major drive of French *aliyah*, many immigrants cite a broader mix of reasons for choosing to leave, including Zionist sentiment and alienation from an adamantly secularist society increasingly intolerant of the religiously devout."

Shimon Samuels notes that a new phenomenon that has come to the surface in the last several years is that many French Jews commute to work on Sunday to Israel and return to Paris on Thursday night, a four-hour flight. And the reverse, many French Jews live in Israel and work in Paris. Yet, there is the group that maintains concerns about the Israeli job market and their place in it. Apparently, a significant amount of French Jewish emigrants chose countries, like Canada and even the UK, for instance, over Israel for this reason.

So while there is *aliyah*, it must be kept in mind by travelers or armchair travelers that the vast majority of European Jews, including France, Belgium and Italy are staying put; it certainly is not an "exodus." "If 100,000 Jews leave, France will no longer be France. The French Republc will be judged a failure," the Prime Minister of France, Manuel Valls, told *The Atlantic Magazine.* January 10, 2015.

So tourists who will not let terrorism defeat them in their pursuit of travel, will feel welcome and at home with their brothers and sisters in France and indeed in other countries of Europe.

Rabbinical School of Paris, 9, rue Vauquelin, 75005, Paris. Tel: 47-07-21-22. FAX: 43-37-75-92 American students may want to contact this Orthodox, rabbinic seminary for a schedule of activities, classes, and religious services. A synagogue is located here as well.

MUSEUMS

The Jewish artists Soutine, Pascin, Chagall, Pissarro, Modigliani, Mane-Katz, Benn, and Lipchitz worked and created masterpieces in France. Many of their works are exhibited in various Parisian museums.

Centre National d'Art et de Culture Georges Pompidou, better known as Beaubourg, on rue Beaubourg, 75004, Paris. Tel: 01-44-78-12-33. www.centrepompidou.fr. **The Centre National d'Art et de Culture Georges Pompidou** was refurbished in the late 1990s. Repairs were needed as attendance at this museum far outstrips other popular institutions. In its first 20 years, Beaubourg served over 160 million visitors and is far more popular than the Versailles Palace and the Louvre Museum. Paintings by Jewish artists, such as Chagall, Soutine, and Modigliani. Hebrew and Yiddish language lessons available on taped cassettes. Numerous books on Jewish history, Judaica, Israel, and Jewish literature. The Pompidou Centre, which is visited by about 25,000 persons daily, is not far from the Pletzel in the Marais section.

Musee d'Art et d'Historoie du Judaïsme, Hotel de Saint-Aignan, 71 rue du Temple, 75003, Paris, Tel: 1-53-0186-60, FAX: 01-42-72-97-47; info@mahj.org. www.mahj.org. A half-century in the making; the Jewish Museum has moved from its perch high above Montmartre to the wonderful **Hotel de Saint-Aignan**, 17 rue due Temple. Located near the Pompidou Centre, the Metro stop is Rambuteau, Hotel de Ville. Hours are Monday to Friday: 11:00 a.m. to 6:00 p.m.; Sunday, 10:00 a.m. to 6:00 p.m. **The Museum of Jewish Art and History** is housed in one of Paris' most palatial mansions in the historic Marais quarter, for many years considered the Jewish quarter. The museum traces the historical evolution of Jewish communities from the Middle Ages to the 20th Century through their cultural and artistic heritage. Although the focus is on the history of the Jews in France, Jewish communities in Europe and North Africa are also represented. Here one will see religious items, textiles, manuscripts, and documents depicting Jewish history, including the archives of the Dreyfus Affair. Some of the artists represented here are Chagall, Modigliani, Soutine, Kikoine and other Jewish painters.

Built in 1650, the Hotel de Saint-Aignan first served as the home of

In the courtyard of the Museum of Jewish Art and History stands a statue of Capt. Alfred Dreyfus, framed and unjustly court-martialed in 1894. He was later pardoned. (Photo by Larry Colby photography)

Comte d'Avaux, Mazarin's superintendent of finance. The Duc de Saint-Aignan bought the house in 1688. During the Revolution, the mansion became the town hall of Paris's 7th district. After 1842, it housed workshops, with Jewish craftsmen moving in at the end of the century. In 1962, the Hotel de Saint-Aignan was bought by the City of Paris who made it available to the Museum of Jewish Art and History. The mansion's restoration and conversion into a museum were financed by the Ministry of Culture and Communication and the City of Paris.

Exhibitions of photography, graphic arts highlight the presentations of the Museum. Cultural events occur here, too. One can see that no expense was spared in setting up the museum

Library of the Alliance Israelite Universelle, 45, rue la Bruyere, 75009, Paris. Tel: 1-53-32-88-55. More than 100,000 books of Judaic interest, including manuscripts. Permission to visit needed.

Musée Carnavalet, 16, rue des Frances Bourgeois, 75003, Paris. Tel: 42-72-21-13. www.carnavalet.paris.fr. Open 10:00 a.m. to 5:40 p.m. every day except Monday. (Closed for repairs until the end of 2019.)

The aim of the museum is to illustrate the history of Paris from its origins to the present day. The building and mansion display a number of personal souvenirs and artifacts of Rachel, one of France's most famous Jewish actresses.

The building houses the Museum of the History of Paris, which covers the sixteenth to the nineteenth centuries. The museum has branched out into a new addition next door, the Hotel le Peletier-St. Fargeau, which includes the bedroom of the famous Jewish writer Marcel Proust. Open 10:00 a.m. to 5:40 p.m. every day except Monday.

A wonderful exhibit entitled "The French Revolution" enhances this inspiring structure and is well worth seeing. At the time of the French Revolution, about five hundred Jews resided in Paris. Many had bribed the chief of police for permission to settle there. Looking back to the days of the French Revolution, we learn that the Jews of that time were indebted to liberal Count Mirabeau and a liberal Catholic cleric named Abbe Gregoire, who supported Jewish equality. The Declaration of Human Rights was passed in the summer of 1789. The Jewish question did not come up for debate until December 24, 1789. The revolutionary Count Mirabeau simply did not possess the votes. The matter was tabled until the next month. On January 28, 1790, Talleyrand brought in a report by the Committee of the Constitution in favor of "equality."

On that day, however, only the Sephardic Jews, those "who were known in France by the names of the Portuguese, Spanish, and Avignon-nais Jews," would henceforth enjoy the rights of active citizens. Twenty months would pass until equal rights were given to the Ashkenazic Jews. On September 27, 1791, after much debate and many delays, the Ashke-nazim who lived in Alsace and the surrounding area were emancipated.

Regarding the impact of the French Revolution on the Jews, "for the first time in the modern history of the West, all the Jews within the borders of a European state were united with all its other citizens, as equals before the law," writes Arthur Hertzberg in *The French Enlightenment and the Jews*. A new era in Jewish history was born.

Robespierre himself was one of the first to demand citizenship for the Jews. True, some synagogues were closed during the Revolution because of the anti-religious policy, which the Jacobins directed against the powerful Catholic Church. But the Jacobins fought against all religious symbols. Although there was anti-Jewish discrimination, neither during the Reign of Terror nor during the Thermidor was a Jew executed solely because he was a Jew.

Soza Szajkowski, author of *Jews and the French Revolution of 1789, 1830, 1848*, says that "the vast majority of Jews did favor the new regime, but because of their diverse economic and regional attachments, Jews were active in all factions of the Revolutionary regime."

A Jewish Jacobin Club sprung up in the "Jewish suburb" of St-Esprit in Bayonne. A synagogue still stands in that very section—at 35, rue Maubec in Bayonne.

The armies of the Revolution and, later, of Napoleon himself carried the banner and, more important, put into practice "Liberty, Equality and Fraternity." For Jews, the cry meant freedom. Napoleon was the liberator of the Jews of Europe.

While on the one hand the French gave Jews human rights, virulent anti-Semitism existed in the philosophical writings of such Frenchmen as Voltaire and Diderot. While the Enlightenment helped the Jews, these French thinkers were widely read and their anti-Semitic writings would in the end harm the Jewish people.

Still, the Republic attracted Jews from all over the world. Because of the country's liberal immigration policy, Jews from Eastern Europe poured into France. In the nineteenth century, this flow would increase. One outcome of the Revolution of course was the Sanhedrin. In 1806, Napoleon convoked a Grand Sanhedrin which codified religious decisions. It met in 1807. Napoleon was determined to provide the Jews of France with a central organization supervised by the State and loyal to the government. He followed the example of the arrangements he had already introduced for other religions.

The emperor possessed an ulterior motive. He wanted Jews assimilated. He felt their emancipation had not produced the anticipated results. Jews, he said, were really a nation within a nation. But because of its group nature, the Sanhedrin was distorted by anti-Semites as an international conspiracy plotting ritual murder.

The Consistoire Central in France was established on July 17, 1808, along with the institution of the chief rabbinate. Following the Revolution of July 1830, the French government proposed that the Jewish religion have equal status with the Catholic Church and Protestantism. One year later it was done.

Musée Cluny, 6, Place Paul-Painleve, 75005, Paris. Tel: 43-25-62-00. Contains furniture, Jewish engagement rings, sculpture, and fragments representing kings of Judea. Displayed here are the famous Strauss-Rothschild collections of Jewish ritual objects.

Musée du Louvre, rue de Rivoli, 75001, Paris. Tel: 42-60-39-26. www.louvre.fr. Every day in Paris, thousands of tourists from around the world enter the **Musée du Louvre** by way of an enormous glass pyramid. Standing 70 feet high and constructed from 200 tons of glass and steel, **La Pyramide du Louvre** welcomes more than five million tourists each year. The pyramid was designed by American architect I.M. Pei and is located in the center of the Napoleon Courtyard. On March 30, 2000, the pyramid celebrated its 10th anniversary. The entrance designed by I. M. Pei and Partners leads from ground level down to the welcoming area. From below ground level, one proceeds to various pavilions, such as the Sully, Danton, or Richelieu Pavilions, or to the museum's cafeteria or bookstore. The Palais du Louvre contains many Jewish archeological items and antiques from Israel, such as a terra-cotta ossuary discovered in a funeral cave in Azor near Tel Aviv. The museum itself contains about six thousand paintings. In 1993, part of the collection was housed in the Richelieu Pavilion in the rue de Rivoli. This pavilion had been used for offices by the

French Ministry of Finance. Open Thursday, Friday, Saturday, and Sunday, 9:00 a.m. to 6:00 p.m.; Monday and Wednesday, 9:00 a.m. to 9:40 p.m. (Closed Tuesday). The Pyramid is open every day except Tuesday. (Metro: Palais Royal Musée du Louvre).

Musée d'Orsay, 62, rue de Bellechasse, 75007, Paris. Tel: 45-49-48-14. A former belle époque railroad station was renovated in 1986 to become a modern museum of nineteenth-century art, including the works of two well-known French Jewish artists, Pissarro and Modigliani. Contains impressionist paintings by Manet, Monet, Van Gogh, Degas, Sisley, Renoir, Cezanne, Seurat, Signac, and Gauguin. Open daily from 10:00 a.m. to 6:00 p.m. and until 9:45 p.m. on Thursday. Closed Monday.

Bibliothèque Nationale (The National Library), 58, rue de Richelieu, 75009, Paris. Tel: 47-03-81-26. Magnificent Hebrew manuscripts, Dead Sea Scroll fragments, Bibles, Haggadoth, ketubot. More than 30,000 volumes are in the Hebraic section. A regular exchange with Israel has ensured the acquisition of all books published there since 1953. One must write for permission to see the manuscripts or use the library.

Musée National Picasso Paris. Hôtel Salé, 5 rue de Thorigny. Paris. Tel: 01-42-71-25.21. www.museepicasso.fr. From Tuesday to Friday, 10:30 a.m. to 6:00 p.m.; Saturday and Sunday, 9:30 a.m. to 6:00 p.m. and public holidays, 9:30 a.m. to 6:00 p.m. Closed Mondays and December 25th, January 1st, and May 1st. During public holidays, 9:30 a.m. to 6:00 p.m. This 17th century palace contains the largest collection of Picassos in the world.

Fondation Louis Vuitton. This museum supports French and international contemporary artistic creation. Frank Gehry designed the building. Louis Vuitton firm has been plagued by rumors of posting signs that said "Jews Need Not Apply." Writing in the *New York Times*, on February 25, 1988, Ari Goldman noted: "In 1974, the Anti-Defamation League of B'nai B'rith investigated and found the rumor groundless."

MEMORIAL SITES

Memorial in Le Drancy, Ave. Jean-Jaures, Le Drancy. Drancy is a town three miles from Paris, a short express ride on the RER train (suburban express subway). Located here is one of the most befitting memorials to the six million Jews who were murdered by the Nazis and to those Jews deported from France, often with the help of the collaborationist Vichy government. Drancy was the site of an internment camp that supplied the concentration camps with inmates.

More than 12,000 Jews were held in this transit camp before being transferred to their death in the East. Drancy was "the ante-room of Auschwitz," say French Jews.

Established in 1940, it was an unfinished housing project with apartment buildings on three sides of a rectangular court. Jews were quartered in the large, grim buildings that still stand today as part of a municipal housing project. The outdoor monument in the form of a statue was dedicated in 1976. It bears a quotation from Lamentations 1:12: "Behold, and see if there be any pain like unto my pain." Just behind the monument is an old railroad boxcar once used in the deportation process. Inside the railroad car is a pictorial exhibit showing the roundups of Jews, their boarding the railroad cars, and their crowded quarters in camps.

The monument is dedicated to the martyrs, victims of the barbaric Nazis. One poster reads, "Never Again a Camp at Drancy. Never Again Auschwitz."

The town of Drancy itself was a stronghold of the Resistance.

The key to the railroad car exhibit must be obtained in advance from the town hall, except on Saturday. However, travelers can visit the railroad boxcar from 2:00 p.m. to 4:00 p.m. every Saturday, except when Saturday falls on a bank holiday. On other days, one may be able to obtain the key from the Cultural Department of the Mayor's Office located in the town hall at Place Maurice Thorez, 93700, Le Drancy. Take the RER at Gare du Nord. At Drancy station, take bus number 148, direction Pantin, to the memorial. If it is not Saturday, ask to get off at City Hall to obtain the key to the boxcar. Tip: Arrangements should be made in advance.

If the collapse of France and the ultimate establishment of the Fascist state of Vichy under Pétain and Laval were painful to France, they were far more tragic for Jews. And yet over 70 years after the war, France is coming to grips with the collaborationist Vichy regime role in deporting some 76,000 Jews. In 1994, at least one Frenchman, Paul Touvier, who was then 79, was brought to trial for crimes against humanity during the war—the first Frenchman brought to trial for crimes against humanity. He served in a pro-Nazi militia during the German occupation of France. Touvier was a key aide during World War II to Gestapo chief Klaus Barbie, who was tried in 1987 for war crimes and sentenced to life imprisonment. Barbie died in 1991.

Touvier picked at random seven Jewish prisoners and lined them up in front of the cemetery wall at Rillieux-la-Pape, outside of Lyon. They were shot by a firing squad. In April 1994, a French court convicted him of the charge of crimes against humanity and he was sentenced to life imprisonment. Writing in the *New York Times*, on April 20, 1994, Alan Riding stated, "The trial assumed special significance because it was the first time a French court had examined any aspect of French persecution of Jews when the country was under German occupation between 1940 and 1944." Touvier died in a prison hospital in July 1996. He was 81.

Another Vichy aide accused of war crimes, Rene Bousquet, had been shot dead by a lone gunman at his home in Paris in 1993, thus precluding a long-promised public trial.

Also accused of complicity in crimes against humanity was Maurice Papon, a former high-ranking French official. Condemned on April 2, 1998, to 10 years of criminal detention, he had been found guilty on two counts of having helped organize the arrest and the deportation of Jewish men, women and children from Bordeaux where he was a young official of the Vichy regime between 1942 and 1944. Papon rose to be the powerful head of the Paris police, a member of parliament and then finance minister under President Giscard d'Estaing (1978-81). His career was halted when a newspaper alleged he was behind the deportation of more than 1,500 Jews while administering the southwestern province of Gironde whose center was Bordeaux. At liberty pending an appeal, Papon appeared in the news in October, 1999 when it was discovered he had fled to Switzerland. He was returned to France and convicted of crimes against humanity. He was subsequently released from prison in 2002 on the grounds of ill health. He died in 2007.

To this day, the memory of Vichy remains a stain on the nation. All the trials force the French more and more to assign responsibility to Vichy France for its "complicity" with the Nazis in the deportation of Jews from France, a fact that many in France have known but have preferred to remain silent about. As Susan Zuccotti has shown in her book, *The Holocaust, the French, and the Jews*, Vichy was overtly and actively chauvinistic and anti-Semitic.

Some believe that President Charles de Gaulle may have inflated the role of the Resistance in liberating France in 1944 in order to expunge the memory of Vichy. In his memoirs, he called Vichy null and void. He argued that "real France" had not capitulated to Germany.

In the Holocaust, about 250,000 Jews, or two thirds of the community, survived, while 76,000 were sent to the death camps. At first, Vichy, which was subservient to Germany, turned over only foreign Jews to the Nazis. Later, when the Germans seized all of France, Jews—French-born or not—were seized. Still, of the approximately 75,000 Jews deported to the concentration camps, only 15,000 were of French descent. The remaining 60,000 were either naturalized or immigrants. If we include all the other Jews who found themselves on French soil when the Armistice was declared, we find that 10 percent of French Jews died. This contrasts with the death of 40 percent of immigrant or recently arrived Jews. France lost about 25 percent of her Jews, including foreigners, in comparison to 55 percent for Belgium and 86 percent for Holland. French Jews played an outstanding role in the Resistance. Some say that one-quarter of the Resistance was Jewish. The **Association of Conservatoire Camp de Drancy**, reminds men and women everywhere of the camp, which was liberated on August 17, 1944. One of the apartments has been made over into a flat just as it was during the war. For further information on the former camp and the model apartment, contact the **Association du Conservatoire Camp de Drancy**, Cite de la Muette, 15, rue Arthur Fontaine, 93700 Le Drancy. Tel: 1-48-95-35-05. FAX: 01-48-95-97-82. chcd@tiscali.fr. A **synagogue** in Drancy is located at 15, Blvd. St. Simon, 93700, Drancy. **Memorial de la Shoah**, 17, rue Geoffroy l'Asnier, 75004, Paris. Tel: 42-77-44-72. FAX: 01-53-01-86-53. contact@memorialdelashoah. com, www.memorialdelashoah.org. The Holocaust Museum in Paris. (Metro: Pont-Marie or Saint-Paul.) This four-story memorial is one of the most moving Jewish sites in Paris and a tribute to the six million Jews who perished in the Holocaust. The museum displays documents and photographs of Nazi camps and prisons and contains material devoted to the Archives of the Centre Documentation Juive Contemporaine. Before one enters the building, however, one passes through a massive courtyard that actually is the roof of an underground crypt. In the street-level courtyard is a large bronze cylinder shaped in the form of a burial urn. On it are engraved the names of some of the notorious concentration camps and the Warsaw Ghetto. Below the courtyard-two flights down-is a tomb of black marble in the form of a Star of David. An "eternal flame" flickers at its center. Erected in 1956, the memorial building contains archives, books, and a library reading room.

The museum is open every day except Saturday: from 10:00 a.m. to 6:00 p.m. Thursday until 10:00 p.m. The multimedia learning center and the reading rooms are open every day except Saturday: from 10:00 a.m. to 5:30 p.m., Thursday until 7:30 p.m.

Regarding the Holocaust, mention also should be made of Varian Fry who went to France as the agent of the American Emergency Rescue Committee. He rescued not only the two hundred persons he had been sent to save, but nearly two thousand more in France. According to Andy Marina in *A Quiet American: The Secret War of Varian Fry*, Fry smuggled out of France such noted professionals and personalities as Hannah Arendt, Franz Werfel, Heinrich Mann, Walter Gropius, Marc Chagall, Lion Feuchtwanger, and Enrico Fermi.

Memorial to the Deported is located in a garden behind Notre Dame on the tip of the Ile de la Cité, not far from the Pletzel. This memorial is dedicated to the 200,000 French men and women of all races and religions who died in the Nazi death camps during World War II.

Vél' d'Hiv, located at 8, boulevard Grennelle, Paris, 15th Arrondissement (Metro: Bir Hakeim). A plaque on this monument commemorates the imprisonment of Jews rounded up by the French police and placed in the Vélodrome d'Hiver Stadium on July 16, 1942. This was a huge indoor sports arena for winter bicycle races, eventually torn down in 1989. When a large-scale manhunt was conducted in Paris on July 16, 1942, about 13,000 Jews, including 4,000 children, were arrested and corralled at the sports facility. "The operation was poetically christened 'Spring Wind' by the French Police, who executed the German orders with almost excessive zeal," writes Annie Cohen-Solal in *Sartre: A Life*. Later they were moved to Drancy, a gathering camp, and sent to Auschwitz. More Jews were rounded up during the summer. The July and August transports included 25,000 French Jews. In the Holocaust, some 75,000 Jews were deported from France to death camps, and only 3,000 of those survived. A square located at the intersection of quai de Grenelle and boulevard de Grenelle, near the former stadium, has been named "Place des Martyrs Juifs du Vélodrome d'Hiver" (Square of Jewish Martyrs of the Winter Velodrome).

The late, former President Francois Mitterrand proposed that bygones be allowed to be bygones regarding France's past. But by this time, Mitterrand had himself been badly compromised by revelations

Memorial to the Jewish Martyrs rounded up by the French police in July, 1942 and held in the Velodrome D'Hiver, Paris. (Photo by Dr. Joshua Fogelman)

that during World War II, he did a stint with the Vichy regime, before joining the Resistance.

On July 16, 1995, French President Jacques Chirac's admission of national guilt for deporting Jews to Nazi death camps during World War II was received as a "significant historical step," and Jewish leaders throughout the world praised the French President's commentary on Vel d'Hiv. Chirac said in his speech, "Fifty-three years ago, 450 French police officers, acting under the authority of their chiefs, complied with the Nazis' demands." He added, "the criminal insanity of the occupier was assisted by the French people, by the French state." Until then, no French leader had acknowledged the state's role in collaborating with the Germans in deporting Jews.

In 2012, President Francois Hollande addressed France at the sight of Vel d'Hiv roundup. He recognized that the event was a crime committed "in France by France."

OTHER SITES

Hotel de Castille, 37, rue Cambon. This is the building in which Theodor Herzl, the father of modern Zionism, wrote his famous tract, The Jewish State. The spark was the trial of Capt. Alfred Dreyfus. Nearly 100 years after emancipation, the Jews of the Republic and the world were shocked by the Dreyfus Affair. For most of the nineteenth century, anti-Semitism had been a weapon in the hands of the royalists, the clergy, and the military. These forces also opposed successive Republican governments. The battle lines were being drawn. Usually, the conservative anti-Republican forces disliked the Jews.

Incidentally, research shows that the Hotel Castille itself was once part of the Ritz. The Hemingway Bar is directly across from the hotel building which counts107 rooms. Located in the fashion district, the hotel's neighboring streets include the rue de la Paix and the Faubourg St. Honoré. Electrifying to shoppers and costly, too, are the shops on this street. Chanel is next door to the hotel. The legendary **Place Vendome**, **Louvre** and the **Palais Royal** are nearby as are **Hermes**, 24 rue Faubourg St. Honoré and **Lancel** is at 8 place de l'Opera.

Statue of Capt. Alfred Dreyfus, on the boulevard Raspail in a small park near the intersection with Notre Dame de Champs. Captain Dreyfus, a Jew, was a member of the general staff of the French Army. The victim of a forgery, he was framed and unjustly court-martialed in a secret trial in 1894. There were many reasons to go after Dreyfus: "he was rich, he was snobbish and he was a Jew."

The charges, the trial, and the resultant riots tore France asunder. They unleashed a wave of anti-Semitism. Every family was affected.

The French were split down the middle; you were either for, or against, Dreyfus. A crisis of conscience had penetrated France and the repercussions caused an upheaval in political life that translated into serious consequences for Jewish life. Shock waves rocked Europe. Found guilty of treason, Dreyfus was relegated to Devil's Island, where he spent almost five years. However, some citizens of France rallied to his side. Among them was the writer Emile Zola (1840-1902), who on January 13, 1898, published an open letter to the president of the Republic. It appeared on the front page of the newspaper L'Aurore and was entitled, "J'accuse." Proclaiming Dreyfus's innocence, it accused his attackers of libel. Zola is buried in the Pantheon.

Dreyfus was retried by a military court. But again, he was found guilty by army officers who just could not admit the army was guilty of conspiracy. Later, after he had been exonerated and pardoned, Dreyfus was reinstated in the army. On July 28, 1906, he received the Order of the Legion of Honor. In World War I, he served with dignity and honor. He died in the 1930s as a colonel in the French Army. He is buried in the Montparnasse Cemetery, Division 29. As a result of the trumped-up charges against Dreyfus and the new anti-Semitism, Theodor Herzl, then a Viennese journalist in Paris, founded the Zionist movement, which brought about the State of Israel. In the cobblestone military courtyard, as Dreyfus was being marched around the square and drummed out of the army, Herzl heard the captain shout: "I am innocent." Stefan Zweig wrote that the incident "convulsed Herzl's soul." Herzl knew Dreyfus was innocent: "He had brought the horrible suspicion of treason on himself merely by being Jewish." Subsequently, Herzl wrote his famous pamphlet, *The Jewish State*, in the Hotel de Castille.

CEMETERIES

Père Lachaise, Blvd. de Menilmontant, Paris. (Another entrance is at rue des Rondeaux, and for this, take the Metro to the Gambretta stop). This is Paris's most impressive cemetery and many famous Jews are buried here, including many of the Rothschild family (Division 7). Some of the more noted Jewish persons buried here are the actresses Rachel (Division 7) and Sarah Bernhardt (Division 44), the painter Rosa Bonheur (Division 44), and writers Marcel Proust and Gertrude Stein (Division 85). The cemetery was opened in 1803.

Sephardic Cemetery, 44, rue de Flandres. Many Sephardic Jews who lived in Paris before the Revolution are buried here. Apply at the office of the Consistoire Central of Paris for the key. 17. rue St-Georges, 75009, Paris. Tel: 40-82-26-26.

The French Countryside

For all the splendors of Paris, France itself is "predominantly a country of villages". Yes, Paris dominates the cultural, business, governmental, and entertainment life of France. But that certain French "sweetness of life" is also found in Angers and Avignon, Biarritz and Bordeaux, St-Tropez and St-Jean-de-Luz, Lyon and Limoges, Strasbourg and St-Malo, Nice and Cannes.

THE LOIRE IS HEARTLAND FRANCE

A good place to start is the fabled valley of Loire, the Garden of France, and its special section, Touraine, which encompasses the famous town of Tours.

Step back into a magnificent past. Visit the amazing chateaux at **Amboise** with its sumptuous setting and wonderful views, **Brissac** with its two round defensive towers on a building standing in a fine park, **Chambord** with its rich Renaissance decoration, **Chaumont-sur-Loire** with its beautiful site on the Loire, and **Chenonceaux** with its gardens and edifice astride the gentle river. It is indeed a horticultural delight.

Follow the majestic river Loire through the heart of France. Travel alongside it from Orleans westward to Angers and Nantes on to the Atlantic Ocean. Jews settled in Touraine at the time of the Romans. They lived along the river and were active in shipping, commerce, and boating

Centers of Jewish life flourished in the Loire Valley in the towns of Orleans, Tours, Chinon, and Angers. Today a Jewish community thrives again because thousands of Sephardic Jews from North Africa have migrated here to give the area new energy.

Visit a few of these Loire towns.

Angers

Angers is a town to roam around. The counts and dukes of Anjou made it their cultural center. Throughout the ages, it has remained the gateway to the west of France and to Brittany.

Angers is a major hub of commerce, transportation, and culture. Its gastronomy and wine cellars, parks and gardens, proximity to the chateaux at Brissac and Saumur, as well as its galleries, museums, and modern new library, make it a wonderful stop.

This capital of the Maine et Loire boasts a very fine, hospitable Jewish community.

The Jewish traveler will probably have a rewarding experience attending a Friday night service. At the Orthodox synagogue, there is usually a small

A view from Angers, France. (Photo courtesy of the French Government Tourist Office)

minyan (quorum of 10 men) on the Sabbath eve. The congregation welcomes you with warm informality; they are extremely friendly. **Synagogue and Community Center,** 1, place du Tertre Saint Laurant, 49000, Angers. Tel: 02-41-87-48-10. acc49@orange.fr

Today, two town streets are named after two notable Jewish personalities: Place Pierre Mendes-France, one of France's prime ministers, and Place Anne Frank (formerly known as de la Juiverie).

Orleans

"Paris is the head of France, Orleans is its heart," they say. Once Orleans was the second most important city in France. On May 8, 1429, Joan of Arc entered the city as its deliverer from the English and persuaded Charles VII to claim his throne.

Jews lived in Orleans before the sixth century. During the Middle Ages, its Jewish community was an important center of Jewish learning. In the fourteenth century, the Jews were expelled, not to return until the beginning of the nineteenth century.

The Synagogue and Community Center are located at 14, rue Robert-de-Courtenay, 45000, Orleans. Tel: 2-38-62-16-62. FAX: 38-77-97-71. cjorleans@free.fr. The synagogue is the heart of the Jewish community. This house of study, meeting place, and sanctuary is not difficult to find. It is next door to the cathedral, which dates from the Middle Ages.

Tours

This is the home of Rabelais, Descartes, and Balzac—the home of good books, fine food, and distinctive wine.

Tours is probably one of the best starting points from which to see the impressive chateaux of the Loire. It is a convenient place from which to make excursions. Tours possesses one of the oldest Jewish communities in France. The first Jews probably arrived here in 570. Later, in medieval times, a Jewish quarter and synagogue thrived in this market town and provincial capital. Today, about 200 Jewish families live in Tours.

Well worth a visit is the **Musée des Beaux-Arts**, 18, Place François-Secord, 37000, Tours. Tel: 47-05-68-73.

Historial de Touraine, Musée Grevin, Chateau Royal, Quai D'Orleans, 37000, Tours. Tel: 47-61-02-95. Brought to life here is the history of Touraine from the Gallo-Roman period to the mid-twentieth century. In almost lifelike scenes, painters, doctors, writers, and politicians are all on view: in one scene, French Jewish Prime Minister Leon Blum, and in another, Nobel Prize-winner Henri Bergson, the French Jewish philosopher.

Synagogue, 37, rue Parmentier, 37000, Tours. Tel: 47-05-56-95.

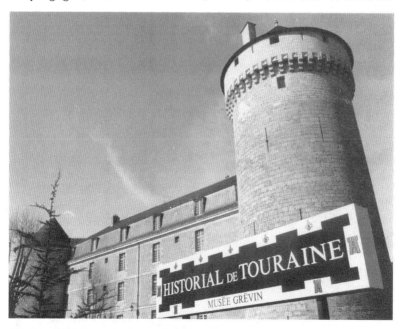

The historical museum, Musee Grevin, in Tours, France. (Photo courtesy of the French Government Tourist Office)

Services are held at 6:30 Friday evenings in the winter and 7:00 p.m. during the summer. Saturday morning services are at 9:00 a.m. A study class conducted by the rabbi takes place every Saturday evening at 7:00 p.m. The synagogue was founded in 1908.

For those needing to stock up on or replenish kosher food for their journey through France, go to the store at 38, rue Parmentier, which sells kosher items. Open five days a week. Call the synagogue first for more information as to exact hours.

REIMS

All the kings of France were crowned in Reims, now conveniently a less than two-hour drive from Paris. It was in the **Reims Cathedral** in 1429 that Joan of Arc, after a legendary ride, achieved her wish of seeing Charles VII crowned king of France.

Reims proudly possesses one of the most beautiful and unique synagogues in the northeast part of France. Built in 1879, its architecture is imposing indeed. A synagogue functioned here in medieval times. After the expulsion of the Jews from France in the fourteenth century, they did not reside in Reims for about 500 years. In 1820, a small group settled in the city.

Fifty years later, Jews from Alsace-Lorraine began to arrive in Reims, which is famous for its champagne wineries, its historic cathedral, as well as the schoolhouse where Supreme Allied Commander Dwight D. Eisenhower's representatives accepted the German surrender in May, 1945.

The Germans made a complete and unconditional surrender to the three Allied powers at 0341, the morning of May 7, 1945. A more formal ratification of the surrender by the German High Command took place in Berlin on May 9; but May 8 is celebrated as V-E Day because the act of the May 7 became effective at 0001 on the 9th of May, Zone B, which in Central European Time, (Zone A) was 2301, May 8, according to *The Invasion of France and Germany, 1944-1945*, by Samuel Eliot Morison.

Today about 150 Jewish families live in Reims.

The **synagogue** at 49, rue Clovis, Reims, also has a community center. Tel: 26-47-68-47.

acsirinfo@free.fr, www.cjreims.free.fr/

STRASBOURG

Known as the Jerusalem of France, Strasbourg is an active, highly organized, intellectual Jewish community of about 16,000 persons. Most of the chief rabbis of France have come from this center of

Jewry, which has deep roots in the province of Alsace. No wonder then that Alsace is considered the cradle of Judaism in France. The large, beautiful **Synagogue de la Paix** with its community center is located on la rue du Grand-Rabbin-Rene-Hirschler (Ave. de la Paix), 67005, Strasbourg. Tel: 03-88-14-46-50. FAX: 03-88-25-12-65 webmaster@wanadoo.fr, www.cisonline.org. Dedicated in 1958, the synagogue features a bronze menorah and a bronze grill which grace the front of the structure. Visitors have included the late President of the Republic Charles de Gaulle, Moshe Dayan, and Golda Meir. This new synagogue replaced the historic Synagogue Consistoriale du Quai Kleber, which was destroyed by the Nazis in the war. The city has yeshivot and Talmud Torahs.

Of course, some great personalities hail from Alsace, such as Leon Blum, the first Jewish prime minister of France, as did the Marx Brothers and mime Marcel Marceau. Cerf-Berr, ancestor of publisher Bennet Cerf was the brother-in-law of Rabbi David Sintzheim, who was appointed president of the Sanhedrin by Napoleon in 1807.

Jews and non-Jews here share many common memories. How would you like to live in a city that has changed hands four times in a little more than 100 years? That is why a war memorial in Strasbourg depicts Alsace as an allegorical mother cradling her lost sons. One of them is French, the other German. Erected in 1936, it shows what an ancient frontier city, this truly is. In 1871, the city became German for almost a generation; then French again in 1918; and then German again in 1940. In 1939, the city had been completely evacuated because a German attack was expected. Many Jews, victims of the Holocaust, would not return. And many of the Jewish survivors settled in the south of France where they were able to hide during the war. Since 1945, the city is French and it truly stands as a European city, for it is the location of the Council of Europe and shares with Brussels, the home of the European Parliament.

As the capital of Alsace, Strasbourg leads the region in business, culture and intellectual pursuits. But today in the 21st century, the Germans also contribute to the shaping of the city, which, after all is in a strategic location—it sits among a dense system of water and land paths.

More than 50,000 students attest to Strasbourg being a university town, made famous by the prestigious University of Strasbourg, founded in 1538.

Strasbourg is situated in northeastern France, nestled between the Vosges Mountains and the Rhine River. The city borders Germany to the north and east and shares many links to the country across the Rhine River. While French is the official language, many inhabitants speak German as well as the regional dialect Alsatian, a mixture of the two.

A rich gastronomical center, this city boasts many beautiful gardens, parks, buildings and museums, and a famous Cathedral.

The first item on my agenda is wandering along the winding streets lined with half-timbered houses and covered bridges. I gaze at the skyscrapers with their multinational flags. I listen to the babble and realize that, not only is Strasbourg the capital of the French province Alsace, but it is also, as we have seen, the capital of Europe.

As in many French cities, hate crimes can occur in Strasbourg. In the summer of 2016, a sixty-two-year-old man and active member of Chabad was stabbed. Described as an anti-Semitic attack, the elderly man survived the knifing.

Later commenting on the attack, Rabbi Mendel Samama, a member of the rabbinical team in Strasbourg, offered words that were meaningful in describing the situation that most Jewish communities find themselves in the second decade of the twentieth century. "We do *not* live in a city with tension and fears. Everyone lives together. We have a Jewish area that is very nice. We have a strong and united community. And it is a very peaceful city. I believe that we will have the strength to overcome this, and be stronger and more united. This is the main thing," he told a writer of Chabad.org.

Akiba, 9-10, quai Zorn, 67000, Strasbourg. Tel: 88-35-48-58. Seven hundred students are enrolled in this famous day school.

Beth Chabad, 59 Faubourg de Pierre, 67000, Strasbourg. Tel: 88-75-66-05. A Chabad youth group also meets here.

Jewish National Fund, 1a rue Rene Hirschler, 67000 Strasbourg. 88-35-54-26.

Union Juive Liberale de Strasbourg, Ibis rue du Puits, 67000, Strasbourg. Tel: 33-952-12-59-30. ujls@free.fr, www. ujls.org.

Alsatian Museum, 23-25 Quai Saint-Nicolas, 67000 Strasbourg. Tel: +33-3-68-98-51-52. This site has a rich collection of Jewish ritual objects in an exhibit entitled "History of the Jews of Alsace-Lorraine."

Worth visiting is Strasbourg's **"La Petite France,"** an ancient quarter of 400-year-old houses.

Kosher Restaurants in Strasbourg

King, 28, rue Sellenick, Strasbourg. Tel: 88-52-17-71.

Aux Mills Saveurs, 17, rue Finkmatt, 67000, Strasbourg. Tel: 3-88-32-44-62.

Café de la Paix, 4, rue Strauss Durkheim, 67000 Strasbourg. Tel: 3-88-36-35-05.

Sushiburger, 42 Blvd. Clemenceau, 67000 Strasbourg. Tel 3-88-36-35-05.

Restaurant Au Coins des Savers, 13 rue Orphelins. 67000 Strasburg.
Restaurant Universitaire, 11, rue Sellenick, Strasbourg. Tel: 88-76-74-76.

This is a good place to note that few Jews populate the towns near Strasbourg; most have moved to that city. But efforts are being made to preserve and promote Jewish heritage in museums and art galleries housed in abandoned synagogues throughout Alsace. To appreciate Strasbourg Jewry, one might want to visit a rural area in the province.

Stop in the cultural and tourist center of Colmar, the province's wine capital and the second largest city in Alsace. The Synagogue is at 1, rue de la Cogogne, Colmar.

Tourists can see more than 200 Jewish sites in Alsace.

Also, note that the annual **European Days of Jewish Culture** is very popular. The 2017 event was held on September 3, 2017. Many European countries and cities participate in this annual event; hundreds of thousands attend exhibitions, conferences and concerts. www.jewishheritage.org. Also contact: aepj@jewisheritage.org. Tel: 34 629-77-84-48

Struthof Concentration Camp. F67130 Natzweiler Struthof. Located on Route D 130, 50 kilometers west of Strasbourg in Alsace. On this site stands the only concentration camp built by the Nazis in France. They called it the "Konzentrationlager Natzweiler Elsass. Set up on May 12, 1941, its victims were from throughout Europe and included French, German, Dutch, and Russian prisoners of war. Horrible medical experiments were conducted on 87 Jewish victims, including 30 women, all of whom perished. The camp was liberated by the First French Army and the Sixth American Army Corps on November 23, 1944.

A Memorial to the Deported was inaugurated by President Charles de Gaulle on July 23, 1960. The 41.5-meter-high concrete shaft spirals. Designated by architect B. Monnet, it not only symbolizes the flame of the crematorium, but also infinite freedom. The emaciated silhouette sculpted on the memorial by Lucien recalls the hunger that precedes death. An inscription honors an "unknown deported prisoner." Another commemorative tablet reads: *Aux heros et martyrs de la Déportation, la France reconnaissante," (To the heroes and martyrs transported, The French Republic is grateful).* A visitor to the camp sees barracks, memorial stones, a national cemetery and the crematorium. The crematorium has been preserved as well as an ash pit located between the two huts and down close to the forest where the ashes of the victims were spread. A commemorative tablet with the Star of David memorializes the 87 Jews who were killed in this camp's gas chambers as well as the *Six Million Jews* who were murdered by the Nazis throughout Europe during World War II. A museum has been placed at the entrance of the camp. Located close to the camp is the sand quarry where camp inmates were forced to toil. Three kilometers down the road back toward Struthof, visitors can view the gas chamber where they were put to death. For further information, on the Struthof Concentration camp, contact the camp at Tel: 88-22-01-02.

DIJON

Visit Dijon, provincial capital of Bugundy, the home of the legendary dukes. Here are the palaces of the dukes who in 1196 placed the Jews under their protection. Here is a small Arc de Triomphe in a city that is an important rail link in one of Europe's technologically advanced train systems.

About 250 Jewish families live in this charming university town in central France, 200 miles southeast of Paris. This fifteenth-century city of clean, winding pedestrian streets, of quaint shops, cafes, and homes, is also the headquarters of famous Dijon mustard and cassis. No wonder Dijon is often called the gastronomical capital of France, and, of course, boasts rare wines to go with delicious cuisine. Dedicated in 1879, the synagogue in Dijon is the focal point of the Jewish community. It is located at 5, rue de la Synagogue 21000, Dijon. Services are held Friday evenings and Saturday mornings. Activities for young people are held in the synagogue on Sundays. For information about kosher food and services, contact synagogue officials at Tel: 80-66-46-47.

Many Jewish tourists visit Dijon for wine tasting and begin week-long vacations on the popular barge waterway program on the Bugundy Canal and Saone River.

LYON

To inhale the quality of French life outside of Paris, visit Lyon. This 2,000-year-old city on two rivers should be a stop on any tour of France. All roads lead to Lyon for culinary delights, and it is, after all, France's second largest metropolitan area.

About 30,000 Jews call Lyon home, a unique location along the banks of the Saone and Rhone Rivers. They live in the Lyon area, including Villeurbanne. They support 35 synagogues of which 10 are in Lyon, 10 in the suburbs of the city, and 15 in nearby Villeurbanne. Of those, one is Ashkenazic and 22 are Sephardic. A further breakdown of the Jewish houses of worship in the area shows that eight are Orthodox, three are Chabad and one is Reform movement of Judaism.

Happily, Lyon keeps the charm of a great provincial city. This city of bridges is noted for the manufacture of silk. Lyon boasts pleasantly paced living with parks, an extraordinary rose garden, sweeping pedestrian malls, a giant shopping center, plus 24 major museums. **Savor Lyon.** It is the financial and cultural hub of the Rhone-Alpes region, the jumping-off point for skiing in the Alps or for visiting vineyards to the north and south of this city. If it is great cuisine you want, this is the place to visit. This city is the gastronomic center of La Belle France. Good food is a fact of life. The area boasts more top chefs honored with little guidebook stars, forks, and tongues than any other part of the country.

You can reach Lyon in just two hours by nearly 20 daily TGV trains speeding from Paris. After arrival you can have your pick of 20 museums, including an excellent Fine Arts Museum.

Make sure you take the funicula, or cable car, to the top of a high hill, an exceptional view of the city of bridges and two rivers.

I like Lyon even if, as Ted Morgan notes, it "has always been in the shadow of Paris." It sports the Palace Bellecour, one of the largest public squares in France. It stands as a prosperous trading center and, let us face it, Lyon means serious gastronomy; it is, after all, a city of "haute cuisine," with its superb restaurants.

Many consider Lyon the capital of the French Resistance in World War II. Significantly, Lyon broke into the news headlines in the 1980s as the city that hosted the trial of the Gestapo commander, the late Klaus Barbie, otherwise known as "The Butcher of Lyon." This city not only served as the base for the French Resistance, but as a center of French Jewry. Barbie was stationed in Lyon and was responsible for the sending of area Jews—including the homeless, orphaned children at Izieu—to the gas chambers, as well as the torture and killing of French Resistance leaders, including Jean Moulin. Twice condemned to death in absentia after the war, Barbie lived in Latin America for several decades until he was tracked down by Beate Klarsfeld, who searches for Nazis, in Bolivia in 1972 and brought to France 11 years later. He was convicted in 1987 as the chief enforcer of a Nazi reign of terror. Sentenced to life imprisonment, he died a prisoner in a French hospital in Lyon in the fall of 1991.

Musée Memorial des Enfants Juifs d'Izieu (Izieu Childrens Home and Museum) The Village of Izieu. Sortie autoroute: Chimilin A 43. Telephone for reservation: 4-79-87-20-00. FAX: 4-79-87-25-01

I kept focusing on the staircase of this farmhouse in the village of Izieu, about 60 miles from Lyon. That was the set of steps that one of the young leaders in the house raced up to escape the German seizure of the children of Izieu. He had been walking down the steps, when a young girl, who could have been his sister we are told, yelled to him to go back up because the Germans were there. He ran up the steps; opened a nearby window; jumped to the ground below and fled through a nearby field. He survived, but for the rest of his life he would remember the children of Izieu who were rounded up by the Germans. The world learned about the children from the trial of Klaus Barbie, otherwise known as "butcher of Lyon." Stationed in Lyon, this Gestapo officer was responsible for the torture and killing of the children. The museum, known as the **Izieu Childrens' Home and Museum,** remains a site that should be visited. While not per se a Holocaust Memorial; it certainly could be. For here in a former modest farm house and in a large building on the premises, the traveler will soon know the story of the 44 children who spent the final year of their lives in this building in the farm area above the Rhone River. It is quiet here. The visitor naturally asks, how this could be the site where one day in April, 1944, the Germans captured the 44 unarmed young children and a half dozen or so adults. It is also a question asked by the thousands of today's French children from the surrounding area and beyond who come here every day. More than 20,000 people visit the museum every year and they certainly see the 44 trees planted behind the memorial.

The displays in the museum consist of drawings and letters the children wrote to parents who probably had been sent to Nazi concentration camps. Also exhibited are the photographs of the 44 youngsters who were seized. Audio-visual displays record the fate of the 11,000 French Jewish children who were sent from France to the death camps by Vichy and its German officials, a small fraction of the more than one million Jewish children murdered in Europe.

In the 1970's Serge Klarsfeld, the French historian, activist and Nazi hunter, began a 20 year-campaign to identify these children whose murderers "had wished them to die anonymously. Klarsfeld went on the radio in France, the U.S. and Israel to request family photographs and testimonials. He sifted through French archives. He went to court to force the French police to produce photographs of the victims. And in 1996, he published the results of his labors in French, in *Children in the Holocaust,* a book that contains photographs and descriptions of more than 2,500 of those children. The Jewish Welfare Organization, OSE, saved children in homes such as that at Izieu. OSE became an underground organization providing children with false identity papers and housing them with Christian families and organizations. OSE would then smuggle them across the border to Switzerland. The method saved more than 1,000 children.

While OSE sponsored 14 homes in France, they hid more than 1,000 of these children until the organization's American branch obtained visas for them. Under OSE's auspices, 253 children were able to leave France before the Vichy government began blocking emigration in the summer of 1942.

In France today, it is important to study and view the horrors of the Nazi era; to sort out the sins of Vichy and to honor the courage of those righteous French citizens. For example, in Le Chambon-Sur-Lignon, local Protestants shielded thousands of Jews from arrest and deportation. An example of another town—and there were many more—which saved Jewish children was Chabannes, an isolated and insulated rural village in the Creuse region of central France. In August, 1942, Vichy had rounded up 10,000 Jews for deportation. But only six of Chabannes 400 Jewish students were deported and just four perished, thanks to various artful dodges, schemes and ploys by a man named Felix Chevrier who ran a chateau that housed a school.

Centre d'Histoire de la Resistance et de la Deportation. Centre of the History of Resistance and Deportation, 14 Ave., Berthelot, Lyon. Dimly lit corridors, films, photographs and biographies of the hundreds of men, women and children who fought the Germans in France are displayed here. Many of these freedom fighters were arrested. Mention should also be made here of the more-than-above-the-call-of-duty of French Jews who flocked to the Resistance. "Charles de Gaulle was reputed to have been bitter that among the few Frenchmen who joined him during the first days in London many were Jews—not because de Gualle was anti-Semitic, but because he knew and felt that the presence of so many Jews in his small patriotic grouping would make it unrepresentative and unpopular," according to John Lukacs. Jews were among the first and all alone in the Resistance. The proportion of Jewish participation in the war and the Resistance in all its forms is by far the highest, comprising approximately a quarter of the Jewish population capable of action.

Sites in Lyon

Fonds Social Juif Unifié, 113 Blvd. Vivier Merle, 69003 Lyon, Tel: 4-78-85-82-96.

Kosher Restaurants

Comptoir 43 Mayoca, 43 rue Boileau, 69006, Lyon. Tel: 06-27-12-50-51.

Boutargue and wine, 166 rue Cuvier 69006, Lyon. Tel: 04-26-72-17-04.

Mika Sushi, 115 rue Cavier, 69006, Lyon. Tel: 04-37-24-00-00.

Pat's Café, 110 Cours Gambetta, 69006, Lyon. Tel: 09-50-68-13-13.

Synagogues in Lyon

American visitors will find a warm welcome at the synagogue-office of the Grand Rabbinat de Lyon and Rabbi Richard Wertenschlag, at the historic **Great Synagogue**, 13 Quai Tilsitt, 69002, Lyon, Tel: 4-78- 37-13-43. FAX: 78-38-26-57. aci@9online.fr, www.consistoiredelyon.fr. Write in advance to the rabbi for information regarding services and kosher food. This synagogue was built in 1864. Many American Jewish tourists attend services here.

Community Center, 97 rue de la Pagere, 69500 Bron. Tel: 4-78-41-88-33.

Charre Tzedek, 18, rue St-Mathieu, 69008, Lyon. Tel: 78-00-72-50.

Synagogue and Community Center Beth Hamidrash de La Fraternité, 4, rue Malherbe, 69100, Villeurbanne. Tel: 4-78-84-04-32. FAX: 4-78-68-62-67. civmalharbe@yahoo.fr. www.consistoirevilleurbanne.org.

Neveh Chalom Synagogue and Talmud Torah, 317, rue Duguesclin, 69007, Lyon. Tel: 78-58-18-74. Cis99@free.fr. This is a beautiful Sephardic synagogue and community center. Many activities are held here. This synagogue also has a mikva.

Keren Or: la Synagoguge Liberale de Lyon, 15 rue Jules Valles, Villeurbanne, Lyon, 69100. Tel: 33-4-37-72-30-19. contact@kerenor.fr. www.kerenor.fr.

Oratoire Etz Hayim Yechouron Chabad, 60, rue Crillon, 69006, Lyon. Tel: 4-78-89-08-32.

Beth Chabad Loubavitch of Lyon, 203 rue Francis De Pressense, Lyon-Villeurbanne, 69100, 78-89-08-32.

BORDEAUX

Bordeaux, France's fifth largest metropolitan area, has a special place in Jewish history. Bordeaux is important in Jewish history because many of the Marranos—secret Jews—escaped from Spain and Portugal to this port city.

There are many interesting individuals in the area who know much about the Sephardic Jews of Bordeaux. If you're not in a hurry and would like to learn about a rich Jewish past which dates back to the sixth century, Bordeaux is a prime place to begin. On the eve of the French Revolution, only a few thousand Jews lived in France. Most were Sephardic Jews in Bordeaux and Bayonne.

On January 28, 1790, the leaders of the French Revolution declared that all Jews in France who were known as "Portuguese, Spanish, and Avignonnais Jews shall enjoy the rights of citizens." Twenty months later on September 27, 1791, after debate and delays, all the other Jews of France, including Ashkenazim, were emancipated. France became the first European state to grant its Jewish residents the rights of citizenship.

Today, this active city of about 650,000 boasts eighteenth-century architecture, with an elegant Grand Theater in the very center of town. Outside the city are the celebrated vineyards of Mouton Rothschild, Chateau Lafite, Chateau Margaux, and many others.

More than 15 Jewish organizations meet at the **Jewish Community Center** at 213 rue Sainte Catherine, 33000, Bordeaux. Tel: 56-52-62-69. acig33@gmail.com. www.synagogue-bordeaux.com. There are active B'nai B'rith and B.B.Y.O. groups who meet in the center.

The **synagogue**, built in 1882 in the Spanish-Portuguese style, is at 8, rue du Grand Rabbin Joseph-Cohen, 33000, Bordeaux. Tel: 5-56-91-79-39.

The **Consistoire** is located at 213, rue Ste. Catherine, 33000, Bordeaux. Tel: 56-91-79-39. acig33@gmail.com. www.synagogue-bordeaux.com Further information on services and kosher food can be obtained by calling: Tel: 56-91-79-39, at the synagogue.

THE SOUTHWEST

Three towns, Biarritz, Anglet, and Bayonne, located in the southwest, are known as the "BAB" towns. About 250 Jewish families live in these municipalities. Most of the Jews who came here after the Inquisition and expulsion from Spain and Portugal were Marranos. They were called the "Portuguese Nation," for it was safer to be called Portuguese than Jew. They settled in the BAB town area, which is about 25 miles from the Spanish border. In 1619, there were 2,000 Jewish congregants here. They and their descendants flourished in the area. Today, these "Basque-Country" Jews continue to prosper. Let us go first to Biarritz.

Biarritz

Biarritz is a resort town made famous by the monarchs of Europe, including Napoleon III, who built what is now the luxurious **Hotel du Palais** for his wife, Eugenie. The aristocracy summered in this city of nineteenth-century charm, and it remains an attractive summer place.

Synagogue, 9 rue Pellot, at corner of rue de la Russie and rue Pellot, 64200, Biarritz. Services during summer and on holidays only. Kosher food is available through the synagogue in nearby Bayonne. Tel: 59-55-03-95.

Bayonne

During the early sixteenth century, the Marranos from Portugal and Spain, who practiced Judaism secretly, were fearful that the long arm of the Inquisition would reach across the border from Spain and snare them in Bayonne, if they revealed their identity. They had settled in Bayonne because it was a thriving port and the commercial capital of Gascony. But when they came here, they were forced to live in the St-Esprit section of the city. Today they still live there, voluntarily of course. The neighborhood of St-Esprit, which supports a synagogue, is called Little Jerusalem.

Synagogue, 35, rue Maubec, 64100, Bayonne. Tel: 5-59-55-03-95.

Musée Basque de Bayonne, 37 Quai de Corsaiers, 64100, Bayonne. Tel: 59-59-08-98. The museum, dedicated to Basque history, draws visitors from all over the world. A room is devoted to Jewish religious objects, mezuzoth, prayer books, lithographs, and candles. It is well worth a visit.

St-Jean-de-Luz

Because the beach resort of St-Jean-de-Luz has a small Jewish population of less than 100, visiting it will be a delightful experience. The town harbored many Jews who fled from Spain in the sixteenth century.

During World War II, Jews escaping the Nazis crossed here into Spain. Today the small Jewish community in this fishing village resort attends services in nearby Bayonne.

Pau

Gateway to the Basque Country, this nineteenth-century resort, popular with the English, was made famous by Henry IV, a Protestant king of France. Here in southwest France, Pau (pronounced "Po"), with a population of about 85,000, beckons every visitor to begin a sojourn by walking along the attractive boulevard des Pyrenees and marveling at the imposing mountain range.

About 160 Jewish families live in Pau. They support an active synagogue and a kosher butcher shop. The **synagogue** is located at 8, rue Trois-Frères-des-Bernadac, 64000, Pau. Tel: 5-59-62-37-85. A community center and Talmud Torah are part of the synagogue building, which survived World War II.

Services are held Friday evenings, Saturday mornings, and Saturday evenings.

Montpellier

Montpellier is a city rich in architecture, with charming eighteenth-century houses, the famous neoclassical pavilion Chateau d'Eau, and the Musée Fabre, one of the best museums outside of Paris. Rabelais once studied medicine here in the city's fine medical facility, part of one of France's most famous universities. Many Jewish doctors and Talmudists resided in medieval Montpellier and contributed to the medical faculty. Today, Montpellier is considered a resort town with sandy beaches.

The Musée Fabre, at 37, Blvd. Sarrail, is located in a district which boasts beautiful seventeenth- and eighteenth-century palaces.

Synagogue Ben-Zakai, 7, rue Général-Lafon, 34000, Montpellier. Tel: 67-92-02-07.

Synagogue, 18, rue Ferdinand-Fabre, 34000, Montpellier. Tel: 67-79-09-82.

Jewish Radio Station, 45, rue Proudhon. 34000 Montpellier. Tel: 4-99-58-35-80. FAX: 4-99-58-35-81.

Communaute Juive Liberale de Montpelier, 5, rue Rondelet, BP 41026. Montpelier. CEDEX 1 34006. Tel: 33-4 67-92-73-40. FAX: 33-4-67-92-25-24. frederic.calfond@wanadoo.fr.

Kehilat Kedem, 34000. Tel: 33-6-14-56-0076. slm.kedem@gmail.com, www.kehilat-kedem.com

Jewish Community Center, 500 Blvd. d'Antigone, 34000, Montpellier. Tel: 4-67-15-08-76.

Synagogue Lubavitch, Blampiers, Montpellier. Tel: 33-467-92-86-93.

Toulouse

When an Islamic terrorist on March 19, 2012, murdered four Jews in a Jewish school, Ozer Hatorah Toulouse, three of whom were young children, it set off a wave of indignation, fear and an even larger movement of *aliyah* to Israel among French Jews. One French Jew was quoted in JTA as saying he "had to decide between sending his son to a Jewish school guarded by a soldier with a machine gun or a secular public school." Since then the French government posted armed guards at French Jewish schools. The terrorist who killed the Jews was an al-Qaeda fanatic who was killed by French police.

The 2012 attack was the deadliest attack on Jews in France since a shooting in 1982 at a restaurant in Paris, Goldenbergs', when six people were killed and 22 injured. (In January, 2015, four people were murdered in the terrorist attack on Hyper Cacher market in Paris.)

Toulouse is called La Ville Rose, "the pink city," and rightly so, for the sights, the gourmet restaurants, the architecture, the unhurried pace, the atmosphere of a university city (one-third of the population are students) spell out a cultural and intellectual city. During World War II, Toulouse was one of the principal centers for resistance to the Nazi invaders. Not only did Jews find refuge in this city steeped in history, but the Organisation Juive de Combat was founded in Toulouse and its leaders would often meet there.

One Jewish historian says Jews have resided in the area ever since the destruction of the second temple. Today, more than 23,000 Jewish residents call Toulouse their home. This is a city that has 30 to 40 active Jewish organizations; 6 kosher butcher shops; 3 day schools, including a technical school sponsored by ORT; and 9 synagogues, with 3 functioning every day.

Only an hour's flight from Paris and located in the Midi Pyrenees in the heart of France's Southwest, this region of open spaces, unique and prestigious, stands as an area where everything is possible. And it is right smack in the middle of the old trade routes between Montpellier and Bordeaux. For those interested in Jewish history, this is the road that makes its way from Beziers to Narbonne, to Carcassonne, to Toulouse, the principal cities of Languedoc, this delightful province bordering on the Mediterranean.

Centre Maimonide, 14, rue du Rempart-St-Etienne, 31000, Toulouse. Tel: 61-23-36-59. Located here is the synagogue called the Old-New Synagogue because many of the Jews of Toulouse came from North Africa and brought from those lands some of the synagogue's fixtures, such as the chandeliers.

The Synagogue and Community Center, are located in the same building at Espace du Judaïsme, 2, place Riquet, 31000 Toulouse. **Synagogue:** Tel: 5-62-76-46-46. FAX: 5-62-73-46-47, acit@acit31. com. Telephone for the Community Center is 5-62-76-45-73. For information regarding services, contact ACIT (Association Cultuelle Israelite de Toulouse,) acit@cedj.org. A restaurant is also located here in this Center.

Les 12 Tribus, 2, place Riquet, Toulouse. Tel: 62-73-56-56.

Synagogue Adath-Israel, 17, rue Alsace-Lorraine, 31000, Toulouse. Tel: 5-61-21-27-87.

Communaute Juive Liberale-Toulouse, 4 rue des Feuillants, Toulouse, 31300. Tel: 33-56-16-15-756. contact@ajlt.com, www.ajlt. com

A kosher restaurant is also located at the University. **Restaurant Universitaire,** 14, rue du Rempart, St. Etienne, Toulouse. Tel: 61-23-36-54.

THE SOUTHEAST

Jewish communities dot the Southeast of France in Provence and the Alps. A comfortable way to reach such centers as Avignon, Nimes, and St-Etienne is the speedy and on-time French National Railways, especially TGV, the world's fastest train.

Moving southward, a visitor sees and feels the warmth of Provence with its luminous sun, sleepy Roman towns, and striking antiquities. Its bright blue sky has inspired French artists, including Vincent Van Gogh, Paul Cezanne, and Marc Chagall.

Provence is so named because it was the Province of Rome. Towns that attract the traveler are classic Aix-en-Provence, medieval Avignon, Carpentras, Cavaillon, and the great port of Marranos.

Keep in mind that a mere two hours from Marseilles or Avignon are the celebrated ski slopes of the French Alps at the foot of Mont-Blanc, Europe's highest peak.

Provence was once an important European Jewish center—a place where Jews have lived continually in spite of persecutions and expulsions. The earliest evidence of Jews in Provence dates from the fifth century in Arles and the sixth century in Marseilles. Five centuries later, Jews lived in many towns of Provence.

While Rabbenu Gershom and Rashi were the products of Judaism of northern France during the tenth and eleventh centuries, Provence in the south was undergoing its own renaissance of learning. When Benjamin of Tudela visited Provence in 1160, he found renowned scholars teaching hundreds of students.

Much has been told about the Jews of Avignon, who with their fellow co-religionists of Carpentras, Cavaillon, and L'Isle-sur-la-Sorgue comprise the four communities of the Comtat Venaissin, where Jews established important centers of learning. These towns were the cities of the Papal States. Here Jews were given protection by the popes and served as financiers and merchants. They were called the "Pope's Jews," and as will be noted in the chapter on Italy, the thinking of the church leaders often was to protect the Jews as a reminder to those who might reject the Catholic Church that they would also be punished.

Nimes

Historically a major center of Jewish life in this part of France, Nimes is proud of two famous native sons, both French Jewish personalities. Isaac-Adolphe Cremieux (1796-1880), French lawyer and statesman, was minister of justice in the Government of National Defense in 1870.

He issued the Cremieux Decree by which the Jews of Algeria received French citizenship. This decree was very meaningful, as it enabled Jews of Algeria to settle in France as French citizens in the 1960s

Bernard Lazare (1865-1903), liberal publicist, helped obtain the freedom of Capt. Alfred Dreyfus, who had been unjustly accused of espionage.

This handsome city has some of the most remarkable Roman structures outside of Italy—the **Roman Arena** and Maison Carrée—as well as magnificent gardens, fine museums, and a colorful medieval quarter.

Synagogue, 40, rue Roussy, 30000, Nimes. Tel: 4-66-29-51-81. FAX: 66-21-60-68. Built in 1794, it is still used as a house of worship.

Community Center, 5, rue d'Angouleme, 30000, Nimes. Tel: 66-76-27-64.

Avignon

Mention Avignon, and artists come to mind, as well as the medieval walls of the city and the children's song, "Sur le pont d'Avignon" ("On the Bridge at Avignon"). After 1309, Avignon became the residence of the popes. Joanna, countess of Provence, sold the city to Pope Clement VI and it belonged to the French states of the Holy See until the French Revolution. Thus, Jews were able to stay there even when they were excluded from the rest of France.

Discover the city's festive ambiance from the vantage point of a café along the **rue de la République** or on the **Place de L'Horloge.**

Another major site is the **Petit Palais Museum** of medieval painting and sculpture. Savor art and music festivals staged in the municipal theater, or performances of choirs in the Palace.

From the nineteenth century onward, Jewish life almost ceased, until it was revived in the 1960s by Sephardic immigrants. There is a very narrow street called **rue de la Vieille Juiverie,** the old Jewish Quarter. Avignon has a small Jewish community of about 2,500.

The **synagogue** is located at 2, Place Jerusalem, 84000, Avignon. Tel: 04-90-85-21-24. contact@aci-avignon.com. Services are at 6 Friday night, at 7 in the summer, and on Saturday mornings at 9. This unusual circular synagogue was built in the Roman manner. It was erected on the site of the old Jewish quarter of the thirteenth century.

A **community center** is located at 18, rue Guillaume-Puy, Avignon. Tel: 90-82-64-87.

Arles

According to a Jewish legend, one of three rudderless ships

bearing Jewish exiles arrived in Arles, 27 miles south of Avignon, after the destruction of the Second Temple in 70 C.E. The first evidence of Jewish life here dates back to the fifth century. Rome made Arles famous. An ancient Roman theater and a vast arena still stand in the city. Benjamin of Tudela, the famous Jewish traveler, notes in the twelfth century that a Jewish community of 200 existed in Arles. Jews were expelled in 1481. After the French Revolution, some Jews from the Comtat Venaissin settled in Arles, the city to which the famous artist van Gogh brought fame.

The **Musée Arlaten**, located in the Palais de Laval-Castellane at 42, rue de la République, founded by the famous Provençal poet Frederic Mistral, preserves the relics of Old Provence. It contains a collection of Jewish religious and cultural objects. The **Arles Museum** houses the Lunel collection.

Cavaillon

Association Culturelle des Juif du Pape, Musée Judeo-Comtadin, rue Hebraique, 84300, Cavaillon. Tel: 90-76-00-34. A short drive from Avignon is the wonderful, provincial town of Cavaillon, "known throughout France for the succulence of its melons."

Jewish history can also be inhaled and seen in Cavaillon by a visit to this synagogue and Jewish Museum of the Comtat Venaissin on rue Hebraique, between rue Chabran and rue de la Republique. Built in 1772, this elegant rococo building is a national monument. This museum-synagogue was built above the gateway to the old "carriere," a single street similar to a ghetto area. The rue Hebraique still shows slightly modified features of the "carriere."

The museum retraces Jewish history. On exhibit are prayer books, Torah scrolls, candelabras, shofars, and an oven used for baking matzoh. Many of these relics date from the 14th and 15th centuries and were housed in a 15th century house of prayer which was on the same site. A small synagogue remains upstairs above the museum. A velvet chair reserved for the Prophet Elijah is located in a niche on the wall high above the wooden circumcision chair.

The story as to how the synagogue survived the Nazi occupation explains that when the Jewish trappings were removed from the house of prayer, it took the appearance of a tearoom. Scheduled to be open from 10:00 a.m. to 2:00 p.m. to noon and from 2:00 p.m. to 5:00 p.m. every day except Tuesday. If the museum and synagogue are closed, contact Mr. Mathon at 23, rue Chabran of Maurice Palombo, Magasin Gigo, 36 rue Raspail, Cavaillon. Tel: 90-78-02-46.

About 50 to 75 Jews make Cavaillon their home.

Carpentras

Synagogue, place de la Synagogue, 84200, Carpentras. Tel: 90-63-39-97. Contact Mme. Jenny Levy. This synagogue opposite the Town Hall is open Monday to Thursday from 10:00 a.m. to noon and from 3:00 p.m. to 5:00 p.m. and Fridays, 10:00 a.m. to noon, and 3:00 p.m. to 4:00 p.m. **Services are not usually held in this synagogue.** Please contact the other **Synagogue and Community Center** in place Maurice Charretier, for information re services. Tel: 90 63 39 97. Call here for information and schedule of events and services.

Synagogue and Community Center, place Maurice Charretier, BP190, 84206, Carpentras. Tel: 90-63-39-97. Once Jews sought temporary asylum within the borders of Carpentras. In this town, which boasts a bustling commercial life, stands a **Synagogue** which may well be the oldest in France. Erected in 1367, it was repaired in 1677, 1730 and 1885. Several more restorations were completed in this century. The synagogue of 1367 contained a men's area and a separate women's section in a cellar. In the two basement levels are a matzoh factory and a ritual bath.

Situated in what was the old "carriere," the restricted area, the synagogue was constructed from 1741 to 1743 by architect Antonine d'Allemand. The synagogue contains two levels, the sanctuary on the first discloses a high, light blue ceiling with gold stars. The bimah is

The historic synagogue at Carpentras. (Photo courtesy of the French Government Tourist Office)

situated in the middle of the prayer hall. There is also a miniature velvet armchair for Elijah the Prophet. It occupies a niche on the wall above the ark. It is said that the chair used to be taken to every house when there was a circumcision, but, obviously, it is too small for anyone to sit in. A mikveh and matzah oven are being restored.

Carpentras has about 100 Jewish families and sponsors special activities, such as holiday celebrations.

The synagogue here, too, survived because the curator took out all the Jewish elements and then brought in coffins, thus giving it the appearance of a church. The Germans believed this, it was reported.

COTE D'AZUR

Mention the names Cannes, Nice, Monte Carlo, Cap Ferat, Antibes, Juan-les-Pins, and St-Tropez and you picture beaches, villages, sun terraces on high-rise apartments, promenades, modern art museums, fireworks, flowers, and Mardi Gras carnivals. Mention the words delightful climate, clear sky, refreshing breezes, deep-blue waters, orange groves, and cassia plantations and you bring up before your eyes the French Riviera. Picasso, Matisse, and Renoir succumbed to this azure coast that now boasts film and folk festivals, as well as a vibrant landscape dotted with red tiled roofs and Mediterranean trees and gardens. It is one of the most beautiful areas in the world. The Riviera lies between the Maritime Alps and the Mediterranean Sea. Swathed in sunshine, a monument to leisure, its inviting hills are an open-air atelier for artists, with all the ripe pleasures of summer and sea.

About 35,000 Jews live and work in this vacationland from Toulon to Menton, Cannes, Antibes, St-Tropez, Nice, and Juan-les-Pins. The area offers tourists an exciting visit in scenic luxury.

Monte Carlo

Over the years, Americans, Canadians, and English, many of them retired, have added vitality to the **Sephardic Synagogue**, which is located at 15, Ave. de la Costa, 99000, Monaco. Tel: 377-93-30-16. FAX: 377-39-50-64. accimc@libello.com. www.synagoguemonaco.net. A community center is located there, too.

Half of the congregation is English-speaking and Ashkenazic. The Ashkenazim have joined with their Sephardic counterparts in attempting to improve the organization of the congregation.

A kosher butcher shop under the supervision of the Beth Din of Nice, a Talmud Torah, and several Jewish organizations make up the community.

Nice

In the spring of 2017, one could rightly say, "they're coming back to Nice, the capital of fame and celebrity, the beautiful city on the Riviera." Nice remains one of the most romantic and beautiful vacation lands in the world.

Seven months after a truck attack by terrorists on Nice's seaside promenade during the 2016 celebration of Bastille Day, the southern French city welcomed in February 2017, 250,000 ticket holders among the estimated 600,000 who would crowd into the city for the famous Nice Carnival.

In the terrorist attack, a large truck was deliberately driven into crowds celebrating Bastille Day on the Promenade des Anglais in Nice, resulting in the deaths of 86 people and injuring 434. A least six members of France's Jewish community were among the wounded.

Maurice Niddam, president of the Jewish Community in Nice, said at the time he was horrified by the attack and called on Jewish communities to send condolences and pray for the wounded victims of the massacre to recover. He added that saying prayers for the victims would be at the heart of Shabbat prayer services, according to the *Jerusalem Post.*

The Jewish community took part in three days of national mourning, and members of Chabad in Nice were busy visiting the hospitalized victims and making food for them for Shabbat, the *Jerusalem Post* reported.

Tourism dropped sharply in the months following the attack, but rose again towards the end of 2016, though by the spring of 2017, it still had a ways to go to catch up to the numbers Nice had before the killing, according to Niddam.

Nice would not give into terrorism and the Carnival Parade took place in February 2017. It was the first time, however, that the parade was changed from the traditional *Promenade des Anglais.* The parade took place on one of the new markers of the city, known as, *The Promenade du Paillon,* 30 acres of park running from the city center to the sea.

As for people watching, the *Promenade des Anglais* remains one of the best in the world. On Sundays especially, you will spy bicyclists, baby strollers, and whole families out for a stroll. I agree with those writers and travelers who say and write that this pathway moves alongside the loveliest urban seafront in Europe.

Whenever I travel to Nice, the capital of the Riviera and of international tourism, I enjoy partaking in its festivals and jazz concerts, old districts, casinos, markets, and fine hotels.

Even in December, the temperatures can rise above 57 degrees Fahrenheit. Yet, it's in summer that Nice flaunts its tourism.

Sauntering along the promenade should not be your only preoccupation when spending time in Nice. For instance, I like to amble through the old town. This is where you find the real Nicois, and oh yes, again, one of the finest flower markets in the country in the outdoor market in Cours Salyea. In old Nice, I like to revisit bistros and galleries, and those little French shops.

In general, security is tight at Jewish institutions, so let the Jewish site you are visiting know of your arrival ahead of time.

Yes, do travel to Nice, the capital of the Riviera and of international tourism. Another reward of traveling to Nice is its festivals and jazz concerts, its colorful old districts, casinos, markets, and fine hotels.

The museums of Nice contain fine collections of impressionist and contemporary art. Outstanding French artists such as Dufy, Matisse, and Picasso worked along this Mediterranean coast.

In Nice, which sits beside the beckoning blue waters of the Mediterranean, about 20,000 Jews support a dozen synagogues, about 20 kosher butcher shops, several Talmud Torahs, a yeshiva, and a headquarters for the Lubavitch movement including a youth hostel. In summer, of course, Nice flaunts its tourism. It is close to other resorts along the shore and is a few minutes' drive from the wonderful scenic mountain Corniche-drives to Monte Carlo.

Nice likes to say that it remains one of the homes of the Jewish artist Marc Chagall in the form of **The National Museum Biblical Message of Marc Chagall**, located at avenue Docteur Menard and boulevard Cimiez. Tel: 93-81-75-75. It contains the most important permanent collection ever assembled that is devoted to Chagall, including large paintings, preparatory sketches, gouaches, and engravings. Chagall once said, "Perhaps in this abode, one will come and seek an ideal of fraternity and love such as my colors and my lines have dreamt." He commented on his famous Bible paintings hanging in the museum: "I want to leave them in this house so that people may find here a certain peace, a certain spirituality, a religious atmosphere, a feeling for life." Other media include stained-glass mosaics, lithographs, sculptures, and tapestries.

The Maeght Foundation, a major museum of contemporary paintings and sculpture, is set in a pine grove of St-Paul-de-Vence.

Then there is the *Musée d'Art*, 65 rue de France, and the *Musée des Beaux Arts*, at 33 Ave. des Baumettes, both in Nice.

Synagogues and points of interest in Nice include:

Consistoire de Nice ACIN, 3 Ave. Jean Medecin, 06000, Nice. Tel: 4-93-92-11-38, consistoire@consistoirenice.org. www.consistoirenice.

org. According to the Consistoire, the community holds community wide celebrations and activities for 30,000 people including those from the Alpes-Maritime.

There probably is less assimilation among Jews in Nice than in Paris because there obviously are fewer Jews and they are concentrated in a smaller area.

Jewish tourists who seek information regarding synagogues and kosher food in Nice and the area should contact the office of the Grand Rabbi, 1, rue Voltaire. Tel: 93-85-82-06.

Grand Rabbi of Nice, 3, Ave. Jean Medecin, 06000 Nice. 04-93-85-82-06.

Grand Synagogue, 7, rue Gustave-Deloye, 06000, Nice. Tel: 4 93-92-11-38. Sephardic service. For those seeking an Ashkenazic service, attend Synagogue Ezras Achim, 1, rue Blacas, 06000 Nice. Tel: 4-93-62-38-68.

Synagogue, 8, rue Marceau, 06000, Nice. Tel: 6-13-55-33-39.

Oratoire, Nice-Nord, 96, Ave. St-Lambert.

Union Libérale Israelite de France, 24, rue de France, 06000, Nice. Tel: 93-82-26-15

Synagogue Massorti of Nice, 17 Ave. Shakespeare, Nice. 33-4-93-88-25-20. www.masorti-nice.com

Organizations in Nice include:

Centre Jean Kling, 3 Ave. Jean Medecin, 06000 Nice. Tel: 4-93-92-11-38.

Centre Michelet, 22, rue Michelet. Tel: 4- 93-51-89-80. This Jewish center contains a modern synagogue, library, rnikveh (ritual bath), classrooms, and a hall for weddings and bar mitzvahs.

Fonds Social Juif Unifié, 55, rue Clement Roassal, 06000 Nice. Tel: 4-93-87-51-72.

Beth Lubavitch-Chabad, 22, rue Rossini, 06000, Nice. Tel: 93-82-46-86. FAX: 4-93-88-29-18. Sponsored by the Lubavitch movement. habadnice@gmail.com. www.habadnice.com. Rabbi Yosef Yitzchak Pinson is the rabbi here.

Chabad Center, 73 Blvd. Edouard Herriot 06200 Nice. Tel: 06-13-67-62-08. Rabbi Reouven Ouanounou is spiritual leader. habadnice@gmail.com. www.habadnice.com.

Kosher restaurants in Nice

The following two establishments are for kosher dairy diners:

Lechem Chamayim, 22, rue Rossini, 06000, Nice. Tel: 33-4-93-82-55-76.

Le Keter, 41, Ave. Georges Clemenceau, 06000, Nice. Tel: 33-4-93-76-02-87

The following are kosher meat restaurants:

Kineret, 37, bis Ave. Georges Clemenceau, 06000, Nice. Tel: 33-4-93-87-56-36.

Meat Bar, 13, rue Andrioli, 06000, Nice Tel: 33-4-93-44-11-94.

Le Dauphin Bleu, 24, rue Meyerbeer, 06000, Nice. Tel: 33-4-93-81-61-36.

Amouyal, 1, Blvd. Joseph Garnier, 06000, Nice. Tel: 33-4-93-51-71-30.

Cach' Crout, 4 Blvd. Gambetta, 06000, Nice. Tel: 33-9-84-12-49-25.

As noted, Nice is an excellent base from which to take day trips.

Cannes

If you are in Nice or Monte Carlo, certainly travel on to Cannes, the radiant city of the French Riviera with its sandy beaches, blue sky, and the beckoning Mediterranean, casinos, yacht harbors, palm trees, and the renowned Palm Beach Club, Cannes, is the largest yachting center of the Riviera.

Cannes has a major Jewish community of about 10,000. Many are involved in enhancing this city known for its film festivals and attractive boulevard La Croisette, as well as Old Port Quarter.

Synagogue, 17- 20, Blvd. d'Alsace, 06400, Cannes. Tel: 93-38-16-54. **FAX: 4-93-68-02-81. cannes.aci@wanadoo.fr, www. consistoireisraelitedecannes.fr.**

Centre Communautaire, Centre Culturel Moos Kahn, 17 Blvd. d'Alsace, 06400 Cannes. Tel: 4-93-38-16-54.

Kosher restaurants in Cannes

Pizza Yam (dairy), 22, rue Commandant Vidal, Cannes. Tel: 6-02-40-85-99 (Summer time only).

New Tovel Restaurant, 3, rue Gérard Monod, Cannes. Tel: 4-93-39-36-25.

Snack Bagel Rouvi, 18, rue Louis Nouveau, Cannes. Tel: 6-22-12-65-59.

Coté Croisette, 3, rue Latour Maubourg, Cannes. Tel: 4-93- 43 51 33.

Le 5 (meat) 62, rue Jean Jaures, Cannes. Tel: 6-65-56-62-90.

Cannes Cacher. 9, rue Marceau, Cannes. Tel: 4-92-98-80-80.

Cannes Cacher (grocery, caterer), 10, rue Louis Braille. Cannes. Tel: 4-93-39-85-08.

Chez Sylvie, 15, rue Maréchal Joffre. Cannes. Tel: 4-93-39-57-92.

Premium Kosher, 11, rue Commandant Vidal. Tel: 6-52-16-83-06.

St-Tropez

Visit this wonderful resort town, a place of beaches, boutiques, cabarets, cafés, and countless yachts. St-Tropez has provided inspiration for so many artists, including Andre Lhote and Raoul Dufy. For those visiting St-Tropez, there is a synagogue at nearby **Frejus-St-Raphael**, in rue du Progrés, 83600, in Frejus-Plage. Tel: 94-52-06-87, 94-53-20-30, or 94-53-14-04.

Antibes—Juan-les-Pins

Two towns, joined into one, sport a super night life and good shops.

Visit Antibes to see the famous castle of the Gromaldis, now the **Musée Picasso**. Juan-les-Pins, as the storybooks say, is a very popular international resort. It became famous after World War I, popularized by Jay Gould, the American railroad magnate who lived here.

Kosher restaurants in Juan Les Pins

Le Natania, 6, Ave. du Dr. d'Auteville, 06160, Juan-Les-Pins. Tel: 4-92-93-94-06.

l'Aquarium Pizzeria Sushi 30 Ave. de l'Esterel . Juan-Les-Pins. Tel: 6-15-22-96-36.

Le Carmel, 25, Ave. de l'Esterel, 06160, Juan-Les-Pins. Tel: 4-92-93-16-01.

Burger One 30 Ave. de l'Esterel 06160. Juan les Pins. Tel: 6-46-48-72-56.

Tipat Mazal (snack-pâtisserie kasher), 3, Ave. Louis Gallet, Juan-les-Pins. Tel: 6-60-46-55-57.

Chez Rico (Sandwicherie), 5, Ave. Louis Galet. Juan-les-Pins. Tel: 6-27-29-35-12.

Coco, 3, rue Louis Galet. Juan-les-Pins. Tel: 4-92-93-82-49.

Casse Croute. 24 Ave. de l'Esterel. Juan-les-Pins. Tel: 7-82-29-62-92.

Le Lev's, 12, Ave. du Maréchal Joffre, Juan-les-Pins.Tel: 4-93-61-6-53.

Seven Seventy, 5, Blvd. Charles Guillaumont. Tel: -6-34-18-38-63.

Antibes-Juan-les-Pins Synagogue, 30, chemins des Sables Villa "La Monada," 06000, Juan-les-Pains, Tel: 4-93-61-59-34. consistoireantibes@gmail.com. A Torah scroll is considered holy, sacred, and venerable. To save a Torah scroll is a great mitzvah. The Antibes-Juan-les-Pins synagogue houses a famous Torah scroll, the story of which follows.

A while back I interviewed Leon Allouche, and for the first 23 years of his life, Allouche lived in Algeria, that wonderful former North African Jewish community, in the city of Bonne. As a result of the

Cremieux Decree of the nineteenth century, Algerian Jews were French citizens. So when war clouds broke over Europe in 1939, Allouche was conscripted into the Army of the Republic of France and shipped off to Europe. When France capitulated to the Nazi onslaught in 1940, Allouche was taken prisoner. He escaped four months later and made his way back across the Mediterranean to Algeria, where he lived briefly until that hero of modern France, Gen. Charles De Gaulle, rallied the nation.

Allouche, like French Jewish men and women throughout the French Empire, immediately joined the ranks of General de Gaulle. Once again Allouche sailed across the Mediterranean.

As the Allied armies fought their way across eastern France, Allouche would stop and ask residents along the way, "Is there a synagogue here? Where is it?"

Nearly all Jewish houses of worship were gutted or completely destroyed. Many towns had no Jews. One day in 1944, in a small town in Alsace, Allouche asked several townspeople if there were a synagogue in the area. A civilian who had been jailed previously led him to a shattered building that was stripped bare and from which the Holy Ark had been ripped right out of the wall.

The Germans had transformed this house of worship into an army barracks and dumped all the religious items they could find into a garbage heap 100 yards away. Allouche then commandeered several German prisoners of war to locate the garbage site, and soon his group found it. There, sticking out of the refuse, were the two poles of a single Torah. The POW crew quickly cleared away the area and found three other Torah scrolls.

Because Allouche and his unit had to move out, he left three Torah scrolls at the liberated synagogue for the future Jewish community and took a small one with him on his journey across Nazi Germany. It protected him, he recalled 43 years later.

Discharged in 1945, Allouche carried the Torah back to his home in Bonne, Algeria. In 1962, when France pulled out of Algeria, the Jews departed with the French who lived in Algeria and were known as pieds noirs (black feet). About 100,000 Jews fled this North African country and came to France as part of a modern exodus. More than 10,000 went to Israel.

Allouche took the Torah with him to Antibes-Juan-les-Pins where, like his fellow Algerians, he could resume his life as a French citizen. (He would later become police chief of Antibes-Juan-les-Pins). This beautiful municipality is described as "one of the flashiest places on the Riviera," such is the quality of nightlife and its beaches. Here rests the Torah now, in a town with a timeless Mediterranean charm.

Other synagogues along the Riviera near Antibes-Juan-les-Pins include:

Cagnes-sur-Mer, 4, Imp. Douce-France, 35.

Draguignan, 15, rue de l'Observance.

Hyeres, Chemin de la Ritorte, 1, Lot Payraud.

Menton, centre "Altyner," 106, cours du Centenaire.

St-Laurent-du-Var, Villa "Le Petit Clos," 35, Ave. des Oliviers.

Marseilles

Some of my happiest and best travel experiences have occurred in the thriving port city of Marseilles, France. Called "Europort of the South," the "City of Conventions," "Gateway to the Riviera," it remains a tough harbor city and its history stretches back more than two thousand years to its foundation by the Greeks in the sixth century, BCE.

Whenever I travel to Marseilles, I ramble along the *Quai du Port, Quai des Belges, Quai de Rive-Nive,* I munch on salted peanuts, the warming sun and the smell of the harbor invigorate me as I gaze at *the Chateau d'If,* the tiny island that houses the 16th century prison portrayed in the book, *Le Comte de Monte Cristo* by Alexandre Dumas.

Marseilles remains the second-largest Jewish community in France and the fifth-largest in Western Europe. About 65,000 Jews reside there, amidst the city's metro population of nearly two million, a city which counts about 220,000 Muslims, of whom 70,000 are practicing.

Is this how Jews live in North Africa? Is this Oran? Fez? Cairo? I asked myself. No, it is Marseilles.

Here are Arab men carrying long spits with roasted lamb. The guttural sounds of Arabic permeate the air as the bearers wail haunting Arabic melodies of the Sahara.

I must have attended several hundred bar mitzvah ceremonies in my life, opulent ones and frugal ones. Held in the summer house of a very successful professional, this one certainly belonged to the former category. Cocktails were served poolside, tables were set out on the veranda, champagne flowed, and food abounded-course after course of exotic Sephardic dishes. There even was the familiar bar mitzvah candle-lighting ceremony similar to the one in the United States, where the boy is joined by various relatives as they light each of the 13 candles to signify the boy's thirteenth birthday. Gathered here were many successful, educated North African Jews who would never go back to the continent across the Mediterranean. They were French. They mixed with French society. They were business persons and professionals: they lived well, dressed well in the latest Paris fashions, and belonged to clubs. Many had fashionable apartments on the affluent avenue Parades and other upper middle-class thoroughfares.

Marseilles, it is said, is a mix of Catholics, Communists, socialists, free thinkers, Armenians, Corsicans, Africans, Arabs, Jews, and Gypsies. Many are newcomers, including repatriated pieds noirs from Algeria, Tunisia, and Morocco. Marseilles has one of France's largest concentrations of Arab immigrants. Lately the newest group are refugees from Vietnam.

Marseilles remains bustling and cosmopolitan. The famous Canebière Boulevard is always full of sailors and crowds at cafes. The city boasts the **Longchamps Palace**, with its **Fine Arts Museum** and the **Natural History Museum**. Atop a hill, **Notre Dame de la Garde Basilica** offers a breathtaking panorama of Marseilles.

Walk around the old port at night. Visit the restaurants, which offer rich gastronomic rewards. The dining establishments, cafes, and fish houses are filled with tourists who come here for a meal that may include bouillabaisse, turbot, white wine, and Chianti. Just southwest of the port lie the islands of Rattonneau and Pomegues. Between them and the mainland is the isle of Chateau d'If, which was the scene of part of Alexandre Dumas's *Le Comte de Monte Cristo.*

As an emporium, Marseilles trades with the Levant and the Near and Far East. The smell of the sea is everywhere.

Through this ancient harbor in the late 1940s passed thousands of Jews on their way to their homeland in Palestine. The late former president of France, François Mitterrand, helped pave the way for Jewish ships to go to Israel. In the three years following the end of World War II in 1945, the French embarrassed the British in Palestine just as the British were trying to keep the French out of the Middle East. France lost Syria and Lebanon. Perhaps the British should lose Palestine, thought a few in the Quai d'Orsay, the French Foreign Office.

As one walks up and down the busy Canebière Boulevard or strolls around the Old Harbor (the Vieux Port), one cannot help but visualize those post-World War II days, when old, unseaworthy Staten-Island-ferry-type boats, their beams bursting from the overcrowding of humans literally stuffed on board, sailed out secretly at night into the blue Mediterranean to run the gauntlet of the British Navy in order to reach the Jewish homeland. The British and the world called them "illegals," these survivors of the Holocaust. They maintained they were neither displaced nor illegal.

As noted above, Marseilles had been my stomping ground during the days of the recovery of France after World War II, as well as the days of the nightmare following the Algerian War. Some of my happiest and best travel experiences occurred in this thriving seaport. Algeria, they say, was France's Vietnam. In the late 1950s and early

1960s, Jews fled Algeria because they knew that the country would revert to Moslem rule, and they were not sure Moslems would allow them to live in peace.

During the Algerian War, Jews in France leaned toward the French view. After all, they were French citizens according to the 100-year-old Cremieux Decree. While some Jews fought on the Algerian side, they would never feel comfortable in an Arab society, even though, throughout history, the Arabs treated Jews relatively well compared with Christian Europe.

They were beginning a new life in a new land, and even though they knew the language, they struggled to settle in. But unlike other Jewish immigrants from the North African countries, Algerian Jews were French citizens. This instant citizenship granted them rights to health benefits, to the vote, and to hold political office.

The first stop of the North African Jews who came to Marseilles was the **Place de la Bourse,** a large downtown square, a place that has witnessed revolutions, demonstrations, financial crisis, peaceful gatherings, and celebrations. Now new activity began on the square: the welcoming of refugees, newcomers, people looking for jobs. When fighting in Algeria had ended, the OAS went underground in clandestine headquarters here.

Today, about 65,000 Jews live here, many from Morocco and Tunisia. They sponsor about 20 synagogues, day and vocational schools, and youth centers. Marseilles is now the second largest Jewish community in France.

Marseilles is a city of Sephardic Jews with names like Chiche, Dahan, Zana, Solal, Amsellem, and Zemmour. They are committed to Judaism. They are proud and active as they try to keep a community alive, fighting assimilation and anti-Semitism.

Their community organizations are enough to boggle the mind: the Fonds Social Juif Unifié, the social welfare agency; community centers; WIZO; ORT; B'nai B'rith; Zionist groups; sports clubs. Many work under the umbrella organization known as **CRIF**, which makes representations to the government.

A Jewish radio station in Marseilles broadcasts cultural programs to the people of all religions. The radio serves an educational purpose; it brings Judaism into the home.

For the Jewish community in France, whether it be Marseilles, Nice, Lyon, or Paris, where nearly two-thirds of the country's approximately 500,000 Jews live, there is a new page in the annals of history.

In the final analysis, the French Jewish community can no longer be called a group of newcomers or of an immigrant generation.

But times have changed. According to Rabbi Michael Rosenthal of

A view of the Canebiere Blvd., Marseilles. (Photo credit: Atout France-France Tourism Development Agency, Pascal Micalef, photographer.)

Beth Chabad Chateau Gombert, "there's not much anti-Semitism on a daily basis," but there is a large Muslim population and that creates, the rabbi added, an "uncertain future."

And William Labi vice president of the Consistoire Israelite de Marseilles, declares that "we have a median level of anti-Semitism, no more than other big towns in France or in Europe." But he and the rabbi stress it is more difficult in certain neighborhoods.

Because of terrorist attacks in Nice and Toulouse in southern France, extra precautions in guarding Jewish schools, synagogues and institutions have been taken.

Despite the fact that the number of synagogues increased over the last three decades, one synagogue is scheduled to be converted into a mosque, reflecting demographic shifts in southern France. The Or Thora synagogue is being used less and less by Jews who have actually moved from that neighborhood near the main railway station. The synagogue is being sold to a Muslim cultural association.

But for now there are eight Chabad centers in the city and "Marseille may be one of the world's most vibrant Jewish communities when you speak about engagement in the everyday Jewish life," added Chabad Rabbi Rosenthal, referring to "Jewish weddings, kosher observance, bar mitzvahs and of course Jewish schools."

The Jews of Marseille sponsor about 50 synagogues, as well as several dozen kosher restaurants and grocery stores.

Five decades after their arrival, Algerian Jews have entered various professions and have done well economically. Unlike their fellow Sephardic Jews in the United States, Sephardic Jews are in the majority in Marseilles and throughout France.

For information while in Marseilles, contact the following:

Appel Unifié Juif de France, 173, rue Paradis, Marseilles. Tel: 91-37-03-21. Similar to the American United Jewish Appeal, this organization is interested in meeting Americans and exchanging views.

B'nai B'rith, 22 place aux huiles, 1300, Marseille.

C.A.S.I.M.-Espace Reussite, 109 rue Breteuil, 13006 Marseilles. Tel: 4-96-10-06-70. casimas@voila.fr.

Consistoire Israelite de Marseilles, 117, rue Breteuil, Marseilles. Tel: 91-37-49-64. www.consistoiredemarseille.com.

Coopération Féminine, 67, rue Breteuil, 13006, Marseilles. Tel: 91-81-79-59.

Fonds Social Juif Unifié (FSJU), 67, rue Breteuil, 13006, Marseilles. Tel: 91-37-40-57.

K.K.L. (Jewish National Fund), 2, bis rue Farges, 13006, Marseilles. Tel: 4-91-53-39-74.

Beth Chabad, 112, Blvd. Bary, 13013 Marseilles. Tourists should contact Rabbi Labkovsky. Tel: 33-6-20-51 43-53. www.bethabad8eme. com. Another contact for tourists is Rabbi Bitton at a new Chabad center located at the tourist beach area. Tel: 33-6-65-22-6012. For prayer service, American visitors can go to the Temple Breteuil, 117, rue Breteuil, 13006, Marseilles. Tel: 4-91-37-49-64. For update information on prayers and events at this synagogue, contact the Consistoire's website, www.consistgoiredemarseille. This main synagogue conducts a Sephardic service. The chief rabbi, Rabbi Reouven Ohana, has his office at 119, rue Breteuil, 13006, Marseilles. An Ashkenazic service is held in the Synagogue at 8, impasse Dragon, 13006, Marseilles, just nearby.

Other synagogues include the following:

Chalom Rav, 8, impasse Dragon, 13006, Marseilles.

Maguen David, 31, Ave. des Olives, 13013, Marseilles (La Rose, a suburban area). Tel: 91-70-05-45.

Ozer Dalim, 8, impasse Dragon, 13006, Marseilles. Tel: 4-91-53-33-73.

Union Libérale Israelite de France, 21, rue Martiny, 13008, Marseilles. Tel: 4-91-71-97-46. FAX: 4-91-37-54-31. ulifmarseille@free.fr.

Masorti Olami Judaica, 71, Ave. de Hambourg, Marseilles. Tel: 30-6-22-25-3695. www.masortiolami.org.

There are several community centers in Marseilles:

Centre Communautaire Edmond Fleg, 4, impasse Dragon, 13006, Marseilles. Tel: 91-37-42-01. mail@centrefleg.com

Centre Communautaire le Rosa, 31, Ave. des Olives, 13013 Marseille. This community center is located on the outskirts of Marseille and has a dairy restaurant known as "Gan Shoshanim."

Kosher Restaurants in Marseilles

The Jews of Marseille sponsor 32 kosher restaurants and 18 kosher groceries.

The following are kosher meat restaurants:

Jackinot, 9, rue Sainte-Victoire, Marseilles.

Le Huitieme sud, 51, Ave. Georges Pompidou, Marseilles.

Au Falafel, 352 Ave. du Prado, 13008, Marseilles. Tel: 4-91-36-04-93.

La Table de Chine, 143 Blvd. Paul Claudel, Marseilles. 13010. Tel: 4-91-75-19-00.

The following are dairy restaurants:

Gan Shoshanim, Centre Communautaire le Rosa, 31, Ave. des Olives, 13013 Marseilles. Tel: 4-91-70-05-45.

Au Pizza Tova, 359, Ave. du Prado, 13008, Marseilles. Tel: 9-80-460-460.

Le Kikar, 35, rue Saint Suffren, 13006 Marseilles. Tel: 4-91-81-13-68.

AIX-EN-PROVENCE

Just a half-hour from Marseilles—only 20 miles—rests the quiet but stimulating municipality of Aix-en-Provence. This delightful academic town is known as the town of spas and arts, of music and fountains. A scholastic center, it boasts three universities and many institutes and it hosts music and art events.

An American school where students from the United States study French language, history, and culture adds to the cultural impact of Aix as it is fondly called. Stroll along the **Cours Mirabeau**, the most celebrated avenue in France and called one of the "most beautiful main streets in the world." At the head of the avenue is a noted fountain, La Rotonde, a monument to nineteenth-century romanticism. Most travel writers advise that the best time to experience the life and sites of the Cours is early morning or late at night.

In spite of wars, construction, and other threats to the landscape, Aix has managed to hold on to its lively fountains along the middle of its lovely streets. It is this music of culture and scenic beauty that keeps many tourists in rapture.

Enjoy the cool, shady plane trees and the eighteenth-century facades of elegant manor houses. Stop at the cafes and watch the world go by. Paul Cezanne and Emile Zola did when they lived here.

Once the capital of Provence, the city has existed for more than 2,000 years. Jews have a long history in Aix. They have lived here since the fifteenth century. Darius Milhaud, the famous French Jewish composer, was born here. His great grandfather helped establish a synagogue in Aix in 1840.

The Aix Jewish community of 600 families nearly ceased to exist after World War II. However, with the influx of North African Jews in the early 1960s, especially those from Algeria, the Jewish community was renewed.

A modern **synagogue** is located at 5, rue de Jerusalem, 13090, Aix-en-Provence. Tel: 4-42-26-69-39.

Visitors are welcome to attend services each morning at 6:45 a.m. Evening services depend on sunset. On Saturday mornings, services are conducted at 8:30 a.m.

A Jewish community center, named Centre Culturel Darius Mihaud, is at 3, bis rue de Jerusalem, 13090 Aix-en-Provence. Tel: 4-42-27-37-94. centremihaud@hotmail.fr. A kosher community restaurant is located in this center.

Or **Shalom Jewish Masorti Community of Aix-en-Provence**. orchalom@gmail.com, www.masortiolami.org.

NORMANDY

For centuries, Jews have lived in the serene and peaceful countryside of Normandy. Because of its scenery, splendid architecture, contrasting landscapes, rich agricultural lands, and historic past, it is one of the most attractive French provinces.

Actually, Jewish presence in Normandy goes back to the days when Julius Caesar completed the conquest of Gaul in 50 BCE.

The towns of Normandy have retained their character despite wartime destruction and postwar building. In Normandy, too, are the D-Day beaches that are part of American and French history: Utah, Omaha, Gold, Juno, and Sword. Farther east is Arromanches, where the British landed. And from the beautiful seaside town of Honfleur, Samuel de Champlain set sail to Quebec to explore the American Great Lakes.

Normandy is considered the home of the best cheese in the world, apple cider, strong Calvados, and tasty duck. It boasts lush, green fields, farmhouses, and estates. Today the Normans, active, friendly people, welcome tourists of all races and religions, just as they greeted the American GIs with glasses of cider following the D-Day invasion.

This is the place that recalls the voice of our former president, then General Dwight D. Eisenhower, who on June 6, 1944, declared, "Peoples of Western Europe, a landing was made today on your beaches."

Rouen

This municipality is one of the most interesting in Normandy; its main street remains the River Seine. Devastated in World War II, the city was rebuilt in such a way that one is constantly reminded of its rich history, art, and architecture. It was at Rouen that the peasant girl, Jeanne d'Arc, (Joan of Arc) inspired France to oppose the invading English.

An archeological discovery in 1976, was made beneath the parking lot of the **Palace of Justice**. Uncovered were the remains of a medieval Jewish building, apparently the only Jewish institution of higher learning in Europe whose walls have survived from either antiquity or the Middle Ages. This would account for the fact that the present Palace of Justice fronts on rue aux Juifs (Street of the Jews). Uncovered in the excavations dedicated that day were graffiti— Hebrew inscriptions—on the walls of the medieval academy. This discovery meant that Rouen was a most important medieval center in France for Jewish studies, overshadowing even Paris

The Jewish school of learning dated back to about the year 1090. (Some believe the building was a synagogue or a *yeshiva*, a monument to France's Jewish culture and history.)

For Prof. Norman Golb of the University of Chicago, a specialist in Hebrew and Judaeo-Arabic studies, this find means that the Jewish presence in northern France was not only economic and commercial, but cultural as well. What makes the story even more exciting is that the location of the structure had been predicted by Golb, who reached his conclusion from a study of medieval manuscripts.

Months before the Romanesque building was discovered, the professor had published his hypothesis about the yeshiva in a book entitled History and Culture of the Jews of Rouen. It appeared in Hebrew in the spring of 1976.

He had researched 150 manuscripts which he studied in Jerusalem, the British Museum, the Bibliothèque Nationale in Paris, and libraries in Budapest, Amsterdam, and New York, as well as the Vatican Library.

His selection of the site of the yeshiva on Rouen's rue aux Juifs was based on the fact that references to the building stop with the sixteenth century. This was the point at which the highly ornamented Palais de Justice was built. "I surmised that they had razed the Jewish center to make way for the new construction," Golb told me in an interview.

Equally fascinating is the fact that Golb may have discovered why Rouen was overlooked as a center of Judaism during the Middle Ages. It may have been bypassed because Hebrew references to the city were misread by Latin scholars of the Middle Ages. Until the fourteenth century, Rouen was known as Rodom.

In surviving Hebrew manuscripts, the name Rodom is written like Rhodoz, a medieval city in southern France. What happened was that scholars, in recopying the manuscripts, often mistook the Hebrew letter samech for a final mem. Golb said he was fascinated by the possibility that the city they were really talking about and writing about as a "thriving Jewish community" was really Rodom or Rouen.

"I went back to the original manuscripts at the British Museum, and my suspicions were immediately confirmed," he said. Subsequent studies of manuscripts in Paris, Amsterdam, and Jerusalem revealed detailed maps, as well as descriptions of the Jewish quarter and of life in the city.

Today in Rouen, there are less than a thousand Jews engaged in professions and academic life, as well as industry and commerce. The Jews who came to Rouen in the 1960s from Algeria and Tunisia brought a Sephardic presence to the area.

With the archeological discovery, more people will be visiting Rouen. Since that day when the find was made, Rouen and the

The Palace of Justice in Rouen. (Photo courtesy of the French Government Tourist Office)

government of France have spent about $1 million on its restoration. It is a Jewish historic landmark in France not to be missed.

The Jewish Monument is open to the public. There are guided religious and spiritual tours for Rouen each Tuesday at 3:00 p.m., but reservations are necessary. For information contact the Rouen Tourist Board: 33-2-32-08-32-47 Read more at: http://us.france.fr/en/information/yeshiva-rouen-medieval-jewish-house.

Synagogue, 55, rue des Bons-Enfants, 76100, Rouen. Tel/FAX: 2-35-71-01-44.

St-Lô

St-Lô was one of the towns that Gen. George Patton made famous. It was from here in June 1944 that his forces broke out of German encirclement, and the enemy front facing the West collapsed. (Behind the roads traveled on by the rabbi are the D-Day beaches).

True, there probably were no Jews here when Patton's Third Army moved out against the Germans. But a few Jewish families have now settled in this historic town.

Like the countryside around it, Normandy contains small Jewish communities tied together by joint activities and by visiting rabbis.

There are a few Jewish families in **Evreux**, about 10 families in

Lisieux, 15 families in **Cherbourg**, 200 families in **Le Havre**, and 400 families in **Rouen**. And in **Caen**, almost entirely rebuilt after the war, there are about 100 Jewish families. After World War II, the Jews of Caen built their own **synagogue** at 46, avenue de la Libération. Tel: 2-31-43-60-54. Caen has a small but active Jewish community. Many arrived here from that cultural center of Jewish life in France, Strasbourg.

Memorial: A Museum for Peace, Esplanade Dwight Eisenhower, Caen, in Normandy. On April 26, 1992, a new and very moving exhibit citing the World War II deportations and acts of genocide was opened. The exhibit includes maps of the camps, items from deportations, a painting by Andre Roth, and a scenographic creation of shadows and vacillating lights dramatizing and highlighting the shameful place that the deportation occupies in the history of World War II. Museum hours: Open daily 9:00 a.m. to 7:00 p.m.; from July 11 to August 31, open until 9:00 p.m. Closed January 1 to 15, March 20, and December 25. Tel: 31-06-06-44.

The Jews of Normandy are a close-knit group. New superhighways and high-speed trains offer them the opportunity to go from Caen to Paris in two hours, from Rouen to Paris in a little more than an hour. But there are also intercity happenings. The Jews of Le Havre and Caen hold joint activities: seminars, lectures, and films.

During summer months, thousands of Jews also come to **Deauville**, which is the world-renowned resort of casinos, polo matches, and horse racing. In the summer, I was told, there is even a minyan in Deauville, whose summer population rises from about 10,000 persons to more than 100,000.

RENNES

Rennes is the capital of Brittany, the French province that is west of Paris and juts out into the Atlantic Ocean. Damaged in World War II and liberated by American GIs, the city boasts a beautiful town hall, with curved facades designed by Jacques Gabriel, as well as two important museums, **Musée de Bretagne** and **Musée des Beaux-Arts**, at 20 Quai Emile Zola. Artists such as Gaugin painted here, and writers such as Chateaubriand wrote here.

Rennes existed in the days of Gaul, the capital city of the Celtic tribe of the Redones. In the ninth century, Rennes became part of Brittany and gained prestige as a grand duchy.

There never have been many Jews in Brittany. Jews lived in nearby Nantes in the fifth century and were found in Brittany at the end of the twelfth century.

By an agreement of February 23, 1222, Pierre Mauclerc, Duke of Brittany, confirmed the jurisdiction of the bishop of Nantes over the Jews living in his area. In 1236, many Jews in Brittany were massacred by Crusaders. The remainder were expelled in April 1240 by Duke Jean le Roux, who declared a moratorium on all debts owed to Jews and ordered them to return all pledges of chattel or real estate. For several centuries, therefore, only converted Jews were found living in Brittany.

From the beginning of the seventeenth century, many Marranos settled in Brittany, mainly in Nantes, a little more than an hour from Rennes.

During the eighteenth century, Jewish traders from Bordeaux, as well as Alsace-Lorraine, began to visit area fairs and markets. But in 1780, Jews were expelled. After the French Revolution, Jews returned to Brittany. In 1808, when Jewish community consistories were established in France, only 300 Jews lived in Rennes. Historically, one reason there may never have been many Jews here is that Brittany, unlike Paris, Strasbourg, Lyon, and Marseilles, is not a "gateway" or port city. The thinking goes: you needed a port city to attract Jews who were tradesmen.

What makes Rennes an interesting place to visit is its ancient ramparts with watchtowers and gates, narrow streets, little squares, and half-timbered houses.

Located in the heart of an agricultural region and surrounded by areas of beautiful beach coastline, Rennes maintains a fine university and an excellent medical center. As a French Army administrative center, the city attracts many civil servants or, as the French call them, "fonctionnaires." The municipality is also the headquarters of the prefect, the official who supervises the whole region of Brittany.

There are usually jobs available here, and that is why many Jews settled in during the wave of the North African Jewish immigration in the 1960s.

What will possibly preserve the Jewish communities in the region is the T.G.V. high-speed train of the French National Railways, which makes the Paris-Rennes run in about two hours instead of three.

The Jews in Brittany feel that their ties to Paris (where one-half of France's approximately 500,000 Jews reside) will obviously be much stronger because the trip is now two hours instead of three. A one-day journey from Paris to attend a lecture on Jewish subjects or a visit to attend Jewish program will help stimulate this small community.

When you visit Rennes, head towards the Synagogue and **Jewish Community Center,** 5 allee du Mont Dol, 35000, Rennes. Tel: 7-82-89-27-23. contact@accisafra-rennes.fr www.accisafra-rennesfr.

Jews must have lived here before World War II, although people don't know too much about the old community. There is a monument in the synagogue reading, "Mortes en Déportation, 1942-1945." I counted more than 60 names on the memorial plaque, victims of the Holocaust.

Services are Friday at 7:15 p.m. They always have a minyan. One of the large community gatherings occurs on the Day of Remembrance, of the Holocaust. The municipal authorities of Rennes attend.

According to Mary Elsy and Jill Norman in Travels in Brittany, Brittany contributed more men and women than any other province in France to the Free French Resistance movement. Some of World War II's fiercest fighting took place in Brittany, in such ports as Brest, Lorient, St-Nazare, and St-Malo.

On Yom Kippur, several hundred Jews pray in the synagogue's large room.

There are regional activities with Jewish communities in Nantes, Brest, and Lorient. One gets the impression they have many joint gatherings. The community is friendly and welcomes visitors.

Here in Rennes, this city of art and history, the second trial of Capt. Alfred Dreyfus took place at the turn of the century. Here again, Dreyfus was unjustly found guilty. But at his Rennes trial it was clear that this Jewish army officer had been framed and several of the judges wavered. The trial took place in the **red brick schoolhouse** that still stands. Later it was named after Emile Zola, the noted French writer who was instrumental in focusing world attention on the injustice to Dreyfus. It was his famous newspaper article that shouted out in a banner headline style, "I Accuse."

Obviously, Jews don't live in a vacuum. They are part of a city and a people with a rich history, and live in a land that should be explored. Brittany offers sandy seaside beaches, rivers, fishing, natural sites, and wildlife. You can live on a boat. You can play golf or ride a horse. You can camp out or stay in a fine hotel. And of course, you can visit a friendly Jewish community.

FRENCH SYNAGOGUES OUTSIDE OF PARIS

There are synagogues and community centers in more than 120 cities and towns in France. Further questions should be directed to the **Consistoire Central**, 19, rue St-Georges, 75009, Paris. Tel: 49-70-88-00.

Here is a partial listing:

Agen, 52, rue de Montesquieu.

Amiens, 30, rue du Port d'Amont.

Annecy, 18, rue de Narvik.

Annemasse, 5, rue du Dr. Coquand.
Arcachon, 36, Ave. Gambetta.
Bastia, 3, rue du Castagno.
Beauvais, rue Jules-Isaac.
Belfort, 6, rue de l'As-de-Carreau.
Beziers, 19, Place Pierre-Semard.
Brest, 40, rue de la République.
Chalons-sur-Marne, 21, rue Lochet.
Chalons-sur-Saone, 10, rue Germiny.
Chambery, 9, impasse chardonnet.
Clermont-Ferrand, 6, rue Blatin.
Colmar, 3, rue de la Cigogne.
Compiegne, 4, rue du Dr. Charles-Nicolle.
Creil, 1, Place de la Synagogue.
Dunkerque, 19, rue Jean-Bart.
Elbauf, 29, rue Grémont.
Epernay, 2, rue Placet.
Epinal, 9, rue Charlet.
Evian, Ave. des Grottes.
Grenoble, 11, rue Andre-Maginot.
La Ciotat, 1, square de Verdun.
 La Rochelle, 40, cours des Dames.
Le Havre, 38, rue Victor-Hugo.
Le Mans, 46, Blvd. Paixhans.
Lille, 5, rue Auguste-Angellier.
Limoges, 25-27, rue Pierre-Leroux.
Luneville, 5, rue Castara.
Macon, 1, rue Bauderon de Seneca.
Melun, corner of rues Branly and Michelet.
Metz, 39, rue du Rabbin-Elie-Bloch.
Montauban, 12, rue Sainte Claire.
Mulhouse, 2, rue des Rabbins.
Nancy, 17, Blvd. Joffre.
Nantes, 5, impasse Copernic.
Perigeux, 13, rue Paul-Louis-Courier.
Perpignan, 54, rue Arago.
Poitiers, 30, Blvd. Jeanne d'Arc.
Roanne, 9, rue Beaulieu.
St-Etienne, 34, rue d'Arcole.
St-Louis, rue du Temple.
Sedan-Charleville, 6, Ave. de Verdun.
Sens, 14, rue de la Grande-Juiverie.
Sete, 136 chemin de l'Anglore.

Tarbes, 6, rue Gaston Manent Cite Rothschild.
Toulon, 184, Ave. Lazare-Carnot.
Troyes, 5, rue Brunneval.
Valence, 1, Place du Colombier.
Valenciennes, 36, rue de l'Intendance.
Verdun, impasse des Jacobins. Versailles, 10, rue Albert-Joly.
Vichy, 2 bis, rue du Marechal-Foch.
Vitry-le-François, 29, rue du Mouton.
Vittel, rue Croix-Pierrot.

England, which we shall visit in the next chapter, is now closer to France. The Channel Tunnel linking the two countries and the Continent with the British Isles brings the two large Jewish communities closer together. Closer links between French and British Jewry will continue to be forged in tourism. It takes about two and a half hours to go by train from London to Paris. However with Brexit, the political and economic ties will surely suffer.

Suggested Reading

Adler, Jacques. *The Jews of Paris and the Final Solution.*
Ben-Sasson, H. H., ed. *A History of the Jewish People.* Cambridge, Mass.: Harvard University Press, 1969.
Bernstein, Richard. *Fragile Glory: A Portrait of France and the French.* New York: Alfred A. Knopf, 1990.
Courthion, Pierre. *Paris in the Past.* Paris: Editions d'Art Albert Skira, 1957.
Culbertson, Judi, and Tom Randall. *Permanent Parisians: An Illustrated Guide to the Cemeteries of Paris.* Chelsea, Vt.: Chelsea Green Publishing, 1986.
Eban, Abba. *Heritage: Civilization and the Jews.* New York: Summit Books, 1984.
Halter, Marek. *The Book of Abraham.* New York: Henry Holt, 1983.
——. *The Jester and the King.* New York: Little, Brown, 1988.
Hertzberg, Arthur. *The French Enlightenment and the Jews.* New York: Columbia University Press, 1968.
Hyman, Paula. *From Dreyfus to Vichy: The Remaking of French Jewry, 1906-1939.* New York: Columbia University Press, 1979.
Johnson, Paul. *A History of the Jews.* New York: Harper & Row, 1987.
Jones, David Pryce. *Paris in the Third Reich.* New York: Holt, Rinehart and Winston, 1981.
Josephs, Jeremy. *Swastika Over Paris: The Fate of the Jews in France.* New York: Little, Brown, 1989.

Krinsky, Carol Herselle. *Synagogues of Europe: Architecture, History, Meaning*. Cambridge, Mass.: MIT Press, 1985.

Liebling, A. J. *Between Meals: An Appetite for Paris*. New York: Simon & Schuster, 1962.

Marrus, Michael R., and Robert O. Paxton. *Vichy France and the Jews*. New York: Basic Books, 1981.

Morgan, Ted. *An Uncertain Hour: The French, the Germans, the Jews, and the City of Lyon, 1940-1945*. New York: William and Morrow, 1990.

Posner, S. *Adolphe Cremieux: A Biography*. Philadelphia: Jewish Publication Society of America, 1940.

Roth, Cecil. *A History of the Jews: From Earliest Times through the Six Day War*. New York: Schocken Books, 1970.

Schnapper, Dominique. *Jewish Identities in France: An Analysis of Contemporary French Jewry*. Chicago: University of Chicago Press, 1983.

Szajkousky, Soza. *Jews and the French Revolution of 1789, 1830, 1848*. New York: Klav Publishing House, 1969.

Vital, David. *A People Apart, The Jews in Europe, 1789-1939*. Oxford: Oxford University Press, 1999.

Wilson, Derek. *Rothschild, the Wealth and Power of a Dynasty*. New York: Charles Scribner's Sons, 1988.

Zuccotti, Susan. *The Holocaust, the French, and the Jews*. New York: Basic Books, 1993.

England

Cromwell, Disraeli, and the Rothschilds

London casts a spell on the American visitor with its parks, museums, art galleries, and history. England was America's "mother country" and London, its capital. In our day, we recall World War II, when Great Britain stood alone against the Nazi tyranny. Bombed at night, the English rose in the morning to meet the day. They never surrendered, neither during nor after Dunkirk and the blitz.

"Surrender?" a British sergeant asked his men when he heard of Belgium's 1940 collapse in World War II. "Let them all surrender; we never will!" And in modern times Britain has stood as an ally with America.

A Brief History

Jews came to England with William the Conqueror (1027-87), who, in 1066, invaded England, which then was a Saxon-Scandinavian land. Those first Jews who arrived along with William hailed from France. Even in those days, one did not give up speaking French easily; in fact, we are told, French continued to be the language of the Jews until they were expelled in 1290.

Jews counted themselves among the few Londoners to own stone houses. They lived in that square mile of central London called "the City," which ironically is located next to the East End. Centuries later it would again become the "old Jewish neighborhood," though by then a poorer area. A street called "Old Jewry" survives to this day in this section of central London; it is one of the area's most famous lanes, and contains much history. Located in EC3, it was once known as "Poor Jewry."

An English travel writer described the Jewish merchants of London long ago as having "the ageless eyes of the Jews." Others would translate "Jew" to mean "moneylender." The first impression of Jews in England was that of a peddler with a pack on his back.

As Jews were to become proprietors, and Christians could not float loans, Jews financed these non-Jews, offering capital with payment of interest. The church condemned moneylending as the "heinous sign of usury." Aaron of the town of Lincoln, a leading Jewish European financier in the twelfth century, became one of the wealthiest persons in England.

While Jewish tax collectors thought they were protected by royalty, they actually were "chattels of the King" and possessed few legal rights. Although the king and his associates were heavily in debt to the Jews, royalty soon discovered ways to renege on their payments by canceling the debts or by killing or expelling the Jews.

Another way to wipe out debts was the fable of ritual murder, followed by blood libel. Jews were supposed to have murdered Christians, then to have used the blood of the victims to make matzoh on Passover.

In 1275, King Edward I prohibited Jews from collecting interest. That measure strangled the Jewish community. Later, on July 18, 1290, Edward I banished the Jews from England. By November 1, 1290, All Saints Day, most of the 16,000 Jewish refugees had made their way across the English Channel to France, Flanders, and Germany. Their descendants would not return for 400 years.

After four centuries, what finally would move England to readmit its Jews? British pounds and shillings would play a major role in bringing Jews back onto English soil. The return of Jews to England has its origin in Amsterdam. Working together would be the Puritan dictator Oliver Cromwell and a Dutch Jew named Manasseh Ben Israel (1604-57). As Winston Churchill wrote, "It was left to a Calvinist dictator to remove the ban which a Catholic king had imposed."

Until 1616, a small colony of secret Jews, mostly Marranos who came to England around 1500, managed to keep Judaism alive. Toleration of the Jewish return to Britain was due in part to the fact that the English read the Old Testament. With Manasseh Ben Israel's pleading and Cromwell's "unwritten permission," Jews began arriving in England in 1656.

During the Revolution of 1688, William of Orange captured the throne of England and sparked the influx of additional Jews to England. The restored Stuarts protected the Jews, who could now earn a living among their Christian neighbors. But it would take 200 more years for them to obtain political rights.

The newcomers were Sephardim from Spain and Portugal. They had names like Pereira, de Castro, d'Oliveira, de Veifa, Mendes da Costa, Gomes, Nunes, Henriques, Alvares, and Lousades.

By the end of the seventeenth century, about 20,000 Jews lived in Great Britain. The majority settled in London. Besides the Bevis Marks Synagogue, three Ashkenazic synagogues were organized. Jews of this era made their living as peddlers and small traders, opticians, physicians, and teachers.

Indirect parliamentary recognition came in 1698. Later, with the Jew Bill of 1753, foreign-born Jews were permitted to acquire privileges enjoyed by native children. Still, despite commercial success, Jews were not permitted to hold political office; nor could they serve in Parliament, vote in municipal elections, or attend the universities. Finally, in 1826, Jews were at least able to become naturalized.

As in many countries, the Jews of England were expected to govern themselves. The Board of Deputies was established in 1760 as the representative house of British Jewry. To this day, it maintains de facto government recognition.

After the Napoleonic Wars, Jewish families, like the Goldsmiths and Rothschilds, played an important role in English finance and society. By 1830, 30,000 Jews lived in England, two-thirds of them in London. But English Jews looked across the channel and saw that their French co-religionists were already emancipated. They wanted similar rights. By 1840, the last of the so-called disabilities for Jews in England had disappeared, with the exception of the right to sit in Parliament. At that time, the swearing-in ceremony for members of Parliament was taken "on the oath of the true faith, of a Christian," an oath a Jew obviously could not take.

In 1858, Lionel Nathan Rothschild became the first Jew to be admitted to the House of Commons. He was not forced to "take the oath of a Christian." Since then, one or more Jews have served in every Parliament.

In 1860, the Orthodox "United Synagogue" came under the jurisdiction of a chief rabbi. This group consisted of the vast majority of synagogues. Reform and Sephardic groups established their own units.

In the 1880s, Jews began to move from Eastern Europe to the west. A vast wave of immigrants from the east arrived in England. In 1880, 60,000 Jews lived in Great Britain. By 1905, there would be 150,000 Jews.

To Jews, London and the British Isles will always mean a land of temporary refuge. For many on the way to the United States in the nineteenth century, it was a stopping-off place. The first Jewish mayor of New York City, Abraham Beame, was born in England and came to New York City as a young child.

The new Jewish immigrants were Yiddish-speaking proletariat and middle-class Orthodox. They were tailors, boot and shoe manufacturers, and furniture suppliers. As immigrants, they set up their own life-style in the poor neighborhoods of British cities.

By the start of World War I, 300,000 Jews lived in Britain. About 50,000 Jews fought with the Allies during the war and suffered 10,000 casualties. Approximately 1,500 Jews were decorated. Six persons were awarded the Victoria Cross, Britain's highest order.

During World War II, about 90,000 Jews fled from Hitlerism to the British Isles, of which 75,000 came from Germany and Austria, Czechoslovakia, Poland, and Italy. Friction between Britain's Jews and His Majesty's government would increase over the country's League of Nations mandate in Palestine, especially since Britain tightened Jewish immigration to the future Jewish State.

In 1944, with the assassination of Lord Moyne and the 1947 hanging of two British Army sergeants, tensions rose in England, which pursued a pro-Arab policy.

Ernest Bevin, the post-World War II British foreign secretary, followed a Palestine policy that "virtually abrogated" the 1917 Balfour Declaration. The latter called for a Jewish national home in Palestine. He imposed severe restrictions on Jewish immigration. Nothing moved Bevin, not even the thousands of Jewish survivors still held in displaced persons (D.P.) camps. His anti-Semitism blinded him.

Although they felt betrayed, English Jews rallied and, on May 14, 1948, they celebrated the establishment of the State of Israel. In those years, Jews moved to the suburbs, mainly to the northwest to Wembley, Harrow, Stanmore, Edgware, Finchley, Palmers Green, Ilford, Golders Green, and Stamford Hill. Today, Jews are less than one percent of the British population.

About three-quarters of Great Britain's estimated 290,000 'core' Jews live in and around London, which boasts nearly nine million persons, according to Sergio DellaPergola in 2016. One suburb, Golders Green, stands out as a comfortable middle-class residential area of northern London. There—and in Stamford Hill—you will find a Jewish neighborhood with Jewish stores and synagogues. While probably not as high as in the United States, the frequency of intermarriage in England is about one out of three. Intermarriage and assimilation are becoming common in Jewish society here, for England, since World War II, has become freer and less stratified.

Today, Jewish citizens of the UK are a central part of British life and contribute greatly to British culture, history, and heritage.

Terrorism

Jews, too, have joined the battle against Islamic terrorism which has hit the British Isles.

As in other countries in Europe, the threat of terrorism is a way of life. More than 330 people were arrested on suspicion of terrorism offences in the UK in the first part of 2015—a third more than the previous year.

The 9/11 attack on the US World Trade Center is lodged forever in its long history. England has 7/7 in 2005 as its day of mass murder, suicide bombings and terrorism. The July 7, 2005 London incursions, sometimes referred to as 7/7, were a series of coordinated terrorist suicide bomb attacks in central London, which targeted civilians using the public transport system during rush hour.

What happened on the morning of Thursday, July 7, 2005 will not be forgotten. Four Islamist extremists' separately detonated three bombs in quick succession aboard London Underground trains across the city and later, a fourth on a double-decker bus in Tavistock Square. Fifty-two people were killed and over 700 more were injured in the attacks, making it, not only Britain's worst terrorist incident since the 1988 bombing of Pan Am Flight 103 over Lockerbie, Scotland, but also the country's first ever Islamist suicide attack.

And then in March 22, 2017, the anniversary of the attack on the Brussels Airport in 2016, a man using a car as a lethal weapon mowed down people on Westminster Bridge, crashed into gates outside Parliament, and used a large kitchen knife to murder a policeman before being shot dead himself. A terrorist, he managed to have Parliament locked down inside the House of Commons. In the final count, five people were killed and 50 injured. His name was Khalid Masood; London was shaken.

Later, the British police said they believed that Khalid Masood may have acted alone. According to reports, the Islamic State group claimed one of its "soldiers" carried out the attack, the worst in Britain since the July 2005 bombings that left, as we have seen, 52 people dead.

On May 22, 2017 an attack took place in Manchester which we shall discuss later in this chapter under Manchester. Twenty-two people were murdered by terrorists and 59 injured.

On June 3, 2017, a terrorist attack left seven people dead and 48 injured when a van hit pedestrians on London Bridge. Three men got out and began stabbing people in nearby Borough Market. The suspects were shot dead.

On June 19, 2017, a group of Muslim worshippers were hit when a van mounted the pavement and drove into them in Finsbury Park, London. One man died.

And yet the British toughness, "stiff upper lip," displaying fortitude in the face of adversity, enters the picture in England's long history, as shown in the police statement declaring: "Terrorists have tried to tear this city apart before and they have never succeeded. A very small minority of people have tried to use this as an opportunity to stir up hate, but once again we stand together in calm defiance. We will not allow them to divide us."

Notable English Jews

The Jewish Chronicle, the first permanent Anglo-Jewish newspaper, was established in 1841. Located at 28 Albans Lane, London, NW11 7QE, Tel: 44-20-7415-1500. www.thejc.com, it has the honor of being the oldest Jewish newspaper in the world in continuous publication. On its pages often appeared notices and reports on outstanding Jewish personalities who contributed much to Great Britain and British Jewry.

Many times, of course, mention was made of Sir Moses Montefiore (1784-1885), a famous son of British Jewry. He was probably the outstanding figure in the Jewish community and the most celebrated Jew in England; he lived until the age of 101. Sir David Salomons became the first Jewish mayor of London in 1855; he was also the first Jewish sheriff in 1835, and the first Jewish alderman in 1847. Sir George Jessel was the first Jew to become a member of the government and was appointed solicitor in 1871.

Benjamin Disraeli (1804-81) was born a Jew, and he became one of the United Kingdom's greatest prime ministers.

Herbert Samuel, later viscount, became a British cabinet minister in 1909. He also was named as the first High Commissioner for Palestine in the 1920s. Solomon Schechter, rabbinic scholar and founder of Conservative Judaism, later took the post of president of the Jewish Theological Seminary in the United States, where he served from 1902 until his death in 1915. Sassoon Siegfried was a famous Jewish poet and author of Memoirs of an Infantry Officer.

LONDON

"London!—that great large place . . ." Charles Dickens, *Oliver Twist.*
"London is not said to be in England, but rather, England to be in London."
(Source: *Thomas Platter.*)

Thirty-two boroughs exist in London and each has its own character. Yes, all different. That's what makes the capital of the UK so different. Amble through the City of Westminster, Kensington, and Chelsea; you will find the variety and the spice of life in this stately metropolis.

"To be in London these days is to be endlessly entertained by art, by the museums that show it, the multiplying galleries that sell it and the masses who have become weirdly fascinated by it," wrote Michael Kimmelman in the *New York Times*, June 6, 2000.

Actually, at the turn of the recent century, London began to reinvent itself.

Sites which are a must on a trip to England and London include

Shakespeare's Globe Theater, the reconstructed playground of England's greatest bard; the restoration of Windsor Castle, after the devastating fire of 1992; the Tate Gallery of Modern Art, on Bankside, 25 Sumner St., now linked to the City of London and St. Paul's Cathedral on the Thames' north bank by the new Millennium Bridge.

Awaiting tourists are the Houses of Parliament, Big Ben, the changing of the Guard at Buckingham Palace, Her Majesty's Tower of London, the National Gallery, Hyde Park, the Victoria and Albert Museum, Westminster Abbey, Westminster Bridge, Whitehall, the Strand, and Trafalgar Square.

Even the venerable British Museum on Great Russell St., which we have noted earlier, has created London's first covered public square, the Great Court. Visit, too, the Royal Opera House in Covent Garden, at Bow Street. Finally, the new Millennium Dome on Peninsula Square, a vast white edifice and the world's largest dome which looks like an upturned dinner plate. The building in which you can take a wondrous journey from one end of existence, that is, the Big Bang to the present, opened on January 1, 2000.

Also, as in Shakespeare's day, London remains a world city. That's why the English today are leaving the countryside and flocking to the capital in droves. And even though they constantly complain that the city is extremely expensive, they'll tell you, "I wouldn't live anywhere else."

And then, there's that weather. The whole world knows the English climate is "fickle." Indeed, Londoners still carry an umbrella even on sunny days. In the words of the great English novelist, Charles Dickens, when you come upon a day when "up came the sun, steaming all over London. Rejoice!"

Rain or shine, London is a city washed in history. And that history includes the momentous decision that the UK took in 2016: *Brexit!*

Brexit

History indeed! In June 2016, Britain chose decisively to "cast off" its forty-three-year-old membership in the European Union. Meaning that Britain, "whose storied history has encompassed the birth of constitutional government, global empire, royal pageantry and heroic defense against fascism, is entering unknown territory," wrote Steven Erlanger in the *New York Times,* June 24, 2016. The vote was a severe shock to Britain and beyond.

In March, 2017, Prime Minister Theresa May filed formal Brexit divorce papers, "pitching the United Kingdom into the unknown and triggering years of uncertain negotiations that will test the endurance of the European Union," according to Reuters.

Now in 2017, the UK is faced with a two year clock on negotiations, "a period in which Britain (including millions of European citizens living in Britain and British citizens living in the European Union) will be in limbo," reported the *New York Times.*

After Brexit, there are those who dissent, such as commentator Baghot of the *Economist*, who noted in that publication's July 23, 2016 issue that Britain is "now seen less as a solution than a problem," adding . . . "Britain's stature in the world is shrinking."

Thus, after Britons voted to leave the EU—the bloc it joined in 1973—it was clear that Europe was facing a crisis. That may be. But going forward, any British government will have a difficult job of holding Britain together in the face of renewed Scottish independence demands, while the UK talks with 27 other EU states on finance, trade, security, and a host of other complex issues.

Whatever one's views on Brexit are today, at the time of the break, the feeling was that "with far-right, anti-bloc (EU) politicians in France and the Netherlands riding high in the polls ahead of the elections in 2017, there is widespread speculation that Britain's departure may be the start of a great unraveling of the European Union," noted the *New York Times,* on December 27, 2016. However, both in France and Holland, the far-right was defeated.

As we shall see in other countries in this guide, especially in Western Europe, critics of the EU complain of distant and unfeeling technocrats in Brussels who enforce arcane rules to the letter, with little understanding of local nuances and needs. Britain's vote to leave the bloc "struck a stinging blow against regional unity at a time when confidence was already flagging in the European Union," wrote the *New York Times.*

Be that as it may, on March 29, 2017, Prime Minister Theresa May informed the European Council that Britain was setting into motion Article 50; that negotiating process with a two-year limit for the UK to leave the European Union. The countdown to Brexit had begun.

Jewish London

THE EAST END

The first Jewish word that a Jewish traveler hears in the London of Disraeli, Rothschild, Adler, Schechter, and Balfour deals with Jewish food. The word is *heimisch,* "homey, informal, comfortable."

"*Heimisch* mushroom barley soup," says a man between spiels in the weekly Sunday market in Petticoat Lane. During the week, it is known as Wentworth Street.

London's East End—with its flavor of New York's Lower East Side—deserves a stroll. This neighborhood has changed. Once it boasted many clubs, theaters, shelters, yeshivas, and schools. Today, there are few Jews, and fewer institutions, but the neighborhood is still exciting and vibrant, and it is good to begin a visit to London here in White Chapel and at such streets as Whitechapel High Street, Osborne Street, Brick Lane, Fournier Street, and Greatorex Street.

"The Asians are here now," says Mr. Meyers, the peddler in Petticoat Lane. "The newcomers want to succeed, so they go where the Jews began," he points out as he looks around at fellow hawkers who sell—from their stalls—leather bags, coats, umbrellas, jeans, mirrors, sweaters, and orange juice squeezers.

Or, put another way, "they're speaking Hindustani where *mamaloshen* used to be spoken," according to the late Member of Parliament Grenville Janner.

The East End can be reached by taking the Underground. Take the "tube" to Liverpool Street, Bethnal Green, Aldgate, Aldgate East, or Shoreditch. Several bus lines also serve the area—6, 8, 15, or 25 from Oxford Circus or the 6 or 15 from Charing Cross.

By the way, the area houses several streets and buildings of interest to Jewish travelers, including the home of Abe Saperstein, who founded the Harlem Globetrotters in the United States; the Jewish Working Men's Club on Alie Street, where in 1896, Theodor Herzl launched the Zionist movement.

TOURS

A tour in the East End, the location of the original Jewish settlement, and elsewhere in London, is conducted by **Londinium**, 6 W. Heath Ave., London, NW11 7QL. Tel: 44-20-8458-2288 or FAX: 020-8455-6612. valandsal@virginmedia.com www.londiniumtours.com.

Call Sally Pitel, Tel: 44-208-964-5540.Valerie Sussman and Sally Pitel conduct the Jewish tour by means of a private car. The tours can be tailor-made to the traveler's interests.

Historic Tours, 3 Florence Rd., South Croydon, CR2 0PQ. Tel/ FAX: 44-20-8668-4019. This is a historical walking tour tracing Jewish history in England from the time of William the Conqueror to World War II. The tour is conducted on Sundays and Tuesdays at 11:00 a.m. from Aldgate Underground Station. Please call for details.

JEWISH SITES IN LONDON

The J.F.S. Comprehensive School, The Mall, Kenton, Harrow HA3

9TE, London. Tel: 44-20-8206-3100. This is a wonderful sight to see regarding Jewish life in Britain. I visited this excellent school and marveled at the sight of about 2,000 Jewish boys and girls, ages 11 to 18, reciting the mincha (afternoon) service in the school's synagogue. The youths were dressed with blue-knit yarmulkes; blue blazers, grey slacks, and school ties for the boys; and blue blouses and grey skirts for the girls, the much-seen school clothes of British youth. The school is Orthodox and its subjects include Hebrew, Bible, laws, and Talmud, along with math, chemistry, history, tradition, and athletic events in fine facilities. At one time, this institution was the largest Jewish school in Europe, with more than 4,000 pupils.

The Office of N. M. Rothschild & Sons is located at New Court, St. Swithin's, EC4N 8AL, in the heart of London. Tel: 44-20-7280-5000. The headquarters of this remarkable Jewish family was responsible for many loans aiding the British government, including funds for the defeat of Napoleon, the relief of the Irish famine, the Crimean War, and, of course, the purchase of the shares of the Suez Canal owned by the khedive of Egypt. After the battle of Waterloo, the Rothschilds became bankers to the Holy Alliance of Christian Monarchs of Russia, Austria, Prussia, and Britain.

The Rothschild family moved to various European capitals to direct financial matters. James made Paris his base; Solomon moved to Vienna; Carl went to Naples; Mayer Amschel remained in Frankfurt. The main center of operations emerged at New Court, London, where the English branch was directed by Nathan Mayer Rothschild (1777-1836). He was the son of founder of the Rothschild dynasty, Mayer Amschel. The son, too, was a financial genius, a creative business person. Nathan Mayer Rothschild, "N. M.," as he was called, had been the first Rothschild to leave Frankfurt. He came to England, entered the textile importing business, and was an agent for his father. He became a British citizen in 1806 and married Hannah Cohen, whose sister married Moses Montefiore. The latter's brother married Nathan's sister, Henriette, and this liaison connected N.M. to the Salomons, Goldsmiths, and other prominent families. He helped establish the Jews' Free School. He was in the government loan business, especially since London was the financial center of the world. He transformed the Rothschilds into "the world's leading business house."

It took ten years of effort, but finally the son of "N. M." was the first Jew to sit in Parliament. You see, time after time, Lionel Nathan Rothschild had been elected by the City of London as its parliamentary representative. But the British Parliament refused to admit him to the House of Commons because, as a Jew, he refused to take the oath of office, which contained the words "on the true faith of a Christian." Ten years later, the House of Commons ended that oath. Even more time elapsed before a Jew could take his seat in the House of Lords. In 1885, Lionel's son, Nathaniel ("Natty") Mayer Rothschild, became the first "professing" Jew to be raised to the peerage of a Lord and became a member of that august body. He was head of the British Jewish Community and president of the United Synagogue.

Anti-Semitism

There is no doubt that in the last decade there has been an increase in prejudice and violence against Jewish communities in the UK, along with an increase in far-right extremist activity.

"Reported rates of anti-Semitism have risen in the UK since 2000, with some fluctuations in line with significant trigger events in the Middle East," reported a Parliament committee in 2016. The committee went on to state:

"The first half of 2016 saw an 11 percent rise in reported anti-Semitic incidents compared with the same period during the previous year. This was the second highest total ever recorded during the first six months of the year . . ."

"In London, reports of anti-Semitism rose by 62 percent between the first six months of 2015 and 2016."

The Home Affairs Committee of Parliament charged that the Labor Party had not done enough to stamp out anti-Jewish sentiment in the party. In the spring of 2017, the Labor Party "failed to expel former London Mayor Ken Livingstone over his claims that Hitler initially supported Zionism and other allegedly anti-Semitic comments," according to *The Times of Israel*, April 6, 2017.

Adding to the above, Chief Rabbi Ephraim Mirvis charged that British universities are turning a blind eye to "Jew hatred." Rabbi Mirvis added that "Zionist bashing on campus has gone unchallenged."

At the end of 2016, the new Prime Minister of Great Britain, Theresa May indicated the government was adopting a definition of anti-Semitism to combat hate crime against Jews and that Britain was among the first countries to use the new definition that includes over-sweeping condemnation of Israel.

KOSHER RESTAURANTS IN LONDON
Kosher Establishments under the
Kashrut Division of the London Beth Din

The head office of Kashrut Division of the London **Beth Din**

(KLBD) is housed at Adler House, 305 Ballards Lane, London, N12 8GB. Tel: 44-20-8343-6255, FAX: 44-20-8343-6254. info@klbdkosher. org. www.kosher.org.uk

Ayelet, 87 Brent St., Hendon, NW4 2DY Tel: 44-20 8202 2327.

Bagels Bar, 84 Brent St., Hendon NW4 2ES. Tel: 44-20-8202-6540. info@bagelsbar.comwww.bagelsbar.com

Burger Bar, 1 Bridge Ln., Golders Green NW11 0EA. Tel: 44-20 8455-8080

Eighty Six (glatt), 86 Brent St., Hendon, NW4 2HH.Tel: 44-20-8202-5575,

Hummus Bar. 82 Golders Green Rd., Golders Green NW11 8LN. Tel: 44-20-8455-4011. hummusbaruk@gmail.com

Isola Bella, 111a-113 Golders Green Rd., Golders Green, NW11 8HR. Tel: 44-20-8455-2228. gg@isolabella.co.uk, www.isolabella.co.uk.

Kaifeng, 51 Church Rd., Hendon, NW4 4DU. Tel: 44-20-8203-7888. info@kaifeng.co.uk, www.kaifeng.co.uk.

Tasti Pizza, 23 Amhurst Parade, Amhurst Park, London N16. Tel: 020-8802-0018. Also, 252 Golders Green Rd., London N11. Tel: 020-8209-00023.

White Fish, 10-12 Bell Ln., Hendon NW4 2AD Tel: 44-20-8202-8780. info@whitefishrestaurant.co.uk, www.whitefishrestaurant.co.uk.

Kosher Take-Away Delis and Shops under the supervision of the Kashrut Division of the London Beth Din

Kosher Deli, 132 Golders Green Rd., Golders Green, NW11 8HB. Tel: 44-20-8731-6450. Order line: 020-8381-4450. info@kosherdeli. co.uk, www.kosherdeli.co.uk.

Kosher Kingdom, 7-9 Russell Parade, Golders Green Rd., Golders Green, NW11 9NN. Tel: 020-8455-1429. info@kosherkingdom.c0.uk., www.kosherkingdom.co.uk

Manna Deli, 149 Brent St., Hendon, NW4 2DR. Tel: 44-20-8201-7575. Manna.orders@mannakosherdeli.co.uk, www.mannakosherdeli.co.uk.

Tapuach, 108-110 Brent St., Hendon, NW4 2HH. Tel: 44-20-8202-5700. sales@tapuach.co.uk. www.tapuach.co.uk.

Hillel Restaurant, ½ Endsleigh St., London WC1 H 0DS. Tel: 0208-7388-0801. A fine place that caters to university students in a marvelous college atmosphere in the area around Euston Station.

Kosher Establishments of the Sephardi Kashrut Authority under the auspices of the Sephardi Beth Din

Orli Café (dairy), 96 Brent St., Hendon, NW4 2HH Tel:44- 20-8203-7555.

Taboon, (dairy), 17 Russell Parade, Golders Green Road, Golders Green, NW11.9NN 1. Tel: 44-20-8455-7451.

Kosher Establishments under the Federation of Synagogues
(All meat restaurants are glatt and all dairy restaurants are cholov yisroel, according to the Federation of Synagogues)

Aviv Restaurant (meat), 87/89 High St., Edgware, Middlesex, HA8 7DB Tel: 44-20-8952-2484. www.avivrestaurant.com
Beit Hamadras (meat), 105 Brent St., Hendon, NW4 2DX. Tel: 44-20-8203-4567. www.beithamadras.co.uk.
Headroom Café (dairy), 89 Golders Green Rd., London, NW11 8EN. headroomcafe.org.
K Grill (meat), 60 Edgware Way, Edgware, HA8 8JS. Tel: 44-20-8958-9087. kgrill.co.uk.
K Pizza/Fishchips (dairy), 60 Edgware Way, Edgware, HA8 8JS. kpizza.co.uk.

SYNAGOGUES

Many British Jews, like their co-religionists in the United States, do not want to forget their heritage; hence their many synagogues.
Bevis Marks Synagogue, St. Mary Axe, London EC3. www.sephardi. org.UK/bevis-marks. In the East End, this is the oldest Jewish synagogue in England. If you have only one day in London to see Jewish sites, you should make sure to visit this landmark. Services are held on Mondays, Thursdays, and Saturday mornings.

Built in 1701, Bevis Marks is modeled after the Portuguese synagogue in Amsterdam, Holland. It is now a national monument worthy of preservation and located in St. Mary Axe (pronounced "Simmery Axe"). Here is a symbol of the resettlement of the Jews in England in 1656, after having been expelled for 400 years.

Dutch Jews brought the central chandelier from Amsterdam in the late 1600s. On the lectern in front of the Holy Ark are ten great brass candlesticks symbolizing the Ten Commandments. The twelve columns supporting the gallery in the three sides signify the twelve tribes of Israel. Worshippers can sit on the old, highly polished oak benches from the very first synagogue of the resettlement, which was then in Creechurch Lane, a short distance from the present site. The gates are often locked, so visitors wishing to see the Bevis Marks Synagogue should phone ahead. Telephone 44-20-7621-1188 to check opening hours. Be sure to ask for directions and which entrance to use. The vestry office is at 4 Heneage Lane and the gates are on Houndstitch Street.

Bevis Marks Synagogue, London. (Photo courtesy of the British Tourist Office)

Interestingly, according to Carol Herselle Krinsky in *Synagogues of Europe: Architecture, History, Meaning,* Bevis Marks Synagogue was built in a lane because Jews were not allowed to erect a synagogue on Bevis Marks Street. Joseph Avis, a Quaker, built the synagogue. When the building costs came to less than the estimate, he returned the difference. Finally, Queen Anne herself is said to have donated a wooden beam for the Bevis Marks Synagogue.

An Ashkenazic synagogue that stood in Duke's Place just next door to Bevis Marks was London's chief Ashkenazic place of worship. Called the Duke's Place Shul, it was considered the country's best-known synagogue, and a popular choice for marriages, until it was destroyed in September 1941. The Rothschilds attended services here. A plaque is affixed to International House, which replaced the Duke's Place Shul.

Marble Arch Synagogue, 32 Great Cumberland Pl., West End, London W1. This synagogue is located in a beautifully designed area by a charming semicircular terrace of houses. Located near many hotels, it is difficult to tell that the building is a house of worship. This Orthodox synagogue took the place of the Great Synagogue on Duke's Place, which was destroyed by German bombers in 1941.

Sephardic Synagogue, Lauderdale Rd., Maida Vale, London W9.

The Holy Ark of the Bevis Marks Synagogue, London. (Photo courtesy of the British Tourist Office)

Sephardi.org.uk/Lauderdale. This famous Spanish-Portuguese synagogue was established in the nineteenth century in a residential section near Paddington Station. A huge dome in the Arabesque style summons Jewish worshippers to prayer. During the service, rabbis and some congregants wear the traditional top hats.

Sephardic Synagogue, 8 St. James Gardens, London W11. Tel: 44-20-7603-7961. Many of the congregation's members are from Greece and Turkey.

Central Synagogue, Great Portland St., London W1W 6NW. Tel: 44-20-7580-1355. Here is another synagogue that was destroyed in the blitz of World War II. Today, a modern Orthodox building stands in its place.

Spanish and Portuguese Jews Congregation, 2 Ashworth Rd., London W9 1JY. Tel: 44-20-7289-2573. http://www.sandp.org This is also the headquarters of the Sephardic community and here the synagogue authorities showed me the registration of circumcision of Benjamin Disraeli, the great British prime minister who shortly before his bar mitzvah was converted by his father to the Church of England (see Statue of Disraeli in "Other Sites" section).

In Stamford Hill, many small Chassidic synagogues dot the area. These congregations sponsor many members who were born in Morocco, Iran, and India. Others are descendants of those who emigrated from those countries.

Synagogues of the United Synagogue
(Orthodox)

The United Synagogue maintains its executive offices at 305 Ballards Ln., North Finchley, London, UK, N12 8GB. Tel: 44-20-8343-8989. info@theus.org.uk, www.theus.org.uk. It is the largest synagogue movement in the United Kingdom. Its Chief Rabbi, Rabbi Ephraim Mirvis, and its Beth Din, administer large sections of London and provincial Jewry from these headquarters.

The new United Synagogue website, www.theus.org.uk, gives up-to-date information on kashrut, the calendar, community development, education, the Chief Rabbi and a wide range of other news and views, including help lines and useful synagogue location information: www.theus.org.uk

The **London Beth Din** is located in the same building as the United Synagogue, 305 Ballards Ln., North Finchley, London, N12 8GB. Tel: 020-8343-6270, FAX: 020-8343-6257. info@bethdin.org.

Rabbi Ephraim Mirvis' official title is Chief Rabbi of the United Hebrew Congregations of the Commonwealth. His website is www.chiefrabbi.org. Although the United Synagogue is the umbrella body for mainstream

Orthodox congregations based almost entirely in and around London, there are two member synagogues outside the capital. One is in Sheffield and the other in Birmingham. The United Hebrew Congregations refers to all the congregations that accept the authority of the Chief Rabbi. This includes communities across the UK and around the Commonwealth.

For information on *kashrut*, contact the Kashrut Division of the London **Beth Din** at 305 Ballards Ln., North Finchley, London, UK, N12 8GB , Tel: 44-20-8343-6255, FAX: 44-20-8343-6254. info@kosher. org.uk. www.theus.org.uk

Chelsea, **Affiliate**, Smith Terrace, Smith St., London, SW3 40L. Tel: 44-20-7351-6292. golda.chelseasynagogue.co.uk.

Edgware, Parnell Close, Edgware Way, Edgware, Middlesex. HA8 8YE. Tel: 44-20-8958-7508. office@edgwareu.com, www.edgwareu.com

Finchley, Kinloss Gardens, London N3 3DU.Tel: 020-8346-8551 office@kinloss.org.uk. www.kinloss.org.uk.

Golders Green, 41 Dunstan Rd., London NW11 8AE. Tel: 020-8455-2460. office@ggshul.org.uk. www.goldersgreenshu.org.uk

Hendon, 18 Raleigh Close, Hendon. www.hendonsynagogue.com

Ilford, 24 Beehive Ln., Ilford, Essex. Tel: 44-20-8554- 5969. office@ ilfordsynagogue.co.uk. www.ilfordsynagogue.co.uk

New, 90 Egerton Rd., London. N16. Tel: 44-20-8880-2731.

New West End, St. Petersburgh Pl., London W2 4JT. Tel: 44-20-7229-2631. newes@newwestend.org.uk, www.newwestend.org.uk

St. John's Wood, 37-41 Grove End Rd., London NW8 9WA. One of Britain's largest synagogues. Tel: 44-20-7286-6333. office@ shulinthewood.com, www.shulinthewood.com.

South London, 45, Leigham Court Rd., London, SW16 2NF. Tel: 44-20-8677-0234 admin@sis.1.org.uk, www.sis.1.org.uk.

Chabad Centers in London
(For more centers, check out chabsd.org.uk,
then to centers, then London and Region)

Lubavitch Foundation, United Kingdom Headquarters, Merkos Menachem, 107-115 Stamford Hill, London, N16 5RP. Tel: 44-20-8800-0022. FAX: 44-20-8809-7324.

Beis Chana, Jewish Women's Centre, 19 Northfield Rd., London, N16 5RL. Tel: 44-20-8809-6508. FAX: 44-20-8800-9467.

Central London: Bloomsbury, Tel: 44-20-7060-9770.

Heichal Menachem-Golders Green, 8 Boardwalk Ln., London. heichalmenachem@gmail.com.

Chabad House-Southgate, 33 Osidge Ln., Southgate, N14 5JL. Tel: 44-20-8361-3044. FAX: 44-20-8361-6107.

Chabad House South London, 42 St. Georges Road, London SW19 4ED. Tel: 44-20-8944-7770
Lubavitch of Edgware, 230 Hale Lane, Edgware, HA8 9P7. Tel: 44-20-8905-4141. FAX: 44-20-8958-1169.
Chabad Ilford Centre, 10-17 Sevenways Parade, Woodford Ave., Grants Hill, Essex, 1G2 6JX. Tel: 44-20-8554-1624.

Independent, Liberal, Progressive, and Reform Synagogues
(Liberal is equivalent to the American Reform Movement of Judaism and British Reform is similar to the American Conservative Movement of Judaism.)

Barkingside Progressive Synagogue (Union of Liberal and Progressive Synagogues), 129 Perrymans Farm Rd., Barkingside, Ilford, Essex. Tel: 44-20-8554-9682. Friday service, 8:00 p.m. Saturday, 11:00 a.m.
Belsize Square Synagogue (ULPS), (IND), 51 Belsize Square, Hampstead, London NW3 4HX. Tel: 44-20-7794-3949. office@synagogue.org.uk, www.synagogue.org.uk. Friday service, 6:30 p.m. Saturday, 11:00 a.m.
Ealing Liberal Synagogue (ULPS), Lynton Ave., Drayton Green, London. Tel/Fax: 44-20-8997-0528. els@liberaljudaism.org, www.ealingliberal.org.uk.
Edgware and District Reform Synagogue (Reform Synagogues of Great Britain), 118 Stonegrove, Edgware, Middlesex HA8 8AB. Friday service, 8:00 p.m. Saturday, 11:00 a.m. Tel: 44-20-8238-1000.FAX: 020-8905-4210.
Finchley Progressive Synagogue (ULPS), Hutton Grove, Finchley, London N12 8DR Tel: 44-20-8446-4063.
Finchley Reform Synagogue (RSGB), Fallow Court Ave., Finchley, London N12 OBE. Tel: 44-20-8446-3244. frs@frsonline.org, www.frsonline.org
Hendon Reform Synagogue (RSGB), Danescroft Ave. Hendon, London, NW4, 2NA. Tel: 44-20-8203-4168. office@hendonreform.org.uk
Kol Chai-Hatch End Jewish Community, (RSGB), 434 Uxbridge Road, Hatch End, Middx,
Liberal Jewish Synagogue (ULPS), 28 St. John's Wood Rd., London NW8 7HA Tel: 44-20-7286-5181. FAX: 44-20-7266-3591.ljs@ljs.org. www.ljs.org. Friday service, 8:00 p.m. Saturday, 11:00 a.m. Located near Regents Park, this is the chief Liberal Synagogue and probably has the largest seating capacity of any British synagogue. Similar to American Reform.
Since the UK decided to exit the European Union in 2016, growing numbers of British Jews of Sephardic descent have applied for

citizenship in Portugal, under a law making amends for the expulsion of Jews from the Iberian peninsula more than 500 years ago. The number of Sephardic Jews in the UK is estimated in the thousands, although there are no official figures.

At the same time, Jews from other parts of Europe are seeking a new home in the UK. As we mentioned in our previous chapter on France, Jews are emigrating from that country. A number are going to the UK. Reports indicate, for example, that on Holocaust Memorial Day, in London's Liberal Jewish Synagogue in St. John's Wood, a service was held on Friday night to welcome the large number of French Jews who have moved to the area, especially after the Charley Hebdo and kosher supermarket shootings in 2015. No figures were given in the report, but according to Marc Meyer, the French chairman of the Hendon United Synagogue and director of the Conference of European Rabbis, French Jewish children now make up 50 percent of the intake at London's Jewish schools.

North Western Reform Synagogue (RSGB), Alyth Gardens, Golders Green, London NW11 7EN. Tel: 44-20-8455-6763. Friday service, 6:30 p.m., Saturday, 10:30 a.m. mail@alyth.org.uk. www.reformjudaism. org.uk

Northwood and Pinner Liberal Synagogue (ULPS), Oakland Gate, Green Ln., Northwood, Middlesex. HA6 3AA Tel: 44-20-1923-822-592. admin@npls.org.uk, www.npls.org.uk.

Shir Hayim, Hampstead Reform Jewish Community, (RSGB) Hashomer House, 37A Broadhurst Gardens, London, NW63BN. Tel: 020-8959-3129. secretary@shirhayim.org. www.shirhayim.org

South London Liberal Synagogue (ULPS), Prentis Road, Streatham, London SW16 1QB. Tel: 44-20-8769-4787. Friday service, 8:15 p.m. Saturday, 11:00 a.m.

Southgate Progressive Synagogue (ULPS), 75 Chase Rd., London N14. Tel: 020-8886-0977. office@sps.uk.com, www.sps.uk.com. Friday service, 8:15 p.m. Saturday, 11:00 a.m.

West London Synagogue (RSGB), 33 Seymour Pl., London, WIH SAU. Tel: 44-20-7723-4404 FAX: 44-20-7224-8258. admin@wls.org. uk, www.wls.org.uk. Friday service, 6:00 p.m. Saturday, 11:00 a.m. Located near Hyde Park, this Reform synagogue for Ashkenazim and Sephardim is a fine example of Victorian architecture, and was founded by affluent West End London Jews. It celebrated its 150th anniversary in 1990. Having changed little, it remains one of the prime movers behind the Foundation of the Reform Synagogues of Great Britain, similar to the American Conservative Movement of Judaism. The Foundation consists of 30 other congregations in various parts of the country. The synagogue says its Holy Ark is famous for its open grillwork, which enables one to see the scrolls throughout the service. (Most synagogues cover their arks with a curtain). In the main entrance hall to the synagogue, known as the Goldsmid Hall, there are Memorial Tablets dedicated to the memory of congregants who fell in the world wars.

Westminster Synagogue (Ind), Kent House, Rutland Gardens, London SW7 1BX. Tel: 44-20-7584-3953 FAX: 020-7581-8012. secretary@westminstersynagogue.org, www.westministersynagogue. org. Friday service, 6:30 p.m.; Saturday, 11:00 p.m. A total of 1,564 Torahs from the Jewish Museum in Prague, Czech Republic, in the Czech Memorial Scrolls Center, which is open to visitors on Tuesdays and Thursdays from 10:00 a.m. to 4:00 p.m. and at other times by appointment. Please let the center know you are planning a visit.

Wimbledon & District Synagogue, (RSGB) 1 Queensmere Rd., Wimbledon Park Side, London, SW19 5QD.Tel: 020-8946-4836. enquires@wimshul.org, www.wimshul.org.

Assembly of Masorti Synagogues and Conservative Synagogues in England

Edgware Synagogue, Baker Path, Edgware, Middlesex, HA8 7YA. Tel: 44-20-8905-4096. FAX: 44-20-8905-4333. admin@edgewaremasorti. org.

New Essex Congregation, Roding Valley Hall, Station Way Buckhurst Hill, Essex. Tel: 44-20-8506-6873.

New London Synagogue, 33 Abbey Road, St. John's Wood, London, NW8 0AT. Tel: 44-20-7328-1026. FAX: 44-20-73-72. office@ newlondon.org.uk, www.newlondon.org.uk.

New North London Synagogue, The Manor House, 80 East End Road, London. Tel: 44-20-8346-8560. office@nnls-masorti.org.uk.

New Whetstone Synagogue, Henriques House, 120 Oakleigh Road North, Whetstone, N20. Tel: 44-20-8445-2671. FAX: 44-20-8346-9710.

Hendon Masorti Minyan, Bell Ln., JMI School, Hendon NW4. Tel: 44-20-8202-9058.

Headquarters of Synagogue Governing Bodies

Adath Yisroel, 40 Queen Elizabeth's Walk, No. 16, London N16 0HH. Tel: 44-20-7802-6226/7.

Assembly of Masorti Synagogues. 3 Shakespeare Rd., London. Tel: 44-20-8349-6650. enquiries@masorti.org. uk

Edgware Adath Yisroel, 261 Hale Ln., Edgware, Middlesex.

Federation of Synagogues, 65 Watford Way, Hendon, London, NW4

3AQ. Tel: 44-20-8202-2263. FAX: 020-8203-0610. Info@federation.org. uk. www.federation.org.uk. The second largest synagogue body in England is the Federation of Synagogues, boasting a membership of 17,000 in some 50 branches. As an Orthodox group, it set up independent courts of Jewish justice, as did the Union of Orthodox Hebrew Congregations and the Reform and Liberal movements of Judaism.

The Movement for Reform Judaism, The Sternberg Centre for Judaism, 80 East End Rd., London, N3 2SY Tel: 44-20 8349 5640. http://www.reformjudaism.org.uk. Member of the World Union for Progressive Judaism.

Spanish and Portuguese Synagogue, 2 Ashworth Rd., London W9 1JY. Tel: 44-20- 289-2573. Located here is the Sephardic Kashrut Authority.

Liberal Judaism, The Montagu Centre, 21 Maple St., London, W1T 4BE, Tel: 44-20-7580-1663 website: http://www.liberaljudaism.org. Member of the World Union for Progressive Judaism

Assembly of Masorti Synagogues, Conservative Synagogues in England, 1097 Finchley Rd., London, NW 11 0PU. Tel: 020-8201-8772. FAX: 020-8201-8917.

ORGANIZATIONS

Agudas Israel, Golders Green Rd., London NW11. Tel: 020-8458-8424.

B'nai B'rith, ORT House. 128 Albert St. London, NW1 7NE. Tel: 44-20-7446-8660. office@bnaibrithuk.org.

Jewish Agency, Central House, 1 Ballards Ln., London N3 1LQ. Tel: 44-20-8371-5250. Gci-en@jafi.org.

Jewish Historical Society of England, 129-131 Albert St., London, NW1 7NB. info@jhse.org.

WIZO, London Office, Tel: 020 7319 9169. central@wizouk.org

MUSEUMS AND LIBRARIES

British Museum, Great Russell Street, Bloomsbury, London WC1. Tel: 44-20-7636-1555. (Tube stop: Tottenham Court Road.) The Hebrew Library here contains about 50,000 volumes and 3,000 manuscripts including material from ancient Palestine. At times, letters from Benjamin Disraeli are shown. Also permanent exhibits contain archeological finds from the Middle East as well as a philatelic collection of early twentieth-century stamps, including pre-Israel Independence Palestine stamps.

The British Museum contains the Balfour Declaration. On

November 2, 1917, Foreign Secretary Arthur James Balfour wrote a
letter to Lord Rothschild declaring, "His Majesty's Government view
with favor the establishment in Palestine of a national home for the
Jewish people." Lord Balfour was interested in Zionism, perhaps as a result of a
meeting with Dr. Chaim Weizmann in Manchester. Weizmann had
persuaded the British government and influenced Lord Arthur
Balfour to favor the establishment of a Jewish state in Palestine. A
distinguished scholar and scientist, Weizmann studied chemistry in
Germany and Switzerland and as a British subject, he admired England
and English ways. A leading British chemist, he had served as director
of the laboratories of the British Admiralty and was instrumental in
the "perfection of the most subtle and complex method of obtaining
alcohol from wood, at a time when this material, absolutely vital for
the production of explosives, was becoming impossible to obtain
in sufficient quantities, because of the submarine campaign of the
abnormal conditions of war"! After the Balfour Declaration, he became
the leader of the World Zionist Movement and is considered a great
Jewish statesman. He was named the first president of the State of Israel.

The **Jewish Museum**, Raymond Burton House, 129-131, Albert
St., Camden, London, NW1 7NB. Tel: 44-20-7284-7384. www.
jewishmuseum.org.uk. A wonderful exhibit of British Jewry covers the
history of the Jews on this island from 1066 until the expulsion by
King Edward I. Also shown is an exhibit of British Jewish history from
the days of Oliver Cromwell. Artifacts are displayed. Portraits of Jewish
leaders are shown.

Browsing through the framed documents, you might ask museum
officials to show you etchings of Levi Salomons, father of Sir David
Salomons, the first Jewish lord mayor of London, who was elected to
his post in 1855. This and other pieces are representative of British
artifacts.

Ask to see an etching or painting of Manasseh Ben Israel. He led
the fight for readmission to England. Born to Marrano parents in
Madeira in 1604, he was baptized Manoel Dias Soeiro. His family
moved to Amsterdam. Upon their arrival, they announced they were
Jews. After studying with Rabbi Isaac Uziel, Manasseh was ordained
a rabbi. He taught, wrote essays, and edited books, many of them for
Christian audiences. He even corresponded with English religious
leaders and intellectuals. Much of his motivation was mystical. You
see, Manasseh had met a Jew named Antonio (Aaron) de Montezinos,
who had told him that he had discovered Jews in America. Manasseh
theorized that since Jews were now living in America, they were
residents of every country on earth except one, that one of course

being England. To make the dispersion cycle complete, and help the Messianic movement reach fulfillment, the Jews needed to reside in Britain. Then the Messiah would come and the Jews would return to their homeland—Palestine. During the conference to decide whether to admit Jews, Manasseh made a logical case for Jewish admission. He argued that wherever Jews live, they develop new branches of economy and trade flourishes. The meeting ended in a so-called compromise, with no official declaration, but it meant Jews were allowed to enter. However, Manasseh, who had fought so hard, took it as a personal defeat. He felt the compromise was a sham. He called for a formal recall of the Jewish people to England. When this did not happen, he returned to Amsterdam, where he died a broken man. He was buried in the cemetery at Ouderkerk, close to the Amstel River, not far from his father, Joseph Ben Israel, and near his teacher, Rabbi Isaac Uziel.

The museum notes that thousands of visitors enter its doors each year. During a bomb scare in early 2017, Abigail Morris, director of the Jewish Museum, told the London Jewish Chronicle, "This incident underlines how vital our work is. We welcome thousands of visitors to the Jewish Museum every year, including 20,000 schoolchildren—95 percent of whom are not Jewish. We challenge prejudice and combat anti-Semitism by breaking down barriers and building bridges."

The museum features The Holocaust Gallery and Judaism: A living Faith which features rare ceremonial art objects in the Jewish Museum.

The Sternberg Centre for Judaism: The Manor House, 80 East End Rd., Finchley, London N3 2SY. Tel: 44-20-8349-5700, The Sternberg Centre for Judaism is located on a seven-and-a-half-acre site in North London. The Manor House itself dates back to the early 1700s and is a Grade II listed building. Various organizations can be found here, including: The headquarters of the Movement for Reform Judaism; The Leo Baeck College; the Akiva Primary School; the New North London (Masorti) Synagogue; a biblical garden; the offices of the European Union for Progressive Judaism (EUPJ); the Art Stables; Manor House Centre for Psychotherapy and Counselling; and the Manor House bookshop.

The Freud Museum, 20 Maresfield Gardens, Hampstead, London. NW3 5SX Tel: 44-20-7435-2002

This museum houses mementos of both Sigmund Freud, founder of psychoanalysis, and his daughter, Anna Freud, a leading authority on child psychoanalysis. In 1938, Sigmund Freud fled the Nazis in Vienna and settled in this house as a refugee. He brought with him his household furnishings, his books, and a collection of about 1,800 classical Egyptian and Oriental antiques. During his last days in 1939, he often asked that his bed be brought downstairs so he could enjoy the garden view. Anna Freud died in 1982. The museum is open Wednesday through Sunday, from noon until 5:00 p.m.

The Weiner Library, 29 Russell Square, Bloomsbury, London, WC1B 5DP. Tel: 44-20-7636-7247. This library probably contains more than 50,000 books and periodicals and hundreds of thousands of newspaper clippings on Nazism and the Holocaust.

Jews' College, Albert Rd., Hendon, London NW4 2SJ. Founded in 1855, coursework at this college leads to graduate degrees as well as rabbinical ordination. Includes a magnificent library of more than 80,000 volumes.

Leo Baeck College, The Sternberg Centre, 80 East End Road, London N3 2SY Tel: 44-20-8349 5600 website: www.lbc.ac.uk. Rabbinic training seminary for UK and European progressive (Reform and Liberal) rabbis and educators

Library of the Spanish and Portuguese Synagogue, Lauderdale Road, London W9.

Mocatta Library and Museum, University College, Gower St., London—WC1E 6BT Tel: 44-20 7679 7793. Sponsored by the Jewish Historical Society, it contains a wonderful Hebraica and Judaica section in the Guild Hall Library. Abraham Mocatta was a leader of the Bevis Marks Synagogue. The family originally came from Spain and the Mediterranean area. The Mocattas were among the first Jews in England, as well as founders of the Bevis Marks congregation. West London Synagogue. They were active on the Jewish Board of Deputies.

OTHER SITES

Selfridge's Department Store, 400 Oxford St., London W1, maintains a Jewish book section, as well as a scrumptious kosher food department.

The Statue of Benjamin Disraeli in Westminster Abbey. One of the most popular tourist sites in England is Westminster Abbey, which is the burial site, as well as house of statues, of Great Britain's greatest heroes, scholars, and politicians. In the Statesmen's Corner of the Abbey, next to former prime ministers Peel and Gladstone, stands a statue of Benjamin Disraeli (1804-81). The guides usually tell you that Benjamin Disraeli was born a Jew, but he was converted by his father.

He was born at **No 22. Theobalds Rd**. There is also a statue of Benjamin Disraeli facing Parliament. He died at 19 Curzon St., London W1, in 1881. A plaque was erected on the building. Disraeli was a statesman, one of the greatest prime ministers of the United Kingdom, and a prolific writer and novelist. Among his books were Vivian Grey,

Alroy, Sybil, and Coningsby. There are Jewish themes in many of his books. In the novel Tancred, Disraeli spoke out in favor of national independence of the Jews.

Just before his bar mitzvah, he was baptized by his writer-historian father, Isaac D'Israeli, after the latter had a quarrel with the Sephardic synagogue. The congregation had asked Isaac to serve on the board of trustees and Isaac refused. In those days, if you turned down your position, you had to pay a fine. Isaac refused again and left the congregation.

Even though Benjamin Disraeli was one of the most brilliant diplomats, and even though he was a regular church communicant, he never hid his Jewish origin and sympathies. As Disraeli liked to tell it, the family actually came from Italy, not Spain. "He believed that the Jews, by their virtue and their glorious past, were entitled to special esteem, and he devoted his tremendous audacity and imagination to securing it for them," writes Paul Johnson. Many say that, in Parliament, he spoke as if he were a Jew. He did much to improve the general social and political position of the Jews. As a young man, he had visited the Near East and Jerusalem.

Disraeli boasted of the "superiority of the Jewish race" as a storehouse of energy and vision. He believed Jews were the "aristocrats of mankind." He is quoted as saying, "The most inspiring singers, most graceful dancers and most delicate musicians are the sons and daughters of Israel." He once told Montefiore, "You and I belong to a race that can do everything but fail."

He was a great friend of the Rothschilds. With the financial help of the Rothschilds, he acquired the Egyptian khedive's shares in the Suez Canal to make sure England controlled the vital route to India. This action brought England right smack into the Middle East, next door to Palestine, which the British, under General Allenby, conquered in 1917 during World War I.

Perhaps Disraeli had indeed studied the map. Some historians say that in his bringing England into Egypt and closer to Palestine, perhaps he actually had in mind eventually to plant Britain in Palestine and thus be able to establish a Jewish state. Farfetched? Did not General Allenby invade Palestine from Egypt a half-century later?

His other great diplomatic victory was at the 1878 Congress of Berlin, when he prevented war in Eastern Europe.

Benjamin Disraeli presided at No. 10 Downing Street, the office of the Prime Minister, when it was the seat of the greatest empire the world had ever seen.

He got along splendidly with Queen Victoria, who laid a wreath upon his tomb. The marble tablet placed in the chancel of

Hughenden Church after his death says, "To the Dear and Honored Memory of Benjamin, Earl of Beaconsfield. This memorial is placed by His Grateful Sovereign and Friend, Victoria, R.I. Kings love him that speaketh right."

The Statue of Cromwell. In Parliament Square stands the statue of Oliver Cromwell, the "Lord Protector" of England. He had a great deal to do with the Jewish return to England in 1656 after a 400-year absence. Indeed the *Standard Jewish Encyclopedia* states that Manasseh Ben Israel's mission to England to petition for the readmission of Jews was probably undertaken at Cromwell's suggestion. Manasseh realized that Cromwell, a Puritan, viewed the Jews favorably and supported their readmission. To Cromwell it made good business sense. Cromwell had hoped to extend Britain's influence and its wealth, and to make England "number one" in Europe. He knew that Jews, as well as Marranos (secret Jews), had enriched other nations, including Holland, whose ships were out-trading the English. He hoped the Jews would do the same for England.

In December 1656, Cromwell convened the Whitehall Conference to consider the matter of the Jews. He himself presided over the opening session. He liked Manasseh Ben Israel, whose speech before the council was one of the most eloquent in Jewish history. It was called "Esperanca de Israel" ("The Hope of Israel"). But Cromwell later dissolved the conference when he realized the council's decision would be a resounding "no" to allowing Jewish immigration. Since he had the power, he could have rammed an admission bill through the meeting. Instead, he connived to allow the Jews to enter the country and stay, giving up attempts to permit their immigration on a formal basis—in short, a compromise.

Soon Jews were permitted to hold services in rented rooms. Later, they would be allowed to build their first synagogue in Creechurch Lane. In the spring of 1656, Cromwell received and granted a petition from the Marranos to establish a cemetery outside of London. Under Cromwell, Marranos obtained seats on the London Stock Exchange. From these trader families, the Jewish community created a network of other families who were prominent in banking, finance, and commerce.

The Statue of Winston Churchill. Near Parliament stands the statue of Winston Churchill. During World War II, Churchill was the voice of the free world. He uplifted men and women all over the globe. He was a leader. As you look at his statue, you cannot but admire this great man who rallied the people all over the world against Nazism. His patriotism, it is said, "was rooted in the very soil of the history of England."

Churchill was an ardent Zionist. His influence established the Jewish Brigade of Palestine in World War II. Churchill once wrote to Franklin

D. Roosevelt, "I am strongly wedded to the Zionist policy, of which I was one of the authors." He was a bitter opponent of England's White Paper, which, in 1939, severely limited Jewish immigration and closed off Palestine as a refuge.

But, as William Manchester notes, he was "unrepresentative of England's upper class, for even England was not free of anti-Semitism."

John Lukacs writes in his book, *The Duel*, which in 1938, when Churchill was in such debt that he was about to sell his beloved country house, Chartwell, Sir Henry Strakosch, a London financier of Jewish ancestry, "paid off his debts." Jewish groups would often cite Churchill for his "courageous defense of freedom and denunciation of Nazism." But even with Churchill's sympathy, it was always an uphill battle to establish the Zionist dream of a Jewish homeland. European Jews who were trapped during the war could not emigrate because most countries refused to admit Jews. And several ships, such as the Patria, were sunk because the English refused permission to dock in Palestine. Even after World War II, when Churchill was out of power, the British Labor Party resisted the establishment of a Jewish nation. It appeared that nothing could sway them, not even the death of the six million Jews.

Yet in the face of world opinion in favor of a Jewish state, the British finally relented. After the U. N. Partition Plan of November 1947, they left Palestine forever in 1948, bitter to the end. Almost seven decades later, many Israelis say the British treated them not as colonial subjects but as human beings. Aspects of the Israeli parliament, judiciary, and bureaucracy are all patterned after the British, under whom the Jews developed self-government

Wingate and Chindit Memorial. Victoria Embankment, outside the Ministry of Defense, London. This monument stands in honor of Maj. Gen. Orde Wingate and his Chindit forces of the Burma campaign during World War II. Wingate, friend of the Jews, some say "hero" of the Jews, helped train the Palmach, the "shock troops," of Haganah, the self-defense army of Israel during the British Mandate in Palestine. The Jewish people did not forget Wingate. They named a sports training and physical training facility, the Wingate Institute, just south of Netanya, Israel, after the general.

Brighton and Hove

Perhaps it is the Royal Pavilion, which houses a museum and art gallery; or the Dome area, which is used for concerts and conferences; or the Lanes and those famous antique shops that attract thousands. Maybe it is the boardwalk, the beaches, and the piers, but whatever the specific attraction, tourists are lured to this wonderful seaside resort on the English Channel, 51 miles south of London.

Many Jews commute from here to London each day, vacation here in the summer, and are active in the community, which has about 12,000 Jews, including a large number of retirees originally from London.

In the middle of the eighteenth century, the town became famous as a resort and wealthy Jews settled here, including the Goldsmids and Sassoons. But the bulk of Jews probably did not settle here until about 1800.

SYNAGOGUES IN BRIGHTON AND HOVE

Synagogue, 66 Middle St., Brighton. Tel: 27785. Brighton is also famous for this synagogue. It is a lovely, small synagogue consecrated in 1875, well known for its interior design.

Brighton & Hove Progressive Synagogue, 6 Landsdowne Rd., Hove Sussex. BN3 1FF. Tel: 44-1273-737-223. bhps@liberaljudaism.org, www.bhps-online.org/

Reform Synagogue, 65 Palmeira Ave., Hove Sussex. Tel: 44-1273-735-343. FAX: 44-1273-734-537. accounts@bh-rs.org, www.bh-rs-org.

Brighton and Hove Hebrew Congregation, 31 New Church Rd., Hoave BW3 4AD. Tel: 44-1273-888855.

Chabad House, 15 The Upper Dr., Hove, East Sussex BN3 6GR. Tel: 1273-321-919. FAX: 1273-821-518. rabbifune@hotmail.com. Rabbi Pesach Efune is *shaliach*.

Chabad at SE Coast Universities. Brighton, BN2 9SA. Tel: 44-1273-693-15.

Manchester

Manchester is often considered the prototypical city of the Industrial Revolution, and the first Jewish settlers arrived here from Liverpool in the eighteenth century. Nathan Mayer Rothschild's first residence in England was in Manchester, from where he exported cotton goods from 1798 to 1805. The large Jewish immigration came here between 1881 and 1914, generally tailors and capmakers. Lord Marks, founder of Marks and Spencer and one of the greatest leaders of the Zionist movement in Britain, was born in Manchester. In addition to the Manchester Jews who came to the city from Russia and Poland, a large number came here from the Middle East and established the important Sephardic congregations of South Manchester. From 1904 to 1917, Manchester was the home of Dr. Chaim Weizmann, the great Zionist leader and first president of Israel. Here he conducted his early scientific experiments and met the future leaders of the Zionist movement.

Many synagogues dot the Manchester urban area, the second largest Jewish community in Great Britain, with a Jewish population of about 35,000.

Lest We Forget: An attack in Manchester left 22 people dead and 59 injured after a male suicide bomber targeted children and young adults at the end of a concert by U.S. singer Ariana Grande at the Manchester Arena. The alleged bomber, Salman Abedi, 22, was born in Manchester and was arrested, according to the BBC.

The Manchester Jewish Museum is located on the premises of the former Spanish and Portuguese Synagogue at 190 Cheetham Hill Rd., Manchester M8 8LW. Tel: 44-161-834-9879. The building, completed in 1874, is listed as being of historical importance. The ground floor of the structure has not been altered in any significant way, and is no longer used for worship services. A traveler can visit this remarkable synagogue. The former ladies' gallery now houses the permanent exhibition in which the history of Manchester's Jewish community, now more than 200 years old, is vividly brought to life. Homes, schools, and workshops of long ago have been recreated in detail to portray the lives of ordinary people. The museum opened in 1984. It is open Monday through Thursday, 10:30 a.m. to 4:00 p.m., and Sunday, 10:30 a.m. to 5:00 p.m.

The first Jewish school was founded in 1842.

An interesting site is the library in St. Peters Square, which has an excellent Jewish collection.

Fulda's Hotel is a kosher hotel located at 144 Bury Old Rd. in Salford Rd., Manchester. Tel: 44-161-740-4551. FAX: 44-161-741-2450.

Lubavitch House Manchester, 62 Singleton Rd., Salford, Manchester M7 4LU. Tel: 44-161-740-9514.

Chabad, Salford, Mancheser, M7 4JD. Tel: 44-300-302-0132. www. beismenachem.org. uk.

Lubavitch of South Manchester, 2a Old Market Place, Altrincham, Cheshire WA14 2TN. Tel: 44-161-929-9999, 161-929-9020. www.lubavitchsoutmanchester.org.

Cheetham Hebrew Congregation, 453-455 Cheetham Hill Road, Manchester, M8 9PA, Tel: 44-161-740-7788

Chabad of Cheadle-Chai Network, 3 Milton Crescent Cheadle SK8 1NT.

Manchester Reform Synagogue, Jacksons Row, Albert Square, Manchester M2 5NH. Tel: 44-161-834-0514 FAX: 44-161-834-0415. admin@jacksonsrow.org, www.jacksonsrow.org/

Manchester Jewish Museum. (Photo by Dr. Gene Sosin)

A special notice of the Manchester Beth Din as shown in the Manchester Jewish Museum. (Photo by Dr. Gene Sosin)

Since religious Law is so central to Jewish life, it has always been necessary for Jewish communities to find means of facilitating its observance.

In England, control of orthodox religious practice had become centralised by the 1840s in the Chief Rabbi's office in London, and each provincial community was expected to affiliate itself to the Chief Rabbinate in order to receive the religious seal of approval. Although this centralisation has been opposed over the years by several groups, gravitating towards stricter orthodoxy or Reform, the Chief Rabbinate has remained the central religious authority of orthodox Anglo-Jewry.

Within the general framework of the Chief Rabbinate, each community found it necessary to organise its own religious affairs. In Manchester for

Rabbinical supervision of the work of the Board and the religious affairs of the community in general was formalised in 1902 by the establishment of a Manchester *Beth Din* – an Ecclesiastical Court, appointed by the Shechita Board and under the jurisdiction of the Chief Rabbi. The Beth Din consisted of 3 local Rabbis, called *Dayanim* (Judges), whose duties were to deal with matters relating to *shechita*, marriages, divorces, conversions, civil cases, and to decide on other religious questions. This ecclesiastical court constituted the highest local authority on religious affairs.

The provision of a *Mikvah* or ritual bath was another religious facility deemed necessary for the community. The Mikvah, used mainly by

A plaque commemorating Dr. Chaim Weizmann, the first President of Israel, who resided in Manchester from 1904 to 1917. (Photo by Dr. Gene Sosin)

Manchester Liberal Jewish Community, Cross Street Chapel Cross Street, Manchester, M@ 1NL. Tel: 44-8709-917-327. mljc.org.uk, www. mljc.org.uk.

Sha'arei Shalom North Manchester Reform Congregation, Elms Street, Manchester Whitefield M45 BCQ. Tel: 44-161-796-6736. office@ shaareishalom.org.uk, www.shaareishalom.org.uk/

Jewish Agency, 72 Singleton Rd., Salford, Manchester M7 4LU. Tel: 44-161-795-7800. aliyahman@jafi.org

Oxford

There is an old British expression that everyone journeys to Oxford sooner or later. Oxford is a city of all seasons, a city of learning and scholarship, and above all, a city built upon books, "books being read, books being written, books being published." This "sweet city with her dream spires" supports a labyrinth of libraries and dozens of bookstores.

About 800 to 1,000 Jews are on the university campus, and several hundred at a second university in Oxford.

The Oxford Center for Hebrew and Jewish Studies, Clarendon Institute Walton Street. Oxford OX1 2HG. Tel: 44-1865-619442, enquiries@ochjs.ac.uk. Mix together a former British country estate, one of the world's greatest universities, nine cottages for Israeli and American Jewish writers, and a college junior-year-abroad program in Jewish studies, and you have an advanced research institute of Judaic studies. The university is Oxford, in the town of Oxford, 56 miles by road from London. The Jewish institute, located just four miles outside the City of Oxford, is the Oxford Center for Post-Graduate Hebrew Studies.

Yarnton Manor, a seventeenth-century manor house that once belonged to the Spencer family from whom Diana, Princess of Wales, was descended, is used for lectures, symposia, seminars, and conferences. At the manor are the Kressel Library and Archives. The library contains 35,000 volumes; the archives contain approximately one-half-million newspaper clippings.

Oxford still remains one of the great centers of England. Historically, Jews came down here from London to sell hats, frocks, and shoes. And now, too, Jewish scholars and students of Judaism are coming to Oxford University, to the Oxford Center for Post-Graduate Hebrew Studies.

These scholars have produced more than 350 academic and literary items, including 80 books, as a result of their stay. Such famous works of Hebrew literature as A. B. Yehoshua's *The Lover* and T. Carmi's

The Penguin Book of Hebrew Verse were written, in whole or in part, at the center. Other writers who have worked here include Benyamin Tammuz, the Israeli novelist, who wrote Minotaur in the Apple Loft, one of the Yarnton Manor's estate cottages. In its English translation, Minotaur was chosen by the late Graham Greene as one of the three best novels of 1981.

The late Dr. David Patterson, founder and president of the center, Cowley Lecturer in Post-Biblical Hebrew, and fellow of St. Cross College in Oxford University, stressed that, during World War II, about 750 institutions of Jewish learning in Europe were lost forever. He recalls that when he started the center, he received the warm support of such leading scholars as Sir Isaiah Berlin and Professor David Daube, the former Regius Professor of Civil Law at Oxford University.

In an interview before he died, Dr. Patterson told me that he knew that Oxford was exceptionally well qualified to serve the needs of an international center for Jewish learning. After all, the chair in Hebrew was established by Henry VIII, and Hebrew has been taught there in an unbroken tradition for more than 450 years since then.

Bodleian Library. Thousands of Hebrew books, handwritten Bibles, priceless Judaica, and manuscripts are located in the Bodleian Library, one of the outstanding libraries in the world.

One estimate quotes that more than 30,000 Hebrew volumes are housed here.

Oxford Jewish Congregation, 21 Richmond Rd., Oxford.

Synagogue and Jewish Center, 21 Richmond Rd., Oxford OX1 2JL. Tel: 44-1865-514-356, Tel: 44-7525-785-200. connections@ojc-online. org. www. ojc-online.org. World Union of Progressive Judaism.

Chabad House, 75 Crowley Road, Oxford OX4 1HR. Tel: 44-1865-200-158. FAX: 44-7772-079-94. info@oxfordchabad.org.

B. H. Blackwell, Ltd., 48-51 Broad St., Oxford OX1 3BQ. This impressive and large bookshop contains a Judaica section.

York

Clifford's Tower of York Castle. A tragic episode occurred in York on the Sabbath before Passover, March 16, 1190, the day preceding Palm Sunday. It took place at Clifford's Tower, located just across from the museum. The tragedy was described thusly: At Easter, villagers launched a whispering campaign that Jews were killing Christian children so they could use their blood for Passover rites. Frightened, the Jews of York, headed by Rabbi Yom Tov of Joigny, fled to the castle. Rather than surrender, they decided to kill each other. Given a so-called safe conduct, a few survivors left the castle. "Kill the Jews," yelled the villagers. After butchering the survivors, they quickly burned the financial debt notes owed to the Jewish moneylenders. York Jewry never recovered from the killings. Today, only about 45 Jews live in York. For an admission fee, one can climb to the top. Open March 15 to October 15, Monday through Friday, 9:30 a.m. to 6:30 p.m. Sundays, 2:00 p.m. to 4:00 p.m. in summer.

On one trip as I departed England, I realized I was leaving London as the mist of a crisp fall afternoon hovered above this capital on the Thames. Nothing unusual about that, for I had walked about the city. I also met and talked to several RAF pilots, now seniors, who during the days when England stood alone during the World War II blitz, stopped the dreaded Luftwaffe. I realized that in many ways each tourist comes away from London with thoughts about great periods in the city's history.

For me, it was those young men who did as Winston Churchill said of them as they were halting the Nazis in the Battle of Britain: "Brace ourselves to our duties, and so bear ourselves that, if the British Empire and Commonwealth last for a thousand years, men will still say, this was their finest hour."

Suggested Reading

Bermant, Chaim. *The Cousinhood.* New York: Macmillan, 1971.

Blake, Robert. *Disraeli.* London: Methuen, 1969.

———. *Disraeli's Grand Tour: Benjamin Disraeli and the Holy Land,* 1830-31. New York: Oxford University Press, 1982.

Corbett, W. *Jews and the Jews of England.* Gordon, 1976.

Hyamson, Albert M. *A History of the Jews in England.* London: Chatto and Windus, 1908.

Litvinoff, Barnet. *The Burning Bush: Anti-Semitism and World History.* New York: Dutton, 1988.

Morton, H. V. *In Search of London.* New York: Dodd, Mead, 1951.

Wasserstein, Bernard. *Britain and the Jews of Europe,* 1939-1945. New York: Oxford University Press, 1979.

Weintraub, Stanley. *Disraeli: A Biography.* New York: Truman Talley Blochs/Dutton, 1993.

Ireland
Dublin Has Had Jewish Mayors

They call it "Bloomsday" and it remains the major literary festival of Ireland. It celebrates the birthday of Leopold Bloom, the son of a Hungarian Jew and the hero in Ulysses, James Joyce's novel that depicts certain elements of Jewish life in Dublin at the beginning of the 20th century. Joyce stands as Dublin's most famous writer and Dublin remains the center of the Jewish community of Ireland.

Walking the streets of Dublin, the birthplace of James Joyce, W.B. Yeats, George Bernard Shaw, and Samuel Beckett, one realizes that Dublin has more literary landmarks than most cities. Stop at Dublin Writers Museum, James Joyce Center, Trinity College, the National Library of Ireland. No wonder UNESCO added the Irish capital to its list of Cities of Literature. Some say it is a "book lover's nirvana."

The Jews of Ireland, most of whom live in the Dublin area, conduct a meaningful Jewish life with many activities. This Jewish community supports Orthodox synagogues, a large variety of religious, charitable, Zionist, and educational institutions, a religious school, and a museum. Relations between the Jewish community and the Catholic and Protestant populations are good.

A Brief History

The Irish love to link Ireland with biblical tradition, as well as to the ancient Jews. "Legends that the Irish are the Ten Lost Tribes of Israel can prove very convincing when delivered in the midst of a peat bog and when shown the genuine Jacob's ladder to heaven in a secret cave near the Lakes of Killarney," wrote Asher Benson, Dublin correspondent for the London Jewish Chronicle.

The earliest known reference to Jews in Ireland is in CE 613 when St. Columbanus penned an epistle to the pope of Rome, and smugly reported, "None of us has been a heretic, none of us a Jew." In the year 1079, five Jews came over the sea with gifts and were refused entry. Jews were forbidden to land in Ireland in the fifteenth and sixteenth centuries, although Marranos probably resided there. After an absence of several hundred years, a number of Jewish families of Spanish and Portuguese descent and two or three of Polish or German origin settled in Dublin around 1660.

But Jews did not flock to Ireland in large numbers until after Cromwell permitted them to return to England in 1656. Marranos from London were the first Irish Jewish settlers. In the middle of the seventeenth century, more Marranos settled in the city. Thus, by the first quarter of the eighteenth century, Dublin was the only city in Ireland that had an organized Jewish community. And they came, according to author Louis Hyman, because Dublin was the second city of the British Empire and the city was an excellent trading post, with a high society rivaling the heyday of Paris. Eighteenth-century Dublin was a vital, innovative capital.

In 1717, a Jewish cemetery was set up and a synagogue was founded in 1746.

Throughout the eighteenth century, the Irish tried often to convert the Jews of Dublin. According to one testimonial, "the people of this Kingdom constantly rejoice when they see a Jew convert." About 200 Jews lived in Dublin in 1750. But the failure of the Irish banks in 1727 and the famine of 1748 would hurt the city, including the Jews. Many Jews fled the severe famine, leaving only a few Jewish families in Dublin in the early nineteenth century. In 1816, the Irish Naturalization Act of 1783, from which the Jews had been excluded, was repealed: Jews could now be naturalized in Ireland. Dublin grew again in 1822 with the arrival of Polish and German Jews, most of whom had lived in England, writes Hyman. "In their struggle for political emancipation, the Jews of England found many a champion in Ireland," he adds.

But in the winter of 1845-46, Ireland again was stricken by a potato famine, which left a giant graveyard. One million persons fled to America. The relief measures taken by an unprepared government were almost useless, but there was outside aid in which British and American Jews were prominent. An Irish famine-loan of 8 million British pounds was negotiated by Baron Lionel Rothschild of London, who waived all commission.

After 1882, the Russian Jews arrived and firmly established the Jewish community. They settled in Cork, Limerick, Londonderry, and Waterford. In 1881, there were 472 Jews. By 1901, that figure rose to 3,769.

While the Jewish community maintained neutrality during Ireland's fight for independence, Dublin Jews sheltered many Irish revolutionaries and individual Jews took a leading part in the rebellion, Robert Briscoe among them. Briscoe later became lord mayor of Dublin.

In 1918, the office of the chief rabbi of Eire was established and Rabbi Isaac Herzog (1889-1959) was appointed. He later served as the first Ashkenazi chief rabbi of Israel. Rabbi Herzog was recognized as one of the great rabbinical scholars of his time. He was rabbi in Belfast from 1916 to 1919 and in Dublin until 1936, receiving the title of chief rabbi of the Irish Free State after 1921. He was a friend of Eamon deValera, the Irish leader and prime minister. His son, Chaim, was president of Israel from May 1983 to May 1993.

Belfast-born Chaim Herzog also served Israel as a former intelligence officer, military commentator, military attaché to Washington, and Israel's ambassador to the United Nations. When Ireland became independent in 1921, the Jews set up their own community council. The 1937 Constitution of the Republic recognized Judaism as a minority faith and guaranteed Jews complete freedom from discrimination.

Israel's independence occurred on May 14, 1948. But, Ireland waited until February 12, 1949, to accord de facto recognition of Israel. In 1995 Ireland finally established diplomatic relations with Israel.

Jewish Dublin

Jews live in Dublin because it is a business center, vacation destination, and port city. It is a city of writers, revolutionaries, and talkers—a city of memories possessing a tragic and yet glorious history.

About 2,500 Jews live in Ireland, and probably more, because of the influx of Israelis in recent years. The Jewish population is rising. Most Jews live in Dublin and what the Irish call "collar counties." According to *The Times of Israel*, the one-way traffic of young Jews out of the country in search of partners and careers may be over. Dublin-based Israeli lawyer Mattan Lass, pointed out that "the Emerald Isle now has one of the fastest growing Jewish communities in Europe. "The story of Irish Jewry has too often been depicted as a community in decline," says Lass, "but not anymore. There are now more than 1,500 new Israeli Jews here working in the IT sector."

Other reports note that 30 percent of Ireland's Jewish community consists of recent arrivals from France, the UK, and the US.

A few Jewish families reside in Cork. Once, during World War II, more than 15,000 Jews lived in the country, most of them in Dublin. When there was a large Jewish community, Jews lived in the South Circular Road section. That area was called the Jewish "Little Jerusalem." In 1961, there were 3,255 Jews in Ireland. That number declined to 2,633 in 1971, mostly because of a fall in the birthrate and emigration to Israel.

JEWISH SITES IN DUBLIN

Birthplace of Leopold Bloom, 52 Upper Clanbrassil St., Dublin 8. This building is supposedly the birthplace of James Joyce's famous character in *Ulysses*.

Bloomfield House, Bloomfield Ave., Dublin 8. This was formerly the Jewish Day School.

Clonyn Castle, Delvin, County Westmeath. More than 100 Jewish orphaned children from concentration camps had a temporary home here until 1948.

The Irish Jewish Museum, 3 and 4 Walworth Rd., Wood Quay, Dublin 8. Tel: 353-85-706-7367. The museum is near Circular Road. Phone ahead to make sure the museum is open. The facility is known to keep irregular hours.

Do not be shocked, dear reader, when you enter the **Jewish Museum** at 4 Walworth, near Circular Road, Dublin. Two photographs stare at you: the Lubavitch Rebbe and James Joyce. The Museum contains photos, articles, and documents. The Irish Jewish Museum officially was opened on June 20, 1985, by the then-president of Israel, Chaim Herzog. The building is located in the former Walworth Road Synagogue, which has been completely restored.

In planning the layout of the museum in the existing premises, a division was made between the secular and religious. The secular exhibition has been mounted downstairs in the reception hall of the former synagogue. The displays trace the history of the Jews in Ireland beginning with their arrival, their various commercial and professional activities, the development of their institutions, and their integration to their present position and status.

Upstairs, at the rear of the synagogue in the Harold Smerling Gallery, there is a display of ritual and religious items.

Some of the exhibition topics are James Joyce and the Jewish characters and references in his novels; Jews in Irish provincial cities; anti-Semitism; the Holocaust; Irish Jews and families in public life, in the professions, and in business; the Jewish wedding; women in Judaism; and ritual objects.

Most people, when they think about Irish Jews, do not consider their artistic achievements. Perhaps the most unique aspect of a visit to this museum is to discover that Irish Jewry, which never numbered more than 6,000 persons, and now numbers about 2,500, produced talented painters. Works by Harry Kernoff, David Eichenstein, Estella Solomons, Gerald Davis, and others, are on display. A cabinet of books written by Irish Jews is a highlight of the exhibit.

The museum abounds in material regarding families and personalities.

The lives of the chief rabbis are also portrayed. A favorite exhibit is "Irish Jews in Public Life." One such personality, of course, is Robert Briscoe (1894-1969), the first Jewish member of the Irish Parliament and the first Jewish lord mayor of Dublin. He fought for Irish independence in the IRA from 1917 to 1924. One of the few Jews in the IRA, he was a member of Eamon de Valera's party from 1927 to 1965. He supported Revisionist Zionism. Briscoe wrote a book, *For the Life of Me*, which was published in 1958, the year he was elected mayor of Dublin. "All the time I was growing up," he states, "I was being steeped in the dark, stormy, racked, light, short history of my country of Eire."

Through the Easter uprising, the terror, the Black and Tans, the controversial treaty with England, and the civil war, Briscoe—who claimed he was the only Jew in the IRA—fought for Irish independence. Some say he taught Vladimir Ze'ev Jabotinsky, Revisionist Zionist leader, guerrilla tactics he learned while fighting the British. He had listened to Jabotinsky address groups in Ireland. In his book, he tells how he pioneered and helped raise money for the famous "coffin ships" that smuggled thousands of Jews into Palestine. He said he regarded Zionism as a magnificent inspiration.

His son, Benjamin Briscoe, was Dublin's lord mayor from 1988 to 1989. He was then elected to Parliament from his father's constituency.

Recalling Robert Briscoe moves one to think he would have commented on Ireland's attitude toward Israel.

On one aspect of Irish Israel relations, BDS "has a presence" in progressively left-leaning nations like Ireland. Actually, Kinvara is the only town that makes BDS an official town policy.

In any case, Ireland has been the European country most critical of Israel, according to Alex Grobman, PhD, in an article entitled, *Why Is Ireland So Hostile to Israel, Why Do the Irish Support BDS, What Is It About Israel That Upsets Them?*

Grobman noted that "As early as 1989, Ireland invited the PLO to open an office in Dublin and followed up by later elevating it to a diplomatic mission. In 1995, the Irish government declined to condemn Arab and Islamist terror attacks, even while other European countries were expressing their outrage. In October 2014, the Irish parliament passed a motion calling on the government to recognize a Palestinian-Arab state. The motion was proposed by Irish Senator Averil Power of the center-right Fianna Fáil (Republican Party). According to the *Times of Israel*, he said he did so to "create pressure on Israel to pursue a genuine peace process that has a real prospect of delivering peace and justice for both Israelis and Palestinians alike," wrote Grobman.

But even into 2017, Ireland it seemed was bent on recognizing Palestine, a move certain to anger the Jewish state as well as millions of its supporters throughout the world.

While most Jewish leaders note that "anti-Israel sentiment has a strong popular acceptance," they add, "Ireland is probably one of the least anti-Semitic countries in Europe." **The Jewish Old Aged Home**, Denmark Hill, Leinster Rd. West, Rathmines, Dublin 6. Tel: 353-497-6258. This home was founded in 1950. Services are held here; times vary according to season and needs of senior citizens.

Memorial to the Six Million Jews, in the synagogue grounds between 32 and 34 Rathfarnham Rd., Dublin 6. This monument remembers those Jews who perished in the Holocaust.

Office of the Chief Rabbi and Jewish Community Office. Herzog House, 1 Zion Rd., Dublin 6. Tel: 353-492-3751. office@jewishireland.org. Rabbi Zalman Lent, rabbilent@jewishireland,org. www.jewishireland. org. He is considered the Communal Rabbi, the post of Chief Rabbi has remained vacant.

Rabbi Herzog's Home, 33 Bloomfield Ave., Dublin 8. The first chief rabbi of Ireland resided here. Not open to the public.

Stratford College and Dublin Talmud Torah, 1 Zion Rd., Dublin 6. Tel: 967351. This college incorporates kindergarten, primary school, and college secondary school.

SYNAGOGUES IN DUBLIN

The Dublin Hebrew Congregation, (DHC) 32a Rathfainham Rd., Terenure Crossroads, Dublin 6W. Tel: 761734 or 766745. Dedicated in 1892. In a nearby structure, one finds the office of the chief rabbi of Ireland, the community center, as well as the headquarters of various Jewish organizations and Zionist groups. DHC has services seven days a week. During the winter months, weekday *mincha* services are suspended as nightfall occurs so early in the working day, and *maariv* is called for 7:00 p.m. In the summer, service times for *mincha/maariv* are fixed at 8:00 p.m., Friday included. In the spring and autumn, times of worship vary. Check times of worship on www.godaven/Ireland.com.

For further information regarding Jewish tourism in Ireland, consult www.jewishireland.org

Tourists are asked to please fill out a form at www.tinyurl.com/shabbat-in-dublin if they plan to attend services. In addition, Rabbi Zalman Lent, rabbilent@jewishireland.org, gives a weekly *gemara shiur* after *maariv* on Wednesdays.

Currently, Dublin Hebrew Congregation is closed to private tours. Instead, visitors to Dublin are encouraged to attend the morning and evening worship services.

Services are Fridays at 8:30 p.m. in summer and at sunset in other seasons; every Saturday morning from 9:15 to 11:15 a.m. Rabbi Zalman Lent, a shaliach of Chabad to Ireland, serves as rabbi of this congregation. For access to the mikvah, contact Karen Walsh or the community office: 353-492-3751.

Dublin Jewish Progressive Congregation, 7 Leicester Ave., Dublin 6. Tel: 490-7605. Services are held Fridays at 8:15 p.m. and first Saturdays in every month at 10:30 a.m. Rabbi Emeritus Charles Middlebrough visits this congregation each month. dublinjpc@gmail. com, www.djpcireland.com. He commutes from the UK, a 35-minute hop. This congregation holds Friday evening services every week, and when the rabbi is in town, they sponsor Saturday morning services.

Please contact the congregation at dublinjpc@gmail.com to inquire about proper arrangements for security and Sabbath observance.

Machzikei Hadass, rear of 77 Terenure Rd. North, Dublin 6. Tel: 490-8413. Services are held every Saturday at 9:30 a.m. Times for all other services vary according to season. Rabbi Zalman Lent serves as rabbi here, too. This synagogue is the oldest surviving Dublin Jewish Institution having been founded in 1883.

Most Jewish tourists who visit Dublin Jewish sites stop by because of a challenge they face or are planning to stay over the Sabbath. Of those that do visit, half of those travelers are Israelis and one-quarter of them are U.S. citizens.

The Israeli presence has gained in recent years.

Dublin Tour Guides, as provided by the *Irish Jewish Travel Guide:* Peter White Tours gives you Jewish Dublin through the eyes of a native Jewish Dubliner. Whole and half-day tours. Walking tours and multiday tours are also available, Fees upon request. Tel: +353-87-2681509 or email peterwhitetours@gmail.com

Neil Hogan is a professional tour guide who has a designed a tour of Jewish Dublin. He can do a tour combining Jewish attractions with popular Irish ones. Whole and half-day tours. Fees upon request. Contact: neilhogan1@gmail.com

It is said that Ireland, once visited, is never forgotten. The traveler certainly will find this to be so.

Suggested Reading

Briscoe, Robert, with Alden Hatch. *For the Life of Me.* Boston: Little, Brown, 1958.

Hyman, Louis. *The Jews of Ireland, from Earliest Times to the Year 1910.* Shannon, Ireland: Irish University Press, 1972.

Italy
Jews Sell Cameos in St. Peter's Square

"All Italians look like Jews and all Jews look like Italians," said the Italian writer, Luigi Barzini.
When I stroll through St. Peter's Square in Rome, I watch Italian men selling religious cameos. At least they look Italian. I soon realize that if these salesmen thought you were Jewish, they might greet you in Yiddish with, "Hello, landsman." Considering that Jews have lived in Europe for hundreds of years, it is not strange to hear Yiddish on the Continent. However, it is uncommon to hear a Yiddish greeting from Jews in Italy who, by and large, are of Sephardic origin, or indigenous Italians who do not know Yiddish.

Anyway, what were Jews doing selling religious cameos in St. Peter's Square in the first place?

Believe it or not, the concession is said to be held by Jews, who know that most American Jewish tourists are Ashkenazim. Like all good business persons, those Italian Jews also get attention by shouting out a Yiddish word in the Vatican, of all places. Incidentally, you will probably meet these Jewish salespersons at the Colosseum and the Pantheon, too.

A Brief History

Welcome to Italy, where beauty reigns supreme and where Jews have lived longer than in any other country in Europe. Italy was one of the first European countries to which Jews migrated from the Holy Land; today it is home to about 30,000 Jews, out of a population of about 62 million.

Ambassadors of Judah Maccabee set foot on Italian soil in 140 BCE seeking alliances, and indeed found a warm welcome.

Italy, the only nation in Western Europe in which Jewish settlement has been continuous from the second century, is considered the oldest Jewish community in the Western world. Few towns or regions in Italy stand without a trace of Jewish presence: catacombs from first-century

143

cemeteries, medieval and baroque synagogues, Jewish quarters and ghettos. Italy's museums and churches contain countless Jewish relics, and history's first Hebrew printing press was started here. In 70 CE, thousands of Jews were massacred in Palestine. Thousands more were deported to Rome. At one time, 1,500 Jews arrived in Rome in chains. Roman Jewish slaves worked on the Colosseum, one of the monumental symbols of the Eternal City, until they could buy their freedom. They would continue suffering at the hands of Tiberius, Claudius, and Nero.

When Rome fell and Christianity was accepted as the official religion, Jews were persecuted. The Church wanted the Jewish people preserved, however, as "witnesses of ancient truths." Jews were seen as the enemies of Jesus, responsible for his death and were therefore looked upon as second-class citizens, excluded from public offices and from various professions. While Jews were persecuted by the Byzantines, these conditions ceased when Pope Gregory I (590-604) began his reign. He protected them and provided safety for Jews in Rome and other cities. After this, it becomes evident that Jewish history in Italy is linked with the papacy. Some popes safeguarded Jews. They even hired Jewish financiers and doctors. On the other hand, many popes were bitterly anti-Semitic.

By the end of the eleventh century, Jews lived in northern Italy in such towns as Verona, Pavia, and Lucca. Talmudic academies existed in Rome. Hostility of the popes erupted in the twelfth century and culminated in the Fourth Lataran Council in 1215, which along with other discriminatory regulations forced Jews to wear a distinguishing badge on their clothes. In the thirteenth century and the beginning of the fourteenth, Jews were allowed to become moneylenders as the Church prohibited Christians from lending money for interest. After the Catholic monarchs of Spain expelled the Jewish people from Spanish soil in 1492, many Jews, as well as Marranos, found their way to Italy. But the Spaniards invaded the south late in the fifteenth century and forced the Jews to leave Sicily and the Italian south. In 1555, Pope Paul IV issued his infamous "*cum nimis absurdum*," banishing Jews to the ghetto. The document also prohibited them from engaging in any business except the sale of rags and other items. During the Counter-Reformation, an Inquisition was instituted. Jews were burned at the stake. Many fled to the north or out of Italy to North Africa, Greece, Turkey, and the Levant. Throughout the years, even as late as the eighteenth century, Jews, forced to listen to sermons, were often baptized against their will.

When Napoleon overran Italy in 1796, the Catholic Church's political rule was taken away. Implementing the ideals of the

Revolution, the French army freed the Jews. For the first time, Jews became Italian citizens. On July 9, 1798, the yellow badge that Jews had been forced to wear was abolished by an edict of the French general St. Cyr.

With Napoleon's abandonment of Italy and his downfall at Waterloo came reaction. Pope Pius VII returned to Rome in 1814 and re-introduced the Holy Inquisition. Jews would have continued to suffer, except for the Risorgimento movement for freedom that started in the Piedmont region in 1820-21 and culminated in the 1848-49 revolution in Milan, Rome, and Venice, the latter under the leadership of Daniele Manin, a Jew. In 1848-49, the walls of the ghetto of Rome came down. They had stood longer than any other in Western Europe. Yet again a wave of repression occurred. Finally, in 1861, when the united Italian kingdom was established, Jews received equal rights.

Cecil Roth points out in *The History of the Jews of Italy* that after 1861, there was no country in either hemisphere where Jewish conditions "were or could be better," at least until the late 1930s. The 1938 racial laws against Jews restricted Jewish life and devastated the Jewish community.

As Germany's ally, Italy invaded France in 1940. Still, the Jews in Italian-occupied southern France, as well as in Italy itself, were reasonably safe. However, when Italy surrendered to the Allies on September 8, 1943, Jews immediately faced danger from the Germans, who rushed troops into central and northern Italy. At this time Mussolini's puppet regime cooperated with the Nazis. The Gestapo also quickly moved against the Jewish community. On September 24, 1943, they blackmailed the Jewish community, demanding 50 kilos of gold within 36 hours, otherwise 200 Jews would be murdered. Four days later, they got their money. Pope Pius XII offered to provide as much as needed, but enough had been collected by the Jewish community. Nothing was taken from the Vatican. Contributions also came from non-Jews.

On October 16, 1943, "Black Saturday," the Germans surrounded the Jewish quarter and arrested more than 1,000 Jews, who were then shipped to Auschwitz, where all but 16 died. "Until that mass roundup the Jews of Rome believed themselves immune to crimes they heard were being committed by the Nazis against the Jews of other countries," writes Robert Katz.

The number of Italian Jews murdered in the Holocaust is estimated at 7,750 out of a total Jewish population of about 30,000 at the beginning of the German occupation, an 85 percent survival rate, second to Denmark.

According to Susan Zuccotti, in her book *The Italians and the Holocaust*, the Holocaust began relatively late in Italy, in September 1943, when the Germans swooped south. Therefore, the danger period was shorter. The Italian Jews were one-tenth of one percent of the population. Financial resources as well as hard cash helped Jews survive. Physical appearances also mattered, for assimilated Jews could pass as non-Jews. Ordinary Italians, moreover, tried to help the Jews during the German occupation. Italy ranks with Denmark as one of the nations that rescued Jews during the dark years. After the war, Italy was the main "highway for Jewish refugees en route to Palestine," although some went to America. In 1945, the post-Holocaust era of Italian Jewry began with lives that had been disrupted. "Those who remained began a slow and painful reconstruction," wrote Emily Braun in *Gardens and Ghettos*. But they were soon to be joined by Jews from Hungary and North Africa, especially Egypt, who lived in more than 200 Italian cities and towns. By the 1990s the Jewish population was estimated at about 30,000, including about 2,000 Israeli students, out of a total Italian population of 62 million persons.

A high rate of assimilation and declining enrollment in Jewish schools, as well as an aging population, plagues present-day Italian Jewry. According to the Institute of Jewish Affairs in London, 56 percent of Italian Jews have a diploma or university degree; 34 percent are engaged in trade or business; 13 percent are professionals; 5 percent are workers; and 4 percent are teachers.

In the 1980s there were some anti-Semitic incidents, a number of which were sparked by the war in Lebanon, but the then Chief Rabbi Elio Toaff spoke out and relations between Christians and Jews in Italy are still good. In 1965, the Second Vatican Council repudiated the notion that the Jews collectively were responsible for the death of Jesus and subsequently affirmed the enduring importance of Judaism. And in 1993, the Vatican and Israel established diplomatic relations.

Over the years, ties between Italy and Israel have strengthened. Daniel Funaro, a member of the board of the Rome Jewish Community, believes that Italy-Israel relations are good and calls Italy a good friend of Israel. But, of course, there are down moments. Italy annoyed Israel by abstaining in an October 2016 resolution that failed to acknowledge Judaism's connection to Jerusalem. The UNESCO resolution criticized Israeli policy surrounding religious sites in East Jerusalem and the West Bank and, again, used language that Israel says denies Jewish ties to the region's holy sites. Still, Israel's Prime Minister Benjamin Netanyahu met with Foreign Minister Angelino Alfons in Jerusalem and discussed expanded cooperation between the two nations.

Notable Italian Jews

Within one or two generations, the Jews moved from crafts and small commerce to industry, the army, and government. Here are some examples. Luigi Luzzatti (1841-1927) was minister of Finance and prime-minister of Italy in 1910. Camillo Olivetti founded the famous typewriter company and Ernesto Nathan served as mayor of Rome in 1907.

The Italian cultural scene included such contributors as Primo Levi (1919-1987), renowned novelist and writer of books on the Holocaust. A chemist, a member of the antifascist resistance, and a survivor of Auschwitz, Levi died in Turin in April 1987—an apparent suicide. Carlo Levi (1902-1975) was a painter, doctor of medicine, political leader, and author of *Christ Stopped at Eboli*. Natalia Ginzburg (1917-1991) was a novelist and playwright. She was a leader of the Italian Resistance and her husband was a victim of the Nazis. Giorgio Bassani (1916-2000), author of *The Garden of the Finzi-Continis*, wrote many stories dealing with the Holocaust. Novelist Alberto Moravia (1907-1991), born Alberto Pincherle, was one of Italy's outstanding writers; he was estranged from Judaism. Amedeo Modigliani (1884-1920), the painter, was born in Leghorn and studied art in Florence and Venice. At 21 he went to Paris; his brother, Victor Emmanuel, was an active Socialist leader who fought Mussolini. Roberto Melli (1885-1958) was a sculptor forced into hiding during war; painter Mario Cavaglieri (1887-1969) was born in the Jewish quarter of Rovigo and lived in Padua. Tullia Zevi, who died in 2011, was a noted leader of the Jewish community and had been mentioned as a future presidential candidate of Italy. Rabbi Dr. Elio Toaff, (1915-2015) was born in Leghorn. He was rabbi of Ancona and Venice before being called to Rome to succeed David Prato as chief rabbi of that community in 1951.

Jewish Rome

In Rome, you will find that several streets contain Jewish-owned stores. One survey has reported that 70 percent of Rome's clothing shops are operated by Jews. The young people of Rome often go straight from school into their parents' businesses. However, Italy has in recent decades become a "heavily industrialized nation via American-style capitalism," and more and more young Jews are moving into industrial and technological professions.

Between 13,000 and 15,000 Jews call Rome their home. Some

Italian Jews have noted that the community in Rome supports more than 20 kosher restaurants, many of which have opened in the past decades. One eatery, Ba'Ghetto has opened two branches in the past seven years to meet demand from locals, not tourists. The capital has three kindergartens and one K-12 school, according to JTA.

Renzo Gattegna, president of the Union of Italian Jewish Communities is quoted as saying in the press that "the vibrant Jewish cultural offerings in Italy offset its declining numbers." As an example, he cited the launch a few years ago of the Balagan Café, a bi-weekly series of cultural events in Florence. In Milan, he pointed to the local Chabad outpost hosting an annex to the EXPO Milan 2015 food fair that focused on kashrut. In Florence and Torino, Jewish student associations have formed and organized cultural events and celebrate holidays.

Describing the Italian Jewish Community, Daniel Funaro, who is also chief of staff to the director of the Rome Jewish Community, recalls a phrase by the late President of Israel Shimon Peres that can relate to Italian Jewry: "small in size, great in spirit." Funero believes that "Jewish education for our children is crucial for the future of the Jewish community in Italy."

Still, chances are that Jews will be in Rome for many centuries to come.

As Fiamma Nirenstein put it in a news article:

"Over the millennia, the Jews always remained proud Romans, even if then they were confined in the ghetto until 1869 , and once a year the Pope used to ritually kick and roll some of them around in pitch and feathers. Some people say," she wrote, "that the Jews are the only true ancient Romans left."

JEWISH SITES IN ROME

The Ghetto of Rome. To find the ghetto in Rome, take buses 44, 56, 60, or 75 to Ponte Garibaldi near the Great Synagogue (see "Synagogues in Rome" section). Walk to the synagogue and then proceed to the area behind the temple.

Another way to reach the ghetto is to circle the Pantheon, going across the Via Botteghe Oscure and past the Caetani Palace, until you reach the winding, narrow cobbled streets and alleyways. Small piazzas are the hallmark of the ghetto, which is on the left bank of the Tiber. The ghetto once was bounded by the Campo di Fiore, the Piazza di S. Croce, and the Piazza Guidea, ancient streets that still exist today.

A small group of Roman Jews still lives in the old ghetto adjacent to the main synagogue.

Before the ghetto was erected in 1555, and even as far back as the days of imperial Rome, Jews lived in the Trastevere section on the right bank of the Tiber. There may have been about 15 synagogues in that sector. A medieval house of worship can still be seen on Vicolo dell'Atleta, No. 13-14. It is located in a narrow alley behind the Cinema Esperia. That synagogue was founded by Rabbi Nathan ben Yehiel in the beginning of the twelfth century. He was the author of Arukh, the famous dictionary of the Talmud and the Midrash.

No Italian ghetto was said to be as severe, in regards to living conditions, as the one in Rome. Wrote Jewish historian Cecil Roth, "The ghetto was situated in the fetid, low lying quarter on the left bank of the Tiber, frequently inundated by the overflowing of the river and heavily visited at the time of plagues."

The civic rules specified that Jews could have only one synagogue; they got around that stricture by maintaining five synagogues with different rites under a single roof. Needless to say, their whole life revolved around the ghetto. Today it seems to be the "in" place to live. But if you really want to see what a ghetto street looked like, head for the **Via della Reginella**. Gloomy and oppressive to this day, it is witness to the "misery that once dwelled here." This area of the Tiber at one time contained between 5,000 and 10,000 persons in one-third of a square mile. Another description says the enclosure was seven acres with 130 houses.

Today, Jews still live in the main street of the quarter, the Via del Portico d'Ottavia. The portico (gate), now in ruins, was built twelve years after the first Jews came to Rome from Palestine. Later this gate and others would be the only entrance and exit of the Jewish ghetto. On this street, you can see old buildings with stores, excellent restaurants that serve Jewish dishes alla Romana, kosher butcher shops, and bakeries.

Marmertine Prison, Rome. This memorial near the Roman Forum contains the tablet of Gen. Simon Bar Giora, defender of the Jews against the Romans in Jerusalem (70 CE). Titus captured him and dragged him before the populace in Rome; he died in this prison.

A **monument** memorializing the massacres at the Ardeatine Caves is located just off the Porto San Paolo, a few yards from the main synagogue. This is an impressive memorial to the 335 persons, including 100 Jews, murdered by the Germans on March 23, 1944. The incident took place in the Ardeatine Caves just beyond the ancient walls of Rome. These lives were ended in retaliation for the killing of Nazis in the Via Rasella by Italian partisans. Thirty-three Germans were killed in that street near Rome's famous boulevard, the Via Veneto. Ten for one was the Gestapo retribution. The 335 hostages were rounded up, taken to the Ardeatine Caves beyond the catacombs, and murdered by the S.S. The Germans tried to conceal the site, but it was soon discovered. In 1998, former Nazi SS Captain Erich Priebke 85, was sentenced to life in prison. Priebke was found guilty of helping carry out the massacre of 335 civilians in German-occupied Rome in 1944. On March 7, 1998, the court also handed down a life sentence to former SS Maj. Priebke died in prison in 2013. He was 100 years old. The late Karl Hass, also 85 at the time, was sentenced for helping to carry out the 1944 massacre. He died in 2005.

While the monument is here, the dead are buried nearby in **The Mausoleo delle Fosse Ardeatine Fine, Rome,** a mausoleum situated just off the Via Appia Antica between the Via Ardeatine and the Via delle Sette Chiese, a short distance from the catacombs of San Sebastian. Three huge figures are shown tied together. Dedicated in 1957, the mausoleum is in a courtyard. The caves are cut into the Ardeatine Hill. The Jewish graves are inscribed with a Star of David.

JEWISH RESTAURANTS IN ROME

Before dining in Rome, do check to see if the eating establishment is kosher and has rabbinic supervision. Below are some recommended spots. A number of kosher restaurants can be found in the via del Portico d'Ottavia, the main street of the Old Ghetto, and a few are listed here. For more information on kosher facilities, check out, www.jewishrome.org.

Little Tripoli, (glatt) (meat) Via Polesine 16, 00161 Rome. Tel: 39-06-6840-398. Certified by Beth Din Rome and Rabbi Itzchak Haan. jewishrome.org.

Ba'Ghetto, via del Portico d'Ottavio, 57, Rome. Tel: 39-06-6889-2868. (Beth Din Rome).

Bella Carne (grill) via Portico d'Ottavio, 53, Rome. Tel: 39-06-683-3104.

Daruma Sushi Kosher, Piazza Bologna, 8, Rome. Tel: 39-06-440-4962. (Beth Din Rome).

Kosher Bistrot, (kosher products and fast food) via Marie del Planto 68, 00186, Rome. Tel: 39-06-686-4398.

LODGING

Pensione Carmel, Via Gioffredo Mameli 11, Rome. Tel: 580-9921. Many Orthodox Jews stop at this hotel, as it is near the synagogue. Call for reservations. Pensione Carmel offers kosher breakfast.

SYNAGOGUES IN ROME

The Great Temple (Tempio Maggiore), Lungotevere Cenci 9, on the banks of the Tiber. Tel: 39-06-6840-0661. Built in 1901, the synagogue, which follows the Italian rite of worship, is Orthodox. There are daily services. A mikveh is located in this synagogue, which is situated between the Via Catalana and Lungotevere Cenci.

The synagogue itself was built on the ruins of the ancient Jewish quarter. Imposing in its Assyro-Babylonian style of architecture, it is set behind wrought-iron gates on the northern side of the Tiber River.

The synagogue interior possesses an Oriental motif. The visitor can see rows of varicolored glass in the top of the dome, stately marble columns and pillars that rise to form wide arcades, windows embellished with cornices, and walls richly painted with stylized floral motifs. Biblical inscriptions adorn the walls. In the synagogue, the Holy Ark comes from the destroyed Sicilian synagogue and bears the

The Great Temple of Rome.

date 1586. The six Assyrian columns that surround it are admired for their volutes and elaborate gilded friezes. There are several annexes, such as the Spanish temple, where the Holy Ark was once part of the city's old synagogue. Memorial tablets of Jews who fell in battle during World War I and of Jews who were deported in World War II grace the walls. A third memorial recalls the Jews who, along with many Christians, were slaughtered by the Nazis in the Ardeatine Caves.

Sephardic services are held in a separate hall of the synagogue as the main service is in the "Italian rite."

The offices of the Jewish Community of Rome are located in the Great Temple. Lungotevere Cenci 9, Rome. Tel: 06-684-00-641. info@romaebraica.it However, the legal address is Largo Stefano Gay Tache, which is the address of the square at the synagogue.

A memorial plate has been placed at the entrance to the synagogue in commemoration of this dastardly attack.

Stefano Gay Tache was the two-year-old toddler murdered in a terrorist attack by Palestinian gunmen at the entrance of the Great Synagogue of Rome which took place at 11:55 a.m., on October 9, 1982. Thirty-seven civilians were injured, including Stefano's brother, Gadiel Tache, at that time four years old.

The Italian Jewish community was shocked that this terrorist murder could occur in Italy. At the time, the Jews accused the government of "flirting" with Arab terror groups. On February 3, 2015, Judge Sergio Mattarella, upon taking the oath of office as President of the Republic, said, in his address to the Italian Parliament, "Italy has paid several times, in a not too distant past, the price of hate and intolerance. I want to remember only one name, Stefano Tache who was killed in the cowardly terrorist attack on the synagogue in Rome in October 1982. He was only two years old. He was our baby, an Italian baby."

Security

As in other synagogues, Jewish community centers and museums, and Jewish institutions throughout Europe, security is an issue. This is especially true in Rome where, as noted above, a two-year-old infant was murdered by terrorists in 1982 in the Great Temple. Visitors should consider a five to ten minute or more wait to clear security. The same procedure exists for visitors to The Great Temple and other Jewish institutions in Rome. It is best to advise officials at Jewish institutions ahead of time that you are planning to visit their building and always important to bring your passport or a copy of same.

The Jewish Museum is located in the same building as the Great

Temple. Lungotevere Cenci 9, Rome. www.museoebraico.roma.it. http://lnx.museoebraico.roma.it/w/?page_id=580&lang=en.

The museum receives about 86,000 visitors each year, including approximately 30,000 American tourists.

In 2005, the museum was totally renovated. The ticket of the museum includes a short guided tour of the Main Synagogue, which starts every hour from inside the museum. The museum can also be visited with an audio guide included in the ticket. Audio guides are available in Italian, English, French, German, Spanish, Hebrew, and Russian language.

Private tours are available by booking in advance. These select tours have a Jewish guide who explains the seven rooms of the museum and two synagogues. The tours last 90 minutes and have to be prepaid.

The Jewish Museum is open from October 1 to March 31: Sunday through Thursday, 10:00 a.m. to 5:00 p.m. (last admission at 4:15 p.m.), and Friday, 9:00 a.m. to 2:00 p.m. (last admission at 1:15 p.m.). Summer hours last from April 1 to September 30: Sunday through Thursday, 10:00 a.m. to 6:00 p.m. (last admission at 5:15 p.m.), and Friday, 10:00 a.m. to 4:00 p.m. (last admission at 3:15 p.m.). The museum is closed on Saturdays and Jewish holidays.

The museum is proud of its exhibits dealing with "Two Thousand Years of Jewish History," as well as pages from the Talmud that refer to Italian Jewry. Rare prayer books, reprints of statements of the popes, maps and drawings of the Ghetto of Rome, Torah pointers, rimmonim (Torah ornaments), Hanukkah menorahs, Torah crowns, and candelabra round-out the collection.

Inside the museum, one finds manuscripts and Jewish ceremonial objects. The collection includes Torah finials made by Roman goldsmiths in the eighteenth century, when Jews were not allowed to touch gold.

Official German records listing the names of some of the approximately 2,000 Jews who were deported from Rome during the Holocaust can be found here.

A significant event was the visit of Pope John Paul II to the synagogue in April 1986. It was the first recorded pontifical visit to a Jewish house of worship in Rome in 800 years. Moreover, in 1994, the Vatican highlighted the Roman Catholic Church's commitment to the fight against renewed anti-Semitism. Pope John Paul II joined with Holocaust survivors at a concert in the Vatican commemorating the Holocaust. The concert marked the first time in the 50 years since the end of World War II that the Vatican had officially commemorated the Holocaust. Among the guests was the late Chief Rabbi Elio Toaff.

Synagogue Sephardic, via Garfagnana 4, Rome.

Synagogue, Via Balbo 33, Rome. Tel: 39-6-6840-0651-2. There are two separate synagogues here. The Ashkenazic service is downstairs in this building, where there is a daily *minyan*. On the main floor, Italian rite services are conducted, but only on Shabbat. This synagogue is near the Piazza Popullo.

Chabad Center: contact for tourists, "Beth Chabad of Rome," Via Berengario 26, 01161 Rome. Tel: 39-06-9436-8049. chabad@lazar.it, chabadPBRome.com. Tourists should contact Chabad at the above address during office hours via phone or email to plan attendance at meals or services and receive instructions regarding locations of Chabad centers throughout Rome. Names and contact information of other Chabad centers in Rome and other Italian cities can be obtained at: http://www.chabad.org/centers/default_cdo/country/Italy/jewish/Centers.htm, email: chabad@lazar.it.

Beth Hillel Roma, via del Salumi 51, Rome. Tel: 39-3899-691-486. bethhillelroma@gmail.com, www.bethhillelroma.org.

ORGANIZATIONS

The Cultural Center, Via Arco de'Tolomei, Rome. This center for the Jewish community of Rome is open from 9:00 a.m. to 1:00 p.m., but not on Saturdays.

The office of the Grand Rabbi, Rome's chief rabbi, Riccardo Di Segni, is located here at the Synagogue at Via Catalana 1, Rome. Tel: 687-5051. ufficio.rabbinico@romaebraica.it

Nearby at Lungotevere Sanzio is the Italian Rabbinical College.

The Jewish Agency, Keren Hayesod, and the Zionist Federation, Corso Vittorio Emanuele 173. Rome. Tel: 65-15-14. This is a good place to discuss *aliyah*, for the Jewish Agency for Israel is the primary Jewish organization responsible for the immigration and absorption of Jews from the Diaspora to Israel.

In the last three years, Italy joined France and Belgium as nations observing an unprecedented increase in *aliyah*. "The prevalence of anti-Semitic incidents have increased dramatically in all three countries since the early 2000s, according to a study by the London-based *Institute for Jewish Policy Research.*

In an article in the *Times of Israel*, December 11, 2014, Fiamma Nirenstein noted that in the first ten months of 2014, for instance, 300 Italian Jews had immigrated to Israel. That is, she noted, "a considerable number if you think that it represents around one percent of the very small Jewish community living in Italy."

Daniel Funaro believes that *aliyah* is up because of a downturn in the Italian economy and that Israel offers more opportunity regarding jobs and business opportunities. Besides, Italians of all ages are wary of whether Italy will ever have a stable government or that the economy will improve quickly. They may be correct. Italy, moreover, is in constant recession. The European Commission forecasts Italian growth at 0.9 percent in 2017, the slowest in the Euro zone. Youth unemployment stands at 38 percent. Italy's chronically low growth, low inflation, and gigantic public debt burden (133 percent of GDP) are factors that could easily send its economy into a tail spin. And then there's always the possibility of a banking crisis. Still there are those that tout the prediction that Italy is the one country that could "bring down the EU."

The Union of Italian Jewish Communities (UCEI), Lungotevere Sanzio 9, Rome. 00153. Tel.: 39-6-4554-2200 Fax: 39-6-5899 569. Email: info@ucei.it http://ucei.it/ucei/contatti/. The Rabbinical College is also located here. The UCEI serves as the umbrella organization for Italian Jewry and as such it represents all 21 Italian Jewish communities. It also coordinates Jewish organizational activities and represents the Jewish community with the government on certain issues.

And one issue is obviously anti-Semitism.

Most officials with whom we discussed anti-Semitism in Italy believe that since the year 2000, hatred against Jews is on the rise, especially in Rome.

"Sixty-three percent of the country's Jews believe anti-Semitism to be either a 'very big' or a 'fairly big' problem, while 68 percent say their personal feeling is that anti-Semitism has increased over the past years (42 percent say that it has 'increased a bit' and 26 percent say it has 'increased a lot,')" according to the London-based Institute for Jewish Policy Research (JPR) study entitled *From Old and New Directions: Perceptions and Experiences of Anti-Semitism among Jews in Italy.* The poll was coauthored by Israeli demographer Prof. Sergio Della Pergola.

Officials at The Union of Italian Jewish Communities agree. And regarding anti-Semitism, Italy's Foreign Minister, Alfano, spoke of Rome's obligation to defend the Italian Jewish community against incidents of anti-Semitism. From what this writer can determine from interviews with the Jews of Italy, that nation will need the government's commitment to combat hate crimes.

OTHER SITES

The Arch of Titus. This arch was erected in 81 CE by Emperor Domitian (81-91) to celebrate Titus's victory in 70 CE in Palestine. A triumphal arch, it symbolically recalls the destruction of the Temple in Jerusalem and shows the Jewish spoils swallowed up by the victors.

For centuries, Jews did not walk under the arch. After all, it had been erected to praise Titus for destroying Jerusalem and the Temple. Titus, the son of Vespecian, deported thousands of Jews to Rome and its western provinces, including Sardinia. On one display on the arch, Jewish prisoners are portrayed carrying the booty of the seven-branched menorah, the candelabrum that was taken from the Temple in Jerusalem, as well as the Holy Ark and silver trumpets, the golden shewbread table—all part of the Temple rituals. According to H. V. Morton, "these are the only contemporary sculpted representatives of these objects in existence, and their ultimate fate is even now a mystery."

The prohibition of walking under the arch ended in World War II, when the Jewish Brigade from Palestine, a unit of the British Army, walked under the arch to signify the liberation of the Jewish people.

Another report says the ban was broken when the United Nations declared a Jewish state in 1947 and again when Israel was declared a state on May 14, 1948.

On another visit to Rome, I saw scrawled in chalk the words, "*Am Yisrael Chai*," "the Jewish people live."

Today Jews are alive throughout the world. There is silence in the Roman Forum!

Piazza Navona. After you visit the Roman Forum, the Seven Hills, the monuments, the amphitheaters, the Colosseum, the Campo di Fiori, the Spanish Steps, the Trevi Fountain, and the Pantheon, walk around the horseshoe-shaped Piazza Navona, where artists and craftsmen display their wares. But did you know that from the fifteenth to seventeenth centuries, it was a carnival sport and comic spectacle to beat and chase half-naked Jews around this square? Yes, the same Piazza Navona used for bullfights, tournaments, jugglers, tightrope walkers, and other entertainment was the scene of a degrading clownish show. Under Paul II in the fifteenth century, public sport was made of the Jews by forcing some to eat a heavy meal and then run in carnival races. As late as 1667, a guide to Rome noted that during the races "the asses ran first, then the Jews marched with only a band around the loins, then the buffaloes, then the Barbary horses." Clement IX modified the custom the following year: "The victims were allowed to pay a heavy fine to avoid racing," writes E. R. Chamberlain in Rome: The Great Cities.

But it was the papacy again, especially during the years of the Holocaust, that aroused a great deal of controversy. Pope Pius XII was silent during the years of mass murder. The **Vatican** argues that he said nothing in order to prevent even greater slaughter. Others claimed he did so to protect the Catholic Church in Germany. The pope did not want to encourage communism by attacking the Nazis, says this argument. Robert Katz maintains in Death in Rome that the pope "interpreted the fall of Fascism as a victory for Communism." In The Catholic Church and Nazi Germany, Guenther Lewry writes, "Finally, one is inclined to conclude that the Pope and his advisors— influenced by the long tradition of moderate anti-Semitism so widely accepted in Vatican circles—did not view the plight of the Jews with a real sense of urgency and moral outrage." According to Rolf Hochhuth in *The Deputy*, Pope Pius failed to protest the roundup of Roman Jews for deportation to Auschwitz.

"For years, Jewish and Catholic leaders alike have warned that the beatification of Pius XII could harm reconciliation efforts begun during Vatican II" and cemented by the Pope John Paul II, wrote Alissa Stanley in the *New York Times*, November 3, 1999.

Moreover, evidence has since come to light that the Vatican aided and abetted the escape of "scores if not hundreds of S.S. and other Nazi genocidists . . . and it did nothing to bar their flight from justice," according to Charles R. Alien, in the magazine *Reform Judaism* (1983).

Pope John Paul has on several occasions apologized for some Catholics' failure to protect Jews during the Holocaust and repeated that regret in a sweeping apology for the historic sins of his church. In Israel at Yad Vashem, in March 2000, the Pope expressed sadness at "hatred, acts of persecution and displays of anti-Semitism directed against the Jews by Christians at any time and in any place." While the Pope stopped short of an outright apology on behalf of the Roman Catholic Church for what some Jews consider the Vatican's silence, inaction and complicity in the Holocaust, he said in Yad Vashem: "In this place of solemn remembrance, I fervently pray that our sorrow for the tragedy which the Jewish people suffered in the 20th century will lead to a new relationship between Christians and Jews."

At that time, Israel Prime Minister Ehud Barak called the Pope's visit and declarations, a "noble act" of reaching out to the Jewish people: "You have done more than anyone else to bring about the historic change in the attitude of the churches toward the Jewish people, initiated by the good Pope John XXII, and to dress the gaping wounds that festered over many bitter centuries."

Rabbi James A. Rudin, the American Jewish Committee's former national inter-religious affairs director, has noted "the extraordinary positive advances in Catholic-Jewish relations," during the last decade of the 20th Century. In the last analysis, since he became Pope in 1978, John Paul was widely credited with advancing the Catholic Church towards reconciliation with the Jews.

San Pietro in Vitcoli (Church of St. Peter in Chains). Here is the famous Moses of Michelangelo, sculpted in the early sixteenth century. This Moses has horns because of an error in the translation of the Book of Exodus, where the Hebrew word *keren* was translated as horn, instead of ray of light.

The Vatican. In the Sistine Chapel of the Vatican are wall frescoes about the life of Moses in the Old Testament done by Pinturicchio, Botticelli, and Signorelli, as well as the work of Michelangelo, the creator of the magnificent ceiling with its nine biblical scenes.

Ostia Antica. This town is the beach community close to the Italian capital, one hour from Rome. A Jewish community once thrived here in this ancient port of Rome as evidenced in the ruins of an ancient synagogue discovered here in 1961 by workmen building the Fiumicino Airport.

Among the fragments of columns and pillars uncovered are the outlines of a prayer room, a study hall, an oven for unleavened bread, and a mikveh (ritual bath). The synagogue proper, a large hall divided into three aisles with marble columns, has also been exposed. One of these sections may have been for women. The wall at the back is slightly curved. In the oldest hall, the seats were of stone, set against the walls.

In another building, the tabernacle for the Holy Ark rises behind the pulpit on the left side along its entire length, a few steps leading to it. Carved into the tabernacle are Jewish symbols that can also be found in other synagogues of that period: a seven-branched menorah, a shofar, a lulav, and an etrog. The floor is covered with mosaic. In recent years, many Russian Jews found a temporary home in the town of Ostia, thus bringing Jews back to an ancient site. As Barbara G. Harrison wrote, "In Italy, history is never stale."

Tour Guide

Micaela Pavoncello, Jewish Roma Walking Tours. Available are tours to the Ghetto of Rome and the Jewish Museum. info@JewishRoma.com. Mobile +39 328 8638128.

Milan

What a city! If ever there was a diverse city, indeed Milan is it. There are 37 ethnic origins alone just among the 6,000 to 7,000 Milanese Jews. Milan contains synagogues, kosher butcher shops, a day school, and several Talmud Torahs (Jewish schools). The Jewish community here boasts diverse Jewish elements, including many Ashkenazim, who in the last century found their way to Milan as they moved down from northern Europe. They first concentrated in the wholesale and export business. Whereas the slower-paced southern Italian looks out to the calm Mediterranean, Jews in Milan scan both north and south in this commercial atmosphere.

One often hears men and women speaking Arabic, especially in the Galleria Vittorio Emanuele II, the galleria that inspired numerous North American imitations. The Arab-speakers may be Jews, for there one can often meet Jewish persons who emigrated from Libya and still speak Arabic. In 1948 and again in 1967, several thousand Libyan Jews came to Italy, although the majority went to Israel. They picked this land because they spoke Italian, for until the middle of World War II, Italy controlled Libya. Like Roman Jews, the Libyan Jews in Milan are by and large shopkeepers and traders. Their connections and linguistic knowledge help them develop trade between Italy and the Arab lands. Incidentally, the Galleria located near the Cathedral and La Scala Opera House is one of the world's first shopping centers, replete with outdoor cafés and famous shops. Located here is the notable establishment Biffi.

Part of the reason Jews settle in Milan is the cultural life of this metropolis. Many Milanese say their city begins in the Piazza della Scala, the location of La Scala Opera House. Since its inauguration more than two centuries ago, the legendary opera house, the home of Verdi and Puccini, has remained the pride of this Lombard capital.

Milan, the gateway to Italy, calls itself the money-maker of this republic, the industrial, commercial, and artisan capital of this nation. It is the most "city-like city in Italy," wrote the Sicilian author Giovanni Vergo a century ago.

Once called "muscular Milan," the city has been described as a city of go-getters and materialistic business persons. About 2 million people live in this bustling urban area located 300 miles northwest of Rome.

The Milanese claim their fashion industry ranks with Paris as a trendsetter. Visit Via Monte Napoleone, the main shopping street, and see for yourself.

Because Milan is so close to the borders of Austria, Switzerland, and France, and because its two airports reach out to the rest of Europe, it always has focused its sights on its European neighbors. Many Jewish business persons fly in for the annual trade fair, one of the most important in the world.

"What do you do in Milan?" I asked a stranger. "You eat!" he exclaimed. Eating is synonymous with Milan, which is famous for its delicious cuisine.

And if you can spot Jewish salesmen in the Vatican, what would you expect to see in various Milanese neighborhoods, such as in the Via Spadari where one finds mouth-watering delicacies? Once a kosher butcher shop was located right next door to the Ambrosiana Museum, which is situated at Piazza Pio XI Square. Ironically, the museum contains Judaica and Hebrew books and manuscripts.

In Italy, the northern and the southern parts of the country vie for attention. This is often mirrored in the Jewish community, too. "Milan makes the money, Rome spends it," said one Jewish citizen of Milan.

Jews—professionals and business people—live and work in this trading center that boasts international fairs, a silk market, nearly 1,000 banks, more than 30,000 firms, and more than 26,000 manufacturers. Italian Jewry lives on because what it loses through assimilation and mixed marriages, it picks up in the immigration of new groups. In the 1980s, for instance, Russian Jews settled in Milan in addition to about 1,000 Iranian Jews. The latter maintain their own synagogue and club for young people. They are excellent business persons and are skilled in the diamond and carpet trades.

As a result of the immigration following the 1956 and 1967 Arab-Israel wars, many Egyptian Jews have settled here, too. The visitor observes streets such as Piazza Tel Aviv and Via Sally Mayer, the latter named for a noted industrialist and philanthropist.

Kosher Restaurants in Milan

Senior Citizens Home, Via Leone XIII No. 1, Milan. This senior citizen home has a kosher facility.

Pizza Carmel, San Giminyano, 10, Milan, Tel: 02-416-368.

Cedika, Via Della Braida, Milan. Tel: 02-551-88248. This is a kosher products store.

Synagogues and Day Schools in Milan

AERP Associazione per l'Ebraismo Progressivo-Lev Chadash, Plazza Napoli 35, 20146 Milan. Tel: 39-2-348-410-2080. info@levchadash.it. www.levchadash.it.

Beth Shalom Congregazione Ebraica Reforma, Via Gaio 8, 20129 Milan. Tel: 39-2-3652-1621. FAX: 39-2-3652-1621. FAX: 39-2-3652-4002. bethshalom.milano@gmail.com, www.betshalom.it

The Central Synagogue, Via Guastalla 19, Milan Tel: 39-2-791-892. A Sephardic (Persian) synagogue and a mikveh are located here. An Italian rite service is held usually on Monday and Thursdays as well as Saturday mornings. Sephardic service is held every day, but do call ahead to check time of prayers. This house of worship was erected after World War II. The original was destroyed in an Allied bombing raid in 1943. The Holy Ark in the chapel originated in the ancient synagogue of Persia.

Lebanese Synagogue, Via Dei Gracchi, Milan.

Synagogue at Via Sally Mayer 4/6, Milan.

Ohel Yaakov Synagogue, Via Benvenuto Cellini 2, Milan. Tel: 39-02-545-5076. This synagogue follows the Ashkenazi rite.

Persian Synagogue, Via Montecuccoli, Milan. Tel: 39-02-545-5076.
Synagogue, Via Eupili 8, Milan. Services are held on Sabbath and festivals.
Beth Chabad of Milan, via F Bronzetti 18, Milan. Tel: 39-2-7010-0080. Fax: 39-2-2952-0167.
Beit Hatamud-Heichal Menachem. Via Arzaga 4, Milan. 39-2-4837-5026. FAX: 39-2-2952-0157.
Beit Menachem, via Cola Di Rienzo 38, Milan Tel: 39-2-4895-1815. FAX: 39-2-236-2711.
Josef Tehillot, via Gracchi 25, 20146 Milan. Tel: 39-2-348-410-2080. FAX: 39-2-4398-1088.
Markos L'Inyone Chinuch, via C.Poerio 35, Milan. Tel:39-2-2952-0157.
Tzeirei Agudas Chabad. Via Regina Giovanna 11, Milan. Tel: 39-2-2941-4170. FAX: 39-2-2941-4173.
Re Salomone, via Sardegna 45, 20146, Milan. Tel: 39-02-469-4643.
Denzel, via Washington 9, Milan. Tel: 39-02-48-5193.

Organizations

Jewish Community Center, Via Sally Mayer 4/6, Milan. Many Jewish organizations and groups are situated here, including the Jewish National Fund and Sally Mayer Hebrew School.

At the Documentation Center, I saw young Jews studying the Holocaust period, as well as the history of pre-twentieth century Italian Jewish life.

Venice

The tourist guide usually begins his or her talk to the largely American-Jewish audience thus:

"The Jews arrived in Venice in the tenth century. They came from the Levant, Corfu, Greece, and Turkey. In the sixteenth century, the Venetians gave the Jews an area to live and work. They gave that designated plot the Venetian name, the word 'ghetto.' The Jews had to wear a colorful cap so that they could be recognized as Jews. The five synagogues that exist in the ghetto today are the German, the Canton, the Italian, the Levantine, and the Spanish synagogues . . . "

There is so much history in that introductory talk.

Visitors immediately realize that something memorable occurred in this city that was once called "*la Serenissima,*" "the most serene one." For today, millions of people every year pour into this "dream city of lagoons," probably the most beautiful city in the world.

This magical city is often called the loveliest city on the planet. It floods regularly, its painting rots, its canals are green, but its citizens love it and enjoy the outdoor pleasures it offers.

At one moment in the world's history, fifteenth-century Venice was rich and influential, the leader of the West. But just at the time when Venice was booming, a "new India" was discovered to challenge the Venetians. We call that land "America." Trade patterns changed and the city's power faded.

Once considered the most important Jewish community of northern Italy, Venice involved Jews in "banking, pawnbroking and second-hand dealing."

The Republic tolerated Jews because Jews were useful. They helped "ring the Venetian cash register." Writer Jan Morris believes that Venice could not have gone on to great heights without Jews. They served as bankers, pawnbrokers, suppliers, outfitters to diplomatic missions, agents, and scholars.

The Jews were usually safe under Venetian rule. But no Jew, not even a local resident, could stay in Venice without a permit, which cost a large sum of money. And it had to be renewed every five years. Jews were often segregated; in the thirteenth century, they were forced to dwell on the island of *Spinalunga*. We know it as the *"Guidecca."*

Before 1336, Jews could reside and work only in Mestre, a town just outside of Venice. Only that year did they receive permission to live in the "Lagoon City."

As a *kabbalistic* mystic center, learning and Hebrew printing thrived here.

Venice, The Dream City. (Photo by Larry Colby photography)

Among the most distinguished of the new arrivals from Iberia after the expulsions zand inquisitions was Don Isaac Abravanel. He belonged to Spanish diplomatic corps before he settled in Venice. We shall meet him later in the chapters on Spain and Portugal.

THE VENICE GHETTO

This is the city that gave the world the "ghetto." The Italians invented and set up the ghetto. A tourist spot today, it once contained several thousand Jews who were literally locked up at night.

The word ghetto comes from the Italian word gettare—to cast in metal. When the ghetto was established, it consisted of iron foundries, or geto novo, which means new foundry in the Venetian dialect. Interestingly, some think the word ghetto comes from the Hebrew word get for divorce. These prison neighborhoods served as a way to separate Jews from Christians. Generally, it is not easy to find Jewish sites in a European city, but not so in Venice. Everyone knows the location of the ghetto. Just ask! Say the word "ghetto." As we have seen, it is after all a Venetian word.

Located near the Venice railroad station, the ghetto can be reached by taking the vaporetti (motor bus-boats) via the Grand Canal. Get off at San Marcuolo landing. Walk away from the canal. Then walk toward Rio Terra San Leonardo. Follow the yellow signs. These signs

Inside The Venice Ghetto. (Photo by Larry Colby)

are in Italian and Hebrew, and say synagogue. They will direct you to the ghetto, a lively area composed of Renaissance buildings, medieval houses and columns, and even some wonderful glassmaking shops. Another way to reach the ghetto is via Lake No. 1 Vaporetto, which passes under the Rialto Bridge. Walk a short distance to Calle Rabbia (Rabbi Street), turn right, and there you are.

While Rome's ghetto was crowded and unhealthy, Venice's remained larger. The ghetto district was located on an island cut off from Cannaregio by wide canals. It was also separated from its surroundings by a wall, gates, and drawbridges. Later in 1541, the "geto vecchio" ("the old foundry") was added to house more Jews. By 1663, the ghetto was so crowded that it was allowed to occupy the neighboring "Ghetto Nuovissimo," the site of the last remaining foundry in the district. In the fifteenth and sixteenth centuries, 5,000 people resided there. As street peddlers, rag pickers, dealers in secondhand merchandise, and pawnbrokers, they transformed the ghetto into a thriving beehive.

As a home for refugees, a medieval ghetto provided a certain amount of security. One felt safe from attack; sometimes its walls kept out the mob. On the other hand, when bigots wanted Jews killed, they knew where to find them. Established on April 10, 1516, the second day of Passover, the Venice Ghetto, as an institution, quickly spread throughout various cities of Italy. Unfortunately, it became accepted practice.

As you stand in the large square of the ghetto, remember that this was the meeting place of the community, and also the site of the well where water was obtained and gossip exchanged. A number of outstanding persons were born or lived in the Venetian ghetto. David Reuveni was one. He appeared in Italy in 1524. He asserted that his brother Joseph ruled over the tribes of Gad and Reuben and half the tribe of Manasseh. He claimed to have traveled in disguise as a Moslem through Ethiopia, Egypt, and the Land of Israel. Reuveni said he came to Europe to obtain the military assistance of the Christian powers for the liberation of the Holy Land from the Turks. His "project" failed and he died in a Spanish prison.

When crowding became a problem, Jews always built upwards. Tall houses resembling skyscrapers were erected. Within the ghetto, there were several autonomous congregations. People worshipped in their own synagogues, according to their own rites, and as we shall see there were at least five different synagogues. The synagogue was the center of Jewish communal life in the ghetto.

When Napoleon's armies broke down the gates of the Venetian ghetto in 1797, it contained little more than a few old huts. The walls were torn down on July 10, 1797, the eve of the fast of the 17th of Tammuz. Emancipation came in 1866.

Although the Jews of Italy were guaranteed full civil equality by King Victor Emmanuel II in 1866, a large group of Jews voluntarily lived in the Venice ghetto until the days of Mussolini. During World War II, more than 200 Jews, one-fourth of all Venetian Jews, were deported to concentration camps in Germany. They never returned. Today, a **monument** to the Holocaust, consisting of seven bronze tablets, stands on the western side of the Ghetto Nuovo, with the following message:

Men, women, children,
Masses for the gas chambers,
Advancing toward horror,
Beneath the whip of the executioners.
Your sad Holocaust is
Engraved in history.
And nothing shall purge
Your death from our memories
For our memories are your only grave.
The City of Venice remembers the Venetian Jews
who were deported to the Nazi concentration camps
on December 6, 1943 and August 7, 1944.

Jews still live in the ghetto. But today, most of the approximate 500 Jews of Venice reside outside that neighborhood. The ghetto, however, is both comforting and intriguing to stop and live the history within, while one is touring Venice. One can people-watch and absorb history while sitting in a sunny square. Here the traveler "can feel the warmth of old Venice." Just 10 minutes from the train and bus station, 15 minutes from the iconic Rialto Bridge, and 25 minutes from Saint Marks Square is this fascinating location. And, all the water buses stop in the ghetto.

The ghetto, moreover, is an excellent location to discover original art and Judaica galleries.

Situated in the ghetto is a kosher hotel, "Kosher House Giardino dei Melograni," under the supervision of the Chief Rabbi of Venice, Rabbi Scialom Bahbout. The hotel overlooks Ghetto Square and the canal and is centrally located in front of the Jewish Museum. The building was renovated in 2015. A kosher, dairy buffet breakfast is served in the hotel. Tel: 39-41-822-6131. info@pardesrimonim.net, www.pardesrimonim.net.

A recently opened kosher restaurant, **Ghimel Garden,** is located in the Ghetto. Campo del Ghetto Nuovo, 2873 Tel: 39- 346-473-5061. ghimelgarden@gmail.com, www.ghimelgarden.com. www.facebook.

com/ghimelgarden. On Friday, Saturday, and Sunday a buffet lunch is offered. The restaurant is under the supervision of Rabbi Bahbout. *(halav Israel, kosher lemehadrin, typical fish dishes)*. "**HAY**," cafeteria in the Jewish Museum in the Ghetto is also under the supervision of Rabbi Bahbout. Tel: 39-340-10-46858. calvanicomontell@libero.it.

Kosher Bakery and Grocery "Volpe" Ghetto Vecchio Calle Ghetto Vecchio, 1143, 30121 Cannareggio, Venezia VE Tel. 39-41-715-178 *(halav Israel and Akum, Israel and France salami, parve cookie, all pat Israel)*.

The Jewish Community Center (Comunita Ebraica) Via Cannaregio 1188-A, Ghetto Vecchio. Tel: 39-41-71-50-12. segreteria@jvenice.org. www.jvenice.org. Tourist information: 39-4-171-5012.

Rabbi Scialom Bahbout serves as chief rabbi. Tel: 39-41-71-5012. chiefrabbi@jvenice.org.

Mikveh: By appointment. 39-41-71-5012.

Beth Chabad, 2915 Cannaregio, 30121 Venice. info@jewishvenice. org, www.jewishvenice.org. Rabbi Ramy Banin is the rabbi at Chabad of Venice. Chabad holds daily prayer services, Shabbat and holiday meals, and Torah classes.

GAM GAM Kosher Restaurant Chabad. 1122 Ghetto Vecchio, Venice. Tel: 39-366-250-4505. For information, as to hours, www. gamgamkosher.com. Shabbat meals available. Details at www. jewishvenice.org.

Five Synagogues in the Venice Ghetto

Five synagogues rise within the ancient boundaries of the Venice ghetto. The five are the German, Italian, and Canton, situated in the Campo Ghetto Nuovo; the Levantine and Spanish, located in the Campello delle Scole.

They were erected by various Jewish groups that emigrated to Venice from other nations or other parts of Italy. (Sometimes, not all the synagogues are open to the public because of repairs). Space in the ghetto was limited, so many of the prayer halls are located within a single room. In the synagogues, crystal chandeliers are in sharp contrast with the wooden benches of the worshippers. The *aron hakodesh* (Holy Ark) is usually at one end, the *bimah* at another.

The Jewish Museum of Venice, (Museo Ebraico di Venezia), Cannaregio 2902b, Venice. Tel: 04-1715359. museuebraico@ coopculture.it, www.museoebraico.com, is located on the first floor of the German synagogue building, Scola Tedesca Grande, built in

1528 in the Campo Ghetto Nuovo. The museum features a collection of Jewish ritual silver articles and pieces of woven and embroidered materials as well as a hummash—a Pentateuch—used by Maimonides.

The Jewish Museum of Venice arranges guided tours to the German, French, Levantine, and Spanish synagogues. Tours leave every hour on the half-hour, starting, 10:30 a.m. to 5:30 p.m., the latter, the last tour. Contact:prennotazioni.mev@coopculture.it

German Synagogue. The German synagogue, located in the Campo Ghetto Nuovo, is the popular one. This Ashkenazic house of worship is known as the Scola Tedesca Grande and is the oldest. Highlighting this temple are five interesting windows, three of which are walled up. The arches are in white stone. There is a beautiful gilded Holy Ark and a *bimah*. The women's gallery is an oval balcony. The synagogue was restored between 1890 and 1910.

The Italian Synagogue. The Italian Synagogue, Scola Italiana, was built in 1575. It is located in the Ghetto Nuovo. Crystal chandeliers are common here, and there are simple wooden benches. At one end stands the *aron ha-kodesh* (Holy Ark) dating from the early 1800s, a gift of Beniamino di Consiglio. This building is not in use, but is now being restored by the Italian Committee for Venice and the Committee for Jewish History of Venice.

The Canton Synagogue. Constructed in 1531, this synagogue is named after a German Ashkenazi banking family and is built into the corner of the piazza. Hebrew writing (names of donors) on the steps leading to the Holy Ark is an interesting sight. The seat behind the pulpit is the gift of Benjamin Marina di Consiglio, while a stone in the corner on the left was placed there in commemoration of an offer of 180 ducats made by a Shelomo for the building of the Synagogue in 1532.

Leaving the synagogue, one can read an admonition: "And now you are leaving, go in peace and do no evil." On the wall outside, to the left, there is a small marble tablet saying: "Many sorrows shall be to the wicked: but he that trusteth in the Lord, mercy shall compass him about" (Psalms 32:10).

The Levantine Synagogue. Located in the Campello delle Scole, this synagogue is used in the winter because it is heated. Founded in 1538, it is situated across the square from the Spanish synagogue. A plaque commemorates the visit of Sir Moses Montefiore, British Jewish philanthropist and leader, in 1875. Above the entrance to this synagogue is written: "Happy are they that dwell in thy House. They will ever praise thee" (Ps. 84:5).

Long benches fill the sanctuary. The men's pews have wooden stage cases inscribed with the names of members. Woodcarvings decorate the ceiling, walls are covered alternately with wooded frames and damask panels, and four Corinthian columns surround the Holy Ark. The doors are inscribed with the Ten Commandments; the *bimah* features numerous carvings and wood sculptures. Surrounded by two wide curving stairways, the pulpit is framed by two decorated twisted columns resembling marble. This imitates Solomon's Temple. The women's gallery is above the long entrance side.

Spanish Synagogue. The Spanish synagogue (built in 1555 and restored in 1840), located in the Campello delle Scole, is called the Scola Spagnola. This Spanish-Portuguese synagogue was designed in classical baroque. Summer services are held here. The main sanctuary is an elongated space. The Holy Ark is in a classical-baroque style and is situated along the eastern wall; the *bimah* stands along the western wall. The *bimah* is composed of four Corinthian columns, two of them actually half-columns set against the west wall. The seating runs parallel along the north and the south walls. An oval gallery for women is an outstanding feature of the structure. The women used to sit upstairs, but now they are on the main level.

The building contains memorial plaques for Jews deported from Venice in World War II.

Florence

Hearts often beat faster when the word *Firenze* is pronounced. Here the past and the present meet.

"Hidden in the city that all the world knows and loves is another Florence: a Jewish Florence," notes tour guide Giovanna Bossi Rosenfeld.

Florence was one of the most important communities in Italian Jewish history before the Second World War and to this day, it is not difficult to find the Jewish community of Florence. Head for Via Luigi Carlo Farini 4, not far from San Marco Square, near St. Ambrose Church and off of Via dei Pilastri. Located in a large single compound, the Florence synagogue is one of the most beautiful in Europe. On the grounds of this large house of worship stand a Jewish day school, the offices of the Jewish community, as well as the headquarters of the B'nai B'rith and other organizations.

Italy often is pictured as a museum. Indeed, Florence contains more fine art per square mile than any other city in all of Italy. Laden with antiquity, Florence is inexhaustible.

Thousands of tourists visit Michelangelo's David in the Academy of Arts Museum in Florence in the province of Tuscany. The city stands as the great collector of Brunelleschi, Donatello, and Michelangelo. In one year alone, 1505, Michelangelo, Leonardo da Vinci, Machiavelli, and Raphael were working at the same time and within a few blocks of each other. The city contains more fine art per square mile than any other in Italy; be sure to visit the Uffizi Gallery, the Pitti Palace, the Accademia della Belle Arti, the Bargello, the Duomo, the Baptistery, and the Medici Chapels. Florence is also advertised as a shopping center where Ferragamo and Gucci have their headquarters.

If at one time on your trip you sit in Florence's town center in Florence in an outdoor cafe, you just might be at leisure in what once was the area of the ghetto.

We know that during the Renaissance, the Jews of Florence did not live in a ghetto. That enclosure would come later. The Jewish community of Florence was established in 1437, when some Jewish financiers were invited to open loan banks. During the time of Lorenzo de Medici (1449-92), Jewish intellectual life corresponded to the rich achievements of Florentine culture. The Medici in Florence were well disposed toward the Jews.

The heyday of the Florentine Jewish community was between the years 1437 and 1494, the most resplendent period in the history of Florence "or perhaps in any city in the world since recorded history began." Jewish literature, Jewish poetry, and Jewish learning flourished in fifteenth- and sixteenth-century Florence, even though the community did not number more than 100 families.

On October 3, 1570, Grand Duke Cosimo I, a Medici duke called "the Great," banished the Jews to a ghetto because they allegedly broke the law. He feared the Jews would fraternize with Christians, so he forced them to wear a yellow badge. The ghetto restricted Jewish culture in the city known as the "Athens of Italy" and the cradle of the Italian Renaissance.

In 1799, Napoleon and his army freed the Jews. But a year after the French emperor withdrew, a period of repression set in. In 1859, when Tuscany became part of the Kingdom of Italy, the Jews were recognized as citizens of the new kingdom. Free at last!

There are about 900 Jews in Florence and the surrounding towns. About half that number live in the city itself. And they are active in such organizations as B'nai B'rith, Anti-Defamation League, WIZO, Maccabi and the Italian-Friendship Society. The community still maintains a kindergarten, a Talmud Torah through Bar Mitzvah age, which is located next to the synagogue

The **Jewish Community. (Comunita Ebraica di Firenze),** via Farini 4, 50121 Florence. Tel: 39-055-245-252. www.firenzebraica.it. The offices of the community are located in a building situated inside the city's magnificent synagogue compound, a highlight of which is a beautiful garden. Office hours: Sunday through Friday, 9:30 a.m. to 12:30 p.m. The tourist entrance for the opening hours of the museum and public events such as Balagan Café are at via Farini, 6.

Most of the members of the Jewish community are of Italian or western Sephardic heritage. Others are from the US, Eastern Europe, and North Africa. The services follow the Spanish and Portuguese rituals and are held on the premises of this outstanding Moorish-style synagogue built in 1882. The community sponsors kosher facilities, a mikveh, nursing home, Jewish cemetery, as well as cultural events. This is an active Jewish community, "surprisingly so," considering the small number of Jewish residents. "Bustling with activity," said a Jewish leader.

Like other Italian Jewish communities, Florence has had its share of anti-Semitic episodes. However, it is different than Rome in this respect: there is a strong "collaboration" with the local Muslim community, both at the official level and with community members. Common events are held and an association called "Women for Peace" unites Israeli residents and Jewish and Muslim women. The Balagan Café mentioned below also reduces tension.

JEWISH SITES IN FLORENCE

Beth Haknesset Firenze (The Synagogue of Florence), Via Farini 4. Tel: 39-055-245-252. info@fienzebraica.it. One of the most beautiful synagogues in Europe, this structure is more than 100 years old. Whether seen from an airplane, from another tall structure in Florence, or from the popular tourist vista of Michelangelo Square, this landmark of Judaism in Italy stands out under the city's azure sky. Possessing a distinctive Moorish architectural style of three separate seaweed-green copper (originally gilded) cupola domes and huge arched windows, this house of worship remains a tribute to Italian Jewry. What makes the synagogue so attractive are the elements that make the sculpture and art of Florence so meaningful, that artistic magnet that has drawn thousands of visitors to it each year.

The synagogue in Florence has a Moorish flavor and is the third largest dome in the city. It is said that it was the first edifice in the city to be built with reinforced concrete. This enormous building is impressive, indeed. The large cupola dome stands out along the city skyline. This monument is visible from every panoramic-view location.

Designated a historical museum, the synagogue attracts Jews and non-Jews. Florence remains one of the few cities in Europe where guides point out the local synagogue. It is not that in other cities tour leaders fail to mention Jewish houses of worship because of prejudice; it is because synagogues in Europe are generally not conspicuous.

Inside the Synagogue of Florence. (Photo by Ed Robin)

But the synagogue in Florence is considered a beautiful temple and a tourist site.

Unlike other synagogues, this one possesses its own compound and is not located on a congested street; nor is it hidden behind high walls. Standing tall and proud, surrounded by a garden of flowers and palm trees, it can be seen from distant hills. The synagogue, built in 1882, symbolizes the emancipation of the Jews of Italy and freedom from the ghetto. The Jewish community also wanted to contribute to the architecture of Florence. They wanted a building that would show their pride.

What style should they choose for the religious building? In the early nineteenth century, many of the synagogues built in Europe were in the Gothic style. Florentine Jewry felt that Gothic was too much associated with Christianity. Instead, the Jewish community adopted the Moorish style, with a central cupola. Eastern influence is also shown by its polychromatic decoration. They wanted to portray an association with the Golden Age of Spain, although Carol Herselle Krinsky, in *Synagogues of Europe*, says many of its features are found in Ashkenazic synagogues.

The construction is pure Moorish style, completely covered with frescoes on the inside and rich Venetian mosaics in the Ehal (area of the Holy Ark) and on the vaulted ceilings. The doors on the Holy Ark are gilded. The bulk of the funds for the temple came from a David Levi, president of the Council of the Jewish University between 1860 and 1870. In his will, dated March 15, 1868, he requested that his assets be utilized for the building of a monumental temple worthy of Florence. At Levi's death on February 16, 1870, it was disclosed that he had left 1,492,255 lire. In 1874, the first stones came from Jerusalem and were laid on October 24, 1882, the date the building opened.

This Sephardic synagogue contains 1,000 pews in a beautiful chandeliered hall. As in many Orthodox synagogues, the women sit upstairs in a balcony. On Saturdays, because of a scarcity of worshippers, prayers are conducted in a special section on the right-hand side of the sanctuary. On holidays, however, it is packed.

The temple has survived wars, barbarism, floods, destruction, and plagues. During World War II the synagogue was dynamited by the Germans; sections were severely damaged. One can still see the bayonet marks inflicted by the "Nazi Fascists," as the guides refer to them, on the doors of the Holy Ark. The Germans used the temple as a garage where they repaired trucks.

On November 6, 1943, the first group of Jews was deported from the synagogue to the extermination camps. It was from the temple, too, that the Nazis arrested the beloved Rabbi Natan Cassuto and others.

The pulpit in the Synagogue in Florence. (Photo by Ed Robin)

The rabbi was the son of Umberto Cassuto, who had abandoned his own career as a physician and had assumed the post of rabbi of the community. Ironically, together with a group of Italian Catholic priests, the rabbi forged documents that permitted Jews to escape to Switzerland or sail to Allied lines. His secret cell was caught in 1943, and its members, rabbis and priests, were sent to Auschwitz. On June 6, 1944, 16 old Jews were taken from the Home for the Aged and sent to Germany. The synagogue was occupied, bombed, and heavily damaged. After the war, Jews held services in a theater until the sanctuary was repaired.

A total of 243 Jews were deported from Florence, of whom only 13 returned. Eight more Jews were shot and 4 out of 22 who had taken part in the underground struggle fell.

During World War II, the prayer books and scrolls were hidden in Catholic churches and even in banks.

But it was Alfiero Borghini, the *shamash* (beadle) who had been a member of the Italian partisans, who told me that they had also been hidden in a garden in a small town nearby. The *shamash* later joined the Jewish Brigade, the unit from Palestine that fought its way through Italy in World War II. The destructive flood of November 4, 1966, was another recent traumatic experience for the synagogue and Florentine Jews. The muddy waters of the Arno River inundated the beautiful structure, causing great damage to the sacred objects and the library. More than 90 *Sifrei Torahs* (Torah scrolls) were lost. Fifteen thousand Jewish books were destroyed.

The building raises funds from the donations of people who take the synagogue tour. In the synagogue, the eternal theme of Judaism greets each visitor: "Bless he that cometh, bless he that goeth." A Jewish school is also located here. The two-story building was named after the chief rabbi of Florence, Natan Cassuto, who was murdered by the Nazis. About 35 children attend this school.

The synagogue does not hold a daily *minyan*, but it does have services Friday evenings and Saturday mornings.

Another attraction of Florence's synagogue is its **Jewish Museum**, located inside the synagogue, a sight certainly worth seeing. The phone number for the museum and tourist access to the synagogue is 39-055-234-6654 or 39-055-246-6089. sinagoga.firenze@coopculture. it, www.jewishtuscany.it. Hours: from June to September; Sunday through Thursday, 10:00 a.m. to 5:00 p.m. and on Fridays, 10:00 a.m. to 5:30 p.m. October to May: Sunday through Thursday, 10:00 a.m. to 3:00 p.m., closed Friday. The museum is closed on the Sabbath and Jewish holidays. The museum, situated on the second floor of the synagogue, opened in 1987. Religious articles, such as *rimmonim* and

Beth Haknesset Firenze, the Synagogue of Florence.

kiddush cups; prayer shawls; and a pictorial display are all here to be absorbed. There are other ritual objects, including silver ornaments and embroidered vestments. There is also a small room dedicated to the Shoah.

The museum was founded by the Friends of the Jewish Museum of Florence, a nonprofit association whose aim is to contribute to the maintenance of the exhibition and to the enrichment of the historic and artistic collection.

Balagan Café. www.balaganafe and/or www.firenzebraica.it. Located on the striking green grounds of the beautiful synagogues of Florence and opened on select Thursday nights, Balagan Café is not your usual café. It is more, shall we say, a night of music, lectures, discussions, performances including klezmer bands, rock stars, and kosher meals and kosher wine. And since 2012, this significant event attracts crowds of Jewish and non-Jewish Florentines. On the average 500 to 600 persons attend and that number can spike up to 1,500 on a special night. "These events have had a large impact on the city's awareness of its Jewish community and have contributed to create an atmosphere much less tense than in other cities in Italy," noted Enrico Fink, founder and artistic director of the Balagan Café. The café program is held mid-June to mid-September. The exact program is posted mid-spring on www.balagancafe and/or wwwlfirenzebraica. it. A Balagan Café night opens at 7:00 p.m., with a light kosher dinner usually dedicated to the main theme of the night, then a talk at 8:00 p.m., and a concert at 9:00 p.m. The café usually closes at 11:00 p.m.

By the way, "balagan" in Hebrew means "chaotic, messy." But no chaos here, just a wonderful cultural mix. Don't miss it!

Ruth's Kosher Restaurant, via Luigi Carlo Farini 2a, 50121, Florence. Tel/FAX: 39- 055-248-0888. info@kosheruth.com, www. kosheruth.com. Kashrut under the supervision of the Chief Rabbi of the Jewish Community of Florence. This restaurant, next to the Florence Synagogue and museum, is definitely open for lunch; check on dinner hours with the establishment. It is open on Shabbat and holidays, but prior reservation should be made with the owners.

Chabad Center, via Della Mattonaia 46, 50121, Florence, Italy and Borgo Pinti BR, 50121, Florence. Tel: 39-388-999-0549. jewishtuscany@ gmail.com, www.jewishtuscany.com

While there is no daily *minyan* at Chabad in the winter, the rabbi, Rabbi Levi Wolvovski said that the group will attempt to put together a *minyan* for a Jewish person who needs to say *kaddish*. Chabad holds Torah classes, holiday celebrations, and in the summer, a weekday summer *minyan*. Many tourists who visit the synagogue also stop at Chabad, which offers kosher food for travelers.

Shir Hadash, via Dante Alighieri 6, Florence, 50122. Tel: 39-380-426-9979. Shirhadash.fl@gmail.com. www.shirhadashfirenze.com.

Tour Guides

Tour guide Giovanna Bossi Rosenfeld, info@Jewish-Florence.com, www. Jewish-Florence.com, is a native historian of Florentine architecture and a licensed tour guide. She specializes in tours of Florence from a Jewish perspective. She makes Jewish history come alive through her knowledge, stories, and by taking you to the places where Jewish history was made. "An insider's view of a Jewish Florence not found in guidebooks," she says of her tours.

Another fine tour guide is Francesca Rachel Valle. Tel: 380-7385-327. francesca.valle@yahoo.it, www.francescarachelvalle.com. https://www.facebook.com/pages/Jewish-Rachel-Tour/417428735089725?pnref=lhc. Francesca Rachel Valle conducts Jewish tours, including Florence Synagogue and Jewish Museum. She also features a "Secret Jewish Florence Walking Tour by Night." This guide organizes tours for families and individuals as well as small groups inside Florence museums. Her tours follow "special requirements and needs of her guests." "With prior request I can customize any tour to fit visitors' needs and interests," she said.

And now we turn our attention to the south of Italy where there is a very small Jewish community. Why so small? Rabbi Ariel Finzi of Milan and Naples told me it all stems from back to the Inquisition and later to World War II. In the south of Italy, he added, there are small communities of Marrano families who are of Marrano or later origin who have decided to return to Judaism. Many of these groups are in Trani, Sannicandro di Bari, Catania, Siracusa or Palermo.

Naples

"See Naples and die," is an Italian proverb. Well you certainly won't die from taking in the beauty of this metropolis which has so much history and monuments to celebrate those historic events: its cemeteries, its Roman ruins, its medieval castles, its Renaissance churches.

Naples has a history problem: there's just too much of it.

Naples is home to famous tenor, the late Luciano Pavarotti, who often sang in the magnificent opera house Teatro San Carlo, and who frequently rode on a Vespa motor bike while singing the folk songs of this busy harbor and the arias made famous by him and native son, Enrico Caruso. This is also the home of the famous actress Sophia Loren.

Naples of course has had a bum rap. Like all port cities, it has its dangers. While walking the streets one doesn't carry large sums of cash; one leaves valuables in the hotel. While it remains one of the most chaotic cities in the world regarding traffic, it does have a street life of its own, as part of one of the most beautiful blue bays in the world alongside the superb vacation lands of the Sorrento Peninsula.

Always in the background is the lofty Vesuvius, often considered to be the "emblem" of Naples. Every tourist realizes this, of course, when he or she visits Pompeii, which was destroyed on August 24, 79 CE. Its latest eruption was in 1944.

Naples is famous for its art galleries, its catacombs and of course, the National Archaeological Museum considered to possess one of the richest collections of Greco-Roman antiques in the world.

Metropolitan Naples, which has a population of about 4 million, is the third largest city in Italy. It rests on the beautiful Amalfi coast, with such hill-perched villages as Positano, Ravello, and of course the island of Capri.

Indicative of the survival of small Jewish communities in Europe is the Naples synagogue, with only about 200 Jews, according to Rabbi Ariel Finzi who is from Milan but spends his weekends in Naples. He describes the community as having a "high cultural level, with a strong link to Judaism, Israel and Zionism."

Synagogue, Vico Santa Maria a Cappella Vecchia 31, Naples. Tel: 081-764-3480. Services are held only on Saturday morning. There is a small Talmud Torah. The office is open Monday, Wednesday, and Friday from 10:00 a.m. to noon. All the holidays are celebrated. Call for time of services.

The synagogue, by the way, is located in the building once occupied by Lady Hamilton, who is thought to have been the mistress of Lord Nelson. The congregation also is just off the Piazza dei Marteri (Martyrs Square), which is surrounded by famous designer shops.

It has been reported that the congregation decided to close, only to rescind the measure. Most religious Jews move away from the city because there is no kosher food available, no kosher restaurant, nor services during the week. Rabbi Finzi said in an email that "I'm here because I believe we we'll never close our synagogue."

American Jewish tourists visit Naples in the spring and summer and they can order kosher meals at the synagogue for the Sabbath, holidays, and even during the week.

During World War II, the community was spared because Allied forces landed on the southern beaches of Italy on September 9, 1943, about 30 miles from Naples. The American and British forces quickly raced up the coast towards Naples. On October 31, the day before they arrived in the city, however, a clerk who later was honored by Israel and the Jewish people as "a righteous Gentile," stalled the Germans and Italian fascists who had come to his office for the list of Jewish residents. "Come back tomorrow," the clerk is reported to have said, and they left. The next day, Allied troops arrived in the city and the Jewish community was saved.

Calabria

Synagoga Ner Tamid del Sud, Vico 1, Indipendenza, Serrastretta (Catanzaro), 88040. Tel: 39-0968-81302. rabbi@rabbibarbara.com, www.RabbiBarbara.com. Rabbi Barbara Aiello is the spiritual leader of this congregation which describes itself as "pluralistic." The synagogue has been functioning since 2006, according to Rabbi Aiello who added that "the synagogue is the first active synagogue in southern Italy in 500 years since Inquisition times." This house of prayer was enlarged in 2014. The synagogue sponsors *chavurot* in Sardinia, Palermo, Sicily, and Matera (Puglia).

Speaking of Palermo, an announcement in the *New York Times,* April 24, 2017, was made in that city that a new synagogue was to be established in a former Baroque oratory known as Santa Maria del Sabato. The unused oratory is located in an area once occupied by the Great Synagogue. The restoration was to begin that year. One can visit the *Guidecca,* Palermo's ancient Jewish quarter. About 35,000 Jews were expelled from Sicily in 1492, including 5,000 Jews in Palermo. Few Jews live on the island today.

Suggested Reading

Chamberlain, E. R., and the editors of Time-Life Books. *Rome: The Great Cities.* Amsterdam: Time-Life Books, 1976.

Cornwell, John. *Hitler's Pope: The Secret History of Pius XII.* New York, Viking, 1999.

Harrison, Barbara G. *Italian Days.* New York: Weidenfeld, 1989.

Hochhuth, Rolf. *The Deputy.* New York: Grove Press, 1964.

Hughes, H. Stuart. *Prisoners of Hope: The Silver Age of Italian Jews 1924-1974.* Cambridge, Mass.: Harvard University Press, 1983.

Kahler, Erich. *The Jews Among the Nations.* New York: Frederick Ungar, 1967.

Katz, Robert. *Black Sabbath.* New York: Macmillan, 1969.

Lewry, Guenther. *The Catholic Church and Nazi Germany.* New York: McGraw-Hill, 1964.

Mann, Vivian B., ed. *Gardens and Ghettos: The Art of Jewish Life in Italy.* Los Angeles: University of California Press, 1989.

Michaelis, Meir. *Mussolini and the Jews: German-Italian Relations and the Jewish Question in Italy 1922-1945*. Oxford University Press, 1978.

Morton, H. V. *A Traveler in Southern Italy*. New York: Dodd, Mead, 1964.

Roth, Cecil. *The History of the Jews of Italy*. Philadelphia: Jewish Publication Society of America, 1946.

Segre, Dan Vittorio. *Memoirs of a Fortunate Jew*. Bethesda, Md.: Adler and Adler, 1987.

Vogelstein, Herman. *Rome*. Philadelphia: Jewish Publication Society of America, 1940.

Zuccotti, Susan. *The Italians and the Holocaust: Persecution, Rescue, and Survival*. New York: Basic Books, 1988.

Spain
Columbus, a Jew?

"O Spain, one-half of thy face is fiesta and the other, misery." So wrote novelist Perez Galdos of his nineteenth-century homeland. Spain is the home of Cervantes, El Greco, flamenco and castanets, the bullring, and the conquistadors.

The enchanting cities of Castile and Andalusia are found here, as well as the Alhambra of Granada and its surrounding gardens that recall the Arabian Nights. The Moors and the Jews, the Christians and the Inquisition make up Spain's history. Hemingway and the Spanish Civil War, Franco and the Lincoln Brigade—there is no question that many world-famous events and figures are linked to this country.

We can visit Spain to recount our glorious past, when one-third of the population of Iberia once contained Jewish blood.

No wonder a tourist official in northeast Spain told me: "Sepharad is your home. Spain is your home." She used the Hebrew word "Sepharad," a symbolic reminder that 500 years of exile had not dimmed the memory of Spain's Jewish past.

Those soothing, welcoming words were pleasant to hear, especially from a non-Jewish Spanish official, the head of tourism in the small town of Castello d'Empuries in Catalonia.

The welcoming and work being done in Spain goes a long way toward honoring those nameless Jews exiled in 1492.

But to understand Jewish life in Spain today, we must remember and never forget the past.

A Brief History

The Jewish people still recall their "Golden Age" in Spain. To this day, Jewish history does not record a similar success story anywhere else in Europe, as Jews have rarely lived as "harmoniously or creatively" as in Spain.

For in Spain, moreover, the people of culture were Jewish. They contributed to the developing societies of both Muslim and Christian

181

Spain. Jews who had been in Spain since the destruction of the First Temple lived peacefully with the Arabs on the Iberian peninsula ever since that wintry night in 711 when Tarik Ibn Ziyad ferried an army across the Strait of Gibraltar and freed the Jews from the barbarous Visigoths.

The Muslims went on to cultivate science, medicine, philosophy, and poetry. The Spanish Jewish communities produced doctors, mathematicians, philosophers, court advisors, diplomats, and military leaders.

Nearly 1,000 years ago, there were cities in Spain where most of the inhabitants were Jewish. Spain contained the largest Jewish community in Europe.

In the Middle Ages, several hundred thousand Jews, one-half of world's Jewry, lived in Spain. To this day, we call these Jews "Sephardim," after "Sepharad," the Hebrew word for Spain. Some of the greatest Hebrew scholars in Jewish history, who devoted themselves to studying both the written and the oral law of Judaism, were from Spain, including Maimonides (1135-1204), known as the Rambam, which stands for Rabbi Moses ben Maimon. These scholars fostered the study of all branches of Jewish literature. They spoke Arabic and established schools and libraries. They wrote the finest Hebrew poetry ever created. The Zohar, the main work of Jewish mysticism, is said to have been written by Moses Ben Shem Tov de Leon (1240-1305) of Guadalajara. He is thought to have been born in Avila. And the works of the Hebrew poets Yehudah HaLevi, Solomon Ibn Gabirol, and Moses Ibn Ezra move us to this day.

But as often happens, history took a turn for the worse for the Jews. By the 1300s, they became vulnerable, no longer needed. In 1391, terrible anti-Jewish riots occurred throughout the country. About 20,000 Jews simply gave up the fight and converted. These "New Christians" were called "Conversos," but many of them only pretended to be Christians; secretly they practiced Judaism. We know them also as "Marranos," the Spanish word for "swine," or "*criptojudios*," "false Jews." They were never trusted by the Spaniards.

Soon one of the most horrible words in the lexicon of the Jewish people was created—the Inquisition. Spain had to be pure Catholic.

Between "4,000 and 8,000 secret Jews and suspects were burnt alive" in the 15 years of Tomas de Torquemada's reign. During the three centuries of its terror in Iberia, nearly 350,000 people were indicted and about 30,000 "Judaizers" were burned at the stake. Another 15,000 were burned in effigy and several hundred thousand were "penanced" because it was thought they were Jews. The burning of New Christians was to be a lesson to the converted: don't dare revert to Judaism.

Tragically, the Inquisition taught many in the world to focus on "pure blood" and "pure race." If you possessed a certificate of *limpieza de sangre* or "certificate of pure blood," you could rise to the top. The others dropped out. In the end, Spain suffered because it excluded too many bright, intellectual persons. It "surrendered itself to the chimera of racial purity", notes Barnet Litvinoff. It never regained the glory it had achieved before it expelled its Jews, who went on to settle in Africa, Turkey, Italy, Portugal, and France. Dr. M. Kayserling maintains, moreover, that the Inquisition and the expulsion had one purpose: to grab the property of secret Jews for the state treasury, even if they had to do it under the guise of religion.

Thus, in 1492, the year Columbus set sail for America, several hundred thousand Jews were expelled, not to return until 1859. The numbers of Jews expelled vary; I have seen estimates from 100,000 to a half-million and upwards. For 400 years, if a Jew was found in Spain, he could be punished by death.

Jews began to trickle into Seville after the Constitution of 1869 decreed liberty for religious faiths. By 1877, there were 406 Jews in Spain. Refugees fleeing from Czarist Russian pogroms reached Madrid in the 1880s. By 1910, a Jewish community had been set up. One of its founders, Ignazio Bauer, was the first Jew elected to the Spanish parliament.

During World War I, many Sephardic Jews of Spanish ancestry moved from Salonika, Greece, and Istanbul, Turkey, to Barcelona and Madrid. Zionist leader Max Nordau, who was an Austrian citizen, was forced to leave France during World War I, and he, too, moved to Spain.

After World War I, Jewish communities existed in Seville, Madrid, and Barcelona. In 1924, Prime Minister Primo de Rivera declared that those who were descendants of the Sephardic exiles of 1492 would be recognized as Spanish citizens. In 1927, Spain offered citizenship to all Sephardic Jews. Under the new Constitution of 1931, Jews enjoyed "full legal equality." This legislation and the Constitution was later nullified by Franco.

About 4,000 Jews resided in Spain when the Spanish Civil War broke out in 1936. "An inner psychic wound" was the way Barbara Probst Solomon described the conflagration. Figures vary, but some say, nearly one million lives were lost in the struggle. Terror reigned; there were excesses on both sides. The overwhelming majority of Jews were on the side of the Republic—10 percent of the 40,000 foreign volunteers who fought for the Republic were Jewish. Lest we forget, the Jewish men and women who fought in the Lincoln Brigade, the American unit of the international brigades against Franco and his fascist cadres.

Franco bombed cities into rubble, tortured citizens, killed POWs, machine-gunned hospital wards, and used the garrote as a punishment tool. No wonder a shiver of terror ran through Spain during those next three years.

But Franco and his fascist generals, aided by Germany and Italy, were victorious.

At the start of the Second World War, Spain was closely tied to Nazi Germany but was nonbelligerent. As the war progressed, she quickly became neutral; obviously the Axis powers were losing.

By 1940, Jews were trying to return to Spain and Portugal as Hitler engulfed the Continent. Large numbers of refugees from Nazi-occupied France fled across the Pyrenees into Spain. Although most were interned by the Spanish, they were not deported.

Stanley G. Payne, in his book, *The Franco Regime*, 1936-1975, writes: "Altogether, during the first part of the war, some 30,000 Jews had received safe passage through Spain, and there is no indication of any Jew who reached Spanish soil being turned back to German authorities. Approximately 7,500 more may have passed through between 1942 and 1944, and during the latter phases of the S.S. roundup in Hungary and the Balkans, Spanish consular officials managed to provide protection (through citizenship status) to more than 3,200 additional Jews, many of them Sephardic."

But Spain never exhausted its capabilities in saving Jews during the Holocaust. At times it allowed Jews to cross the border from France to safety. In the second half of the war, it saved more than 10,000 Jews, according to Haim Avni in *Spain, the Jews and Franco.*

Post-World War II Jews moved cautiously as Franco continued to tighten his grip over Spain.

A number of people claim Franco had direct Jewish ancestry that could be traced back to the Inquisition. Perhaps! But many people in Spain, it is said, have "Jewish blood."

After World War II, Spain followed the lead of the Vatican, which failed to recognize Israel as a state in 1948. In 1950, Israel voted against Spain in the U.N. when the world body revoked a resolution condemning Spanish actions during the war. This hardened Franco's position not to recognize Israel.

After the death of Franco in 1975, a new life began for all Spaniards, including Jews. Today dynamic, vibrant Spain, with its approximate 46 million citizens, has molded itself into a democracy. Spain, a member of the European community, is often called Europe's "moveable feast," with its famous dress designers, rock stars, and chic café people.

A decline in religious observance has marked post-Franco Spain. Although the 1492 expulsion edict has never been officially annulled (it is still "on the books"), the Constitution of 1978, which guaranteed non-Catholics "the right of religious freedom and religious equality," abrogated it de facto. On February 21, 1990, the government signed an accord that officially placed Jewish and Protestant faiths on par with Roman Catholicism. In 1992, King Juan Carlos I signed a royal decree officially canceling the 1492 Edict of Expulsion of the Jews.

In 2014, King Juan Carlos I abdicated and Felipe VI became King of Spain. Two years later, the Conference of European Rabbis honored King Felipe VI with the 2016 Lord Jacobovits Prize for European Jewry. The group praised the Spanish monarch for the "immense contribution that the king has made in his willingness to embrace the many religious faiths present throughout the continent." King Felipe VI has declared that it is Spain's "duty in the name of justice" to work towards reviving Jewish life in Spain.

After a long and arduous diplomatic effort, Spain and Israel established diplomatic relations in 1986, and, in the same year, Spain became a member of the European Union. Spain joined NATO in 1982.

Yes, there are Jews in Spain today. Indeed, a renascence of Jewish life has occurred. Schools and synagogues serve about 15,000 to 20,000 Jews—most of whom live in Madrid and Barcelona. They are devoted to leading a full Jewish life. They are building a vibrant community, the likes of which were not seen even 50 years ago when this writer first visited Spain.

Andalusia

Fly to Andalusia in the south of Spain. The Moslems called it "Al-Andalus," their appellation for the conquered lands of Iberia. For millions, the image of Spain is Andalusia.

In the days of Moslem Spain, the heart of Andalusia was represented by three great cities: Seville, Cordoba, Granada. They are Moorish cities, and even today Moorish traditions remain strong. But they were also Jewish cities with literary salons, Talmudic schools, and synagogues. Visit Andalusia and your eyes will view luscious landscapes, singing birds in olive groves, and fertile valleys.

SEVILLE

Let us begin our journey with Seville, the capital of Andalusia—city of romance, poetry, and art; Spain's fourth largest urban area, and the largest city in southern Spain.

Seville, with its approximately 700,000 persons, is the mythical home of Don Juan, Carmen, and Figaro; the Alcazar, the fourteenth-century palace for Christian kings built like the Alhambra; the Columbus Archives of the Indies, a museum: the Torre del Oro, Tower of Gold, and the huge, imposing Seville Cathedral; and the spiritual home of flamenco, bullfights, and Gypsies.

Today there are 15 Jewish families in Seville. A **synagogue** is located at Bustos Tavera 8, 41003, Seville. Tel: 34-95-427-4299. In the summer, services are at 8:30 p.m. on Friday. What is remarkable is that there is a synagogue at all in Seville and that there are Jews here: 70 at the latest count.

Some 600 years ago, there were 23 synagogues (all destroyed), thousands of Jews, and a Jewish quarter whose remnants we can see today. This Jewish section is called **Barrio de Santa Cruz**, a tourist attraction in this city that Columbus helped to make famous.

Tragedy, of course, came to Seville, in the form of riots, pogroms, conversion of synagogues into churches, and the Inquisition.

Today, in this Santa Cruz section of Seville, you can stroll through the narrow lanes of whitewashed homes and realize that the "Sephardim" (Spanish Jews) lived a full, comfortable life and that members of the Jewish community were even advisors to the vizier.

The Santa Cruz quarter contains the remains of the old Jewish quarter, which may have run as far as the Alcazar. There is indeed a new hotel called **Las Casas de la Juderia** (The Houses of the Jewish Quarter), made up of individual apartments and located in the midst of the labyrinth of the old Jewish quarter. Located near the Plaza Santa Maria la Blanca, near the Murillo Gardens, the address is 7 Callejon de DOS Hermands. Tel: 441-5150. FAX: 442-2170.

One legend that came out of that time concerns a street in the Barrio de Santa Cruz called **Calle Susona**, street of Susona. Once it was named Calle de la Muerte, street of death.

Visit it; it has an interesting tale. Don Diego Suson, a Marrano whose ancestors originally had converted to Catholicism in 1391, organized a group of Marranos who were trying to halt the Inquisition. Don Diego's daughter, who was called "Beautiful Susanna," may have betrayed a secret meeting of the Marrano group to her Christian lover, who in turn reported it to the authorities. Don Diego and his associates were burned to death as "false Jews." Shocked beyond grief, Susanna placed herself in a convent. But when she was about to die, she repented. She asked that her corpse, and later her skull, be hung in front of the house she had betrayed. The street was known as Calle de la Muerte for many years.

Within a decade, Jews were expelled from Spain. Romantic Seville became a tragic port of embarkation for Jewish refugees from western Andalusia, most of whom left for North Africa.

Today, interestingly, most of the Jews in Spain (and in Seville) are also from North Africa, from cities across the Mediterranean Sea, some of whose exotic names are Ceuta and Melilla, the latter still governed by Spain. These Moroccan Jews, besides having a synagogue, hold a Passover Seder in Seville, celebrate Jewish holidays as best they can, teach their children Hebrew, and bury their dead in a Jewish cemetery. They face the same problems as Jews all over the world: assimilation, intermarriage, and a desire for Jewish education and knowledge.

But they are not that isolated at the end of the twentieth century. The Jews of Seville belong to a National Federation of Spanish Jewish Communities; they visit Jewish communities in nearby Malaga. It is only an hour's flight on Iberia, airline of Spain, to Madrid where there are about 7,000 Jews. And, of course, there is Israel, which most of them have visited.

Sites in Seville

In the **Seville Cathedral**, Jews of Seville presented a symbolic key to Fernando III when he conquered the city from the Moors in 1248. The key is still located in the cathedral treasury, engraved in Hebrew: "The King of Kings will open, the King of the Lord shall enter." The silver tomb of Fernando III rests in the cathedral, with an epitaph written in Latin, Arabic, and Hebrew.

When the Moslems ruled here the cathedral was the city's main mosque. Today, it stands as one of Christendom's most spectacular houses of worship; only the squares of Rome's St. Peter's and London's St. Paul's are larger.

Interesting to both Jews and non-Jews is **Columbus Archives of the Indies** at 3 Avenida Queipo de Llano, which contains the account books of Luis de Santangel, a descendant of a Marrano family. A supporter of Columbus, he has been called the "Disraeli of Spain." He held the posts of chancellor of the Royal Household and controller general of finance in Aragon. He made a private loan of 17,000 ducats to Columbus, "money out of his own pocket," writes Dr. M. Kayserling. Without Santangel's enthusiastic support, "the first voyage of Christopher Columbus would never have taken place," says Cecil Roth. Incidentally, Columbus's first letter telling of his trip was written to Santangel, who with "his kinsman Gabriel Sanchez were the most zealous patrons of Columbus," according to Dr. Kayserling. Other Marranos may have pitched in to help Columbus, but Abraham Seneor, the crown rabbi of Castile, a go-between in the royal marriage of Ferdinand and Isabella, also supported Columbus, as did Don Isaac

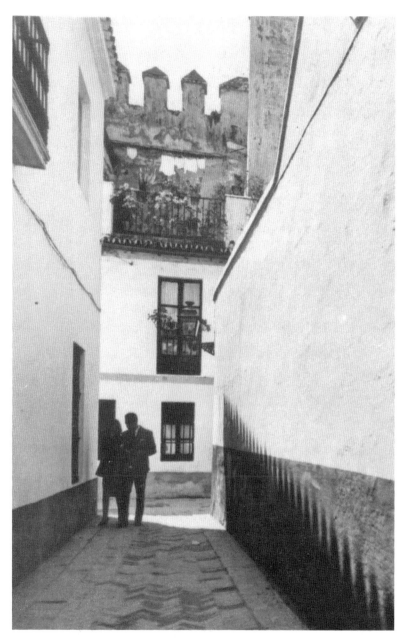

Passageway in the Barrio de Santa Cruz, the old Jewish quarter in Seville.
(Photo courtesy of the Tourist Office of Spain)

Abravanel, formerly of Lisbon, now the Jewish spokesperson in Spain, says Litvinoff. Seneor himself would eventually convert. Santangel, though a devout Catholic and counsel to the king and queen, also tried to alleviate the situation of the Jews.

The 1992 world's fair in Seville celebrated the 500th anniversary of Columbus's discovery of America. Columbus returned often to Seville; they like him here.

Was Columbus descended from a Jewish, or ex-Jewish, family? Was he a Marrano, a secret Jew? We simply do not know. Evidence exists on both sides. He could have been a converted Jew and/or Marrano. The famous writer Blasco Ibanes was convinced that Columbus was indeed a Marrano—i.e., ostensibly a Christian, but actually of Jewish descent. Other Spanish authors have said he was of Iberian Jewish stock.

Why did Columbus begin the account of his famous voyage with a reference to the expulsion of the Jews from Spain, scholars ask. Others say the expulsion of Jews and Columbus's voyage are a coincidence: "In the same month in which their majesties issued the edict that all Jews should be driven out of their kingdom and its territories, in the same month they gave me the order to undertake with sufficient men my expedition of discovery to the Indies."

Finally, other scholars note Columbus was mysterious about his religion. He seemed to have something to conceal. He had a strange affinity for Jewish and Marrano society. He deliberately postponed the day of his sailing until August 3, 1492. Why did he wait one day? Perhaps it was that the previous day, August 2, was the "unpropitious fast day of the Ninth of Av known as Tisha B'Av," which commemorates the destruction of the Second Temple. As Cecil Roth notes in *Responsibilities and Events in Jewish History.* "One who does work on the Ninth of Ab, the rabbis say, will never see a blessing therefrom."

Professor Roth maintains Columbus had an obsession with Jewish matters. He points to the theory that the Colombo family were Spanish Jews who settled in Genoa and who, "following the traditions of their race, had remained faithful to the language of their country of origin." "He indubitably had a curious mystical Jewish obsession and was always referring in his notes to the facts of ancient Jewish history," writes Professor Roth.

Also, letters that Columbus wrote to his son, Diego, have been preserved. In the corners were written the Hebrew letters *Bet Heh,* for "*B'ezrat Ha Shem*" (with the help of God). According to the *Encyclopedia Judaica,* Columbus "boasted cryptically about his connection with King David."

Columbus may have studied Jewish literature firsthand. But Professor Yosef Yerushalmi is quoted as saying: "There is not a shred of convincing evidence that he was either a Jew, a Marrano, or a proto-Semite, although many Conversos helped fund his ventures. After all, it was a business." In part, the voyage can be considered a Jewish enterprise because exploration was a business, and Jews were involved in efforts to find new lands. Those who overwhelmingly supported Columbus were "men of Jewish extraction," such as Luis de Santangel, Gabriel Sanchez, and Alfonso de la Caballeria.

Luis de Torres, a Marrano, was Columbus's interpreter on his historic journey. A linguist, he spoke Hebrew. Luis de Torres may have been baptized just before Columbus set sail. "He was the first European on these expeditions to step upon American soil," says Erich Kahler in *The Jews Among the Nations.* Dr. Kayserling also notes that Luis de Torres was the first European who discovered the use of tobacco and "was the first person of Jewish stock who settled in Cuba." There may have been other Jews among Columbus's crew. We know that, in his journeys, the explorer used the nautical instruments perfected by Joseph Vecinho, who was Jewish.

Navigation was traditionally a Jewish trade. Abraham Zacuto compiled the navigational almanac. Zacuto, who had ties to the University of Salamanca, went to Portugal at the time of the expulsion and apparently died in Damascus. One of his major contributions was the invention of the copper astrolabe.

The key mapmakers were all Jews. The most famous, of course, were Abraham and Yehuda Cresques, who established a school of cartography in Palma de Mallorca.

Jewish sites of those days still stand, like the **Plaza de Santa Cruz**, the **Arco de laJuderia**, and the streets with Jewish names: **Calle de Cal** (Kahal)—street of the congregation; **Calle de Cal Major**—street of the large congregation; **JuderiaVieja**, the Old Jewish Quarter; **Calle de dos Tintes**—street of the dyers. In 1492, there were three events that changed the world. The Moslems were defeated in their last battle with Christianity at Granada and Spain was reunited under the Catholic kings. Then Jews, who were seen as the "traitor burrowing from within," were expelled and would not return for 400 years.

And on August 3, 1492, Columbus sailed for America, a day or two after the last Jews left the soil of Spain and one day after Tisha B'av, the Jewish holiday that laments the destruction of the Temple.

With 1492 being so important, it is no wonder that the International Jewish Committee Sepharad '92 was formed to commemorate the 500th anniversary of the expulsion of the Jews from Spain, and celebrate the rebirth and subsequent growth of the Sephardic heritage and its place in Jewish history. And so as one walks through Seville, one thinks of Columbus, the Jews, and the Inquisition. But the sounds and sights are of the present. This is a city to tour and absorb. The Moors and the Jews loved Seville. A proverb says, "If one were to ask for bird's milk in Seville, one would be able to get it."

As I walked through the open areas of the middle of the city, I recalled that 500 years ago, 700 Conversos were burned at the stake and more than 5,000 were reconciled with the Catholic Church, all within seven years. Even in 1484, Tomas de Torquemada, a converted Jew himself, chaired a convention of the Inquisition in this city to define the procedures of the torture process used to obtain so-called truth. A Spanish Jew once told me, "They tried to kick us out, but we're still here; we were stronger than they were."

CORDOBA

It is good to visit Cordoba after Seville. About 100 miles separate the two cities. To those Jewish travelers interested in Jewish history and culture, Cordoba evokes memories of a brilliant Jewish intellectual center in the Golden Age of Spain. Today one can visit one of the three existing Jewish synagogues of ancient Spain; gaze at the statue of Maimonides in Tiberias Square; or walk in the narrow alleys of the famous Juderia (Jewish Quarter) near the cathedral and the alcazar, where tourists and students sit in the Plaza de Juda Levi and sip coffee or a soft drink.

Cordoba, where once lived Averroes, the Arab philosopher who was a contemporary of Maimonides, is a Moorish city with narrow winding streets, gardens, olive and orange groves, and a population of one and a quarter million. The capital of the caliph, it contained 200,000 buildings, 3,000 mosques, 27 free schools, and a university that attracted scholars from throughout the world. In the Middle Ages, Cordoba, a scientific center, possessed a vibrant economy that made it the largest city in the world, and the wealthiest and most civilized city in Western Europe. Stanley G. Payne, professor of history, says: "In size, services, culture and economy, the city was without a peer in Western Europe and was rivaled in the East only by Constantinople."

Famous for its libraries and bookshops, Cordoba was the high-water mark of the Arab civilization in Europe. It once contained a library of 400,000 catalogued volumes.

The past and its rich cultural and religious mix can be seen in La Mezquita (mosque) building, which shares the same foundation as the cathedral. The combined structure—not far from the Jewish Quarter—boasts a Muslim forest of pillars and white Moorish arches with a domed ceiling, a testimonial to the dauys when Cordoba was the capital of Islamic Spain. But after the Christian conquest ended in

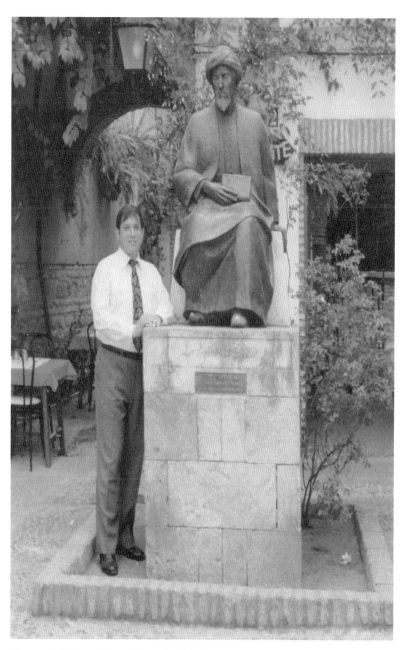

Statue of Maimonides. (Photo by M. Serels)

1492, 60 columns were torn out of the mosque to make room for the cathedral in the mosque's center.

Today, once again, Jews live in Cordoba, which the poet Antonio Machado y Ruiz called "Roman, Moorish and silent." To be sure, there are only a few Jews here in this Andalusian city of about 330,000 the birthplace of the genius scholar, Maimonides. Once, too, it was the temporary home of Yehudah HaLevi, one of the great Hebrew poets. It was the home of Hasdai ibn Shaprut (915-70), physician, diplomat, and advisor to the caliph, who established the first Talmudic school here. This city contained a galaxy of Hebrew scholars, philosophers, and poets who attended the court of Abd-al Rahman III (912-61).

In 1985, the 850th anniversary of the birth of Maimonides brought much attention to the Jewish past in Spain, and there were symposia held, bringing about increased Jewish consciousness.

The Jewish Quarter in Cordoba

When you enter the Moorish gateway known as the **Puerta de Almodovar** (it was once called "Bab-al-Yahud"), you are in the **Juderia,** which is located between the Plaza de las Tendillas and the River Guadalquivir. Turn right down the **Calle de los Judios** in the Jewish Quarter. You have to imagine that Cordoba was once the "New York City of Europe," that along these narrow passageways of flower-laced streets and whitewashed abodes, of gardens and orange groves, a population of one and one-quarter million thrived and lived in this capital of the caliph. The Jews flourished in Cordoba. Under the Moors, the Talmudic school of Cordoba was famous throughout Europe. Jews served in high positions as ambassadors and advisors. Many of the caliphs hired Jewish physicians.

The Statue of Maimonides, erected in 1964, is located near the synagogue on Calle de los Judios. Actually, it is just down the street from the synagogue in a square named **Plaza Tiberias** to perpetuate the ties between his Spanish birthplace and Tiberias, the city in Israel where he is buried.

Maimonides was one of the greatest Jewish thinkers and scholars of all time, author of the Guide of the Perplexed, and a doctor who lived from 1135 to 1204. Barnet Litvinoff says Maimonides "stands as the most significant Jewish intellect and teacher from the time of the Prophets until Spinoza."

Born Maimonides, this remarkable figure in post-biblical Jewish history fled from his native Cordoba because of persecution from the Almohad sect, whose military forces rampaged Andalusia in 1146. He mastered medicine and, through tireless study, absorbed many other fields of knowledge, such as mathematics and astronomy. By 1185, he was already a leading physician at Saladin's court in Egypt and knew Richard Coeur de Lion. In 1180, he compiled the Mishneh Torah, "Repetition of the Law." His 13 articles of belief would be incorporated in the creeds of Judaism, and his Guide of the Perplexed scrutinized the revelation at Sinai through the lens of reason. It is not hard to imagine Maimonides walking through the old Jewish Quarter in Cordoba.

The courtyard is small and the statue of Maimonides, sitting in the middle, dominates the area of plain, whitewashed walls. The sage sits on a marble bench atop an attractive cube. He is wearing the robes and twisted turban of the desert. In his lap, he holds a book, his right thumb marking the spot. His face, his posture, and his robes are those of a philosopher and, as you look at the statue, you understand why his admirers said, "From Moses to Moses there was no one like Moses."

Just up the street from the statue of Maimonides is the small, "cubicle-in-shape" synagogue built in 1315. On the east wall of the small Moorish-designed building is a vacant niche that once held the Ark of the Law. On the south wall can be seen intricately designed Scripture and prayers in Hebrew. In his book, Travels in Jewry, Israel Cohen writes that one of the verses in Hebrew says: "A little sanctuary and a house of testimony which was built by Isaac Mehab, son of the wealthy Ephraim, erected in the year 75 as a temporary structure. Arise, O Lord and hasten to rebuild Jerusalem." Upstairs, in the upper part of the south wall, you can clearly make out a women's gallery. The building later served as a church, the Church of Saint Crispin.

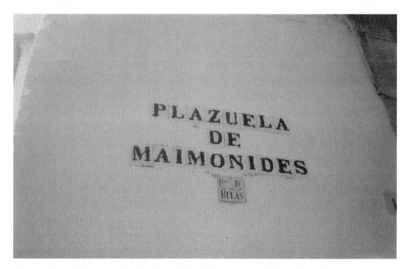

Plazuela de Maimonides in Cordoba. (Photo by Malke Frank)

The spirit of Maimonides is everywhere. Right in the Juderia, not far from the statue of Maimonides, you will find a square called **Plazuela de Maimonides**. This may have been the site where Maimonides lived when he resided in Cordoba. Visualize silversmiths, silk embroiderers, and leather-goods makers who sold their products. Extending from this street is **Calle Rambam Maimonides**.

Walk to 5 Calle de los Judios, along the street that was the main street of the medieval ghetto. This is *Casa Maimonides*, the actual spot (if not the house itself) where the great Maimonides was born. In 1935, the Spanish government sponsored an 800th birthday celebration of Maimonides. Jews came from all over the world. For the first time in 443 years, a Jewish prayer service was held in Cordoba. In the synagogue courtyard, the municipality of Cordoba erected this plaque: "On the occasion of the eight-hundredth anniversary of the birth of Rabbi Moses ben Maimon, the Spanish government, in the name of the entire nation, expresses its recognition of that immortal Jewish spirit. Cordoba, his birth place, honors his memory.

During the Muslim period, the Jewish Quarter was located near the alcazar (fortress) in the northwest section of the city. It continued in existence after the Christian reconquest.

Walk down **Juda Levi Street**, named for the Jewish poet who was born in Tudela in 1075, but who lived for a number of years in Cordoba.

On one of my visits, the proprietor of the cafe in the Plaza de Juda Levi spoke to me about the poet, philosopher, and physician for

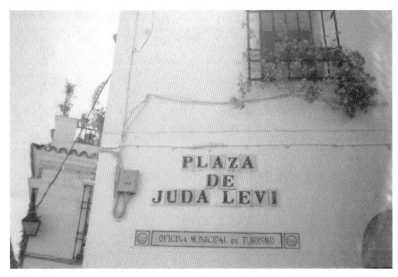

Plaza de Juda Levi in Cordoba. (Photo by Malke Frank)

whom this historical square is named. Born in Tudela (1085-1140), he traveled south to the literary salons of Andalusia and passed through Cordoba on his way, with the intention of going on to Granada. In Cordoba, HaLevi participated in a poetry writing contest and won the competition for imitating a complicated poem by Moses Ibn Ezra, who invited HaLevi to his home. HaLevi lived in many communities in Spain. When he lived in Toledo, he practiced medicine.

"His was the sweetest and most poignant of all the nightingale voices of that time," writes Chaim Raphael. He gave the Jewish people the electrifying "Ode to Zion"; "Songs of Exile"; and "Poems of Zion," or as we know them, "Zionides." "He was the most beloved poet in post-Biblical Hebrew literature," says Raphael. He dreamed of reaching the Land of Israel and freeing himself of the enslavement of Exile. One of his most famous lines is "My heart is in East, and I in the uttermost West." Finally, he did leave Toledo. According to legend, HaLevi reached Jerusalem, which was occupied by Crusaders. He bowed down and kissed its stones. As he recited the opening words of one of his elegies, "Zion, wilt thou not ask if peace be with the captive," an Arab horseman pierced his heart with a lance.

But the more likely story is that he died six months after reaching Egypt and was buried there. His "Ode to Zion" expresses Israel's yearning for its homeland. He said the ideal existence for the Jew was attainable only in his own homeland. A Spanish writer, Filipe Torroba Bernaldo de Quiros, says that he united "Sefardite nostalgia of Spain with Palestinian Zionism."

The café owner, too, decries the decision 500 years ago of the Jewish expulsion. "Spain today is not racist," she says. "It is not possible to have one people; we have to have many peoples."

Today, the Spanish people are still remarkably hospitable. Spain has passed through a peaceful transition from repressive dictatorship to parliamentary government.

GRANADA

Once it was called "Gharnata' al-Yahud," "Granada of the Jews." It was also known as "Villa de Judios," the description of the city by the first great poet of Hebrew Spain, Samuel haNagid (Ibn Nagrela). This poet, "the Prince," was also a philosopher-soldier, who lived in Granada.

"Whoever has not seen the splendor of the Jews of Granada, their fortune and their glory, has never seen true glory for they were great with wisdom and piety."

The best place to find Granada's Jews is the **University of Granada**, at the Cartuja Campus.

On a visit to Granada a number of years ago, I met dynamic Dr. Maria Jose Cano, a Catholic who teaches in the Department of Semitic Studies. Dr. Cano, who studied at the Jewish Theological Seminary in New York and who attended the Hebrew University and Tel Aviv University, speaks and reads Hebrew and has written scholarly papers on the poetry of Solomon Ibn Gabirol and Maimonides. Here is her story. When she was a young girl, at Easter time the children of her village would travel to a nearby village and make papier-mâché targets depicting Jews. They would then throw stones at them. Her father told her this was wrong, so she never participated in this hatred. Her father explained to her that Jews are people like all people—not the devil as depicted by the children. She believed her father was an upright, honest man and what he said must have been true. So she pursued her interest in this people, the Jews, because her father had shown kindness toward them. She went to Israel and studied Hebrew in a kibbutz ulpan as well as at the Hebrew University in Jerusalem.

"Interest in Jewish studies and Israel is rising in Spain," she said in an interview in her office at the university, "especially with the finalization of diplomatic relations between Spain and Israel in early 1986." For example, the town in which she grew up commissioned her to write a paper on Jewish life in that village as it was centuries ago. Dr. Cano hopes her students will also engage in research into the Sephardic past.

I met a number of Spanish students who were eager to visit Israel. They talked about Israel and the Jewish people.

The Alhambra Palace and the Jews

The Alhambra, the palace of paradise, is also of historic significance to Jews. It is the "apex of Moorish design extravagance." All routes led to the Alhambra Palace, which is one of the most beautiful monuments in all Spain. The royal palace—which is a fortress—was constructed on a 35-acre plateau atop a last spur of the Sierra Nevada to express the spirit of the civilization that was Moslem Spain.

It is said that the best time to view Granada is when the colors of the sky are lilac, rose, gray, blue, hazel, aquamarine, red, and dusty-gold. Surrounding the Alhambra are flowering gardens, courtyards, and splashing fountains. The scene brings to mind an idea of what life must have been like under the Arabs. Nightingales sing in the Alhambra Gardens, a wonderful legacy of the Moors, who "designed their gardens not only in the visual sense, but also aimed to catch a visitor's ear, arouse his taste buds and coax him into touching all that summoned him."

Looking up at the Alhambra, one recalls that the Ibn Nagrela family may have had something to do with building part of the structure. Joseph Ibn Nagrela was the son of the famous Samuel Ibn Nagrela, "The Nagid" (933-1055). Samuel, the vizier of Granada, achieved the highest position as a Jew in medieval Moslem Spain. Joseph, who succeeded his father, built a huge palace. It is believed that this was later destroyed, and the present Alhambra built on that site.

Joseph came to an untimely end as a result of a palace intrigue. He was assassinated on December 30, 1066, and a day after his murder, a Moslem mob stormed through the Jewish Quarter of Granada in what was one of the few recorded pogroms of Moslems against Spanish Jews.

The Moors who conquered Spain in the eighth century believed that the fertile plain of Granada would be heaven, as told in the Koran. They built a grand city here and created the impressive fountains of the Alhambra, whose walls owe their redness to bricks made from ferrous mud. The "Red Fort" is still one of the most admired monuments in Spain.

The guides who take you around the Alhambra cite Jewish influence in the "ruddy hue" of the palace. Some say the famous "Lion Fountain," "Court of the Lions," was a gift of the Jews of Granada. Others say the 12 lions are patterned after 12 oxen of King Solomon's Temple, which Joseph Ibn Nagrela had copied for his palace.

The Alhambra is history. Perhaps that is why two million persons visit here each year. The Alhambra, a symbol of Moorish surrender to the "Catholic kings," still stands as the last bastion of Islam in Spain. It fell on January 2, 1492. But this Moorish architectural gem contains within its silent walls much of Jewish history in Spain.

Let us go first to the **Hall of the Ambassadors**. Under its 60 feet high domed ceiling, the Catholic kings, on March 31, 1492, signed the document expelling the Jews. The huge square room contains nice large windows from which one can look down to the city of Granada.

In the very same room, Ferdinand and Isabella signed an agreement allowing Columbus to sail west to America.

Here in this hall, Don Isaac Abravanel (1437-1508), Jewish philosopher, statesman, and supporter of Columbus, and Abraham Seneor of Segovia tried to change the minds of their Catholic rulers about the expulsion of the Jews in 1492 by offering a large bribe. They almost succeeded, but as Litvinoff writes: "Tomas de Torquemada, Confessor to the Queen, Inquisitor General of the Inquisition and converted Jew, is said to have taunted Abraham Seneor, a confidant of Isabella, who then converted." Torquemada stopped any wavering on the part of the "Catholic kings," and the Jews were forced out.

After the expulsion decree, incidentally, Don Isaac Abravanel left Spain on May 31, 1492, first to Italy, then to Corfu, and finally to Venice in 1503, where he wrote mystical works and biblical commentaries. He died in 1508 at the age of 71 and was buried in Padua. The expulsion edict was promulgated at the end of April, and the Jewish exodus began in May and continued until August 2, 1492. More than 100,000 Jews went to Portugal, just across the border. They were seeking a haven. Instead, they ran right smack into danger once again. In Portugal, they would soon be forced into baptism and sold into slavery.

Like Abravanel, thousands of Sephardim moved eastward to the Levant: to the Tuscan coast at Loghorn and Grosseto as guests of the Medici; to the realms of the Ottoman Empire where they were welcomed by the Sultans. They settled in trading ports like Constantinople, Salonika, Smyrna, and Rhodes, "landing, it is said, with nothing but the scrolls of law and the massive keys of their homes in Cordova, Granada or Cadiz," noted Patrick Leigh Fermor in his *"The Broken Road, From the Iron Gates to Mount Athos."* Very few Jews, as we have seen, live in Cordova, Granada or Cadiz, but they live today in Madrid.

Jewish Madrid

It is only about an hour's flight from Granada to Madrid, a city of bullfights and "machismo." Hemingway called it "the most Spanish of all cities, the best place to live in, the finest people."

Madrid is busy and active; the energy is addictive.

Walk down the Calle de la Fe, the "street of the faith." Some say it was once called "Calle de la Synagogue." On this street, Jews once owned stores and real estate. In the riots of 1391, many Jews were massacred here. Others were converted on the spot. A synagogue destroyed during those disturbances stood next to the San Lorenzo Church. Other streets in the old Jewish quarter, called the Juderia, are Calle de Bailen, Plaza de Oriente, and Plaza de Lavapies.

Greater Madrid boasts about 6.5 million Madrileños, who traverse wide boulevards and bask in the sun at dramatic fountains and statues of heroes. Here Cervantes wrote Don Quixote, Lope de Vega wrote plays and El Greco painted.

Madrid, which became the capital in 1561, lies almost in the center of the Iberian Peninsula, the highest capital city in Europe. Situated in the Meseta, this somewhat isolated city rests on an undulating plateau of sand and clay. Because it suffered severe damage in the Civil War, which ended nearly 80 years ago, many of its buildings and homes were rebuilt. Rarely seen is a piece of physical damage of the two-and-a-half-year civil war that ended on March 28, 1939, when Franco's troops entered the capital.

SITES IN MADRID

Centro de Estudios ibn Gabriol-Colegio Estrella Toledano, Direccíon: Paseo de Alcobendas 7, 28109, Alcobendas, Madrid. Tel: 916-50-12-29. www.colegiogabiroltoledano.com/
Arias Montano, Institute of Jewish Studies, 4 Calle del Duque de Medinaclli, in front of the Palace Hotel and American Embassy. Located in the heart of Madrid, this library contains more than 16,000 volumes, manuscripts, and publications about Sephardic Jewish history. It was opened in 1940, during World War II, at a time when Franco was an admirer of Hitler.
University City offers courses in Hebrew and Sephardic studies.

BETH YAAKOV SYNAGOGUE

Beth Yaakov Synagogue and Jewish Community Center, 3 Calle Balmas, Madrid. Tel: 34-915-91-31-31. info@cjmadrid.org. www.cjmadrid. Located near the Plaza Sorolla. Sephardim from Europe and North Africa began settling in Spain after World War II, but it was not until the public dedication of a new synagogue in Madrid on September 17, 1968, that recognition and a new era began for the Jews in Spain. It was 476 years after the Jews were expelled from Spain. Today, laws in Spain grant Jews the legal right to observe their religion. Present at the historic ceremony were the archbishop of Madrid and representatives of the Foreign and Justice ministries. Rabbi Moshe Bendahan is rabbi of the JCC.

Actually, the nucleus for this congregation was established after World War II. Later, when many Ashkenazi Jews arrived in Spain, they began to meet in a room at **Calle del Cardinal Cisneros**.

This building on Calle Balmas serves as religious and cultural center and contains a library, a kosher catering facility, a youth lounge, and another small synagogue. Downstairs there is even a letter from President George Washington of the United States of America. Arrangements for kosher meals can be made here, but write and order in advance. There is a kosher kitchen that even dispatches wine and matzah to other Jewish communities at Passover.

The synagogue maintains a mikva. Direct number: 34-652-13-1888, or 34-591-3135.

The synagogue, which is Orthodox, contains a separate women's gallery, as well as a meeting hall for youth groups.

The community center section of the building also includes a rabbinical office and a Talmud Torah of about 200 children and a Sunday school of 40 also function. Youth activities include summer camps and a growing Maccabi sport movement.

The Jewish Community Center sponsors a Friday night Shabbat dinner. Make sure you make a reservation in advance. Tel: 34-91-591-31-31. Madrid Jewish Community: Tel: 932-00-85-13.

Friday night services at the synagogue are usually at 7:30 p.m., 8:30 in summer; on Saturday morning they are held at 9:30 a.m. Services are daily and on holidays, but do call to check on times.

When I first went to Spain in 1964, I searched and searched for the synagogue. I had difficulty finding it, for in those days, a Jewish house of worship could not display exterior signs.

I remember I walked up a long flight of steps in an apartment building to reach the nearly hidden synagogue.

The synagogue at 3 Calle Balmas, is not difficult to find. You might easily spot it from a distance because of security. When I visited the congregation, for example, a police car was parked in front of the building.

The Sunday morning I attended services, a small minyan of Moroccan Jews had gathered. As we talked about life in the Spanish capital, cake was served. At the synagogue, I also talked to a Lubavitcher Chassid, Rabbi Yitzchak Goldstein. A teacher, he is the brother of a Lubavitch rabbi at the University of Michigan, Rabbi Aaron Goldstein. Rabbi Yitzhak Goldstein has been a rabbi in Madrid for 40 years.

The cornerstone of the new synagogue building reads: "This house of prayer is the first ever to be built in Madrid. May it be a symbol and a memorial for the Jewish communities that existed in this land until 1492 and a portent for the revival of Judaism in Spain."

Chabad. Tel: 34-91-029-1269, www.chabad.org. jabad770@gmail. com. For correspondence, website or write to: Chabad, Apartado De Correos (POB) #10. 117, Madrid. 28080. Rabbi Yitzchak Goldstein represents Chabad which as noted does not maintain a center in Madrid.

Bet El Masorti Congregation, Plaza Castilla area, administracion@ bet-el.org, www.orhayeladim.org.

Or **Haheyladim Synagogue**, Artura Soria Area, info@orhayeladim. org, www.orhayeladim.org.

Rambam Synagogue, Alcobendas Area-North Madrid. rambam@ cjmadrid.org.

Comunidad Judia Reformista de Madrid. Reform Movement of Judaism in Madrid. Tel: info@javurareformista.org, www. javurareformista.org.

Kosher Restaurants in Madrid

Kosher food can be obtained at the following listed below. But again, Chabad does not endorse these facilities. And Rabbi Yitzhak Goldstein of Chabad urges shoppers to check for known, reliable kosher seals. He adds that one must be cautious with milk and milk products, as well as bread and pastries in Spain as they may contain non-kosher ingredients.

Elias Susana Butchery, Calle Viriato, 35, 28010 Madrid. Tel: 34-91-446-7847.

Shalom Susana, Calle Medellin 13, 28101 Madrid. Tel: 34-91-445-5296.

Gourmet Kosher S.L, Calle Anastro 9, 28033 Madrid: Tel: 34-91-383-1186, 34-628-190-708, 34-630-534-859.

El Corte Ingles, (Castellana) Raimundo Fernandez Villaverde 79, Madrid. Tel: 34-91-418-8800.

Restaurant **"La Escudilla C/Santisima"** Trinidad 16, Madrid. Metro Iglesia. Tel: 91-445-73-80. Info@laescudilla.com, www.laescudilla.com

Restaurant **Café de Oriente**. (Kosher service supervised by the Rabbinate of the Jewish Community) Direccíon: Plaza de Oriente 2, 28013, Madrid. www.cafedeoriente.es

ORGANIZATIONS

Federation of Jewish Communities of Spain. Tel: 34-91-700-1208 or 34-91-446-6232. fcje@fcje.org. www.fcje.org. The Federacion de Comunidades Judías de España, which unites Jewish Spanish communities from different parts of the country, acts as the liaison for presenting Jewish interests to the government and also works with Jewish communities to provide religious, cultural, and educational services. It offers a weekly program in official radio and TV stations and owns www.radiosefarad.com, with cultural and religious program. Radio Sefarad also has a French, Hebrew, and English corner.

Centro Sefarad-Israel, Calle Mayor, 69. Madrid. Tel: 34-91-391-10-02. centro@sefarad-Israel.es/ www. Casasefarad-israel.es/

Centro Hebreo Vivo, Plaza de Emilio Jimenez Millas No. 2, Madrid. Tel: 91-050-27-44. info@hebreovivo.com, www.hebreovivo.com

Centro de Estudios ibn Gabirol Estrella Toledano, school, Direccíon: Paseo de Alcobendas 7, 28109 Alcobendas, Madrid. Tel: 916-50-12-29. www.colegiogabiroltoledano.com/

Heritage Tours, Private Travel. www.htprivatetravel. New York City. 1-800-378-4555.

Sefarad Connection. Jewish Legacy Tours. Tel 34-627-26-41-28. info@sefaradconnection.org, www.sefradconnection.org. Contact: Ziva Freidkes Szeinuk.

MUSEUMS

Museo Sefardito de Madrid, 18 Calle Zorilla, one block from the

American Express office. This museum has an interesting display of Jewish historical documents, art replicas, and other objects related to the history of the Jews in Spain.

National Archaeological Museum, 13 Calle de Serrano. This museum contains castings of Hebrew inscriptions from medieval buildings.

The Prado, Paseo del Prado, Madrid is the home of one of the world's outstanding art museums, the Prado, also called the National Museum of Painting and Sculpture. In 1994, it celebrated its 175th birthday and interestingly, one and a half million persons visited it in 1993. Hemingway wrote that if the city "had nothing else than the Prado, it would be worth spending a month in Madrid every spring, if you have money to spend for a month in any European capital." There are about 2,000 paintings by Spanish and foreign masters, including more than 30 works by El Greco, 100 by Francisco Goya, and 50 by Diego Velazquez.

Of special Jewish interest in the **Museo del Prado** are Titian's famed Moses Saved from the Waters and Murillo's painting of Rebecca and Eliezer, as well as two works depicting an autoda-fé of the Inquisition.

Barcelona

Barcelona rocks.

Barcelona makes noise and money.

Barcelona is one of the most cosmopolitan cities in Europe.

Barcelona, a popular Mediterranean port, welcomes thousands of cruise passengers every day.

Even with the threat of terrorism facing every traveler, thousands of tourists pour into this port city by air and by sea. "Visitor numbers have grown exponentially in recent years. In 2016, an estimated nine million people stayed in hotels and a further nine million in holiday apartments. In addition, the city received around 12 million day-trippers arriving by car and train or on cruise ships," according to the Guardian publication in the UK. A large portion of visitors are from the US and Israel.

Even in the twelfth century, that world traveler, Benjamin of Tudela, mentioned the prosperity and beauty of Barcelona, according to Dr. Kayserling.

Before Franco came to power, Barcelona was one of the most creative cities in the world. It still is. Since the Olympics in 1992—a turning point for the city—tourism has become a fast-growing industry. One of the city's biggest tourist attractions is the Sagrada Familia church.

Miguel de Cervantes of Barcelona once wrote, "Barcelona was the fatherland of all valiant men." A beautiful city, it is conveniently situated, and it once welcomed Columbus home from a long journey to the Americas.

Even at midnight, there is a difference between Madrid and Barcelona. Hardworking and energetic, Barcelonians walk fast as if going somewhere in a hurry. Madrid is slower.

The second city in size and 2,000 years old, Metro Barcelona, with its approximate five million citizens, stands as the great metropolis of the northeast coast. Indeed, Barcelona is considered the most populous metropolitan area on the Mediterranean coast and one of the largest in Europe.

No wonder some observers of Spain say that it would make a better capital than Madrid. As one of the oldest and largest Mediterranean seaports, it is the capital of Catalonia Autonomous Region of Spain.

The Statute of Autonomy of Catalonia provides Catalonia's basic institutional regulations under the Spanish Constitution of 1978 and again approved in 2006. It defines the rights and obligations of the citizens of Catalonia (Spain), the political institutions of the Catalan region, their competences and relations with the rest of Spain, and the financing of the Government of Catalonia.

A huge issue in Spain today is the possible secession of Catalonia, including of course Barcelona.

In recent years, the drive for independence for the state of Catalonia has increased. In effect, Catalonia is a state within a state: it has its own language and institutions. Like other regions in Spain, Catalonia already has the power to run its educational and healthcare systems, as well as limited freedoms in the area of taxation. It accounts for a fifth of the country's GNP. A quarter of all forms of investments end up in Catalonia. If Catalonia were an independent country, it would count among the most prosperous states on the European continent.

The stand-off between the Spanish state and the north-eastern region of Catalonia is intense; Catalan leader Carles Puigdemont set the tone in a New Year message, saying a planned referendum would go ahead by October 2017. That would defy the Spanish government's warning that any vote organized by Catalonia's regional authorities would be illegal, according to the BBC.

Traditionally the Jewish community has been seen as unsupportive of independence, but with the passing of time and with another generation of Catalan Jews, there are changes, according to observers in Barcelona. The younger generation seems more favorable.

After what the Madrid government termed an illegal referedum held in the fall in 2017 demanding independence for Catalonia, Madrid continued to clamp down on any independence more. Whether Barcelona leaves Spain or not, the city will probably always be cosmopolitan.

Historic Barcelona flaunts itself as an international city and looks across the Mediterranean to Alexandria, Genoa, Pisa, and Venice. Visit the **Ramblas** (long avenue) with its stalls and outdoor cafés; "it's always gay and lively." It was especially so in 1992 when the city was the site of the summer Olympics and with the commemoration of the 500th anniversary of the discovery of America and the expulsion of the Jews. But tragedy struck the Ramblas on August 17, 2017, when a devastating terrorist attack involving two separate vehicular assaults. One swept through Barcelona and the other in the seaside resort town of Cambrills, Fifteen persons were murdered in Barcelona and scores wounded. The attack on the Ramblas took place quite near the kosher restaurant Maccabi, Las Ramblas 79, 08002, Barcelona. Tel: 34-93-317-95-45. info@restaurantmaccabi.com. www.restaurantmaccabi.com. The other attack took place in Cambrills. Until this terrorist assault, Spain had been spared terrorist incidents, although in 2004, Madrid was the scene of Spain's worst attack in which passenger trains were bombed and 192 people died and more than 1,800 were injured.

Once a center of Talmudic learning, Barcelona is known for the great disputation between Rabbi Moses ben Nachman, known as Nachmanides, and members of the Dominican and Franciscan orders. (We shall meet Nachmanides in Gerona, where he was born).

In 1391, Spain's Jewish community was almost destroyed. Barcelona's Jewry never recovered—by 1396 not a single Jew lived in the city. Since Barcelona was a harbor, many of the Jews who were expelled left from this harbor for safer lands. This was the port, too, where Columbus briefed the "Catholic kings" after his first voyage to America.

By 1887, however, about 20 Jewish families lived in Barcelona, mainly businessmen, originating from France and central Europe, notes Victor Sorenssen.

At the beginning of the twentieth century, a few Jewish peddlers from Morocco and Turkey settled in Barcelona.

After Salonika was taken from the Turks by the Greeks in 1912, more Jews arrived. The Spanish government encouraged settlement of Spanish Jews on its territory, and another wave of Jewish immigration moved in from the Balkans after World War I.

In 1917, the *Communidad Israelita de Barcelona* was born, notes Sorenssen. To this day it represents the Jewish community.

More than 100 Jews lived in Barcelona in 1918. By 1932, the number rose to about 3,000, mostly of Sephardic origin. German Jews, fleeing Hitler, began arriving in 1933, and they brought the figure to more than 5,000 Jews, mostly Ashkenazim. During the Spanish Civil War of 1936-39, however, many of Barcelona's Jews left for France and Palestine. Some of the city's German Jews emigrated after the defeat of the Republic in 1939. But ironically many, if they had not been able to get to America or England, quickly came back, for Barcelona became a center for refugees. The city became "a precarious refuge from Nazi barbarism."

After World War II, the government granted permission to open a synagogue in Barcelona.

In 1965, together with leaders of the Madrid Jewish community, Barcelona's Jewish community officers were received by Franco in the first meeting since 1492 between a Spanish head of state and Jewish leader.

Estimates of the Jewish population of this capital of Catalonia vary: probably 4,000 to 5,000, but it could be higher. There are hundreds of Israelis who have settled in Barcelona for business and work. The actual number is unknown. According to Victor Sorenssen, a political science expert and student of Semitic philology, and director of the Jewish community in Barcelona, many Israelis work at Hewlett-Packard (HP) Spain Corporate Headquarters in the city.

The world is very cognizant that five centuries after Spain expelled the Jews, the country has invited their descendants—Sephardim—to return. Up to 3.5 million people around the world are thought to have Sephardic Jewish ancestry.

In 2015, Spain passed an "unprecedented law" granting citizenship to the descendants of the hundreds of thousands of Jews who fled Spain after 1492 when the Catholic Church and the King and Queen of Spain instituted a campaign of persecution, forced conversion to Christianity, and dispossession against Jews known as the Spanish Inquisition.

A few years after the new law came into force in Spain allowing dual citizenship for the descendants of Jews forced out of Spain in 1492, it was clear that the process for final citizenship is more difficult than previously thought.

Unlike the open-ended law in Portugal, the Spanish law set a three-year window for applications. The Spanish law is also stricter than the Portuguese one, as it requires passing tests attesting to cultural or language ties to Spain by applicants.

Spain has naturalized nearly 5,000 applicants for citizenship by Sephardim since the law went into effect in 2015. However, only three applicants were granted citizenship based on the actual law. Others were naturalized by a royal decree and not through the nondiscretionary procedure devised by the law, according to the Jewish Telegraphic Agency. One of the reasons for the paltry numbers of applications through the law is the obstacle that the language and sociocultural knowledge tests represent, according to the Sephardic community in Turkey.

Therefore, in an effort to encourage more Sephardic Jews to

exercise their right to become Spanish nationals, Spain, in early 2017, announced that individuals of 70 years of age or over will be waived of taking tests in the Spanish language and of their knowledge of Spanish culture and constitution.

Most of the Turkish Jews applying speak very little Spanish to take the examinations for citizenship and the little Spanish they speak is derived from the version which was spoken in the 15th century and is not useful for testing.

Adam Yedid, an Israeli lawyer specializing in international citizenship law, estimates that up to three million Israelis are eligible for Spanish citizenship, according to Raoul Wootliff's writing in the *Times of Israel* on Feburary 11, 2016.

Interestingly, Argentinians head the list, followed by Israelis and Venezuelans, according to BBC News. Other countries from which persons are applying to Spain for citizenship are Morocco, Israel, the U.S., and Pakistan.

"Potential applicants have described the procedure, which involves a Spanish exam and a trip to Spain, as expensive and time-consuming. But they have also praised the fact that it no longer requires them to relinquish their existing nationality, as the previous Spanish 'law of return' had," according to the BBC News.

JEWISH SITES IN BARCELONA

Mountain of the Jews. Much of the Jewish history of Barcelona evolves around two hills called Tibidabo and Montjuich. The latter is on the southern side of the city. Vast amounts of land lie between these two mountains. In Catalan, "Montjuich" means "Mountain of the Jews," where obviously Jews once owned much land. Here again, we meet the old Jewish neighborhood.

In the eleventh and twelfth centuries, Jews helped establish Barcelona's commercial greatness. "Jews helped forge the Catalan personality. Medieval Catalan Jews and Christians not only shared a space, but also a language, a taste for business affairs, a characteristic form of government," writes Victor Sorenssen.

A Jewish cemetery about 1,000 years old is kept up with a special section still set aside for Jewish graves. Located on Montjuich is the outstanding **Museum of Art**, with its excellent collection of Romanesque art.

Comunidad Israelita de Barcelona, the overall community group which owns and manages Synagogue Maimonides and Community Center, info@cibonline.org. www.cibonline.org.

Synagogue Maimonides and Community Center, 24 Avenir, 08021,

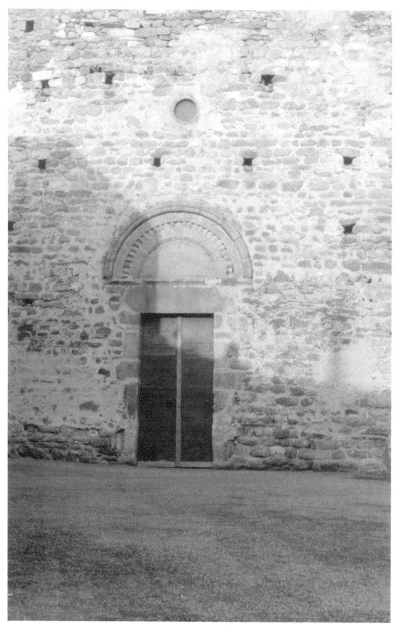

Synagogue of Vilajuiga (Jews' Village) near Barcelona. (Photo by Ruth Serels)

Barcelona. Tel: 34-93-200-8513. info@ciboline.org. Located near the President Hotel, it was established in 1954. From that date one can realize that it was the first synagogue to be built in Spain in almost 500 years. The first floor is the Sephardic prayer hall; the second floor is Ashkenazic, which holds services on Rosh Hashanah and Yom Kippur. The Sephardim hold services every day and there is a minyan every day in this synagogue at 7:30 a.m. and evenings at 8:15 p.m. Friday night services are held at 8:00 p.m. and Saturday mornings at 9:00 a.m.

The building maintains recreational rooms and classrooms, and many activities are offered. In the entrance lobby of the five-story edifice, just beyond the outside iron gates, is a tablet in Hebrew and Spanish dedicating the building to Maimonides. For kosher food, call or write the center office. There is also a store at Avenir 29 that sells kosher products, including kosher meat. It is usually open from 10:00 a.m. to 1:00 p.m. and 3:00 p.m. to 7:30 p.m. Friday, 10:00 a.m. to 1:00 p.m. Closed Saturdays.

Check on times when it is open by calling **Chabad**, Tel: 34-93-200-85-13 or 34-93-439-99-34. For kosher meals, please call ahead of time.

Kosher products can be obtained at the **Corte ingles** on Calle Diagonal. This store has a section of kosher products.

Maccabi Restaurant, Las Ramblas 79, 08002, Barcelona. Tel: 34-93-317-95-45. info@restaurantmaccabi.com

Taim, kosher catering. Carrer de la Ciutat de Granada, 44, Barcelona 08005. Tel: 34-934-61-96-42.

Program for Tourists

Mozaika is part of the Synagogue Maimonides and Community Center, info@mozaika.es. www.mozaika.es www.facebook.com/Revista Mozaika. It was created in 2008 and promotes the spread of Jewish culture from its fundamental pillars: publications, artistic happenings, literature festivals, exhibitions, and ongoing research into the Catalan Jewish legacy.

Toldot. Carrer Sant Domenech del Cal, 3, Barcelona. www.toldotbarcelona.com. Facebook: www.facebook.com/toldotbarcelona. Toldot, located in the center of the old Jewish quarter in Barcelona, is a branch of the Mozaika cultural program, which is dedicated to uncover the Jewish legacy of the city in an original, innovative and young way.

The building dates from the 14th century and offers guests a "gastronomic experience" of Jewish cuisine along with a story as well as enjoying other Jewish cultural activities. The group offers different guided routes to explore this program, ranging from the medieval history of the Catalan Jews to the contemporary history from 1918 to the present. The routes are endorsed by the University of Barcelona. The focus is to explain this rich history through its characters, places and the cultural and artistic expression of Catalan Jews.

Until recently, according to Victor Sorenssen, the Synagogue Maimonides and Community Center did not offer a program to attract tourists. But that has now changed, according to Victor, because of the Mozaika. A new cultural program will organize guided tours that will offer tourists visits to the old medieval Jewish quarter and to the contemporary history of the Jewish community since 1917, with a special emphasis on the Spanish Civil War and the role of the Jews in it. Also covered will be Spain and World War II. A visit to the synagogue is also planned. Invited are tourists who are passing through, but want to take part in cultural activities, exhibitions, and concerts.

Chabad Lubavitch de Barcelona, Calle Montnegre 14, Barcelona 08029. Tel: 34-93-410-0685. Info@chabadbarcelona.org, rabbi@chabadbarcelona.org, www.chabadbarcelona.org. Daily minyan 7:30 a.m.; Sunday, 8:30 a.m.; Friday night, at time of candle lighting; (Friday night dinner) Saturday morning 9:30 a.m. Rabbi Dovid M.M Libersohn, director, and Mrs Nechama Dina Libersohn, co-director.

Chabad Center is located at Calle sant honorat, 9, Barcelona, 08001. This site is not in use as a synagogue.

Bet Shalom-Comunidad Judia Progresista de Barcelona, Sardenya 414, Bajos, Barcelona, 08025. Tel: 34-696-810-863. Comunitat@betshalom.cat, www.betshalom.cat. The temple says in its mission statement, it is "egalitarian, participative, friendly and supportive community."

Comunitat Jueva ATID de Catalunya. Calle Castaner 27, Barcelona, 08017. Tel: 34-933-482-705. secretaria@atid.es, www.atid.es. The congregation is known as **ATID**, or future. Rabbi Ruben Sternschein heads this. Reform congregation of about 200 newcomers, many from South America.

Calle del Call. From the end of the eleventh century, the Jews of Barcelona lived in a special quarter in the heart of the old city, near the main gate and not far from the harbor. The main street of the quarter is still called "Calle del Call" or "Carrer del Call," "the quarter of the kahal." In the Catalan language, call is the equivalent of the Hebrew kahal, community. A part of the old ghetto wall is built into a Gothic house at **No. 5 Calle del Call.**

Maccabi Restaurant, Las Ramblas 79, 08002, Barcelona. Tel: 34-93-317-95-45. info@restaurantmaccabi.com

Taim, kosher catering. Carrer de la Ciutat de Granada, 44, Barcelona 08005. Tel: 34-934-61-96-42.

Girona: "The Pearl in the Oyster"

If ever there was a place where the footsteps of Jews still seem to echo in the streets, it is Gerona. This Spanish municipality lies in the province of Catalonia in the northeast corner of Spain between the Pyrenees and the Mediterranean Sea. Just 30 miles from the French border and 60 miles from Barcelona, Girona can be considered one of the spiritual resting places for "the wandering Jew." Little known is the fact that this city was one of the most important Jewish communities in the area, and that once it was the first center of Kabbala (mysticism) in Spain. Some people consider the well-preserved and old Jewish Quarter here to be the most representative in Europe after that of Prague.

In any analysis of Spain's attitude toward Jews today, it must be noted that reconciliation is the word in 21st century Spain. In booklets and documents, Spanish officials point out that "their history would be incomplete without the history of the Jewish community."

Probably for the first time in hundreds of years, a few Jewish families live in Gerona, a historic city for the Jewish people before they were expelled from Spain in 1492.

Spain is no exception to the European phenomenon whereby non-Jews care for and preserve old Jewish sites. Driven and organized in most cases by non-Jews—and financed by municipalities, Madrid's main government and the European Union—the rediscovery of Jewish sites includes not only uncovering a mikvah, but also collecting and preserving tombstones, or saving and restoring 500-year-old Hebrew parchments. Yes, history is being preserved in Catalonia and throughout Spain.

The *Red de Juderias de Espagna,* popularly known as the Red Network, is a network in Spain of 24 cities with Jewish quarters. www. redjuderias.org. Known as Routes of Sefarad, this association tells the story of the inheritance of Jewish communities that inhabited them. Officials hope that restoring Jewish sites will attract Jewish and non-Jewish travelers interested in learning about Spain's Jewish past.

Thus, changes are continuing in Spain concerning the Jewish past, present, and future. Catalan cities, for instance, are rapidly creating a new network called "Xarxa de Calls." And in terms of Jewish history and Jewish preservation, Gerona, as noted, is the "pearl in the oyster."

The Call or Jewish Quarter of Girona

An interesting area to visit is the Call itself, the Jewish district in Gerona, which probably had its origins back in the ninth century. Renovated in the early 1980s, it may, without doubt, be one of the most interesting visits in Jewish Spain. There were about 300 Jews in the area, also known in Arabic as "Aljama" (or Alsima).

The steep, narrow streets surrounding the broad avenue, **Carrer de la Forca**, were home to the Jewish community of Girona in medieval times. The life of the "Aljama," was concentrated around the synagogue which, over time, was housed in different locations.

Today visitors can go to the **Centre Bonastruc ca Porta**, a complex of buildings in an enclosure that preserves the essence of the former Jewish presence. The complex contains the **Institut d'Estudis Nahmanides** (Nahmanides Institute of Jewish Studies), which includes a book and gift shop, an attractive library rooms for lectures and special programs, and a **Jewish Museum** which opened in July 2000. Tradition has it that the center, which is covered with the mystery of history, is built on or near the site of a former synagogue.

Further information can be obtained at the Patronat Municipal Call de Girona for the above mentioned Museum and Institute. Tel: 34-972-216-761. callgirona@ajgirona.cat.

Since 1992, the city council of Girona manages The Patronat Municipal Call de Girona, www.girona.cat/call/eng/index.php, which sponsors a series of lectures on Jewish topics, which are also designed to reflect the various cultures existing in feudal Catalonia, as well as today. Experts on culture, philosophy, art, and literature share their knowledge at monthly sessions held at the Institute, mostly in Spanish or Catalan.

Another site to visit is **The Monastery of St. Pere de Galligants** built between the 11th and 12th centuries. This was a Benedictine monastery and now houses the Archeological Museum. It contains a large collection of prehistoric objects as well as those from the Greek and Roman periods. Its unique collection of Hebrew tombstones, inscribed in Hebrew, will be moved to the **Jewish Museum.**

Further information can be obtained at the **Centre Bonastruc ca Porta**, Bonastruc ca Porta, Girona. Tel/fax: 34-972-216-761, or e-mail: secretaria@redjuderias.org.

Girona also participates in the European Days of Jewish Culture. www.Jewishheritage.org/web/

Perhaps Girona's best-known citizen is Rabbi Moses ben Nachman (Nachmanides) who was born here and often called the "Rabbi of Gerona." He has been described as the outstanding personality in Jewry during the thirteenth century. Nachmanides' halachic works rank among the masterpieces of rabbinic literature and many of them have become classics. We also know Nachmanides as a philosopher, Kabbalist, biblical exegete, poet, and physician. As we have seen, there is a street named after him, Bonastruc da Porta, his name in the Catalan language.

Nachmanides was chief rabbi of Catalonia. He is famous for the disputation in Barcelona in July 1263, when at the request of King James I, he debated several Dominicans, including the convert Pablo Christiani. Permitted to speak as he wished, Nachmanides (also known as the Ramban) took full advantage of the opportunity and spoke frankly, for which the king rewarded him. The distinguished historian Yitzhak Baer says of him, "His personality was the product of diverse influences: the Spanish cultural background, French talmudist, German pietism, the mysticism of the Kabbala and an acquaintance with Christian theological writings." He wanted Jewish thought to embrace mystical ideas.

After the Barcelona Disputation, Nachmanides codified his views at the request of the local bishop. Still the Dominicans attempted to put him on trial. Even with the king's help in obtaining his release, Nachmanides barely succeeded in escaping from Spain to Israel.

Toledo

Experts say that if you have only one day to visit Spain, spend it in touring Toledo, once the ancient capital of Spain. Like Florence in Italy, the city is preserved as a museum.

Historic Toledo boasts that it is the most fascinating, aristocratic metropolis in all Spain and among the most interesting cities of Europe. It still stands today just as the great Spanish artist El Greco painted it centuries ago. Indeed, this city of about 84,000 persons houses his masterpieces, as well as those of artists Goya and Velazquez. Toledo, 40 miles from Madrid, rests on a mountain. A deep-etched gorge caused by the winding Tagus River surrounds it on three sides.

In the Civil War of 1936, the streets of Toledo actually "ran red with blood." The alcazar, which housed an infantry academy, was held by the Fascists. For 72 days, Franco's forces withstood wave after wave of fierce attacks from the Republic's troops and survived.

As the seat of the Spanish primate, Toledo records Catholic history. Its main cathedral, a Gothic masterpiece with paintings by El Greco, stands at the top of the hills of the city. Joseph L. Andrew, Jr., observed in The Jewish Advocate of February 23, 1989: "It is apparent even from the city's geography that the Jews had a less lofty status than the Catholics, as you must descend from the summit of Toledo's hills with their cathedrals down to the Jewish Quarter, near the bottom, through narrow lanes, past weathered golden-hued limestone buildings."

Toledo is one of the few towns in Spain where remnants of Jewish edifices have been preserved. Jews came to Toledo in the fourth and fifth centuries. By the seventh century, Toledo possessed a large Jewish population that helped the Moors capture the city from the

Visigoths. By the eleventh century, 40,000 Jews resided in Toledo; one-third of the city was Jewish and they lived in peace with the Moors and Christians. The name Toledo comes from "Toledoth," the city of "generations." Legend has it that Toledo was founded 4,000 years ago by a direct descendant of Noah. Others say that the first Jewish exiles to Toledo were members of the tribe of Benjamin.

What we do know for certain, however, is that, because of its outstanding Jewish scholarship and community structure during the Middle Ages, Toledo became known as the "second Jerusalem." Perched on a hill and surrounded by walls, it still resembles Jerusalem. Some say it was the "most important Jewish city in Spain."

As a center of Spanish Jewry, Toledo, with its schools and libraries, attracted poets, translators, and writers. Yehudah HaLevi, the great Hebrew poet, resided here. Surely not all Jews in Toledo were scholars. They served as tailors, felt makers, masons, butchers, farmers, and craftsmen. The Jewish Quarter in Toledo, a spacious area, functioned virtually as a city in itself. For about 600 years, Jews lived in peace. In the twelfth century, there were 12,000 Jews there. But in 1391, mobs attacked and nearly slaughtered the entire Jewish community of Toledo. In a moment of weakness, many wealthy Jews sought to save their lives by converting; they became New Christians. Expulsion followed. Today, the Cathedral of Toledo, completed in 1477, contains, on an interior wall, a plaque memorializing the Expulsion of the Jews in 1492. Despite its sad history, Toledo has been named the "World Sephardic Capital."

Recent reports indicate there are nine Jewish families in Toledo, but they are not organized. When I visited Toledo, I found a restaurant that is run by a Moroccan Jew. This eating spot was not kosher, but it had a Jewish-Israeli atmosphere. Many Israelis came here. The owner said he conducts a Passover Seder for 140 friends and their families every year. The establishment is near the El Transito Synagogue (see below). He told me he knew a man who lights candles every Friday night and does not eat pork. The man did not know the religious significance of what he did, but he said he was told to do it by a grandparent. Shadows of the Marranos, the secret Jews, over and over again are perceptible in modern democratic Spain.

SYNAGOGUES IN TOLEDO

Once Toledo housed numerous synagogues. Today, there are only two. But these two are famous and a "must" on a tour of Jewish sites in Toledo. They are located in the eastern side of what was once the Jewish Quarter. Indeed, Santa Maria la Blanca and El Transito are considered two great architectural treasures of medieval European Jewry.

Santa Maria la Blanca, with its inspired Almohad art, was founded in 1203—the oldest Jewish monument in Toledo. Like all medieval synagogues, it is unimpressive on the outside. But the inside is a forest of 32 pillars supporting a long vista of horseshoe-shaped arches, surrounded by limestone block walls. The octagonal columns are richly decorated with designs of a Moorish-Jewish motif. There are arched galleries and you can see signs of a separate women's upper gallery. In the fifteenth century, it was converted into a church by Vicente Ferrer, who stirred up many riots against Jews and was responsible for many conversions. The church later became a military barracks, a warehouse, and even a dance hall. Now it is a national museum.

In 2017, the Federation of Spanish Jewish Communities officially called for the restitution of this city's main synagogue that was turned into Santa Maria la Blanca. The request was made to the Toledo diocese.

Santa Maria la Blanca greets nearly a half million visitors per year, making it the third most visited monument in Toledo after the cathedral and the Church of Santo Tome.

El Transito Synagogue got its name from a church that the building housed after the Inquisition. Samuel Levi Abulafia built the structure in about 1360. He was a finance minister and advisor to Pedro the Cruel, king of Castille, who ruled from 1350 to 1369. He not only managed Pedro's finances but, as a diplomat, defended his interests. His reward was the king's permission to build a new synagogue despite clergy and city opposition. Barnet Litvinoff writes that Abulafia "maintained a style in Toledo almost as regal as the masters." He wanted the building to be a private synagogue for his own house, which still stands and supposedly from which there was an entrance to the synagogue. The artist El Greco lived in this house, which some say is the Casa El Greco (House of El Greco), now known as the **El Greco Museum.**

To build the synagogue, Abulafia, it is said, imported cedars from Lebanon, as did Solomon when he built the Temple in Jerusalem. The graceful Moorish arches, the artistic designs, and the quotations from the Torah that line the entire length of the synagogue walls at ceiling level, bring the entire Golden Age back to life. The building boasts alabaster columns, a wall with stone tracery, and 54 elegant windows.

The building of El Transito Synagogue contains the **Sephardic Museum and Library** and is located on the **Calle de Samuel Levi**, an old ghetto lane named after Samuel Levi Abulafia. The museum contains Sephardic relics, documents, other pieces of Judaica, reproductions, and manuscripts. Abulafia hid his wealth here in the house. He had a long tunnel dug out connecting his home in Toledo with the Tagus River so that, in case of a popular uprising, he and other Jews could escape. It did not help him. Pedro the Cruel tortured and executed him.

El Transito served successively as a church, a monastery, a hospital, a military storehouse, and army barracks. But in 1877, it was designated a national monument. The building cannot be restored to its original state because no one knows what it looked like.

In 1964, the El Transito Synagogue became a museum for the history of the Jews in Spain. A synagogue service celebrating the opening of the museum holds the distinction of being one of the first public Jewish meetings in Spain since Jews were expelled.

Marbella

Synagogue, Beth El, 21 Calle Jazmines, Urbanizacion El Real, Km. 184. Marbella.Tel: 34-952-82-49-83. FAX: 34-952-778-243. cimarbella@yahoo.es. This synagogue has an Ashkenazic prayer service and a Sephardic one and is the headquarters of the Marbella Jewish community. Beth El also has the distinction of being the first synagogue built in Andalusia after 1492. The building was consecrated in 1978.

Tudela

There are no Jews in Tudela. At least that's what I was told.

But I went there anyway as it is the birthplace of the great Jewish travel writer Benjamin of Tudela, one of the greatest travelers that ever lived, certainly of the greatest Jewish travelers. Rabbi Benjamin of Tudela wondered over the greater part of the civilized world in the second half of the 12th century.

The tourist will find various plaques and statues in the public square, plaques that the city put up in 1960, the 800th anniversary of his journey.

Jewish authors come to Tudela for inspiration, for it was also the native city of two other famous Jewish writers of previous generations: Judah Halevi, born about 1075, and Abraham Ibn Ezra, born 1092.

Tudela, a several hour drive northwest form Barcelona, reminds one of the history of the Jews in Spain. This author went to see the area of the old *juderia*, the Jewish quarter located in the fortified part of the city. It was amazing to walk the narrow streets in the bright, hot Spanish sun.

Tudela in the province of Navarre, in Spain. With the final expulsion of the Moors from Granada in 1492, religious intolerance became the policy of Christian Spain. Jews were faced with a choice between conversion and banishment. Several hundred families in the city were baptized. Those *marronos* (secret Jews), however, were subject to scorn, their names being published in a great roll called, "*La Manta,*" and exposed in the nave of the Cathedral of Tudela. Many of them immigrated to France, ending Jewish life here.

But 850 years later, neither Jews, nor the City of Tudela, have forgotten. As I ended my trip to Spain, it was with a deep heart at those who were exiled, but a smile that day, for Jews were returning to Spain and even promised citizenship. "The Jewish people live."

Suggested Reading

Ashtor, Eliyahu. *The Jews of Moslem Spain.* Philadelphia: Jewish Publication Society of America, 1973.

Avni, Haim. *Spain, the Jews and Franco.* Philadelphia: Jewish Publication Society of America, 1982.

Baer, Yitzhak. *A History of the Jews in Christian Spain.* Philadelphia: Jewish Publication Society of America, 1966.

Cohen, Israel. *Travels in Jewry.* New York: Dutton, 1953.

Kayserling, Dr. M. *Christopher Columbus and the Participation of the Jews in the Spanish and Portuguese Discoveries.* New York: Hermon, 1968.

Lipschitz, Rabbi Chaim U. Franco. *Spain, the Jews and the Holocaust.* New York: Ktav, 1984.

Litvinoff, Barnet. *Fourteen Ninety Two: The Decline of Medievalism and the Rise of the Modern Age.* New York: Charles Scribner's Sons, 1991.

Morris, Jan. *Spain.* Oxford University Press, 1979.

Morton, H. V. *A Stranger in Spain.* New York: Dodd, Mead, 1955.

Netanyahu, Benzion. *The Marranos of Spain.* Millwood, N.Y: Kraus Reprint Company, 1973.

Payne, Stanley G. *The Franco Regime, 1936-1975.* Madison: University of Wisconsin Press, 1989.

———. *A History of Spain and Portugal.* Madison: University of Wisconsin Press, 1973.

Pritchett, V. S. *Marching Spain.* London: Ernest Benn, 1928.

Raphael, Chaim. *The Road from Babylon: The Story of Sephardic and Oriental Jews.* New York: Harper & Row, 1985.

Roth, Cecil. *A History of the Marranos.* New York: Hermon Press, 1974.

———. *The Spanish Inquisition.* New York: Norton, 1964.

Wiesenthal, Simon. *Sails of Hope: The Secret Mission of Christopher Columbus.* New York: Macmillan, 1973.

Yahil, Leni. *The Holocaust: The Fate of European Jewry, 1932-1945.* New York: Oxford University Press, 1990.

Portugal
Saying the Mourner's Prayer
In Rossio Square

Think of Portugal and you think of the sea, explorers and navigators, and weather-beaten faces of fishermen hauling in the day's catch.

"With its shoreline facing the Atlantic Ocean to the west and to the south, the Portuguese had a long tradition of seafaring as fisherman and traders," says Miriam Estensen in her book *Discovery: The Quest for the Great South Land.* Its location soon determined its vocation to the sea and let us remember that two-thirds of the earth is converged by water.

Think of Portugal and you consider driving up to Estoril, the fashionable resort, and Cascais, "the town of fishermen and kings." You see yourself sitting in the coffeehouses, drinking smooth port wine and strong coffee, and listening to moody *fados*, those melancholy songs of the Portuguese fishermen. Think of Portugal and you think of Lisbon, the city that attracts many tourists. "By day Lisbon has a naïve theatrical quality that enchants and captivates, but by night it is a fairy-tale city, descending over lighted terraces to the sea, like a woman in festive garments going down to meet her dark lover," wrote Eric Maria Remarque, in his novel, *The Night in Lisbon.*

Some people label Portugal an anachronism. Long ago, Prince Henry the Navigator, Vasco da Gama, Magellan, and Cabral, who sailed uncharted waters, led Portugal into its golden age as a great power. Few European countries reached such seafaring heights. But then it crumbled and lost its colony, Brazil, and later was ruled by a dictatorship. Finally, a peaceful revolution, "the Revolution of Flowers" of 1974, would install a democracy.

Portugal is one of the smallest countries in Europe. Containing 35,516 square miles, or one-sixth of the Iberian Peninsula, it is located on the far western edge of the peninsula. Because Iberia was isolated from Europe for centuries, people said Europe began and ended at the Pyrenees. No longer! A free, democratic atmosphere envelops the country today, bringing tourists to Portugal.

Portugal is a founding member of NATO and is committed to European integration and good transatlantic relations.

Let us also remember that Portugal is a member of the European Union since 1986. A steady economic growth was the hallmark of Portugal, that is, until 2000 when henceforth its economy grew by one percent between 2003 and 2012. Portugal suffered badly as a result of the global recession of the late 2000s. In 2011, the government applied to the European Commission for financial assistance to avoid a debt default. By 2014, however, the economy was recovering, according to the International Monetary Fund, (IMF).

As we shall see, Portugal, like Spain, has offered Sephardim all over the world, an opportunity to become citizens of their country. As President of the Portuguese Republic, Marcelo Rebelo de Sousa said in a visit to the Lisbon Synagogue: Portugal "should recognize and cherish its Jewish heritage, emphasizing its role in shaping national identity." He was correct in declaring the above, for the Portuguese Inquisition in 1538 was at times crueler than its earlier Spanish one. Portugal "persecuted, tortured and burned at the stake thousands of Jews."

For Jewish travelers, the Jewish connection lies just beneath the surface, more in knowledge of the past than in the sites themselves. Most of the cities and towns contained an area that was assigned to the Jews and known as *"Juderia."* Today, many of them can be found. For starters in your visit, ask if there is a "street of the Jews."

A Brief History

Some sources say the Jews migrated to Portugal after the destruction of Jerusalem by Nebuchadnezzar, settling there before the establishment of the first Portuguese kingdom. By the year 900, with the Muslims in control, Jews worked as winegrowers. In the reign of Sancho I in the twelfth century, Don Solomon Jachia, a Jew, was a field marshal commanding the Portuguese Army.

For a long time Portugal befriended Jews. Before the sixteenth century, most of the rulers of Portugal considered the Jews a valuable resource, especially their financial and commercial talents. Christian noblemen often married daughters of wealthy Jews.

Until 1497, no profession or occupation was barred to Portuguese Jews. They were active in government, philosophy, botany, finance, medicine, and astronomy. They improved Portuguese typography so that it could compete with Italy and Germany. A Hebrew printing press was set up in Lisbon at the end of the fifteenth century. Vasco da Gama, who discovered the sea route to India, was advised by Jewish scholars and financed by Jewish businessmen. He also followed maps and instruments made by Jewish manufacturers. Jewish physicians were on board his ships. Jews possessed a great reputation in the sciences. Portuguese Jewish doctors rivaled their co-religionists in Spain.

During the thirteenth to fifteenth centuries, Portugal's rulers even allowed a synagogue to develop in Lisbon. By the end of the fifteenth century, Portugal's 200,000 Jews made up one-fifth of the population. Included were many of the several hundred thousand Jewish refugees who had been expelled from Spain in 1492. The reception, while not warm, was tolerant. Jews were forced to pay a poll tax of eight cruzados per adult and agree not to remain longer than eight months.

Romance, intrigue, and expulsion now entered the history of the Portuguese Jewish community in the person of Emanuel I, the Fortunate (1495-1521). He was an unfortunate monarch for the Jews. Ambitious, he soon initiated Machiavellian scenarios. Assuming power in 1495, he hoped to rule all of Iberia. He would do this simply by marrying the Spanish princess Isabella, the daughter of Ferdinand and Isabella. But as a condition for marriage, the Spanish king and queen demanded that Emanuel expel the Jews from Portugal. He had to "purify" his kingdom, and then, as Barnet Litvinoff writes, he could "Christianize Portugal."

Emanuel reluctantly banished the Jews and Muslims in December 1496, a month after the royal marriage, but soon changed his edict—because he needed their revenues. He tried to persuade them to convert to Christianity. He then went so far as to strike at the parents through the children. "Be baptized or die," he decreed. On March 19, 1497, all Jewish children between the ages of 4 and 14 were forcibly baptized in one single day in an attempt to keep the parents in Portugal. On another occasion, shortly thereafter, when 20,000 parents were forced to gather in Lisbon, only seven or eight badly beaten persons escaped the forced baptism. But like their Spanish brothers and sisters, these Jews would become Marranos and flee the country. By 1499, however, Marranos were denied emigration and had to revert to subterfuge to leave.

For several decades, Jews in Portugal managed to ward off the Inquisition. However, a papal brief on May 23, 1536, ordered Portugal to establish a Holy Office of the Inquisition to be patterned after the Spanish model.

An auto-da-fé was held in Lisbon on September 20, 1544. Sebastion Jose de Carvalho e Mello halted the Inquisition in 1821. History knows him as Marqués de Pombal. During the three centuries of the Inquisition, more than 40,000 persons were indicted, of whom 30,000 were sentenced at autos-da-fé in Portugal.

About 1,200 persons were actually burned at the stake. Sir George Young suggests that had the Jews been left alone, Lisbon might have become the commercial capital of Europe, a position the country was firmly headed toward a hundred years before London.

The Portuguese Jews who left Iberia between 1540 and 1800 would establish communities or join their Sephardic brothers and sisters in such cities as Venice, Hamburg, Amsterdam, London, and Bordeaux in Europe; Recife in Brazil; Surinam in South America; Curaçao, Jamaica, Barbados, Nevis, and St. Thomas in the West Indies; and New York City and Newport, Rhode Island; in the New World. Some of them became international Jewish personalities. One son of a Portuguese Marrano whom we know as Baruch Spinoza, the seventeenth century philosopher, later would be excommunicated by his own people in Holland.

Trade caused the return of Jews to Portugal after 400 years. It is said that an admiral invited two Jews from Gibraltar to come to Portugal to create a commercial outlet. The two merchants, Isaac Aboab and Moses Levi, accepted the offer. Thus began the return of the Jews to Portugal.

By 1820, the city of Faro had a small Jewish community. Jews began to arrive as merchants when foreigners were allowed freedom of worship under the Charter of 1826. In 1868, the Jews were recognized as a colony. At the turn of the century, Eastern European Jews found in Portugal a haven from persecution.

Official recognition permitting religious services was granted to Jews in 1892. A synagogue was erected in 1902. The new Portuguese republic, established by the revolution of 1910, finally gave the Jewish community official status in 1912.

During the Holocaust, neutral Portugal adopted a liberal immigration policy, with about 45,000 Jewish refugees entering the country. Later, Portugal would at times withhold asylum because of its concern that the country would be overrun with refugees, and sailings across the Atlantic were limited. Still, it granted consular protection to Jews in occupied countries. Indeed, Portugal, with other neutral countries in 1944, managed to save many Hungarian Jews. Ironically, even as late as the Holocaust, some Christians or descendants of Marranos would help Jews. One such person was Aristedes de Sausa Mendes do Amaral e Abranches, a Portuguese consul in Marseilles. He issued 10,000 visas to stranded Jews in defiance of his own government. He did the same thing in Bordeaux. (With a Portuguese visa you could travel through Spain). Ousted from the diplomatic corps, where he worked around the clock to save Jews, he was never reinstated, according to Rabbi Chaim U. Lipschitz, but was helped by a Jewish organization. He died in 1954, forgotten and impoverished. In 1961, Israel and Yad Vashem planted 20 trees in the Martyrs Forest in his memory, and in 1967, posthumously awarded him a medal in deep appreciation and gratitude.

The story of Portuguese Jewry makes it seem like a miracle that this Jewish community is still alive. After World War II, 12,000 Jews resided in Portugal, which has a population of slightly more than 10 million. After shrinking in numbers, the Jewish community has grown and is active. About 800 Jews call Lisbon their home.

Lisbon is the capital, chief port, and largest metropolis of the country. Strategically, it is "the most splendidly situated capital in Europe," says V. S. Pritchett in *At Home and Abroad: Travel Essays*. Lisbon—called the quintessence of Portugal—is home to over two million Portuguese. This city, whose sea aroma wafts from the Atlantic Ocean, may pale next to expansive Paris or London. Yet, there is much for the tourist to see and do, including the Sao Carlos Opera House, Castle of Sao George, Tower of Belem, the Museum of Ancient Art, the city's many public squares, statues of national heroes, tree-lined avenues and small parks, and the 25th of April Bridge, one of the longest suspension bridges in the world.

One of the most recent developments in events regarding the "Sephardic world," was that Portugal, seeking to make amends for past wrongdoing, joined Spain in adopting laws allowing citizenship for descendants of Sephardic Jews—the term commonly used for those who once lived in the Iberian Peninsula—persecuted during the Inquisition.

Portugal approved a law in March 2015 that grants citizenship rights to the descendants of Jews it persecuted 500 years ago. The rights apply to those who can demonstrate a 'traditional connection" to Portuguese Sephardic Jews, such as through "family names, family language and direct or collateral ancestry."

Applications must be vetted by the Portuguese Jewish community institutions in Lisbon or Porto. Those communities are responsible for checking existing documentation of the applicants' ancestors, often written in Ladino. Portuguese authorities have approved only 7.5 percent of the nearly 4,000 applications filed since March 2015, it was reported by JTA in the fall of 2016.

The Portuguese citizenship was granted to applicants whose families were integrated into communities known as "Sephardim: Turkey, Greece, old Palestinian, former Yugoslavia, Bulgaria, Syria, Lebanon, Macedonia, Morocco, Tunisia, Libya, Egypt, etc," according to the Porto Jewish Community website.

A newspaper report in *Ynet News*, based in Israel, indicated that

3,546 applications for Portuguese citizenship had been submitted and remain pending at the end of 2016 and 292 approved.

Since the UK decided to exit the European Union in 2016, growing numbers of British Jews of Sephardic origin have applied for citizenship in Portugal under the law making amends for the expulsion of Jews from the Iberian Peninsula more than 500 years ago, according to the Guardian newspapers. The reason for such a rush for Portuguese citizenship is that many desire to obtain a European Union passport which "has its advantages" while others wish for a recognition of their Sephardic routes and their "wider European identity." A rise in racist, post-referendum attacks across the UK is also adding to fears.

Notable Portuguese Jews

While the Jewish schools of Portugal may not have produced a Maimonides, they could boast of their Abravanels, as well as many others whose names resound among great literati.

Other Jews contributed much to Portugal. Abraham Zacuto, innovator of navigational instruments such as the first astrolabe in copper and astronomical tables, also emigrated from Spain to Portugal at the time of the expulsion and went on to become royal astronomer to advise Vasco da Gama on his voyage to India. In 1497, when King Emanuel forced the Jews to convert, Zacuto left Portugal and went to Spain. Cresques headed the Academy of Navigation founded by Prince Henry the Navigator. Pedro Teixeira explored South American territories in the early seventeenth century. Joseph Vechino was a court physician and advisor to Joao II. The nation's first printing press was set up by Samuel Porteira. And of course Jewish scholar Judah Abravanel served as royal treasurer of Joao I.

Jewish Lisbon

ROSSIO SQUARE

Imagine landing in the middle of Lisbon's main square and reciting "kaddish," the Hebrew prayer for the dead. That is what a group of Jews would do if they stood in the Plaza Rossio (Rossio Square) in this busy capital of Portugal. Here in the center of the city, not far from the Royal Palace in 1506, between 2,000 and 4,000 New Christians, known as Marranos, were butchered.

In the Plaza Rossio stood the Palace of Estaos, which housed the Inquisition. The building was destroyed by the earthquake of 1755, and the National Theatre of Dona Maria was constructed in its place.

During the Inquisition, Jews were forcibly baptized at the Church of Sao Domingo, which is located in the adjacent square. Rossio Square is a good spot to stand and reflect on the world of the Marranos, a world in which no one could trust anyone.

Plaza Rossio, or *Pracal ldo Rossio,* is actually the popular name of the Pedro IV Square. Located in Pombaline Downtown of Lisbon, it has been one of the main squares since the Middle Ages. Popular revolts and celebrations, bullfights, and executions have been held here. Today, it is the place where Lisbon natives and tourists meet. The Column of Pedro IV stands in the middle of the square.

A vast difference existed between Spain and Portugal in terms of the Inquisition. Portuguese Jews had 20 to 30 years longer to adjust to Christianity and practice Judaism secretly before the Inquisition came on the Portuguese scene. This meant that crypto-Judaism in Portugal contained deep roots and enabled these New Christians to revert to their former Jewish faith whenever they managed to escape to free lands.

But Elias H. Lindo writes in *History of the Jews of Spain and Portugal* that the Inquisition of Portugal exercised the same cruelty as that of Spain towards the New Christians. Those who were discovered or suspected of practicing Jewish rites, and under torture confessed their Judaism, suffered death and expired in the flames of the autos-da-fé.

The Inquisition concentrated on rooting out all traces of Judaism. Basically it succeeded. In fact, many of the victims of the Inquisition were not guilty. There are those historians who claim that the purpose of the Inquisition was really to enrich church coffers. But it never completely crushed the Marrano movement, which is important to understand.

The visitor on a trip to Portugal keeps hearing and seeing the word Marrano. The term Marrano is derived from a Spanish word meaning swine; it was an ugly, contemptuous word. Jews prefer to use the Hebrew word *anussim,* meaning those whose change of religion was forced upon them, but "who lived according to the precepts and laws of their ancestral faith," writes Dr. M. Kayserling.

In Portugal and Spain, they were also called New Christians, or "Conversos." The church was suspicious of the Conversos. They suspected that these newcomers had not given up their Sabbath and holidays, assembled in subterranean or other secret synagogues, and practiced Jewish rites in their homes. The true-born Christians, the old Christians, "who were free from any taint of Moorish or Jewish blood," frequently participated in riots against the New Christians.

These secret Portuguese Jews, some believe, are considered the first modern Jews of the Diaspora. They set the stage for the center of world trade, moving from southern to northern Europe. The Marranos were always looking for a home where they could openly proclaim their religion. Many of them, joined by their Spanish and Portuguese brothers and sisters, settled in the West Indies, but especially in Brazil. They also tried to get to Holland, which had turned Protestant and welcomed persons of all religions. Remember, Marranos were valued because European businessmen perceived them as having connections with relatives and friends throughout the world. These Jewish merchants and entrepreneurs knew Spanish and Portuguese. They had helped make Lisbon the commercial center of the continent. They maintained contact with Jews who had settled in North Africa after the 1492 expulsion from Spain. They controlled more than a quarter of the stock of the Dutch East India Company. But even though they were respected traders outside of Portugal, many were still afraid to say openly that they were Jews. So they called themselves Portuguese. Thus, "Portuguese" became synonymous with "Jewish." Others, as soon as they felt secure, openly professed Judaism. To understand the story of the Marranos is to understand Portuguese Jewish history.

Revival. That is the best way to describe the Jewish community of Lisbon, which a decade and a half ago many would have said was in its last throes. Its Jewish population has grown by over a hundred; there is a continual influx of Israelis moving in to the Portuguese capital. Best estimate for the Jewish population in Portugal itself is about 800, with 300 in Lisbon, 200 in Oporto, 60 in Algarve, 50 in Belmonte and several hundred in the rest of the nation.

KOSHER FOOD IN LISBON

Kosher meals can be obtained by calling **Mrs. R. Assor,** rua Rodrigo de Fonseca, 38, Lisbon. Tel: 386-03-96. FAX: 351-21-386-63-36. Also private kosher meals at Mrs. Patricia, lisbon.kosher@clix.pt.

Kosher food can be obtained at **El Corte Ingles Department Store** Av. António Augusto de Aguiar 31, 1069-413 Lisbon. Tel: 351-21-371-1700. Kosher food is located in the store's supermarket.

Liberty Supermarket, Largo de Sao Sebastiao, da Pedeira 90, Lisbon. Tel: 351-213-545-243. www.jojasliberty.

For more on kosher food in Lisbon, check out www.cilisboa.org/rel.kosher/httm.

SYNAGOGUES AND ORGANIZATIONS IN LISBON

Shaare Tikvah Synagogue, rua Alexandre Herculano, 59, Lisbon.

Tel: 351-213-931-130. administrativo@cilisboa.org. www.clisboa.org. Facebook: https://www.facebook.com/cilisboa. For those travelers who wish to join the congregation for Shabbat services, contact the administrative services to make prior and necessary identification, no later than Friday, noon, before the Sabbath. E-mail: seguranca@cilisboa.org.

Sabbath services are held on Friday evenings and Saturday mornings. A *kiddush* is held on Saturday. The cornerstone bears the Hebrew name, Kehilla Kedusha Shaare Tikvah, in Portuguese, Portas da Esperanca (Gates of Hope). On the Holy Ark, it says in Hebrew, "Know before whom thou standest."

The building contains 20-foot wooden gates and high concrete walls that enclose the synagogue. A beautiful courtyard extends behind the building. There are several candelabra, common to Sephardic houses of prayer, in the sanctuary. Services are Friday night at 8:00 p.m. and Saturday morning at 9:00 a.m. The service is Sephardic ritual.

In the year 2002, this famous synagogue underwent renovation as a tribute to its 100th anniversary. The second floor of this house of worship serves as a museum and includes memorabilia of the community.

Within walking distance from hotels, the building features a blend of Eastern and North African styles inside. In 1948, the congregation rebuilt sections of the building. The then chief rabbi of France, Jacob Kaplan, attended this public dedication ceremony that symbolized the rebirth of the Portuguese Jewish community. "After an interval of 500 years, the inhabitants of Lisbon looked on with curiosity and admiration at the procession of the sacred Jewish scrolls, which their forefathers had outlawed, despoiled and put to flames," wrote one reporter. In 1949, a second balcony and additional seats were added to the synagogue. As you walk into the synagogue, on the left-hand side you will see a memorial room to victims of the Holocaust. Refugees from Nazi-occupied France knew that neutral Portugal was their best hope of fleeing the Germans in World War II.

Chabad: Chabad holds activities and classes in Cascais and Lisbon. Contact Chabad at Tel: 351-910-345-754. info@chabadportugal.com. chabadportugal.com. Chabad also sponsors its annual Chanukah celebration in Cascais at Cascais Bay known as praia dos pescaddores. Chabad Portugal holds the event in partnership with the Municipality of Cascais. In Lisbon, the ceremony is held at Park Eduardo VII in partnership with the Communidade Israelita de Lisboa, Chabad Portugal, and the Municipality of Lisbon. At press time, Chabad did not possess their own building.

Chabad sponsors events in Lisbon at different venues.

To visit Chabad, best to email ahead of time. Info@chabadportugal. com. Chabad invites tourists to join them for Shabbat dinners. At press time, a daily *minyan* had not been established.

Rabbi Eli and Raizel Rosenfeld arrived in Portugal at the end of 2010, the first full-time Chabad emissaries in one of the few countries at the time that had yet to see a permanent Chabad House. The rabbi notes that business travelers, tourists or residents in the small community join each other for holidays and other celebrations.

Maccabi Country Club, Quinta da Luz-R. Gonçalves Correia, 8 Albarraque-Conselho de Rio de Mouro. Lisboa Tel.Fax (+351) 21-911-11-88. maccabicountryclub@gmail.com

Embaixada de Israel-Israel Embassy Rua Antonio Enes 16-1000 Lisboa. Tel: (+351) 21-045-5500 www.http://embassies.gov.il/lisboa/Pages/default.aspx.

Synagoga Ohel Jacob-Communidade Judaica Hehaver, Lisbon, Tel: 351-217-975-283. info@hehaver-oheljacob.org, www.hehaver-oheljacob, org.

Progressive Ritual Synagogue, the only Askenazi synaggogue in Portugal, founded in 1934. Affiliated Member of the EUPJ / WUPJ (European Union of Progressive Judaism / World Union of Progressive Judaism) since April 2016.

Comunidade Israelita de Lisboa, Rua do Monte Olivete 16, r/c -1200-280 Lisboa–Portugal. Tel: (+351) 213 931 130. FAX: (+351) 213 931 139E-mail: administrativo@cilisboa.org. www.cilisboa.org, https://www.facebook.com/cilisboa.

The Lisbon Jewish community has been trying for years to combat opposition to a Jewish Museum in Lisbon in the neighborhood of Alfama. That neighborhood is opposed to the ongoing construction of the four-story Jewish museum being built there. Residents say they were not consulted about the plan to erect the Jewish Museum of Lisbon in Alfama, whose signing in 2016 ended decades of lobbying on the part of Portuguese Jews for the construction of a Jewish museum in Lisbon—one of the few capital cities in Western Europe without such an institution, according to JTA. Still, **The Jewish Museum** was expected to be opened late 2017 or 2018.

Belmonte, Guarda, and Covilha

Visit the towns of Belmonte, Guarda, and Covilha. Marranos live here as well as in **Monsanto** and **Castelo de Vide**. Samuel Schwartz, the Polish Jewish mining engineer, discovered these villages in 1919.

Belmonte Jewish Museum, Rua da Portela 4, 6250, Belmonte. Tel: 351-275-0888-698. Museujudaico.belmonte@net.vodafone.pt. www.

cm-belmonte.pt/museumudaco.html This museum reopened in August, 2017 after renovation. **Belmonte** is a farming and wine area in the northern province of Beira Alta. In 1988, Michael Fink reported a community center of two cramped rooms: "On the walls are a tiny Israeli flag, a roster of the members of the community and a generic synagogue dedication in Hebrew." Recent reports indicated that there are 200 Marranos in Belmonte, with a rabbi from Israel to lead them.

Schwartz said that Marranos in Belmonte "were completely ignorant of the existence of other Jews with different religious rites." The old Marrano women who acted as "keepers of the faith" did not recognize Schwartz's Hebrew prayers and rejected him. Obviously, these Marranos lived outwardly as Christians—they attended Catholic Church services and joined in Catholic sacraments—but kept alive secretly some form of Jewish rites. Observers say their distrust of outsiders made them wary even of fellow Jews. (They seemed to believe that they were the only remaining pure Jews).

More and more, conversos or crypto-Jews, are formally converting to Judaism, such as in Belmonte. Even today, Belmonte's Jews find it hard to be open about their religion. They still attend Mass with their Catholic neighbors at the village church where, for so many generations, they have been baptized, married, and buried under marble tombstones, writes Paul Ames of the Associated Press in *The Jewish Week* of June 22, 1990. According to Colette Avital, Israel's former ambassador to Portugal, "They've lived on the outside like Christians. On the inside, in their houses, they were not Christians, they were Jews, and they have transmitted this from father to son.

Descendants of the original Marranos who still live in and around Belmonte are uncircumcised and baptized, but otherwise practice Judaism in secret, lighting their Sabbath lamps in the cellar. They do not eat pork; they marry amongst themselves and are known by their neighbors as Judeos—Jews. They are not officially recognized by world Jewry. Although they were discovered in 1919, attention was not drawn to them until the neighboring town of **Guarda** was "twinned" with the Israeli town of Safed in 1982.

According to *Time* magazine of April 11, 1977: "The Marranos shun all Saturday work: a telltale sign of their identity. But paradoxically, most of the men have not been circumcised because that could disclose their secret."

Here is another description in *The Jerusalem Post* of these descendants of Jews who fled from the Inquisition: "They get together for Yom Kippur eve services; they observe the Purim eve Taanit Esther fast, but not the Purim celebration. They observe baking their own *matzot*, according to a generations-old recipe, reciting certain traditional blessings at various stages of the process; they have a short seder meal that includes bitter herbs, but they do not read the *haggada*."

When Marrano communities were discovered, Jewish organizations began to raise money to bring them back into the fold. But success has been limited. The Marranos have been difficult to reach.

Anthropologists have found the Marrano communities living in semi-isolation and cut off from most of the developments in the world and from their own religion. The estimate of the number of these Marranos has been revised downward. They seemed to be disappearing. Decades and even centuries of intermarriage were noted in the poor health of community members. Most were poor and earned their livelihoods as wandering tradesmen. Those who had managed to achieve upward mobility had achieved it through marriage outside the group and subsequent departure from Jewish tradition.

While discussions continue, of course, the Jewish Community of Oporto has declared:

"It is the opinion of the Religious Committee of the Jewish Community of Oporto, as well as of reputable scholars, that there are no longer any *Bnei Anousim* (Crypto-Jews) in Portugal, just as there are no longer any samurai warriors in Japan, and it is misleading to imply that there are. The matter is now one for the history books, local culture and tourism."

The community in Oporto pointed out that:

"All the Portuguese people have "Jewish roots" as far as after the Edict of Expulsion of the Jews from Portugal (1496), the overwhelming majority of Jewish families were prevented from leaving the country and generally, in the following centuries, joined the Christian population by marriage. If all the descendants of Jews were to be expelled from Portugal, this would be the equivalent of depopulating the whole country. (Lúcio d'Azevedo, "História dos Cristãos-Novos portugueses", 1921)"

"The fact that Portuguese citizens are descendants of Jews (and descendants of many other people) does not confer on them the status of *Bnei Anousim*. In fact these were the descendants of Jewish converts who secretly continued to pray to Hashem and maintained the Jewish spirit and Jewish family matrilineality in marriages, as happened with the Bnei Anousim of Belmonte in Portugal."

"The current Jewish Community of Oporto would welcome within the congregation true *Bnei Anousim* if they still exist today in the Portuguese territory, whose existence has for long been unknown and not credible, and those interested must prove the contrary. Ben Anousim is currently a false statute that applicants take on for their own convenience, as an effective way to greatly simplify their "conversion processes."

Jewish Museum of Belmonte, rua da Portela, No 4, Belmonte. Tel: 351-275-088-698. Belmonte.em@netvisao.pt. In 2017, this museum which was founded in 2005 was opened after being refurbished. It holds the title of the largest museum in the world about crypto-Jews. The opening was designed to be ready for the annual European Days of Jewish Culture project in September. Included in this fabulous collection are reconstructed murals and individual stories of Belmonte Jews.

Synagogue Belmonte Portugal, rua da Fonte da Rosa 41, 6250, Belmonte.

Faro

A decade ago, a Jewish community in the Algarve did not exist. Today, there are about 30-40 Jews living this beautiful area.

Faro is the capital of the Algarve and even possesses a medieval wall and a large number of monuments, museums, and Roman ruins. Traces of the Moorish presence are also still seen in the area's unique architecture, terraces, chimneys and whitewashed houses. Faro was a famous center of Hebrew printing in the fifteenth century. The first printed book in Portugal, a Hebrew edition of the Pentateuch, was published here in 1487 by Samuel Porteira.

For information on the Jewish community in the Algarve, contact: info@ciasp.org. Today in Faro, the Jewish traveler will find a medieval **Jewish cemetery** dating from about the fourteenth century. A new cemetery was started in 1820.

Oporto

Oporto is indeed picturesque, especially looking down on it; settled peacefully on the Douro River. One cannot but be impressed with homes replete with red tile roofs that line the riverbank. This metropolis is one of the Portugal's largest cities, chief seaport, and commercial, industrial center of the northern part of the country. The Dom Luis Bridge links Oporto with the city of Vila Nova de Gala.

About 1,000 American Jews visit Oporto each year.

Oporto is also a city known for its contrasting baroque architecture and modern commercial center.

About 200 Jews live in Oporto and the synagogue is proud to state that its community hails from 21 countries. This is one community is growing, according to Michael Rothwell, a member of the Board of Directors of the Jewish community.

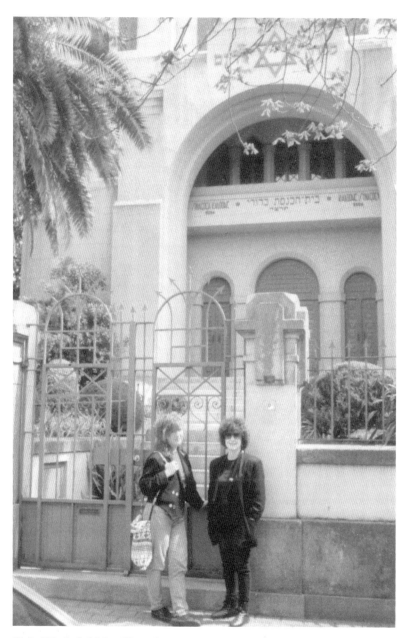

Kahal Kodosh Mekor Haim Synagogue, Oporto. (Photo by Ed Robin)

"Oporto had some 20 Jews over a decade ago; today about 200."

Today, this community, like others throughout Europe, is engaged in fighting the "Boycott, Divestment and Sanctions," (BDS) movement against Israel. Rare in Portugal are attacks on Jews or non-Jews who support Israel. In 2016, however, anti-Israel activists vandalized a restaurant in this city and posted signs on it reading "Free Palestine."

Kahal Kodosh Mekor Haim Synagogue (Kadoorie Synagogue), rua Guerra Junqueiro 340. 4150-386 Porto. Tel: 351-911-768-596. info@comunidade-israelita-porto.org, www.comunidade-israelita-porto.org, tourism@comunidade-israelita-porto.org.

This was the first synagogue built by and for native Portuguese Jews in more than 400 years. The cornerstone for the synagogue was set on June 30, 1929, and the dedication ceremony took place on January 16, 1938. It is the largest synagogue in the Iberian Peninsula. This house of worship contains two prayer halls, a mikveh, a grocery, restaurant, library, community dining room for 200 persons, a kitchen, and a patio to build a *sukkah for Succot.*

The synagogue was opened under the initiative of Capt. Barros Bastos, Portuguese hero of Marrano descent. The synagogue received funds from the famous Kadoorie family of Baghdad. For more than 20 years, Bastos led this synagogue. He hoped to bring the Marranos back to Judaism.

But there is more to the story of Arthur Carlos de Barros Bastos. As we know, in the 1930s Antonio de Oliveira Salazar served as dictator of Portugal. His dictatorship promoted Catholic conservatism and nationalism. Barro Bastos made powerful enemies for his efforts to establish a Jewish community made up of descendants of *anusim,* (Jews who had been forced to renounce their faith to escape religious persecution during the 16th century Portuguese Inquisition and after). Wrongfully accused of sexually abusing men he circumcised, Barros Bastro was in 1937 dishonorably discharged from the army, where he had served with distinction. According to JTA, the initiative to reinstate Barros Bastos who died in 1961, was restarted by the Jewish community of Porto. The community wanted Barros Bastos reinstated to the rank of colonel with all benefits.

In 2012, the Portuguese Parliament officially declared that Captain Barros Basto (the founder of the Jewish Community of Oporto) "was separated from the Army due to a general climate of animosity against him driven by the fact that being a Jew. The conviction of Captain was motivated by religious intolerance and an anti-Semitic prejudice."

In 2013, the Chief of the Portuguese Army recognized Captain Barros Basto as Colonel since 1945 and decided that "the reinstatement of Captain Barros Basto's career can be materialized as follows: Second Lieutenant (15 Nov 1912), Lieutenant (1 Dec 1916), Captain (17 Aug 1918), Major (5 Sept 1938), Lieutenant-Colonel (28 Jan 1943), Colonel (22 Nov 1945), Reserve (26 Mar 1947)"."For our community, this is enough," said Michael Rothwell, a member of the Board of Directors of the Jewish community.

The synagogue is open every day for religious services. The congregation maintains a regular *minyan* and *kiddush* every Shabbat.

At the synagogue of Oporto, which is the largest on the Iberian Peninsula, it is said, kosher meals are sold under the supervision of Rabbi Daniel Litvak, who is the spiritual leader of the congregation. The location is called Kosher Kadoorie Vending Store. Also, a kosher community grocery is located here. A Kosher Kadoorie Restaurant exists, but only for Jewish groups by request.

"Low cost" kosher meals are also available; kosher.catering.porto@ gmail.com

Kosher Restaurant of the Hotel de Musica. Just a kilometer from the synagogue. The restaurant was certified by Rabbi of the Oporto community following rigorous training of the employees of the hotel, so that they are able to welcome Jewish tourists. info@hoteldamusica. com. Also, a kosher product store is located here. portokosherstore@ hoteldamusica.com.

The Jewish Museum of Oporto is located on the first floor of the synagogue and is operated solely by the Jewish community. Open every day except for the Sabbath and holidays. The museum's collection is replete with Jewish artifacts and relics and aims to promote Jewish culture, tradition, religion, and history. It is worth noting here that the Jewish Community of Oporto played a vital role in the sheltering of hundreds of refugees during the Second World War. Refugees from Germany, Poland, Austria, Belgium, Czechoslovakia, France, Netherlands, Bulgaria, Luxemburg, and many other countries passed through this city, some stateless and some originally from Argentina and Iran. One of the Jews who passed through France and ended up here in Oporto was Ralph Baruch, who later became the Chairman of the Viacom Media Group in the USA. He embarked on a ship from Portugal to the United States, where he stayed and settled.

Suggested Reading

Bradford, Sarah. *Portugal.* New York: Walker, 1973.

Estensen, Miriam. *Discovery, The Quest for the Great South Land.* New York: St. Martin's Press, 1998.

Mocatta, Frederic David. *The Jews of Spain and Portugal, and the Inquisition.* New York: Cooper Square, 1973.

Austria
Where Jews Have Memories

"Something out of the dim past . . . when Vienna was a free city, where Herzl lived and worked and created the Zionist movement, where the *Neue Freie Presse* was one of the great liberal newspapers in the world; where Freud developed his ideas; where Yiddish writers . . . could be found . . . "

This passage by Joseph Leftwich comes to mind as the car leaves the city of Vienna and heads toward the green forest around the capital. The tourist guide-driver turns on the cassette tape and the music of Strauss's "Tales from the Vienna Woods" bursts forth. You can visualize the majestic, uniformed men and the gowned ladies waltzing in the grand ballroom. All you need is a piece of *sacher torte mit schlag*, cake with whipped cream. But that comes later when you are back in Vienna and after you visit Stadtpark, that pleasant place where the statues of Strauss and Beethoven lure you back to the city's heyday where Haydn, Mozart, Brahms, and Schubert also composed.

Vienna remains a center of European culture, with more than 100 art museums, which, combined, attract more than eight million visitors annually. This capital also boasts architectural masterpieces, with its magnificent palaces and world-class museums, such as the Hofburg complex, the Kunsthistorisches Museum. And do stare at the imposing façade of Vienna's Opera House, Statsoper.

Vienna's city center is easily explored by foot.

So do walk over to the Ringstrasse, one of the world's most beautiful boulevards. On this main thoroughfare are situated the university, the town hall, the Parliament buildings, the National Library, the Museum for Natural History and the History of Art, the State Opera House, the famous hotels, and stately offices.

The "*Inner Stadt*" is home to the most of Vienna's points of interest and historical buildings. It is surrounded by the "*Ringstrasse*," which separates the center of Vienna with the surrounding districts.

In Vienna you practically inhale nostalgia. Where else can you still buy picture postcards of Emperor Franz Joseph or books on the Hapsburg Empire of 100 years ago?

But like other Jewish communities in Europe, 70 years after the fall of the Nazis, Vienna for some still may no longer be a popular place for Jewish settlement. Some feel the Holocaust actually began in this capital. Here lived the art student Hitler, who became insane with the idea that he had to murder Jews; and this city, say some commentators, is "the cradle of modern political anti-Semitism."

Says author Judith Miller, Austria also has become synonymous with the country of Kurt Waldheim, the former United Nations Secretary General President of Austria, who lied about his past for 40 years, who told Austrians that he had only done his duty in yielding so willingly to the Third Reich. Waldheim, who did not run for a second term in 1992, was shunned by virtually every Western European leader after it was disclosed that he had covered up his service in a German Army unit that was accused of atrocities in the Balkans in World War II. His 1986 political campaign was marked by anti-Semitic overtones that obviously affected the small Austrian Jewish community. Throughout Waldheim's presidency, Austrian-Israeli relations remained strained and were reinstated only after Waldheim left office.

In 1993, Austrian Chancellor Franz Vranitzky was the first head of the Austrian government to visit Israel.

After the late Chancellor Bruno Kreisky, who served as federal chancellor from 1970-1983, left office, Austria once again veered to the far-right. First there was Jorg Halder, of the reactionary Freedom Party, which actually became part of the cabinet in the Austrian government. Chancellor Kreisky, who was Jewish, was among the first to make the Freedom Party respectable. His Austrian socialist government joined with the Freedom Party between 1983 and 1986, when it was not led by Haider. That party then was headed by a former member of the Waffen SS.

In May 2016, the far-right Freedom Party, headed by Norbert Hofer, challenged the establishment. In addition to its historical baggage, the Freedom Party features an anti-Muslim agenda that includes a ban on the construction of mosques, a shutdown of immigration and a prohibition on ritual slaughter and public prayers. It lost by just 31,000 votes, less than a percentage point, to a left-wing candidate. But because of miscounted ballots, there was a rerun in December 2016. Then, in the latter Presidential election, Austrian voters defeated a candidate vying to become the first freely elected far-right head of state in Europe since World War II, halting at least temporarily the wave of populism sweeping Western democracies. However, by the late fall of 2017, the center right People's Party, which won the election was expected to include the far-right Freedom Party in the government.

Still, anti-Semitism in Austria remains on the upswing. The Forum Against Anti-Semitism reported that "a record number of anti-Semitic incidents, ranging from verbal and online threats to assaults," were recorded in Austria in 2016. The report follows a finding by Austria's BVT domestic intelligence service in 2015 that incidents involving xenophobia, Islamophobia and anti-Semitism were in the rise in Austria, "swept up in Europe's migration crisis."

Within the last decade, Austria for the first time has acknowledged that Austrians were responsible for crimes against Jews. The country has passed legislation setting up a National Fund that provides token sums to Austrian Jews who suffered as a result of Nazi rule. The Austrians also have passed a law establishing ways to return Jewish artworks seized during war to the proper owners or their heirs. The government has called on banks and insurance companies to settle claims put forward by Jewish organizations that deal with the restitution of money.

Today about 90 percent of the Austrian Jewish community lives in this capital of 1.8 million, although small Jewish communities exist in Salzburg, Linz, Graz, and Innsbruck.

Nine-tenths of what the world celebrated as Viennese in the nineteenth century was "promoted, nourished and created by Viennese Jewry," wrote novelist Stefan Zweig (1881-1942). Zweig was to take his own life in Brazil because he could not stand the horrible crimes being committed against the Jewish people.

A Brief History

Jews probably arrived in Austria with the Roman legions. By the tenth century, they are mentioned as "paying tolls on merchandise." An early Jewish tombstone dating from 1130 was found near St. Stephan (Carinthia) and is the earliest evidence that exists of a permanent Jewish settlement is 1194.

A synagogue was built in Vienna in 1204. By the thirteenth century, Austria had become a center of Jewish learning, and a ghetto would grow around the Judenplatz square. The ghetto is gone but the square still exists today near the main synagogue.

At the end of the thirteenth century and during the fourteenth century, Vienna was recognized as the leading community of German Jewry. In 1421, the Jews were expelled from most of Austria, including Vienna. In the fifteenth and sixteenth centuries, only a small number of Jews remained in Vienna; they were restricted to ghettos.

Community life was revived at the beginning of the seventeenth century, especially in the Leopoldstadt section, named after Leopold I. At one time, about 500 Jewish families occupied 136 houses.

During the Turkish War of 1683, the Imperial Armies were financed by court Jews Samuel Oppenheimer and Samson Wertheimer. The latter was called the "Jewish Emperor." They helped stop the Turks at the gates of Vienna. Wertheimer's home in Eisenstadt, capital of the State of Burgenland, 60 miles south of Vienna, where many Jews once resided, became the site of the Austrian **Jewish Museum** in 1982.

By 1753, about 500 Jews lived in Vienna, many in the provinces. The ruler of Austria was Maria Theresa (1740-80), who hated the Jews—unless they converted to Christianity, that is. Maria Theresa once wrote of Jews: "I know no worse plague than this nation, therefore, as far as possible they are to be kept away from here and their numbers kept down." But the financial motive was so strong during her reign that she was forced to cultivate wealthy members of the Jewish community. Her son Emperor Joseph II, known as the "lover of mankind," brought about Jewish emancipation. In 1782, this enlightened monarch issued his Toleranzpatent, which guaranteed Jews certain rights, such as allowing them to attend general schools and to engage in agriculture and handicrafts.

The Revolution of 1848 altered the course of Jewish and Hapsburg history when the ghetto walls came down. Modern Austrian Jewish history begins with this period. Jews had been very active in the Revolution, including Adolf Fischer, who was chief of the new police force, and Ignaz Kuranda, the first Jewish parliament member.

Only 197 Jewish families lived in Vienna in 1848. The very next year, thousands arrived from Czech lands, as well as from Galicia. The Austria-Hungary Constitution of 1867 extended basic civil and religious rights to all in the Hapsburg Empire, including Jews.

In the early 1900s, Vienna had the largest Jewish population in Western Europe, 175,318 by 1910 with only Warsaw and Budapest having greater numbers of Jews. Every tenth Viennese was Jewish. Sixty percent of Vienna's physicians were Jews, reminiscent of fifteenth-century Spain. Vienna was said to be a "land-locked version of New York City."Jewish travel from Eastern Europe to Western Europe went via Vienna, still a transfer point.

World War I began the process that led to the destruction of European Jewry. During that war, thousands of Jews died for Austria.

It was Serbia's refusal to allow Austro-Hungarian police onto its soil in 1914 to investigate the murder of the Habsburg crown prince that precipitated World War I. About 10 million persons died in that war, which swept away the great empires of Central and Eastern Europe. As John Keegan points out in his book, *The First World War*, remaining was "a legacy of political rancor and racial hatred so intense that no explanation of the causes of the Second World War can stand without reference to those roots."

After 1918, the powerful Hapsburg monarchy shrank and Austria became the state no one wanted. Vienna became the capital of a "rump state." It's monarchy had lasted about a thousand years.

The Jews became the scapegoat for its defeat. No matter what they did, even reminding the Austrians of the part they played in the country's development, "they could do nothing to counter the violent hatred against the Jews ingrained in wide sectors of the Austrian population."

Still, Jews there considered themselves Austrians, first. Even in 1933, few could foresee that the disaster that would soon crush German Jewry would be repeated in Austria five years later. "The Jews underestimated the danger of persecution by Hitler," said Nazi-hunter Simon Wiesenthal.

On the morning of March 12, 1938, the German Wehrmacht centered Austria and marched into Vienna. They were met by "huge and enthusiastic crowds." Jewish life was doomed by the German annexation of Austria, the Anschluss. But as Stephen Brook says in *Vanished Empire*, "The idea that staunch little Austria was brutally invaded by the Nazi hordes in 1938 is a fiction, for the ground had been prepared ever since 1934 for closer ties with Germany." The vast majority of Austrians not only welcomed Hitler, but unleashed "a violent explosion of race hatred the like of which even the Jews of Germany, who had already endured five years of Nazi rule, had not experienced," wrote George Clare. Fortunately, about 120,000 frightened Viennese Jews would escape Austria between 1938 and 1941.

World War II soon erupted and engulfed the world. Ironically, the Allies, hoping Austria would resist Nazi occupation, made the mistake of calling Austria "the first victim of the Nazis." It left the Austrians believing they were innocent.

During that war, one-third of Austria's Jewish population, about 60,000 to 65,000 out of approximately 180,000, was killed.

"My Fuehrer, I report to you that Vienna has been cleared of all Jews." Baldur von Schirach, Vienna's Nazi gauleiter, sent that message to Hitler. In 1945, 29 Jewish children remained in Vienna and only a few hundred adults. After the Holocaust, between 250 to 500 persons, the remnants of Vienna's original 180,000 Jews, survived. But it was not the end.

Even though after World War II Austrian Jewry began a fresh start, the naysayers in the early 1980s were predicting the demise of the Austrian Jewish Community. Bad bet. For we now have a community that publishes several Jewish newspapers and maintains about a dozen synagogues, a community center, a day school that includes primary and secondary education, Talmud Torahs, kosher facilities, and a modern senior citizens home is not dormant.

The present Jewish population is composed of those who returned from Western countries where they had fled from Hitler or those who emigrated from former Iron Curtain cities, including 3,000 to 4,000 Soviet Jews, Polish and Romanian Jews, as well as Iranian Jews. Today, about 10,000 Jews are members of the Jewish community of Austria. A large percentage of the community consists of Jews who arrived here during the Hungarian Revolution in 1956. Austrian Jewry is a very heterogeneous community as far as its origins and today's culture of the people are concerned.

Between 1945 and 1952, 400,000 Jews from Eastern Europe passed through Vienna en route to Israel. And between 1968 and 1988, more than 270,000 Soviet and Iranian Jews used Austria as a gateway to freedom.

Notable Austrian Jews

Some prominent Jews of Austrian culture include Gustav Mahler, composer; Arnold Schoenberg, initiator and creator of the Vienna School of Music; Solomon Suizer in religious music; and Sir Rudolf Bing, general manager of the New York City Metropolitan Opera. In drama, there are the well-known Max Reinhardt, founder of the Salzburg Festival; and Berthold Viertel and Billy Wilder, producers.

Jewish Nobel Prize winners of Austrian origin were Alfred Hermann Fried, Nobel Prize for Peace, 1911; Karl Landsteiner, 1930, and Otto Loewi, 1936, Nobel Prize for Medicine; Robert Barany, Nobel Prize for Physiology, 1914; and Elias Canetti, Nobel Prize for Literature, 1981. Isidor Isaac Rabi won a Nobel Prize for Physics (1944).

Jewish contributions to psychiatry included Sigmund Freud; his daughter, Anna Freud; Alfred Adler; William Reich; and Theodor Reik. In the field of politics, Kreisky.

Austrian Jews prominent in journalism and literature were Hugo Bettauer, Martin Buber, Hans Habe, Franz Kafka, Franz Werfel, Stefan Zweig, Arthur Schnitzler, and Hugo von Hofmann. Arthur Koestler, although born in Hungary, was educated at the university in Vienna.

JEWISH SITES IN VIENNA

Community Headquarters, Seitenstettengasse 4, 1010 Vienna 1. Tel: 43-1-531-040, FAX: 43-1-531-04-108. office@ikg-wien.at. www.ikg-wien.at. The Jewish Community of Vienna, the only representative body of Viennese Jewry "recognized by the authorities," naturally comprises all religious and political organizations. The 24 members of its governing board are elected to a four-year term by the members of the community. A newspaper called *Die Gemeinde* is published once a month. In the foyer of the headquarters is an exhibit of Jewish religious items.

Leopoldstadt, now the Second District, is indeed an interesting neighborhood. The area holds 1,500 of Austria's approximate 10,000 Jews. In 1937, one-third of Vienna's Jews, about 60,000, lived in Leopoldstadt, where they were one-half of the district's total population. For Jews, Leopoldstadt meant home, even if it was a ghetto. Even as far back as the seventeenth century, it was known as the Metropolis of Learning. Especially famous were the district's doctors.

Rossauer Cemetery, Seegasse 9, 1090 Vienna. Recently, this First Vienna Jewish cemetery, the oldest Jewish cemetery in the city, was completely renovated and rededicated. The cemetery was restored with funding by the City of Vienna along with the local Jewish community. About a third of the destroyed tombs and headstones have been restored. The oldest tombstone is dated 1582, with the last funeral taking place there in 1783. Later the cemetery became a historical monument.

Buried here is Samuel Oppenheimer, along with other famous eighteenth-century Jewish financiers. Open Sunday through Thursday, 7:00 a.m. to 5:00 p.m.; Friday, 7:00 a.m. to 3:00 p.m.

The Vienna Central Cemetery, Simmering Hauptstrasse, Vienna XI. Tel: 76-62-52. Graves of famous rabbis, authors, and artists can be found here. Gate 4 is an entrance to the Jewish section; Gate 1 is for an older section. At the Simmering Hauptstrasse entrance, the hours are Sunday through Thursday, 8:00 a.m. to 5:00 p.m. and Friday, 8:00 a.m. to 3:00 p.m.

KOSHER DINING IN VIENNA

Alef-Alef kosher restaurant, Seitenstettengasse 2, 1010, Vienna 1. Tel: 535-25-30. This restaurant next to the synagogue entrance on the Judengasse (the old ghetto) is strictly kosher and under Orthodox kosher supervision. It opened in early 2001.

Kosher Bakery, Hollandstrasse 7, (1020 Wien) Vienna 2. Tel. 214-5617.

Kosher Shop, Tempelgasse 8, 1020 Vienna 2. Tel: 24-83-94. This store sells kosher food.

Kosher Supermarket and Kosher Bakery, Hollandstrasse 10, 1020 Vienna 2. Tel: 216-96-75. Also located here is a Jewish bookstore.

SYNAGOGUES IN VIENNA

Stadttempel, Seitenstettengasse 4, 1010 Vienna 1. Tel: 43-1-531-04–111.

For a guided tour, telephone the Jewish Community Center, Tel: 531-04-105 or 531-04-16. Guided tours Monday to Thursday, 11:30 a.m. and 2:00 p.m. The synagogue serves as a rallying point for the community, which has maintained and centralized facilities that consist of a community center, and Alef-Alef restaurant often frequented by Jewish travelers to Vienna. There are two buildings that compose the complex: The synagogue and the offices of the Jewish community are located at 4 Seitenstettengasse and the community center hall and the restaurant, Alef-Alef, are situated at 2 Seitenstettengasse. Rabbinat@ ikg-wien-at.

Also, the Library of the Jewish Museum is at 4 Seitenstettengasse. Tel: 43-1-535-04-312. www.jmw.at. Open Monday, Tuesday and Wednesday, 10:00 a.m. to 3:00 p.m. This reference library contains over 41,000 works in German, English, and Yiddish spanning four centuries.

The Stadttempel, located in one of the oldest sections of the city, opens Monday through Friday at 7:00 a.m., Sunday at 8:00 a.m., and Sabbath morning, Saturday, at 9:00 a.m. Daily services are held in the afternoon for mincha and in the evening for maariv. The pale blue and gold sanctuary is a fitting tribute to a once very large congregation.

Although badly damaged by the Nazis during Kristallnacht in 1938, the synagogue remained the only house of worship not destroyed by the Germans. (The Nazis leveled 22 synagogues and 40 small prayer houses).

This synagogue, the oldest existing Jewish house of prayer in Vienna, was founded on April 9, 1826. The builder was Josef Kornhausel. The structure is also noted as the burial place of the founder of modern political Zionism, Theodor Herzl (1860-1904), who died in Vienna on July 3, 1904. After World War II, Herzl's remains were taken to Jerusalem for final burial.

Thousands of Viennese lined the streets. Thus, it is difficult to walk through the streets around the Judenplatz and not think of Herzl, that "black-bearded prophet of the Jewish people who led them back to Zion restored." Vienna was the headquarters of the Zionist movement under Herzl. His book The Jewish State called for a sovereign Jewish nation for those who wished to go there.

Herzl, born in Budapest, was a student of law in Vienna from 1878 to 1883. He wrote journals for the Vienna newspaper *Neue Freie Presse* and became the Paris correspondent for the paper in 1891. *Neue*

Freie Presse was comparable to The Times in England or Le Temps in France. Writers such as Anatole France, Ibsen, Zola, and Shaw were associated with this journal.

Herzl had earlier experienced a tide of economic anti-Semitism in 1891 and in 1894. He was appalled to see France in an alliance with Russia when pogroms were killing Ukrainian Jews. Witnessing the degradation of Capt. Alfred Dreyfus framed by the French military, Herzl was moved by the need to create a Jewish state. He became the hero of the Jewish world, especially to the East European masses, although the term "Zionism" had been coined in May 1890 by a Vienna-born journalist, Nathan Birnbaum (1864-1937).

Agudas Yeshurun, Riemergasse 9, 1010 Vienna 1. Orthodox.

Bet Hamidrash Torah Etz Chayim, the former Schiffschul, Grosse Schiffgasse 8, Vienna Orthodox. Tel: 43-1-216-36-99.

Mizrachi Synagogue, Judenplatz 8, 1010 Vienna 1. Tel: 43-1-535-64-60. www.misrachi.at. Open for prayer Monday through Friday, 7:00 a.m.; Sunday, 8:00 a.m.; Sabbath, 9:30 a.m. The sanctuary and banquet hall are on the second floor. Here also are the headquarters of the Zionist religious youth, Bnei Akiva. Call for information on activities and lessons.

Nearby is **Judenplatz** or Jews Square, where there are plaques recalling the site of an older synagogue, hospital, and place where Jews lived in medieval times.

Ohel Moshe, Lilienbrunngasse 19, 1020 Vienna 2. Tel: 43-1-216-51-94. Orthodox.

Shomre Haddas, Glasergasse 17, 1090 Vienna. Orthodox.

Synagogue Agudas Israel, Grunangergasse 1,1010 Vienna 1. Tel: 512-83-31. This synagogue opens Monday through Friday at 7:00 a.m., Sunday at 8:00 a.m., and Sabbath at 8:00 a.m.

Synagogue Agudas Israel, Tempelgasse 3, 1020 Vienna 2. Tel: 43-1-512-83-31.

Synagogue Machzeke Haddas, Desider Friedmann-Platz 22, Vienna 1. Tel: 512-52-62. Services are held Monday through Friday at 6:30, 7:30, and 8:00 a.m. in summer; 7:00, 7:30, and 8:00 a.m. in winter; Sunday at 7:00 and 8:00 a.m.; and on Sabbath at 8:30 a.m. Call to confirm hours.

Or Chadasch, Robertgasse 2, Vienna-A-1020. Tel/FAX: 43-1- 967-1229. office@orchadasch.at, www.orchadasch.at. This is a Reform congregation and member of the World Union for Progressive Judaism.

Sephardic Center, Tempelgasse, 7, 1020 Vienna. Tel: 43-1-276-44-68. www.bucharische-gemeinde.at.

A recommended hotel in the Second District, but only a 10-15 minute walk to the main synagogue, is **Hotel Stefanie**, Taborstrasse 12, 1020 Vienna, Tel: 43-1-21-150-0. FAX: 21-150-160. www.schick-hotels.com. Kosher breakfast upon request.

ORGANIZATIONS

Jewish Welcome Service Vienna. Judenplatz 8/8, 1010 Vienna. Tel: Tel: 43-1-535-04-31-500. Office@jewish.welcome.at. www.jewish.welcome.at. http//www.Facebook.com, Jewish Welcome Service, http//www.facebook.com/DasJuedischeEcho, http//www.instagram.com/JWS_Vienna1#

Susanne Trauneck is Secretary General of the Jewish Welcome Service.

Located in the heart of the most cited area of Vienna, the Judenplatz (Jews Place) is the Jewish Welcome Service that serves as a communication and mediation function between Vienna and those expelled Jewish citizens and their descendants.

The main task of the Jewish Welcome Service is to look after Jewish visitors. "This is done," points out the group, "by way of a variety of projects and activities and through the invitation program for expelled Jewish citizens." The group was founded by the mayor, Leopold Gratz and city councellor Heinz Nittel, with the late Dr. Leon Zelman, himself a shoah survivor. Today the mayor of Vienna serves as president of the organization.

Today, the Jewish Welcome Service is the link between the City of Vienna, Vienna Tourism, The Jewish Museum Vienna, the IKG and the ESRA, and the Psychosocial Center for Victims of Nazism.

The late Dr. Zelman pointed out to this author on a number of occasions that no one dreamed that a Jewish community would ever again exist in the land of the Anschluss. Jewish leaders saw no future for the Jews in Austria. Young people immigrated to other lands. But Dr. Zelman was convinced that the Austrian Jewish community will continue as a vital and viable entity. His theory about the Jews of Vienna may be extended to other Jewish communities in Europe. He disagreed with those Jews who say that after World War II, Jews should have abandoned Europe completely, leaving for good. "Many of us who stayed sometimes feel that we have done so because we didn't want to give Hitler his victory." The task, as Dr. Zelman saw it, remains to keep the light of Judaism shining in Vienna.

Jewish Students Organization, Wahringerstrasse 24, 1090 Vienna 9. Tel: 317-54-99. www.joeh.eu. Jewish Center Vienna: info@jcv.at.

Club for young Jewish Adults. Wahringerstrasse 24, 1090, Vienna. Moadon@moadon.at.

Jewish Youth Home, Krummbachgasse 8, 1020 Vienna 2.

Chabad House defines itself as a non-profit organization aimed at strengthening the young. www.cbabadvienna.com.

The IKG Campus

The Jewish Community of Vienna (IKG, www.ikg-wien.at), revived decades ago, is today a flourishing institution in cosmopolitan Vienna. One of the IKG's focuses was the campus that it established and opened in 2009 in the Prater.

IKG Campus includes the Hakoah Sport and Leisure Center, the Zvi Perez Chajes School, and the Maimonides Home for the Elderly. These institutions were opened in 2009 on the campus, which includes private schools. That same year, the Austrian Government decided to establish the Vienna Wiesenthal Institute for Holocaust Studies. Also located here is the Lauder Chabad Campus and the Jewish Vocational Education Center.

This magnificent campus is located in the Second District where one will find Jewish shops, kosher supermarkets, butchers, snack bars, and restaurants. And in the area around Tempelgasse, the Sephardic Center and Synagogue. Tempelgasse 7, 1020 Vienna. Tel: 43-1-276-44-68.

MUSEUMS

Vienna Wiesenthal Institute for Holocaust Studies. (VWI) Desider-Friedman Platz, 1/18. 1010 Vienna. Tel: 43-1-189-01-51-40. office@vwi.ac.at. www.vwi.ac.at.

The Vienna Wiesenthal for Holocaust Studies, was founded in 2008 after the death of Simon Wiesenthal. His unique archives are stored and processed here. On September 8, 2014, the foundation stone was laid for a new research and communications facility at Rabensteig 3. The new center for Holocaust Studies will house the IKG archives.

Before Simon Wiesenthal's death, the **Jewish Documentation Center** was located at Salztorgasse 6, 1010 Vienna 1. Tel: 533-91-31. This primary source of information on Nazism was the original headquarters of Nazi hunter Simon Wiesenthal.

Seventy years after World War II, there must be many who were afraid of the man whose office and small staff now are located in the building at Salztorgasse 6.

Simon Wiesenthal spent more than half his life tracking down evidence against living Nazis. As founder and head of the Jewish Documentation Center, Wiesenthal had acted as the nemesis of the Nazis. He guided more than 1,000 cases to trial.

Melodramatic but true: no Nazi war criminal rested in peace with Wiesenthal's staff stalking him. His most famous conquest was Adolf Eichmann. Through the collaborative efforts of Wiesenthal and Israeli agents, Adolf Eichmann was located in Buenos Aires, Argentina, in 1959, where he was living under the alias of Ricardo Klement. Captured and brought to Israel for trial, Eichmann was found guilty of mass murder and executed on May 31, 1961.

Wiesenthal grew up in a small town in Galicia at the easternmost extremity of the Austro-Hungarian Empire. His mother perished in the Holocaust. Most of his wife's relatives did not survive the concentration camps. A total of 89 members of both families perished. He ended up in the Mauthausen concentration camp located near Vienna. Weighing less than 100 pounds and lying helplessly in a barrack where the stench was so strong that even hard-boiled S.S. guards would not enter, Wiesenthal was barely alive when Mauthausen was liberated by an American armored unit on May 4, 1945.

His main point hits home: the trials of ex-Nazis remain an educational experience for the world. Wiesenthal was often at loggerheads with the late Bruno Kreisky, a Jew, who was prime minister of Austria from 1970 to 1983. Kreisky was described as "born a Jew, but he became a hater of Israel and a front-line activist against the Jewish state," according to Edmund Schechter in his *Viennese Vignettes: Personal Recollections.* Obviously, Kreisky's relations with Israel were tense because of his policy of talking with the PLO. In view of the famous "handshake" in Washington, D.C., in 1993 between the late Prime Minister Yitzhak Rabin of Israel and the late Yasir Arafat of the PLO, some say they admire "Kreisky's foresight." History will tell.

In 1993, Wiesenthal, who was 85 years old that year, became embroiled in charges that he discovered and concealed evidence of alleged World War II crimes committed by Kurt Waldheim. But Wiesenthal wrote that the accusations being made against him "have no basis in fact." He denied the author's allegations.

Meanwhile, even into 1994, Wiesenthal was often invited to speak to schools and university audiences in Austria, where he is regarded as a leading representative of survivors of the Holocaust and he rarely refuses. Indeed, all of the city's high school students were offered a free screening of the movie *Schindler's List,* and then the students were given the chance to question Holocaust survivors. The first witness was Weisenthal, according to a report by the Austrian Information Services.

Sigmund Freud Museum, 19 Berggasse, 1090 Vienna 9. Tel: 43-1-319-15-96. office@freud-museum.at, www.freud-museum.at. The apartment building at 19 Berggasse where Dr. Sigmund Freud lived and worked for 47 years looks like any multi-unit building in this section of North Vienna, except it was the home of the man whom author Peter Gay calls the "Columbus of the mind."

The Sigmund Freud Museum is open daily, 10:00 a.m. to 6:00 p.m. Guided tours by prior arrangement. The house and the study on Berggasse (berg means mountain) have been restored and the consulting rooms converted into a museum. The site is sponsored by the Sigmund Freud Society and the Vienna Municipality.

The staircase to the 14 rooms where Freud lived from 1891 to 1938 has not been changed. The rooms contain memorabilia, some 420 items on display in four museum rooms. There are 60 items from Freud's own archaeological collection. Much of the museum is devoted to the history of psychoanalysis.

On a visit to Freud's apartment you see his rooms, his desk, his collection of Greek, Roman, and Egyptian antiques, pieces of sculpture, his books, and his Oriental rugs. The traveler will see Freud's walking cane, his hiking flask, his hat, a suitcase, as well as his comprehensive library. Near his study, note that Freud's youngest daughter Anna set up her office dedicated to the psychoanalysis of children in the mid-1920s. The displays in this memorial room, accessible to the public from late 1991 on, show original documents from Anna Freud's psychoanalytic work with children.

Sigmund Freud, the founder of psychoanalysis and the best-known Austrian throughout the world after Johann Strauss, was born to Jewish parents on May 6, 1856, in Freiberg, a small town in Moravia, now the Czech Republic. He attended school in Vienna and entered the university as a medical student where, it is said, he encountered anti-Semitism. Because of his Jewishness, he was sometimes excluded from the academic community of Vienna, the center of world medicine. However, he found a haven in Ernest Brueck's psychological laboratories. The rest is history.

Freud was not a practicing Jew. He wrote that he did not understand Hebrew. Some would accuse him of being estranged from Judaism. But author Amos Elon asserted in the *New York Review of Books* that "Freud was attached to the Jewish world with ties he knew to be indestructible," and is even said to have contemplated briefly, in 1922, settling in Palestine. He remained a steadfast member of the Jewish community and of the Vienna B'nai B'rith lodge, which author George E. Berkley says he had helped found. Freud once wrote: "My parents were Jews, and I remained a Jew myself."

Sigmund Freud Park and Memorial, located in front of Vienna's Votive Church, only steps from the Medical School of the University of Vienna and from Berggasse. Freud lectured at the university. The park was dedicated in 1985. In the park, which adjoins the University on one side, Vienna's Mayor and Governor, Dr. Helmut Zilk, unveiled a memorial to Freud. It is a simple stone facing the university and bearing the Greek letters, psi alpha, and the inscription, "The voice of reason is soft." Freud himself had used the Greek letter combination psi alpha as the logogram of psychoanalysis and it has become worldwide scientific shorthand.

Jewish Museum of the City of Vienna, Dorotheergasse 11, 1010 Vienna. Tel: 43-1-535-04-31. info@jmw.at. www.jmw.at. Located several blocks away from the Museum in the Judenplatz and the Holocaust Memorial is the Jewish Museum in the Palais Eskeles. This museum has developed into one of the most important Jewish museums in Europe and one of the most innovative cultural establishments in Vienna. Having said that, it is incumbent on a tourist to Vienna, if possible, to visit this museum, for it is an essential and prominent communicator of the past and present day history of the capital. Here, too, the history of the Jews of Vienna is comprehensively documented. So, take a somber trip into Vienna's Jewish past. The Jewish Museum was completely designed in 2011 and reopened in 2013 with its new permanent exhibition, *Our City! Vienna Then and Now,* which relates the 800 year history of Jewish Vienna. "The Jewish Museum of the City of Vienna is a place of encounter, confrontation, and understanding, which seeks to raise awareness of Jewish history, religion, and culture," says part of its mission statement.

A highlight of the museum is the Berger collection, which with its approximate 10,000 items includes religious and ritual objects, medals, paintings, prints, and archive material. The exhibit covers the entire spectrum of Ashkenazi art.

A collection on the Jewish community of Vienna contains material from the old Jewish Museum, which was closed in 1938 by the Nazis. Another important collection is that of Martin Schlass, which was donated to the Jewish Museum in 1993. This collection contains 5,000 items of anti-Semitic objects such as figurines, household utensils, manuscripts, prints, and postcards.

The first Jewish Museum was opened in 1897 and lasted until the Nazi era. Where were all the objects now housed in the new museum? After the war, all the Jewish objects found in different parts of Austria and Vienna itself were handed over to the Jewish community for keeping.

A municipal Jewish museum was located in the Vienna Jewish community center-synagogue until the museum opened in Dorotheergasse.

The new museum building was originally a palace that dates back to the sixteenth century when it was separated from the adjacent Dorotheestift convent. After frequent changes of ownership over the centuries, it finally became in this century an art gallery and in the last decades, it has housed the art department of Vienna's biggest auction house. In 1993, the auction agency put the palace at the disposal of the Jewish Museum of the City of Vienna.

The museum has made it clear that the Jewish Museum "will always have to be aware of the fact that the Nationalist Socialist policy of persecution and annihilation has created a traumatic counterpoint in the history of Jews and non-Jewish Austrians." It added, "the memory of the Holocaust will therefore permeate all activities undertaken by the Museum; at the same time, the Museum also represents a new beginning, by employing the methods available to a museum of cultural history to reconstruct and preserve the past.

The Jewish Museum, Dorotheergasse, is about a 10 minute walk from the Museum in the Judenplatz and the Holocaust Memorial in the same square. The director is Dr. Danielle Spera.

Jewish Museum Vienna, Dorotheergasse 11, is open Sunday through Friday 10:00 a.m. to 6:00 p.m. Closed on Saturdays.

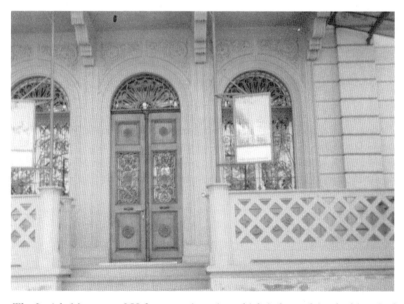

The Jewish Museum of Hohenems, Austria, which is housed in the historical Villa Heimann-Rosenthal built in 1864. One room is dedicated to the music of Hohenems-born Solomon Sulzer (1804-90), who composed religious music. (Photo by Monica Wollner of New York, great granddaughter of Malwina Rosenthal, whose family owned the Villa.)

Museum Judenplatz. Judenplatz 8, 1010. Vienna. Tel: 43-1-535-04-31. info@jmw.at. www.jmw.at. Hours: Sunday through Thursday, 10:00 a.m. to 6:00 p.m. Friday, 10:00 a.m. to 5:00 p.m. During the summer, closing at 5:00 p.m. This museum houses the foundation of the medieval synagogue uncovered in 1995. Many cultural events and temporary exhibits take place here in the Museum Judenplatz, which is opposite the Holocaust Memorial.

One of the highlights of this museum is a computer animated reconstruction of the synagogue and a virtual tour of the medieval Jewish quarter. This gives tourists a better understanding of life in the Middle Ages.

Another new museum in Vienna is the Arnold Schoenberg Center, (Palais Fanto) Schwarzenbergerplatz 6, Zaunergasse 1, 1030 Vienna. This building documents the life and work of the eminent, modern Austrian composer. Exhibitions are also held here.

MEMORIAL SITES

Memorial to the Victims of the Shoah, in the Judenplatz, Vienna. Designed by Rachel Whiteread, the monument recalls the 65,000 Jews of Vienna murdered during the Holocaust.

This Holocaust Memorial, in the middle of Judenplatz, is located on the site of the burning of a medieval synagogue and resembles an inside-outside library. It honors the memory of about 65,000 Austrian Jews killed by the Nazis. The sculpture is about 12 feet high, 24 feet wide, and 33 feet long. The double doors on the front do not open and the names of the Nazi death camps are inscribed around the base.

Gestapo Victims Monument. The monument in Morzinplatz honors hundreds who were murdered here, including many Jews. The Gestapo headquarters were located in the Hotel Metropole. Although Austrians accounted for only 8 percent of the population of the Third Reich, about one-third of all people working for the S.S. extermination machinery were Austrian. Almost half of the six million Jewish victims of the Hitler regime were killed by Austrians.

The Mauthausen Concentration Camp, A-4310, Mauthausen-Marbach 38. Tel: 07-238-2269. The Mauthausen memorial site consists of watchtowers, barbed wire, and a gas chamber. Mauthausen is located 17 miles from Linz and 80 miles west of Vienna. About 200,000 persons perished here, and one-third were Jews. Methods of execution included pushing inmates from one of the 186 steps that they had to climb while carrying rocks from the quarry or ordering them to run to the barbed wire and then shooting them as escapees. The University of Stuttgart concluded its report on Mauthausen with, "deliberate extermination played a more significant role in this camp than in other concentration camps."

According to James E. Young, author of *The Texture of Memory: Holocaust Memorials and Meaning in Europe, Israel, and America,* "Mauthausen has been transformed from a hellish scar on the landscape to a clean, beautifully maintained state memorial."

There are 20 national monuments here, and the Jewish memorial monument is one of them. It consists of a menorah and a stylized Hebrew lettering spelling out zachor "remember."

Young points out that the former Soviet Union's monument to victims of fascism at Mauthausen, "seems inspired partly by Nathan Rapoport's Warsaw Ghetto Monument."

The visitor can see all the buildings of the former concentration camp and its museum with 133 pictures and exhibits. A guide is available or you can obtain a tape as well as a film. Additional exhibits show the fate of Austrians in the concentration camps of Dachau, Buchenwald, Sachsenhausen, Ravensbruch, Auschwitz, and Theresienstadt. Every May 4, ceremonies are held to honor the camp's liberation by the Americans.

Sculpture Monument. A sculptured figure of a Jew forced to scrub political slogans off the street, a common scene during the 1938 Anschluss, when Nazi Germany marched into welcoming Austria, can be viewed. This stone ensemble is located on a square behind the Opera and the Sacher Hotel. The late Alfred Hrdlicka is the sculptor. The sculptural ensemble by Mr. Hrdlicka, one of Austria's most prominent sculptors, was meant to guide the viewer through Austria's suffering under Hitler, through its participation in the German crime, and finally its liberation from the Nazi hell.

Recommended Guides

Dr. Brigitte Timmermann, Brigitte@viennawalks.com and Walter Juraschek, walter.juraschek@chello.at.

Suggested Reading

Bassett, Richard. *A Guide to Central Europe.* New York: Viking, 1987.
Berkley, George E. *Vienna and Its Jews: The Tragedy of Success 1880-1980s.* Lanham, MD: Madison Books, 1988.
Fraenkel, Joseph, ed. *The Jews of Vienna, Essays on the Life, History and Destruction.* London: Valentine Mitchell, 1967.
Herzstein, Robert Edwin. *Waldheim: The Missing Years.* New York: William Morrow, 1988.

Hofmann, Paul. *The Viennese: Splendor, Twilight, and Exile*. New York: Doubleday, 1988.

Lengyel, Emil. *The Danube*. New York: Random House, 1939.

Magris, Claridio. *Danube: A Journey Through the Landscape, History and Culture of Central Europe*. New York: Farrar, Straus and Giroux.

Miller, Judith. *One, by One, by One: Facing the Holocaust*. New York: Simon & Schuster, 1990.

Sands, Phillippe. *East West Street, On the Origins of Genocide and Crimes Against Humanity*. New York: Alfred A. Knopf, 2016.

Schechter, Edmund. *Viennese Vignettes: Personal Recollections*. New York: Vantage Press, 1983.

Wiesenthal, Simon. *Justice Not Vengeance*. New York: Grove Weidenthal, 1989.

Young, James E. *The Texture of Memory: Holocaust Memorials and Meaning in Europe, Israel, and America*. New Haven: Yale University Press, 1993.

Switzerland
Home of the First World Zionist Congress

Welcome to Switzerland, one of Europe's most popular tourist destinations. An Israeli I once met said that the most beautiful place in the world is Switzerland, the country of the Alps, of civilized behavior, famed for cheese, chocolate, clocks, and watches. Many Jewish travelers favor Switzerland because for 700 years it has remained without conflict and seems calm and content. Golda Meir, the former prime minister of Israel, once said that Jews were the most nervous people in the world. So there is Switzerland, a place to soothe their nerves.

This "heart of Europe" covers 15,941 square miles or about one-third the area of France. Switzerland's population of 7,275,467 includes about 18,000 Jews, who live mostly in the big cities. Actually, half of the Swiss Jews live in the Zurich area. To be more precise regarding where the Jews reside in this Alpine nation, some 61 percent of the Jews live in the German-speaking part of the country and 36 percent in the French-speaking part, according to the World Jewish Congress.

Five large cities dominate Switzerland: Zurich has 366,445 citizens; Basel, 165,000; Geneva, 177,500; Bern, the capital,140,228; and Lausanne, 129,273. Sixty-five percent of the people speak Swiss German; 18 percent speak French; 12 percent speak Italian; and 1 percent speak Romansch.

A traveler to Switzerland will see that its people are both orderly and literary. Zurich, Basel, Bern, Lausanne, and Geneva have more bookstores than other big cities in the world. Two of the world's greatest educators, Jean Jacques Rousseau and Henrich J. Pestalozzi, hail from this land-locked state.

Well-known Swiss painters include Alberto Giacometti and Paul Klee.

Switzerland is an independent nation, supporting an economy based on international trade and banking.

The Swiss banker is known the world over. It is said that "the responsibility of the Swiss is to prosper."

In World War II, while Europe destroyed itself, neutral Switzerland was untouched. Only the Swiss resisted involvement in two world wars. With a freely convertible currency, Switzerland served as an international finance and communication center. After New York and London, Swiss Banks are rated third in the world. But the Swiss banking industry became tarnished when the World Jewish Congress led an investigation into banks that had accepted Nazi-looted gold. At stake were millions of dollars of gold from Jews who had perished in the Holocaust, as well as Swiss accounts that belonged, but were no longer accessible, to Holocaust survivors after World War II. After several years of investigation and prodding by several groups including the U.S. government, New York state officials, and the World Jewish Congress, Swiss banks in 1998 agreed to a settlement of $1.25 billion with respect to most of Holocaust-related financial claims against Switzerland and Swiss industry. Specifically, this agreement will cover the bank accounts that Holocaust victims placed in Swiss banks for safe-keeping and were unable to recover after the war, according to the World Jewish Congress.

A Brief History

The Swiss date their origin from 1291. Men from Uri, Unterwalden, and Schwyz gathered to form the nucleus of the Swiss Confederation. To this day, a Swiss's first loyalty is to his or her canton, of which there are 23. In 1315 the Hapsburg invaders were defeated; the cantons were united to form a confederation.

During the sixteenth century, Switzerland was considered the headquarters of the Protestant Reformation.

In 1798, the French occupied Switzerland. The Confederation set up a formal constitution that established the Helvetian Republic. The Congress of Vienna recognized Switzerland's "perpetual neutrality," a condition that has endured to this day. A new confederation was established in 1848, with Bern as its capital. The Swiss have the peculiar distinction of being the only country in the Western Hemisphere to delay the right of women to vote until the 1970s. (Before the modern era, some cantons allowed the vote, while others did not).

A Jewish presence in Switzerland appears in the thirteenth century. Jews first settled in Basel in 1213, in Lucerne in 1252, followed by Bern in 1262, and finally in Zurich in 1273. A French expulsion edict in 1306 caused French Jews to move here, only to experience the Black Plague (1348). For allegedly having poisoned the wells, a common medieval anti-Semitic accusation, Jews were tortured.

In 1622, Jews were expelled again. Later, only a handful of Jewish physicians was allowed to remain in some towns, with a few in the canton of Baden. Until the French Revolution, Jews lived mainly in the canton of Aargau in northern Switzerland. Two Jewish villages, **Endingen and Lengnau,** actually became the cradle of today's Swiss Jewry. If you have a half-day's time in Switzerland, you should definitely visit the two villages and their synagogues, not quite an hour's drive from Zurich. Endingen, by the way, is the only village in Switzerland that has a synagogue and no church, although there are practically no Jews living there anymore. The **Jewish cemetery** located between the two villages, its oldest section romantically secluded in a small forest, is one of the most touching in Europe. But in the 1850s, the United States, England, Holland, and especially France pressed Switzerland to end its discrimination against Jews. Again under French pressure, the Federal Constitution of 1866 was revised to allow Jews to live anywhere in Switzerland. The cantons followed suit and finally, in 1879, Endingen at last granted emancipation to Jews.

Today Zurich is home to about 8,000 Jews; Geneva, 4,321; Basel, 2,577; and Lausanne, more than 1,000. The *"Schweizerische Israelitische Gemeindebund"* (SIG), "Union of Swiss Jewish Communities," is the umbrella organization of Swiss Jewry and has 22 member communities. The majority of Swiss Jews are Ashkenazic, but since 1945, Sephardic Jews from the Mediterranean area have arrived. "The community is largely middle class, its members increasingly employed in the specialized professions, large corporations and the civil service," according to the Institute of Jewish Affairs' book. The Jewish Communities of the World.

Most Jews in Switzerland are members of Jewish communities and most belong to the Swiss Federation of Jewish Communities (SIG), located at Gotthardstrasse 65, CH-8027 Zurich. Tel: 41-43-305-07-77, FAX: 41-43-305-07-66. info@swissjws.ch, www.swissjews.ch. A few Orthodox and Reform communities operate independently. The two Reform communities of Zurich and Geneva are members of the Platform for Liberal Jews in Switzerland (PLJS), according to the European Jewish Congress.

Approximately 40 synagogues ranging from Orthodox to Liberal operate in Switzerland. Synagogues conducting services regularly are located in Zurich, Geneva, Berne, Basel, Lausanne, Lucerne, St. Gallen, Baden, and Lugano.

There are also nine Jewish schools functioning in Swiss cities: Zurich, Lausanne, Basel and Kriens-Obernau.

A silver Torah ornament from Endingen. (Photo courtesy of the Swiss National Tourist Office)

Notable Swiss Jews

Switzerland has been known to be a refuge to many expatriates and to the persecuted. Here are the tombs of Rainer Maria Rilke, Thomas Mann, James Joyce, Robrt Musil, George Kaiser, and E. Weicher. Goethe, Byron, Franz Liszt, Johannes Brahms, Stefan Zweig, Eric Maria Remarque, Albert Einstein, Thomas Mann, and Paul Klee all found peace and a chance to carry on their work in Switzerland after they had been forced to flee their own native countries. Ernest Bloch lived in Switzerland, as did Wolfgang Pauli, physicist, and Tadeus Reichstein, the medical researcher who won Nobel Prizes in Physiology and Medicine in 1950.

The President of Switzerland at the beginning of the new millennium was Ruth Dreifuss. She became the first Jewish head of state in the nation.

Basel

Basel Stadt Casino, 14 Steinenberg. In the story of Zionism and the State of Israel, Basel looms large. The Basel Program—"to create a publicly recognized secured home for the Jewish people"—was adopted here. Theodor Herzl would later write in his diary: "In Basel I found the Jewish state. If I said this out loud today, I would be answered with universal laughter. Perhaps in 5 years, certainly in 50, everyone will know it."

The First World Zionist Congress began on August 29, 1897. Frankfurt Jewry had refused its city as the site of the Congress, so it was held in the Basel Stadt Casino, which in 1938 was replaced by a new concert hall on Steinenberg Street. Today a plaque commemorates the Congress. The English Jewish writer Israel Zangwill referred to the First World Zionist Congress when he wrote: "By the rivers of Babylon we sat down and wept as we remembered Zion. By the rivers of Basel, we resolved to weep no more."

In this city of museums on the Rhine River, Herzl was elected president of the World Zionist Organization. The year 1997 was the 100th anniversary of the first Zionist Congress and a celebration was held.

Centuries ago, Jews were not allowed to live in Basel. They had to live outside the city walls. Indeed, still standing is a city gate where Jews were required to pay a special fee. Ironically, Basel became a center for Hebrew printing.

People enjoy living in Basel, the second largest Swiss city. It is an academic as well as chemical/pharmaceutical center. An aura

A view of the Basel Town Hall. (Photo courtesy of the Swiss National Tourist Office)

of scholarship, history, humanism, publishing, and love of the arts permeates the place. The city likes to be known as the "cultural heart" of Switzerland.

Three Kings Hotel (Hotel Drei Könige/am Rhein), 8 Blumenrain, is not only a hotel, but it is a symbol for Jews. Every American tourist is familiar with the claim, "George Washington slept here." Well, Theodor Herzl, the founder of modern Zionism, did sleep here during the First World Zionist Congress in 1897 and several times afterward. Mounted on many a wall throughout the world is the famous photo of him standing on the balcony of his room in the Three Kings Hotel overlooking the Rhine and its bridges in the background.

The synagogue, known as the Israelitische Gemeinde Basel, is located at 24 Leimenstrasse. Daily services are held. A Hebrew school and a day school are housed here.

The Jewish Community Center adjoins the synagogue and houses a kosher restaurant known as Jewish Restaurant & Catering TOPAS, Leimenstrasse 24 CH-4051 Basel, Tel: 41-61-206-95-00. Info@ restaurant-topas.ch, www.restauranttopas.ch/

According to Swiss law, ritual slaughtering of animals is forbidden and kosher meats are imported from France.

As for most Jewish residents in Europe, assimilation remains a major problem. New leadership is hard to find and often one leader serves for many years in many roles.

Still, Basel Jewry is active: B'nai B'rith, a local World Zionist Organization, a UJA group, and Bnei Akiva are the main groups. The community sponsors kosher meals on wheels for its senior citizens.

The Jewish Museum, 8 Kornhausgasse. Tel: 261-95-14. This museum is the only Jewish museum in Switzerland and is certainly worth visiting. It reflects the Jewish population of more than 2,000 in Basel and exhibits the history of Swiss Jews, who now number approximately 18,000. Although a small museum, it exhibits some exceptionally rare and remarkable items, such as tiny tefillin and rare books of Esther (the story of Purim), as well as *havdalah* candles, a Polish-Jewish Hanukkah menorah and other Judaic items, and memorabilia from the First World Zionist Congress of 1897. Open from 10:00 a.m. to noon and from 2:00 to 5:00 p.m., Monday, Wednesday, and Sunday.

Kosher Restaurants in Basel

Restaurant Topas, (meat) Leimenstrasse 24, 4051 Basel. Tel: 41-61-206-95-00. Info@restaurant-topas.ch, www.restauranttopas.ch

Restaurant Holbeinhof. (dairy) Leimenstrasse 67, 4051. Basel. Tel: 41-61-270-68-10.

Lugano

The whole world seems to come to Lugano, a summer resort whose city population is about 30,000. They call it the "Rio de Janeiro of the Old World," because of its subtropical vegetation and the peaks of San Salvatore.

Located on Lake Lugano on the southern edge of the Alps, this town has a distinctive Mediterranean character. It "dances in sunshine and is fringed with palms and mimosa trees," making it one of Switzerland's most popular summer holiday resorts. Most of the tourists walk along the calm, cool lakeside promenade. Others visit the sector known as Castagnola. The Villa Favorita, perched at the town's border, contains one of the finest private art galleries in Europe. Day trips on the lake round out the visitor's trip to this garden city.

About 400 Jews reside in the Canton, including the area to Ticino; many are black-coated, black-kneesocked, bearded Chassidim who are seen in the city streets. The community boasts Jewish Orthodox families, many of them Chassidim, a Talmud Torah (afternoon school), a day school, and a synagogue. About 50 Orthodox families live and work in Lugano.

The Lugano Community Shul, a synagogue, is located at 11 C Via Maderno. Tel: 23-61-34.

Chabad of Greater Lugano,via Lambertenghi 2, Lugano. Tel: 41-91-921-3720, 41-78-839-9271. rabbi@jewishlugano.com, www. jewishlugano.com. Rabbi Yaakov Kantor told me Chabad provides services from "A to Z."

Kosher Facility in Lugano

There are no kosher hotels or restaurants in Lugano. But a "Kosher Corner," a kosher grocery, operates out of the Chabad Center at Lugano,via Lambertenghi 2, Lugano. A variety of kosher products are available at this facility open Tuesdays, 5:00 p.m. to 7:00 p.m. and Fridays, noon.

Geneva

Old-fashioned elegance is one way to describe the setting of Geneva, often called "the city of God" or "the city of Calvin." A "geographic crossroads" and "peace hub of the world," it takes international crises in its stride, although it is the seat of many peace and disarmament conferences and administrative headquarters of the International Committee of the Red Cross and 150 other global organizations.

Here is Geneva, Switzerland's most cosmopolitan city, where the art and jewelry dealings are endless; where one out of three residents is a foreigner. On the banks of a beautiful lake, the sights are attractive, including a new Red Cross Museum and the Opera at the Grand Theatre. Here stands the Palais des Nations, with architecture similar to Versailles. Here sat the League of Nations from 1936 to 1939. And here is the European headquarters of the United Nations.

When Philip Augustus expelled the Jews from French soil in 1182, many businessmen and doctors resettled in Geneva. They were not welcomed with open arms, for, if you were Jewish and passing through the city, you had to pay a poll tax.

Officially recognized in 1853, the Geneva Jewish community founded a synagogue in 1859.

The World Jewish Congress was set up in Geneva in 1936. In August 1939, the last Zionist Congress before World War II took place here. During that war, Geneva served as an important center for information regarding the fate of Jews in Nazi-occupied Europe.

After the war, Eastern European Jews arrived in Geneva. Later came Jews from North Africa and the Middle East. In 1945, the Jewish population was 2,245, by 1968, 2,700. Now it has passed the 4,000 mark.

Kosher Restaurants In Geneva

Le Jardin, Ave. Dumas 21, Geneva, Tel: 22-317-8910.

Ketori (Japanese cuisine) 5 Ave. King, 1208 Geneva. Tel: 22-700-31-55.

Les Marronniers, 9 ch DeLa Bessonnette, 1224. Geneva. Tel: 22-344-87-60

SYNAGOGUES IN GENEVA

The Liberal Synagogue. Communaute Israelite Liberale de Geneva. 43, route de Chene. (Bet Gil), CH-1208, Geneva. Tel: 41-22- 732-32-45. FAX: 41-22-738-2852. info@gil.ch www.gil.ch. Services on Friday evening at 6:30 and Saturday morning at 10:30. Beautiful sanctuary. There are Talmud Torah classes, activities, conferences, community dinners, and a sisterhood. Many people here speak English. Established in 1984, the congregation has about 400 family members of Reform or Conservative movement backgrounds. Services are in French and Hebrew; some are in English. During the community *seder*, prayers are in English. Rabbi François A. Garai, originally from France, speaks excellent English. A friendly atmosphere invites visitors.

The Great Synagogue, now known as Beth Yaakov, in memory of the late Jacob Safra. Place de la Synagogue 11, 1204 Geneva. Tel: 41-22-311-4815. A memorial plaque stands in front of the courtyard at this 100-year-old synagogue honoring the six million Jews who died in the Holocaust.

This would be a good place for the Jewish traveler to consider the Holocaust and the Swiss role in that event.

There are many sides of the debate as to how much Switzerland could or could not have done during the Holocaust. What is true is that by 1942, the situation of the Jews in Europe became extremely dangerous. Yet to understand the problem, we must go back to 1938. On July 6 of that year, in nearby Evian, which is located on the French side of Lake Geneva, an international conference was called to solve the refugee problem. Nobody "lifted a finger." There was only silence. Some even reduced the refugee quota. No one wanted Jews. Switzerland maintained it could only be a transit country for fugitives from Germany. "This was by no means a glorious chapter in Swiss history."

Wartime Swiss officials refused entry to thousands of Jewish refugees, even after "it was known that they faced almost certain death in Nazi Germany," wrote Elizabeth Olson in the *New York Times* of December 11, 1999. Citing an announcement of a group of independent international historians who had issued a 350-page report, she noted that Swiss authorities were aware that Jews were being annihilated by the Third Reich. By its sending thousands of Jews to their death, Switzerland helped the Nazi effort. Yes, Switzerland saved 21,000 Jews, but it abandoned more than 25,000 and in 1942 closed the border because it was afraid Germany would invade.

The historians said there was no evidence that accepting many more asylum seekers would have put neutral Switzerland in danger of "invasion by the Axis or caused insurmountable economic difficulties." They rejected an argument advanced in Switzerland's defense after earlier disclosures of the country's treatment of Jews trying to escape the Holocaust.

Switzerland did not reverse its policy of keeping out Jews until July 1944, when it declared that persecution for being Jewish was a valid ground for granting asylum.

Remember, too, that it was a Swiss—the head of the police administration in the Ministry of Justice—who concluded that 'J' *for Juden*' inscribed in German, in passports held by Jews, would help Hitler control the flight of Jews from Germany. Four years later in August 1942, Switzerland closed its borders. Leni Yahil says Switzerland "took the position that the right of asylum is the sole prerogative of the State—not that of the refugee." A Swiss official compared Switzerland to a lifeboat, with thousands of drowning people clamoring to get into that only available lifeboat with very limited space and provisions. In

August 1942, at about the time of the sealing of the borders, he said that the lifeboat was full.

From 1939 to 1945, a total of 295,381 fugitives received asylum in Switzerland, some for only a short time. But about 25,000 Jews were refused admission. Many did not even hazard an attempt to get across the freedom line. During the war years, about 21,000 Jewish refugees were saved and taken care of in Switzerland.

Nearly 1,700 Jews from Hungary were brought to Switzerland via Bergen Belsen, 1,200 Jews from Theresienstadt were rescued, as well as the 400 children who came from the Buchenwald concentration camp. After the war, many left for other lands.

The Machsike Hadass Synagogue, 2, Place des Eaux Vives. 1207 Geneva.Tel: 76-342-37-56. Call ahead for times of services as they may change, depending of course, on the season.

Hekhal Haness, 54 ter, route de Malagnou.Geneva. Tel: 78-655-46-61. Sephardic.

Chabad Geneva, Ave. Theodore Weber, 12, 1208 Geneva. Tel: 41-22-860-86-13-41. Chabad is housed in a four-and-a-half story building on Ave. Theodore Weber, between rue de Rhone and Malagnou in the heart of the Jewish neighborhood.

ORGANIZATIONS

Macom, The Jewish Community Center, 21 Ave. Dumas, 1206, Geneva. Tel: 41-22-317-8900. FAX: 41-22-317-89-91. servsoc@comisra. www.comisa.ch. This is Geneva's principal Jewish community center, which offers a sanctuary, a main Jewish library, and Le Jardin, a kosher restaurant.

World Jewish Congress, Geneva Office, Tel: 212-755 3770. geneva@worldjewishcongress.org

Mission of Israel to the United Nations in Geneva, 1-3 avenue de la Paix, 1202 Geneva. Tel: 41-22-716-05-00, FAX41-22-716-05-55.

Zurich

"Athens on the Limat River" is how Zurich is described. This is Switzerland's largest city and the commercial and financial capital. It is a Swiss "New York City," known for its efficiency and exactness. This second city of psychoanalysis stands as a prime gateway to Europe.

Even if it is a communications and industrial center, Zurich is still one of Europe's most beautiful cities because of the hills surrounding it, the fresh air blowing down from the mountains, and the red geraniums, roses, and begonias that decorate this urban area.

Zurich is a city for strollers, especially on the luxurious and prosperous Bahnhofstrasse, where one might just by chance meet one of the city's 6,000 Jews.

Jews first arrived in Zurich in 1273 and were mainly moneylenders. But eventually came bad times and bad memories, among them the Black Death of 1348 when Jews were burned at the stake, as well as the expulsion from Switzerland in 1634. After the French Revolution in 1789, a few Jews returned to Zurich. The Swiss waited until 1866 to grant civil and legal equality, and only then did a new Jewish community arise. Swiss Jewry, and especially Zurich's Jews, are very well organized into the 22-member SIG, the umbrella organization of Swiss Jewry.

A must for the first-time or even second-trip visitor is the city's attractive section across the river, "the East Bank." This area is fast becoming a preserved area of guildhalls and medieval houses. These charming Old World structures are still among the most precious landmarks in the old town.

Located in Zurich is the Swiss Federation of Jewish Communities, (SIG) Gotthardstrasse 65, PO Box 2105, CH-8027, Zurich. Tel: 41-43-305-07-77. FAX 43-3-5-07-66. Info@swissjews.ch. www.swissjews.ch.s

Half of Switzerland's Jewish population of 18,000 Jews live in the Zurich metropolitan area.

The Zurich skyline. (Photo courtesy of the Swiss National Tourist Office)

JEWISH SITES IN ZURICH

Marc Chagall, France's famed Jewish artist, is also well known in Zurich. His five stained-glass windows are located in the chancel of the **Fraumunster Church**. There is the Prophets Window, Jacob Window, Christ Window, Zion Window, and Law Window.

The Jewish ghetto here was once called the *Judengasse*. You would never know it now; there isn't very much left. We do know, however, that one small street now called **Froschaugasse** was located in the ghetto. Book and antique stores give the street a peaceful shopping appearance. Nearby is the building where Nikolai Lenin lived from February 1916 to April 1917. The sign on the building calls him "the Father of the Russian Revolution."

SYNAGOGUES IN ZURICH

The main address of the Zurich community is the **Cultural and Community Center** at 33 Lavaterstrasse, 8027, Zurich. Tel: 044 283 22 22. 201-1659. info@icz.org, www.icz.org. The building contains an extensive library and meeting halls. A synagogue is located here, too, as well as a kosher "cafe-restaurant," called **Schalom**. Tel: 201-14-76. The library is open Monday, 10:00 a.m. to noon, and 3:00 to 6:00 p.m. Closed Tuesday. On Wednesday, noon to 5:00 p.m.; Thursday, 10 a.m. to noon. Closed Friday. Sunday, 10:00 a.m. until noon. It is closed the last Sunday of the month.

Placed just off the fashionable Bahnhofstrasse and its designer stores is the oldest **synagogue** in Zurich, at 10 Lowenstrasse, 8001, Zurich. Built in 1883 in a Moorish style, it has two magnificent cupolas and an exterior of brown and whitish stone. While the rabbi is Orthodox and the service is Orthodox, many non-Orthodox Jews attend services here, I was told. Around the corner at Nuschelerstrasse 36, Zurich, is the entrance to the **prayer hall of the synagogue**. Tel: 41-43 211-68-80.

Agudas Achim, Erikastrasse 8, 8003 Zurich. Mikveh telephone for appointment: 41-43-7925.

Beth Chabad Lubavitch, Rudigerstrasse 10, 8038, Zurich. Tel: 41-43-201-0770. rabbi@chabad.ch.

Chabad Esra, Rehalpstrasse 89, 8008 Zurich. Tel: 41-43-383-9304. rabbi@chabadesra.ch

A traditional **German Orthodox Congregation** stands at 37 Freigutstrasse, 8002, Zurich. Tel: 41-43 201 49 98

Or Chadasch, a Liberal or Progressive synagogue, is at Hallwylstrasse 78, 8004 Zurich. Tel: 41-43-322-03-14. FAX: 41-43-322-03-16. info@jlg.ch. www.jlg.ch.

The Orthodox community here is the third largest in Europe after London and Antwerp.

Kosher Restaurants in Zurich

Bagels and Co. (dairy), Bederstreasse, corner Klopstocksrasse, 8002 Zurich.

Ma'adan, bakery and kosher groceries, Schimmelstrasse 13, 8003 Zurich. Tel: 44-762-4060.

Restaurant Olive Garden (meat), Cultural and Community Center, Lavatrstrasse 33, 8002, Zurch. Reservation: 41-43-283-22-13.

Fein & Shine (dairy), Schonpalstrasse 14, 8004 Zurich. Tel: 41-43-241-3040. FAX: 41-43-241-21-12

Suggested Reading

Hasler, Alfred A. *The Lifeboat Is Full: Switzerland and the Refugees, 1933-1945.* New York: Funk and Wagnalls, 1969.

Martin, Lawrence and Sylvia. *Switzerland: An Uncommon Guide.* New York: McGraw-Hill, 1965.

Schwarz, Urs. *The Eye of the Hurricane: Switzerland in World War Two.* Boulder, Colo: Westview Press, 1980.

Sorell, Walter. *The Swiss: A Cultural Panorama of Switzerland.* New York: Bobbs, Merrill, 1972.

Belgium
Diamonds, Rubies, and the Most Luxurious Ghetto in the World

Belgium does not have to boast it is the heart of Europe. Everyone knows it is. With its capital city, Brussels, designated as headquarters of both the European Union and NATO, this small country has achieved that goal.

Belgians not only speak English, they openly solicit and welcome English-speaking travelers. They have turned their beautiful canal and seashore cities and towns into tourist attractions. Explore Bruges, Ostend and Ghent and you will marvel at Belgian skills in welcoming visitors. Certainly Belgian cooking is giving the French a run for their money. We even found what probably is the best kosher restaurant in Europe in Antwerp at Hoffy's, which we shall discuss when we visit that city, which contains a vibrant, Orthodox Jewish community.

You can spend a week in this urbane country and enjoy every minute of it, including shopping for lace and tapestry and savoring world-renown, delicious Belgian chocolate.

Sandwiched between Germany and France, bordering, too, on the Netherlands and Luxemburg, and facing Britain across a narrow strip of the North Sea, this kingdom has seen wave after wave of invading armies. When you talk to these citizens about their role among nations, some bitterness creeps into the conversation. As they say, the whole world marched onto this tiny land to fight on Belgian battlefields: Waterloo, where Napoleon ended his military career; Flanders Fields in World War I, where a generation of English and French lads were wiped out halting the invading Germans; at Bastogne in World War II, where American troops withstood a last-gasp attack by the German Army.

So let us begin our journey to Brussels, Ghent, Bruges, Antwerp and Mechelen. After all, "if it is Tuesday, it must be Belgium."

Here along the North Sea lies Belgium, a rich nation of 12,000 square miles—the size of the state of Maryland—with outstanding cultural and artistic complexes blanketing the country.

As nations go, Belgium is a youngster, becoming an independent entity only in 1830. Its nineteenth-century creators hewed out an "artificial state" that had been ruled previously by Rome, Burgundy, Spain, Austria, France, and the Netherlands. It was also to be overrun by Nazi Germany in the twentieth century.

With its 11.5 million citizens, Belgium also holds the distinction of being the second most densely populated nation in Europe—after its neighbor, the Netherlands, that is. Belgium is flat—trisected by the Scheldt and Meuse rivers with the hills and forests of the Ardennes in the south.

A Brief History

The area came to be known as Belgium because it was settled by Belgic tribes of Celtic origin who were known as Belgica. Much of Jewish settlement in Europe began with the Roman conquests; Jews followed the path of those Roman legions in Belgium in the years 53 to 57 CE. A group of Jews may have reached the country just after the destruction of the Second Temple in the year 70 CE. Even with limited evidence, we know that Jews lived in Belgium from the ninth through the thirteenth centuries.

As in most countries of Europe, Belgian Jews were sometimes tolerated and at other times persecuted, depending on who ruled. Jews who were expelled from England in 1290 and from France in 1306 settled in Belgium and Holland. But in 1309, crusaders rampaged the area. Then came the Black Death of 1348, with its scapegoat, the Jews, who were charged with poisoning the wells and the Christians massacred nearly the entire Jewish community of Belgium. In 1380, Jews were accused of desecrating Christian religious symbols. They were dragged from their homes and burned at the stake.

Belgium remained Catholic; Holland had become Protestant. The Belgians never welcomed the Jews as warmly as did the Dutch. And so, the Jews did not come in any significant number until the sixteenth century. Attracting them to Belgium and Holland were the commercial cities of Zeeland and Flanders. The latter needed skilled newcomers for the lively markets of Antwerp and Bruges.

Enter the Marranos, the "secret Jews" who arrived in the Belgian cities in the early sixteenth century. Antwerp's star was rising and the Marranos were sharp businessmen. Because Antwerp needed them, the city fathers gave these Iberians or "New Christians" safe-conduct passes. The Marranos accepted the offer, settled down, and introduced the flourishing silk trade in 1526.

Marranos could not go directly from Spain or Portugal to southern lands in the Mediterranean, so some would pass through Antwerp en route to, of all places, "hospitable" Turkey. An underground railroad from Spain and Portugal via Antwerp to Holland and Turkey was set up. For example, Joao Miguez, a famous Jewish personality of the day who became the future Duke of Naxos and known as Joseph Nasi, came to Antwerp to reach Turkey. He maintained many important commercial contacts. Antwerp also became the first stop on the long odyssey of the Marranos over the Alps into Italy or the Balkans. The clergy, enforcing the Inquisition, watched every move of these New Christians, many of whom secretly practiced Judaism and sought religious freedom.

Later, with the establishment of a free Jewish community in Amsterdam, the main tide of Marrano settlement from Iberia moved from Antwerp toward Amsterdam, which then became the metropolis of the Marrano Diaspora. Still, because Belgium displayed a high quality of life, it would continue to attract Jews.

But waves of unrest surfaced in the seventeenth and eighteenth centuries. Holland and Belgium were split when the northern provinces under Maurice of Nassau won their independence from Spain in 1609. That division continues to this day.

Belgians have learned that they must get along with each other in order to survive. The country exists as a bicultural, bilingual state. People here speak both Flemish and French and some German.

One group, the Flemings, speak Flemish (a dialect of Dutch). They outnumber the other group, the Walloons, by about two million. The Flemings live in Flanders, along the North Sea and on the northern plains, in an area rich in agriculture. The Walloons live in Wallonia, which is in the southern plains and in the hills of the Ardennes. Bordering on France and Luxembourg, they speak French.

When Belgium, which had been governed by Spain since 1519, was turned over to Austria in 1713 according to the Treaty of Utrecht, the Jewish community began to live in relative freedom and attracted Eastern European Jews.

In 1794, the French invaded the Netherlands, which then included Belgium, and immediately introduced religious equality for the 800 Jews. In 1808, Napoleon established the Consistoire Central Israelite, which to this very day stands as the representative body of Belgian Jewry.

After Napoleon was defeated in the Battle of Waterloo, the great powers, meeting at the Congress of Vienna in 1815, did not feel France should rule Belgium. The British pushed for a single state for both the Dutch and Belgians. Nobody bothered to ask the people of Holland and Belgium what they thought about a unified state. The union lasted 15 years.

In 1830, Belgium began its revolt against Dutch rule and soon won its independence. In the new state, religion received official recognition and Jewish religious freedom was written into the constitution guaranteed by the Concert of Europe.

Throughout the nineteenth century, the Jewish population in Belgium increased. By 1900, Antwerp contained 8,000 to 10,000 Jews, including many who would soon be on their way to the United States. Others were attracted to the city by the diamond industry. Jewish life, however, was interrupted by World War I, as Belgian neutrality was scrapped by the invading Germans.

Between World Wars I and II, the Jewish population in Belgium continued to grow, reaching about 100,000, a quarter of them refugees from Nazi Germany. After the Nazis' rise to power in 1933, Antwerp counted 55,000 Jews and Brussels, 30,000. When the Germans unleashed their blitzkrieg strike on the Western front on May 10, 1940, many Belgian Jews fled to France. But they were not safe there, as France, too, was conquered and large numbers of Jews would later be rounded up and returned to Belgium, which itself capitulated to the Germans in May 1940.

By August 1942, the Nazis began transporting Belgian Jews to Auschwitz. Within a year, about one-third of the Jews in Belgium were murdered. By war's end, about 40,000 of the 85,000 Jews who had lived in Belgium perished. After the war, thousands of Jewish refugees from Eastern Europe, many of whom awaited permission to enter the United States and Israel, poured into the country. By the 1960s, both immigration and emigration decreased. The community stabilized.

Today, the majority of Belgian Jews are middle class and are active in the fur, textile, and diamond industries. Total Jewish population is approximately 40,000. About 18,000 to 20,000 Jews live in Brussels, 15,000 to 18,000 in Antwerp. In addition, about 2,000 Jews reside in smaller Jewish communities such as Charleroi, Ostend, Ghent, Liege, Mons, Arlon, Knokke, and Namur.

But times have changed: Fear of attack is the new norm among Belgian Jews. One reason is that Belgium has become a "per capita contributor of fighters to Syria, and its capital has become an incubator for radicalism."

Belgium, as other countries in Europe after World War II, was considered "safe" for Jews. No longer. When Muslim terrorism explodes in Europe, Jews are often the target. Many Belgian Jews have already left for Israel or the United States. Some of the killers in the 2015 Paris attacks were radical Muslims living in Belgium. They were also violently anti-Semitic.

If there is one incident in Belgium that rocked the Jewish

community into an insecure mental state, it was the May, 2014 terrorist attack at the Jewish Museum of Belgium in Brussels. Four people were killed; three died at the scene; a fourth was taken to the hospital and later died. Mehdi Nemmouche was later captured. He was initially extradited to Belgium from France after his arrest. No trial is likely before September 2018.

French prosecutors filed a European arrest warrant to have him prosecuted in France on charges of terrorism and kidnapping. In 90 seconds, the shooter, Mehdi Nemmouche, struck fear into the hearts of the Jewish community, so much so that people who never thought of immigrating to Israel or other countries were now seriously considering it.

The list goes on: Belgian jihadist Abdelhamid Abaaoud, suspected of organizing the November 13 attacks in Paris in 2015, is killed on November 18.

During a police raid on an apartment where he had been hiding in the Saint-Denis area north of Paris, Salah Abdeslam was arrested in the Molenbeek area of Brussels on March 18, 2016. The most wanted man in Europe was hiding in a building a few hundred metres away from his parents' house. The capture occurred four days before the Brussels airport attack. Molenbeek is said to be a predominantly Muslim neighborhood often searched for terrorists by the Belgian police.

Fear among Belgium Jews reached new heights when, on March 22, 2016, three coordinated suicide bombings occurred in Belgium: two at Brussels Airport in Zaventem, and one at Maelbeek metro station in central Brussels. The perpetrators belonged to a terrorist cell which had been involved in the November 2015 Paris attacks.

Belgian Jews are now accustomed to fearing for their safety. Every morning when parents drop off their children at Jewish schools across the country, they are greeted by heavily armed soldiers, stationed to protect the students. Jews know not to be too open about their faith, avoiding wearing kippahs or Stars of David on the streets. Jews in Belgium seem like they are always on "high alert."

"The Jewish community feels more threatened because we remain a target of those attacks. The fact that we have not been specifically targeted this time does not mean that we will not be in the future," Serge Rozen, president of the Coordinating Committee of Belgian Jewish Organizations, told the *Forward* in March 2016.

Even after the terrorist attacks, the *aliyah* numbers are relatively stable—about 250 a year, though in 2015, 287 Jews immigrated to Israel from Belgium. From 2010 to 2015, an average of 234 Belgian Jews made *aliyah* annually—56 percent increase over the annual average of 133 new arrivals from Belgium to 2005-2009, according to Israel government data.

Community leaders now speak with alarm of a rising tide of anti-Semitism in a country that has been home to Jews since Roman times. Sad indeed! As one Jewish leader put it: "There is a very strong feeling of fear and uneasiness about the situation of Jews in Belgium," though he implied, "not as dramatic as sometimes presented in the US media."

Still in 2017, as in Germany and France, anti-Semitic attitudes dropped again significantly from 2016, it was reported. In that year, 28 anti-Semitic reports were registered in Belgium. But, as was pointed out, many victims do not report incidents.

An example of difficulties facing the Belgian Jewish community is the question of ritual slaughter and the move by regional parliaments to ban the non-slaughter of small animals, a move which would outlaw the provision of kosher meat produced in the country. Such a ban exists in various countries in Scandinavia. European Jewish communities are adamantly against the proposal. Brussels chief rabbi Albert Guigui noted that the Nazi occupiers had banned *"shecita"* even prior to enacting other anti-Jewish measures.

In Europe, the Jewish and Muslim customs have united opponents both from liberal circles who cite animal welfare as their main concern and right-wing nationalists who view the custom as foreign to their countries' cultures, it was reported. Thus, Walloon intends to effectively ban ritual slaughter in June 2018.

In another matter, again, as in other countries in Western Europe, immigration of Belgian Jews to the US and Canada is "trending upward." The highly educated members of the community "can settle anywhere in Europe and have little trouble getting visas to the US, Canada, and Australia," wrote Cnaan Liphshiz, of JTA, adding, "Unlike French Jews, who tend to speak only one native language, Belgian Jews speak two and often three languages fluently." This could mean Belgian Jews have an easier time than their French counterparts immigrating to destinations that are not Israel.

Jewish Brussels

The city welcomes, shelters, and entertains diplomats. No wonder this ancient metropolis employs thousands of civil servants and "ex-pats," many of them American. Flocking to the cobble stone Grand Place, tourists gape at this lovely square; they focus on the superb architecture of these Old World buildings, and they enjoy its fine cafés, restaurants, and nearby shops.

The city of 176,000 stands as the nation's fifth largest city. But if you count the suburbs, it becomes the country's largest metropolitan area.

The Grand Palace, Brussels (Photo by Ben G. Frank)

People have been moving to the outlying suburbs, such as Waterloo.

Brussels is shaped like a heart. The oldest section, called the lower city, is in the center. This area includes the Grand Place, which is surrounded by elaborately decorated buildings built in the 1600s to house merchant and craft guilds. The Brussels town hall actually dates from the 1400s.

Jews probably arrived here in the mid-thirteenth century. The Black Death nearly wiped out the entire Jewish community in 1348. Further unrest and exclusion kept the Jewish population at a low level.

From time to time, Marranos found their way here, and in 1713 the Treaty of Utrecht brought Austrian rule and the return of some Jews. In 1757, the Jewish community of Brussels consisted of 21 men, 19 women, and 26 children, many of whom had moved here from Holland. But with the French annexation of Belgium in 1794, Jews again began flocking to Brussels in large numbers. Over the next 150 years Jews came from Holland, Germany, and Eastern Europe. By 1939 10,000 Jews lived in Brussels.

JEWISH SITES IN BRUSSELS

These "Little Belgians" as the French call them, have welcomed and absorbed Jews into their country. When Belgium became independent in 1830, Jews became equal citizens.

Travelers need to recognize that two separate Jewish communities existing in the same country could not be as different as Brussels and Antwerp.

Let us visit the Brussels Jewish community first.

Chabad representatives in Brussels explained that the Jewish community lives in neighborhoods throughout the city, whereas in Antwerp, Jews live mostly in one area.

Jewish leaders agree that assimilation is high among Jews in Brussels. Whether it is higher or not, "it is true that both cities look different. The perception is that Antwerp Jews are more visible and religious, while Brussels Jews are more secular," notes Yohan Benizri, president of the CCOJB.

Still Benizri adds that "both Brussels and Antwerp have very active communities, a strong sense of belonging and collective responsibility, and a very strong bond both to Belgium and to Israel."

Coordinating Committee of Belgian Jewish Organizations, Comite de Coordination des Organizations Juive de Belgique (CCOJB,) Ave. Ducpétiaux 68, 1060 Saint-Gilles. Brussels. Tel: 32-2-537-16-91. FAX: 32-2-539-22-96. www.ccojb.be.

The Union of Deportees Organization and the World Jewish Congress (Belgian Section) are also here.

Consistoire Central Israelite de Belgique, (C.C.I.B.) rue Joseph Dupont, 1000 Brussels. Tel: 32-2-512-21-90. FAX: 32-2-512-35-78. www.jewishcom.be. Since Belgium became a nation in the 19th Century, the C.C.I.B. acts as the representative of the Belgian Jewish community to the Belgian government.

Communaute Israelite de Brussels, rue Joseph Dupont 2, 1000 Brussels. Tel: 32-2-512-43-34. FAX: 32-2-512-92-37. This group respresents the Jewish community of Brussels.

Communaute Israelite Orthodoxe de Brusells, 67 a rue de la Clinique, 1070 Brussels. Tel: 32-2-521-12-89.

Communalite Sephardite de Brussels, 47 rue du Pavillon, 1020 Brussels. Tel: 32-2-215-05-25.

Synagogues, Schools, and Organizations

The Great Synagogue, 32 rue de la Regence, 1000, Brussels. Tel: 32-2-512-43-34. This is a magnificent synagogue on a magnificent, stately boulevard, a boulevard that contains important Protestant and Catholic churches. Built in 1878, it was not damaged during the Holocaust. The building was described by a Belgian writer in the 19th century as "one of the most successfully carried out buildings of modern Brussels." Today, the chief rabbi maintains his office here. There is a minyan every day: Services on weekday mornings are held at 8:00 p.m. and in the evening depending, of course, on sunset.

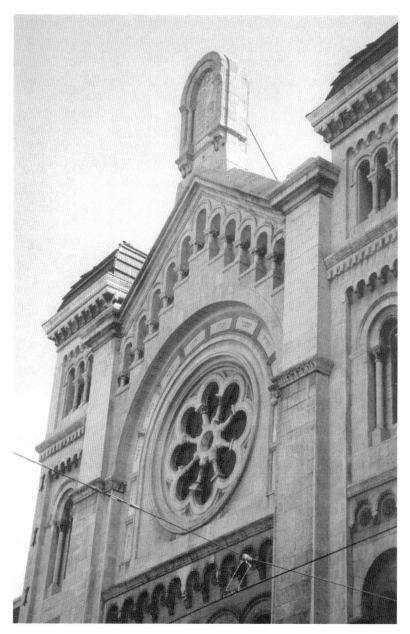

The Great Synagogue, Brussels. (Photo by Ben G. Frank)

Friday night services are held around 6:00 p.m. or 7:00 p.m. and on Saturday mornings, prayers begin at 9:30 a.m. Call the synagogue for exact times.

The architect for this synagogue, which was constructed between 1875 and 1878, was Desire DeKeyser. On the façade, there are ornamental features, such as a rose window. A feature of this house of worship is the three-storied gabled central section flanked by slightly recessed four-storied towers which conceal low-glass-covered passages running along the north and south sides of the building, according to Carol Herselle Krinsky, author of *Synagogues of Europe: Architecture, History, Meaning.*

Nearly a million francs was spent on building the synagogue and the community administration building which is next door and whose entrance is on **rue Joseph Dupont**. Use this entrance for weekday services as well as services on some Saturday mornings.

Beth Chabad, 87 Ave. du Roi, 1190, Brussels. Tel: 32-2-537-47-70. shlasker@gmail.com, www.chabadbrussels.com. Beth Chabad offers Shabbat meals every Friday night.

Chir Hadach, (Masorti Olami) 89 Chauser de Vleurgat, Brussels. Tel: 32-4-75-38-6944.

Shaarei Tsion, rue Boetendal 147, 1180 Brussels.

Beth Israel, Ave. Stalingrad 74, 1000 Brussels.

Congregation Israelite, Sepharde Unifiee (CISU) rue Roosendael 154, Brussels. Tel: 32-2-346-34-87.

Ohel Eliezer, rue Froissart 109, 1040 Brussels. Tel: 32-2-335-57-71.

Maale, 11 Ave. de Messidor, 1190 Brussels.

Foyer Sepharade, Ave. Winston Churchill, 150, 1180 Brussels. Tel: 32-4-75-24-54-99.

Communaute Israelite Liberale de Belgique, Beth Hillel, rue des Primeurs 80. 1190 Brussels. Tel: 32-2-332-2528. FAX: 32-2-376-7219. info@beth-hillel.org. www.beth-hillel.org. Tourists passing through Brussels often contact this synagogue, which welcomes tourists. As in most synagogues and Jewish institutions, best to let their office know of your arrival ahead of time.

International Jewish Center. Reform and English-speaking. info@ijc.be. www.ijc.be. With its description as Progressive Jewish Community of Belgium, this group meets at neighbor's homes in central Brussels as well as in other organization's facilities in the suburbs of the capital.

Musee Juif de Belgique, Ave. de Stalingrad, 1000 Brussels. The Jewish Museum is open Monday to Friday, from noon to 5:00 p.m.; Sunday, from 10:00 a.m. to 1:00 p.m. In 2002, a new Jewish museum opened in the rue des Minimes 21, 1000 Bruselles, 10:00 a.m. to 5:00 p.m. every day, closed on Mondays. On 24 May 2014, a gunman opened fire at the Jewish Museum of Belgium, killing four people. Three died at the scene; a fourth was taken to the hospital and died on June 6th.

B'nai B'rith, 68, Ave. Duepetiaux. Tel: 02-537-39-17.

Fédération Nadonale des Anciens Combattants et Résistants Juifs Armés de Belgique, 148, Chaussée d'Ixelles.

Jewish Community Center, Centre Communautaire Laïc Juif, 52, rue Hotel des Monnaies. Brussels. The Federation of Jewish Youth is also here. Tel: 32-2-532-82-16.

FAX de Jerusalem, semi-monthly review of the Zionist organization of Belgium, 66-68, Ave. Duepetiaux, Brussels. At 68, Ave. Duepetiaux is The Zionist Federation (Tel: 32-2- 538-56-29) and the

Institut d'Etudes du Judaisme—Institut Martin Buber, 17, Ave. Franklin Roosevelt, Brussels. Tel: 02-650-33-48. FAX: 02-650-33-47. iej@ ulb.ac.bl. This is part of the Free University of Brussels. Conducting studies in Judaism at the university level, it is also known as Institut Universitaire d'etudes du Judaisme Martin Buber. The Centre National des Hautes Etudes Juives (the National Center of Higher Jewish Studies) is also located here. Tel: 32-2-648-81-58, ext., 3348.

An impressive **National Monument to the Jewish Martyrs of Belgium** is at rue Emile Carpentier and rue de Goujons in the district of Anderlecht. The square is called Square of the Jewish Martyrs, and 23,838 names are inscribed on the wall. A small museum is also located here. Office: U.D.J.B. 68 Ave. Duepetiaux. Tel: 32-2-538-98-66.

KOSHER DINING IN BRUSSELS

La Mozzarella, Ave. Brugmann 522, 1180 Brussels. Tel: 32-2-217-74-67.

Kosher supermarket. Eatanous, rue H. Wafelaerts 12, Brussels. Tel: 32-2-343-18-48

Kosher supermarket. Gel Tov, rue Vanderkindere 381, 1180 Brussels. Tel: 32-2-346-8700. Only open various hours. Call ahead.

Ghent

"Welcome to Flanders," the guides will tell you.

They do not have to add, "enjoy your stay in Flanders," because you will. Not only is Ghent one of the most beautiful historic cities in Flanders, it was its capital. Today it is less than an hour from Bruges, Antwerp, Brussels and the airport. I found it a quiet city with high-quality events.

Americans will realize that here in the early 19th century, peace talks were underway at Ghent, with the aim of ending the War of 1812 between the U.S. and Great Britain. The final treaty did exactly that and was signed on December 24, 1814. Among those representing the U.S. were Henry Clay, John Quincy Adams and Albert Gallatin. I recalled that when I entered college I was shocked to learn that the U.S. actually lost the war itself, but won a victory at the peace table at Ghent.

Here I was in the city where the Treaty of Ghent in reality settled none of the disputes that caused the war, but merely restored the situation that existed previously, without the British boarding our ships.

The waterways right in the center of the town are quite attractive and add to the peace of the municipality. At one time Ghent had 76 bridges. This city once was a power in Europe and you can still see the spirit of enterprise in the facades of the guild houses.

The flower markets, the fruit markets, the vegetable markets add to the atmosphere of a city that is in effect part museum.

Jewish Ghent

There is no synagogue in Ghent. Nor is there a kosher butcher shop or a single kosher restaurant. But there is a Jewish community and there are Jews in Ghent—perhaps 100 live and work in the area. Non-Jews will lead you to one of the town's leading citizens who is Jewish: if you stop a native of Ghent on the street and ask if there's a synagogue in Ghent, chances are he or she will send you to Blochs Bakery, J Veldstraat 60, 9000 Ghent. Tel: 32-9-225-70-85. This concern has had a presence in this town for many, many years. It is a fine establishment and the minute you enter you know you are in a Jewish establishment. There, facing you on the shelves of this bakery and tea room (non-kosher), are several Jewish National Fund boxes.

Ghent is an historic Jewish community. It was founded at the end of the 19th century, and grew between World Wars I and II. Many Eastern Europeans study at the university here.

The synagogue is not the center of Jewish life here and the Jewish community is not religious. Judaism here is "not linked to religion."

A very important site in Ghent is the **Holocaust Memorial, Coupure rechts and Linden lei**. This Holocaust memorial is in the shape of a dreidel and is located at the confluence of a major canal. But it is not easy to locate. Often tourists are told about it when they are walking in the area or come upon it by accident. More than half of the Jewish population of Belgium survived the war, according to Holocaust historian Yehuda Bauer. He explains that the Christian population and the activities of various Jewish underground groups helped save

The Holocaust Memorial in Ghent. (Photo by Ben G. Frank)

Jews. Unlike the Dutch, the Belgians did not follow the orders of the Germans or of the Jewish leaders to register and report for assignments in work camps elsewhere, which, as we know, turned out to be located in the killing fields of Poland.

Another memorial to the Holocaust is located on a wall of the city's university building. There is a memorial plaque citing the deportation of Jewish students during World War II.

Ghent Jewish Community. Blochs Bakery, J Veldstraat 60, Ghent. Tel: 09-225-70-85.

Bruges

As long as I can remember: mention Belgium, and travelers answer, "Bruges."

And they are right. This sophisticated, small, pretty city will not let you down.

As far as we can tell, there are no Jews living in Bruges. We were told Jews work there, but they are commuters, driving in from Antwerp or Ghent or other nearby cities.

Bruges long ago figured out exactly how to attract tourists and went about doing it. The city sports canals, excellent eateries, from fine, gourmet restaurants to moderate establishments, and historic structures that invite exploration. The shops and stores here are geared for tourists, especially for keen shoppers. Even in the rain,

A familiar sight in Bruges. (Photo by Ben G. Frank)

True, you can jump onto a little yellow minivan for a city tour. Or you can see Bruges by boat or bike or horse-drawn cab. All this is fine as long as some place along the line, as they say, you get out of a car and become a pedestrian. You see, Bruges is a walking town and the traveler will just love the shops, the museums, the banks of the Lake of Love and the picturesque canals. Walking is the best way to discover Bruges. The city is rather small. You can easily walk across it in a half-hour.

Don't forget to visit the City Hall, the Old Country House, the Fish Market and the city's many museums.

Bruges was once a world-famous trading center and a cradle of Flemish art. It started as a Gallo-Roman settlement in the Second and Third centuries. From the 11th Century, Bruges became an international commercial center, thanks to its direct access to the sea. Around 1350, Bruges had about 45,000, twice the amount it counts today. In the 15th Century, Flanders became part of the Burgundian state. But at the end of the 15th Century, the Burgundians left Bruges and the city's "Golden Age" ended. First, the city lost its outlet to the sea because of the silting up of the coastal area. Then, Antwerp pulled ahead of Bruges and took over the wool trade. It took several hundred years, but Bruges finally regained its position as an art and tourist city. Europe still thinks that it is a fine place to visit. In 2002, Bruges bears the title of "Cultural Capital of Europe."

Travel is much faster today in Europe. For example, you can take high-speed trains in direct runs between Brussels and Charles de Gaulle Airport in Paris. This journey takes about 1 hour 25 minutes to travel between the Paris airport and Brussels. But now let's hop a train to that inviting port city of Antwerp.

Antwerp

A proverb says: "Antwerp owes the Scheldt to God and everything else to the Scheldt River."

The latter made Antwerp the business and commercial capital of Northern Europe and the second largest city of Belgium.

Antwerp is Antwerp and here they speak Flemish, which is basically Dutch. Only Flemish has less guttural sounds than the Dutch they speak in Holland. (In Brussels, they speak both French and Flemish). Antwerp with its 463,000 citizens is Belgium's second largest metropolis. It thrives as a lively commercial center and a very active harbor. Busy as it is during the week, on Sundays, the city's populace goes outdoors and strolls on the promenade along the Schelde River or sits in the cafes in Old City. The natives, joined by the tourists, love to devour mussels and frites (french fries).

In the age-old tradition of one of its major occupations, that is, diamonds of course, Antwerp's art also dazzles, for this city is also Rubens, Van Dyck, Jordaens, Bruegel and Plantin. The city owes much of its cosmopolitan atmosphere to its art, its diamond business and its shipping center.

Antwerp is proud of its many museums: the **Plantin Moretus Museum** and the **Fine Arts Museum** are the best known.

The old Plantin Moretus Museum in the Vrijdagmarkt has examples of Jewish printing, as well as the Polyglot Bible.

This was the home of the great sixteenth-century printer Moretus and of his descendants. In 34 years, he published about 1,500 different works, a phenomenal achievement. Included were editions of classical authors, Hebrew Bibles, and liturgical pieces. The pressroom, foundry, proofreaders' room, and bookshop are still in their original state. The Plantin Moretus Museum also contains an exceptional collection of manuscripts, books, wood blocks, copperplates, and tapestries, as well as paintings by Rubens and others. It is well worth a visit.

The Jewish traveler to Antwerp, a world port and a mecca for art lovers, has no problem whatsoever in finding Jews. Head for the streets called **Pelikaanstraat** or **Hovenierstraat**. You'll find synagogues, bookstores, restaurants, kosher bakeries, and, of course, diamond marts. The area just looks Jewish.

"This is the most luxurious ghetto in the world," said one Jew who lived on **Belgielei Street**, where many Jews reside. He quickly added, "It's a free-will ghetto, of course." No doubt the Jews of Antwerp are very tightly knit. They live together and work together. After all, about 90 percent of the Antwerp Jewish population of 18,000 is involved in the diamond industry.

Antwerp always has been a "Jewish" city. As one Jewish leader put it, "The non-Jews of Antwerp are so used to living with Jews, they don't see them as Jews." Non-Jews know that their Jewish friends like to live alone and are not too involved in the political and social life of the city.

Most of the Jews of Antwerp are of Polish origin and Orthodox. They admit they just don't mingle.

One must remember that the letters forming the name Antwerp spell "diamonds" and "Orthodox Judaism."

And the diamond industry is built on everyone knowing everyone else; reputation and trust are paramount. This breeds a certain amount of introversion, to say the least. They live in a "diamond world." More Chassidim live here than in any other city in Europe, five or six different sects, such as Belz, Gur, Lubavitch, Satmar, Chortkov, and Vizhnitz. In fact, some say the Lubavitch are not that active in Antwerp, because at least 75 percent of the community is

Orthodox. "It is another life and another world, a religious world," a Jew in Antwerp told me.

Ninety percent of the Jewish children of Antwerp go to Jewish day schools, which include yeshivot of such sects as Belz, Satmar, and Vizhnitz.

Others point out that, unlike other cities in Europe, intermarriage is not high here because obviously people are religious. "If you are in the diamond business, you don't want people to think of you as one married outside the religion," said one merchant.

A Dutch-language weekly is published in Antwerp, as are various Yiddish publications. The Anti-Defamation League in Antwerp publishes a monthly called *In de Naam Van de Vrijheid (In the Name of Freedom)*.

American Jews, religious or nonreligious, who want to inhale the "shtetl" life of Europe before World War II, can still find a shining example in Antwerp. The signs and the institutions are here.

Shabbat (Sabbath) morning here resembles a scene out of B'nei Brak, Israel, or Williamsburg, Brooklyn, USA: Chassidic fathers and sons walking to synagogue or to a shtibel. No business is conducted in the Antwerp Diamond District on Saturdays. The Diamond Exchange employs a large number of the chassidim; you can easily believe you are walking on the street of diamond exchanges on West 47th St. in Manhattan.

Orthodox Judaism is very well organized in Antwerp. Two large Orthodox groups in Antwerp, Shomre Hadass and Machsike Hadass, are active in the city. No problem of obtaining a minyan here. No problem of children attending Jewish studies, albeit a strictly religious one, here. No problem of intermarriage here. No problem of finding kosher food here. There are other problems, of course: Unemployment and Jews disagreeing with each other. Undoubtedly, as one diamond worker once told me, a number follow religious observances so as not be excluded. Still, Antwerp has been described as "a Jewish ghetto."

JEWISH CENTERS AND SCHOOLS

The Romi Goldmuntz Center, Nerviersstraat 12-D14. Tel: 03-239-39-11. Built in 1968, this beautiful, modern structure maintains a library, meeting rooms, a catering hall, sports facilities, and a kosher snack bar.

Tachkemoni School, Lange Leemstraat 313. Tel: 03-239-04-67. This Jewish day school with about 780 pupils is Zionist oriented.

Yesodei Hatora Beth Jacob, Lange Van Ruusbroeck Straat. This day school has about 1,100 pupils. Some say about 90 percent of the Jewish children in Antwerp attend this school or the Tachkemoni one. The Jewish day schools of Antwerp are unique in Europe, and the Jewish Board of Education maintains good relations with the government's Bureau of Education.

KOSHER RESTAURANTS IN ANTWERP

Nearly a dozen kosher restaurants and delis exist in Antwerp. Here are a few:

Hoffy's, Lange Kievitstraat 52, 2018 Antwerp. Tel: 32-3-234-35-35. info@hoffys.be. They are three Orthodox brothers. And they are called Yumi, Yankele and Moishe. But can they cook? It is this author's opinion, that this by far is one of the best strictly kosher restaurants in all of Europe. The restaurant which is open from 11:00 a.m. to about 10:00 p.m. at night, serves up stuffed cabbage, schnitzel, chicken, roast. Fish is also served with zucchini, carrots, potatoes etc. One great feature of this superb establishment is that you can go up to the

The three brothers of Hoffy's kosher restaurant in Antwerp. (Photo by Ben G. Frank)

counter and pick what you like; a little bit of this, a little bit of that. Obviously closed on the Sabbath and all holidays.

Moszkowitz, Lange Kievitstraat, 47, 2018 Antwerp. Tel: 323-232-03-49. FAX: 32-3-226-04-71. This is a fine take-out facility.

Blue Lagon, Lange Herentalsestraat, 70, 2018, Antwerp. 32-3-226-01-14.

Beni Felafel, Leemstraat, 188, 2018 Antwerp.

Mama Mia, Plantin Moretusle, 10, 2018 Antwerp.

Rivi's, Isabellalei 51, 2018 Antwerp. Tel: 32-3-281-23-00

Time Out, Lange Herentaslsestraat, 58, 2018 Antwerp.

A snack bar is located at the **Romi Goldmuntz Center**, Nerviersstraat 12, Antwerp.

SYNAGOGUES

There are more than 20 synagogues here in Antwerp, plus many "shtieblach" (small prayer halls).

Americans usually pray at the **Romi Goldmuntz Synagogue**, not located at the community center, but at Van den Nestlei 1.

Beth Jacob Synagogue, Jacob Jacobstraat 22, Antwerp. Tel: 32-3-231-40-39.

Beth Hamidrash Hagadol Synagogue, Oostenstraat, 43, Antwerp. Tel: 32-3-230-92-46.

Beth Lubavitch, Belgielei 20, 2018 Antwerp. Tel: 32-3-218-41-96. www.chabadantwerp.org.

Communaute Israelite du Rite Portugais d'Anvers, Hoveniersstraat 32, 2018 Antwerp. Tel: 32-3-232-53-39.

"Hollandse" Synagogue, Bouwmeesterstraat 7. Moriah Synagogue, Terliststraat 35. Antwerp. Tel: 32-3-232-01-87.

Sephardic synagogue, Hovenierstraat 31, Antwerp. Tel: 32-232-5339.

ORGANIZATIONS

There are many Jewish cultural, political, and youth organizations in Antwerp.

Communaute Israelite Shomre Hadass d'Anvers, Terliststraat 35, 2018 Antwerp. Tel: 32-3-232-01-87.

Communaute Orthodoxe Machsike Hadass d'Anvers, Jacob Jacobstraat 22, 2018, Antwerp. Tel: 323-233-55-67. This is the headquarters of this Orthodox community.

Agudath Israel, Lamorinierestraat 67, Antwerp. Tel: 03-230-85-13. Keren Hayesod, Schupstraat 1, Antwerp. Tel: 03-232-97-74/232-05-28.

Mechelen

Jewish Museum of Deportation and Resistance, Goswin De Stassartstr 153, 2800 Mechelen. Tel: 32-15-29-06-60. FAX: 015-29-08-76. info@kazernedossin.eu, www.kazernedossin.eu. This museum tells in part the story of the Holocaust in Belgium. Located in the Dossin Barracks which were used in World War II as an assembly point; this facility served as a holding pen for Jews and gypsies prior to deporting them to the concentration camps, This is one of the few Holocaust museums located in a place which was an "ante-room" in the extermination process of Jews.

From these barracks, 25,124 persons including 5,430 children, were dispatched, mostly to Auschwitz. The first convoys left the Dossin Barracks on August 4, 1942. Between that date and July 31, 1944, the Nazis organized twenty-five more convoys.

Nearly half of the Jewish population of Belgium was murdered during the Holocaust. Belgian Jews indicate that while every country had its collaborators, Belgium was one of the countries that tried to save its Jewish citizens.

The museum was opened on May 7, 1995 by the King of Belgium.

First, the visitor to the museum will learn about the early history of the Jews of Belgium. Step by step, the museum will show the methods the Germans employed in transforming the Jewish community into a pariah and then moved to destroy every last vestige of Belgian Jewry. But in Belgium, there was resistance, armed struggle, overt or clandestine action. Shown in the museum is "Belgium under the German Occupation of 1940-1942." One can also see drawings made by detainees in the Dossin Barracks.

Open Sundays to Thursdays from 10:00 a.m. to 5:00 p.m., Fridays from 10:00 a.m. to 1:00 p.m.

The museum is closed on Friday afternoons and Saturdays and on the Jewish holidays of Rosh Hashanah and Yom Kippur as well as on the holidays of Christmas Day and New Year's Day. Also closed during the annual summer holidays in the second and third week of August.

Suggested Reading

Krinsky, Carol Herselle. *Synagogues of Europe: Architecture, History, Meaning,* Cambridge, Mass.: MIT Press, 1985.

Lerman, Anthony, ed. *The Jewish Communities of the World: A Contemporary Guide.* London: Macmillan, 1989.

Pilkington, Roger. *Small Boat through Belgium.* London: 1957.

Holland
The European Jewish Grandees and Anne Frank

Amsterdam conjures up water, canals, and an active port. Sit and watch the barges ply the canals. Stare at gleaming diamonds in polishing factories. Stroll on streets strewn with leaves as the cool sea breeze bites your face. Then follow the path of nearly 200 canals that were created by the dredging of infected marshes.

Visit the city's museums; Van Gogh and Rembrandt are just two Dutch masters to see. Inhale the spirit that covers the home of the young Anne Frank, whose name will live forever.

A Brief History

This is Amsterdam, the Netherlands, a place that has always welcomed political and religious refugees. For centuries, Jews have carried on a love affair with Holland, a relationship that began in the twelfth century. Called "Little Jerusalem" and "Mokum, the place," Holland has never persecuted Jews.

In this country of harbors, the first large-scale immigration of Jews came here via the sea from Spain and Portugal in 1580. The newcomers were Marranos, secret Jews, who had escaped to Holland and were no longer forced to hide their religion. They could also apply their financial acumen to careers in banking, importing, and exporting in the city that was founded about 700 years ago and which, by the second half of the fifteenth century, was the "emporium of Europe," a commercial capital, a melting pot. This was the place to be, especially for Jews who thrive in a pluralistic society.

These grandees, the aristocracy of Dutch Jews, came here for economic opportunities, religious freedom, and culture. Their names still resound through Jewish history: Spinoza, Cardozo, Pereira, de Castro, Da Costa, Lopes Mendes, Suasso, Teixerira de Mattos. They worked as silk manufacturers, sugar refiners, printers, book dealers, tobacco merchants, brokers, and doctors.

Legend has it that Uri Ha Levi, a rabbi from Emden, came to Amsterdam about 1600 and met his fellow Jews at a tower that still stands, the **Montel-baanstoren Church.** The first Jewish neighborhood was said to have begun here.

Amsterdam would later become the "metropolis of the Marrano Diaspora." With freedom to worship and unrestricted economic choice, most became entrepreneurs. They became involved in the Dutch West and East Indies companies and, as a result, they became plantation owners and merchants in Brazil, Dutch Guiana, Curaçao, and the Dutch East Indies.

Yet, they did not live by bread alone. As heirs of Spanish, Portuguese, and Moorish culture, Dutch Jewry, made up mostly of Sephardim, would become one of the most important "cultural conveyors" of Jewish life in Europe.

In 1601, the Amsterdam Municipal Council approved a law that Jews could live anywhere in the city they desired. Jews held religious services in a home in 1607 and, the very next year, a congregation was established. In 1610, Jews were already living in The Hague, Rotterdam, Haarlem, Amersfoort, and Alkmaar. Two years later, a synagogue was built in Amsterdam.

In 1616, authorities officially sanctioned the community as members of the Hebrew nation, and Rabbi Isaac Uziel writes that the Jews "live peacefully in Amsterdam." A basic law was passed in 1619 declaring that each city in the provinces could adopt its own local policy toward the Jews.

In 1627, the first Hebrew book was printed. Fifty years later came a Spanish-language paper and Yiddish biweekly, the *Kurant,* according to Jules B. Farber in his *Amsterdam, City of the Seventies.*

In some localities, Jews were singled out, excluded from many trades, guilds, and professions. But compared with Jews in Catholic countries, here was "exceptional liberty" granted by liberal-minded Protestants.

And one man who was on particularly good terms with the Christian community was Manasseh Ben Israel (1604-57), alias Manoel Dias Soeiro, a Marrano, born in Madeira. He was one of the most illustrious rabbis of his age and of world Jewry. His parents brought him to Amsterdam in 1605. At age 18 he became rabbi at a synagogue no longer in existence in Waterlooplein. He acquired fame for his knowledge of Hebrew and the classical languages, enabling him to build contacts with many Christian theologians in Holland and abroad, with whom he discussed religious and philosophical matters. His Hebrew printing press in Amsterdam printed more than 70 books.

In 1650, he wrote *Hope of Israel.* In this volume, he discussed a report dealing with the so-called discovery in South America by Aaron Levi Montezinos of the Lost Ten Tribes. He worked day and night to obtain permission for Jews to live once more in England, an event which he maintained had Messianic implications because it would complete the dispersion of the Jews to *Kezeh ha Arez.* (the end of the earth; *Kezeh ha Arez* is the medieval Hebrew term for Angle Terre or England). He believed that the Jews would not be redeemed until they were scattered over the four corners of the earth.

His trips to England and his appeals in 1655 to Oliver Cromwell had effect, although Manasseh Ben Israel felt he had failed because neither Cromwell nor the conference had made it official. Even though he had induced Cromwell to admit the Jews to England, he returned to Holland a broken man, and died in 1657.

The year 1648 was a milestone: the Treaty of Westphalia brought an end to 80 years of fighting between the Spaniards and the Dutch. Holland (the United Provinces) was now free, meaning less restrictions on Jews. In 1657, Holland officially recognized the Jews as subjects of the country. Related to independence was the fact that Amsterdam had topped Antwerp as the chief port in northwest Europe and captured the Belgian city's lucrative trade. Jews immediately moved north to their new Dutch home. The Treaty of Westphalia also closed the navigation of the Scheldt River and almost reduced Antwerp to a dormant city, a condition that would last for two centuries. Jews soon realized that Holland was "where the action was."

With their trading contacts in Spain, Portugal, and the Ottoman Empire, Jews also became very useful. They played an important part in Holland's economic growth. They were involved in the East and West Indies companies. Obtaining control of 25 percent of the shares of the East India Company, they brought in capital and established new enterprises

By 1672, there were 7,500 Jews in Amsterdam, out of a total population of 200,000. In those days, the Jewish quarter resembled a small Lisbon and Madrid. Spanish and Portuguese was spoken on the streets. The city became a center throughout the Jewish world, the mother community of London, New York, and West Indian Jewry. Many of the 10,000 Jews in Amsterdam, at the close of the seventeenth century, served as academicians, teachers, and rabbis in this city of Jewish printing and learning.

In 1780, the Ashkenazim had by far overtaken the Sephardim, so that only 10 percent of Holland's Jews were Sephardim. (By the early twentieth century, it would be only 6 percent Sephardim).

By the middle of the eighteenth century, Amsterdam possessed the largest Jewish community in Europe, and the French Revolution would dramatically alter Jewish life in Holland. In 1795, the French conquered the Netherlands and its 23,400 Jewish residents. On September 2, 1796, the Batavian National Assembly gave Jews full civil rights. Louis Napoleon, Napoleon's brother, ruled the country until 1815.

Holland became the first country in Europe to elect Jews to its parliament. Here was a precedent, for Holland would become one of the few European nations where Jews would hold many government posts.

Rulers and governments might come and go, but for the Jews of Holland, "unqualified religious equality was the rule until the Nazis entered in 1940." Like other countries in Europe in the nineteenth century, however, assimilation and discrimination would eat away at the vitality of the Jewish community.

Still, many Jews embraced Zionism and the Eighth Zionist Congress was held at The Hague in 1907. By 1940, 1,500 Dutch Jews had settled in Palestine.

In 1933, many German Jews crossed the border into Holland to escape the Nazis. Few realized that seven years later Hitler would follow them there.

Of all the countries in Western Europe, Dutch Jews in Holland suffered proportionately the most in the Holocaust. Holland, after all, was close to Germany, and the Jews were concentrated in the large cities. From the day the Nazis swallowed up the Netherlands in 1940, until the very end of the war five years later, Jews were hunted down and deported to death camps.

At the beginning of World War II, 156,000 Jews lived in Holland. About 107,000 would perish in the Holocaust. "The Dutch Jewish death rate was the highest in Western Europe. In the East, only Poland had a higher kill ratio," writes Judith Miller, in *One, by One, by One.* By 1943, "about the only way a Jew was seen now was floating down in a canal," wrote Miep Gies in her book, *Anne Frank Remembered.* Interestingly, "the percentage of Jews deported from France did not exceed 24 percent in contrast to Holland, whence 76 percent were deported," writes Leni Yahil. In Belgium, the percentage was 40 percent in Denmark it was two percent.

Perhaps because of their naiveté and slavishness to rules, many Dutch Jews obeyed deportation call-ups. Feeling very at home in Holland, they may have been lulled into a false sense of security when the Nazi threat hovered. Some, according to Judith Miller, felt the Dutch Jewish councils "let themselves be used for the liquidation of Dutch Jewry," said a Dutch Commission finding, reported by Ms. Miller in her book. "They collaborated with the Germans by compiling registers of deportees and in many other ways, all of which facilitated the final murder of the Jews." What has happened of late is that the Dutch, too, are being forced to confront their past. More than 80 percent of the Dutch Jewish population had been murdered. This constitutes the highest percentage in Western Europe. Elise Friedman in the May-June 2000 issue of the *B'nai B'rith International Jewish Monthly* explores the question of how the Dutch can account for the orderly disappearance of more than 100,000 Jews in 1943 and 1944.

When we visit the Anne Frank House, we might want to pause and think about Ms. Friedman's argument that for non-Jewish Holland, Anne Frank "embodies the myth of the heroic nation-in-resistance." What is forgotten is the fact that Anne Frank was betrayed, as were thousands of other Jews in the country. There are 800,000 visitors annually at the Anne Frank House, but only 19,000 visit the former theater where the Germans processed most Dutch Jews for deportation, the Hollandse Schouwburg Museum.

"Onderduikers" or "divers" was the name given to those hidden underground. They lived in cellars or secret rooms. Often, Jews who became fugitives or resistance fighters were supported by clandestine organizations. Only 25,000 Jews went into hiding and of those, only 8,000 of them survived the war, according to writer Elise Friedman.

After the war, between 20,000 and 30,000 Jews returned to their former homes. About 30,000 "core" Jews out of a total population of 17 million, live in Holland today, and two-thirds of them reside in Amsterdam.

The Netherlands survived the war. Most of the Jews did not. Anne Frank, the Jewish proletariat, the rabbis, the Jewish doctors and lawyers, and the diamond cutters did not. But as Jules B. Farber wrote, "Unlike the Dutch, who tallied their war dead, the Jews counted those who were alive."

Over the years, Jews in Holland and other nations have recognized that populists and extremists are dangerous to the stability of democracy. It was not surprising, therefore, that European Jewish leaders breathed a sigh of relief after voters in the Netherlands rejected the far-right challenge of Geert Wilders. Wilders had vowed to bar Muslim immigrants, close mosques, and ban sales of the Quran. He has pledged to close the Netherlands' borders, leave the Eurozone and EU if he gained the election victory.

Men and women of goodwill realized that the populist revolt could happen in Holland as well. It is doubtful if many Jews in the end voted for Wilders' right-wing Populist Party for Freedom. Yet according to one prestigious poll, The Party for Freedom had the vote of 10 percent of Dutch Jews, reported JTA. Still, despite the support of some Dutch Jews, the Party for Freedom angered many Jews with its support of a ban on Jewish religious slaughter. Wilders' 2011 decision to support a ban on religious slaughter, aimed primarily at Muslims but also including kosher slaughter, left many Jews skeptical of his oft-stated commitment to "Judeo-Christian values." His promise in 2014 to make sure the Netherlands has "fewer Moroccans" alienated even some of his right-wing supporters from within a Jewish community sensitized by the Holocaust.

And, if Wilders had won, that presumably would have added momentum to the campaigns of anti-immigrant, far-right movements around Europe. He did flirt with other far right groups, including France's National Front. A Wilder's victory would have been the latest blow for Europe's liberal order. But he did not win. Prime Minister Mark Rutte's centrist party emerged victorious in the March 2017 contest by a clear majority, leaving Wilders in distant second, just in front of progressive and green parties.

Chief Rabbi Pinchas Goldschmidt, who heads the Conference of European Rabbis, said it was "encouraging" and "a good day for Europe," adding: "We will continue to pray for the future of the European Union, its ideals, liberties and values," reported the *Jewish News* in the UK.

But time will tell for the EU. Populists in the end could crack the European Union because Europe's "economic mood is so glum." That's why the Dutch were now watching the French and German elections in 2017 for the fate of the 60-year-old EU.

JEWISH SITES IN AMSTERDAM

The Anne Frank House, 263 Prinsengracht, 1016 GV Amsterdam. Tel: 31-20-556-7105. www.annefrank.org. @annefrankhouse, http// twitter.com/annefrankhouse. Trams 13 and 17, buses GVB 21 and 33, or a five-minute walk from Dam Square will take you here. This site is near Westermarkt. Open from November to March, every day from 9:00 a.m. to 7:00 p.m. (until 9:00 p.m. on Saturdays.) Open from April to October from 9:00 a.m. to 10:00 p.m. The Anne Frank House is open every day. From 9:00 a.m. to 3:30 p.m. However, the museum is only open to visitors with an online ticket for a specific timeslot. From 3:30 p.m. until closing time, you can buy a ticket at the museum entrance. A word to the travel wise, book on line months in advance. Check on other possible closings, for the museum is not open on Yom Kippur.

Now an international center against discrimination, this is the four-story house where teenager Anne Frank (1929-45) hid from the Nazis and kept a diary. A million Jewish children died in the Holocaust. She became their voice and their symbol. The secret annex, consisting of two upper floors and an attic, is the building behind the structure on 263 Prinsengracht.

The building would turn out to be a good hiding place, since Mr. Otto Frank sold herbs and spices and the inventory had to be stored in the dark. It looked natural, therefore, when the windows at the back of the building were blacked out and painted over. Miep Gies, who died in 2010, would risk her life and bring food to the Frank family and the others. Her husband Jan, helped hide the Frank family. He died in 1993 at the age of 87.

The entrance to the hiding place was hidden behind a hinged bookcase. The top of the door was hidden by a map. When you pass through, make sure you watch the brief video tape in the first room, after you pay admission.

The first room you see is the room of the Frank family; Mr. and Mrs. Frank and their eldest daughter, Margot, slept here. On the wall, you spy a newspaper map of Normandy. Otto Frank marked the Allied armies' advances with colored pins. Next to the map, you see the pencil marks where the Franks and the Van Daans measured the height of their teenage children.

Anne's room comes next. She shared the room with Mr. Albert Dussel, the dentist. Recently, a collection of letters and photographs belonging to Mr. Dussel were found and are now displayed in the Anne Frank House. Anne cut movie star pictures out of magazines and pasted them on the walls. They can still be seen. As you walk through to the narrow top floor of the house, you think, "What was it like to live in secret?" Privacy was impossible. Emotions had to be contained. Silence was an absolute necessity, even at night and on weekends. Caution was paramount. Garbage had to be burned in the stove.

Visit the next room, the Van Daan family room. The washroom and toilet were next to Anne's room. The facilities could be used only when people were not working downstairs.

A steep stairway leads from the washroom to the room of Mr. and Mrs. Van Daan, which also served as the hideaway's kitchen and living room. There were a kitchen stove and sink. In the evening, all the windows had to be blacked out.

Peter Van Daan's room is preserved, too. Peter's room can be entered by mounting the stairs leading to the attic. The room contained the only window that could be opened safely. A small supply of food was stored here.

Inside the Anne Frank House (Photo by Doris B. Gold)

Downstairs, you see a photo exhibit on Anne Frank and her diary and the Holocaust. Her dairy has been translated into more than 40 different languages. On the other side of the room, you find panels on current events that show modern examples of prejudice, discrimination, and repression.

The end of the story came on August 4, 1944, when the police raided the secret annex and destroyed and plundered the apartments. Simon Wiesenthal claims a Dutchman gave them away; he was never found. All eight persons were arrested and sent to concentration camps.

Anne's father, Otto, was the only survivor. In March 1945, two months before the liberation of Holland, Anne died in the concentration camp at Bergen Belsen. According to Mr. Frank, the SS man who discovered them flung some papers on the floor. Anne's diary was among those papers. "Had he taken the diary with him, no one would have known anything about my daughter." Among the pile of old books, newspapers, and magazines left lying on the floor, Miep Gies and Elli Vossen later found Anne's diary. New revelations in the discovery of the Frank family came out in 2016. According to JTA, the raid on the Frank hiding place may have been over illegal trade in food rations and other issues and not the result of betrayal, according to a Dutch study. The research highlights the story of Anne Frank, whether it is "emblematic both of Dutch heroism during the Holocaust and of collaboration with the Nazis—for which Dutch prime ministers have consistently declined to apologize despite calls to do so." A study in Holland suggested that the house at Prinsengracht 263 was tied to activities punishable under the Nazi occupation in addition to Dutch underground fighters' sheltering of Jews there.

After the war, Otto returned to the annex and was given the diary. The world now knows it as *Anne Frank: The Diary of a Young Girl.*

Antiquariaat Spinoza, Archangelkade 2G, 1013 BE Amsterdam. Tel: 31-20-620-9129.

Bibliotheca Rosenthaliana, 421 Singel, 1012, WP Amsterdam. Tel: 31-20-525-23-66. Known as the Rosenthal Collection of the Amsterdam University Library, it contains 500,000 volumes, including the 5,000 volumes of the Rosenthal Collection of Jewish Literature, one of Europe's greatest collections of Hebraica and Judaica. This library is particularly interesting to those who wish to research some aspect of Jewish history and culture.

Huis de Pinto, 69 St. Antoniebreestraat. Established by Isaac de Pinto, a Portuguese Jew from Marrano ancestry who bought the house in 1651, this house is now used as a public library. This is a wonderful street to walk through, as it has a Jewish past.

Waterlooplein is the old Jewish neighborhood area also known as "Vlooyenburg." Years ago, poor Jews resided around Waterlooplein, which is in the heart of this old section known as "Jodenbuurt" ("Jews' quarter"). By the end of the nineteenth century, the Jodenbuurt had become a slum. It was destroyed between 1941 and 1943. One of its hundreds of famous residents was Baruch Spinoza (1632-77), who lived at 41 Waterlooplein. At No. 33-39 was the synagogue, now demolished, that banned Spinoza.

Who was Baruch Spinoza? He was a Bible scholar and philosopher. Born here in the Waterlooplein area, he was a descendant of Portuguese Marranos. His questioning of ideas angered the leaders of the Jewish community when he criticized aspects of the Bible and refused to consider it as ultimate truth. In 1656, the Jewish community expelled him for his "heretical views." He left for The Hague, where he died in 1677.

The **Waterlooplein Flea Market,** now held around the Town Hall and Muziek Theater complex, was once the daily market in the Jewish quarter from 1886. Originally, Jews were barred from owning shops, and so they bought and sold on the street. Actually, the old Waterlooplein Flea Market replaced the old market that used to stand on St. Antoniebreestraat and Jodenbreestraat.

KOSHER RESTAURANTS IN AMSTERDAM

HaBaron Restaurant, Kastelenstraat 110, Amsterdam—Buitenveldert Tel: 31-20-6-424-555. www.h-baron.nl.

Golan restaurant, Kastelenstraat 265, Amsterdam—Buitenveldert Tel: 31-20-4-044-208.

Pizza & Co. Kastelenstraat 105a, Amsterdam—Buitenveldert Tel: 31-20-4-044-453

Sal Meijer Sandwich shop, Buitenveldertselaan 114, Amsterdam. (Meat sandwiches). Tel: 31-20-673-13-13. www.sal-meijer.com

Carmel, Amstelveenseweg 224, Amsterdam. Tel: 31-20-675-76-36. An Israeli-style restaurant that is open from Sunday through Thursday, from 2:00 p.m. until 11:00 p.m.

Mouwes, Kastelenstraat 251, Amsterdam-Buitenveldert. Tel: 020-661-01-80. A kosher sandwich shop that is open Monday through Thursday, from 9:00 a.m. until 5:00 p.m. Fridays, from 9:00 a.m. until 2:00 p.m. and Sundays, from 10:00 a.m. until 5:00 p.m.

The Dutch Chief Rabbinate, Van der Boechorststraat 26, (POB 7967,) 1008 AD Amsterdam. Tel: 31-20-644-3868. Fax: 31-20-646-46-35. This organization can help with a list of kosher products and other kashrut related matters.

SYNAGOGUES IN AMSTERDAM

The Portuguese Synagogue, 3 Mr. L. E. Visserplein, 1011 RD Amsterdam. Tel: 31-20-624-5351or 31-20-531-0310. This magnificent building is still used as a house of worship. It was just as I pictured it. Still I had to use my imagination to envision the existing huge square building in front of me without the present crisscross of highways and cars, but with several handsome synagogues and thousands of worshippers. This area, this inspirational center of Dutch Jewry, is famous and recognized as the largest historical monument to Jewish Holland.

Like many former Jewish communities in Europe, very few Jews now live in this neighborhood, which includes the street called Jodenbreestraat, the heart of the Jewish neighborhood. They perished in the Holocaust or have moved to other neighborhoods in Amsterdam.

Walk along the heavily trafficked road called Mr. L. E. Visserplein. (Mr. Visser, 1871-1942, was a Dutch Jewish burgher who aided Jews at the beginning of the Holocaust). Here you can see the historic Portuguese Synagogue, the most important building of the old Jewish Quarter. Indeed, it was the first synagogue in Western Europe to be recognized as such and was the model for synagogues in many countries.

Portuguese Synagogue, Amsterdam. (Photo courtesy of the Netherlands Board of Tourism)

At one time, it was the largest Jewish house of worship in the world. It is said to be modeled after King Solomon's Temple in Jerusalem, especially the courtyard around the synagogue.

These Sephardic Jews had waited more than 200 years to pray together openly. They wanted the finest synagogue possible and they achieved it. The synagogue was dedicated with such pomp and circumstance that a contemporary witness observed that the people might have been forgiven for thinking they were rededicating the Temple in their homeland.

When it was consecrated in 1675, the mayor and alderman of Amsterdam attended the festivities, which went on for eight days, just as long as the consecration of the Temple in the days of the Maccabees.

The synagogue is always open for services on Saturday mornings at 8:45. On Sunday mornings at 8:30, and on some Friday nights, services are held, but it is better to telephone ahead to see when services are being conducted, as there are security precautions. Museum hours are Sunday to Friday, from 10:00 a.m. Closed on Saturdays, King's Day, Jewish holidays and during special events for touring.

Across the main entrance is a Hebrew text: "For I shall enter your house through your abundant kindness." This is part of the text said upon entering a synagogue.

Enter the hall and you are struck by its size and its spiritual atmosphere. The synagogue itself is one huge room. Twelve stone Ionic columns support the women's galleries and symbolize the 12 Tribes of Israel. Low-hanging brass chandeliers hold 1,000 to 1,500 candles, all of which still have to be lit for services. Seventy-two bow-shaped windows adorn the walls and the light easily shines upon a magnificent ark.

Designed by Elias Bourman in 1675, this house of worship took four years to build and cost 186,000 guilders, an enormous sum in the seventeenth century.

The congregation today consists of 500 to 600 members, but attracts some 25,000 visitors a year. It houses unique works of art, many from the sixteenth and seventeenth centuries, and exquisite antique silver. In 1993, a major restoration was completed and the building regained much of its original beauty.

Officials still wear traditional dark garb with tall hats. When evening services, bar mitzvahs, and High Holiday services are held in the main synagogue, the candles are lit. In the winter, a small attached synagogue is used for prayer when the main hall itself is too cold, as the latter is not heated.

The Ets Haim Library, at the Portuguese Synagogue, is open Sundays from 9:00 a.m. to 1:00 p.m. Check visiting hours by telephoning 622-6188. This is the library of the Jewish community, one of the major Jewish libraries in the world. It began in 1616 as the library of the Portuguese-Jewish Seminary, an institute that trained rabbis. Its collection contains many remarkable Jewish books, manuscripts, and drawings. There are also copies of famous editions of Hebrew books, such as the books produced by Rabbi Manasseh Ben Israel, one of Dutch Jewry's earliest leaders.

Today, the active synagogues and Jewish center are in the south of the city. Here is a list:

Rav Aaron Schuster Synagogue—Obrecht Heinzestraat 3, 1071 Amsterdam Tel: 31-206-719-383.

Synagogue, 238 Gerard Doustraat is in Jacob Obrechtplein, Amsterdam. Tel: 31- 20-6-750-932.

AMOS—Amsterdam Modern Orthodox Synagoge, Kalfjeslaan 376, 1081 JA Amsterdam. info@amossjoel.nl.

Kehillat Yaakov Synagogue–The Gerrit. Gerrit van der Veenstraat 26 Amsterdam Tel: 31-20-6-763-602.

Beit Medrash "Etz Chaim" Merckenburg 3, BT Amsterdam Buitenveldert 1082 Tel: 31-65- 4-781-641

Liberal Synagogue, 8 Jacob Soetendorpstraat, 1079 RM Amsterdam. Tel: 642-35-62. Services are at 8:00 p.m. on Fridays and at 10:00

a.m. on Saturdays. Phone for correct prayer times. This is also the headquarters of the **Union of Liberal Jewish Congregations in the Netherlands**.

Dutch Union for Progressive Judaism, Zuidelijke Wandelweg 41, Amsterdam, 1079 RK. Tel: 31-20-540-0140. info@verbond.eu, www. verbond.eu.

Liberal Joodse Gemeente Amsterdam, Zuidelijke Wandelweg 41, Amsterdam, 1079. RK. Tel: 31-20-540-0120. secretariat@ljg.nl. www. ljgamsterdam.nl.

Synagogue, 26 Van der Boechorststraatm, Buitenveldert. Amsterdam. Tel: 31-20-86-460-046.

Beit Knesset "Nidchei Yisrael Yechaneis" Nieuwe Kerkstraat 149 Amsterdam. Tel: 31-20-6-712-345

ORGANIZATIONS

B'nai Akiva, 665 Amstelveenseweg, 1081 JD Amsterdam. Tel: 31-20-646-38-72.

Beth Chabad, Chabad Central Amsterdam, Albert Cuypstraat, 165-167, 1073 BG Amsterdam. Tel: 31-20-42-12 770 info@ chabadamsterdamcenter.com. www.chabadamserdamcenter.com. Daily morning service at 9:00 a.m. in Chabad House. Mincha at 2:00 p.m. Erev Shabbat services and dinner.

Student Center, Chabadamsterdamsouth.com,

Masorti Olami Netherlands, 3-5 Nieuwstraat Almere, Amsterdam. Tel: 31-36-523-9888. Fax: 31-36-537-5351. D.daniels4@kpnplanet.nl. www.masortiolami.org.

The Organization of Jewish Communities in the Netherlands, (N.I.K.) Van der Boechorststraat 26, Amsterdam, POB 7967, 1008 AD, Amsterdam. info@nik.nl.www.nik.nl. This is the headquarters of the Dutch Jewish community. Also located here are the Ashkenazic community offices. **N.I.H.S., Jewish Community of Amsterdam**, 26 Van der Boechorststraat, 1081, AD, Amsterdam. Tel: 31-20-646-00-46. Fax: 642-8135. Call for information on services.

MUSEUMS

The Boas Building, Uilenburgerstraat. Amsterdam. This is part diamond museum and part showcase, where diamond cutting is observed by visitors who can view exquisite diamonds and jewelry. Most of the original workers were Jews. In the eighteenth century, observant Jews turned Amsterdam into a fine international diamond center. Many still consider it a "city of diamonds." They became involved in diamond finds in Brazil in 1844.

World War II was the darkest period for these men and women. In 1985, the fortieth anniversary of Holland's liberation from Nazi occupation was observed. Ceremonies were conducted at Westerbork, the deportation site from which more than 100,000 Dutch Jews were sent to the death camps by the Nazis in World War II, including more than 2,000 diamond workers.

Today, only about a third of Holland's diamond workers are Jews.

Our visit to **the Portuguese Synagogue** above reminded us of the wonderful **Jewish Cultural Center,** *(Joods Cultureel Kwartier),* Postbus 16737, 1001 RE, 2-4 Jonas Daniel Meijerplein St., 1011 RH Amsterdam. 31-20-531-0310. www.jck.nl.

Stunning synagogues, striking buildings and impressive memorials grace the streets of Amsterdam's old Jewish quarter. In the heart of this great neighborhood, in an area less than one square kilometer, is the **Jewish Cultural Quarter** which includes the Jewish Historical Museum with the engaging Jewish Historical Museum, Children's Museum and two other museums, as well as the stately Portuguese Synagogue, the moving Holocaust Memorial and the National Holocaust Museum. Here visitors can find out all about Jewish culture, history and traditions—all with just one ticket. To arrange group visits and guided tours it's best to contact the Sales & Events department. Tel: 31-20 5310380. service@jck.nl. www.jck.nl.

The Jewish Historical Museum (Joods Historisch Museum), 2-4 Jonas Daniel Meijerplein St., 1011 RH Amsterdam. Tel: 31-20-531-0310. info@jck.nl. www.jck.nl. Here we see that several synagogues have been restored to their pre-1828 state, and are connected by modern steel bridges and a glass-covered courtyard. Regarding the four synagogues, the Jewish Historical Museum is located in the Great and New Synagogue which we shall now discuss. The Children's Museum is situated in the former Obbene Sjoel. The Dritt Sjoel is now part of the offices.

The entrance is on the side street, *Nieuwe Amstelstraat*, once also a heavily populated Jewish street. Queen Beatrix attended the opening ceremony on May 3, 1987, as did Austrian Chancellor Franz Vranitzky and Nazi-hunter Simon Wiesenthal. It is hard to believe that this, an area now crisscrossed by highways, was, during the eighteenth century, the heart of the Jewish community and the site of four Ashkenazic synagogues that adjoined one another and faced the great Portuguese Synagogue. All that hustle and bustle over the centuries, particularly on Friday nights and the holidays, must have generated warmth and inspiration.

The new museum is a complex of Ashkenazic synagogues connected by passageways and is now said to be the largest center of Jewish culture in Europe. The street is named after Mr. Jonas Meijerplein, a jurist. He was the first Jew in the Netherlands to be admitted to the bar. He reconciled the differences between conflicting Jewish congregations during the rule of the French king Louis Napoleon.

Standing in the square facing the Jewish Historical Museum, we are reminded, according to Hebrew scholar Naftali Herz Weisel that it all began in 1671, when the Jewish community borrowed the equivalent of $8,000 from the City of Amsterdam to build the large and luxurious Grote Shul (Great Synagogue). Facing the museum, this is the synagogue on the right. Adjacent to the shul were a *mikveh* and study rooms. But the community soon outgrew the large synagogue. In 1686, on an adjacent plot, the community built the Obbene Shul (the Upstairs Synagogue) so named because of the kosher butcher hall constructed under it. It is now a kosher coffee shop and bookstore. In 1700, the Dritt Shul (Third Synagogue) was established. This synagogue is now used as administrative offices for the museum. Finally, in 1730, the expensive Neie Shul (New Synagogue), which could seat close to 1,000, was constructed. (This is the synagogue on the left). These four synagogues functioned separately.

The Jewish Historical Museum has a remarkable history of its own. It was founded in 1932 on a floor of the Historical Museum of the City of Amsterdam, which was in the Waag (Weighing) House, built in 1488. When the Nazis invaded Holland in May 1940, the Waag was closed. In 1943, all the Jewish Historical Museum materials were hauled off to Germany. After the war, however, the majority of the artifacts were recovered. They were not damaged because the Germans wanted to furnish a future Nazi museum for remnants of the "extinguished race." The museum was reborn in 1955, once again on a floor of the Waag. In 1974, the City Council designated the city-owned synagogue complex, deserted and dilapidated since the war, as the future home of the museum. In the last year of the war, after the Germans had looted the synagogue buildings, the Dutch people, cold and starving, scavenged for any speck of wood and literally ripped up planks from the buildings. After the war, the Amsterdam city government granted restoration permits. The $14 million project began with the synagogues being integrated into what we know today as the **Jewish Historical Museum.**

Inside the Jewish Historical Museum is another museum, just for children, six to twelve years of age. Six rooms where children can play games that will teach them about Jewish culture. Every week, the JHM Children's Museum hosts special activities like painting workshops and birthday parties.

Inside the New Synagogue of the Jewish Historical Museum. (Photo by Jeroen Nooter, courtesy of the Jewish Historical Museum)

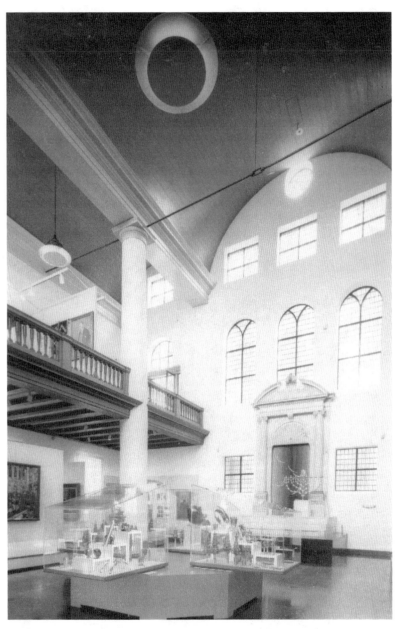

The interior of the Great Synangogue, in the Jewish Historical Museum.
(Photo by Jeroen Nooter, courtesy of the Jewish Historical Museum)

Jewish Historical Museum. (Photo by Jeroen Nooter, courtesy of the Jewish Historical Museum)

The Ashkenazic Synagogue complex, now a museum, remains a memorial not only of the past, but also a monument to the future. The information in the Jewish Historical Museum buildings is divided into three headings: Jewish identity, elements, and aspects; Jewish religion and culture, illustrated through the Jewish festivals and daily life; and then history of the Jews in the Netherlands. Included in the collection are Torah scrolls and a selection of seventeenth-century Hebrew books printed in Amsterdam. The most beautiful objects in the collection of the Jewish Historical Museum date from the seventeenth and eighteenth centuries. Glass showcases display ritual silver objects. One item that brings interest to all is a silver candelabrum with three oranges. It was a gift from the monarch of Holland. In 1688, Prince William III of Orange obtained a loan of two million Dutch gold pieces without interest from a Jewish merchant, Francisco Lopez deSuasso. William and Mary thus proceeded to England to be joint rulers.

Seen throughout the museum will be exhibitions and photos showing the "gash" in the history of Amsterdam and the Netherlands caused by the Holocaust. And yet, the museum shows that Jewish life has not died but has been rebuilt and is remembered.

The Museum Route for the Jewish Historical Museum begins in the renovated eighteenth-century New Synagogue. This synagogue was probably designed by city architect G. F. Maybaum. The most impressive part of this building is its glass-domed roof, beautifully decorated both on the inside and outside. The inventory, as well as the richly ornamented ark dating from 1750, was lost in World War II. In the New Synagogue, the visitor is introduced to the theme of Jewish identity. A Holocaust display is located here.

The new section inside the synagogue, the Gallery is used for temporary exhibitions. From here you can reach both the Hans Jaffe room and the extensive "mediatheque" or resource center. The well-stocked mediatheque with its 5,000 books, 4,500 photographs and slides, hundreds of video and sound tapes, and 3,000 documents is open to the public on weekdays from 1:00 p.m. to 5:00 p.m.

The Great Synagogue is the oldest public synagogue in Western Europe. The plan and elevation resemble the Protestant churches of city architect Daniel Stalpaert. When this synagogue was restored, the original shades of blue and green were used. A striking feature is the marble ark dating from 1671, placed against the eastern wall. Also noteworthy are the galleries for both men and women, which have been restored to their original state. During restoration work, the original ritual bath, or mikveh, was found and can now be seen.

The objects of the Great Synagogue emphasize Jewish rituals and prayer: Portuguese silver, a prayer book that Manasseh Ben Israel printed in 1654, and a magnificent silk and satin curtain that hung in front of the ark during circumcisions. The oldest item is a large thirteenth-century holiday prayer book. In the **galleries** of the Great Synagogue, attention is focused on the social history of the Jews in the Netherlands. The main theme deals with the concept of "tzedakah," the Hebrew word meaning "generosity and righteousness." This gallery has been linked via a bridge to the gallery in the New Synagogue, which is used for temporary exhibition.

Rembrandt House Museum ("Het Rembrandthuis"), 4-6 Jodenbreestraat, 1011 NK Amsterdam. Tel: 31-20-520-0400. This house stands across the street from the home of Manasseh Ben Israel, who lived there from 1639 to 1657. That latter structure is gone today. But this charming Rembrandt museum is located in the house of Rembrandt's family and it contains about 250 of his etchings and paintings. The house is open daily from 10:00 a.m. to 6:00 p.m. Sundays and holidays from 1:00 p.m. to 4:00 p.m. Directions: From the Central Station, ride to the Nieuwmarkt subway stop or take Tram No. 9 to Waterlooplein.

As a friend of the Jews, Rembrandt van Rijn (1606-69) is deeply involved in Dutch Jewish history. Rembrandt had a special sympathy for the Jews as "biblical heirs and the patient victims of persecution," according to art historian H.W. Janson. A friend of Ephraim

Rembrandt House Museum.

Bueno and Manasseh Ben Israel, Rembrandt, who lived in a Jewish neighborhood, painted Bueno and Ben Israel's portraits. He rarely painted everyday scenes without biblical allusions and the influence of the Jewish neighborhood clearly can be seen in his work. He was often asked by Jews to do their paintings and he loved their biblical faces. He could even mix Ashkenazirn with Sephardim. Rembrandt also studied Jewish law and lore. Biblical prints include Nebuchadnezzar's Dream and The Triumph of Mordecai. There is also a sketch, Jews in the Synagogue. Scholars have estimated that almost one-fifth of the artist's male subjects were Jewish. Some say Jozef Israels, Dutch Jewish painter, saved the house from being torn down.

Resistance Museum, Plantage Kerklaan 61A, 1018 CX Amsterdam. Tel: 31- 20-20-2535. Tram 4, 25. Housed as part of a synagogue, this museum is open Tuesday to Friday, 10:00 a.m. to 5:00 p.m.; Saturday, Sunday, and holidays, 1:00 to 5:00 p.m. Closed Mondays.

The Rijksmuseum, Stadhouderskade. Amsterdam. There are many paintings of Jewish interest here, including a number by Rembrandt, most famous of which The Jewish Bride (room 221) is and Jeremiah's Lamentations (room 220). Also in room 221 is A Portuguese Synagogue by Emmanuel de Witte. Jewish Wedding by Jozef Israels is on view in room 148. A highlight in this museum of course is Rembrandt's Night Watch.

MEMORIAL SITES

The Dutch Playhouse, 24 Plantage Middenlaan. Amsterdam. Tel: 31-20-531-03-10. www.jck.nl. Once a building of joy, then a place of pain and humiliation, today this is a monument. The Nazis took this 1892 structure, a former Dutch theater, at the time called the Jewish Theater, and used it as a detention center before they shipped the Jews off to a concentration camp. Today, only the facade of the playhouse and part of the jagged stone walls are left. The site has been made into a memorial garden. A *Ner Tamid* (eternal flame) burns in the foyer, and a mourning chamber is filled with paintings from Israel. A plaque commemorates "our Jewish compatriots who were deported between 1940 and 1945 and did not return." The children taken to the theater were often housed in the kindergarten across the street. Many escaped and a plaque on the school building commemorates the fact. The story of the Holocaust is told in temporary exhibitions and events. The theater is open Monday to Saturday, 10:00 a.m. to 4:00 p.m.; Sundays and holidays, 11:00 a.m. to 4:00 p.m.

The Dockworker Statue ("De Dokwerker"), Jonas Daniel

Meijerplein Square. This statue of a strong, hefty dockworker stands between the Portuguese Synagogue and the Jewish Historical Museum. Each year on February 25, Dutch Christians and Jews come out and commemorate the bravery of the Dutch people. In 1941, these dockworkers stood up for the rights of their fellow Jewish citizens. Their bravery began when, on February 22, the Nazis rounded up about 400 young Jews for deportation. The Amsterdam dockworkers staged a protest strike that was brutally put down by the Germans. This is perhaps the only time that the population of a city rose against the Third Reich. The statue was designed by Mari Andriessen, who wrote about Amsterdam's collective protest: "Not in Moscow, not in Warsaw, but in Amsterdam, and that is what Amsterdam should always be remembered by."

Gratitude Monument Memorial, Weeperstraat. Established to commemorate those who helped the Jews during World War II, this monument was designed by the sculptor Johan G. Wertheim and erected in 1947 by the Jews of Amsterdam.

The Hague

About 2,000 Jews reside in The Hague. Kosher food can be obtained De Kleiner Croon. https://nl-nl.facebook.com/koosjerdenhaag/

Orthodox Jewish Synagogue. Cornelius Houtmanstraat 11, 2593 RD, The Hague Telephone: (070)-347-3201.

Scheveningen Synagogue. Doorniksestraat 152, 2587 AZ. Tel: 31-70-358-6363 www.joodsdenhaag.nl.

Liberaal Joodse Gemeente Den Haag, Prinsessegracht, 26, 2514. The Hague. Tel: 31-70-750-4680. FAX: 31-70-750-4681. info@ljgdenhaag.nl. www.ljgdenhaag.nl.

Synagogue Jan Evertstraat 7, 2514 BS the Hague. Telephone: 31-70-365-6893 www.ljgdenhaag.nl.

Synagogue, 152 Doorniksestraat, 2587 AZ, Amsterdam, The Hague. While Chabad in The Hague does not have its own building, it sponsors many activities throughout the year. @chaij.denhaag. www. joodsdenhaag.nl/ www.chabad.org and search for The Hague.

Rotterdam

About 1,500 Jews live in Rotterdam.

Liberal Joodse Gemeente Rotterdam, Mozartlaan, 99. Rotterdam, (Hillegersberg) 3055 KJ, Tel: 31-10-461-2606. FAX: 31-10218-0333. info@ljgrotterdam.nl. www.ljgrotterdam.nl.

Synagogue and Community Center, 4 A. B. N. Davidsplein, 3039 KA Rotterdam. Tel: 4669765. This is the headquarters of the Jewish community in Rotterdam. www.nigrotterdam.nl/nl. For information on **Chabad**, contact Rabbi Jehoeda Vorst, a Chabad shaliach. Tel: 31-10-265-5530. rabbi.vorst@zonnet.nl. Tourists are invited to join in for meals. Service on Saturday morning is at 9:00 a.m. But do call ahead of time to let them know of your arrival.

Suggested Reading

Barnouw, Adrian J. *Pageant of Netherlands History.* New York: Longmans, Green, 1952.

Bloom, Herbert 1. *The Economic Activities of the Jews of Amsterdam in the 17th and 18th Centuries.* New York: Kennikat Press, 1969.

Farber, Jules B. Amsterdam, *City of the Seventies.* De Haan/Bussum, 1975.

Frank, Anne. *Anne Frank: The Diary of a Young Girl.* Garden City, N.Y.: Doubleday, 1952.

Gans, Mozes Heiman. Memorbook: *Pictorial History of Dutch Jewry from the Renaissance to 1940.* Bosch & Keuning, D.V., Baarn, Netherlands, 1977.

Gies, Miep, with Alison L. Gold. *Anne Frank Remembered: The Story of the Woman Who Helped to Hide the Frank Family.* New York: Simon & Schuster, 1987.

Hillesum, Etty. *An Interrupted Life: The Diaries of Etty Hillesum 1941-1943.* Translated by Arnold Pomerans. New York: Pantheon, 1984.

Koning, Hans, et al. *Amsterdam.* Amsterdam: Time-Life Books, 1977.

Presser, Jacob. *Ashes in the Wind: The Destruction of Dutch Jewry.* New York: Dutton, 1969. Roth, Cecil. *A Life of Menasseh Ben Israel: Rabbi, Printer and Diplomat.* New York: Arno Press, 1975. Originally published by The Jewish Publication Society of America, 1934.

Germany
Jews Do Live There

Who would have dreamed that the Israeli flag would appear on the iconic Brandenburg Gate in Berlin, Germany 70 years after the Holocaust.

The famous landmark in Berlin was lit up in January 2017 with the colors of Israel's flag in solidarity with the victims of the attack that month in Jerusalem, which took the lives of four Israeli soldiers.

The German Jewish community still remains a fast growing Jewish community in Europe.

Population figures of Jews in Germany range from 117,000 core Jewish population, to 225,000 Jewish population with one Jewish parent, to 275,000 population if you cite the Law of the Return, according to Della Pergola, 2016.

Ronnie Golz, a teacher, lecturer, and tour guide estimates that at any given time there are about 250,000 Jews in Germany. He includes visiting students, the diplomatic corps, and Jews who reside here but do not wish to join the Jewish community (some because they would be required to pay a religious tax).

The German Jewish communities are united under an officially recognized umbrella body, the Central Council of Jews in Germany, which receives financial support from the German state.

While the second and third post-Holocaust generation German Jews have come of age already, much of the Jewish population increase was fueled originally by Jews from the former Soviet Union. These Russian Jews gave the German Jewish community a feeling of stability, a sense of permanence and most important—numbers. The doubling of the Jewish community in Berlin, was the result of Russian Jews who arrived here at the rate of about 6,000 a year and who basically came for economic reasons so they could take advantage of Germany's excellent economy and welfare system. They also wanted to escape vestiges of anti-Semitism in the former USSR. Some estimate that at least 85 percent of the Berlin Jewish community is Russian-speaking.

The arrival of Russian and Ukrainian Jews was not without problems for the German Jewish community. Everyone agrees that many of the newcomers knew little about Judaism. Few spoke German. Dependent on welfare, many found it difficult to obtain employment. In all fairness to these new immigrants, however, German state agencies are often very hard on newcomers, who want to work but must meet stringent licensing examinations. Most of the Jews from the former Soviet Union have settled either in Frankfurt or Berlin. But basically, the Russian Jewish immigration to Germany is over.

The German Jewish leadership worked at integrating these Russian Jews into various communities throughout the country. No easy task! To train rabbis, to provide Jewish schools, to set up new institutions remained a challenging undertaking, especially in the eastern part of the country, which is burdened with a high rate of unemployment.

There is a Jewish presence in Germany and you see it in the streets and in the media. On German state radio, you can hear the music of the prayer *kol nidre*. In Berlin, you can see young Jewish lawyers, many of them wearing yarmulkes arriving at the German foreign ministry to settle reparations claims. You can see Jewish books in the stores. You can feel an interest and eagerness of German youth to learn about Judaism. And you see memorials and monuments to the Holocaust nearly everywhere you move in the capital.

Jewish life moves at a fast pace in congregations, day schools, organizations, clubs, WIZO balls, and Jewish community centers.

Ronnie Golz maintains that a somewhat younger German leadership has come into its maturity.

The younger generation grew up with the shadow of the Holocaust around them. The new generation has produced a change in the attitude of those Jews who do call Germany their home. By and large, they no longer feel guilty about residing in this land that murdered six million Jews. Not all Jews are comfortable in the new Germany. There is still anti-Semitism. Many are weary of the increases in xenophobia in recent years, or in the rise of new skinhead groups.

The reader might ask how Jews in more than 65 German communities can live in the country of their murderers. At World War II's end, there were fewer than 100 Jews under the age of 20 in Germany.

Why did Jews return to Munich, Berlin, and Frankfurt after the war? How could they? Many returned to collect German reparations, and stayed. Despite war destruction, Germany became an economic haven even by the mid-1950s. Many Jews also fled the then Communist-ruled East Germany. Some married German spouses and settled in West Germany, where mixed marriages made up a high percentage of the Jewish community.

The Brandenburg Gate, Berlin Germany. (Photo by Ben G. Frank)

Many of the parents of Jewish children born in postwar Germany did not tell their offspring of their suffering in the Holocaust. After the war, these children grew up in a Germany where, at least for a few decades, no one dared to express anti-Semitic thoughts.

For the Jewish visitor flying over Germany, it is hard to forget that one's fellow Jews were gassed and burned by Germans. Upon seeing factory smokestacks, the Jewish traveler may "see" the smoke rising from the ovens in the concentration camps. Even if you try to avoid going to a camp, the subconscious visions and symbols may haunt you.

As hard as it for Jews and non-Jews, there obviously is a Germany before 1933 and after 1945, as Fritz Stern points out: "We should never play down the achievements of German Jewry and the extent to which they were woven into the fabric of German society," he adds. "One quarter of all the Nobel Prizes won by Germans in the first third of this century were won by German Jews" says Otto Friedrich.

A Brief History

It all began when the Romans came to Germany. The Jews tagged along with the centurions as they settled the towns along the Rhine. Jewish traders moved by raft and cart, up and down villages of the Rhine, Rhone, and Danube rivers. By 321, they had settled in Cologne.

In the following centuries, Jewish settlements could be found in

Mayence, Metz, Worms, Trier, Speyer, Regensburg, and Wurzburg.

By the ninth century, the words "merchant" and "Jew" had become synonymous, and later "moneylender" would be added to the vocabulary.

Regarded as a group with initiative and business skills, Jews were given guarantees of rights in various places. For five centuries, the Franks—German pagans who had crossed the Rhine—ruled the Jews but left them alone.

The year 1096 heralded in the First Crusade's murderous wrath against Jews. Jewish communities that lived along the Rhine, however, chose a martyr's death. Rather than allow their children to be baptized, Jewish mothers cut their throats. Jews call that *kiddush hashem* ("the sanctification of the name," loyalty to God).

Disaster and riots plagued Jews in the thirteenth and fourteenth centuries. The Black Plague (1348-50) nearly wiped out one-half of the population of Europe. Jews were accused of having poisoned the wells. By now, Germany was nearly *"judenrein,"* "cleansed of Jews." Still, they would return again and again; they were needed for their financial acumen.

The law forbade usury by Christians so, although excluded from the guilds, Jews served as bankers. "The pecuniary motive explains the continuity of Jewish history in Germany," writes H. G. Adler in *The Jews in Germany*. Emperor Frederick II declared in 1296 that the Jews of Germany were "servants of our treasury."

Not until the seventeenth century, after the disastrous Thirty Years' War, were Jews slowly invited back to help rebuild the devastated north. "Germany could live neither with its Jews, nor without them," according to Marvin Lowenthal.

The institution of "Court Jews," or privileged Jews, began in Germany. They were called *"shtadlan"* (go-betweens) and were the official representatives of the community, so chosen because they were wealthy and influential. Often they put their financial skill to work for the prince and helped prevent anti-Jewish measures. One such leader was Joseph Oppenheimer (1698-1738), known as "Jew Suss." Another was Samuel Oppenheimer (1635-1703), who financed Vienna's military operations against the Turks who had besieged Vienna.

Later the spirit of the French Revolution would move to Germany. In 1812, Wilhelm von Humboldt and Karl August von Hardenberg liberated the Jews of Prussia. Napoleon created the Confederation of the Rhine. But Jewish rights were soon lost when the Holy Alliance defeated the French emperor.

The first Reform Temple was established in Hamburg in 1818.

Abraham Geiger (1810-74) was spiritual father and one of the leaders of the Reform Movement. On the other hand, under the leadership of Rabbi Samson Raphael Hirsch (1808-88), a more modern Orthodox Judaism was launched in Germany.

Banking became a Jewish enterprise, with family branches all over Europe. The Mendelssohn family banking house developed the banking firm of Bleichroeder. The House of Rothschild, the Warburg family, including Max, S. G., Paul, and Felix Warburg, the Guggenheims, the Lewisohns, the Kuhns, and the Loebs contributed much to German economic growth.

The Revolution of 1848 helped emancipate the Jews in Central Europe.

After the German victory over Austria in 1866 and the establishment of the North German Confederation, the Reichstag passed a resolution banning religious discrimination. The Constitution of the North German Federation in 1869 ensured full equality, so much so that many cases of assimilation and conversion soon arose. Only Eastern European Jewish immigration into Germany maintained the population level. But then came the anti-Semites. From 1871-1914, German Jews comprised about 1 percent of the German population, hovering between the 500,000 and 600,000 figure.

More than 100,000 of the 550,000 German Jews fought in World War I, and 80,000 of them were in the front lines. At least 12,000 died in the war. About 35,000 were decorated, with more than 2,000 promoted to officers, and 23,000 received German awards for bravery.

But by the 1930s, "millions of Germans began to believe that Adolf Hitler somehow had the skill and intelligence to solve all the nation's problems," writes Otto Friedrich in his book, *Before the Deluge: A Portrait of Berlin in the 1920's*. As we look back in history, we note the police could have deported him; they did not. Later the democratic world powers could have stopped him; they did not. Many Jews thought Nazism would blow over. People do not just pick up and leave their homes, family businesses, or jobs. They did not foresee the catastrophe of Hitler. Of approximately 500,000 German Jews, about 330,000 would flee between 1933 and 1939. Most of them reached the United States, the United Kingdom, France, and Palestine; the rest would perish.

After the war, the Zionist movement actually opposed Jews returning to Germany, which it called "accursed land." Jews generally do not return to places of tragedy. About 15,000 Jews resettled in Germany. And of these 15,000, only 8,000 would remain; the rest would emigrate to the United States and Israel. By 1986, close to 30,000 German Jews were registered and gave money to the Jewish community.

A law exists in Germany that makes it illegal to spread lies about the Nazi war crimes, lies and crimes that insult the memory of the Jewish dead. Anti-Semitic racism is punishable by law. Millions of Germans under twenty-one still have never known, seen, or spoken to a Jew.

Jewry here makes up five groups: those who survived the Holocaust; those who returned after World War II from other countries such as England, Palestine, and China in which they had found refuge; those displaced persons or camp survivors who took temporary refuge in Germany after the war; those emigrants and refugees who were attracted to Germany by its economic prosperity or who fled from persecution; and finally the Soviet Jews.

Jews in Germany appear to be economically well off. Most do not feel overt anti-Semitism. But they realize that the neo-Nazi extremism has threatened the stability of Central Europe and that means Germany, too.

German Jews praise what they call Christian Jewish societies, which are very active and sponsor various projects. One program invites those who were born or lived in Germany before the war to come and visit their former homes. Some municipalities pay the airfare. Others give the visitors spending money, tickets, and a tour.

Many visitors come from Israel. Indeed, most German Jews have visited Israel; the ties between German Jews and Israel are strong. For example, the Jewish State helps Dusseldorf Jewry by providing and training teachers, principals, and even rabbis.

On September 10, 1952, the reparations agreement was signed by the representatives of West Germany and Israel. Reparations came to about $8 billion or 25 billion German marks to Israel direct, while 15 billion marks were paid to individuals.

Germany has paid more than $50 billion in reparations to victims of Hitler since World War II. In the first half of 2000, negotiators had hammered out details of a compensation for Nazi-era slave workers and other victims. The agreement focused on how a $5 billion fund was to be distributed. In principal, an agreement was reached whereby forced and slave laborers of the Nazis will be able to receive a one-time payment from the fund established by German industry and government.

The two nations established diplomatic relations in 1965. By and large, Germany has positioned itself as the champion of Israel within the European Union. Several decades ago, Germany, it is said, made the decision to back Israel because it felt it had a special obligation to the Jewish state. While Germany remains Israel's key ally in the European Union, a rockier relationship has marked French-Israel ties.

"Relations between Israel and Germany in early 2017, are 'fine,'" noted Professor Dr. Julius H. Schoeps, managing director of the Mendelssohn Center for European Jewish Studies (MMZ) in Potsdam, adding, a great deal of "political, economic, cultural, academic, and security cooperation."

In 21st century international affairs, you cannot leave Germany out of the larger world picture. Because of its financial strength, it stands as the most powerful economic force in Europe. As the world's largest economy, Germany, with its approximate nearly 81 million people, is now even becoming more immersed in Central and Eastern Europe. Berlin, we should remember, is only about 50 miles from the Polish border, giving it significant market potential and political influence in the east. However, according to Professor Schoeps, Germany "is in a difficult situation." It often has to convince its European partners that they have "no ambitions to strive for power." He added that today, "its most important task is to succeed in holding together the European Union."

But for many generations, Germany will remain in the spotlight. The world will watch her because even now there are ultraconservatives among the conservatives who deny the existence of gas chambers and the Nazis' extermination of millions of Europeans, including six million Jews. German Jews have called upon their government to take stricter measures against neo-Nazi groups. But in the final analysis, it all depends on whether Germany continues to defend its democratic rights against terrorism and dictatorship.

"For no people can step out of its own history and disown it. It is a legacy which cannot be denied," said the late Israeli President Chaim Herzog.

Yet a generation of Germans who were not even born when the Berlin Wall went up finds it hard to shoulder responsibility for the Germany of seventy years ago.

Even Jewish leaders point out that the interest of young Germans to learn about Judaism and the Holocaust has never been as great as it is today. "What did you do during the war, Daddy?" is very close to the question young Germans ask of their fathers and grandfathers: "Where were you when all this happened?" They look incredulous when the grandparents tell them they voted for Hitler, although one said, she did not think that they should have killed the Jews, "just ship them off to Jerusalem." One even admitted she liked Hitler; he got rid of the garbage in the streets and he stopped unemployment. This grandmother lost her husband on the Russian front. Another said the years 1933 to 1940 were the "best years of her life."

In the Knesset in February 2000, Johannes Rau, German President said, "I ask forgiveness for what Germans have done—for myself and my generation, for the sake of our children and our children's children." In Germany, the populist Alternative for Germany (AfD) may win seats in parliament for the first time in the September 2017 general election. Chancellor Angela Merkel was expected to be re-elected. She won a fourth term as chancellor in a bitter fight with the AfD which garnered 13 percent of the vote. By the end of 2017, she was finding it difficult to form a cabinet.

Notable German Jews

German Jews "identified with Germany as their homeland," according to Leni Yahil, and contributed much to their country's political, social, and cultural life. Here are some outstanding German Jews.

Ferdinand Lassalle, an adherent of Marx, founded the German labor movement. German shipping magnate Albert Ballin directed the Hamburg American line, and was a close friend and advisor to Kaiser William II. Kurt Eisner was a Jewish socialist who headed a People's Republic in Bavaria at the beginning of November 1918; he was assassinated in 1919. Nobel Prize laureate Albert Einstein (1879-1955), known as one of the world's greatest physicists, discovered the theory of relativity. David Ben-Gurion, first prime minister of Israel, invited Einstein to become president of the Jewish State.

Germany also boasts a great list of Jewish writers: Ernest Toller, Jakob Wasserman, Arnold Zweig, Alfred Doblin, Kurt Tucholsky, and Walter Benjamin. German Jewish musicians include Felix Mendelssohn, Jacques Offenbach, Otto Klemperer, Bruno Walter, Fritz Kreisler, Paul Hindmith, Kurt Weill, and many others.

Jewish Berlin

"Have a nice day in our capital," says the flight attendant as the plane swoops down onto the runway at Tegel Airport in Berlin, built in the Cold War city of West Berlin and surrounded by former East Germany. Tegel should have closed down years ago, but delays on the new Berlin Brandenburg Airport have kept it open.

Only in 1999 has Berlin assumed the mantle as the capital of a united Germany, today very powerful and very rich. And in so doing, Berlin has become a great city of Europe. Berlin offers museums and galleries, monuments, parks and gardens, as well as "the legacy of a divided city."

Jewish population figures for Berlin range anywhere from 10,000 to 25,000, including Israelis, though it could reach 30,000 or even higher. Israelis are flocking to the capital because it is "a cool, hip place, and not expensive." And Berlin is what one might call a "start-up" hi-tech city, and that attracts Israelis. Some observers believe the

Israelis are in Berlin, not to live permanently, but to reside in this very cosmopolitan city for a stay. As we shall see later in this chapter, one can find Israelis in cafes, restaurants, and galleries in Berlin.

Not too many Jews emigrate from economically powerful and democratic Germany, a nation that has represented evil in the last century. But still, there are those Jews who are interested in the Spanish government's offer for citizenship in that country. Germany has reported rises in applications for the naturalization process in Spain and Portugal.

For Jewish travelers to this city, there are three Berlins. The Berlin of the past before 1933 when, despite anti-Semitism, Jews were involved in the artistic and cosmopolitan energy of this capital; the Berlin of Hitler, the dark grotesque capital of the dictator and the brutal murder of Jews; and finally, the post-war Berlin, the Berlin that existed for 45 years in a Communist East German sea but finally became the German capital.

There was an active Jewish life here before 1933 and there is Jewish life in this metropolis in the 21st century. We must remember that Jews—who had no access to the politics of the country—financed artistic and cultural programs. They hosted salons, started new publications, and backed galleries. Jews, including Jewish artists and thinkers, supported the German counter-culture concept of Bildung which was a broad pursuit of humanistic education and inclusion of all human beings regardless of race or religion—all part of the Berlin scene in the 1920s.

Berlin, from whose center emanated so much destruction and death in the 20th century, has reinvented itself and today, stands as a modern and cultural metropolis.

No wonder guide Ronnie Golz compares Berlin to New York, San Francisco, Chicago, and Washington combined.

"New York, because Berlin is the cultural capital with concert halls; San Francisco, because it is the most liberal, open-minded, and tolerant city in Germany, including a large LGBT community; Washington D.C., because it's mainly only a political capital, not industrial nor financial; and Chicago, because it boasts incredibly new architecture by world-famous architects."

Berlin was always avant-garde in the arts, Golz reminded me. Today with more than 3.5 million residents, including an ever-growing Jewish community, the capital remains high on the list of tourist destinations in Europe, including those who cruise the Baltic and are bused down to Berlin for a day of sightseeing.

Others have said that Berlin is always on a journey and yet never arrives anywhere. East and West Berlin were reunited in 1990, bringing together two halves of a city that had functioned separately for thirty years. Even today, one can notice the differences. The West section of the city around the Ku-Dam features noise and traffic, clubs and halls, and movement, which inspired and still inspires urbanites, foreign and domestic. Yes, the western section of Berlin is busy as ever, with its 8,000 bars and restaurants and all-night clubs. Berlin is still Berlin and today's Berlin especially in the western part reminds one of the 1920's exciting city.

In the East, the quiet atmosphere and revival makes one realize that beneath the surface East Berlin, as it was under the Communist regime, is drab no longer. True, you can still see a few gray, shabby buildings, but the area is quickly changing and becoming the trendy, art and in-section of the city. Walk around the Gendarmenmarkt, the most handsome, elegant-looking square in Berlin and you can sense an exciting and business revival here. Standing in the center of the Gendarmenmarkt square is Schinkel's Schauspielhaus a concert hall, as well as several area churches and cafes. Hotels such as the grand and very modern former Four Seasons Hotel, now Regent Berlin, catch the traveler's eye. The area was the heart of Berlin before its twentieth century convulsion. This is the still the historic part of Berlin. Just a few blocks away is the Unter den Linden, the grand imperial avenue which is sure to be the heart of the new, unified city. There is much shopping in the area on the Friedrichstrasse such as Galeries Lafayette.

Like any traveler, I have my favorites in this vibrant and energetic city. I saunter over to Potsdamer Platz, the city's main intersection before World War II and location of Europe's first traffic light, installed in 1924. Here rests a huge plaza, surrounded by modern skyscrapers, that attracts thousands to its restaurants, shops, and outdoor cafés. Yes, in the 21st Century, the "showcase" and the impressive architecture of the Potsdamer Platz section is a sight not to be missed. It contains many important corporations making a construction statement.

Skyscrapers, shopping malls, restaurants and concert halls are reaching up to the heavens. In the Mitte district near the Reichstag, on the Hackesche Hofe, stands an Art Nouveau residential complex that also houses cafés, restaurants, galleries and theaters.

At night especially, the city comes into its own, entertainment-wise, especially in Unter den Linden, the Kurfurstendamm, Kreuzberg, and Prenzlauer Burg.

Once again the city is being reinvented. Splendid art galleries, nightclubs, and a lingering historical presence have made the city attractive to foreigners. The city has again assumed its role as capital of Germany.

According to Deidre Berger, director of the American Jewish Committee's Berlin Ramer Institute for German Jewish relations, German Jews are not in danger, but they are facing challenges such as rising anti-Semitism. Disparagements as "Jews rule the world, those Jewish bankers," are heard more and more, she added in an interview and she cited verbal insults and slurs to Jews on the internet.

Anti-Semitism is rising on the left through the BDS movement and from the right as populism takes hold, she said, adding that "populism disguises anti-Semitism by being pro-Israel."

"AJC has more to do now, serving the AJC community and working with German decision makers," she told this writer, especially in the area of the rising threat of growing hostility to Israel. She explained that Jews and the large Turkish immigration that entered Germany had cooperated and worked together. There were few tensions between Jews and Turks. But now, large numbers of immigrants from Syria, Iraq, and Afghanistan to Germany raise concerns and challenges to the large Jewish community, she indicated.

Challenges facing the Jewish community include rising voices against circumcision and religious slaughter, according to Deidre Berger.

Indeed, the Berlin-based Research and Information Office on Anti-Semitism founded in 2015 reported in March 2107 that the number of anti-Semitic incidents in the city had risen by 16 percent in 2016 over the previous year. "Most of the incidents were nonviolent, but nonetheless threatening," according to JTA, which reported a total of 470 anti-Semitic incidents in Berlin itself, including seven physical attacks.

Noting this new report of a rise in anti-Semitic incidents in Berlin, Jewish leaders in the German capital renewed their call for a federal commissioner to deal with the problem. In this regard, Deidre Berger said a federal commissioner would help ensure the government does not drop the ball on fighting Jewish hatred.

Germany and its capital is not immune to radical Islamist terrorism. The Christmas market attack in December 2016 was tragic: 12 people died and 50 wounded. The killings attest to Germany's resolve in future days to come.

Jews will continue to settle down here for a number of reasons. Berlin is the major city between Moscow and Paris, a bridge between East and West. (Lenin said, "He who has Berlin, has Germany, and he who has Germany, has Europe"). Berlin has joined Paris, Brussels, and Rome as being "where the action is." Jews will come to this creative center, mostly for business, economic, and professional opportunities. How they will live and how they will withstand the pressure of memory cannot be foretold. Russian Jews say that they had it so bad in the former Soviet Union, that the past here does not affect their functioning in society. Of all the cities in Germany, Berlin and its landmarks remind you of the Nazis. It is "an open air museum of the nation's history": Hitler's bunker-grave in the form of a mound of dirt; the Reichstag; Unter den Linden and the Brandenburg Gate under which the jackbooted Nazi hooligan army marched singing "Death to the Jews" and "Tomorrow the World."

Jews who do come here say this city is attractive, scintillating, and creative. Outwardly, it throbs: the opera, the state library, the university, and the Kurfürstendamm, that exciting main boulevard that declares, "Berlin could not be Berlin without me, the Ku-damm."

Berlin, which even then rivaled Paris and London culturally, inspired the Jews in the nineteenth and early twentieth century, as Paris influenced the world, according to Barnet Litvinoff. Henry Adams once described the city as a "poor, keen-witted provincial town, simple, dirty, uncivilized," and Mark Twain named it "German Chicago." This "European New York" of about 3.5 million people evolved over the years along an east-west axis centered by the Brandenburg Gate, that gigantic neo-Grecian portal supported by 12 Doric columns, 65 feet high, and surmounted by a sculpture of four horses drawing the chariot of the Goddess of Victory.

Jews, who never numbered more than five percent in Berlin, arrived there in the thirteenth century. A cemetery was established in 1543. In 1671, Elector Friedrich Wilhelm admitted 50 Jewish families from Vienna and the community grew. The first synagogue was built in 1714.

Moses Mendelssohn (1729-86), philosopher, settled in Berlin in 1743. With access to the king, his home also became a center for intellectuals of the Enlightenment (*Haskalah*). The son of a poor Torah scribe, Mendelssohn was born in Dessau. This eighteenth-century scholar and philosopher helped launch the renascence of Jewish culture. Mendelssohn was a friend of the famous German Christian writer, Gotthold Ephraim Lessing, who immortalized him in the play, Nathan the Wise. Mendelssohn said that Jews should abandon Yiddish, purify Hebrew, and learn German. In 1768, he published his translation of the Pentateuch for his co-religionists. His followers were called "*maskilim*" (the Enlightened). They urged Jews "to broaden their minds by studying the culture of those among whom they lived."

The homes of Henriette Herz, Rahel Varnhagen, and Dorothea Schlegel also became centers of the Jewish elite of Berlin.

After the Franco-Prussian War of 1870, Berlin replaced Vienna as

A memorial to Moses Mendelssohn in Berlin.

the center of the German-speaking world. Jews flocked to Berlin. By the 1930s there were about 150,000 to 180,000 Jews in a city that, before the war, maintained several hundred synagogues and now has seven or eight. About one-third would be murdered in the extermination camps, and the rest would flee. Hitler took power in 1933. Four months later, a boycott of Jewish stores in Germany began; the rest is history. In 1945, Berlin was obliterated by Allied bombing and shelling, with 2.6 billion cubic feet of rubble. Now rebuilt, the city covers more than 550 square miles, is bigger than Chicago, five times the size of the District of Columbia, 15 times the size of Bermuda, and about as large as the five boroughs of New York City. Because Berlin has about 3.5 million inhabitants, it is thought to be one of the least dense great cities of the world. Berlin is Germany's leading city and the gateway to expanding markets in Eastern Europe. And Berlin, considered to be located at the most important crossroads in Central Europe, is no longer vying with Prague as Central Europe's most cosmopolitan city. This point emphasizes the fact that with reunification, Germany has moved from being an Atlantic state to a Central European state.

In the last analysis, Berlin has changed beyond recognition. Many would agree that it has become Europe's major capital and a popular travel destination.

The famous German Jewish writer, Joseph Roth, journalist and author of such classics as *The Rudetsky March,* and *The Collected Stories of Joseph Roth* begins a 1921 essay about Berlin entitled "Going for a Walk." He wrote: "What I see, what I see."

As in 1921, a traveler to Berlin in 2018 and beyond will have much to see.

SITES IN BERLIN

Scheunenvierte—this is one of Berlin's exciting neighborhoods. Once it served as the heart of the city's Jewish district. This old Jewish neighborhood is the sight of one of the liveliest nightlife sections of East Berlin. No wonder it has been called Berlin's Soho or Greenwich Village of New York City; visit it!

Berlin Wall. A 1.3-mile stretch of the Berlin Wall remains. It boasts graffiti and paintings, like an outdoor gallery, with huge, bizarre drawings. By the way, on one of those paintings, there is half a six-pointed Jewish star next to a cracked glass, symbolizing Kristallnacht.

Jewish cemetery, Herbert Baumstrasse 45, Berlin-Weissensee, in the northeast suburbs of former East Berlin. Tel: 365-3330. These graves evoke the days of the mid-nineteenth century when Berlin's flourishing and gifted Jewish community played an influential role in the cultural life of the city. Baum incidentally was a German Jewish resistance fighter executed by the Nazis in 1943.

Jewish Center, Fasanenstrasse 79/80, 1000 Berlin 12. Tel: 30-880-28-0. This is the headquarters of the Berlin Jewish community and is located not far from the Kurfurstendamm, near the Kempinski, Bristol, and Steigenberger hotels. The future of the German Jewish community lies with the young people. A visitor to the Jewish Center can not but notice in a corner of the lobby a computer center alongside a coffee café bar. Here young people can gather information on Jewish subjects and socialize at the same time. This attractive, well-designed Jewish community center was built in 1959 on the Fasanenstrasse site of the Great Synagogue, which seated about 1,700 persons and was completely destroyed on Kristallnacht in 1938. As you face the building, you will see, incorporated right into the facade around the front door, the old portal that once stood above the former main synagogue entrance. The new building was also constructed with a column from the old synagogue, thus showing the crack in human relations on the one hand but also hope for the future.

The center is the focal point of many activities in Berlin, as the community center sponsors lectures, concerts, and dances. A synagogue in the building is used for major holidays such as Rosh Hashanah and Yom Kippur.

In the lobby are photos taken on Kristallnacht, which still sears the minds of German Jews. On November 7, 1938, Herschel Grynszpan, age 17, an exile from Germany who was living in Paris, shot Ernst vom Rath, the third secretary of the German Embassy in Paris. He said he had avenged his parents, who had been among those dumped on the Polish border, a common Nazi tactic and practice. The Germans knew that the Poles would refuse entry to Jews. When vom Rath died, the Gestapo organized a bloodbath designed as a "spontaneous reaction of the people." The date was November 9/10, 1938. Kristallnacht, this "Night of Crystal," derives its name from the shattering of glass, as the Nazis literally went berserk when they broke the stained-glass windows of synagogues throughout Germany. The broken glass littered the streets on the morning of the ninth. Edmond Engelman called it "the glitter of the night's flying glass." About 90 Jews were killed during Kristallnacht, and about 7,500 Jewish shops were destroyed. Around 25,000 Jews were thrown into concentration camps. Approximately 200 synagogues were destroyed, shops and offices were looted, and plate-glass windows were smashed. Yet it was the Jews who were fined one billion Reichsmarks.

The center also contains a library and kosher restaurant:

Library. Nine to 10,000 volumes in all languages, which may be circulated. Most of the 2,000 visitors each year are non-Jewish. The library is open to the public. Open Monday to Thursday, 11:00 a.m. to 8:00 p.m. and Friday, 11:00 a.m. to 3:00 p.m.

Kosher restaurant, second floor. Open every day from 11:30 a.m. to 3:30 p.m. and 6:30 to 11:00 p.m., on Shabbat from 11:30 a.m. to 2:30 p.m., a buffet on Tuesdays. Those who would like to eat in the restaurant on the Sabbath can order and pay for their meals beforehand.

Reichstag. Seared permanently in this author's mind are two famous photos, the raising of the American flag at Iwo Jima in World War II as well as the photo taken in May 1945, of Russian soldiers hosting their country's flag on the top of a burning Reichstag in Berlin. Perhaps others, including the architects and planners of the new Reichstag, also probably remembered that Second World War photo. Germans who are confronting their history should be reminded of the defeat of Nazism by the Allies and the taking of Berlin by one of the major partners in the battle against the Axis powers. How else do you explain the reconstructed interior of the Reichstag where carved into the walls are pieces of Soviet soldiers' graffiti. "Surely no other people would allow itself to be so grossly denigrated in its own Parliament. But then the modern Federal Republic probably places a greater value on a continuous and unabashed confrontation with the past than any other state," wrote Roger Cohen in The Sophisticated Traveler supplement of *The New York Times*, November 21, 1999.

The Reichstag is situated at a critical spot in the city. Beauty and ugliness once enveloped the area. On the one hand always refreshing was the green relaxing Tiergarten. On the other hand for 30 years the infamous Berlin Wall, stood nearby across from the Tiergarten. Because of tight security, visitors should apply to visit several months in advance.

In 1999, the Reichstag became the seat of the German Parliament when the government moved from Bonn. On the western façade of the Riechstag is an old inscription, "*Dem Deutschen Volke*, "To the German People,"

Sitting on the top of this noted structure is a glass dome. Inside, a circle of historic pictures lie below the dome. Much of the Reichstag is open to the public. Its new glass dome and winding ramp were designed by the British architect, Sir Norman Foster. You can walk up the Guggenheim Museum-style ramp to the top of the dome for a magnificent view of the Tiergarten.

Walther Rathenau House, Koenigsalle 65. Now a private building containing offices, this was formerly the villa of the noted Jewish industrialist, philanthropist, and statesman. Born in Berlin in 1867, Rathenau managed A.E.G., the electric light complex that was founded by his father. While foreign minister, he negotiated the Rapallo Treaty with the U.S.S.R. in April 1922, which eliminated the political isolation of Germany. He was assassinated by Fascist sympathizers.

Haus der Wannsee Konferenz, The House of Wannsee Conference Memorial Site, Am Grossen Wannsee 56-58, D-14109, Berlin, in Wannsee section of Berlin. Tel: 49-30-80-50-01-0, FAX: 49-30-80-50-01-27.www.ggwk.de

(Take the S-Bahn subway and when you reach Wannsee station, take the 114 bus to the Center). The Hours are Monday to Friday: 10:00 a.m. to 6:00 p.m.; Saturday and Sunday, 2:00 p.m. to 6:00 p.m. The Reference Library, the videotape collection, audiovisual archives are shown Monday to Friday, 10:00 a.m. to 6:00 p.m. (No charge).

The garden is still there. The villa which overlooks the lake is still there. The lake is still there. The bushes are still there. The little cement cherubs are still there. The boats and the yachts and the various yacht club signs are slightly different than they were in 1942, but they are still here. The boats, though newer, are here. You would never in your life guess that this attractive villa which blends into the neighborhood so nicely and that this recreational center for the Gestapo, was the site where on January 20, 1942, Reinhard Heydrich, head of the NS Reich Security Main Office. He chaired a meeting of 14 high ranking civil servants and SS-officers to organize and implement the "Final Solution." Actually, in a main hall, a long table around which Nazi officials sat and in effect began the execution of the Jewish people in Europe can still be seen. At this table, they took notes on how to conduct the murder of Six Million Jews; then got up and took a break for lunch or walked along the shore.

Called the "Wannsee Conference" because it was held in the Wannsee district of Berlin, these bureaucrats and police offices of the Third Reich made the extermination of Jews of Europe official German state policy. The word, "conference" is a misnomer. It really was a meeting for the killing of European Jewry which already had started during the early stages of the German invasion of the Soviet Union in 1941. John Cornwell notes that a month after the Germans invaded Russia, Heydrich was ordered to make all the necessary preparations for a "complete solution of the Jewish question in the German sphere of influence."

The decision to murder the Jews of Europe had already been made. The significance of the 90-minute meeting at Wannsee was not that a final plan was formulated there, but that decision-making authority was transferred from governmental ministries to the SS hierarchy, assuring the ministries cooperation in a "Final Solution."

A draft had been prepared by Adolf Eichmann. It said that "in the course of the Final Solution, the Jews should be brought under appropriate direction in a suitable manner to the east for labor utilization." Heydrich had expected that his concept of annihilation of the Jews "would meet with misgivings and objections from the ministerial departments," according to a Villa publication." But he encountered only general agreement and readiness to help in its execution. The discussions dealt solely with details.

For example, among the resolutions adopted at the Wannsee Conference was that the Germans were willing to deport to the German east, the Jews of Romania, Slovakia, Croatia, Bulgaria, and Hungary.

Fifty years later, on January 20, 1992, which marked the 50th anniversary of the conference, a memorial and educational center was opened at the Villa.

The permanent exhibition, called "The Wannsee Conference and the Genocide of the European Jews," is certainly worth seeing. The documents the conference, the events leading up to it as well as the consequences are all spelled out. Officials at Wannsee say it "provides basic information on the entire process of the segregation, persecution and genocide of European Jews."

The history of Nazism, the racism, the round-ups of Jews in Germany and then Europe, nation by nation, the story of Jewish resistance, the story of the concentration camps, the story of the murder, the shootings, the hangings, the gassing, the killing, it's all here and displayed very graphically and effectively. Guides lead each group and give talks in German before each set of pictures.

About 80,000 persons visit the Villa each year. The exhibit is certainly worth viewing. But you need to obtain an English-language program as there are just major headlines in English over each exhibit. Narrative information is supplied only in written German, not English.

Besides the permanent exhibits, there are always major displays of topics related to the Holocaust. For example, the story of the "Lodz Ghetto, 1940-44," was told in a display.

In the main hall where the Germans planned the roundup and murder of Jews, are the photos of the 15 officials. Easily recognized is Adolf Eichmann whom the Israelis captured in Buenos Aires in 1962 and who was tried, convicted, and hanged for genocide.

The Villa was built in 1914 by the industrialist Ernst Marlier. He sold it to Friedrich Minoux who was general director of the Stinnes Trust. In 1940, the site was acquired by SS. After the war, it was occupied by the Soviets and then the Americans. From 1952 to 1988, it was a school vacation home for the school district. The Historian Joseph Wulf drew attention to the role of the Wannsee Conference. In 1965, Wulf proposed establishing an "International Documentation Center for Researching National Socialism and its Consequences" at this site.

The World Jewish Congress supported the idea. In 1986, the Berlin

The photos of SS officers and high ranking civil servants who planned the details of the murder of six million Jews when they met at the Wannsee Conference Villa in Berlin. (photo by Ben G. Frank)

The bus stop sign for the Villa of the Wannsee Conference, Berlin. (Photo by Ben G. Frank)

this historical site. On the 50th anniversary of the Conference, the building was opened to the public.

American visitors may have seen some of the photos from previous exhibitions. But put together it is a remarkable visit and well worth the one half-hour subway ride and short bus or taxi trip to the site.

There is a guest book. This author signed it, "Never again."

SYNAGOGUES AND ORGANIZATIONS IN BERLIN

The Ronald S. Lauder Foundation. Rykestrasse 33, 10405 Berlin. Tel: 49-30-440-13-16-10. info@lauderfoundation.com, www. lauderfoundaton.com. This would be a good place to note the wonderful work of the Lauder Foundation. In the words of Ronald S. Lauder: "We help to rebuild Jewish life in Central and Eastern Europe, and we believe that education is the most effective means to achieve that goal." The group supports over a dozen kindergartens and over a dozen schools, nine youth centers and camps, and several institutions of higher learning, a total of more than 30 projects.

Commenting on the schools, Mr. Lauder noted: "Our philanthropy underwrites the future of Jewish life in Europe through supporting excellent Jewish schools. And what is an excellent Jewish school? One that prepares young Jews for personal and professional success and that inspires active participation in Jewish life."

In Berlin, the Ronald S. Lauder Foundation sponsors the Lauder Beth Zion Primary School, the Lauder Nitzan Kindergarten, and two institutions of higher learning, Lauder Yeshurun Institutions: Yeshivat Beit Zion and Midrasha.

Foundation offices include Vienna, Czech Republic, Budapest, Warsaw, and Sofia.

Rabbi Joseph Spinner is executive vice-president and chief executive officer of the Ronald S. Lauder Foundation.

Synagogue, Joachimstalerstrasse 13, Berlin. This Orthodox synagogue, originally built as a Masonic lodge in 1902 and converted into a synagogue after World War II, is the popular house of worship. Also located here are offices of Jewish organizations. Services are at 6:00 Friday evening and 9:30 Saturday morning. The synagogue holds many activities, including a Passover seder. Out-of-town visitors are welcomed at services. In the synagogue you often see Russian Jews coming for help and aid. They are welcomed.

Synagogue, Pestalozzistrasse 14, Berlin. This is a famous synagogue. An organ is used during services. Open only at prayer times.

Synagogue, Frankelufer 10-12, Berlin.

Synagogue, Dernburgstrasse 26, Berlin.

Synagogue, Rykerstrasse 53, Berlin. This red brick Moorish structure, built in 1903, is located in former East Berlin. Services may not take place according to schedule, for this congregation is not always able to obtain a minyan (quorum of 10 men needed for a service), even on a Saturday morning. By the way, the reason the building was not destroyed during Kristallnacht was that the Germans were afraid the apartment buildings next door would catch fire if they torched the synagogue. According to Paul Goldberger in the *New York Times* Magazine on February 5, 1995, during the Nazi era, the Rykerstrasse synagogue "was only a couple of miles from the headquarters of the Gestapo."

Renovations began on the Talmud Torah in the Rykestrasse Synagogue, which will house the new school for Jewish educators founded by the Ronald S. Lauder Foundation.

Adass Israel, Tucholskystrasse 40, 10117 Berlin. Tel: 49-30-78-13-135. Among its many activities, the synagogue sponsors a Passover Seder. To attend the seder call 281-31-35, or FAX: 281-31-22. Services here only on weekends: On Friday nights the start of services depend on sunset, though they usually start at 4:00 p.m. in the winter. Shabbat morning services usually begin at 9:00 a.m.

Leo-Baeck House, Tucholskystrasse 9, Berlin. Once Leo Baeck, Martin Buber taught here. Solomon Schechter and Abraham Joshua Heschel, went to school here. The building, which formerly housed the University of Jewish Sciences, was shut down by the Nazis in 1942. In this house are: **Headquarters of the Jewish Community in Germany (Zentralrat Der Juden un Deutschland)**, Tucholskystrasse 9, Berlin. In 1999, the group moved its office from Frankfurt to Berlin, capital of Germany once again. This organization is in charge of religious, communal, and financial matters for German Jews. The move to Berlin occurred at the same time that the Reichstag reopened in April 1999. The then president of Germany, Roman Herzog said the new Jewish office "opens a new chapter in the postwar history of German Jewry." Also located in the Leo-Baeck House is **Allgemeine Juedische Wochenzeitung**, Germany's main Jewish newspaper, and the **European Jewish Congress**. Another symbolic move occurred in 1999 when for the first time, the European Jewish Congress opened an office in Germany and placed it at the Leo-Baeck House. **Jewish Teachers School** also calls this building its home.

Chabad House, Munstersche St., 6, 10709, Berlin. Tel: 49-30-212-808-30. www.chabadberlin.de. Also, Student Center, Wilmersdorfer St., 96, Berlin. www.berlinjewishstudents.de/about; as well as a Chabad Center geared for Israelis in Kair-Liebknecht St., 34, Berlin.

(Near Alexander Platz). Chabad indicated that they are "happy to assist tourists with any questions."

MILO Restaurant, strictly kosher, is located in Chabad House. 6, 10709, Berlin Tel: 030-212-808-30. www.chabadberlin.de. "As Berlin has become a magnet for Jewish students from throughout the world in recent years, it's time to have a regular home for Jewish students in the city," said Rabbi Yehuda Teichtal, head of the Chabad Lubavitch Educational Center in Berlin. It was announced that at the Chabad Center in the Wilmersdorf section, Chabad plans to build a 75,000 sq. ft. educational campus and center in a seven-story building. Estimated cost, 20.3 million US dollars

Masorti Germany, Eislebener St., 4, Berlin. Tel: 49-30-2101-6551. FAX: 49-30-2101-6551.

Liberal Synagogue. A prayer room has been established in the New Synagogue in Oranienburger St. 49-30-28-30, 10117, Berlin. Tel: 49-30-88-028-300. www.or.synagogue.com, www.cntrumjudaicum.de/en. The prayers are described as "The Egalitarian Service"—the language is "not so male oriented," explained one member. The prayer group is a continuation of the Reform movement which ironically was founded here in Berlin. Services are held at 7:00 p.m. Friday night and 9:30 a.m. Saturday morning. This congregation is growing. Services are also held on holidays when about 200 persons attend.

Synagogengeeinde Sukkat Schalom, Liberal. Huettenwege,V, Herbartstr, 26, 14057, Berlin. Tel: 49-30-2472-0410. FAX: 49-30-8090-3609. info@sukkat-schalom.de. www.sukkat-schalom.de/

Unabhangige Synagogengemeinde, Liberal. Berlin Bet Haskala. Corneliusstr, 15, 12247, Berlin. Tel: 49-30-6606-4586. Bet_haskala@online.de. www.bethaskala.com/startseite/

The American Jewish Committee, Berlin office. www.ajc.org.

AJC Berlin Ramer Institute (AJC Berlin) works to enhance Jewish security while promoting democracy and diversity, combating hatred, and protecting dignity and human rights. Together with a wide range of governmental and non-governmental partners, the Institute advances German US and German Israeli partnership; promotes US European cooperation on Israel, Iran, and Middle Eastern affairs; and counters anti-Semitism and extremism as well as strengthens Jewish security.

Deidre Berger is director of the AJC Berlin Ramer Institute for German-Jewish relations.

Jewish Restaurants in Berlin

MILO Restaurant, strictly kosher, is located in Chabad House, 6,

10709, Berlin. Tel: 030-212-808-30. www.chabadberlin.de.

Hummus & Friends, just next door to the museum and synagogue. Oranienburger St., 27, 10117, Berlin, Germany. Tel: +49-30-55471454 Dairy. Patrons should check themselves regarding kosher status.

Bleiberg's, Nurnberger St., 45 A, Berlin. Tel: 49-30-21-91-36-24. www.bleibergs.de/english/. Located in the borough of Wilmersdorf, near the famous KaDeWe department store. This establishment serves dairy.

In fact, Jewish food is popular in Berlin as witnessed by the first Jewish Food Week held in the capital in March 2017. Seventy establishments participated in the Jewish Food Week.

With the large number of Israelis living in Berlin, there are a number of hummus eateries, such as:

Sababa. Israeli Restaurant, Kastanienalles 50/51. Mitte section. 10119 Berlin, Tel: 49-30-405-05-401.

There are also Israeli and Russian-style eateries scattered throughout the city. Since the Jewish population is only about 30,000, the restaurants count on tourists and the popularity of Israeli and Jewish food.

Located in this area is Beth Café at Adass Israel synagogue, Tucholsky St., 40, 10017, Berlin. Tel 40-30-28-13-135. The café serves Israeli specialties.

Beth Café, Tucholskystrasse 40, 10117, Berlin. This establishment is known as the café-restaurant of the Adass Israel Congregation.

MUSEUMS

Niklas Frank, son of Hans Frank, the governor general of Poland, responsible for the killing of three million Jews, has said, "There isn't a day when I don't think about my father and everything that the Germans did. The world will never forget this. Wherever I go abroad, and say that I am German, people think 'Auschwitz,'" he wrote. "And I think that absolutely just," he added, according to Newsweek, January 24, 2000.

Writer Andrew Nagorski wrote that he feels the Germans are confronting their country's past. "No other country has examined its dark side as fully as Germany has."

"There's a growing fascination with Judaism and Jewish history," wrote Nagorski.

Harvard Professor Daniel Jonah Goldhagen's book, *Hitler's Willing Executioners,* advances the argument that the Holocaust was not perpetrated simply by Adolf Hitler, or by the SS, or by the Nazis— but by the German nation as a whole, with dozens of social elements working together to exterminate an entire people. *The Jewish Exponent* of Philadelphia, points out that "the unique evil perpetrated by Germany was the self-degradation of Europe's most civilized people into the abomination of genocide." That is why every Jewish public building in itself is a memorial to the Holocaust. An example is the new Jewish Museum, which we shall soon visit. Architecturally it towers over all of Berlin and it is only four stories high.

Jewish Museum, Lindenstrasse, 9-14, D-10969, Berlin. Tel: 49-30-25-99-33-00. FAX: 49-30-25-99-34-09.

It's hard to believe I took a tour of the Jewish Museum about 15 years ago and it was empty of exhibits and yet, it was one of the most challenging visits to a museum dealing with the tragedy that befell the Jewish people in the Holocaust.

In a little over one year, 145,000 persons also took a tour through this most remarkable museum building designed by Daniel Libeskind. They all came to tour the structure even before any exhibits were installed.

The museum stands as one of the most remarkable buildings you will ever encounter. It is a must on your visit to Jewish Berlin. Officials here are quick to say that this is not a Holocaust Memorial; it is a Jewish history museum that is going to show the creative role that Jews played in Germany before 1933. Still, as you walk through this new elongated, sharply angled and folded building, the Holocaust probably will always be on your mind—no matter what officials or the printed program says.

Officials here see this museum as the largest Jewish Museum in Europe and stress that it will depict the history of not only Berlin Jews, but of German Jews as a whole. But, again, it is more than that. As Robert Leiter noted in an article in the *Jewish Exponent* of Philadelphia, "one of the great glories of the architectural rebirth of the unified city of Berlin is its new Jewish Museum." He is correct.

This museum and the Reichstag probably stand as the only pieces of 21st century "avantgardistic architecture."

The Museum contains two buildings: the former City of Berlin Museum structure and the new Libeskind designed edifice. For just after you enter the new museum from the old City of Berlin Museum building, the floors you walk on in the new building are uneven. You might even feel a little dizzy. At certain points, you will be disoriented. You will stand in space voids. You will enter a dark angular tower, an oppressive space that obviously stands as a symbol of the Holocaust. The outer walls of the building are covered in zinc, pierced by slashes of window that could be lightning or a shattered Star of David.

Anthony Lewis writing in the *New York Times* on October 19, 1999 said that he found the tower "more powerful than museum images of the reality."

You will walk along three museum streets, or axis, that express "historic continuity, emigration and exile and Holocaust and extermination," said one guide. And always light and darkness and black and white, and hope and fear are with you.

All tours are guided.

Three quarters of the visitors here are German, one quarter are Swiss, Dutch and American. In the guest book are quotes in Japanese, Chinese, French, Hebrew, and English. They range from "with great admiration," to "I think my grandparents would sigh with relief and grief if they could visit this place. I will lend them my eyes," wrote a woman from the Netherlands. The Jewish Museum Berlin has "lent us its eyes."

The exhibits began in 2001.

New Synagogue Berlin, Centrum Judaicum Foundation, Oranienburger Str. 28/30, Mitte District, Berlin. For tours in English: Tel: 49-30-880-283-00. They stare at you. The men in the photo, the dignified German Jewish men, bedecked in fedoras, black hats, bowlers and suits. They are wearing their overcoats. Either the heat was off or it was very cold that day. A rabbi stands to one side. But more than anything, this huge blown up photo shows us the faces of the men in 1935. Not smiling; not panic either. Their hands were folded in front of them. Already Jews were suffering indignities. This was the Great Synagogue on Oranienburger strasse, designed by Eduard Knoblauch who patterned this house of worship after the Alhambra in Spain. Its Moorish style dome was covered with gilded buttresses and was more than 50 meters high.

When you enter the synagogue and view the exhibit in the remaining part of the structure, you will be standing in the remaining one-third of the original synagogue building. Damage from Kristallnacht, damage from the War, damage from the Allied bombing, damage from the post-war construction blasting after the war, left only about one-third standing. The synagogue was set ablaze in 1938 during Kristallnacht. When the Nazi gangs torched the building the police immediately arrived on the scene. They forced the arsonists to leave and even alerted the fire department. The last service of the congregation was held on September 14, 1939. Even though this temple is no longer used for services, thousands come to see and inhale this former center of Jewish life in the capital.

The synagogue also boasts that it once hired the first and only female rabbi in Germany. Her name was Regina Jonas, 1902-1944.

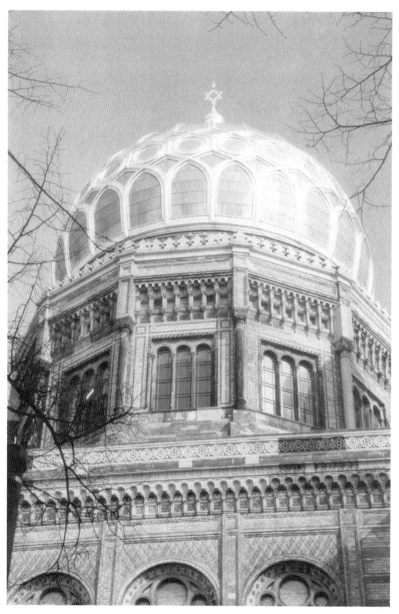

New Synagogue Berlin, Centrum Judaicum Foundation, on Oranienburger Str. 28/30 in the Mitte District, Berlin. This museum is located in the former Oranienburger Strasse synagogue. (Photo by Ben G. Frank)

Although she did teach, she was never allowed to preach from the pulpit of the New Synagogue. On November 6, 1942, she was deported to Terezin. On October 12, 1944, she was sent to Auschwitz where she perished.

This was once the heart of Jewish life in Berlin. It is intended to be used as a museum and research center. According to Carol Herselle Krinsky, writing in *Synagogues of Europe: Architecture, History, Meaning*, it was the largest synagogue in the world when completed in 1866. "The fact that the Jews could build a synagogue that was as visually impressive as a church, located in central Berlin and on a street rather than a lane, marked a significant victory," she says, adding, "the synagogue, representing the achievements of modern technology and civilization, remained as a skeletal presence besides the Jewish community office building in the former East Berlin." The reworked facade was completed in 1991, the 125th anniversary of the original dedication. The synagogue's exotic dome, topped by a gilded Star of David, was restored. Over the main entrance of the structure is an inscription in Hebrew, "Open ye the gates, that the righteous nation which keepeth the truth may enter in" (Isaiah 26:2).

The hours for viewing the exhibition are Sunday through Thursday, from 10:00 a.m. to 6:00 p.m.; Friday, 10:00 a.m. to 2:00 p.m.

As we have seen, this edifice now houses an exhibit about the synagogue and Jewish life in Berlin. But it is also home to administrative offices and institutions of the Jewish community.

Library of the New Center is located on the second floor and is open on Mondays from 10:00 a.m. to noon and 1:00 to 6:30 p.m.; and on Thursdays, from 10:00 a.m. to noon and 1:00 p.m. to 4:00 p.m.

Checkpoint Charlie, The Museum and the former Checkpoint, Friedrichstrasse 44, 10969 Berlin. If you are a traveler to Berlin as this writer was on several occasions, you will enjoy a sign at Checkpoint Charlie that says in part, "Wanderer! Stay and reflect. At this place, the "Western World," ended and the power of the Moscow Kremlin started, from here to Vladivostok. For 40 years, the world experienced the "cold war" and no two words better describe the memory of those four decades in Berlin than "Checkpoint Charlie." The sentry point that separated East and West Berlin is today a noteworthy museum. It shows how the famous Berlin Wall went up in August 1961, and came down in late 1989 and early 1990.

Today, travelers flock to "Checkpoint Charlie," now strictly a tourist site. Actors dressed in Allied uniforms pose for foreign photographers, many of whom were born after Berlin was divided during the Cold War.

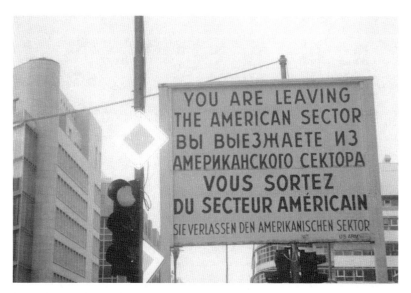

"Checkpoint Charlie," a relic of the Cold War, when Berlin was a divided city. (Photo by Ben G. Frank)

MEMORIAL SITES

Holocaust Memorial, Behrens strasse, corner Friedrich-Ebertstrasse, Berlin, behind the Aldon Hotel and across from the Tiergarten Park, Berlin. In the year 2000, it was a 4.9 acre empty dirt plot with a wire fence near the Brandenburg Gate in the center of the city.

About 2,600 stone pillars were placed in the empty field creating the impression of a huge graveyard and a "documentation center."

The dedication for the Holocaust Memorial was held was held in January 2000 and was attended by German Chancellor Gerhard Schroder, President Johannes Rau, Nobel Laureate Elie Wiesel and other dignitaries. The ceremony finally ended a debate over what type of memorial should be implanted there.

Speaking at the opening in the huge field which is a stone's throw from the final suicide bunker of Hitler, Elie Wiesel pointed out that: "No nation, no ideology, no system has ever inflicted brutality, suffering and humiliation, on any people, as yours has on mine, in such a short period."

There is indeed much symbolism in the site.

Designed by Peter Eisenman, the monument ended up consisting of 2,711 concrete blocks or pillars of different sizes, set in a wave-like pattern on a five-acre field.

Holocaust Memorial, Berlin (photo by Ben G. Frank)

Across the street from the middle of the block on Ebertstrasse, there is an entrance to Tiergarten Park. At one entrance stands a remarkable statue of Germany's greatest poet, Goethe, whose gaze manages to spy a corner of the memorial, underscoring what many have asked before: How could a nation that produced Goethe and Schiller and hundreds of other great cultured, civilized human beings, commit the genocide of a nation, simply because, as in this case, they were Jews?

German Resistance Memorial Center, Stauffenbergstrasse 13. Also known as the Bendeerblock. The victims were those generals who rose against Hitler on July 20, 1944. At the wall in the courtyard, a number of generals were shot. A memorial is located at the spot. On the second floor of the former Army High Command building is a museum devoted to the entire range of the German resistance, including the White Rose movement. The White Rose movement was founded by two Munich students, a brother and sister, who were arrested and executed. Each of the 26 rooms has an exhibit dedicated to a different aspect of the Third Reich and its opponents. Also on display is a section devoted to resistance by Jews.

A Rosa Luxemburg plaque stands alongside the Landwehr Canal in Berlin, not far from the zoo garden area. Gartenufer/ Katharina-Heinroth-Ufer, Berlin. The memorial to Rosa Luxemburg is behind the Hotel Intercontinental. You can see the sign displaying the letters, "ROSA LUXEMBURG" from the boat on the canal.

There is also a square and a street in former East Berlin named after Rosa Luxemburg, who was born on March 5, 1871, in Russian Poland and who emigrated to Germany in 1888. Imprisoned during World War I, she and Karl Liebknecht formed the Spartacus Union.

In October 1918, two German battleships mutinied and hundreds of thousands of Berliners, joining the sailors, poured into the streets calling for a revolution. Liebknecht, who led radical left-wing Spartacus Union, which became the Communist party at the end of 1918, prepared to proclaim a Soviet Republic, with Rosa as a co-founder. Near civil war atmosphere existed; some called it the German Revolution of 1918. But the Free Corps Army crushed the workers and the army picked up Luxemburg and Liebknecht.

The case against them was shaky. Both had moderated their stand and neither seemed to be murderous Bolshevik types, it is said. "Red Rosa," who had taken part in the 1905 Russian uprising, had urged an end to violence. But the army, while moving them to a prison, shot them and dumped their bodies into the Landwehr Canal. A stamp was issued by the East German government in 1955 that depicted Luxemburg as "leader of the German Workers Movement."

"Some of the older men and women in the Communist Party in East Berlin were Jewish. Their ties to the Party and its orthodoxies had to do with the 1930s and with an anti-Nazi movement that found a home and a raison d'être in the Communist underground," writes Jane Kaplan. Until the Communist regime fell over the winter-spring of 1989-90, the East Germans never apologized for the Holocaust. On April 12, 1990, the East German Parliament admitted "joint responsibility on behalf of the people for the humiliation, expulsion and murder of Jewish women, men and children. We feel sad and ashamed and acknowledge the burden of German history. We ask the Jews of the world to forgive us. We ask the people of Israel to forgive us for the hypocrisy and hostility of official East German policies toward Israel and for the persecution and degradation of Jewish citizens also after 1945 in our country."

Sachsenhausen Concentration Camp

Sachsenhausen Memorial and Museum, Strasse der Nationen 22, Oranienburg. Tel: 49-3301-2000. More than 200,000 political prisoners were interned at Sachsenhausen Concentration Camp. Half of them died from starvation. There was one gas chamber at the camp, which was built in 1943. At times there were more than 6,000 Jewish prisoners. The camp was a training ground for the Nazi SS. In 1942, Himmler ordered the Jews to be deported to Auschwitz. The story did not end in 1945 when Germany surrendered. From 1945 to 1950, the Russians converted this camp into a political prison for about 60,000 Nazi functionaries and opponents of the Communist regime. Under the Soviets, about 12,000 prisoners died here at Sachsenhausen known as the "Camp of Silence." Relatives and friends of prisoners were not allowed to talk about the camp. Two barracks, numbers 38 and 39, remain at the site. A museum nearby can also be visited. In 1992, the late Israeli prime minister, Yitzhak Rabin, visited the camp. Immediately afterwards, an arson attack on the two Jewish barracks occurred. In 1998, about 265,000 persons visited the camp. The museum can be visited from April 1-September 30, 8:30 a.m. to 6:00 p.m. Daily; October 1 to March 31 from 8:30 a.m. to 4:30 p.m. 4:30 p.m. Exhibitions are not shown on Monday.

Famous Cemeteries

Jewish Cemetery. Schonhauser Allee in Prenzlauer Berg, 10435 Berlin. Tel: 030-965-33-30. Many of the gravestones still lie smashed or overturned by the Nazis or Allied bombs. The remaining stones remind one of the remarkable success of German Jewry in the late 19th century and early 20th century.
Jewish cemetery in Charlottenburg, Heerstr am Scholzplatz, 14055, Berlin. Tel: 030-304-32-34.
Weissenssee Cemetery, Herbert-Baum St., 45, 13088 Berlin. Tel: 030-965-33-30. Considered as Europe's largest Jewish cemetery, it contains 115,000 graves. This cemetery open for visitations from Sunday through Thursday, from 8:00 a.m. until 4:00 p.m. in the winter and until 5:00 p.m. in the spring and summer, Fridays until 2:00 p.m.

Guides

Recommended Guide: Ronnie Golz, Tel: 49-30-321-76-86. Mobile: 49-177-321-76-86. E-mail: rgolz@t-online.de. Would you expect a guide in Berlin to speak with an English-accent? Meet Ronnie Golz—guide, lecturer, and teacher. He conducts private limousine tours to Jewish Sites in Berlin in the Past, Present and Future, and Art and Memory of the Holocaust in Berlin. His Jewish tour takes the traveler to synagogues, community buildings as well as Holocaust memorials, including Wannsee Villa, and if requested, Sachsenhausen Concentration Camp. He also offers a private walking tour through the Jewish Quarter, including a visit to the Centrum Judaicum Museum and if desired he will research possible grave sites on Jewish Weissensee Cemetery and take visitors on a tour of the cemetery.
Recommended Guide: Nirit Ben-Joseph. Tel: 0049-177-797-3892,

nirit@snafu.de. http//nirit-berlin.de/home-english.html. Besides being a freelance guide for Berlin and the area, Nirit lived in Israel and speaks Hebrew. In addition to tourists from throughout the world, she conducts tours for Israeli groups. Moreover, she is a guide for the House of the Wannsee Conference, Jewish cemeteries whose families were from Berlin. She is available to find addresses of former residents of the German capital.

Potsdam

A half hour by express train from Berlin brings you to the peaceful town of Potsdam—no longer located in the former Communist state of East Germany but in a united Germany.

For the traveler, for the student, for the history buff, a visit to this thriving tourist site of Potsdam, this "summer-time" capital of Berlin, is a nice reprieve from the hectic schedule of Berlin. The tour guides like to call this city "Berlin's Versailles"—to walk through Potsdam is to walk through history, exquisite gardens, and palaces.

But it should also be emphasized that Potsdam and Potsdam University have become "an excellent place for higher Jewish education."

Every summer, this municipality flew the flag of the summer home of the Hohenzollerns and other German royalty. Frederick the Great (1712-1786) had his castles built in this mecca of the German

The Conference table used at the Potsdam Conference, attended by the U.S., Britain, and the USSR. (Photo by Ben G. Frank)

military. Indeed, the bones of Frederick the Great, which the Nazis had evacuated to West Germany to keep them out of the hands of the Russians at the end of World War II, were brought back to Potsdam in 1991. With Chancellor Helmut Kohl standing by, they were ceremoniously reinterned next to the emperor's greyhounds in the park of Sanssouci Palace. The creations of Frederick the Great define the character of the city. As a patron of culture and art, he created the world-renowned Sanssouci Palace as well as Sanssouci Park.

There are only about 1,000 Jews and they are mostly Russian Jews and you see them in the streets of this prestigious town. There were 400 Jews living here before the war.

One of the monuments declared "historic" by UNESCO is the New Gardens with the Cecilienhof Palace and its memorial to the Potsdam Conference held in 1945. The hall in which the conference was attended by President Harry S. Truman, British Prime Minister Winston S. Churchill and Soviet Premier Joseph Stalin can be seen with its original furnishings. Interestingly, Churchill was replaced at the final meetings of the conference because the results of the British election were announced and Clement Attlee was victorious and arrived at Potsdam as the new prime minister. The Potsdam Conference ran from July 17 to August 2, 1945 and was the longest of the Allied war time conferences. The French were excluded. The Conference dealt not only with Germany with whom hostilities had ceased, but with the continued war with Japan. Regarding Germany, three practical issues faced the conference, according to Gerhard L. Weinberg in his book, *A World At Arms: A Global History of World War II.* "One was the establishment of a government machinery, the second was that of borders, and the third reparations."

Jewish Potsdam

Abraham Geiger College at the University of Potsdam campus, Am Neuen Palais 10, 14469, Potsdam. Tel: 49-331-977-1191. Fax: 49-331-977-1193. Mr. Kujawa, gkujawa@uni-potsdam.de, office@geiger-edu.de, www.abraham-geiger-kolleg.de.

As noted, Potsdam is emerging as the new nucleus of Jewish Studies in Germany, especially since the **Abraham Geiger College** was founded in 1999, in order to develop progressive Judaism in Germany. It is the first liberal rabbinical seminary in Continental Europe since the Shoah and was founded to meet an "urgent, unfilled need for rabbis and cantors" . . . "and to give women the chance to study Jewish theology as an academic subject so as to equip them to pursue the rabbinate or cantorate as their life's calling . . ."

"In response to the urgent need for academic rabbinical and cantorial training, the school provides progressive, enlightened and modern spiritual leadership for Europe and beyond," the school says in its literature.

The college is named after Abraham Geiger (1810- 1874), a German Reform oriented rabbi and scholar. Rabbis Walter Jacob and Walter Homolka are co-founders of the college.

In 2016, the Abraham Geiger College and the World Union for Progressive Judaism (WUJP) signed a cooperation agreement in order to enhance the training of rabbis in Russia. Graduates of the college are members of the Central Conference of American Rabbis.

In 2017, there were 20 students enrolled at Abraham Geiger College, while 162 students were enrolled at the School of Jewish Theology at the University of Potsdam. www.juedischetheologie-unipotsdam.de/en. This new School of Jewish Theology was founded in 2013.

The Zacharias Frankel College is affiliated with the Conservative Movement of Judaism/Masorti. www.zacharias-frankel-college.de "The Zacharias Frankel College is dedicated to training a new cadre of Masorti/Conservative rabbis in Europe who are deeply versed in Jewish texts, committed to a life of mitzvoth and the love of the Jewish tradition, and who are capable of transmitting the beauty and wisdom of Judaism to others," wrote Rabbi Professor Dr. Bradley Shavit Artson, dean of the Ziegler School of Rabbinic Studies at American Jewish University

Chabad House is at Kiezstrasse, 21A, Potsdam, 14467. Tel: 49-331-270-50-90. Rabbi Nahum Presman is the director, rabbipresman@gmail.com, www.chabad.org, www, chabad-brandenburg.com. Ohr Avner-Chabad School is just one of a plethora of programs offered by Chabad. Rabbi Presman conducts prayer services, officiates at funerals, and organizes Torah learning and holiday programming. The only kosher food available in Potsdam is at the small kosher grocery Rabbi Presman opened for the community; contact Chabad for kosher meals.

The Jewish Gemeinde of Postdam (Jüdische Gemeinde Stadt Potsdam), is located at Werner-Seelenbinder Straße 4, 14467 Potsdam. Tel: 49-331-88714493. Tel: 49-331 88714494. Fax: 49-331-201-95-55. kontakt@jg-potsdam.de, http://jg-potsdam.de/. Prayers are held here, but call for exact times. Rabbi Daniel Naftali serves the Jewish Gemeinde Stadt Potsdam which has about 400 members. This is the largest of four Orthodox Jewish congregations in the city of Potsdam. Gesetzestreure Jüdische Landesgemeinde Brandenburg and Synagogengemeinde Potsdam and Mitzwa. Also, a branch of Hillel is in the city. Each group meets at its own headquarters.

In April 2017, the Judische Gemeinde Stadt Potsdam and the Synagogenmeinde Potsdam agreed to support a joint building program for a synagogue.

Former Jewish Synagogue, Platz der Einheit, Potsdam. Directly in back of and across the street from the Victims of Fascism Monument was the site of the Jewish synagogue. A plaque informs the visitor that: "On this spot stood the synagogue of Potsdam. On the night of November 9, 1938, it was plundered and destroyed by fascists."

The first synagogue in the city was built in 1748 on Ebraer strasse or "Hebrews Street." In 1934, the Nazis tore down that street sign and put up a new one with an "aryan" name." But in 1992, the old Jewish name was restored. In 1768, the congregation had moved from the Ebraer strasse location to a new synagogue on the Nauner Plantage, later called Wilheimsplatz. Today that square is known as Platz der Einheit, or "Unity Square." The original synagogue building had

Former Jewish Synagogue, Platz der Einheit, Potsdam. (Photo by Ben G. Frank)

to be torn down because of the swampy ground conditions which enveloped the area. So a new synagogue was constructed between 1901 and 1903. After Kristallnacht, the Nazis used one undamaged room of the synagogue as a radio broadcast center.

The Jewish Cemetery. This Jewish burial ground was once called Judenberg, or Jewish Mountain. In the 19th century it was named Finksburg or Pentacostal Mountain. Opened in 1743, the burial spot was closed by the Nazis in 1943 and never reopened until the fall of the Berlin Wall in 1989. In 1992, it was once again used as a Jewish cemetery. Today, the cemetery is open from 10:00 a.m. to 1:00 p.m. only on Sundays. A sign tells visitors, one must wear a yarmulke or hat.

Monument Against Fascism, Platz der Einheit, Potsdam. This wall monument still stands. A relic of the Communist days, the following words were inscribed on it: "Our sacrifice, our struggle against fascism and war. Remind the living of their responsibility." A ceremony

The Jewish Cemetery at Potsdam. (Photo by Ben G. Frank)

is held here every January to mark the liberation of the Auschwitz concentration camp.

The **Moses Mendelssohn Center**, Am Neuen Markt 8, 14467 Potsdam. Telephone: 49-331-280-94-0. FAX: 49-331-280-94-50. moses@mmz.uni-potsdam.de. www.mmz-potsdam.de. An attractive remodeled building on a quiet street is the headquarters of this important research institute for European Jewish Studies. Prof. Dr. Julius H. Schoeps is managing director. The Moses Mendelssohn Center for European Jewish studies (MMZ) in Potsdam was founded in 1992 on the 15th anniversary of the Wannsee Conference and named after the philosopher of the Enlightenment, Moses Mendelssohn (1729-1786). The Moses Mendelssohn Center is an interdisciplinary scientific facility, which carries out basic research in history, philosophy, religion, literature, and social science.

The MMZ is an institute affiliated with the Potsdam University and involved in the university's Studiengang Jüdische Studien/Jewish Studies course. A special emphasis is on the history of the relations between Jews and their non-Jewish environment. The Jewish Studies course is set out to be interdisciplinary and is one of the latest of its kind offered at university facilities in Europe.

Einstein's Tower, Telegraphenberg, Potsdam. Tel: 49-331-288-23-33. Built by Erich Mendelssohn in 1923, the Einstein Tower has been declared a technical monument, a major example of expressionist architecture. The structure was used by Einstein for experiments so he could provide practical evidence of his theory of relativity. It still serves as a sun observatory. Every architectural student in the world is familiar with this building. The "Albert Einstein Science Park" which includes the Potsdam Institute for Climatic Effects. Research, the Potsdam Astrophysical Institute, the Potsdam GeoResearch Centre and the Alfred Wegener Institute for Polar and Marine Research, is open to visitors on the weekend. The tower is about a 20-minute walk from the Potsdam train station. A tour of the tower can be arranged by calling (0331) 288-23-33.

The Einstein House, Waldstrasse 7, Caputh. Einstein himself spent the summer months between 1929 and 1933 in nearby Caputh, about five miles southwest of Potsdam. This "Einstein House" is also known as the lakeside cottage where he vacationed. The Potsdam suburb of Babelsberg is the home of one of Europe's oldest feature film production facilities.

Dusseldorf

Dusseldorf includes an "old town" section: tourist pubs, boutiques, art galleries, and an area where one can hear languages from all over the world.

The "desk of heavy industry," Dusseldorf is home to many large corporate headquarters. The region is a very highly industrialized part of Germany, which now has one of the highest standards of living in the world.

Jews have gone back to this urban, vibrant, cosmopolitan, and charming Rhine River city. There are about 7,000 Jews in Dusseldorf out of a total population of about 600,000. This metropolis contains the fourth largest Jewish community in Germany, following Berlin, Frankfurt, and Munich.

What strikes one immediately about the community is that 90 percent of the Jewish population is not made up of German Jews, but mainly of Jews who emigrated from Eastern Europe. In recent years, too, a number of Israelis and Russian Jews also took up residence in Dusseldorf.

Jews are attracted to Dusseldorf because it is an artistic and cultural center. It is known as the Paris of Germany because of its fashion industry and famous boulevard of designer shops called the Koenigsallee, which is the heart and showplace of the city. The chic avenue is called the "Ko." Dusseldorf has been described as a "brash town flush with new money and the financial center for the industrial Ruhr."

Here are a few places to visit in Dusseldorf.

Heine Statue, in a small park at Schwanmarkt (a square and park) on Haroldstrasse. Heinrich Heine (1797-1856), the famous Jewish writer and poet who lived in both Germany and France, once wrote that his birthplace, Dusseldorf, "is very beautiful. When you are far away from it, you think of it and you get a strange feeling that says, 'I was born there and I feel as if I would have to go back there immediately.'" Heine was one of Dusseldorf's distinguished citizens.

Heinrich Heine Institute, Bilkerstrasse 14. Original manuscripts of "The Lorelei" and "The Rabbi of Bachrach" are housed in this museum. A great poet, Heine accepted baptism, the "entree card into European culture." Still, he wrote, "I make no bones about my Jewishness to which I have not returned because I never left it." Heine was born in Dusseldorf. In 1831, he emigrated to Paris, where he died in 1856.

In "The Lorelei," he wrote, "When I think of Germany in the night, I am robbed of my sleep." Heine also said, "What we now call the hatred of the proletariat against the rich was formerly called Jew hatred." Except for the French Jewish writer Marcel Proust, there was no Jew who could hold a candle to Heine. He feared grave developments in the near future: "Germany is still a little child—but the sun is its nurse. The sun does not suckle it with soothing milk, it suckles it with wild flames." Perhaps he knew that violence would continue forever in Germany, as in the summer of 2000, when a bomb wounded nine immigrants, six of them Jews.

Synagogue and Jewish Community Center, Zietenstrasse 50, Dusseldorf. Tel: 46912-0. info@jgd.de, www.jgd.de. Before the war, there was only one synagogue in Dusseldorf, which then had a population of about 5,000 Jews. The synagogue, then located on Kasernenstrasse, was destroyed in 1938 and it is now the site of the Handelsblatt, the Wall Street Journal of Germany. A stone monument recalls the synagogue. Kosher food can be obtained in the Jewish Community Center.

The synagogue in Dusseldorf is modern Orthodox. Friday evening services are at 6:00 p.m. in the winter, Shabbat morning services are at 9:15 a.m., and morning services during the week are at 7:30 a.m.

The Düsseldorf JCC has an ambitious cultural program of concerts, lectures, youth and adult education. Its beautiful white-stone synagogue opened in 1958. It has virtually no straight lines—everything, from its facade, to its pews, chandeliers, and arch, is circular, curved or arched. Düsseldorf's largest pre-war synagogue, on Kasernenstrasse, was destroyed on Kristallnacht; a stone Synagogue Memorial marks the site.

The Dusseldorf Jewish Community also sponsors a Jewish kindergarten (150 children); a Jewish elementary school named after the late Prime Minister of Israel, Yitzhak Rabin, (160 children); and a Jewish high school, which opened in 2016, named the Albert Einstein Gymnasium (80 children).

Dusseldorf Memorial Center, Muhlenstrasse, 29, Dusseldorf. Open Tuesday through Sunday. Exhibits and memorials focus on how the Nazi era affected the city. Opened in 1987, it shows the visitor how the Germans themselves remember. There is a memorial book of 2,213 names, the names of Dusseldorf Jews who were deported. Exhibits are in German.

Rohr Chabad Lubavitch Familien-und Bildungszentrum, Bankstraße 71, 40476 Düsseldorf. Tel: 49-211-420-96-93. Fax: 49-211-514-4190. info@chabad-duesseldorf.de

Nelly Sachs House, a senior citizens residence, Nelly-Sachs-St., 5, 40474, Dusseldorf. Tel: 49-211-43843-0. FAX: 49-211-43843-101. nelly. sachs@jgdus.de.

Frankfurt

Located at the center of Western Europe is Frankfurt-am-Main, the financial capital of Germany. Just gaze at the modern all-glass high-rise offices and you can see why Germany is the economic: colossus that it is. Although Frankfurt has about 725,000 people, this Rhine-Main industrial area takes in nearly 400 banking concerns. But then, Frankfurt always has been a center of trade and commerce. Just stand on one of the bridges over the Main River and you can see why trade flourished here.

Frankfurt is also the home of Goethe. His home, **Goethehaus,** is open to the public at Grosser Hirschgraben 23. He lived in this house—now a wonderful museum—from his birth until the age of 26.

Some of the famous Jewish native sons of Frankfurt include, of course, the Rothschilds, as well as the artist Moritz Oppenheim, Erik Erikson, Nahum Goidmann, and Daniel Cohn-Bendit. Martin Buber was a professor at Frankfurt University during the Weimar Republic years. Buber, who later emigrated to Israel, sought to resurrect the heritage of Chassidism for the modern Jew and offered his mystical view of the Jewish people. Leopold Sonnemann was the Jewish founder of one of Germany's most prestigious newspapers, Die Frankfurter Zeitung.

The book fairs of Frankfurt were always attended by Jewish printers and booksellers. Jewish book people from the United States and Israel still come to the Frankfurt Book Fair, which attracts nearly 250,000 persons. In fact, Sohar, the kosher restaurant here in Frankfurt, is usually the scene of a dinner of Jewish book dealers sponsored by the city's Jewish community.

Jews probably already traded in this flourishing city in the twelfth century. We know that a massacre occurred in 1241. But to Jews, Frankfurt meant the Rothschilds and the ghetto.

JEWISH SITES IN FRANKFURT

The Ghetto. In 1462, the Jews of Frankfurt were transferred to a specially constructed street, known as the Judengasse. It was a ghetto that was enclosed within walls and gates. The Jews possessed their own quarters, but the area could not be enlarged.

The Rothschilds once lived in the ghetto. In the 1560s, Isaac Elchanan, the first Rothschild, obtained a house here that displayed a red sign on the board of a shield, "rot schild" meaning "red sign." While those descendants might have moved, the name Rothschild stuck. On February 23, 1743, Mayer Amschel Rothschild was born. He later established a relationship with William of Hanau, who loved coin collecting. Mayer Amschel would offer him coins and William in return offered a patronage that eventually blossomed into the Rothschild financial empire.

By 1750, there were 3,000 men, women, and children in the Frankfurt ghetto—all crammed into 200 houses. The building regulations made it impossible to see into the houses of Christians. The side windows of the Jews were walled in and pasted over. The Jews were restricted to the *Judengasse*, afterwards known as the Bornestrasse; the street still exists. The Jews were locked in after sunset on weekdays and as early as 4:00 p.m. on Sundays. On certain holidays and festive public occasions, they were forced to remain indoors during the day and were let out only in the evening.

The *Bornestrasse* is near the Zeil, a pedestrian mall. To get to the Judengasse (Bornestrasse) from the Zeil, head south on Fahrgasse and make a quick left to Ander Staufenmauer. You'll pass through the arch of what was the city wall in the twelfth century and became the ghetto wall in the fifteenth century.

In 1796, the French Revolutionary Army liberated the Jews of Frankfurt, and in 1798, the prohibition on leaving the ghetto on Sundays and holidays was abolished.

Frankfurt became a center of Reform Judaism. In 1845, a conference of rabbis sympathizing with the Reform movement was held there. A leading member was theologian Abraham Geiger, an early German Reform rabbi, first in Frankfurt and then Berlin. Emancipation of the Jews of Frankfurt came in 1864.

Before the Nazis came to power, Frankfurt had a higher percentage of Jewish citizens than any other German city, including Berlin; and Jewish patronage was responsible for the establishment of many of the city's internationally known institutions, including its university and its paper, *Die Frankfurter Zeitung*.

The Bornestrasse Synagogue occupied the same site as the ghetto synagogue until it was destroyed on Kristallnacht. A plaque on the building that now houses a city statistical office identifies the site.

The configuration of the street was changed by the Allied bombings of World War II—it now comes to a dead end at a parking lot. Just past the synagogue plaque, the street now curves in the opposite direction from the old Judengasse. The Rothschild home probably stood in a place that is now one block over, near the Canon Copier store on Kurt Schumacherstrasse.

The Frankfurt Municipal Library contains the largest collection of Judaica in Germany, about 25,000 volumes and 325 manuscripts.

The Ignatz Bubis Gemeinde Centrum (Community Center) stands as one of the most impressive Jewish structures built in postwar Germany. Located at Westendstrasse 43, 60325, Frankfurt-am-Main. Tel: 49-69-76-8036-1000. One should actually enter the other side of the building on Savignystrasse 66. On this impressive side, one sees a menorah set high above the entrance. But to the left is a single, blank tablet of law with cracks to symbolize the break between the Germans and the Jewish people. There are about 10,000 Jews in the Frankfurt metropolitan area and most make this their center of activity. The community sponsors a day school. Lectures, movies, senior citizens' clubs, and talks by Israeli leaders all add to this program mix offered by this facility. It also contains a gym.

Sohar Kosher Restaurant is located in the Community Center. The establishment serves Israeli-style dishes. Shabbat meals can be ordered in advance. Ms. J. Marstaeller is executive director of the Community.

A few blocks away is the grey-stoned Westend Synagogue, the only Frankfurt synagogue to survive Kristallnacht. (see below under synagogues).

Jewish Museum Frankfurt, Untermainkai 14-15, 60311 Frankfurt-am-Main. Tel: 49-69-212-35000. FAX: 49-69-212-30705. info@juedischemuseum.de. Open Tuesday to Sunday, 10:00 a.m. to 5:00 p.m.; Wednesday until 8:00 p.m. Closed Mondays. The museum is closed until 2018 for construction work. The Jewish Museum Frankfurt will construct an extension building and have a new enhanced permanent presentation. The permanent exhibitions at the Jewish Museum and Museum Judengasse, will be new and modern. From March 20, 2016, the Museum Judengasse will present Jewish History until 1800. From 2018 on, the Jewish Museum at Rothschild Palace will cover the period after that until the present. Significantly, the museum was opened on November 9, 1988, in the former Rothschild Palais on the occasion of the fiftieth anniversary of Kristallnacht. The Jewish Museum is the largest of its kind in the German-speaking world. It features a history of Jews in Germany from the Middle Ages to the present with the Jewish community as the main example. The building was the home of Baron Carl von Rothschild and housed a vast library now in the Municipal and University Library. In the words of Georg Heuberger, the director, "the aim of the Jewish Museum is to provide the knowledge relating to the history, culture and religion of the Jewish people necessary for a dialogue between Jews and non-Jews." The museum, one of the finest in Europe, includes exhibits on Jewish life, rituals, festivals and holidays, a 1731 Haggadah, and portraits of Gotthold Ephraim Lessing and Moses Mendelssohn.

A videotape shows the history of the Jews of Frankfurt.

The exhibit on the Holocaust is outstanding. A memorial wall bears the names of 11,000 Jews of Frankfurt who lost their lives. It is quite moving!

The museum contains a wooden scale model of the Frankfurt

ghetto. The model of both sides of the Judengasse (street) shows Jewish life in the Middle Ages, and was made from plans drawn in 1711. There is an exhibition on the architecture of the synagogue, as well as on Jewish holidays and religious items. Other exhibits are about achievements in the area of civil rights, the development and social structure of the Jewish community, integration (a superb exhibit), assimilation, and anti-Semitism. There is a well-documented section on the Nazi era. Many non-Jews visit this building; it is in effect a learning center.

Museum Judengasse, Karl-Schumacher-Strasse, 10, at *Battonnstrasse*, 60311 Frankfurt. The museum reopened in 2016 after renovations. This museum located in the old Jewish quarter covers 300 years of Frankfurt's Jewish history. Highlights of this new building are a computerized infobank and other audiovisual instruments. The museum is open from 10:00 a.m. until 5:00 p.m. every day, except Mondays. On Wednesdays, the building is open until 8:00 p.m. In 1987, the city of Frankfurt began constructing a building for the public utilities company. The workers discovered the foundations of houses from the city's former Jewish quarter, the *Judengasse*. After considerable protest parts of the archeological excavations were reconstructed and made accessible to the public in a museum. The museum has now been redesigned. Its entrance was moved to *Battonnstrasse* so that the museum, the old Jewish cemetery, and the memorial to the deported Jews of Frankfurt are now visible as a historical ensemble.

Book-café is a very popular institution in the Jewish Museum in Frankfurt. Hanna Solomon manages this bookstore where one can find German-Jewish and Israeli newspapers and magazines on the racks.

In a room whose theme is the struggle for the Jewish State, Americans will be pleased to see the American flag flown high in a photo exhibit of the liberation of the concentration camp at Dachau. A poster in the display says, "Freedom can only be with the realization of a Jewish National Home in Palestine."

An electronic encyclopedia on Jewish subjects and a bookshop and cafeteria are included in this impressive building.

The Jewish Museum is not the only museum on what is called the Museum Row, Museum Mile, or Museum Embankment. In recent years, Frankfurt, which in 1994 celebrated its 1,200-year anniversary, embarked on much museum construction and it now also is considered a city of art. It has established a Museum Embankment containing a number of museums on Schaumainkai, the tree-lined avenue along the left bank of the Main River. The Jewish Museum is always mentioned as part of this museum complex, although technically, it is located across the river, on Untermainkai, 14-15. Included in the museums that are in the area are the Museum of Applied Arts, Museum of the City of Frankfurt, German Film Museum, German Architecture Museum, Stadel Art Institute, Liebreghaus, an extensive collection of sculpture, and the Jewish Museum. It is also not far from the excellent Franidurter Hof hotel, Bethmannstrasse 33.

Rothschild Park. The affluent Jews of Frankfurt lived in the westend and this is still the home of many Jews, and their cultural and religious center. The park once housed the mansion of the Goldschmidt-Rothschild family and was located behind the Opernplatz.

Senior Citizen Center, Bornheimer Landwehr 79b. Tel: 43-96-02. The **Atereth-Zvi Synagogue** is also located here.

SYNAGOGUES IN FRANKFURT

Synagogue Baumweg, Baumweg 5-7. 60316, Frankfurt.

Synagogue, Henry and Emma Budge-Stiftung, Wilhelm-shoherstrasse 279. 60389, Frankfurt. Tel: 49-69-47-87-10.

Westend Synagogue, Freiherr-vom-Stein-strasse, 30, 60323, Frankfurt. Tel: 49-69-7680-360. This is the only Frankfurt synagogue to have survived Kristallnacht. The grey stone building features vaulting stone arches on four sides under a massive cupola, with Star of David stained-glass windows in blue and white. Although a Liberal Synagogue before the war, it is now Orthodox, as are all the Frankfurt synagogues.

Munich

About 4,000 Jews now live in the Bavarian capital. One thing is certain: they want, and work for, an active Jewish community. And they don't like to be asked, "How can Jews live in Germany?" To them, and the approximate several hundred thousand Jews, including Israelis, in Germany, this is their home. Most of the young people are professionals and of the middle class. Only one-third of Munich's Jews are native-born; Israelis and Polish and Russian Jews make up the rest. Many of the Russian Jews who emigrated from the former U.S.S.R. did not go on to Israel.

Following Berlin and Hamburg, Munich is Germany's third largest industrial city. This warmhearted metropolis is famous for its art collections, its theater, the largest museum of science and technology in the world, and the largest university. Over a million people reside here in Germany's "secret capital." It is said that 60 percent of all Germans would like to live in this area. Surrounded by green valleys and dark green forests, the Muncheners are not poor in nature or wealth; on the contrary, they are probably the richest in all of Germany.

This city of Old-World elegance is a center of art and culture. Alongside its art galleries and museums are open-air beer gardens and the Hofbrauhaus. The Oktoberfest was once described as a Teutonic drunk scene. Fine buildings of every period, grand boulevards and squares, and the Marienplatz all highlight this city. Theodor Herzl, father of modern Zionism, wanted Munich as the seat of the First World Zionist Congress. But the local Jewish community protested because its German patriotism might be questioned. And that is how Basel, Switzerland, came to be the site of the Congress.

In the Schwabing district, the center of European intellectual life, lived Brecht, Mann, Klee, Kandinsky, Trotsky, and Spengler. Munich was the site of the Red Commune in 1919, as well as the birthplace and center of the Nazi movement. In 1923, it was the scene of Hitler's Beer Hall Putsch. In spite of this failed attempt to overthrow the government, Hitler made Munich the headquarters of the Nazi party. In the spring of 1913, Hitler had arrived in this city as a "young artist and German nationalist," according to Stephen Kinzer in the *New York Times*, January 4, 1994. Then, and after World War I, Munich was the scene of great political upheaval. To this day, the area around Munich—the capital of the state of Bavaria—remains one of Germany's most conservative regions.

Munich also has become synonymous with appeasement. In 1938, British Prime Minister Neville Chamberlain signed the Munich Pact with Hitler at the then Fuhrer Ban (headquarters). "Peace in our time," it was called, but it was clear, outright appeasement, the sellout of Czechoslovakia, and the tragic forerunner of Hitlerian victories.

JEWISH SITES IN MUNICH

Munich's Olympia Park, is the site of the 1972 Olympic Games. A Memorial to the 11 Israeli athletes murdered by terrorists at the Games stands in front of the apartment where they were held hostage, Connollystrasse 31.

Ludwig-Maximilian University was home to the anti-Nazi White Rose Movement, one of the most idealistic and effective German attempts at resistance during World War II. Led by students Hans and Sophie Scholl and their professor, Kurt Huber, the White Rose distributed anti-Nazi leaflets in 1942 and 1943, publicizing details of the Final Solution and German battlefront reverses. The Scholls and Huber, were caught, tried and executed.

Today, the east side of the main university square is named Professor-Huber-Platz, and the left side, Geschwister-Scholl-Platz (Scholl Siblings Square). A memorial plaque to the White Rose Martyrs is in the university's main lobby. The White Rose Information Center is near the university's Lichthof Hall. www.weisse-rose-stiftung. de.

The **Neuer Israelitischer Friedhof cemetery** on Garchinger Strasse 37 (Alte Heide subway stop) was opened in 1908.

The **Alter Israelitischer Friedhof cemetery** is on Thalkirchner Strasse 240.

SYNAGOGUES AND JEWISH CENTERS IN MUNICH

Israeli religious community Munich and Oberbayern Kdö. R. St. Jacob's Place 18, 80331 Munich, Germany Tel: 49-89-20-24-00-100. Fax: 49-89-20-24-00 -170. info@ikg-m.de

Jewish Community Center, St. Jacobs Place 18, 80331 Munich. Tel: 49-89-20-24-00-100. FAX: 49-89-20-24-00. info@ikg-m.de.

The main synagogue, Ohel Jacob, is located here as is Einstein kosher restaurant. Tel: 89-20-24-00-333. FAX: 89-20-24-00-334. restaurant@kik-g-de, www.Einstein-restaurant.de. Call ahead for information on prayer times, kosher food, and community activities. A mikveh is also located here.

Recently, the Youth and Cultural Center of the Jewish Community moved to the above Jakobsplatz building and offers recreation, education and adult education. Programs include lectures and talks, discussions and exhibitions, as well as Hebrew language instruction

Located in the new Jewish Center on St. Jacob Place is the Jewish Museum. Tel: 49-89-233-96096.

Chabad House, Prinzregentenstr, 91, 81677 Munich. Tel: 89-470-6355. info@chabad.de, www.Chabad.de.

Chabad for Jewish Students and Young Professionals. Schumannstr, 7, 81679, Munich. rabbifreedman@chabad.de. Rabbi Levi Freedman is the rabbi here.

Liberale Judische Gemeinde Munchen Beth Shalom, Munich, Hermann-Hummel St., 18, Grafelfing, 82166, Munich. Postfach 75-05-66. Munich 81335. Tel: 49-89-7670-2711. info@beth-shalom.de. www. beth-shalom.de.

DACHAU

Dachau, nestled in the rolling hills of Munich, is the site of the infamous Nazi death camp and is the fourth most visited site in

Germany, with one million visitors in a year, and not all foreigners or school groups.

There are complaints that the Germans have prettied up the camp. But as Thane Rosenbaum notes in a book review of The Last Survivor, by Timothy W. Ryback, "no amount of natural scenic beauty can camouflage the death museum that brings a million tourists a year to Dachau."

Dachau boasted the first concentration camp, the first crematory oven, the first gas chambers, the first medical experiments. The author and journalist Robert St. John described Dachau as "an ugly little word." Dachau was opened on March 21, 1933, in what had been a World War I munitions factory. Between 1933 and 1941, the camp was finished and actually had a reputation among inmates as "relatively luxurious," according to James E. Young in his book, *The Texture of Memory: Holocaust Memorials and Meaning in Europe, Israel, and America.* He writes that while several thousand Soviet Army officers were executed here, and Jews were killed at Buchenwald, "the only extermination centers on German territory were Mauthausen and Hartheim Castle in Austria, with their operational gas chambers." But as the war ended and the Soviet troops moved in from the East, "the Germans evacuated masses of starved, diseased ravaged Jews from the death camps in Poland to Germany," according to Young. Dachau became a death camp. "It was inundated with open cattle cars of dead and dying prisoners." Today, there are memorials in Dachau—the sculpture by Nandor Glid of a 45-feet long, black bronze grid of human forms enmeshed in barbed wire, is well-known throughout the world.

There is also a Jewish monument of a stone vault. A path descends downward to the vault and on both sides of the path is a barbed iron gate with Stars of David on either side. Inside, one gets the feeling of being in the pit of a furnace looking up through the chimney—it "mirrors the shape of crematorium ovens."

Officials say that Americans are among the most numerous of the foreign visitors to Dachau. Many of the visitors wear yarmulkes. There are German youth from the schools, as well as students arriving on tour buses from Italy. There are English men and women on holiday. They all come to Dachau. An excellent historical museum that traces the brutal rise of Nazism and tells what went on here in the first death camp occupies the premises. Some of the camp's original structures still stand, and two of the barracks have been reconstructed.

What goes on in the visitors' minds? While they say Dachau is not as gruesome in its preservation as, say, Auschwitz, they get the message. Perhaps they hope that the world will be better, that there were righteous Christians even in Germany who saved Jews.

The entrance to the concentration camp at Dachau. (Photo by Scott Michaels)

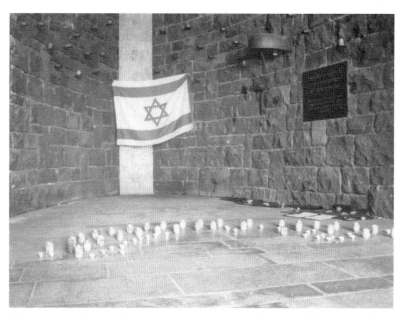

Memorial candles at the concentration camp at Dachau. (Photo by Scott Michaels)

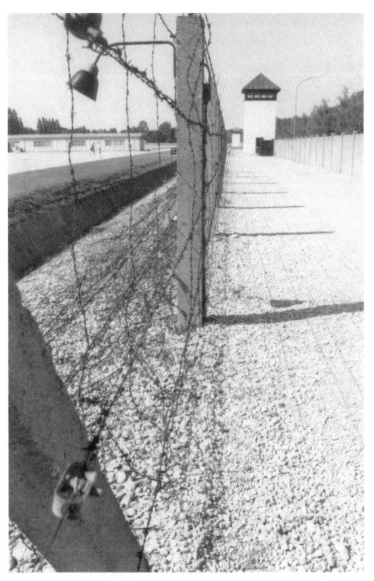

Dachau. (Photo by Scott Michaels)

A number of years ago, I met a man who was dedicated in his way to heal wounds. Johann Waltenberger, served as principal in the Josef Effner High School, whose student body numbers 1,500. It seems that Waltenberger, who is not Jewish, was moved by the television film Holocaust. He immediately set out on his own to bring two peoples, Germans and Israelis, together "to remember the past."

Waltenberger is a religious man. He always has been interested in the Bible and in the Holy Land. He has visited Israel several times and is fond of it. He talks like a Zionist. A number of years ago, with some help from the Jewish community of Munich, he wrote a long letter to a number of Israeli schools and asked them if they would be interested in an exchange program of students and teachers.

The Israelis answered back politely, in effect, "Thank you, but no thank you." Waltenberger said the Israelis wrote that he should teach the Holocaust in his class and drop the matter.

Waltenberger says he understood their reaction but was not deterred. On his next trip to Israel, he visited several of the Israeli educators and personally talked to them about the program.

He was persistent. He says he had to try. After a year of negotiations, six Israeli teachers were scheduled to come to Dachau for a week to exchange ideas, discussions, and methods regarding teaching the Holocaust.

In Waltenberger's school, of course, the Holocaust is taught. His pupils visit the camp, which contains a museum, a sample barracks, several memorials, as well as a synagogue and two churches.

"Emotions," Waltenberger says, "are not enough; dialogue is important. We must do these things." He set up the whole program himself. All of this could be brushed aside as infinitesimal compared to the thousands upon thousands who perished at Dachau. But there are those in the American Jewish community and the German Jewish community who believe that Jews should never cease to remind the world about the Holocaust. As emotionally trying as a visit to Dachau becomes, homage should continue to be paid to the six million Jews on the soil where they died. The world must remember!

Dresden

On a trip to Europe, I took a tour heralded by the travel industry: Berlin, Dresden and Prague. Linked to Berlin and Prague and smack right in the middle lies Dresden, the capital of Saxony—a gem on the Elbe River, 100 miles southeast of Berlin and 20 miles from the Czech Republic border.

On my visit, I learned that the city likes to be called, "Florence of the Elbe," and rightly so. Its array of art is dazzling: 35 museums, including the Old and New Masters Art Galleries, as well as a unique Dresden Hygiene Museum. Also, 34 theaters and stages, including the Saxon State Opera, a Saxon State Orchestra, a Dresden Philharmonic and a Dresden Symphony. If you are into music and art, this city should be on your itinerary.

The world famous Frauenkirche Church has been restored and reopened.

And there is more:

The 18th century Zwinger, known the world over for its fine collections of porcelain; the Semper Gallery, contains some of the world's finest paintings; The Old Masters Art Gallery houses several thousand noted paintings.

The city is famous for porcelain, often called, "Dresden china." Actually, it is Meissen porcelain, produced in nearby Meissen.

World War II lies deep in the psyche of anyone who enters here. Reminders are everywhere. Seventy years ago, near the end of the war, both the U.S. Army and Red Army raced for Berlin. At 10:00 p.m. February 13, 1945, 1,100 American and British heavy bombers dropped more than 4,500 tons of high explosive bombs and incendiary devices, leaving the city in flaming ruins and claiming the lives of between 25,000 and 40,000 persons.

A Brief History

A Jewish community existed here in the early 14th century. Its members were massacred in the Black Death persecutions in 1349. Jews are not mentioned in Dresden again until 1375. A synagogue and cemetery were opened in the middle of the 18th century and by the end of that century there were about 1,000 Jews. The community numbered approximately, 2,300 in 1886; 4,300 in 1913; and over 6,000 in 1925. After the Holocaust, few Jews returned. A new synagogue was opened in 1950. But by the end of the 1960s, when the Communists were in power in East German, only 199 remained.

Synagogue, Hasenberg 1, Dresden. On Kristallnacht in 1938, the original Dresden Synagogue, which served 6,000 Jews was leveled. It had been consecrated on May 8, 1840. Gottfried Semper, the city's most famous architect—who drew up the plans for the famous Semper Opera House—designed that synagogue. In the 1840s, that house of worship was the largest Jewish congregation in Germany. Today, a new synagogue and JCC stand at the exact spot as its predecessor. Modern, impressive, with several rows of memorial trees in its courtyard, with a kosher kitchen, the synagogue and community center serve about 600 Jews, most of them from the former Soviet Union.

Old Jewish Cemetery, Pulsnitzer st., Dresden, is the oldest in Saxony, with graves dating back to 1750.

Chabad, Dresden. www.Chabad-Sachsen.de.

Guide: A recommended guide for city tourinbg and Jewish points of interest is Susanne Reichelt, Tel: 49-351-2513152. info@tourguide-dresden.de. Website, www.tourguide-dresden.de. For tours of the synagogue itself, Ms. Reichelt noted that she puts travelers in touch with the association known as Hatikvah, www.hatikva,de.

Worms

A number of Jewish scholars lived in Worms.

Jewish cemetery. Located just beyond the southwest corner of the city wall is this Jewish cemetery, one of the oldest in Europe. Comprised of 2,000 tombstones, it was probably founded in 1076. Many great scholars are buried in Worms. A section of the cemetery designated as the "Valley of the Rabbis" has directional signs in Hebrew to guide visitors. The municipality tends to the grounds.

Rashi Haus, Worms. This is a Jewish museum as well as the city archives and is located next to the synagogue. It was opened in 1982 on the site of a yeshiva where once stood a hospital and an old age home. And just to remind us where we are, there was once on this very site an assembly of Jews, half of which were dispatched to the concentration camp.

Rashi Synagogue, Worms. This is one of the most significant Jewish historical sites in Germany. Built first in 1034 and destroyed several times thereafter, it is one of the oldest Jewish houses of worship in Europe. The mikveh (1186) and the Rashi Chapel (1624) were destroyed by the Nazis in 1938, but they have been reconstructed. Although Rashi lived here for only five years, his disciples still come to inhale the atmosphere in which he lived and thrived. The Rashi Chapel has a chair that may have been used by the venerable scholar. A large room to the left of the bimah was a separate women's synagogue built in the thirteenth century. The wall between the two buildings was removed in the nineteenth century and the room now stands empty, except for a memorial marker for the 500 Worms Jews who died in the Holocaust.

Synagogueplatz. This is the square just off the Judengasse that runs parallel to the remnants of the city's north wall.

Suggested Reading

Adler, H. G. *The Jews in Germany: From the Enlightenment to National Socialism.* Notre Dame, Ind.: University of Notre Dame Press, 1969.

Berenbaum, Michael. *The World Must Know: The History of the Holocaust As Told in the United States Holocaust Museum*. Boston: Little, Brown, 1993.

Bolitho, Hector, ed. *Twelve Jews*. Freeport, N.Y.: Books for Libraries Press, 1934.

Cornwell, John. "*Hitler's Pope, The Secret History of Pius XII*, Viking, New York, 1999.

Fest, Joachim C. *Hitler*. New York: Vintage, 1973.

Friedrich, Otto. *Before the Deluge: A Portrait of Berlin in the 1920's*. *New York: Harper & Row, 1972*.

German National Tourist Office. "*Germany for the Jewish Traveler*." New York.

Herz, Emil. *Before the Fury: Jews and Germany Before Hitler*. Philosophical Library, 1966.

Katcher, Leo. *Post-Mortem: The Jews of Germany Today*. New York: Delacorte, 1968.

Kempe, Frederick. *Father/Land: A Personal Search for the New Germany*, New York, G. P. Putnam's Sons, 1999.

Kramer, Jane. *Europeans*. New York: Farrar, Straus & Giroux, 1988.

Krinsky, Carol Herselle. *Synagogues of Europe: Architecture, History, Meaning*. Cambridge, Mass.: MIT Press, 1985.

Lowenthal, Marvin. *The Jews of Germany: A Story of Sixteen Centuries*. New York: Longmans, Green, 1936.

Meltzer, Milton. *Never to Forget: The Jews of the Holocaust*. New York: Harper & Row, 1976.

Nelson, Walter Henry. *The Berliners, Their Saga and Their City*. New York: David McKay, 1966.

Rabinbach, Anson, and Jack D. Zipes, eds. *Germans and Jews Since the Holocaust: The Changing Situation in West Germany*. New York: Holmes &; Meier, 1986.

Rothschild, Joseph. *East Central Europe between the Two World Wars, Seattle and London*, University of Washington Press, 1974.

Roy, James Charles. *The Vanished Kingdom: Travels Through the History of Prussia*, Boulder, Colo.: Westview Press, 1999.

Ryan, Cornelius. *The Last Battle*. New York: Simon & Schuster, 1966.

Schalk, Adolph. *The Germans*. Englewood Cliffs, N.J.: Prentice Hall, 1971.

Serotta Edward. *Jews, Germany, Memory: A Contemporary Portrait*. Vienna: Central Europe Center for Research and Documentation. 1996.

Shirer, William L. *The Rise and Fall of the Third Reich*. New York: Fawcett Crest, 1959.

Shlaes, Amity. *Germany: The Empire Within*. New York: Farrar, Straus & Giroux, 1991.

Sichrovsky, Peter. *Strangers in Their Own Land: Young Jews in Germany and Austria Today*. New York: Basic Books, 1986.

Smyser, W. R. *From Yalta to Berlin: The Cold War Struggle Over Germany*. New York, St. Martin's, 2000.

Weinberg, Gerhard. *A World At Arms: A Global History of World War II*. New York: Cambridge University Press, 1994.

Young, James E. *The Texture of Memory: Holocaust Memorials and Meaning in Europe,   , and America*. New Haven and London: Yale University Press, 1993.

Zweig, Stefan. *The World of Yesterday: An Autobiography*. New York: Viking, 1943.

Greece
Grandeur at the Jewish Museum

The colors are blue and white. The flag is blue and white. Even the Greek color scheme of sea, sky and cloud is blue and white.

Nikos Stavroulakis, the late co-founder and former director of Athens' Jewish Museum, sat back in an interview, and reflectively said: "You know, there always have been Greek-Jewish tensions since the days of the Maccabees. The Greeks have always felt and maintained a strong identity about themselves.

Nikos was right. There was a clash 2,000 years ago between Jewish and Greek culture.

Often, Greek merchants envied their Jewish rivals and sought to restrict their progress. Today tension is not felt in the ancient city of Athens, whose majestic Acropolis looks down on you. Jews still live here. They go to the synagogue and they visit the community center. They come and go as they please to Israel. And above all, they keep Judaism alive.

The Jewish traveler can experience Greek Judaism in Athens. He or she will find Athens to be friendly, warm, and quiet—almost like a little peaceful village—despite the rush-hour traffic around Constitution Square and the congestion in the city. The past permeates the air as tourists descend by the millions on this capital. It is after all, one of the oldest cities in the world that goes back 3,400 years.

Athens prides itself on being located at the crossroads of Europe, the Middle East, and Africa. About four million people live in the Athens area, out of a total population of nearly 11 million. This city contains an old Jewish community that originated probably in the first century, before the Common Era. It is small, but united.

This is a wonderful Jewish community: appealing, warm, welcoming. Greek Jewry has a high rate of intermarriage due to the isolation of young Jews in small communities.

In the first century BC, when the apostle Paul traveled through Greece, active Jewish communities existed in Corinth, Thessaloniki, the ancient name of Salonika, and Patras, as well as on the islands of Rhodes, Somos, and Delos. The original Greek Jews were called Romaniots. Influenced by Greek culture and language, their family names were Greek and their synagogues were known by their Greek names.

Under the Christian rulers of the Byzantine Empire, Jewish rights became limited when Jews were expected to convert to Christianity. Crusaders on their way to the Holy Land would kill Jews living in Greece.

As Christianity spread, substantial legal and economic restrictions were placed on Jews, but they continued to exist. They developed their own variant of Jewish rituals and customs, which came to be known as the Romaniot rite.

Benjamin of Tudela found large numbers of Jews in Greece in 1170 when he toured Jewish communities. He found them in Corfu, Patras, Thebes, Salonika, and other cities, including the Greek islands. They worked in dyeing, weaving, and the making of silk garments. Jews were well off, he reported.

The Turkish conquest in the fifteenth century (Athens was conquered in 1456) ushered in a "Golden Age" for Greek Jewry when the Sephardic migration from Spain and Turkey overwhelmed and absorbed the older Byzantine Jewish communities. The newcomers revived the Sephardic way of life, including the Ladino language.

When Jews were expelled from Iberia, many Spanish and Portuguese Jews settled in Salonika, so much so that by 1553, 20,000 Jews lived there.

The sultan, Bayazid II, had welcomed tens of thousands of Iberian Jews to Istanbul in Turkey and to Salonika, now in Greece but then ruled by the Ottoman Turks, who were to remain in Greece until 1822.

In the sixteenth century, prominent rabbis lived in Salonika. One was Sh'lomo Alqabetz, who wrote the stirring, romantic Shabbat Hebrew song, "L'cha Dodi."

In the seventeenth century "Jewish" Salonika radiated power as the center of rabbinic and Kabbalistic studies and the seat of leading halachic authorities.

Meanwhile, between 1453 and 1821, Greece as a nation-state vanished from history. And it was in 1821-22 that Jews obtained equal and legal rights, even though many Jews lost their lives for backing the Turks.

By 1920 Greek Jews were organized into 24 religious communities with stable institutions and numerous activities. Salonika itself boasted 40 synagogues, which were named after once-famous Jewish communities in Spain. Two newspapers were published in Ladino.

After population exchanges between Greece and Turkey in 1923, and the arrival of 100,000 Greeks from Anatolia, the Jewish communities declined somewhat. In 1940, there were 77,000 Jews in Greece. At war's end, only about 10,000 to 15,000 Jews survived the Holocaust.

Between 1945 and 1955, 3,500 Greek Jews, mostly Sephardim, settled in Israel, and about 1,200 journeyed to the United States. After the war, Greece promulgated a law that makes racism and anti-Semitic criminal acts. Greece stood as one of the few European countries to vote against the 1947 U.N. Partition Plan creating a Jewish state. A disappointment at that time, especially since Greece is a key player in the Mediterranean.

Over the years, Greece and Israel have grown closer! Today in the second decade of the 21st century, Greece and Israel have joined hands in many common ventures. The strengthening of ties with Israel on a political and military level is an important development given the rise of Islamic terrorism, according to Ronald S. Lauder, the president of World Jewish Congress, who visited Athens on the occasion of Holocaust Remembrance Day in January 2017 according to a statement in an interview with the Greek newspaper, *Kathimerini*. Greece is a member of NATO and the European Union. In the last decade improved relations between Greece and Israel have been on the upswing. Victor Eliezar, second vice-president of the Central Board of Jewish Communities, and a correspondent for the Israeli newspaper, *Yedioth Achronot*, believes both countries desire to draw closer together, not because relations of both of them with Turkey are tense, but Greece "has decided that Israel can be a credible ally in the economic and political stability in this part of the Mediterranean." And, he added, Israel and Greece share common interests regarding exploration and development of natural gas reserves in their areas as well as the issue of Cyprus. An example of cooperation between these three countries came in April 2017 when Israel, Greece, and Cyprus pledged to move ahead with the world's longest undersea gas pipeline from the eastern Mediterranean to Southern Europe, with support from the European Union.

The spread of right-wing nationalism has affected Greece, too. In an interview with *Kathimerini's* Sunday's edition, Ronald S. Lauder noted the rise of nationalism and anti-Semitism which, he said, is not just a threat to minorities but to society at large. Lauder said the proliferation of far-right groups in Europe, including Golden Dawn in Greece which openly professes its hatred of Jews and Israel, has taken on alarming proportions. He also noted a rise in anti-Semitism among

Muslim migrants in Europe, as well as among traditional European newspapers and even Britian's Labor party.

JEWISH SITES IN ATHENS

Wonderful things can happen to one in Athens, though it does not win awards for its attractiveness. Like Greece, Athens is beautiful and ugly and someone has to show you the beautiful: A friend, a relative, or a good guide. The same with the countryside in this sometimes "dry and sleepy land."

Still even during a very humid summer day in Athens, when the sun burns as a dry forest suddenly ignited, or at night when the stars shine brilliantly, Athens stands as a symbol of fame.

One must stroll in *Athinai,* its Greek name. Walk and inhale the past, not the smog. Although Athens is a modern city, the sudden twist of a street can land you in an area filled with ancient Greek or Byzantine ruins. Ancient Athens was the leading cultural center of the Greek world. The Athenian statesman Pericles called Athens, the "school of Greece."

In many ways, the city was the birthplace of Western Civilization and the Acropolis remains the heart of the capital, often visible from wherever you are, always reminding you of the glory that was Greece.

Before heading to visit Jewish community sites, walk up the hill under the clear blue summer sky. Stare at the Acropolis and the Acropolis Museum. You will feel the grandeur of Greece, the birthplace of Western Civilization. Like beauty, one never tires staring at the Acropolis and its lit-up Parthenon, white, shiny, some say virginal.

City bus tours will take you to the Acropolis, the Temple of the Olympian Zeus, and Hadrian's Arch.

Welcome to the popular tourist sight Plaka with its outdoor cafes, its bars, its pedestrian streets, its shops. Stroll around the narrow paved streets of Plaka. There you will see how life should be lived and enjoyed. This is the way to spend an Athenian evening.

Another way to the Plaka is to walk from Constitution Square (Syntagma) Square which houses one of the best hotels in the world. Hotel Grande Bretagne, rich in history. This hotel served as the headquarters of Greek, German, and British forces in turn during World War II. On Christmas Eve, 1944, it is said, while British Prime Minister Winston S. Churchill was visiting strife-torn Athens, an attempt to blow up the hotel from the sewers was foiled.

Athens has improved transportation-wise. A subway system, a modern airport, and a ring road were completed for the 2004 Olympics, which were revived in 1896 in Athens.

But even in those days of athletic excitement and world attention, dark clouds were appearing on the economic horizon of the country: recession, bankruptcy, bailout by the European Union, strict controls, riots in the streets of the capital, and a new government.

Many have described Greece as an "economic basket case." Some observers believe Greece will be the next to quit the EU.

Greece's GDP per person has fallen by 45 percent since late 2009, according to *The Economist* on March 25, 2017. Greek economic recovery has been dismal by historic standards.

By 2016, unemployment reached 25 percent that meant one million Greeks were out of work, according to government statistics. And what's worse, notes Victor Eliezer, second vice-president of the Central Board of Jewish Communities in Greece and correspondent for the Israeli newspaper, *Yedioth Achronot*, "the percentage among those between 18 to 30 years old, is 56 percent." He added that during the last 8 years, the number of needy people has dramatically increased. "If Greece does not attract foreign investments, the situation will not change," he declared.

Reforms, reducing the bureaucracy, privatization of public companies, and modernization of the educational system, are all suggestions put forward by Mr. Eliezer.

Will Greece follow the UK in leaving the EU. "Hope not," says Mr. Eliezer, adding, "The great majority of the Greek people do not want a Grexit."

Because of the economic crisis in Greece, the Jewish community, too, has been affected. Its income is down, especially from real estate which is the main financial source of Jewish communities in Greece. At the same time, notes Mr. Eliezer, more members of the community are seeking support from Jewish social departments. "Still," he said, "we try and succeed to keep alive all aspects of Jewish life in Greece, thanks to the solidarity of international Jewish organizations."

Moreover, the hard core of right-wing extremism has shown its ugly head in Greece too. Greece's Golden Dawn party is quite active in the country. Like other extremist parties in Europe, this one also attacks "mainstream politics." It has been dubbed a neo-Nazi and fascist party. And the group has made use of alleged Nazi symbolism and praised figures of Nazi Germany. Anti-Semitism is definitely up in Greece, heated by the extreme right.

However, Mr. Lauder noted, "From what I heard, a lot of anti-Semitic stereotypes persist in Greece, but the actual number of anti-Jewish attacks is lower than in other countries. The way I interpret this is that we need more education to get rid of these stereotypes. Holocaust remembrance is also important."

Ronald S. Lauder is also president of the Lauder Foundation which supports the Athens Jewish Community School.

And now a few Jewish sites in Athens:

Beth Shalom Synagogue, 5 Odos Melidoni, Athens. Tel: 30-210-325-2875. An attractive white building with ample seating. Rabbi Gabriel Negrin is the rabbi of the Athens community

Ets Hayim Synagogue, 8 Odos Melidoni, Athens. Tel: 30-210-3252875, the older Romaniote synagogue of Athens.

Jewish Community Center, Vissarionos St. Athens. Tel: 36-37-092. Activities abound at the Jewish Youth and Community Center: Lectures, a Seder on Passover, Purim celebration, holiday celebrations, Israel Independence Day, Tu B'Shvat.

Jewish Community Offices, 8 Odos Melidoni, Athens, Tel: 30-210 325-2823. Almost the whole Jewish community turns out for High Holiday services. Jews in Athens are: businessmen, merchants, corporate executives, lawyers, doctors, and hold professional and working class jobs.

The members here can tell the traveler about organizations such as WIZO; the Zionist Federation, Bnai Brith. The Jewish Community of Athens organizes summer trips to Israel for teenagers and young adults; and the Panhellenic Jewish Youth movement. A most successful project is the Athens Youth Club.

Central Board of Jewish Communities in Greece, 36 Voulis St. 105 57 Athens. Tel: 30-210-32-44-315. Fax: 30-210-33-13-852. hhkis@ath.forthnet.gr. www.kis.gr. This is the umbrella organization and representative body of the Jews of Greece. The council is composed of representatives of the Jewish communities in Athens and other areas of Greece. More than two-thirds of Greek Jewry reside in Athens This community group makes representations to the government. It also represents Greek Jewry at the international level. KIS also coordinates and assists the nine Jewish Communities functioning in Greece: Athens, Thessaloniki and Larissa host the largest in numbers regarding Jewish Communities, to be followed by Volos, Trikala, Chalkis, Ioannina, Corfu and Rhodes.

The Jewish population in Greece is figured at 4,300 core Jews. When one figures in Jews with one Jewish parent the number rises to 5,500, according to Sergio DellaPergola. "World Jewish Population, 2016," in Arnold Dashefsky & Ira M. Sheskin. (Editors) *The American Jewish Year Book*, 2016, Volume 116 (2016) (Dordrecht: Springer). Total Greek population is just under 11 million citizens.

Holocaust Monument of Athens, between Melidoni Ermou and Evoulou streets, is located near Beth Shalom and Etz Hayim synagogues.

The Jewish Museum, 39 Nikis St., 105 57, Athens. Tel: 30-210-322-5882. Fax: 30-210-323-1577. info@jewishmuseum.org. www.jewishmuseum.gr. Open Monday through Friday, 9:00 a.m. until 2:30 p.m., Closed Saturday and Sunday, 10:00 a.m. until 2:00 p.m. Admission fees charged. Be prepared for security checks before entering the museum. Perhaps the history of Greek Jewry haunted the community. Perhaps it plagued the artist, educator, historian, and co-founder, and director, Nikos Stavroulakis so much that he almost single-handedly created one of the finest Jewish museums in Europe. If you are nearby, it is worth a special visit to Greece to see this wonderful museum. The current curator is Zanet Batinou. She served as curator from 1994 to 2001, Director from 2001 to the present. Nikos created the old museum on Amalias Street. But the new facility on Nikis Street was created through the efforts of Samuel Matsas, president of the board of directors and Sam Benroubi, former president of the Board of Directors. The design used here is based on a concept of Nikos: spaces rise spiraling around a central void.

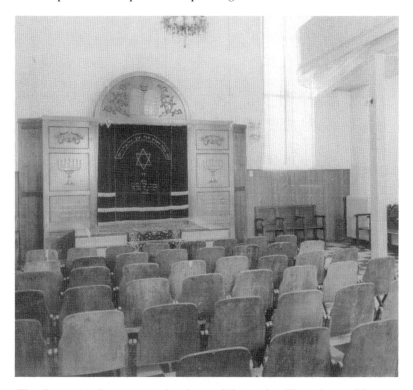

The Romaniot Synagogue of Athens. (Photo by Timothy DeVinney, courtesy of the Jewish Museum of Greece)

Synagogue of Corfu. (Photo by Timothy DeVinney, courtesy of the Jewish Museum of Greece)

The Jewish Museum is located smack in the heart of Athens, convenient to the city's major hotels. It is a good place to begin a visit to the Jewish community of Greece. With much to see and study, it is not unusual to spend a good half-day here. Nikos began his museum project by collecting "war leftovers." He obtained 15 cloth bags from the Bulgarian government. The sacks contained 2,800 items that had been confiscated from Greek Jews during the war. Included were watches, rings, and amulets. You can now look at them in this museum: silver from Rhodes, furniture from the Patras Synagogue, and gravestones from Hania in Crete. He saved and collected and recorded, and today we benefit from his work. Ancient Hebrew books have been preserved.

The Holocaust is remembered and portrayed in the museum. Nearly all of Greek Jewry perished in it, about 80 percent, one of the highest in the Holocaust, according to historian Leni Yahil. The Nazis killed more Jews in Greece proportionately than in any other country except Poland.

During the war, almost all of the synagogues had been destroyed or severely damaged. Exhibits in 2017 were titled: "The Jewish Community of Ioannina—The Memory of Artefacts," and Joseph Eligia, "The Poet of the Lake."

A U.S. Embassy report once singled out the Greeks as one of the

The Holocaust Exhibit in the Jewish Museum of Greece. (Photo by Timothy DeVinney, copyright © Jewish Museum of Greece. All rights reserved.)

few European peoples who not only helped its Jews, but sheltered them at the risk of being killed if they were discovered.

The Jewish Museum houses the culture of Greek Jewry that was part of the birth and rebirth of Greece. Fittingly, when you walk out of the renovated historic building that now houses the museum, head for nearby busy and noisy Amalias Ave. There you will observe the ancient monument, Pillars of Zeus, across the street.

In discussing the Holocaust as it relates to Greece, it should be noted that the Greek government decided to allow descendants of Holocaust survivors to apply for Greek citizenship. The parliamentary amendment follows a call from the Central Board of Jewish Communities for this action. As expected the neo-Nazi Golden Dawn party, the fourth biggest in Parliament, voted against the measure.

Chabad, 10 Aisopou St. Athens, Tel: 30-210-323-3825. info@chabad.gr. Rabbi Mendel Hendel is the spiritual leader of the congregation. Born in Safed, Israel, he informed me that services take place at **Beth Shalom Synagogue,** 5 Odos Melidoni. Chabad maintains the only kosher restaurant in Athens, known as **Gostijo Kosher Restaurant,** www.gostijo.gr. That is the name of this Sephardic-style cooking restaurant in Chabad House, 10, Aisopou, Athens. Rabbi Mendel Hendel said that Chabad hosts Shabbat meals by reservation, www.chabad.gr/shabbatform. The rabbi also noted that Chabad, on its premises, has a grocery with kosher products and catering service that ships kosher meals throughout Greece. www.koshergreece.com.

Thessaloniki (Salonika)

An Oriental air hovers over Salonika, Greece's second city, located on the Aegean Sea. It is a gateway to the Balkans, and right on the road between Athens and Istanbul. Thessaloniki is named for the sister of Alexander the Great. It is a short drive from Pella where excavations have revealed Alexander's capital city of Macedonia and from Veria, another city where Jews flourished. Alexander's brother-in-law, Kassandros, who built Thessaloniki, apparently asked the king of Egypt to send him Jewish artisans. This is supposed to have marked the start of the Jewish community of Thessaloniki (Salonika). By the end of the fifteenth century, Salonika became a melting pot for European Jewish communities. Each brought their own exotic sounding names to the city. Calabria, Majorca, and Lisbon were among its thirty separate Jewish communities. Eventually, all the groups embraced Ladino. Also settling here was a large group of Marranos from Portugal.

In the sixteenth and seventeenth centuries, the city of Salonika, then part of Turkey, became a great center of Sephardic Jewry.

"Salonika in 17th century terms was as Jewish a city as is New York in the 21st century," says Barnet Litvinoff. This Greek metropolis was known throughout the world for its famous rabbinical scholars and seminaries, Hebrew printing presses, and Jewish libraries. Actually, until the mid-twentieth century, Salonika was "a Jewish city." Shabbetai Zevi, the false messiah born in Smyrna, tried to make Salonika his base of operations. But in 1657, he was expelled from the city. By the end of the nineteenth century, 80,000 of Salonika's 120,000 citizens were Jews who spoke Ladino. In 1900, 90,000 Jews made up more than half of the city's population. The community supported hospitals, orphanages, schools, daily newspapers, and rabbinical seminaries where Hebrew, Ladino, and French were spoken. Despite hardships, it remained a center of Jewish learning and culture.

In 1912, Greece conquered Turkish-held Salonika and proceeded to Hellenize the city by settling Greeks within it. According to Israel Cohen, a fire in 1917 leveled the Jewish quarter, destroying 20,000 homes, 30 synagogues, 8 schools, and residential and commercial buildings. Nearly two thousand years of history went up in smoke.

While many people immigrated to then Palestine, the most interesting group who picked themselves up and went to the Land of Israel seems to have been Greek fishermen, relates Cohen. As far as we know, they were the only organized body of Jewish fishermen in the world, descendants of the exiles from medieval Spain. They continued their family occupation and established their own synagogue. For centuries they had been the only fishermen in Salonika. But their monopoly was brought to an end with the Greeks taking over. Some 16 families were transported with all their boats and fishing tackle to a stretch between Atlit and Acre in Palestine.

There are no words to describe the brutal death of Salonika Jewry during World War II. We know 56,000 Jews lived there before the Nazis invaded, with about 85 percent being deported to the death camps, according to Israel Cohen.

The late Simon Wiesenthal estimated that it took 11 or 12 days to transfer these wonderful, stoic, hardworking Jews from Salonika to Auschwitz, where about 60,000 out of 77,000 Greek Jews were murdered. Of that group, 46,000 were from Salonika.

About 13,000 Jews fought for the Greek army when Germany and Italy attacked.

Today, approximately 1,200 Jews live in Thessaloniki (Salonika).

Jewish Thessaloniki (Salonika)

Monastirioton Synagogue, 35 Sygrou St., Thessaloniki. Tel: 30-231-524-968.

Yad Lezikaron Synagogue, Vassileos Irakleiou St. 26, Thessaloniki. Tel: 30-231-223-231.

The Center for Historical Studies, Vassileos Irakleiou St., 26, Thessaloniki. Tel: 30-231-223-231.

"Simon Marks" Museum of the History of the Jews of Thessaloniki, Vassileos Irakleiou St., Thessaloniki. Tel: 30-231-273-767.

The Jewish Community of Thessaloniki, Tsimiski st., 24, Thessaloniki. Tel: 30-231-275-701. FAX: 30-231-229-063. E-mail: jct1@compulink.gr. This center is open Monday through Friday, from 9 a.m. to 3 p.m.

Museum of Jewish Presence in Thessaloniki, Agiou Mina St., 13, Thessaloniki. Tel: 30- 231-250-406 and 250-407. This museum is open from Sunday through Friday, from 9 a.m. to 5 p.m.

Jewish Primary School, "Talmud Torah Hagadot," Fleming st. 7, Thessaloniki. Tel: 30-231-830-347 and 837-177.

Cemetery and Memorial to Holocaust Victims. Located in the suburb of Stavroupolis, opposite the "AGNO" Factory. Tel: 30-231-655-855.

Square of the Jewish Martyrs. Located between Papanastasiou St. and Priamou St. Thessaloniki. This is a new monument for the Holocaust victims of Thessaloniki. It was created by the late Nandor Glid.

Museum and Educational Center on the Holocaust, located on Old Railway Station, Thessaloniki. A six-story circular building made of metal and glass, is expected to be built at the historic spot where 55,000 Greek Jews were deported by the Nazis to their death. The building will rise in the area of the Old Railway Station where the Jews of Thessaloniki started their final trip according to the daily newspaper, *Kathimerini.*

According to the newspaper, the city's mayor Yiannis Boutaris raised the issue several years ago after many years of silence on the part of the city government. The mayor spoke at the Monument when it was erected in a corner of the University Campus which up to that time honored the dead of Salonika. The memorial building is expected to change the skyline of the city's western entrance.

This was an idea of the president of the Jewish Community of Thessaloniki, David Saltiel. The mayor adopted this idea and, in order to promote it, he used its contacts around the world. The Municipality and the Jewish Community of Thessaloniki worked together, methodically, without fanfare, to implement this idea and now, almost three years later, with funding guaranteed, they are setting the project's timelines.

Suggested Reading

Brinn, Herb. *Ich Bin Ein Jude*. Middle Village, N.Y.: Jonathan David, 1983.

Cohen, Israel. *Contemporary Jewry*. London: Methuen, 1950.

—. *The Journal of a Jewish Traveler*. New York: Dodd, Mead, 1925.

Elazar, Daniel J., and Harriet P. Friedenreich. *The Balkan Jewish Communities: Yugoslavia, Bulgaria, Greece, and Turkey*. Lanham, N.Y: University Press of America, 1984.

Keeley, Edmund, *Inventing Paradise: The Greek Journey, 1937-1947*, Farrar, Straus and Giroux, New York, 1999.

Messinas, Elias, "*The Synagogues of Salonika and Veroia,* "Athens, Gavielides Editions, 1997.

Nachmani, Amikam. *Turkey: Facing A New Millennium, Coping with Intertwined Conflicts*. Manchester University Press, 2003.

Patai, Raphael. The Vanished Worlds of Jewry. New York: Macmillan.

Turkey
Jewish History from Constantinople to Istanbul

Despite upheavals in recent years, Turkey still draws tourists. This gateway to both Europe and Asia remains a popular destination, especially for Americans and Israelis.

Turkey, about the size of Texas, shares a border with seven countries that circle this nation of about 80 million. Massive movement of millions of people from country areas to the city has jumped Istanbul's population from about 500,000 in 1920 to about 10 million in 1993. Today, Istanbul, with its nearly 15 million residents, of which about 16,000 are Jewish, stands as the largest metropolis in the nation, followed by Ankara, the capital, and Izmir, the third largest city which counts about 1,200 Jews.

A Brief History

Benjamin of Tudela, who visited Jewish communities in the mid-twelfth century, said of Istanbul (called Constantinople until 1930): "It is a bustling city, with business coming to her from all foreign lands on land and on sea. There is no other city like her except Baghdad. There are the Church of Sophia, and the Pope of the Greeks and as many churches as there are days in the year, and in them, incalculable wealth more than in all the churches of the rest of the world. There is a Hippodrome where the king organizes great games on the birthday of Jesus of Nazareth, and in that place are drawn pictures of all kinds of men in the world before the king and queen with all types of sorcery."

That was eight centuries ago and once upon a time, Istanbul was one of the most important Jewish centers of the world, replete with Jewish schools and scholars. It was even called the Jewish "mother city." Although Jews lived here in Byzantine times, it was not until the Ottoman conquest in 1453 that Muhammad II welcomed Jews. He wanted them to develop business and trade and help Turkey's growth.

Granted asylum after they fled Spain, the Jews who came to Turkey were treated extremely well, especially under Suleiman the

385

Magnificent. They called him "King Solomon," not only because of his name, but also because of his wisdom and legislative programs. During his rule, the Jews of the Ottoman Empire made great cultural and economic strides. Jewish intellectual life rose to new heights. They devoted themselves to secular science, physics, astronomy, math, and medicine.

By the sixteenth century, Istanbul, with 40,000 Jews, had the largest Jewish population in the world. The Jews became a protected minority, although sometimes subject to discriminatory legislation that included dress, taxes, and housing. During this time, the Turkish Jewish community was the home of some wonderful personalities, such as Gracia Nasi and Joseph Nasi. Gracia Nasi (1510-69) was a Portuguese Marrano who openly returned to Judaism. As a stateswoman and patron, she helped Marranos flee Portugal. In 1537, after her husband's death, she left Portugal and went to Istanbul, where she was joined by Joseph Nasi. Nasi, a Portuguese Marrano, married her only child, Reyna.

When Nasi arrived in Istanbul in 1543, she brought with her large amounts of capital. In addition to her banking and economic activities, she founded *yeshivot* (religious schools) and synagogues and continued her efforts on behalf of persecuted Marranos and Jews.

Meanwhile Joseph Nasi (1524-79), who became one of the most influential figures in the Ottoman Empire, had been named duke of the island of Naxos and surrounding isles. Gracia Nasi had obtained a grant to set up a yeshiva in the ruined city of Tiberias, Israel. In 1561, Joseph Nasi extended the grant and began the rebuilding of the ruined walls of Tiberias. This whole enterprise turned out to be one of the practical attempts to establish a Jewish political center in Palestine between the fourth and nineteenth centuries.

In Turkey, too, Joseph Karo (1488-1575) wrote the *"Shulhan Arukh,"* the code of Jewish law. Indeed, Turkey became a great center for the study of Kabbala and was the birthplace of a number of prophetic and messianic movements. Here grew the legend of Shabbetai Zevi. Actually, we cannot visit Turkish Jewry without recalling Shabbetai Zevi, the Kabbalistic mystic who attracted thousands to his following. (See Achrida Synagogue below.)

The visitor to Turkey will also learn about the Karaites and the Dönmeh.

During the eighteenth and nineteenth centuries, Jews began moving westward from Turkey as world trade was shifting from the Mediterranean to the Atlantic coast of Europe. Seeking greater opportunity, Jews now would relocate to Holland, England, and the states along the Danube River.

At the turn of the twentieth century, about 100,000 Jews lived in Turkey. Before World War I, Theodor Herzl approached Constantinople leaders, but could not persuade them to grant a national home to the Jewish people in Palestine. During the reign of the Sultan Abdul Hamid II (1876-1909) the attitude of the Sublime Porte toward Jews was positive. Jews were involved in the economic and political life of the empire. In 1908, the Young Turks overthrew the sultan and Jews actively participated in the Young Turk movement. During World War I, in which the Turks sided with the Germans, the Jews of Istanbul prospered greatly. But after the war, Jews suffered anti-Semitism in former Turkish lands taken over by the Greeks.

Between the wars, Turkey was not fundamentally hostile to Jews; it was anti-foreign and anti-traditional. In 1927, about 82,000 Jews lived in Turkey—46,000 in Istanbul, over 16,000 in Izmir, 5,700 in Edirne, and the rest in 14 other communities. During World War II, however, Turkey was neutral. Many refugees from Nazism found their way here and continued on to Palestine. Indeed, through the aid of Turkish consuls in Marseilles and Vichy in France, as well as the island of Rhodes, the Turks saved thousands of Jews.

After the 1948 Israel Declaration of Independence, Jews began to leave Turkey. Nehemiah Robinson wrote that between 1948 and 1956, about 43,000 Jews emigrated from Turkey The latter was the first major Muslim country to recognize Israel in 1949 and the two cooperated closely for decades even as Israel fought with Muslim Arab nations.

Not only that, but then the two nations in the second half of the twentieth century, had a successful courtship and moved to what might be called the "honeymoon years." The strong military alliance, high volume of civilian trade, tourism between the two nations soared. Israelis flocked to Turkey as if it was their vacation summer house. It was a love affair made in heaven.

"Strategic alliances are built slowly, but their destruction is rapid," notes Amikam Nachmani, retired Professor Emeritus at Bar Ilan University in Tel Aviv, and author of *Turkey: Facing A New Millennium.*

And this Turkey-Israel alliance went down fast.

It may have started when President Tayyip Erdogan, drew world attention with his outburst in Davos in 2009 following a heated debate with the late President of Israel, Shimon Peres. The contentious debate concerned the 2009 Israeli offensive in Gaza. What really caused the breakup—at least outwardly—was the attempt of the ship *Mavi Marmara's* which sailed to breach the blockade to Gaza. As Israeli forces descended from a helicopter to stop the ship, they were attacked by the activists onboard with clubs and knives. The Israelis opened fire and the ensuing fight caused the death of ten Turkish nationals, injured dozens of passengers and resulted in a number of wounded IDF soldiers.

Turkey demanded an apology, compensation, and diplomatic relations were broken. It would take six years until the two nations resolved the issues. Finally, in mid-2016, Jerusalem and Ankara restored full diplomatic relations. Israel agreed to pay $20 million in compensation to the families of the dead and wounded and the families agreed to drop any future claims against the Israeli military. Prime Minister Benjamin Netanyahu apologized for the incident.

So now in 2017, Israel and Turkey have cordial relations, notes Professor Amikam Nachmani. But, he adds, "No security business, no joint military drills, although there could be more business deals, energy sales of Israeli gas to Turkey, export imports. Much less involvement of governmental companies."

Other developments harmed Turkey's position in the world. During recent decades, Turkey also seemed to take a hard line against the Kurdish movement which they say threatens national unity. On the other hand, deadly bomb attacks claimed by or blamed on, Kurdish fighters groups and the Islamic State of Iraq and the Levant, (ISIS) have killed hundreds of Turkish security forces and civilians in recent years. Turkey continues to oppose compromise with Greece over Cyprus, another thorn in the eastern Mediterranean. The Turkish Republic's human rights record also has been criticized.

In 2016 and 2017, Turkey suffered major terrorist attacks. Terrorists hit a nightclub in the center of Istanbul, with at least 39 people killed and 69 wounded, 15 foreigners among them, in the first hours of the New Year 2017. ISIS carried out this and at least eight large attacks in Turkey in recent years, including a suicide bombing that killed more than 100 people in October 2015. Thus, in 2017, we have Muslims killing Muslims; Turkey remains a nation torn apart.

Recently, the European Union suspended talks regarding Turkey's application to the EU. Because of what the EU perceives as lack of democratic rule and values, it seemed unlikely that at least in 2017, Turkey would be admitted to the European Union. And as the *New York Times* put it on April 17, 2017: "Although Turkey is a vital member of NATO, it is increasingly an outlier in the alliance, which was founded on democratic values." Today, one is not so sure Turkey itself wishes to enter the EU. Turkey will have to execute some democratic reforms to assure their full integration into the European Union. One positive aspect of Turkey's situation has changed somewhat and that is tensions between Greece and Turkey have subsided.

But then came the earth-shattering news of an attempted military coup in Turkey on the night of July 15, 2016. Hundreds died when the citizens of Istanbul and other cities rushed out into the streets to confront the rebel soldiers.

Soon, President Erdogan began to destroy the democracy that Turks defended with their lives. Six thousand soldiers arrested, thousands of policemen, prosecutors, and judges sacked. "The purge is so deep and so wide that it affected over 60,000 people," said the *Economist* on July 23, 2016. Erdogan blamed the U.S. for the coup. Turkey demanded that the U.S. extradite Fethullah Gulen, a religious leader who lives in self-imposed exile in the U.S. Turkey insists he orchestrated the coup attempt, which killed around 300 and led to massive purges and arrests within state institutions.

Indeed, by April 2017, according to the *New York Times*, "the government has since fired or suspended 130,000 people suspected of having a connection to the coup and has arrested about 45,000."

Tensions between Turkey and its NATO partners have been running high since last July's 2016 failed military coup. President Erdogan has fired hundreds of senior military staff serving at NATO in Europe and the United States. In the opinion of many, he would have blamed Israel, too, but how could he? He had just reestablished relations with the Jewish State.

But Erdogan continues to stir anger in European capitals. Moreover, the Turkish president, frustrated with the West as he perceives it, has cozied up to the Russian bear, with trade agreements and friendly overtures between himself and Russian President Vladimir Putin. Erdogan also has strained relations with the U.S., an alliance also in disarray. Despite the coup, Turkish disagreements with NATO-member Greece, including the invasion of Cyprus in 1974, and the Turkish alliance with NATO lasted over the years. In 2017, even that tie was in doubt, though Washington needs Turkish airbases to combat ISIS and other threats in the Middle East. In the last analysis, Turkey continues to drift away from America, NATO, and the EU.

In March 2017, Erdogan repeatedly used Nazi comparisons against his perceived enemies in Germany and the Netherlands while comparing Turks today to Jews in the Third Reich. And in the past he has repeatedly compared Israel with Nazism as well as called Zionism a crime against humanity, though he later said he was misunderstood.

Defending German Chancellor Angela Merkel's government for not allowing rallies for Turkish elections in 2017, Josef Schuster, the head of the Central Council of Jews in Germany, the country's European Jewish Congress affiliate, said that Erdogan disrespected the memory of the victims of the Third Reich in accusing German Chancellor Angela Merkel of "using Nazi methods."

In mid-April 2017 to solidify his rule and move Turkey from a parliamentary system to a strong "presidential system," Erdogan narrowly squeezed out a win in the referendum. "Democracy Loses in Turkey," claimed the *New York Times* on April 17, 2017. Suspensions, arrests, and trials continued toward the end of 2017.

Turkey also has been confronted with a cascade of crises that seem to have only accelerated as the Syrian civil war has spilled across its border.

JEWISH SITES IN ISTANBUL

This entrepot, this strategic city, this often mysterious, bustling, metropolis enveloped by mighty dome-covered mosques, this city whose thin, needle-like minarets puncture the sky, this gray, yet golden confluence of great waters—this Bosphorus, this Golden Horn, this Sea of Marmara, it's all here in Istanbul, the city that attracts thousands who arrive here by land, sea, and air.

Back in the days when Israel-Turkey relations were really strong, I had heard that tourism from Israel to Turkey rose to an all-time high. I also knew that the Turks were great salespersons and that Israelis love to shop. But what really convinced me that travel from Israel to Turkey at that time, must be setting records, occurred when the Turkish street hawkers, with leather jackets slung over outstretched arms, and greeted the tour buses picking up passengers at various Istanbul hotels.

"*Esrim dollar*," ($20) would bark these very mobile merchants in Hebrew.

Hebrew on the streets of Istanbul?

Actually this should not shock Jewish travelers. This is not the first time that Jews and Israelis came to this "land-and-water city" in large numbers as newcomers and tourists.

Five hundred years ago, the Sultan of the then Ottoman Empire opened this country's borders to Jews fleeing the wrath of the Spanish King Ferdinand and Queen Isabella who in 1492 expelled their Jewish citizens. Not only did Sultan Beyazid welcome Jews to Constantinople, but he had a chosen barb for the Spanish royal family.

"You call Fernando of Spain a wise king—he who has impoverished his country and enriched ours," exclaimed the Sultan who granted Jews immediate asylum to his kingdom.

Although Jews had lived here in Byzantine times, it had not been until the Ottoman conquest in 1453 that Jews were welcome. The Ottomans wanted these Sephardic Jews from Spain and other lands to help the economy especially in perfecting the use of gunpowder.

This city, by the Bosphorus, remains one of the world's few cities that have a romantic appeal. With the charm of the East reflecting the smells and sights of Istanbul before you, the past projects immediately to the forefront of your thoughts.

Tourists soon realize that from any point of view: history, culture, recreation, lodging, shopping, entertainment, and food, this land awakens your senses. Yes, even if it is a few days, you can manage to see the principal attractions, the Hagia Sophia Museum, the Suleymaniye Mosque which is the largest and most grandiose in the city. Then there is the Blue Mosque, the Hippodrome, and the Topkapi Palace (yes, the diamond is still there!). Drive to the Egyptian or spice market and the Covered Bazaar with its 4,000 shops nestled on 50 acres. Both here and in the Egyptian Bazaar you can purchase spices, dried fruits, tea, and of course baklava and taffee. And in the Grand Bazaar, you will find Turkish specialties: rugs, leather and suede goods, golden jewelry with precious stones as well as traditionally shaped pieces in silver. Add pottery and ceramics and the shopping is complete. Restaurants and food shops serve up mouth-watering kebab and shwama. And if its belly dancing you want, you've come to the right country.

Walk slowly around Taksim Square and peek into the stalls selling bazaar type items, including jewelry, books, posters, postcards. I recalled the words of that great French writer, Pierre Loti who once described the then Constantinople: "The only town in the world, where I have really taken part in the life of the people, the life of this Oriental people noisy, full of color, picturesque, but needy and poor, a life busy with a thousand little trades, a thousand chaffererings."

The so-called "murmur of Constantinople" can be heard in Istiklal Caddesi, the pedestrian street with just an old trolley clinging its bell and moving up and down the street with the flow of the crowd, men, women, children and their pets. Restaurants, fast food spots, shops, art galleries, are at hand.

Of course, don't forget to visit the Dolmabache Palace on the Bosphorus which the travel books tell you is the "richest palace in the world." Your guide should ask you to stand in the magnificent hall of the Dolmabache Palace. Here in this grandeur, the Sultan welcomed visitors to the Sublime Porte as it was called. You will compare it with the Hall of Mirrors in Versailles. Each person decides which is more impressive, the Dolmabache Palace grand room or the mirrored grand hall at Versailles?

I took several boat rides along the Bosphorus, a major strategic waterway. I sailed past the luxury summer homes. The deep Bosphorus links the Black Sea with its dark Russian storms to the Sea of Marmara, to the Dardenelles and then out to the Aegean and the Mediterranean. So much conflict, so much tension, the spot where the roaring Russian bear from the north who has been land locked, shuffles back and forth always trying to break out of her imprisonment. This is the same Russian bear that has always sought a passage through the Dardenelles for her navy. Did not Winston Churchill once describe Russia as "a giant with his nostrils pinched by the narrow exits from the Baltic and the Black Sea"?

This bottleneck of the Turkish straits has certainly been a trouble spot and caused many disputes and even a reason to go to war. "Although the status of the Turkish Straits has been regulated since 1936 by the Montreux Convention, the question of free passage is still topical," says author Nicole Pope.

Throughout World War II, Turkey played such a masterly game of hide-and-seek that they called "active neutrality," the Germans on one side, the Allies on the other. The Turks in World War II suspected that the Russians had designs not only on Turkey and the Straits but on the Balkans, too, according to Pope.

Regarding the Holocaust, the Turkish Jewish community continues to mark that terrible tragedy to the Jewish people. Many Jews tried to escape to Turkey during World War II. Many made it; others did not. Turkish Jews still remember the sinking of the cargo ship *Struma* and the 769 men, women, and children who perished when the British refused to admit the ship to Palestine in 1941. The Turks put the matter to the British and when the British would not take up the plight of the refugees, Istanbul towed the ship to a point outside its territorial waters. The ship was sunk by a Russian submarine for unknown reasons. On February 24, 2017, Istanbul Governor, Vasip Sahin and Turkish Chief Rabbi Isak Halevi attended a ceremony at the Sarayburnu area of Istanbul for the victims of the tragedy which Turkey began to commemorate officially in 2015. At the end of the ceremony, known as the *Struma Commemoration Day*, Governor Sahin and Rabbi Halevi threw wreaths into the area where the vessel was docked for over two months, with its passengers unable to disembark despite a series of diplomatic efforts. According to the *Hurriyet Daily News* in Istanbul, for nine weeks, the passengers were prevented from leaving the boat due to German pressure on Ankara. The boat also was forbidden to depart so it could continue on to Palestine due to British objections. The boat had reached Istanbul from Constanta, Romania. Aided for a short period thanks to the efforts of Istanbul's Jewish community, the passengers struggled to survive on the ship with limited resources for weeks before the vessel departed.

Events on International Holocaust Remembrance Day have been organized by Turkish government since 2011.

With all this history surrounding the area, I was interested in having lunch in a café or fish restaurant, overlooking the only sea passage out of the Black Sea where I could watch a fascinating flotilla of freighters, fishing boats, oil tankers, barges, cruise liners—some coming from Russia to the thriving Mediterranean ports of Athens, Haifa, Cairo, Naples, Barcelona, Marseilles and beyond: some going to the former Soviet Union to the famous and attractive port of Odessa. It was indeed a pleasant, and now, peaceful, relaxing sight.

And now let us visit specific Jewish sites and those associated with Jewish History. An excellent website is www.turkyahudileri.com.

Many Jews live in suburbs, such as Beyoglu, Sisli, Ortakoy, Kuzguncuk, Kadikoy, Sirkeci, Galata, Tunel, Taksim, Nisantas, Macka, and others. There are large summer communities on three of the islands off of the Bosporus in the Sea of Marmara. The largest communities are located in Buyukada and Heybeli Ada.

One neighborhood of course to visit is Beyoglu. During the Ottoman period, Jews arrived here from Spain, from Arab lands, Greece and Armenia.

Headquarters of the Chief Rabbi, Rav Isak Halevi as well as The Jewish Community of Turkey. Tunel, Yemenici Sokak 21, Beyoglu, 34430, Istanbul. Tel: 212-293-87-94/95. Fax: 212-244-19-80. This is the headquarters of the Turkish Jewish community, tourists and visitors would do well to stop off here for information on the Jewish community. The staff is friendly and will help tourists.

As you walk to the office, you are apt to recall that as recently as World War II, Turkey contained one of the most creative and distinguished Sephardic communities in the Diaspora. This may be Turkey, but 500 years after their arrival from Iberia, Jews still speak Spanish here. Once Arabic, Armenian, Greek, French, Italian, and yes, even Ladino, was spoken here. Ladino, an archaic form of Spanish, absorbed a considerable vocabulary from the local language, primarily Turkish and Greek, as well as a Hebraic and Talmudic component. This Judeo-Spanish was commonly used in Turkey and some of the Balkan countries ruled by Turkey, according to Bernard Lewis. Under the Ottomans Jews did not normally speak Turkish-only Ladino, which remains the language of the older generation. Ladino still is spoken and read here, as witnessed by the Jewish weekly, Salom. That newspaper contains seven pages in Turkish and one in Ladino and is helping keep alive the language of the Sephardim that younger Jews here are increasingly unable to speak. Young people now speak Turkish as their first language. Today, Jews are trying to keep Ladino alive here in Turkey.

Here at the chief rabbi's headquarters, I met the Jewish poet and artist Joseph Habib Gerez, a leader of the Jewish community.

Yusef Habib Gerez was born on June 14, 1926, to a middle-class family in the picturesque neighborhood of Ortaköy, along the European shore of the Bosphorus Strait. His mother was a homemaker, and his father worked in textiles.

He still writes in Turkish and describes the glories of Istanbul. He is a man who has traveled the world yet still loves his city, which commands a central position in maritime communications between the Black Sea and the Mediterranean and where you see Russian freighters and cruise ships sailing down the Bosporus. His paintings reflect Jewish life in Istanbul.

The suburb of Galata. Even today, Jews live in Pera and Galata, which is on the heights above the Golden Horn. In Byzantine days, it was a colony of European merchants. The hills north of Galata were favorite places for foreign envoys. The Europeans called that area Pera, from a Greek word meaning "beyond" or "across," i.e., across the Golden Horn from Old Istanbul or beyond the Galata Tower. Many Jews moved to these popular new neighborhoods; at the end of the nineteenth century, half of Istanbul Jewry was living in the Galata and Pera sections. However, the Jews in each quarter maintained their own communal institutions, rabbinical courts, schools, budgets, and councils.

According to Hilary Sumner-Boyd and John Freely, the area in front of the Galata Bridge was once a Jewish quarter inhabited by Karaites, a sect that denies Talmudic rabbinical tradition. The Karaites broke off from the main body of Orthodox Jewry in the eighth century. **The Topkapi Palace**. The Palace of the Sultans "is the most extensive and fascinating monument of Ottoman civil architecture in existence," according to Sumner-Boyd and Freely. Many Jewish women occupied the palace harem. When you tour the palace and see the harem, remember Esther Kyra. She was a Jewish broker, only she did not deal in stocks and bonds. Her exchange was the royal harem. She had free access to it, where she sold jewels, cosmetics, and rich fabrics and generally made herself indispensable to the ladies. She won the favor of Sultan Murad III's mother, Nur Banu, and of his preferred concubine, the Venetian, Safya Baffo, both of whom had enormous influence. Through them, Esther, in turn, exercised considerable influence in imperial appointments and became involved in political affairs. Her power and wealth spawned jealousy and she was murdered. In 1593, her fortune was confiscated.

The Jewish women in the palace bribed the eunuchs who kept the doors, ruled over the women, and bought and sold for them. The Jewish women became rich. Bernard Lewis tells us that when Sultan Murad III learned that Sephardi girls were wearing choice garments and ornaments with precious stones, he issued a decree to exterminate all Jews throughout all the provinces of his empire. Through the influence of the sultan's mother, the decree was revoked, but an order was given that Jews must wear, in place of the yellow turban, a strange tall hat, pointed above and wide below, like those of the Spaniards. Sounds familiar to those who know Jewish history, especially as this book has recalled anti-Semitic events in Spain and Nazi-occupied Europe.

Visiting the office of the chief rabbi, one might also discuss anti-Semitism in Turkey.

Regarding anti-Semitism in Turkey, Cnaan Lipshiz, writing in the *Times of Israel*, November 18, 2016, noted that a 2015 survey by the Anti-Defamation League suggested that 71 percent of the population holds anti-Semitic views—by contrast in Iran the figure was 60 percent.

An added encumbrance for Jewish organizations is that they have to go it alone. Turkish law forbids Turkish citizens to have any formal links or even contact with foreign countries or international organizations. This policy applies to all groups.

By 2017, all these events in Tukey which is slowly becoming unhinged has caused Jews to ponder their future in Turkey, especially since anti-Semitism exists.

"Thousands of Turkish Jews are seeking foreign passports this year amid growing religiosity in a society where civil rights activists and some ethnic minorities are feeling the weight of the increasingly authoritarian politics of Erdogan. Turkey's Islamist president also has used anti-Israel rhetoric," noted Cnaan Lipshiz in *The Times of Israel*, November 18, 2016. An example of possible anti-Semitism, it was believed by some in the Turkish Jewish community, was the murder of a Turkish Jewish writer, Beki Ikala Erikli in 2016. On April 15, 2017, the BBC reported that "Turkey is currently the world's biggest jailer of journalists—with some 150 behind bars. Over 140 newspapers, magazines and television channels have also been banned since a state of emergency was declared after the failed coup."

Two of the countries that Turkish Jews may be heading to are Spain and Portugal which have offered citizenship to Sephardic Jews for those countries expulsion of the Jewish people in 1492. "Sephardim" is the term commonly used for those who once lived in the Iberian Peninsula and who now make up 96 percent of the Turkish Jewish Community, with Ashkenazim accounting for the rest.

Turkish Jews apparently are applying for citizenship in Portugal and Spain. Both the latter two nations passed laws that year on the naturalization of descendants of Sephardic Jews. The passing of the laws of return for Sephardic Jews was described as "an attempt to atone for the state and church-led mass expulsion, dispossession, torture and forced conversion into Christianity of Jews during the Inquisition," a period that began in the 15th century and ended with the disappearance and dispersion of what used to be one of the world's largest Jewish communities. Many of those Sephardic Jews reached safety in Turkey.

It also has been reported that of the 3,500 applications for Portuguese citizenship to descendants of Jews who Portugal persecuted 500 years ago, half were from Turkey.

SYNAGOGUES IN ISTANBUL

The Jewish community is proud of its 19 synagogues in Istanbul as well as one school which goes from kindergarten to high school which is located on the Europe side of Istanbul and a kindergarten on the Asian side. The community told this writer that the Jews of Istanbul consider themselves an "active community which celebrates all the Jewish holidays as well as sponsoring Jewish education classes."

Achrida Synagogue, Kurkcu Cesmi Sokak, 9. Balat section, Istanbul. Tel: 90-212-523-47-29. Once this was a Jewish neighborhood in Istanbul and this house of worship stands as Istanbul's oldest synagogue. Founded before the Muslim conquest of the city in 1453, the synagogue seats about 500 persons. Prior arrangements must be made before visiting the synagogue.

In 1992, in honor of the 500th anniversary of the Iberian Jews' arrival here, the Achrida Synagogue was restored. Many festivities, concerts, the opening of a new Jewish Museum, and major ceremonies highlighted the 1992 celebration of 500 years of Jewish history in Turkey. Built in 1412, it existed when the city was in Byzantine hands. Shabbetai Zevi preached here. Born in Smyrna, July 1626, his birthday occurred on the Ninth of Av, the day in which the First and Second Temples had been destroyed. At age 18, he was honored by the rabbis of his town.

According to Barnet Litvinoff, he was the son of a merchant who traded with England. While bathing in the waters of the Aegean Sea, the idea dawned on him that he was the Messiah, the one appointed by God to save the Jews and lead them back to the Holy Land. Late in 1648, during the synagogue service, he stood at the Holy Ark and pronounced the full name of God, an act that only the priest had the right to perform. He proclaimed himself as the Messiah.

Shabbetai Zevi met Raphael Joseph Chelebi in Cairo, who was known as the "prince of the Jews of Egypt and head of that country's treasury." In Gaza, Nathan Benjamin Levi helped Shabbetai, who sojourned for a while in the Holy Land and attracted followers. In 1665, he returned to an ecstatic reception in Smyrna. There he prophesied the impending defeat and abdication of the sultan. The Jews would usurp his empire, said Shabbetai Zevi, reestablishing the Lord's rule in Jerusalem. He, Shabbetai Zevi, would be the king of kings. The Sultan naturally had to get rid of Shabbetai Zevi—either convert him to Islam or put him to death. To save his skin, Shabbetai converted to Islam. So, he was appointed as chamberlain in the royal palace and received a salary. Later he was banished to a small town in Albania, where he died in 1676. His conversion was a severe blow to world Jewry—a betrayal, demoralizing a great part of the Sephardic world.

Ashkenazi Synagogue, Yuksek Kaldirim 27. Karakoy, Istanbul.

Italian Synagogue, Sair Ziya Pasa Yokusu 23, Karakoy Istanbul.

Turkish Jewry makes every attempt to keep alive its Jewish heritage. On April 2, 2017, a prayer service was held to mark the return to the Jewish community of the Abudaram (or Abudara or Parmakkap) Synaoguge on Haskoy Hahluk St., Istanbul, after it had been used since the 1960s as a workshop, according to the Jewish news website *Salom*, reported by *Jewish Heritage Europe*.

Neve Shalom Synagogue and the Jewish Museum, Buyuk Hendek Caddesi, 39, Galata, Istanbul. Tel: 90 212 244 15 76 www.muze500.com.

On September 12, 1986, more than 20 people were killed in a terrorist attack on the Neve Shalom Synagogue. The incident shattered the peaceful existence of 500 years, but life goes on. You can still see the clock that on that Sabbath Saturday stopped at 9:17 a.m., the time the terrorists attacked the house of prayer. Near the *bimah*, you can see the patched-up bullet holes. Unfortunately, ultranationalist and Islamist protestors attacked Neve Shalom Synagogue in July 2017. The attack was an example of the alarming rise in anti-Semitic incitement and hate crimes in Turkey in recent years.

The synagogue also serves as a community center. A thorough security check is maintained here and in other Istanbul synagogues, checks that are similar to those at airports today. Passports or identity cards must be shown. This is the procedure at Neve Shalom and The Jewish Museum. But for other synagogues, tourists should book an appointment at least a week in advance.

Neve Shalom, probably the most modern synagogue in Istanbul, is close to the Pera Palas Hotel, the last of the old-school grand hotels on the Galata Hill, the section of Galata where the Jews live. Located very near the American Consulate, this hotel sports "Old World charm."

The Jewish Museum, located at Neve Shalom Synagogue, www.muze500.com, boasts a fascinating collection of photographs, documents and Judaica regarding Istanbul's Jewish population. Founded in 2001, the museum concentrates on the traditions and history of Turkish Jewry. A highlight of the exhibition are historical accounts of the Jewish odyssey from Spain to Turkey.

The Museum collects, preserves, and exhibits knowledge about the cultural heritage of the Turkish Jews from the Ottoman Empire to the modern Turkey.

Visitors can visit The Jewish Museum and Neve Shalom on weekdays from Monday to Thursday, between 10:00 a.m. and 4:00 p.m. On Saturday and Sunday, from 10:00 a.m. until 1:00 p.m.

Galata Jewish Cultural Heritage Tours are available to tourists. Those who would like to take a nostalgic trip from Galata to the Kula of 1930's to acquaint yourself with Jewish culture and heritage can contact the Jewish Museum, www.muze500.com. Various synagogues in Istanbul also offer tours to historic Jewish Istanbul.

Kosher Dining in Istanbul

Gerez Café in the Jewish Museum Buyuk Hendek Caddesi, 39, Galata, Istanbul. Tel: 90 212 244 15 76 www.muze500.com. Open only during museum hours, between 10:00 a.m. to 4:00 p.m., Monday to Friday and on Friday and Sunday, 10:00 a.m. to 1:00 p.m.

Caffe Eden is a kosher restaurant in Ortakoy, a suburban neighborhood of Istanbul. This restaurant features Turkish meat dishes, such as pide, lahmacun, and doner. Tel: 90-212-236-36-67. caffeedenortakoy@gmail.com.

La Casa restaurant in the Sisli Synagogue is open for lunch every day of the week except on Shabbat. Location: Sisli Kosher Restaurant Cumhuriyet Mah. Nakliye Elgun Sk. No: 15 Osmanbey Sisli Istanbul Tel: 90-212-246-22-25, metin@lacasa-mb.com La Casa catering provides kosher meals to tourists in their hotels. Tel: 90-212-291-38-12, ext. 123. Fax: 90-212-293-60-22 (0530)405-86-61 (Sabahat Berker) sabahat.berker@lacasa-mb-com.

Akasya Restaurant and Bar, open only in summer. Bufe Ve Satis Noktasi (Denetci Gozetiminde) 23 Nisan Caddesi No: 49 Buyukada, Istanbul. Tel: 90-216-382-10-50.More kosher restaurants and kosher caterers: http://www.denetgida.com.tr/restaurants-and-caterers-serving-kosher-foods.htm.

The Sisli Synagogue, Rumel Cadessi, Efe Sokak No 4, Osmabey, Istanbul. Near the Galata Tower. This was the quarter overlooking the Golden Horn where the Jews lived. Sisli Synagogue is close to the Hilton Hotel.

I completed my tour of Istanbul, packed and realized that it was a lovely day and the sun was shining on the Golden Horn. Like other visitors to Istanbul, I departed with a "lightening of the heart."

Suggested Reading

Fermor, Patrick Leigh, (Edited by Colin Thubron and Artemis Cooper) *The Broken Road, From the Iron Gates to Mount Athos,* New York, New York Review Books, 2013.

Freid, Jacob. *Jews in the Modern World.* New York: Twayne, 1962.

Lewis, Bernard. *The Emergence of Modern Turkey.* London: Oxford University Press, 1961.

—. *Istanbul and the Civilization of the Ottoman Empire.* Norman, Oklahoma: University of Oklahoma Press, 1972.

—. *Semites and Anti-Semites.* New York: Norton, 1986.

Loti, Pierre "Constantinople", New York, Frederick A. Stokes, Co., Publishers, 1928.

Mann, Vivian B. *A Tale of Two Cities: Jewish Life in Frankfurt and Istanbul,* 1750-1870. New York: The Jewish Museum, 1982.

Malcomson, Scott L. *Borderlands-Nation and Empire,* Boston, London, Faber and Faber, 1994.

Pope, Nicole *"Turkey Unveiled: A History of Modern Turkey."* New York: The Overlook Press, 1998.

Nachmani, Amikam. Turkey: Facing A New Millennium, Coping with Interwined Conflicts. Manchester University Press, 2003.

Settle, Mary Lee. *Turkish Reflections.* New York: Prentice-Hall, 1991.

Simon, Joseph. *The Itinerary of Benjamin of Tudela, Travels in the Middle Ages.* Malibu, Calif.: Pangloss Press.

Sumner-Boyd, Hilary, and John Freely. *Strolling Through Istanbul: A Guide to the City.* Istanbul: Redhouse, 1972.

Scandinavia
Something for Everyone

"Scandinavia!" exclaimed a Jewish travel agent. "Why, there are only four Jews there."

Not true; probably about 30,000 is the accurate figure. Since the year 2000, Scandinavian Jewry also has suffered increased anti-Semitism, acts of terror, and in Sweden, a leftist government, that remains hostile to Israel. Yet a visit to four capitals—Helsinki, Stockholm, Copenhagen, and Oslo—will show how that old, dire prediction that Jews will disappear here through intermarriage and assimilation still remains somewhat premature. True, extremely high intermarriage ratios exist; some have put it at 80 percent in Denmark, 75 percent in Sweden, but, there are valiant efforts being made to stem the tide.

Approximately 20,000 Jews reside in Sweden, about 8,000 in Denmark, 1,000 in Norway, and about 1,300 in Finland. Truly, these numbers are miniscule. In fact, as it was once aptly put, there are more Jews in Minnesota than in all of Scandinavia.

And Jews settled in New York City (1654) before their co-religionists moved into Scandinavia.

Years ago, anti-Semitism rarely reared its ugly head in Scandinavia. And Jews needed a place of refuge.

One of the places which welcomed them was Denmark and its "fun city," Copenhagen, where, as the travel brochures declare, "there is something for everybody." Copenhagen, which has a population of over 2 million in the metro area, features Tivoli, the enchanting park next to City Hall in the center of town. Festivities during the season last until the end of September.

Denmark: Jewish Copenhagen

On my "city tour" in Copenhagen, our very vocal guide made his passengers memorize the years of the reign of Christian IV, who did so much for Copenhagen in the way of institutions, fortifications, and palaces. The years 1588 to 1648 were welded into our minds. In fact, we often were instructed to bellow out the dates in hearty unison.

The guide, however, never mentioned that in 1622, Christian IV invited Portuguese Jews from Amsterdam, probably Marranos, to settle in Gluckstadt. Although now in Schleswig-Holstein in North Germany, it was once an area ruled by Denmark.

Most tourists do not, of course, come to Denmark to learn about Christian IV. They come to see the environment immortalized by the Hans Christian Anderson stories and recounted by the late actor-comedian Danny Kaye; to gaze at the Little Mermaid—and she is indeed little—sitting in the harbor; and to inhale and experience Tivoli, the granddaddy of all amusement parks and one of the tourist wonders of Europe.

Denmark is a good land for Jews. Following King Christian IV was King Frederick III (1657-59), who allowed Sephardic Jews to settle in Denmark. Israel David, a goldsmith, and his partner, Meir Goldschmidt, settled in Copenhagen in 1684. Seven merchants and craftsmen followed. They, too, were Marranos, who had obtained permission to leave their country. At first, they all prayed behind closed doors. But soon, not only would the government decree punishment for anyone who harassed those of another religious faith, it also voided its ban on Jewish employment of Christian servants. By 1766, the first synagogue in Copenhagen was erected.

Nearly 2,000 Jews—merchants, craftsmen, and entrepreneurs—lived in Copenhagen in 1782.

In 1834, more than 4,000 Jews inhabited the country. Chief Rabbi Dr. Abraham Alexander Wolff (1801-91) served as rabbi for 62 years and kept the community united. In 1837, Jews were allowed to hold municipal office. Jews achieved full emancipation when Denmark abolished the absolute monarchy in 1849 and adopted a constitution.

Jews administered their own affairs with little or no anti-Semitism holding them back from assimilation into the country's economic and intellectual life. Prominent Jews have included Mendel Levin Nathanson, father of Danish journalism; Georg Brandes, literary critic and historian; Gen. C. I. De Meza, commander of the Danish Army; the late Victor Borge, who often came home to his native Tivoli in Copenhagen to entertain; and Niels Bohr (1885-1962), a Danish physicist and Nobel laureate who also escaped the Nazis by going to Sweden in a fishing boat in 1943. His mother was from a prominent Jewish banking family.

Following the Kishinev pogrom in 1905, several thousand Jews entered Denmark. By the end of World War I, 96.7 percent of the Danish Jewish community lived in Copenhagen. In the 1930s, many Jewish refugees from Germany poured into Denmark, and then went on to Palestine and the United States. The Jews believed that King Christian X would stand by them. As events would prove, they were correct. They remembered that in 1933, Christian X attended services in Copenhagen's synagogue. This was the year when Hitler took over Germany. Denmark and its ruler, however, were one in protecting their Jewish citizens. A "bone" in his throat, was the way Hitler described Jewish freedom in Denmark. Adolf Eichmann himself, the SS officer who put into operation the execution of Europe's Jews, admitted that in Denmark he could not do as he wished. Not only did the Danes resist the ill treatment of Jews; they saved their Jews (as we shall soon see) in one of the most remarkable rescue operations in history, certainly in recent Jewish history.

After the war, between 1966 and 1967, about 2,500 Polish Jews arrived in Denmark. Poland had unleashed another of one of its waves of anti-Semitism; this time aimed at Jewish members of its Communist party. Not all Polish Jews wanted to go to Israel; Denmark was among the few nations to welcome them.

Many Jews visiting Copenhagen head for Israelsplads (Israel Square), where they find a large memorial stone from Israel. A ceremony took place here in 1968. During the event, the name of "Gronttorvet" (the Vegetable Market Place) was changed to "Israel Square." And at the same time, the Beth Hakerem Park in Jerusalem was renamed "Kikar Daniah" (Denmark Square). On weekends, Israel Square turns into a flea market.

In October 1943, the Danish people and the resistance movement defied Nazi occupation of their country to rescue their fellow citizens. During a period of ten nights, almost all of the Danish Jews were carried across the body of water known as Oresund Strait, in fishing boats and other small craft, to safe Sweden. Israel and Jews all over the world will never forget the rescue. If we were editing the Bible in the 21st century, the saving of the Jews from the Nazis in October 1943 would be told in the Scriptures, similar to the Book of Esther. In the latter biblical event, a wicked Haman wanted to kill the Jews, but the Jewish people were spared. Thus, too, were the Jews of Denmark saved. "This modern-day legend will be commemorated for generations to come," writes Aage Bertelsen in his book, *October, 1943.*

Some headline the events of October 1943 a "Jewish Dunkirk." The Danes rescued virtually the entire Jewish community from the Germans and brought it safely to Sweden. The Nazis had planned to deport the Jews on the night of the Jewish New Year, October 1-2, 1943. But at a religious service on September 29, the acting chief rabbi of Denmark, Rabbi Dr. Marcus Melchior, rushed into the Great Synagogue on Krystalgade street in Copenhagen and warned his congregants to hide.

But where could they find shelter? Where could they flee? Where could they find friends? But they managed: they hid in small groups until their turn came to board the small fishing boats to nearby Sweden.

The Danish police had set up a sea escape route and turned a blind eye to the boats leaving the shore. Some Germans even accepted bribes and allowed trucks of refugees to pass, but it has been conjectured that they did this because they knew if they stopped the vehicles, they might incur the wrath of the Danes. About 7,900 Jews escaped, including 686 non-Jews who were married to Jews. About 30 were lost at sea or committed suicide. On the day of the action, the Germans managed to capture 284 Jews and in the next few weeks, 190 Jews were arrested while trying to escape. Thus, 474 were picked up, of which 101 were non-Danish refugees. Fifty-one of the deported persons died in the concentration camp Terezin (Theresienstadt), in the Czech Republic, while the rest returned safely home in 1945.

A shipping expert in the German Embassy tipped off the Jewish community. He was George Ferdinand Duckwitz (1904-73), according to the book *The Rescue of the Danish Jews*. After the war, he served as West Germany's ambassador to Denmark (1955 to 1958).

But not only did the Danes physically help the Jews escape, they never forgot their Jewish brothers and sisters who were arrested by the Nazis and imprisoned in Theresienstadt. Between October 1943 and April 1945, the Danes pressured the Germans to release all those deported and to allow food parcels to get through. These Danes prevented Denmark's Jews from being transferred from Theresienstadt to the death camp at Auschwitz, and those food packages probably saved the Jews from starvation.

Historian Leni Yahil offers five reasons for the success of the sea evacuation: First, the number of Jews was small. Second, Sweden was nearby. Third, conditions in Denmark were different than in other countries in Nazi-occupied Europe. Fourth, the Germans were reeling after their defeats at El Alamein and Stalingrad. The final reason is "the special character and moral stature of the Danish people and their love of democracy and freedom."

Rabbi Bent Melchior also told me in an interview that the organized church in Denmark was very active in helping to save Jews. To the Danes, he asserted, the treatment of its Jewish citizens was "every citizen's business," not just that of a few leaders or "good souls."

During "Little Dunkirk," Acting Chief Rabbi Marcus Melchior was rescued. Today, his two sons, Rabbi Bent and Arne, are prominent.

Rabbi Bent Melchior is former chief rabbi of Denmark. He is the eighth generation of his family in Denmark, the Melchiors having lived there, it is said, for 300 years. A number of streets in Copenhagen are named after this illustrious family. Rabbi Melchior, who fought in

Israel's War of Independence, once told an interviewer, "We have a mission in Denmark. We were saved by the Danes and must continue the community." In 1983, Rabbi Bent Melchior received Denmark's Order of Knighthood.

The late Arne Melchior held a high position in the Jewish community of Denmark and in the government. Having served as a cabinet member and a member of Parliament, he also was in the Haganah in Israel's War of Independence. His nephew, Michael, son of brother Bent, was a former member of the Israeli cabinet, and former Minister of the Diaspora. Another of Rabbi Marcus Melchior's grandsons, Rabbi Uri Schwartz, served in Finland and now is in Israel.   Religiously, Danish Jews belong to the "Mosaic Community," which is governed by a 20-member board of delegates selected every two years.

Denmark like other Jewish communities in Scandinavia faces specific problems regarding religious slaughter. Anti-Semitism, and acts of terror are banned in Denmark, Norway and Sweden. In 2015, a Jewish synagogue guard, Dan Uzan was killed after a gunman opened fire on a Jewish community building behind the synagogue in Copenhagen. The suspect was Omar El-Hussein, later killed in a shootout with police.

JEWISH SITES IN COPENHAGEN

Caroline Skoline, 18 Bomhusvej, Copenhagen. This is a Jewish, co-ed day school founded in 1805. At one time, half of the Jewish children in Copenhagen attended this school. Today about 300 pupils are enrolled. In 2014, the Danish Jewish school, informed parents that its pupils are no longer allowed to wear religious symbols near school grounds, according to an August 8, 2014, JTA dispatch in the *Forward* newspaper.

Jewish Community Center, 6 Ny Kongensgade, 1472 K. Copenhagen. Tel: 33-12-88-68. Located here are Bnei Akiva youth group. Hakoah Sports Club, and the Jewish Youth Club. Adults are active in Keren Kayemet (JNF), WIZO, and the Danish Zionist Federation. A museum and library display Judaica.

Resistance Museum, Esplanade in Churchill Park. Tel: 33-13-17-14. A devastating fire in 2013 destroyed this fine museum. But it is scheduled to reopen at the same spot at the end of 2018 or early 2019. This building should head every tourist's must-see list. Its many exhibits tell the story of the Danish fight for freedom in 1940-45 and there are sections devoted to the rescue of Danish Jews. You will know you have arrived at your destination when you see a tank on the pavement in front of a brown wooden building with the words, "Frit Danmark" ("Free Denmark"). The entrance gives the appearance of a ship; you quickly remember how the Danes rescued the Jews in fishing boats. From May 6 to September 15, the museum is open Tuesday through Saturday, 10:00 a.m. to 4:00 p.m., and on Sunday, 10:00 a.m. to 5:00 p.m. From September 16 to April 30, the museum is open Tuesday through Saturday, 11:00 a.m. to 3:00 p.m.; and on Sundays, 11:00 a.m. to 4:00 p.m. Closed on Mondays. Admission is free.

Exhibition cases 40-42 tell the story of the rescue operation of October 1943, when nearly all of Denmark's Jews were smuggled out on small fishing schooners and ferried to Sweden. Many thank-you letters and plaques grace exhibition cases 83-85 (off to the side and down the steps). Ask the guard if you cannot find these cases.

You will see greetings from many synagogues and Jewish community centers, such as Beth Sholom Mens' Club of Pittsburgh, Adath Jeshurun Congregation in Minneapolis, and other congregations in Spring Valley, New York; Jersey City; and the Boro Park section in Brooklyn. National organizations also have dispatched their thanks, including a large impressive plaque from the Rabbinical Council of America, the largest Orthodox rabbinic group in the world. All voice the sentiment that Israel and Jews everywhere will never forget the rescue of Danish Jews from the Nazis to neutral Sweden. In the courtyard of the museum is a sculpture made by Knud Nellemose; it commemorates those who gave their lives to Danish resistance to the Nazis.

A tank in front of the Resistance Museum, Copenhagen, Denmark.

The Royal Danish Library (Bibliotheca Judaica Simon-seniana), 8 Christians Brygge. 1219 Copenhagen. This library houses one of the largest Jewish book collections in the world. About 80,000 volumes and manuscripts in Hebrew, Latin, Arabic, Aramaic, Ladino, Yiddish, Ethiopian, Persian, and many other languages occupy the shelves. Because it relates history, the library stands as a magnet for scholars from throughout the world. It holds the only illuminated copy of Maimonides' Guide of the Perplexed, penned in Barcelona in 1148.

The Danish Jewish Museum, Proviantpassagen 6, Copenhagen, Tel:45-33-11-22-18. www.jewmus.dk

This landmark museum was designed by the world-famous architect Daniel Libeskind and opened in 2004. Observers say that the design of the building attracts visitors as much as the contents. The emblem and concept of the museum is the Hebrew word *mitzvah*. The floors, walls and ceiling are slanted and disorientating. Videos and artifacts tell the story of Jewish life in Denmark. Hours are in summer include: June 1 to August 31, Tuesday to Saturday, 10:00 a.m. to 5:00 p.m., Monday, closed. Winter: September 1 to May 31: Tuesday to Friday, 1:00 p.m. to 4:00 p.m., Saturday and Sunday, 12:00 p.m. to 5:00 p.m.

KOSHER DINING IN COPENHAGEN

Kosher dining in Copenhagen is not available. There is one kosher shop in Copenhagen. **Kosher Delikatesse** (Butcher) 97 Lyngbyve Copenhagen. Tel: 45-33-18-57-57. It serves up sliced and frozen meats, humus and various cheeses.

Religious slaughtering *shechita* is forbidden in Denmark as well as in Sweden and Norway, though in Denmark, Rabbi Jair Melchior hopes that it can be reversed. Most believe that the decision to suspend kosher slaughtering in Denmark was motivated by animal rights beliefs rather than anti-Semitism. Rabbi Melchior and Rabbi Yitzi Loewenthal of Chabad, believe that the ban is unfortunate. Kosher meat must now be imported from other countries, and thus it is expensive in Denmark. Few kosher-certified products are available in local grocery stores, it was reported.

SYNAGOGUES IN COPENHAGEN

Krystalgade Synagogue, 12 Krystalgade, DK-1172-Copenhagen, 45-33-12-88-68 email: mt@mosaiske.dk, www.mosaiske.dk. This synagogue stands as the main Jewish prayer house in Copenhagen. Most community events occur in this Orthodox house of worship,

Entrance to the Krystalgade Synagogue, Copenhagen. (Photo by Ben G. Frank)

including weddings and bar mitzvahs. Services are held every day of the week. *Shacharit* is at 7:00 a.m., except of course Saturday morning and Sundays as well as Danish holidays when it is at 8:30 a.m. Also, at 8:00 p.m., Friday evenings, though in summer the time changes. Check with the synagogue administration. Important to call ahead when attending services at Krystalgade. Saturday morning service is at 9:00 a.m. in winter, and 9:30 a.m. in summer. There is no mixed seating in the synagogue—women sit in an upstairs gallery. Erected in 1833, this beautifully designed building features inside walls painted white and decorated with gold. The prayer hall seats 650 persons, with standing room for about 100 people.

Rabbi Jair Melchior is the rabbi at Krystalgade Synagogue. Born in Norway, raised in Israel, he is serving as chief rabbi of Denmark. As noted earlier, Rabbi Bent Melchior, former chief rabbi, is the seventh generation of the Melchior family.

Overall, except for the terrorist attack on the synagogue in 2015, Jews feel safe in Denmark, as well as in in Norway and Sweden, too, according to Rabbi Jair Melchior. The Danish government positions itself on the right in the political spectrum and is opposed to settlements in the West Bank. It also supports "a two-state solution." Aliyah from Denmark has increased, according to the rabbi.

The synagogue is near the main shopping area and the pedestrian street, Frederiksbergade, as well as close to major hotels such as the SAS Royal.

Shir Hatzafon, Agnetevel 4, Copenhagen, 2300. Tel: 45-23-70-97-57. shir@shirhatzafon.dk. www.shirhatzafon.dk. This is a progressive synagogue.

Machsike Hadas, 12 Ole Suhrs Gade, 1354 kbh K. Copenhagen. This synagogue maintains ties to Agudath Israel. It sponsors Orthodox services on Saturday and Sunday. 7:45 pm. This is the time for services Friday evening in the summer. Rabbi Yitzi Loewenthal of Chabad serves as spiritual leader. He has been in Denmark since 1996.

Beth Chabad Denmark, Ole Suhrs Gade 10, 1354 kbh K. Tel: 45-3379-3326, or 45-3316-1850, info@chabad.dk, www.chabad.dk. Chabad House is located next door to Machsike Hadas

Many activities are held in the Chabad Center, lessons, a "cheder" for children. Shabbat meals are offered to tourists. Tourists can consult Chabad re catering services and a hospitality apartment. The group offers programs celebrating all the holidays as well as an overnight summer and winter camp for children. Minyanim are not held in Chabad House. Shabbat meal at 5:45 pm. In spring and autumn, check the synagogue's calendar. A mikveh also is located on the premises. Rabbi Yitzi and Rochel Loewenthal are in charge of the Chabad program in Denmark.

Sweden

Stockholm: Latitude 59 19'45.56"N. Longitude: 18 4'6. 89" E. Cold it is, but it also has the largest Jewish community in Scandinavia. Sweden is peaceful. This country has not fought a war since 1814. Once for a brief moment, it wielded great power. Its large towns by and large were peopled by hanseatic merchants who settled in a long and narrow country that today is bordered on the west by Norway, on the north by Norway and Finland, and on the east and south by the Baltic Sea. Peaceful Sweden remains the envy of the Continent. You rarely see poverty or shabbiness.

Sweden encompasses an area of 179,896 square miles of forests and dark lakes. The 1990 population was put at 8,340,000, 94 percent of which is Evangelical Lutheran. Although religious observance is on the wane, the stern Lutheran ethic places high value on discipline, hard work, and achievement.

A BRIEF HISTORY

The story of Jewish settlement begins in 1774. A gem-carver, Aaron Isak, of Mecklenburg, Germany, became the first Jew granted the right to live in Sweden; he was invited by King Gustav III. A year later, his brother arrived. Aaron brought a minyan of ten Jewish men and their families, so he could hold services. Eight years later, the Swedish Parliament passed a law, the so-called Jew Regulations of 1782, authorizing the settlement of Jews, but only in Stockholm, Gothenburg, and Norrköping.

The Jews who arrived at the end of the eighteenth century and first half of the nineteenth century came from Germany. In 1838, the king repealed restrictions that had been passed in 1782 and incorporated the Jews into the Swedish state. After several revisions, all limitations to full citizenship were removed by Parliament in 1870.

Jews were now entitled to hold political office and were emancipated. (The Law of Freedom of Religion in 1951 abolished the regulation of 1838 requiring that citizens affiliate with a religious organization).

In 1880, the Jewish population reached 3,000; in 1910, 6,112. In 1930, nearly 8,000 Jews resided in the country, with nearly half in Stockholm.

During World War II, Sweden sought and won complete neutrality as she had done in World War I. In 1940, the Swedes managed to stay out of the Soviet-Finnish War.

In the decade preceding the outbreak of World War II, Sweden's immigration policy was a restrictive one, according to News & Views, published by the World Jewish Congress. While there were Nazi sympathizers and while Sweden did maintain diplomatic relations with Germany, Jews were not persecuted. As the War went on, Swedish public opinion switched and Jews were admitted into the country. In fact, the Jews of Sweden were directly or indirectly involved in several important lifesaving efforts during World War II, including the rescue of about 7,000 Danish Jews. A booklet put out by the Great Synagogue in Stockholm cites the name of Gilel Storch. The pamphlet says he "is relatively unknown, although he was the driving force behind many projects, the most successful being the supplying of some 170,000 food packages to name given persons in Nazi death and work camps. "Numerous testimonies prove the value of these packages, which were sent from Sweden directly or by way of Portugal." When the Nazis invaded Norway in 1940 and began to round up Jews, about 700 escaped to Sweden, which offered them asylum. Swedish Count Folke Bernadotte and Raoul Wallenberg later saved thousands of Jews from concentration camps.

A panel of historians studying Switzerland's response to saving Jews in World War II, while it did not compare, said at the news conference, that Sweden, also neutral during World War II, had been significantly more helpful than Switzerland. Sweden, like Switzerland, had limited Jewish immigration between 1938 and 1942, but reversed its policy after officials learned of the mass killings of Jews. Every country in Europe is being asked to come to terms with its own action during World War II. Swedish neutrality carried a high moral price. The Swedish government allowed German forces to pass through the country on their way to occupied Norway. When it was clear that the Allies would win, Sweden began its refugee aid.

The largest and most important Jewish immigration to Sweden occurred immediately after World War II, when thousands of survivors were brought from the death camps. About 7,000 remained in Sweden, although the majority soon left for the United States, Canada, and Israel. After the upheavals in Communist Eastern Europe, 550 Jewish refugees arrived here in 1956 from Hungary. In the 1960s, 3,000 Jews emigrated from Poland. By 1970, Sweden had a Jewish population figure of 13,500; it is currently about 20,000, more than double the combined Jewish populations of Norway, Finland, and Denmark. Jews play a major role in the cultural life of Sweden, out of proportion to their numbers, especially in the fields of music, painting, and literary criticism.

Half of the Jews who inhabit Sweden today were victimized by the Nazis or emigrated from Eastern Europe after the war. Today, about 12,000 Jews live in Stockholm, approximately 2,500 in Gothenburg, and 2,500 in Malmö; the remainder have settled throughout the country.

Over the years, tension between Israel and Sweden have risen to the boiling point. The downturn began when Sweden offered long-term and hearty support for the PLO (Palestine Liberation Organization.) The Swedes worked to have the PLO chief, Yasir Arafat, enunciate a so-called moderate position toward Israel and renounce terror in December 1988.

Relations between Israel and Sweden have deteriorated over the years, especially since Sweden recognized Palestinian statehood in October, 2014. Indeed, Israeli government officials have accused Swedish officials of "anti-Semitism." One example, they point to occurred when Swedish Foreign Minister Margot Wallstrom accused Israel in 2016 of carrying out "extrajudicial executions" in response to attacks by knife-wielding Palestinians. Ms. Wallstrom also angered Israel by saying a sense of hopelessness among Palestinians was a factor behind the rise of Islamist extremism in Europe.

Wallstrom suggested, according to the Times of Israel, December 22, 2016, that Israel's response to terrorism was "disproportionate," and equated the Jewish state killing of Palestinian attackers with "extrajudicial executions."

On its part, Israel continues to bar the Swedish foreign minister from visiting the country and accuses her of fostering terrorism.

As of the end of 2016, the left-wing Social Democratic Party continued to be known for its staunch support of the Palestinian cause and its criticism of Israel.

Tied in with the anti-Israel rhetoric is a very left-wing media which is "very biased against Israel." According to Rabbi Ute Steyer, "the Swedish media is more left-wing than the population." She does feel, however, that anti-Semitism exists within the immigrant Muslim minority.

Indeed, hate crimes against Jews were on the rise in 2014, seeing a 38 percent increase in reported anti-Semitic incidents from the previous year, according to a report by the Swedish National Council for Crime Prevention.

Unfortunately, Sweden, too, like many countries in Europe, is also vulnerable to terrorism, as witnessed by a Stockholm truck attacker who was a rejected asylum-seeker and who barreled a stolen beer truck several hundred yards down the bustling pedestrian street, Drottninggatan in the heart of Stockholm in April 2017. In the terrorist attack, four were killed, 15 wounded.

JEWISH STOCKHOLM

Summer light stands for Stockholm—a city of islands, canals, and museums. Stockholm proclaims itself as the most beautiful and cosmopolitan of the Scandinavian capitals, replete with outstanding architecture and charm. Often called the "Venice of the North," the capital is the largest city of Sweden, with a metro population of 2.3 million. With water everywhere, you soon discover the city is built on 14 islands connected by about 50 bridges, under and around which ply more than 100,000 boats.

From downtown Stockholm with its modern business area to the Old Town (Gamla Stan) and its pedestrian streets; to the City Hall and its beautiful surrounding calm waves of water to boat rides in the canals alongside Renaissance buildings, you inhale this relaxing city. Visit the new Vasa Museum featuring the 1628 warship that was raised in 1961 from its watery grave after sinking, or the 75-acre Skansen Outdoor Museum of Swedish Life, a great tourist attraction of 150 reconstructed buildings spotlighting traditional handicrafts and domestic life.

This is Stockholm—clean, pure air and a wonderful traffic pattern. Much of Stockholm can be explored by foot. I immediately took a liking to the area around Nybroplan; the Number 47 bus goes there. Here is the Strand Hotel and its park areas; the Royal Dramatic Theater; the ferryboat to the Skansen Outdoor Museum; the Raoul Wallenberg Square, as well as Bajit, the Jewish center that serves as the headquarters of the Jewish community. And of course, the famous Great Synagogue.

Jewish Sites in Stockholm

The Jewish Museum, was scheduled to open at a new location by the spring of 2018. The new address will be Sjalagardsgatan 19, Stockholm, Tel: 46-8-30-1500. www.judiskamuseet.se. The new facility will focus more on Swedish Jewish history than previously. Here you will still be able to explore the history of the Swedish Jews and their contributions to art, literature and culture of Sweden.

Bajit, the Jewish Community of Stockholm. Riddargatan 3, Stockholm, Operations office Tel: 46-84-091-4044. General questions email to: info@bayit.se, www.bajit.se. This is the new Jewish Community Center of Stockholm, the center of Jewish cultural and social activity. Located in the fashionable Ostermalm section of Stockholm, and near the beautiful Market Hall, the center sponsors many programs, such as Israeli folk dancing and sports clubs.

Kosher food at Bajit.

Kosher store (In the Jewish center) known as Kosherian,

Riddargatan 5, Ground Floor, Tel: 46-8-663-6580. www.kosherian.se. Opening hours: Monday-Thursday: 11:00 a.m. to 6:00 p.m. Friday: 9:00 a.m. to 4:00 p.m. or one hour before Shabbat, 4:00 p.m. Between July 1st and August 15th, the store is only open Wednesday through Friday 10:00 a.m. to 4:00 p.m. At kosher facility, you can get basic kosher food such as, frozen chicken and meat, canned gefilte fish, packaged cold-cuts, snacks, spreads, etc. The kosher establishment can prepare light meals such as, sandwiches, burgers and more. Please contact the store directly for more details and further information.

Tourists: Keep in mind that in order to enter the Jewish Community's premises, you have to bring along some form of identification, such as your passport or ID card.

A kosher dining facility (dairy) functions in Bajit, but check to see if it is open; a gymnasium and Jewish student club meeting rooms are part of the complex. Built in 1963, with a grant from the JDC (Joint Distribution Committee), the center also encompasses a meeting house for such groups as Bnei Akiva, Habonim, Maccabi, Keren Kayemet (Jewish National Home), WIZO (Women's International Zionist Organization), and other organizations. Most of the time, at least one shaliach (advisor and teacher from Israel) resides in Stockholm and maintains his or her office here. Offices, a mikveh, as well as a gift and book shop round out the facilities in the building. But above all, there are many cultural, social, and recreational activities. Please contact the center in advance to see if the cafeteria is open. For info on food and catering, call 46-84-091-4042.

Take the Number 47 bus to Nybroplan and you can walk a few short blocks to Riddagatan 3.

Other Kosher food outlets in Stockholm

Chabad, info@chabadstockholm.com, www.chabadstockholm. com Picked up, delivered, or eaten at **Chabad.** Call for address and directions. Travelers can buy prepared meals at Chabad, Tel: 8-679-7067. Cell: 07-07-908-994. Chabad house. All main courses are delivered double-wrapped and possible to reheat in any oven.

Recommend guide is Marianne Prager Tel: 46-70-497-2783. mariannesguide@gmail.com, www.jewishstockholm.com. Ms. Prager conducts Jewish and general tours. Some highlights of her various tours include, Raoul Wallenberg Square, Jewish monuments including that remembering the Holocaust monument, and the Great Synagogue with its beautiful, folkloristic interior, and Assyrian exterior. Take a ride to the spectacular subway station, "Cave Station," and the "Old Town." Also, the changing of the Royal Guards at the Royal Palace and the new Jewish community center, Bajit. Born in Malmo, Ms. Prager, who is active in the Jewish community, has lived in Israel.

She is a licensed tour guide. A Jewish day school, Hillel, functions in Bajit, www.hillel.nu/. But one should inquire at the Jewish center for permission to visit. Kosher food may be available in the cafeteria when the day school is in session. Call ahead!

Raoul Wallenberg Square. During the six months between July 1944 and January 1945, tens of thousands of Hungarian Jews were saved from the Nazis by a 32-year-old non-Jewish Swede, Raoul Wallenberg. In desperation and fear of certain deportation, the Jews of Budapest appealed for help to neutral embassies. In response, the understaffed Swedish Embassy asked Stockholm to send extra personnel to help them cope with the large number of Jews in need. At the same time, arrangements were being made by the Swedish Foreign Department, the American War Refugee Board, and the World Jewish Congress to initiate a last minute operation to save Hungarian Jews.

Wallenberg, who was unmarried and a skillful organizer and negotiator, volunteered for the job. He was able to save Jews by giving them the famous "schutzpass," a type of protective passport stating that they were under Swedish jurisdiction. After the Russian liberation of Budapest in January 1945, Wallenberg was picked up by Russian soldiers and taken to the Soviet Union, never to be heard from again. The Soviet government told Sweden in 1957 that Wallenberg had died in a Moscow prison in 1947, but witnesses claim to have seen him in prison as late as the 1980s. In 2000, he would have been 88 years old. In recent years, the Russians have acknowledged to the Swedes that Wallenberg had probably been killed in prison. In 2016, the Swedish government formally pronounced Wallenberg, dead. His family requested that he be officially declared deceased. "Let Raoul rest in peace," they said. But in August 2017, Wallenberg's family sued Russia's security services for access to his files.

Synagogues in Stockholm

The Great Synagogue, Wahrendorffsgatan 3A, Stockholm. Tel: 8-679-2900. info@jfst.se, www.jfst.se. This brick building is one of the most beautiful synagogues in Europe and was designed by Fredrik Wilhelm Scholander. The seating capacity is 830 persons. Carol Herselle Krinsky, in her book Synagogues of Europe: Architecture, History, Meaning, claims this house of worship possesses "an Eastern identity." The community's Administrative Building stands at Wahrendorffsgatan, 3B, Stockholm.

In September 1870, Rabbi Ludwig Lewysohn dedicated the synagogue by kindling the gas-burning eternal light (Ner Tamid)

The Holy Ark in the Great Synagogue in Stockholm. (Photo by Ben G. Frank)

over the Holy Ark (aron ha-kodesh). This date is confirmed by the Hebrew inscription over the main entrance to the synagogue. While the lamp is from that time, the cloth decorations around it are traditionally attributed to the time of King Gustav III, although no one is really certain of the truth of this claim. On the other hand, the eight-branched Hanukkah menorah is definitely a gift, according to the Hebrew text on which it stands, that was donated in 1792 after approval by King Gustav III. The legs of the menorah are in the shape of the royal G, which certainly stands for "Gustav." Those of the base upon which the menorah stands are formed in the shape of an S. The queen's name was Sofia Magdalena and the donor was Strelitz, so the meaning behind this letter is unclear.

The Raoul Wallenberg Room in the Great Synagogue is dedicated to Raoul Wallenberg, the Swedish diplomat who saved thousands of Hungarian Jews from the Nazis by issuing them diplomatic passports.

Most Jews here in the synagogue follow what probably is close to the Conservative movement of Judaism in the United States. The synagogue has been described as Ashkenazic, Liberal, and Conservative—with an organ and mixed seating in one section.

Rabbi Ute Seyer, ute.steyer@jfst.se, is the rabbi at The Great Synagogue. She is the first female rabbi in Sweden. Rabbi Steyer received her rabbinic ordination in 2009 from The Jewish

The Great Synagogue. (Photo by Ben G. Frank)

Theological Seminary in New York in 2009. Prior coming to Stockholm, Rabbi Steyer worked as the program director of the Center for Jewish Law of Yeshiva University/Cardozo School of Law and as research fellow and adjunct lecturer at the Jewish Theological Seminary. She also speaks Swedish.

A high rate of intermarriage exists in Sweden. "More rule than exception," points out Rabbi Steyer. In Sweden, she explains, a form of common-law marriage is very wide-spread and outranks formal marriage. She believes intermarriage in Sweden is about 75 percent. Saturday morning services are at 9:15 a.m. Shabbat mornings are an exciting time to be in the synagogue, as the service is rewarding and the kiddush that follows gives travelers a chance to meet the Jews of Stockholm. The kiddush is held in the lecture hall, which features paintings of the past leadership of Swedish Jewry.

Winter brings darkness. Shabbat can begin as early as 2:30 p.m. on a Friday afternoon. A Thursday morning minyan is scheduled for 8:00 a.m., Friday evening services are at 5:30 p.m. in winter; and 6:30 p.m. in summer. 7:30 p.m. in June and July. But check these times by calling the synagogue.

Tourists should note that few activities are scheduled in the summer, as most Swedes go on vacation, especially in July. The synagogue sponsors a popular Jewish summer camp that includes not only several hundred children, but senior citizens, too. Often, both a grandparent and grandchild will meet on the campgrounds.

Regarding visits to the synagogue, email or call the congregation as early as possible in advance of your visit or at least several days ahead of time, as to who is coming, what dates. Do bring proper official documents, photo ID.

Further information on the Jewish Community can be obtained from the Stockholm Jewish Community, Box 7427, 103 91, Stockholm, 46-8-587-858-10.

The SAS Strand, Grand, and Diplomat hotels are near the synagogue. The Royal Viking Hotel, Vasagaten 1, near the central railroad station, is a little farther, but it is an excellent place to stop in the Swedish capital.

Progressive Judaism in Stockholm, 3 Pokalv, Stockholm 117 40. Tel: 46-8-668-4576. jrkleinsbbg@gmail.com. www.progjud.se.

Two small Orthodox synagogues function in Stockholm.

Adas Yeshurun at present is located in Bajit Jewish Center. The address is Riddargatan 3. Tel: 46-84-091-4044. This house of worship was furnished with benches, Holy Ark, pulpit, and table that were in a small synagogue in Hamburg and miraculously survived Kristallnacht. These religious objects were sent to Stockholm's Orthodox Jews by the Orthodox Jewish community in Hamburg. "This synagogue and its furniture have great emotional value for all of Stockholm's Jewry. They express symbolically the faith that Judaism is eternal and that it lives throughout the world and in all ages," says a synagogue brochure. Rabbi Amram Maccabi is the spiritual leader of Adas Yeshurun.

The other Orthodox house of worship, **Adath Israel,** is located at St. Paulsgatan 13. Tel 8-644-1995.

Chabad Lubavitch Stockholm, PO Box 5053. 10242 Stockholm. Tel: 8-679-7067. Cell: 07-07-908-994. info@chabadstockholm.com www.chabadstockholm.com. Holiday celebrations, educational and cultural programs for children, young adults and adults, Torah classes, as well as after-school programs, and "Mommy and Me," are offered as are Shabbat and holiday dinners and events. This Chabad Center does not have a school, synagogue, or mikveh. Rabbi Chaim Greisman represents Chabad in Stockholm.

GOTHENBURG

Jewish Community Center, Ostra Larmgatan 12, 41107, Gothenburg. Tel: 46-31-10-94-00. Fax: 46-31-711-93-80.

Chabad Center. To contact Chabad Tel: 46-7077-11770. Info@ chabad.se. Rabbi Alexander Namdar is the spiritual leader of this congregation. This center sponsors a Shabbat meal and has a guest facility. For the mikveh, Tel: 46-707-408709.

Beth Tifilah, Storgatan 5, Gothenberg. Tel: 46-031-711-78-72.

MALMÖ

Only few hundred Jews live in Malmo a city of over 300,000, but if you ask the Jewish residents of that city, the last decade has seen them face threats and hate mail and even rallies with death chants in Arabic urging the killing of Jews. This in the third largest city in Sweden and according to the Times of Israel, in a December 22, 2015 article, "anti-Israel rhetoric often turns violently anti-Semitic," and a climate of fear exists for the Jews of Malmo. So much so, it has been reported, that Jews have been urged not to wear *yarmulkes* (skull caps). This city, in which one-third are immigrants from Muslim countries, has become known as an example of immigrants' failing to integrate. Frequent expressions of anti-Semitism by the newcomers and some far-left politicians, have left Jews shaken and led to travel warnings by the Simon Wiesenthal Center.

And though attacked several times as far back as 2014, Rabbi Shneur Kesselman of Chabad, remains in Malmo. In one incident, he and a congregant had objects hurled at them and pejoratives uttered at them. Despite the high rate of anti-Semitic hate crimes, which have gone up in recent years, have also gone unchallenged. Rabbi Kesselman remains to "support and strengthen the organized Jewish community and for the Jew of Jewish identity." In 2012, an explosion struck the JCC building No injuries. Today, many fear to wear a yarmulke in public especially since the Jewish community is concentrated in the center of the city as is the Muslim community.

Chabad. 46-40-979-358. www.chabadmalmo.com.

Jewish Community Center, Karmregatan 11, 21156, Malmö.

Synagogue, Foreningsgatan, Malmö.

Norway

The Jewish community in Norway is alive and well and in recent years has a full-time rabbi who spends most of his time in Oslo, but travels long distances to Trondheim, Bergen, and Stavanger.

"The king is in fact giving the Jews the feeling that anyone who lives in this country is part of Norwegian society," said Rabbi Joav Melchior, the spiritual leader of Norwegian Jewry.

The year 1992 was the 100th anniversary of Norwegian Jewry as a congregation, according to Norwegian Jewish leader Herman Kahan. Kahan has written a book, part of which explains Judaism to this "caring," and "friendly" Norwegian society and another section on the history of this young Jewish community, a community that Kahan came to after the war, when he realized his sister was alive and living here. He fell in love with the people and country, which is attractive, clean, and very environmentally conscious. Although Norway can be expensive, it still offers some travel bargains.

You need only one address when you are visiting the city—

Most of Jewish activity is conducted at Bergstien St. 13, 15, 17— which is the Community Center and synagogue (see below).

About 1,300 Jews reside in Norway, with most of them in Oslo, except for about 150 who live in Trondheim.

Actually, because less than four percent of its land is livable, most of Norway's 5.5 million citizens inhabit Oslo, Trondheim, and Bergen.

Today, Norway welcomes tourists to its attractive, picturesque villages and spectacular scenery of fiords, cliffs, rugged uplands, and forests that once were the paths and sea lanes of Viking warriors. They were those hearty warriors who sailed to North America between the ninth and eleventh centuries. Norway covers 125,057 square miles, with a 2,125 mile jagged coastline along the North, Norwegian, and Baltic seas. Norway lies back to back with Sweden along a peaceful

1,000 mile border. Actually, from 1814 until 1905, the country was held by Sweden. In the north, it shares a boundary with Finland and Russia.

Norway boasts the fifth largest merchant fleet in the world—more than 200 shipping companies. So one can see why the sea and the fishing industry remain paramount in Norway. The fiords, which are deep inlets of the sea extending back into the mountains sometimes for more than 100 twisting miles, complete the beautiful picture of this fine nation. Despite latitudes equal to Alaska, Norway's climate remains mild because of warm ocean breezes. A welfare state and the discovery of oil and gas have helped give the country a high standard of living.

A BRIEF HISTORY

For many years the history of Norwegian Jews was linked to Denmark's Jewish community since Norway was ruled by Denmark for 400 years until 1814, when Sweden took over. Norway may have been one of the last countries in Europe to admit Jews. The first Jews arrived here about 300 years ago, but 1851 seems to be the date they settled down. Immigration really got under way after 1881, with an influx of Jews from Eastern Europe. In 1890, 214 Jews lived in Norway, most of them in Oslo. Norwegian Jews erected their first synagogue in 1920, when there were about 1,500 Jewish inhabitants.

Nazi Germany invaded Norway on April 9, 1940. Hitler needed this peace-loving land to secure the transports of iron ore from northern Sweden along the Norwegian coast in the winter when the Baltic Sea is iced. Norway could be exploited as a base to attack northern Great Britain. About 1,800 Jews inhabited the country, including several hundred Jewish refugees. Vidkun Quisling (who gave us the word quisling—traitor) was "minister president" of a puppet regime. He became dictator and turned Jews over to the Nazis. He was executed after the war.

In late 1942, 770 Jews were rounded up and shipped to Nazi death camps. Only 12 survived. Twenty additional Jews were murdered in Norway.

With the help of the Norwegian underground, some 930 Jews escaped to Sweden. This action was carried out with the aid of a group called the Norwegian Lifeboat Society.

After World War II, about 800 Norwegian Jews returned from Sweden. The Norwegian government, however, allowed several hundred Jews to enter from displaced persons (D.P.) camps, under the category of "war casualties." By the mid-1950s, about 1000 Jews resided in Norway, of whom 700 settled in Oslo, and 150 in Trondheim.

A democratic state, Norway fights anti-Semitism and is proud that the first secretary-general of the United Nations was Norwegian Trygve Lee, who helped gain passage of the 1947 U.N. Partition Plan Resolution creating the State of Israel. To fight a 50 percent mixed-marriage rate, many young Jews are sent to Stockholm, Copenhagen, London, and, of course, Israel to find a Jewish spouse. But the rate of mixed marriages here is believed to be lower than in Sweden and Denmark because many Norwegian Jews are newcomers from Eastern Europe and have not as yet assimilated fully. Jews have been involved in the life of the country. Jo Benkow, born Josef Benkowitz, served as the speaker of the Norwegian Parliament from 1985 to 1993. He is said to have been the most influential Jewish politician ever in Norway. According to the Jewish Bulletin, February 11, 2000, Benkow was the head of the opposition Conservative Party in Norway from 1980 to 1984.

A decade ago, the Jewish Community of Detroit grew closer to Norway as one of Michigan's Jewish sons served as U.S. Ambassador to this Scandinavian country. Ambassador David and Doreen Hermelin served from 1998 to 2000 in Oslo. Members of the Jewish community describe Ambassador Hermelin, well-known for his philanthropy as a "total mensh," a wonderful human being.

Norwegian Jewry lauds its religious freedom, the absence of anti-Semitism, as well as government and public support for the Jewish community. The Jewish community here lives in a prosperous environment, so well off that the assimilation process may be accelerated.

Norway played a key role in bringing together Israeli and Palestinian leaders, which resulted in the Oslo Accords. The Norwegian capital has become synonymous with that agreement.

Norwegian society has been especially critical of Israel. At times, elements of the Norwegian press have published material that could fairly be called anti-Semitic.

On the other hand, Norway is home to a large community of active Christian Zionists, according to the World Jewish Congress.

JEWISH OSLO

Oslo, this bright, busy capital city of more than a half-million, situated on 175 square miles and founded nine centuries ago in 1050, is a friendly city. From the new, modern Oslo Plaza Hotel to the comfortable, calm harbor area, the City Hall, the museums and restaurants, Oslo has many sites for the visitor. One of the most fascinating European tourist attractions is the open-air Vigeland

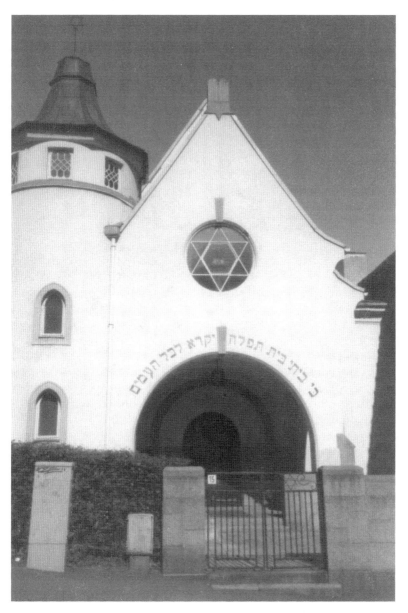

The Oslo Synagogue. (Photo by Ben G. Frank)

Sculpture Park in Frogner Park. There, more than 200 bronze, granite, and wrought-iron statues of men, women, and children, reflecting the relationship between the sexes, draw tourists. Anyone visiting the Norwegian capital should pay a visit to Vigeland's present to the city of Oslo.

Informal Oslo proudly advertises that nearly everyone speaks English in this land of sailors and ships and merchant marines. The museums reflect the sea, especially the Kon-Tiki Museum on the Bygdoy Peninsula, which contains the raft of the anthropologist and adventurer, Thor Heyerdahl. Other museums include the Norwegian Folk Museum, also on the Bygdoy Peninsula. Oslo was also the site of the negotiations that led to Israel and the PLO signing "protocols" in Washington, D.C., in September 1993.

Jewish Sites in Oslo

Community Center and Synagogue, Bergstien St. 13, 15, 17. Three attached buildings—a senior citizen home, a synagogue, and a community center—make up the Jewish community complex on Bergstien Street. Friday evening and Sabbath morning services are scheduled. Prayer times obviously depend on the season in these northern lands. The Sabbath can start at 3 p.m. Friday afternoon in Oslo. Telephone number for the Jewish community: 47-2-2606-826. Fax: 47-2-24-16-5783. adm@dmt.oslo.no. dmt.oslo.com. Rabbi Joav Melchior is the rabbi of this congregation. He also travels to Bergen and Stavangar. Ervin Kohn is president of the community.

The synagogue is located at Bergstien 15, 0172, Oslo, Tel: 22-69-65-70. It is difficult to find as it is in a residential community, situated on the east side of St. Hans Haugen Park. If you are walking, follow Ullevalsveien to Knud Knudsens Plass and follow the east side of the park to Bergstien Street.

No kosher restaurant exists in the city. However, there is a kosher provision store located in the basement of the Jewish Community Center at Bergstien 13, Tel: 2-3205-751, trine@dmt.oslo.no. Tourist groups can order from the caterer of this facility.

The synagogue was founded in 1892 and the present structure built in 1920. After World War II, King Olav V, then Crown Prince, attended the reconstruction ceremony. The building had been miraculously spared by the Nazis in the war. In 1992, the 100th anniversary of the synagogue was celebrated.

Chabad. Rabbi Shaul Wilhelm who arrived in Norway in 2004, leads Chabad in Oslo and travels to distant communities in Trondheim, Bergen, and Stavanger. Shabbat meals are offered both on Friday night and Saturday. Reservations are required via email: chabadnorway@ gmail.com Location of Chabad and further information re its program also are provided by that email: chabadnorway@gmail.com. Tel: 47-22-59-94-63. Large, exciting communal events are held at each of the holidays. Ongoing educational and cultural programs for children, young adults, and adults are held.

The Jewish community is active. Zionist groups, B'nai B'rith, and WIZO meet at the Community Center, which is next door to the synagogue.

Jewish Museum, Calmeyersgate 15 B, 0183, Oslo, Tel: 47-22-20-84-00. post@jodiskmuseumoslo.no, www. jodiskmuseumoslo.no/ The Jewish Museum is located in a former synagogue site which was destroyed in World War II. The new museum was established in 2003. Exhibits offer a survey of Jewish holidays and customs as well as experiences of Norwegian Jews before, during, and after World War II.

Jewish War Victims Memorial, Stroensveten 105, in the Jewish cemetery, an enclave in the municipal cemetery. A large Magen David is engraved on the memorial's panels and it includes the names of 620 Norwegian Jewish men and women who perished in the Holocaust. From the center of the star rises a column in the shape of a truncated tree trunk, on which a memorial plaque is affixed. King Olav V and the Royal Family attended the unveiling ceremony.

The Jewish Memorial Park in the suburb of Hurum, on the Kjerrlgrav Hill, overlooking the Oslo Fjord. A planeload of Tunisian Jewish children crashed on this spot in 1949.

The Resistance Museum. Part of Oslo's Akershus Castle, the medieval stone fortress of the Viking king Harkon, this museum is close to the monument to heroes who lost their lives in World War II. Described as "informative," "interesting," and "stirring," Norway's Resistance Museum deals with Norwegian resistance against the German occupation, 1940-45. The building is known as the Double Battery and The Frame House. The basement consists of two stone vaults built in about 1650 to accommodate six cannons and an adjacent powder magazine. Later, a battery was positioned on top of the vaults, hence the name. The frame building above, erected in the mid-eighteenth century, was used mainly as a military storehouse right down to 1862, when the building was made available for use as a museum. The museum was opened to the public by the then Crown Prince, now King Harald, on May 8, 1970, 25 years to the day after the end of the war in Europe.

The Wergeland Monument. Each year on May 17, which is "Constitution Day" in Norway, Jews, especially Jewish youth, come together at the Wergeland Monument in the Var Frilser's Cemetery to honor Henrik Wergeland, (1808-45) the national poet. They lay bouquets of red and white carnations at the foot of the statue of Henrik Wergeland. Wergeland was instrumental in having the ban against Jewish immigration lifted. Creating a welcome climate for Jews, he wrote a book entitled Jodinden, The Jewess. He did not live to see the ban against Jewish immigration lifted, as he died in 1845. Donated by Swedish Jews, the inscription reads: "To the indefatigable fighter for freedom and the rights of man and citizens." On the other side of the monument it says: "Grateful Jews outside the frontiers of Norway erected this monument to him."

Another monument to Wergeland stands in Studenterluden, a park on Karl Johansgate Street, which is the main pedestrian avenue, replete with shops and restaurants. For further information on sightseeing in Oslo, contact the Oslo tourist office: Tel: 83-00-50.

A recommended guide for Jewish tours of Oslo is Rami Kafarov, Tel: 47-47-25-19-70, info@oslophototour.com.

TRONDHEIM

Norway's third largest city is Trondheim. Originally a railroad station, this imposing synagogue structure is located at Arkitekt Christiesgate IB, near Nidaros Cathedral. The building—used by the Nazis as a warehouse in the war—was enlarged in 1955 by adding a Jewish community center that also includes a Hebrew school. More than 100 Jews live in the city. The sanctuary can seat 150 people, including a women's gallery. The telephone number of the **synagogue** is 47-52-20-30. kontor@dmt.trondheim.no, dmt.trondheim.no.

The Jewish War Victims Memorial in Trondheim is located in the Jewish cemetery. The monument consists of three granite slabs on which are inscribed the names of the 60 Trondheim Jews murdered by the Nazis.

At the end of 2016, Trondheim, approved a resolution to boycott goods and services originating from Israeli settlements in Palestine, according to local publication Adresseavisen.

The resolution is part of a global movement advocating boycott, divest from, and sanction Israeli settlements that are not recognized by international law.

The resolution was reportedly drafted as a suggestion by local transport worker and activist Ole Roger Berg. Berg gathered 340 signatures along with his proposal, which also condemned the Israeli occupation of Palestine and policies that harm the sovereignty and livelihood of Palestinians.

The resolution was supported by the Labor Party, the Socialist Party, the Green Party, and the Red Party. It was opposed by the Conservatives, Progress Party, Pensioner's Party, Christian Democratic Party, and Centre Party.

Finland

Welcome to Finland, land of a thousand lakes, land of the "sauna." Five-and-a-half million people inhabit 130,119 square miles, in some places one person per square mile. Bounded on the north by Norway, on the east by Russia, on the south by the Baltic Sea, and on the west by the Gulf of Bothnia and Sweden, Finland is as beautiful as a picture postcard, with 187,888 lakes—one lake for every 26 persons.

Much of the Finnish population lives in the south and that means they reside in and around the capital, Helsinki, a large industrial city, cultural center, and Baltic port.

This "white city of the North," with its numerous white buildings, rose in the 1550s and was built to be inhabited by humans. Helsinki grows on you. You cannot take in this city in one day. It must be observed and returned to in order to get the feel of it. Even with the end of the Cold War, it still remains a bridge between the West and the vast expanse of Russia to its east. For those flying back from Russia or Baltic countries, Helsinki still positions itself as a welcome stopping-off spot.

Walk around Market Square and watch the people. Look out to the water buses in the south harbor. Stroll along Esplanade Park surrounded by shopping streets and hear the concerts at the bandstand. Buy some fruit in the market near the water.

The Jean Sibelius Memorial in Sibelius Park and Finlandia Hall are sights not to be missed.

The passenger ships of the Silja Line to Stockholm await you. A good way to arrive here from New York is on the daily Finnair jet flights.

A BRIEF HISTORY

In the Middle Ages, Finland was joined to Sweden. But in the eighteenth century, sections of southeastern Finland were ceded to the czar. Moreover, in the Peace Treaty of Hamina in 1809, Finland was formally ceded to the czar, but kept its status of an autonomous grand duchy that retained its previous law and institutions. In 1812, the country's capital was transferred from Turku to Helsinki (Helsingfors). While the Russian Revolution raged in 1917, Finland declared its independence on December 6. An ensuing civil war between Finnish Whites and Reds nearly devastated the country, with the Whites winning the conflict. Peace was signed in 1920.

Until Russia grabbed up Finland in 1809, Jewish settlement in Sweden was forbidden. When the Russians took over the country, a few Jews who served in the army were permitted to reside here. We call these ex-Jewish soldiers "cantonists." These "cantonists" were Jewish boys torn from their parents at a very young age and kept in the czar's military service for 25 years. But after that long quarter of a century of service, these veterans were permitted to settle anywhere in the czar's dominions, including Finland.

The edict of 1858 has been regarded by the Jews of Finland as a "Magna Carta," granting them precious rights and privileges, but still not complete emancipation. By 1880, about 1,000 Jews lived in Finland, but they had to stay in only a few cities, including Turku and Vyborg. When independence was achieved in 1917, Jews were granted full civil rights. After the Russian Revolution, many Russian Jews found a haven in Finland. By 1930, the Jewish population of Finland was about 1,700.

Zionism had a strong hold on Finland's Jewish population. In May 1939, Ze'ev Vladimir Jabotinsky, the leader of the Revisionist group in the Jewish State, visited Helsinki. Twenty years earlier, he had addressed the Jews of Finland. Only this time, with war beckoning, he desperately called on Jews to leave Sweden, Finland, Estonia, and Latvia and settle in the Jewish State. Jabotinsky called for a "clear nationalist feeling and a battle for liberation," according to Hannu Rautkallio. Nobody listened.

A few months later, the Russians attacked Finland in what became the Russo-Finnish Winter War, and Jewish lives were again lost as they rallied to the blue and white flag of Finland. The Finns fought the Soviets with "religious fervor." The Finns drew the admiration of the world as they mounted a desperate defense of their country. Many Jews served in the Finnish Army in that war of 1939-40 as well as during the Continuation War of 1941-44. The losses suffered by Finnish Jews were substantial; of the country's Jewish population, no less than one-fifth had served in the Finnish armed forces (more than 300 men, of whom 26 had been killed or reported missing—nearly eight percent of the total number of Jews who served).

But even more unbelievable was the fact that Jewish soldiers fought in units that were alongside German soldiers in World War II. They actually did, and they did it on the Finnish-Russian border. In fact, during the war, the Finnish Jewish soldiers built a field synagogue by the River Suir, "no doubt, a very exceptional event in an Army fighting on the German's side during the war," writes Tapani Harviainen, a professor at the University of Helsinki.

Finnish Jews serving with Germans? How did it happen? The Finns say they were on the side of the Germans because in this case, the enemy of both nations was the then U.S.S.R. This unique situation actually began on August 23, 1939, with the signing of the infamous Molotov-Ribbintrop pact. Nine days later, on September 1, 1939, Hitler invaded Poland and Russia gobbled up the eastern part of Poland. The Soviets soon made harsh demands on Finland and the Russo-Finnish Winter War broke out on November 30, 1939, with the bombing of Helsinki. "It was naked, unprovoked, inexcusable aggression," wrote William L. Shirer. The war lasted 105 days and Finland, in 1940, ceded much territory to the U.S.S.R. But the fighting between Russia and Finland would start again a year later, in what became known as the "Continuation War."

The way the Finns tell it, Finland joined in the Continuation War in 1941 after it was attacked by Russia during the same time that the Germans launched their June 1941 invasion of the U.S.S.R. Thus, the Finns maintain, the Russians attacked first in 1941, and this was a "separate war." The Finns, continues the argument, were not "allied" to Germany, but merely a "co-belligerent." Therefore, "the Finnish campaign was a defensive struggle separate from the war of the great powers," says Eino Jutikkala.

However, in reality, one must also remember that as the Nazi Blitzkrieg swept across Russia in 1941, the Soviet Union seemed doomed and the Finns saw it as an opportunity to regain their land lost in the 1939-40 war. They did so briefly, but by 1943, the Russians hurled back the German invaders and broke through the Axis lines to assault Finland. Britain had declared war against Finland. The latter was obliged to make peace, once again ceding land and reparations to the U.S.S.R. At the same time, the Germans in their retreat through Finland ravaged Finnish land and killed many civilians.

The Finnish government withstood German pressure to harm Jews. By 1939, the Jewish population had grown to 2,000, and Finland gave temporary sanctuary to fleeing Jews and saved its Jewish residents. It gave shelter to a substantially larger number of westward-bound Jewish refugees than official statistics indicate, Rautkallio says. In 1944, 200 stateless refugees came to Sweden from Finland. Rautkallio states that Finland refused to hand over Finnish Jews to the Germans. The record shows that perhaps less than 20 non-Finnish Jews were surrendered to the Germans, the Encyclopedia Judaica puts the figure at 50 Jewish refugees from Austria and the Baltic countries, and Finnish Jewish publications and leaders today say eight. But it is clear that the Jews of Finland escaped being drawn into the Nazi net. As Raul Hilberg has affirmed, the process of the destruction of Jewry never extended as far as Finland. Finland was the only nation fighting on Germany's side against a common enemy that was never pressured to hand over the Jews, according to Rautkallio. He notes that the Germans were quite aware of the public outcry that would have been raised in Finland if there was so much as a hint of any coercive action against Jews. Persecution or anti-Semitism could hardly be discerned in Finland. Although quite late in the war, on Finland's Independence Day in 1944, Marshall Mannerheim attended a ceremony in the Helsinki synagogue.

Commenting on Rautkallio's book, Irving Abrahamson, in Reform Judaism magazine, said, "If, on the one hand, Rautkallio's book shows that the Finns took no part in the Final Solution, on the other it shows that the Nazis made no effort to impose the Final Solution on them."

In the end, Finland suffered many casualties. She lost 11 percent of her territory to the Russians. As Aini Rajanen points out, the Finns are "people who fought 42 wars with Russia and lost every one of them."

In World War II, there may have been up to 2,300 Jews in Finland, refugees and descendants of the cantonists; by 1949 there were 1,700 Jews in Finland.

Finland was the third nation, after the United States and the U.S.S.R., to recognize the State of Israel in 1948. Twenty-nine Finnish Jewish youths fought in Israel's War of Independence, proportionately the highest number in the Diaspora. More than 100 immigrated to Israel. Today, the Finns display strong support for Israel.

Today, Finland remains nervous once more as Russia flexes its muscles. The Finns feel threatened by Russian flights that tend to stray over Finnish territory. Aligned with the West, Finland joined the European Union in 1995. But Finland is not a member of NATO, though it cooperates with NATO on peace and security operations as well as education and training and development of military capabilities. Indeed, in 2016, Finland and Sweden took part in their first ever NATO foreign ministers' meeting. "Their participation," noted the BBC, "was hailed as a sign that the two nonaligned countries are moving closer to NATO and U.S. security structures."

In 2016, it was clear that Russia's growing military presence in the Baltic Sea region, its nuclear posturing, its undeclared exercises and the provocative actions taken by Russian aircraft and naval vessels, are threat to the peace and tranquility of Finland and the other Scandinavian nations.

In recent years, women have played a leading role in leading the nation. In 2000, Matti Vanhanen became head of the ruling party as well as prime minister. That same year, Finland elected its first woman president, Tarja Halonen, and three years later Matti Vanhanan became head of the ruling center party and prime minister. Mari Kiviniemi replaced Matti Vanhanen in 2010, becoming Finland's second woman prime minister.

About 1,300 Jews live in Finland, most of them in and around Helsinki with small Jewish communities in Turku and Tampere. Those Finnish Jews, recognized as Jews according to halacha or through halachic conversions, are members of the community, which is Ashkenazic and mostly upper middle and middle class. The three Finnish Jewish communities of Helsinki, Tampere, and Turku are united under the Central Council of Jewish Communities in Finland. Its executive board includes nine members, six from Helsinki and three from Turku. The Central Council represents the Jews of Finland, both nationally and internationally. This council is a member of the World Jewish Congress and the World Zionist Organization.

Some assert that at least half the Jewish population intermarries, and that rate is rising. "A marriage of two Finnish Jews has long been a rare exception," wrote Harviainen. Still, Jewish leaders note that many non-Jewish partners convert and the majority of the mixed couples prefer to send their children to the Jewish kindergarten and the Jewish school.

Jews voice their happiness with living in Finland. Why not? Finland's economy generally is good. There are no international problems, and no anti-Semitism hovers over the Jewish community. A very homogeneous society, Finland has no minority problems. Finns don't bother Jews, Jewish leaders told me; and while the people are reserved and not as gregarious as their neighbors, the Swedes, they love their country and their land and are trying to keep their national identity.

As for Finnish Jews, most of the older generations are independent business persons or shopkeepers, while the younger generation enters the professions.

Jews are active in all professions and walks of life. Max Jakobson was former Finnish ambassador to the United Nations and actually ran against Kurt Waldheim of Austria for the post of secretary-general of the United Nations. Jakobson lost when the Soviets vetoed his candidacy. Dr. Simon Parmet is a noted composer and conductor. Sam Vanni is a famous painter, a member of the Finnish Academy and the European Academy of Science, Art and Literature. In 1979, Ben Zyskowicz was the first Finnish Jew to be elected a member of Parliament.

Still active is a Finnish Jewish War Veterans League that was founded in 1979, with a membership in 1991 of 86 members, 70 of whom live in Finland, according to Gideon Bolotowsky.

JEWISH HELSINKI

Kosher Dining in Helsinki

Jewish Community Center. Malminkatu 26, next to the synagogue. Tel: (09) 586-0310. FAX: (09) 694-8916. E-mail: jchelsinki.fl. Kosher meals are available at the center if you phone in your order ahead of time.

Kosher food can be obtained in Helsinki by contacting Avi at 358-400-488-982. www.avicatering.fi He maintains his facility at the community center.

A kosher deli and cafe, **Zaafran & Co.** is located at Malminkatu, 24, Tel: 09-685-4584, info@zaafran.fi, www.zaafranco.com/v1/

Jewish Sites in Helsinki

Synagogue and Jewish Community Center, Malminkatu 26. Tel: (09) 586-0310. FAX: (09) 694-8916. E-mail: jchelsinki.fi. All organizations meet here. The congregation is one of the few in Scandinavia holding daily services. Services at the Synagogue and Community Center are at 9:00 a.m., Sunday 7:45 p.m., Monday 8:00 a.m., Tuesday 8:00 a.m., Wednesday 7:45 p.m., Thursday 8:00 p.m., and Friday 9:00 a.m. on Shabbat.

The synagogue was built in 1906. Renovated and enlarged in 1926,

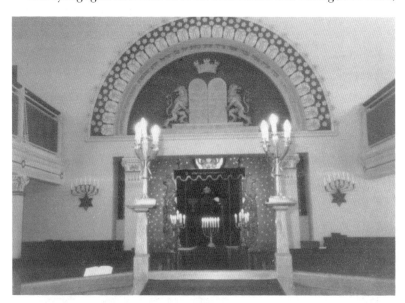

The synagogue in Helsinki. (Photo by Ben G. Frank)

this house of worship added a library to the building that same year. Unlike many synagogues in Europe, this synagogue is very visible. Services in the synagogue follow Orthodox Lithuanian ritual. Chief Rabbi Simon Livson is the spiritual leader of the synagogue.

The synagogue is 30 meters west from the Kamppi bus terminal (one metro stop away from the central railway station). It is located just behind the Royal SAS Radisson Hotel.

The Jewish Community Center, next to the synagogue, was dedicated in 1962. Facilities include a senior citizens home and an auditorium, lounges, meeting rooms, and a mikveh. Here the Helsinki Jewish community sponsors a day school. At one point, 80 percent of the Jewish children in Helsinki attended the school, founded in 1918. Enrollment has gone up because the Israelis send their offspring to the school. About 85 children attend this day school.

Jewish organizations that meet at the Community Center include the 125-year-old Chevra Kadisha, the Chevra Bikur Cholim, WIZO Finland, which has several hundred members, as well as branches of the JNF and Keren Hayesod. Cultural activities are promoted by the Jewish Choral Society, the Club Judaica, and the Hebrew language club, the Chug Ivrit. Sports Club, also located at the Community Center, is the oldest existing Maccabi sports club in Europe. Pictures of its famous athletes adorn the walls of its club room in the Jewish Center section of the complex.

The community publishes a bi-monthly magazine called Ha' Kehila.

Preserved in the synagogue is a wreath presented by Field Marshall Carl G. Mannerheim when he made a visit to synagogue services in 1944. The wreath memorialized the 23 Jewish soldiers who had died in the Russo-Finnish War. Mannerheim was president of Finland from 1944 to 1946. His statue stands tall in several places, including near the Parliament Building in Helsinki. His former home is a museum now.

Chabad Center, Mariankatu 3, Helsinki, 358-9-444-770, email: info@ lubavitch.fi. www.lubavitch.fi. Rabbi Benyamin Wolff is head of the Chabad Center. Chabad conducts a wide range of activities for young people. Trips to Israel as well as a Purim carnival, matzoh baking, trips and visits with other Jews in nearby Tallinn, Estonia. Chabad also sponsors a kindergarten Shabbat dinner which is held Friday evening; time depending on the day of the week.

The Mannerheim Museum, Kalliolinnantie 14, 00140, Helsinki. Tel: 635-443. The guides at this museum are excellent. To the Finns, Mannerheim is George Washington, Abraham Lincoln, and Winston Churchill all rolled into one. Jewish senior citizens maintain it was Mannerheim who saved the Jews.

TURKU

With a population of slightly more than 150,000, this seaport and one-time capital is one of Finland's oldest cities. Often called the "cradle of Finnish culture," for much of the country's early history occurred here, it is surrounded by great forests.

Synagogue and Community Center, Brahenkatu 17. This brick building, located on a corner site, also has a distinctive cupola that can be seen from a distance. The structure was built in 1912, with an adjoining community center erected in 1956. Several hundred Jews support the center. The community maintains a Burial Society, a Bikur Cholim society, and a Makkabi Sports Club. Also, Talmud Torah classes are held here.

Suggested Reading

Bertelsen, Aage. *October, 1943.* New York: Putnam, 1954.

Bradley, David. *Lion Among Roses: A Memoir of Finland.* New York: Holt, Rinehart & Winston, 1965.

Goldberger, Leo, ed. *The Rescue of the Danish Jews: Moral Courage under Stress.* New York: New York University Press, 1987.

Jutikkala, Eino, with Pirinen, Kauko. *A History of Finland.* Translated by Paul Sjoblom. Helsinki: Weilin and Goos, 1984.

Krinsky, Carol Herselle. *Synagogues of Europe: Architecture, History, Meaning.* Cambridge, Mass.: MIT Press, 1985.

Rajanen, Aini. *Of Finnish Ways.* Minneapolis: Dillon Press, 1981.

Rautkallio, Hannu. *Finland and the Holocaust: The Finnish Experience.* New York: Holocaust Publications, 1987.

Shirer, William L. *The Challenge of Scandinavia, Norway, Sweden, Denmark and Finland in Our Time.* Boston: Little, Brown, 1955.

Yahil, Leni. *The Rescue of Danish Jewry.* Philadelphia: Jewish Publication Society, 1969.

The Czech Republic
The Spotlight Shines on Prague

I stand on the banks of the Vltava River—in German, it is called the Moldau. Being in Prague, I naturally start humming Smetna's wonderful symphonic poem, "The Moldau," which salutes Bohemia's noble past and rich culture. Many Jews and non-Jews know that the yearning anthem of Zionism and later the National Anthem of the State of Israel, "Hatikvah," was adapted from the same Czech folk song on which Smetna based his famous E minor melody.

Cities often take on characteristics of their rivers or harbors as the case may be. Prague is such a city. It imitates the embracing calm and serene flow of the Moldau. The tourist wants to hug this Bohemian capital. Mention Prague and we feel good. Jews have a kind word for this capital. It was, and can be again, a shining light of Jewish scholarship. It remains one of the few cities in Europe where Jewish sites have been preserved.

And yet for all our fondness, in our memory there is another side of the ledger that comes to mind.

In a speech to the British people in 1938, that arch-appeaser, Prime Minister Neville Chamberlain, said: how 'horrible, fantastic, incredible, it was that we should be digging ditches and trying on gas masks here because of a quarrel in a faraway country between people with whom we know nothing.'

The "faraway" country was Czechoslovakia and the people were the Czechs and Slovaks. Because the French and British sought to appease Hitler, the Munich agreement sacrificed Czechoslovakia to the Nazis. It would take fifty years for this wonderful country to begin to emerge from the consequences of Fascist and Communist totalitarianism.

In coming to Prague, you journey to the heart of Europe. Photograph Prague as you would a perfectly cut diamond, because Prague is the jewel of Central Europe. And as you travel through this city, remember history. History will tell you that Prague has always vied with Warsaw and Berlin for the title the "heart of Europe."

Prague is in the limelight now because Americans are flocking there

for its beauty, charm, and vibrancy. Young people love it, just as they love Paris, only Prague is less expensive. Once, Paris, too, was the home of the American expatriates: Hemingway, Stein, Crowley, Fitzgerald, and Ford Maddox Ford. Today the spotlight shines on Prague, the "Left Bank of the New Century" the new Paris of American expatriates with writers, tourists, and students arriving here by the thousands to observe its Bohemian culture and patronize its cafes. They crowd Wenceslas Square—the downtown center of shopping and sight-seeing. And they rent apartments in the Old Town, if they can get them or if they can afford them.

A young Jewish man who lives in the new nation of Slovakia told me that while he is a Slovak citizen, whenever he sees the flag of the Czech Republic, he cries. He has good reason: "For 10 centuries, Prague (Praha) and the areas of Bohemia and Moravia ignited the torch of liberty in Central Europe. Sometimes it was the only light in a vast darkness." When it was independent, Czechoslovakia was one of the most progressive countries in the world. Timothy Garton Ash writes in his book, *The Magic Lantern*, "historically, Czechoslovakia was much the most democratic state in the region before the War." He believes culturally that "Prague is the Central European city."

But, like the former U.S.S.R., Czechoslovakia as a united state no longer exists. The year 1993 was a momentous one in the history of the former Czechoslovakia: the divorce between the Czech lands and Slovakia became official. When it was united (between 1918 and 1939, and 1945 and 1993), Czechoslovakia was the size of New York state. Now the Czech Republic has 10.5 million people in 30,000 square miles with 1.3 million persons living in Prague.

The Czech Republic and Slovakia still stand at the major crossroads of Europe. "Not a single major European conflict has left the area untouched in its thousand-year history," wrote Czech President Vaclav Havel in the October 17, 1993, *New York Times*. He added that "wars have started or ended in our territory, and the main threads of history have sometimes been wound together and unraveled here."

Bounded in the west by Germany, in the north by Poland, in the east by Slovakia, and in the south by Austria, the Czech Republic takes pride in its economic progress, with a budget surplus and a healthy export market to the West. By 1994, sixty percent of production came from privatized companies, and unemployment was low.

For the traveler's purpose, Czech history starts when Slavic tribes pushed down from the north, perhaps as early as the first century CE. Then came the Roman legionnaires, who were followed by waves of fierce Avars and Magyars and then Tartars and Turks—all of whom spilled rivers of blood through these lands.

A Slavic empire flourished until the tenth century. While the Slovaks chafed for a thousand years under Hungarian rule, the Czechs briefly enjoyed their own kingdom. Bohemia existed for several centuries. But then came the Hapsburgs who ruled for three hundred years, until 1918. Freedom lasted only twenty years until the flames of Hitlerism raged across this democratic nation. Following the war, Czechoslovakia was stifled by communism for forty years. In 1989, the Czech Communist world collapsed in the wake of the "Velvet Revolution," a peaceful mass revolt in which not one person died.

After the split with Slovakia in 1993, the Czech Republic became one of Europe's youngest states. By 1999 it was a member of NATO, and in 2004 it joined the European Union.

Now a member of NATO and the European Union, Czech Republic faces challenges from its citizens common to East European countries: support for the EU is waning; critics condemn the EU's response to the mass flow of refugees from the Middle East; they feel "the integration of the Muslim community is practically impossible."

A Brief History

Jews have lived in Czechoslovakia—always an important Jewish cultural center—for at least a thousand years. For much of the time, it was one of the richest and most advanced nations in Europe, with a high degree of religious freedom and. cultural development. Jews flocked there. As Jewish merchants moved eastward from the Rhineland in the West to the Fertile Crescent in the East, they plied the trade routes of Central Europe and probably arrived at the end of the tenth century in what we now call the Czech Republic.

Until the twelfth century, Jews lived under favorable conditions. With the Third and Fourth Lateran Councils (1179 and 1215), the Catholic Church cracked down on Jews and Jews lost many of the rights they had enjoyed. By the thirteenth century, sixteen Jewish communities existed in Bohemia and Moravia, all actively seeking religious freedom. It is no wonder that Jews by the thousands poured into these provinces. There they could live in peace and practice their religion. They became moneylenders, and because they also paid higher taxes than most people, they were somewhat protected by the king. But the king often turned against them and cancelled all debts to Jews. At other times, the Jews had the backing of the king and the nobles. During these periods, they were particularly creative: they established the first Hebrew printing house in Prague; they designed and published the *Prague Haggadah*.

Prague took on cultural and economic importance, especially when

Ferdinand I declared that Jews could not live in other towns. Jews owned land and they even farmed. They traded, practiced medicine, and served the court. They excelled in crafts. They contributed to Jewish learning and literature.

A momentous event occurred in Czech history in 1402. That year, the preacher Jan Hus reached the masses with the idea of Church reform. For his criticisms of Church practices, he was burned at the stake on July 6, 1415. The Hussite Reformation shook Europe a hundred years before Martin Luther emerged.

In 1522, 600 Jews resided in Prague. By 1541, the number had risen to 1,200.

A milestone in Czech history was the Battle of Mohacs on August 29, 1526. In that conflict, Louis II of Hungary was defeated and killed, leaving the throne vacant for the ascension of Ferdinand I of Hapsburg as ruler of the Bohemian lands and Hungary. The Golden Age of Prague Jewry appeared on the horizon in that century and early in the next as Jews began to prosper economically. They gained privileges, economic freedom, and the right to live anywhere.

The Battle of White Mountain in 1620 saw the defeat of the Czechs at the hands of the Austrians. In one fell swoop, the Austrians overwhelmed the Czech people and their noblemen, executing 27 members of the Czech aristocracy and exiling 150,000 Protestants. Geoffrey Moorhouse in Prague writes: "The story of Prague since 1620 is essentially the story of alien domination. Unless the outsider can guess this fact, he or she will not understand this city, nor appreciate the wary, stoic temper of its people."

Even in Czechoslovakia as in other parts of Europe in the 18th century, Jews were viewed as an alien people. "But as, regrettably, they had come to be embedded physically within Christendom, it was necessary to ensure that formally, legally, morally and socially they needed in some way to be excluded from it," writes David Vital, in his book, *A People Apart: The Jews of Europe, 1789-1939.*

The Counter-Reformation, which was the response of the Catholic Church to the Protestant Reformation of the sixteenth and seventeenth centuries, "helped destroy religious freedom, national independence, and the educated classes of Czechoslovakia. In the Thirty Years' War, the Counter-Reformation was imposed on the Czechs, and they in effect lost their national independence." On the heels of the good life came oppressive laws, plagues, death, and pogroms. The Jewish quarter was burned to the ground and Maria Theresa (1740-80) banished the Jews from Bohemia and Moravia for three years. They were allowed to resettle, however, despite the anti-Semitism of this Holy Roman empress.

Joseph II of Austria (1780-90), who issued the Toleranzpatent of 1782 ("patents of toleration"), improved the quality of life of the Jewish community. Yet he wanted the Jews to be totally assimilated and to be useful to the state as participants in a modern economic system. Jews took advantage of Joseph's reforms and expanded economic activities. They established factories and even worked in agriculture. Prague joined with Berlin and Vienna to become an important center of Jewish Enlightenment.

By 1848, the number of Jews in Prague reached the 10,000 mark, compared to Vienna, with only 4,000. Just as Jews began to achieve equal rights, the Jewish community of Prague dwindled as new Jewish centers arose in Berlin and Vienna. Yet by the 1900s, half of the Jews of Bohemia resided in Prague. Those Jews were active in the politics and cultural life of the city, which once again became a major center of European Jewry.

After Czechoslovakia gained its independence in 1918, more and more Jews began to speak Czech. In Slovakia and Carpathian-Russia, they spoke Yiddish and Hungarian. Before 1918, the history of the Jews in Bohemia, Moravia, and Silesia was an integral part of the history of Austrian Jews, whereas the Jews of Slovakia and Carpathian-Russia shared their history with Hungarian and Transylvanian Jews.

Jews played an important role in the Czech economy during the years of independence, notably in textiles, food, and paper industries. Estimates vary, but at least thirty to forty percent of the total capital invested in Czech industry in the 1930s was initiated by Jews.

But the independence and the relatively good life would not last. An event took place in Bavaria in 1938 that began the countdown to World War II, although much of the world thought it was a reprieve. In Munich, the British and French appeased Hitler and sold out the Czech people, who then really had little choice but to cave in. But who cared? The world knew little of Czechoslovakia. Hitler gained the "rich rim of Czechoslovakia for nothing," writes John Lukacs, in *The Last European War.* "The ignorance of the Western democracies regarding Eastern Europe was and remains inexcusable."

At Munich on September 29, 1938, 20,000 Jews were literally handed over to Nazi Germany. Another 25,000 fled to the unoccupied part of the country, only to be caught in the Nazi trap within the next few years. The fate of the Jews would be in the hands of the Reich security main office in Berlin and that meant the hands of the notorious Adolf Eichmann, who would organize the deportation of Jews to death camps. As for Slovakia in the east, it became Hitler's lackey after the Nazi dictator told them on March 13, 1939, to proclaim Slovak independence or to suffer occupation. On March 15,

1939, the Nazis seized and incorporated western Czech lands into the Reich as the "Protectorate of Bohemia and Moravia." Slovakia went on its way to fascism under clergyman Jozef Tiso. A government-in-exile was later set up under Dr. Eduard Benes. During World War II, a high percentage of Czech military units consisted of Jews. Almost fifty percent of Czech soldiers abroad were Jews.

When Czech independence ended in 1939, only the Czech Jews out of all the Jews of Europe could "look back warmly on the period between 1918 and 1939," says Charles Hoffman in his book *Gray Dawn: The Jews of Eastern Europe in the Post-Communist Era.* That indeed says a great deal for the people and nation of Czechoslovakia.

After the war and the Holocaust and the Communist coup of February 1948, the surviving Jews greeted the establishment of the State of Israel in May of that year. Between 1948 and 1950, 18,879 Jews left Czechoslovakia for Israel. More than 7,000 departed for other countries. In 1950, the Communist rulers barred Jewish emigration. Only about 18,000 Jews remained. Some 5,500 of them waited for a chance to settle in Israel. Few were allowed to go. And the Jews became fearful of this harsh Communist regime, which they suspected would inflict upon them suspicion and humiliation. The blow would come soon.

RUDOLF SLANSKY TRIAL

In 1951, Rudolf Slansky, the Secretary-General of the Czech Communist Party, and thirteen co-defendants were purged in a trial that was a signal that scapegoats were being sought for the crimes and shortcomings of the regime, which Slansky himself helped create. It was the morning alarm clock ringing and calling for an intensive anti-Semitic campaign. Peter Meyer calls it "the great anti-Semitic show trial."

The 1951-52 Prague show trials were watched with horror and revulsion throughout the free world. The purge even embraced a Nazi type of anti-Semitism. The Czechs actually followed the pattern of Soviet political trials. Staged by the Russians, these shows could easily have played at home to U.S.S.R. audiences.

Many of the accused were branded Zionists. Eleven of the 14 defendants were Jews. Eventually 11 were executed, 8 of them Jews. Paul Lendvai maintains that Slansky "was undoubtedly an innocent victim of the Soviet-sponsored purge since the specific charges against him were patently untrue."

So, after the trial, Czechoslovakia would be ruled as a closed society—except for the fresh air of the "Prague Spring" of 1968, and until communism was dissolved in 1989 and Prague once again basked in freedom.

Much of Czech Republic's recent history as a free republic was formed by Václav Havel, a Czech writer, philosopher, political dissident, and politician. From 1989 to 1992, he served as the last president of Czechoslovakia. He then served as the first president of the Czech Republic after the Czech–Slovak split. Indeed, Havel was a major figure in modern European history, along with Lech Walesa and Mikhail Gorbachev. With his writings, Havel influenced dissidents throughout Central and Eastern Europe who wanted to free themselves from the Soviet yoke. He helped engineer the fall of communism in Czechoslovakia, so much so that the regime that had lasted 40 years toppled in ten days. Although he failed to prevent the velvet divorce between the Czech Republic and Slovakia in 1992, he did ensure that his country "returned to the heart of Europe."

Notable Czech Jews

Jewish contributions to Czech literature and culture were out of all proportion to the small minority of Jews in the country's population. Achieving international recognition were Franz Kafka, Max Brod, Franz Werfel, Oskar Baum, Ludwig Winder, Leo Perutz, and Egon Erwin Kisch.

Eduard Goldstuecker served as president of the Czech Writers' Union during the Prague Spring days of 1968 when the Czechs tried to release the severe grip of the Communist police state. Albert Einstein taught in Prague for a year in 1911. The composer, Gustav Mahler, a native of Bohemia, spent several years in Prague.

Most of these artists spoke German. Often they were middle class, secularized, and assimilated into the larger society.

Jewish Prague

Mother of cities, this elegant city is a chronicle in stone. It is a museum and an art gallery. As a tourist site, Prague is "in." Perhaps travelers flock here now because the Communist regime kept it isolated for four decades; it probably was the most closed of the large Eastern European capitals.

Above all, civilized Prague remains a delight, charmingly laid out on hills and slopes. Not damaged by the war, it remains "Europe's most ravishing city, a perfectly preserved confection of Gothic, Renaissance, baroque and rococo and decorated with an icing of art nouveau," writes one observer. People who visit the city are charmed by the capital's beauty and location, and its architectural gems, cultural traditions, and extraordinary millennium-long history.

One of Europe's "most magical" capitals, Prague boasts cobbled medieval alleys, soaring gothic spires and lively squares.

An interesting fact about the city is that it is in the *Guinness World Records* for having the largest castle in the world—covering 18 acres. Known as Prague Castle, (Czech: Pražský hrad) it stands as a castle complex dating from the 9th century and serves as the official residence of the president of the Czech Republic.

Because of this and other public sites, Prague is a highly recommended tourist destination because many believe it is the soul of Europe. It truly rewards the Jewish visitor.

For centuries, this city has been proclaimed and acclaimed as "Golden Prague," where Jews have lived for at least a thousand years. Indeed, a thousand years ago, a Jewish Arab merchant, Ibrahim Ibn Jacob said this about Prague:

"The town is built of stone and limestone and it is the biggest trade town. Russians and Slavs come here from the royal town with goods. And Muslims. Jews and Turks from the lands of the Turks also come here with goods and trade coins."

Destined to become an important trade route along a major commercial river, Prague attracted Jewish leaders in 995. Rewarded for the aid they rendered to Christians in their fight against the pagans, they set up their own residential area. They built a school in what is now the "Mala Strana," the Little Quarter or Lesser Town, as it is sometimes called.

These Jewish pioneers settled around the area of what is now Dusni Street. Their next move was to the area known as the Old Jewish Town that for the last hundred years or so has been called Josefov, after the Hapsburg Emperor, Joseph II.

Here is what Alois Jirasek said in an old Czech legend:

"Six gates marked the division. And beyond those gates, everything was different. Strange buildings which excluded an air of poverty and neglect. Architecturally, there was all manner of weird additions, balconies, protrusions, dark dilapidated courtyards. The streets were very different, too. They were short and narrow, meandering, seedy and unpaved. And Jews at every turn, people of different customs and manners."

But Prague is not a stagnant city-state. This old city is studded with new retail shops, computer companies, banks, and a visual explosion of restaurants and bars. Alongside these establishments move a well-educated and cohesive population. And Prague trades extensively with its neighbor and one-time bitter foe, Germany.

Today, in Prague, there are only about 4,000 "registered" Jews, out of approximately 8,000 Jews in the Czech Republic, although the latter figure could be much higher. Many Jews intermarried. Since being Jewish no longer carries political stigmas as it did under the Communist regime, the "unregistered" Jews may also participate in community activities. Still, due to a high degree of assimilation, which existed even in pre-war Czechoslovakia, many are simply not aware they are Jews and many of those that are aware do not identify with Judaism in any way. So, cross the crooked medieval span of the Charles Bridge and look down onto the gentle Vltava River, which flows from the Bohemian hills and splits the capital Prague. Then enter into the Jewish Town.

You can stroll through Wenceslas Square, through the Old Town, past medieval architecture, past the big square in front of the city hall, down Pariska Street to the Jewish quarter, and then down the narrow cobblestone streets, through the old Jewish quarter. When you come to the banks of the Vltava River, set back your imagination ten centuries and visualize Jewish merchants traveling the trade routes and arriving at the very spot where you now stand. The Vltava still inspires romantic artists, writers, and historians.

Make sure you visit the Altneuschul. Then go on to the Klaus Synagogue, the Pinkas Synagogue, and the High Synagogue (also called the Town Hall Synagogue), which was built in the second half of the sixteenth century next door to the Jewish Town Hall. The latter is now the headquarters of the Prague Jewish community. Stand in the Maisel Synagogue reconstructed in 1885-1913. And be sure you take some time to wander through the Old Jewish Cemetery.

From November to April, most of the synagogues and sites are open from 9:00 a.m. to 4:30 p.m., Sunday to Thursday. On Shabbat, the museums and offices are closed. On Friday, these institutions usually stay open until 1:00 p.m. In the summer, the hours are from 9:00 a.m. to 6:00 p.m. To obtain a guide, one can call the Jewish community at 2481-0099.

A century ago, there were about 400 synagogues in the Czech Republic. About 70 of them were destroyed by the Nazis and then the Communists demolished about 100 more. Most of the remaining houses of worship were converted into churches and/or residences. Many were used as warehouses or stood neglected and vacant.

Today about 200 synagogues stand in the country, though only a few are active. Dozens, as in other European nations, serve as museums or cultural halls.

THE JEWISH TOWN

Prague may have existed as a settlement for six thousand years, but for the modern traveler, it is the Old Town that draws and inspires the tourist. A living museum of medieval architecture, it contains nearly two thousand historic buildings. Few are more popular with tourists than the synagogues, the Jewish Town Hall, and the cemetery of Josefov, the Old Jewish Town. Actually, these sites still remain central to Prague Jewry and will probably be so for as long as Jews live in this city by the Vltava River. More than 500,000 tourists, predominantly non-Jewish, visit the Jewish quarter or Jewish Town, as it is called, each year. During the peak tourist season, thousands daily stroll through the narrow streets.

Hear the words of Franz Kafka describe this ghetto, which he knew in his childhood: "Living within us are still those dark corners, mysterious corridors, blind windows, dirty backyards, noisy pubs, and closed inns. We walk down broad streets of the newly built towns. But our steps and looks are uncertain."

In 1896, a city-wide development project demolished the Jewish quarter, except for the Altneuschul, the Pinkas, Maisel, and the High (Hoch) synagogues. Many Jews moved out of the Old Quarter to new city areas. In 1870, more than half of Prague Jewry still lived in the Old Quarter. By 1900, less than one-fourth remained. Still, the Jewish ghetto has played an important role in Prague's history.

One million visitors come to the Old Town each year.

The Jewish Museum, Prague. The "exotic museum of an extinct race"—that is what the Nazis had in mind when they spoke of a Jewish museum. In Czechoslovakia, Jewish religious objects were saved because the Germans in their skewed insanity wanted to transform these museums into "museums of hate"—after all the Jews were annihilated by Nazi killer squads, of course.

In an article on JewishHeritageEurope.com, Misha Sidenberg, visual arts curator at the Jewish Museum, noted what she called "an unparalleled example of Jewish defiance against Nazi genocide and cultural plunder—the rescue and preservation of Jewish cultural and material heritage in Bohemia and Moravia during and after World War II."

Two notorious Nazis, Reinhard Heydrich and Adolf Eichmann, sadistically added items to the Czechoslovakia Jewish community's pre-war collection of Judaica by seizing Jewish books, manuscripts, and religious and art objects in Germany and other countries in Europe and bringing them to Prague for storage. This insane behavior saved an immeasurable wealth of Jewish cultural objects. At the end of the war, 8 buildings in the Jewish quarter and 50 warehouses throughout Prague were packed with Torah scrolls, ritual objects, musical instruments, paintings, furniture, and other stolen items.

The Nazis seized these items from Czech and Slovak homes and from at least 168 synagogues that they destroyed in Bohemia, Moravia, and Slovakia.

Today, the Jewish Museum, founded in 1906, is housed in the surviving Prague synagogues that were not leveled by the Nazis. These former houses of worship possess a great collection of religious and secular Judaica, much of it from other European nations—a unique treasury of Jewish history. Actually, it may even be the richest Judaica collection in the world. One estimate is that there are more than 30,000 religious and artistic objects and a library of 100,000 volumes, most of which the Nazis had stolen from synagogues and from the homes of 92,000 Czech Jews who were deported to concentration camps, where 77,297 died.

The Altaeuschul, or Old-New Synagogue (Staronova Synagoga), corner of Cervena and Maislova streets, Prague. If you have time to visit only one site in Jewish Prague, this world-famous early Gothic synagogue should be it. Services are held every day. (The building is closed to sightseers on Shabbat). Erected around 1270, the

Inside the Altneuschul, "the Old-New Synagogue," in Prague. (Photo by Ed Robin)

"Altneuschul" stands in the ancient Jewish Town. Today, architects, artists, and scholars fix their sights on this and other buildings that were not touched by the Holocaust. The traveler should do likewise. Lest we forget, this is the oldest monument of Prague's ghetto and the oldest functioning synagogue in Europe. This synagogue of synagogues is among the most impressive of early European Gothic style. And during the summer tourist season up to 2,500 persons may visit the synagogue in a single day.

News was made in the beginning of 2017 when this medieval synagogue received two new Torah scrolls, the first ones since World War II.

"After years when Torahs were being destroyed, burnt (in World War II), the community celebrates. That is the best expression of the development of the Prague Jewish Community," said deputy head of the Jewish Community of Prague, Frantisek Banyai, according to Reuters.

Located in this city of Gothic, neo-Renaissance architecture, the Altneuschul comes upon you very quickly. Its portrait looks better in photos. When you look closely you may see the marks of age. You realize it contains within its walls seven hundred years of Jewish history and the will to survive. Stories have been told and legends have been created. Thousands of people from all over the world have come to see this synagogue, one of the most important early Gothic brick buildings in Europe, and one of the world's oldest Jewish architectural monuments.

In the past, some sentimental visitors reported that the history of the Jews of Prague flashed on the walls before them. The blood of pogroms became visible to them on its whitewashed walls, they said. Jews were murdered in this building and the bloodstains, they were told, have never been whitewashed off the walls out of respect for the martyrs, according to Carol Herselle Krinsky in *Synagogues of Europe: Architecture, History, Meaning*. However, the stains have apparently faded away.

In 1254, Premysl Ottokar II granted certain Jews "privileges," which meant he would protect their houses, cemeteries, and organizations. Following up on this, Prague Jewry obtained permission to build a new synagogue and to hire masonry workers who were constructing nearby St. Agnes Church, which still stands.

Even the synagogue's name can be considered mythical. Interwoven into the history of how it obtained its name, the "Alneuschul"—the Old-New Synagogue—are numerous legends. Construction of the synagogue was completed between 1270 and 1290. To differentiate it from another older synagogue, it was named "new." At the end of the sixteenth century, or at the beginning of the seventeenth century, another "new" synagogue was built and the former "new" synagogue came to be known in German as the "Alte Neu Schul," or "the Old-New School," a name that was later written in one word, "Altneuschul." Thus we see that the Altneuschul's original name was the New or Great Synagogue (schul). The name, "Old-New" (Altneu in German), came into use only after other synagogues in the ghetto were erected in the late sixteenth century.

Another explanation is given by Jan Lukas, who recounts in *The Prague Ghetto* that "some experts maintain that the name 'Old New' developed precisely from the fact that the new part of the building was built on top of the old one which had been uncovered by the children at play."

Yet another source attributes the unique name to a vague expression that arose from the translation of the German word, alt-neu. The correct term, they say, is the Hebrew al-tnai, "on condition" or "temporarily"; that in fact, Jewish legend says the foundation stones for the construction of the Altneuschul were brought by angels from the destroyed Holy Temple in Jerusalem "on condition" (al-tenai in Hebrew) that the stones would be returned when the Temple was restored.

Still another legend maintains that the Jews were not permitted to change or to repair anything in the Altneuschul. When something had to be fixed or built onto the synagogue, the builder was always punished by misfortune or even death. For this and other reasons, the synagogue remained unchanged for many centuries.

At one time, according to yet another Altneuschul legend, the synagogue was protected against fire in the ghetto by angels who changed into doves.

A different folktale relates that the remains of the golem, the artificial creature made of clay and brought to life by the famous scholar, Rabbi Loew, are deposited in the synagogue—perhaps hidden away in the attic. Even today, it is said, no one dares to go up to the attic and the author was even told that during the Nazi occupation, two German soldiers climbed up to the attic to seek jewels and were never seen again. We shall discuss the rabbi and golem again when we visit the Old Jewish Cemetery.

Today, this oldest preserved synagogue in Europe still serves the needs of Prague's Jews. In the middle of the synagogue waves a historic banner of the Prague Jewish community. The right to have a banner of their own as a symbol of independence was first granted to the Jews of Prague by Charles IV in 1357. Attached to the western pillar of the main nave, the banner was altered to its present form in 1716 on the occasion of the birth of a son to Emperor Charles VI. The center of the banner bears the Star of David and contains a pointed Jewish hat that for centuries was the sign of Prague Jewry. The hat was also one of the traditional items of clothing of Prague's Jews. In certain periods Jews were not allowed to leave the ghetto without the mark of their religion.

There were times when conflict followed conflict. Historically, hatemongers—often incited by the Church itself—blamed the Jews for the Black Death in the fourteenth century, for example, and accused them of poisoning the wells "in order to destroy the whole of Christendom." The largest pogrom in the history of the Prague ghetto took place during Easter 1389. The killing was so onerous that this horrible event is still remembered in a special prayer that is read on Yom Kippur in today's Old-New Synagogue. Rabbi Avigdor Kara is the author of this elegy commemorating the pogrom that overwhelmed the Jews in 1389.

The synagogue's structure is in the shape of a reticulated nave. Its gateway is a portal with plant ornamentation. This original portal with a tympanum is decorated with stylized vine leaves. The hall-type double nave has a five-part rib vaulting supported by two octagonal pillars. The purpose of the fifth rib was to avoid giving a "cross" form to the vault, writes Rachel Wischnitzer in *The Architecture of the European Synagogue*. At the eastern wall stands the aron ha-kodesh (cabinet containing the scrolls of the Torah). The prized bronze chandeliers are from the sixteenth and seventeenth centuries.

"The synagogue is a grayish stone structure composed of a double-naved main room for men." The hall of worship is 49 x 29 feet. On three sides the main building is surrounded by low annexes that serve as a vestibule and a nave for the women. The latter section is connected with the synagogue's main room only by slit openings in the wall to enable the women to hear a service. The floor of the main nave is somewhat lower.

Statue of Moses. Near the Altneuschul is a statue of Moses by sculptor Frantisek Bilek. It is Moses on his knees in despair after his descent from Mount Sinai. When he sees the results of his anger: the fragments of the shattered tablets of the Law, he despairs. He broke the tablets out of anger when he found that his co-religionists had been worshipping idols.

Sculpted at the turn of the century by Bilek, the statue was "meant to be the first of an unfinished series of numerous biblical characters and prophets to demonstrate the spiritual development of mankind." The original sculpture that was placed in the small park next to the Altneuschul in 1935 was destroyed by the Nazis. A copy was unveiled in the same spot in 1948.

Jubilee Synagogue, u. Jeruzalemska, 7, Prague. Located in the Nove Mesto or New Town. This and the Old-New Synagogue still serve the existing Jewish community. Services are held Friday evenings and Saturday mornings. The organ is sometimes used and men and women can at times sit together. The community calls it modern Orthodox. The Jewish community decided to erect this synagogue "at the time of the Silver Jubilee of Franz Joseph l's ascension to the Austrian throne, which is why it is called the Jubilee Synagogue in his honor."

The Jewish Town Hall, 18 u. Maislova, 110 00, Prague. This impressive building is the heart of the Jewish community. This Jewish Town Hall with its distinctive Hebrew clock, with Hebrew numerals moving counterclockwise, serves as the community center and boasts a kosher restaurant (see below). The present rococo appearance of the Town Hall dates from 1763.

The kehila offices, rabbi's study, community archives, and dining hall are all contained here in this early seventeenth century building located just up the street from the Old-New Synagogue. In 2014, Rabbi David Peter became the chief rabbi of the Prague Jewish Community. A native of Prague, he served as rabbi of the city's Jerusalem Synagogue. He replaced Rabbi Karol Sidon who resigned from the post after serving for 22 years. Rabbi Siden remains chief rabbi of the Czech Republic.

The building serves as the headquarters of the Federation of Jewish Communities. 18 u. Maislova, P.O. Box 297, 11001, Prague. Tel: 420-224-800-824. FAX: 420-224-810-912. sekretaria@fzo.cz. www.fzo.cz. Rabbi's office: Tel: 420-224-800-849. FAX 420-222-318-664

Chabad Center, u Milosrdnych 6, 110 00, Prague. www.chabadprague.cz. This center is located in the Jewish Quarter. It houses a synagogue and two kosher restaurants, meat and dairy. Holiday events, Torah classes for men and women. The restaurant website is www.ChanbadGrill.cz. Rabbi Manis Barash is the spiritual leader. Prague has many top tour guides for Jewish Prague as well as outside the area. Chabad is willing to recommend a guide to suit the traveler's needs.

Reform Groups in Prague. There are two Reform movement groups in Prague. Both are members of the World Union for Progressive Judaism.

ZLU. Hatikva. 37 Dlouha, 1-110 00, Prague. Tel: 420-7-397-7660. info@zlu.cz. www.zlu.cz/

Reform synagogue. Maiselova, 4, 110 00, Prague. Czech Republic. Tel: 420-603-393-558. kehila@bejsimcha.cz. www.bejtsimcha.cz.

Masorti Olami Community of Czech Republic, Prague. Tel: 420-608-176-579. info@masortiprague.cz . www.masortiprague.cz, www.masortiolami.org.

Kosher Restaurants in Prague

Shalom Restaurant, located in The Jewish Community Town Hall, 18 u. Maislova, Prague. 110 01. Tel: 420-224-800—06. Offered here is cafeteria-style eating. Shabbat dinners. Open daily from 11:30 a.m. to 2:00 p.m. Closed Sunday.

King Solomon, Siroka 55/8, Prague 1, 110 00. Tel: 420-24-818-752 Open from 11:00 a.m. to 11:00 p.m. This restaurant offers a varied menu during the week and Shabbat lunch.

Charles Bridge

Of the fifteen bridges linking the two halves of Prague, the oldest and best loved is the Charles Bridge. After making Prague his capital in 1346, this Holy Roman Emperor and King of Bohemia, Charles IV (1346-78) built the bridge on the site of an old Slavic fort. Thirty stone saints line the bridge, the oldest stone bridge in Central Europe. Most of the stone saints were carved in the eighteenth and nineteenth centuries. Under Charles IV, a Czech national hero, Prague became an important medieval capital with the first university in Central Europe.

Another important figure in Czechoslovakian history and Jewish history in Bohemia and Moravia is that of Rudolf II (1552-1612), Holy Roman Emperor and King of Bohemia from the year 1576. In 1583, Rudolf transferred his court to Prague. This move improved the position of the Jews, and Jewish culture flourished. Rudolf was in constant touch with Marcus Mordecai Maisel, who served him as a banker and supplier of art objects for his art collection. He received Rabbi Judah Loew ben Bezalel (the Maharal—the Hebrew acronym for "most venerated teacher and rabbi") in an audience, it is said. Rudolf created the category of the Hoflefreiter Jude (1582): Jews who were attached to the court and enjoyed such privileges as exemption from taxes and from wearing the Jewish badge. From them the institution of "Court Jew" developed.

But how King Randolph and Rabbi Judah Loew ben Bezalel met on the Charles Bridge comes from another legend. The Marahal, according to Elie Wiesel's account of the meeting in his book The Golem, was standing in the middle of the bridge waiting for King Rudolf. Onlookers argued that the rabbi might be run over because the king might not stop because "his horses run faster than the wind." "'Not this time,'" said the Maharal. People sneered. Soon, the horses came running as though they would trample the rabbi under their feet, "and then, suddenly they stopped." The king wanted to know why the Maharal risked his life. "I had to,'" said the Maharal. "'My people's lives are in jeopardy. Have you not signed a decree ordering them to go into exile?'" The king invited the Maharal to the castle and they became friends. The Maharal became a frequent visitor in the role of intercessor and defender.

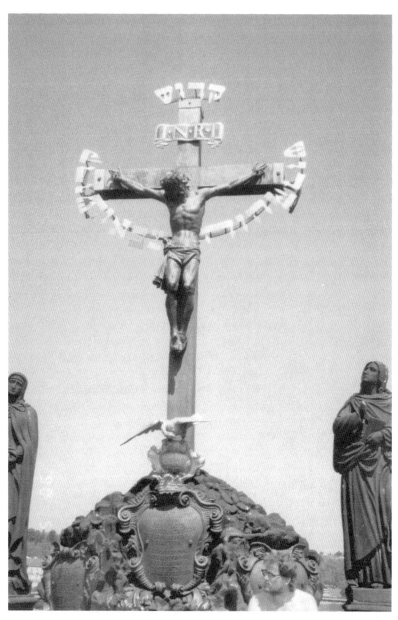

On the Charles Bridge, the crucifix surrounded by huge gilded Hebrew letters that spell the traditional Hebrew sanctification, "Holy, holy. Holy is the Lord of Hosts." (Photo by Sam Urman)

Although Jews were persecuted in Prague, during his lifetime Emperor Charles IV protected the Jews. He was a statesman, writer, scholar, linguist, and builder.

At the end of the bridge named for him, you pass into the "Mala Strana," the Little Quarter-one of the three ancient areas of historical Prague.

On the Charles Bridge, the visitor will observe a great crucifix surrounded by huge gilded Hebrew letters that spell the traditional Hebrew sanctification, *Kadosh, Kadosh, Kadosh Adonai Tzvaot,* "Holy, Holy, Holy is the Lord of Hosts." According to various commentators, this piece, degrading to Jews, came about because in 1609 a Jew was accused of desecrating the crucifix. The Jewish community was forced to pay for putting up the Hebrew words in gold letters. The Nazis removed the gold.

Another explanation is that a Jew spit at the cross and for this he was to be put to death as punishment. When this man begged for his life, the king, seeking to have good relations with the Jews, said the Jewish community had to rectify the offense, and the Jewish man would have to put up a cross.

A Jew is not allowed to put up a cross, but the man was forced to do so. By adding the words, *Kadosh, Kadosh, Kadosh,* the Jew felt exonerated from wrongdoing to his religion because the sanctification contains the words, *Adonai Tzvaot,* so that the man was in effect saying his god is Adonai Tzvaot.

High Synagogue, also known as the **Town Hall Synagogue, VysoKa (Radnicni) Synagoga,** u. Cervena, Prague. This synagogue is located across the street from the entrance to the "Old-New Synagogue," or the "Altneuschul." The High Synagogue, or "Hoch Synagogue," was built in 1565. The name High Synagogue probably comes from its unusual location on the first floor, which suggested its then exclusive and nonpublic character. Originally, it was accessible from a room on the first floor of the Jewish Town Hall. It was used as a prayer house by loaders of the Jewish community.

The High Synagogue and the Maisel Synagogue were financed and built by Mordechai Maisel (1528-1601), the so-called mayor of the Jewish Town Hall. The architect was Panacius Roder. In 1907, the High Synagogue's entrances on the eastern facade were removed and the existing entrance opposite the Altneuschul was constructed.

Like the other synagogues, the High Synagogue today is a museum. Exhibition cases and wall displays will mesmerize the visitor. Significantly, the High Synagogue contains several thousand synagogue curtains, draperies, Torah mantles, and binders that were seized by the Nazis from Czech Jews and from Jewish families throughout Europe.

The Prague Jewish community was especially known for its embroidery workshops. There is an exhibit showing the continuous development of synagogue textiles from the sixteenth to the twentieth centuries. An early baroque stone Holy Ark with combined columns on the sides, a symbol of the Torah crown, and an inscribed cartouche distinguish this synagogue.

When you leave the Old-New Synagogue or the High Synagogue, cross Maislova Street and walk down Stareho Hrbitova Street. On the left side of the street and to the left of the entrance to the Old Jewish Cemetery is the Klausen Synagogue.

Klausen Synagogue (Klausova Synagoga), u. Stareho Hrbitova, Prague. Located to the left of the cemetery entrance on u. Stareho Hrbitova, this synagogue, which stands as a museum, is especially noted for its permanent exhibition of Hebrew manuscripts and prints. The exhibits here contain examples of Jewish cultural and religious items.

Three small buildings that comprised the then-synagogue were destroyed by fire on June 21, 1689. That fire ravaged all of the 316 houses in the ghetto and most of the synagogues and public buildings.

The Klausen Synagogue was completed in 1694, thanks to Shlomo Kohen, a printer. The name "Klausen" may be derived from the Latin claustrum. Another source says the name Klausen comes from those small buildings, which were called "klauses." That is why some call this the Klaus Synagogue. The building was enlarged in 1883-84 and partly rebuilt in 1910, according to Carol Herselle Krinsky.

Interestingly, for lack of open space, the Klausen Synagogue was built on its location even though it faced the Old Jewish Cemetery. Shown in the synagogue is an exquisite baroque Torah Ark consisting of three sections. The vaulted ceiling of the synagogue is decorated with a rococo stucco from the eighteenth century.

By the way, the works of Kohen the printer are highly artistic. Well known are the Prague editions of the Pentateuch of 1518 and 1530 and the so-called "Prague Haggadah" of 1526. Kohen also printed selections from the writings of Rabbi Loew.

Chevra Kadisha Building, u. Stareho Hrbitova, Prague. The Chevra Kadisha building, to the right of the entrance to the Old Jewish Cemetery, once served as a mortuary. Today, it contains a heartbreaking display of poems, drawings, and letters from the children of the Terezin concentration camp. The majority of the Terezin children's material was created under the supervision of an established painter, Friedl Dicker-Brandejsova, to whom the children went to for lessons. Altogether 4,000 drawings survived, along with excerpts from illegal magazines published by the children in the camp. The present building, a Romanesque structure, was built in 1906.

Maisel Synagogue (Maislova Synagogue) u. Maislova, Prague. Originally built in 1592, this is now a neo-Gothic, triple-nave building designed by architect Alfred Grotte and remodeled between 1893 and 1905. It is named after Marcus Mordechai Maisel (1528-1601), who commissioned a number of buildings in the sixteenth-century Prague ghetto, including the High Synagogue (Town Hall) on Cervena Street. However, this synagogue was almost completely destroyed by the fire of 1689. Within two years (1691), it was rebuilt in baroque style.

This synagogue remains one of the most spectacular buildings in the Prague ghetto. A permanent exposition of silver and other synagogue objects from the collections of the Jewish Museum draws thousands of tourists. Here one observes synagogue crowns, shields, spice boxes, *kiddush* cups, and 8,000 silver pieces. The exhibit here is one of the largest collections of silver artifacts in the Czech Republic, with the oldest silver objects dating from the late sixteenth century. The largest part of the collection consists of silver Torah ornaments. The visitor can view Sabbath lamps, pairs of silver candlesticks, and silver *kiddush* cups for benediction over wine. Most interesting, however, are silver spice boxes of various forms. They are used for the "Havdalah ceremony," which concludes the Sabbath.

Marcus Mordechai Maisel was a remarkable man. A Prague Financier, philanthropist, and head of the Jewish community, he was known as the "Maecenas of Science" and "the benefactor hero." A generous and fabulously rich merchant, his clients included the Imperial Court. He has been called the "First Jewish capitalist in Germany." Maisel helped Finance Rudolf II, who appointed him counselor during the Turkish wars. He had the streets of the ghetto paved. He bought a garden so that he could extend the area of the cemetery. He also built an infirmary and public baths. Above all, he organized the construction of the two synagogues—the High Synagogue and the Maisel Synagogue—upon which he lavished grand gifts and generous donations. Toward the end of his life in 1590, Maisel, who had so far been engaged in building public structures, bought a piece of land at the southern end of the ghetto on which to build a synagogue for his own use. In 1591, he obtained a special tax immunity privilege from Emperor Rudolf II to do so. A year later, during the holiday, Sirnchat Torah, the synagogue was dedicated. Architect Judah Tsoref Goldschmied de Herz designed the original building and Joseph Wald built it.

Historian David Gans, Maisel's contemporary, says in his chronicle that the building was unusually impressive. Supported by twenty pillars, its main, vast nave has been acclaimed by architects. Maisel and his wife donated a rich treasure of synagogal textiles, mantles, and curtains to the synagogue. This house of worship also served as the repository for a special banner that Maisel had made for himself on the basis of the privilege granted by Rudolf II in 1592 and kept in the Altneuschul.During the Renaissance period, the Maisel Synagogue was the largest and most impressive house of worship in the Jewish Town.

Spanish Synagogue (Spanelska synagoga), u. Dusni, and Vezenska ulice, Prague. The building exhibits the distinctive Moorish style that flourished in the 1880s. The exterior's design, which corresponds to the interior's Oriental decoration, gave the synagogue its name. Today, this synagogue, which is located opposite the presbytery of the Church of the Holy Spirit, is closed.

This Jewish house of worship is still called by some the "Old Schul," because it was built in the place of the original synagogue and was erected before the pogrom of 1389. The Portuguese rite had been followed there for many years. In 1868, the synagogue was demolished. The rebuilding was undertaken by Prague architect Vojtech Ignats Ullmann. The interior was designed by architect Joseph Nikias and is entirely Moorish.

The synagogue has a square, central ground plan and a large dome over the middle section. On three sides are balconies of metal construction that open into the main room. The interior was decorated between 1882 and 1893, according to a design by A. Baum and B. Munzberger. It includes a low stucco arabesque of stylized Islamic motifs that is richly gilded and polychromed in green, blue, and red. The same decorative elements are used in the carved decoration on the door around the organ, balcony railing, and wall lining with the ground floor. The windows were filled with painted glass in 1882-83.

During World War II, the Germans used the Spanish Synagogue as a warehouse. It was handed over to the State Jewish Museum after it had been partly restored.

In 1960, the first permanent exhibition of synagogal textiles was opened, and it ran until 1982.

The Old Jewish Cemetery, u. Stareho Hrbitova, Prague. Can you imagine a cemetery that some guidebooks call one of the ten most interesting sights in the world? U.S. President Bill Clinton visited the Old Jewish Cemetery on his visit to Prague in January 1994. And thousands of tourists come here each day.

Called a garden, it "evokes the spirit of the ghetto some feel and defies the passage of time." The Old Jewish Cemetery is one of Europe's oldest and best preserved Jewish burial grounds. About 500 years old, the cemetery contains between 12,000 and 20,000 gravestones. All are crowded into a very tight space and teeter at different angles. Slabs and tombstones date to the mid-fifteenth century. These tombstones are a chronicle of the Prague ghetto.

Actual burials took place here until 1787. The oldest-known tombstone—from 1439—is that of the Kabbalist and poet, Rabbi Avigdor Kara.

Because the tiny cemetery was not large enough to contain all the dead, it was necessary to gradually cover older graves with earth to provide a new burial layer. The result was that an uneven area appeared, and in some places it forms twelve burial layers. Parts of the tombstones from the older layers were raised to higher layers, which created the pile of tombstones that is typical of this cemetery.

All the tombstones carry Hebrew inscriptions giving the date of death and in some cases the name of the deceased and the date of burial. Poetic texts recall the merits of the individual and express the sadness of the relatives. On some stones you can see the biblical tribe, family name, and profession of the deceased. Hands outstretched in blessing represent a person from the priestly tribe of Aaron; a jug signifies the tribe of Levi; scissors are for tailors; a book identifies scribes; a violin is for musicians; and a tweezer marks a doctor.

The most significant tombstones are the large tombs confined by two oblique and two vertical stone slabs; most of these are in the central part of the cemetery opposite the main entrance.

The visitor really stands in awe here. Beneath the gravestones lie rabbis and scholars. Every human being is precious and significant. Yet we search for the tombs of the so-called mayor of the Prague Jewish Town, Mordechai Maisel, who died in 1661; the grave of Rabbi Loew; as well as the tomb of Hindel, the wife of Jacob Bashevi of Truenburg who died in 1628.

Rabbi Loew

One cannot really discuss the Old Jewish Cemetery and the Altneuschul, Prague Town Hall without commenting on the legendary, and some say miraculous, Rabbi Judah Loew ben Bezalel or the. In the cemetery you will see the gravestone of Rabbi Judah Loew ben Bezalel, creator of the golem. His tomb, located in the rear of the cemetery, resembles a sarcophagus. This famous rabbi is supposed to have invented an artificial man we have come to regard as the golem, considered by Elie Wiesel to be "the most fascinating creature in Jewish lore and fantasy." As the story goes, Rabbi Loew is said to have constructed a clay figure that he brought to life in the Altneuschul with the help of God.

Owing to his profound knowledge, including the Kabbala, he thus entered popular lore as the miracle worker who could secretly give life and breath to the golem, which became a robot figure serving the rabbi as a reward for his good works. "Without the Maharal and the golem, the Jewish community of Prague might not have survived," Elie Wiesel maintained.

The golem, constructed to represent a human being, was to be the Rabbi's servant and defend the Jews from their persecutors, notably ritual-murder accusers. But it ran amok. Finally, legend has it, the rabbi was forced to destroy his creation by removing the magic name from underneath its tongue. He left the body of the golem in the attic and forbade any access to the attic in the Altneuschul. To this day, no one is to go up to the attic.

Rabbi Loew, who was also known as Der Hohe Rabbi Loew because of his great height, was a rabbi, Talmudist, moralist, mathematician, and philosopher. And he was a philosopher of great originality. His profound wisdom and wide-ranging scholarship influenced not only Jewish religious philosophy, but also ethics and pedagogy. He was the spiritual head of the Jewish community from the end of the sixteenth century until the early seventeenth century.

He was known as the Maharal. Maharal is the Hebrew acronym for "most venerated teacher and rabbi." Some people call him a wondrous magician who vanquished the angel of death. Known throughout the Jewish world as one of the greatest Talmudic scholars, he was acclaimed as the celebrated "Wonder Rebbe of Prague."

Born circa 1525, Rabbi Loew resided in Prague from 1573 to 1584, then from 1588 to 1592, and then again in 1597, until his death in 1609. When he died, he was serving as a rabbi and head of the yeshiva in Prague.

We think he was named after the Kabbalist Reb Yehuda Loew, also of Prague. His tombstone states that he belonged to the royal line of David. We know he left Worms to study in Prague. He later married Pearl, the daughter of Rabbi Shmelke Reich, when he was thirty-two and she was twenty-eight. They had a daughter and one son.

He lived during the reign of Rudolf II, a time supposedly of the supernatural, which gave rise, obviously, to many of the legends surrounding him.

He is best known as the author of commentaries, essays on ethics, and mystically oriented writings. In his scholarly works he emphasized a logical progression from the simple biblical texts and post-biblical religious and legal writings called the Mishnah to the more difficult Talmud.

Rabbi Loew died at the age of ninety-seven, leaving behind a legacy of works covering every aspect of Jewish religious life and a legend that "consoles the hunted, the persecuted," according to the late Elie Wiesel.

Prague Town Hall. An impressive statue of Rabbi Loew adorns the entrance of the Prague Town Hall. It portrays a tall, severe figure with a high cylindrical hat and a long flowing beard fending off a naked woman who appears to be holding him. This statue was sculpted by Ladislav Saloun, a non-Jew who also designed Jan Hus's monument in the Old Town Square.

While working on the statue when the town hall was created in 1910, Saloun was inspired by a legend of Rabbi Loew's death: "Unable to approach the almost century-year-old scholar who was always absorbed in the study of holy books, death hid in a rose that was offered to the rabbi by his unsuspecting granddaughter."

After you walk through the cemetery, you can visit the Pinkas Synagogue, where a further treasure awaits you.

Pinkas Synagogue (Pinkasova Synagoga), u. Siroka, Prague. At the other end of the cemetery in the heart of the old Jewish quarter is the Pinkas Synagogue. It was originally set up on the site of a Jewish house of prayer that existed before 1492. At that time, the house belonged to the Horowitz family. A descendant of the family, Zalman Munka Horovic, also known as Aaron Meshullam, financed the construction of the synagogue. Built in 1535, it was modeled after a late-Gothic, partly Renaissance synagogue built in 1479. One of the oldest and most valuable houses of worship in Prague, it was founded by Rabbi Pinkas and enlarged in 1535 by his grandson, Aron Meshule. The construction contains rib vaulting on Renaissance supports. The women's section was added in 1625 by Judah Tsoref Goldschmied de Herz

Between 1954 and 1959, the interior of the Pinkas Synagogue was turned into the memorial for the 77,297 Bohemian and Moravian victims of the Holocaust, about 85 percent of the community. The names, and family names arranged according to communities, were inscribed on the walls of the main nave, balcony, and anteroom. Today when you enter the Pinkas Synagogue, you see craftsmen painstakingly inscribing the names of the 77,297 murdered Czech Jews. The engraved names had been inscribed previously, but the Communists allowed the Jewish names to fade away. The memorial to the victims of the Nazi persecution under the Communists, it was closed to the public for more than twenty years. The names have to be inscribed again so they can live in memory.

Although the location of a synagogue near a cemetery is quite unusual, the Pinkas Synagogue was built close to the Old Jewish Cemetery because there was not enough space in the ghetto.

A memorial to Franz Kafka, the great Czech Jewish writer of universal fame, is located at his native house, No. 5, u. Radnice, Old

Town of Prague. Kafka (1883-1924) attained worldwide respect and readership. He was born in the Old Town of Prague, in a house at that time located in Jachymova Street. This corner house next to the St. Nicholas Church was destroyed by a fire in 1897 and rebuilt in 1902. Only the portal of the old house was preserved. On July 3, 1966, a memorial tablet by academic sculptor Karel Hiadik was unveiled on the house standing at the corner of Kaprova, Maiselova, and Uradnice streets. A Kafka museum is located at this site of his birth.

Nearby is the Golz Kinsky Palace, a large, pink and white rococo structure that played an important role in Kafka's life. There, he attended school in the Palace and often visited his father's dry-goods store located on the ground floor. Kafka studied law at the German university and worked First in a law office and then for an insurance company. He wrote only in his spare time.

Because he was sensitive to noise, Kafka stayed and worked for some time in a small house on the Golden Lane in the area of the Prague Castle. The building was rented from its owner, Mrs. Michlova, by Kafka's youngest sister, Ottla. In the winter of 1916-17, Kafka wrote during the evenings and nights a number of shorter prose works and stories that he published in 1919.

In 2000, the area of the Old Town Square where the famous Jewish writer was born over a century ago, was renamed after Kafka, the author of such classics as The Trial, The Castle and Metamorphosis. It took a 37-year campaign for the naming to occur. Eduard Goldstuecker, 87, who led the drive, was a former Czech ambassador to Israel. In 1953, Goldstuecker began the campaign for the "best-known son Prague has today," he has said. He escaped death during the country's show trials of the 1950's. When released in Prague Spring, he fled to Britain. In 1992 he returned to Prague and began the campaign again.

Kafka did not live to bear the pain of the Holocaust. His works were suppressed by the Communists as "subjective and pessimistic." Now, of course, his writings are in great demand.

Kafka is buried in the New Olsany Cemetery alongside his parents. A stone marks their burial spot. A plaque also remembers his three sisters who died in the Holocaust. Located in Nad Vodovodem Street, this new Jewish cemetery includes prominent Jewish community leaders, such as the founder of the Jewish Museum, Dr. Salomon Hugo Lieben.

Hradcany Castle (Castle Hill) or Prague Castle—Look up to Prague Castle. Below the castle wall are hanging gardens and ancient roofs descending to the water's edge. Built by Bohemian kings, the castle was also the residence of Czech kings of old as well as of modern Czech leaders, such as Thomas Garrigue Masaryk and Eduard Benes.

The Jews who came to Prague probably lived around the marketplaces in what is now Hradcany, a popular tourist attraction and a must-see on any visit to the Czech capital. It is a labyrinth of castles, churches, and museums perched on one of the seven hills on which Prague is built. Head for the sprawling edifice that dominates the city, the Hradcany or Prague Castle. Everyone looks to the castle for leadership as a symbol of strength.

After the Jews settled near the castle, they ran up against difficulties from the community and invaders torched the oldest Prague synagogue as well as the Jewish quarter that was located just below the castle. As a result, the Jews moved to the right bank of the Vltava River, which became the Jewish quarter we know today.

One occupant of the castle, Thomas Garrigue Masaryk (1850-1937), a profound writer and thinker, was certainly a friend to the Jews and to men of goodwill everywhere. Without Masaryk, "there would have been no Czechoslovakia," according to Josef Korbel in *Twentieth Century Czechoslovakia: The Meanings of Its History.*

By 1918, Masaryk and Czech leaders had convinced the French, the British, and U.S. President Woodrow Wilson that the Austro-Hungarian monarchy must be dismembered and that an independent Czech-Slovak state be set up. A declaration proclaiming the new nation of Czechoslovakia was signed in 1918 by Czech and Slovak émigré politicians in Pittsburgh, Pennsylvania.

Throughout his life, Masaryk fought anti-Semitism. Emil Ludwig writes that Masaryk had "a life-long sympathy for the Jews. As a Czech, he himself knew what it meant to be a member" of a downtrodden people. After World War I, anti-Semitism existed in most parts of Eastern Europe; it was much less of a problem in Czech lands.

During the Hilsner affair—a blood libel case occurring at the turn of the century—Masaryrk wrote pamphlets declaring anti-Semitism an uncivilized and slanderous attitude. The Hilsner case involved trumped-up anti-Semitic charges against a young Czech Jew, Leopold Hilsner, who was arrested for the murder of a seamstress. Masaryk intervened; he did not have to do this. His pamphlets won the day and Hilsner's sentence was commuted to life imprisonment, and he was pardoned in 1916.

But Masaryk and Eduard Benes, who succeeded Masaryk, were not the only ones to occupy Prague Castle.

Even the hated Nazi invaders walked up the carpet-lined stairways of the castle. Hitler proclaimed from the castle that Czechoslovakia no longer existed. And it was the home of hard line Communist rulers who leaned hard on the people of this country for forty years. The popular playwright and intellectual, Vaclav Havel, a true dissident against the

Communist regime and now Czech president, comes to work here every day, although he does not live here. In February 1990, in one of his First acts as president of Czechoslovakia, Havel re-established full diplomatic relations with Israel, ties that had been broken in 1967. Havel became the first head of state in modern Eastern Europe to visit Jerusalem in 1990. The next year, he hosted the then-Israeli President, Chaim Herzog, in Prague. He called Communist rule "20 years of timelessness."

WENCESLAS SQUARE

Most visitors will tell you that the first place they visit in Prague is Wenceslas Square, an 800-yard-long avenue of shops and restaurants. This is a great place for a leisurely stroll. Not only does stately Wenceslas Square cleave the heart of Prague, not only is it the "Main Street" of this wonderful metropolis, but it is also the symbol of Czech freedom and of a people's desire for liberty.

The square is named after Prince Wenceslas, later the "Good King" of the Christmas carol who lived more than a thousand years ago. His equestrian statue looks down on the square that bears his name. They say that today flowers are placed at its base in memory of those who died or committed suicide in Prague Spring. The statue was a symbol of good during the Velvet Revolution. Here in the middle of the square, President Vaclav Havel addressed the Czech and Slovak people. Here is where the hated Nazi troops entered in 1939. Here in Prague Spring 1968, Czech students hurled rocks at the Soviet armored tanks that crept into Wenceslas Square. And here in 1989, thousands gathered to celebrate the end of communism in what the world knows as the Velvet Revolution.

The 1968 Prague Spring was a symbol of hope and opportunity. The people of Czechoslovakia wanted to ease the toughness of Communist rule. But on the night of August 20-21, 1968, troops of the Warsaw Pact invaded Czechoslovakia. Soviet airborne forces, including tank and artillery units, were landed in Prague and Bratislava. The invasion, said the Soviets, was a domestic affair. But the world did not buy it and was outraged. Telephone lines were cut and soldiers armed with machine guns took over Hradcany Castle. The invasion even then was a testimony to the failure of Marxism-Leninism.

But the Czechs fought back in their own way. They painted swastikas on the Russian tanks. They spat at the Russians. They turned street signs in the wrong direction to confuse the Soviets. They practiced passive resistance. Indeed, the tanks in 1968 were wholly inadequate weapons because in Czechoslovakia, they fired at "ideas with no hope of hitting the target."

The late Alexander Dubcek and other Prague Spring leaders were taken to Moscow, where behind closed doors in the Kremlin, Leonid Brezhnev forced Dubcek's government to surrender to undemocratic experiments. Among the Czechs was Frantisek Kriegel. A dedicated reformer, Kriegel, who had been called "that Galician Jew" by one of the Soviet leaders, was an abstainer to the Communist proposal to stop the reforms. The Russians kept him hidden and claimed that he was sick. The Czechs who were at the airport ready to depart for Prague said they would not leave until the Russians produced Kriegel. The Russians, who had every intention of keeping him, finally freed him and he took off with the delegation, according to Patrick Brogan in his book *The Captive Nations: Eastern Europe, 1945-90.*

But Prague still remained the "city of Kafka and Soviet tanks." Wenceslas Square had the submerged, slow motion quality of a nightmare. As Havel is said to have remarked, "The clocks had stopped." In the 1980s, however, Czechs kept alive the desire for freedom. At this time, 12,000 Jews remained in Czechoslovakia. Their average age was 60; it would stay that way for several decades, for there were only about 1,000 young people between the ages of 15 and 20. Some of these young Jewish persons would be among those who brought about the Velvet Revolution in 1989. In those 21 autumn days, without a drop of blood spilled, the people of Czechoslovakia broke the power of their Communist rulers. "It was a glorious, gentle revolution."

TEREZIN (THERESIENSTADT)

It is not easy to get to Terezin, forty minutes northwest of Prague. And yet they come day after day after day. On the bleak, rainy day I was there, I saw members of a teenage Canadian hockey team, a Danish college student, and an American university professor—all who spent one hour by bus to reach this city in Bohemia, this death station of the Nazis. Horrible things happened here in Terezin, especially to children.

To get there, you travel north from Prague. The fields at first are flat and neatly plowed. Farmland and sweeping highways spotlight a rich farm area that turns hilly as you approach the town of Terezin. The scenery actually gives little idea of the gruesome fortress town of Terezin, the star-shaped garrison town named for the Austria Empress Maria Theresa, who perhaps was a harbinger of the horrible inflictions hurled at the Jewish people there. In German, the town is called Theresienstadt. In the late 1700s, Terezin was a bulwark against the Prussians, who often would barrel their way down from the north.

The name will probably send shudders down the spines of men and women of goodwill everywhere for hundreds of years to come, those who know the story of Terezin and the Holocaust.

About 277,000 Jews who had resided within the pre-Munich boundaries of Czechoslovakia lost their lives in the Holocaust. Approximately 25,000 escaped from Bohemia and Moravia before the war broke out, which left a Jewish population of about 90,000 in those two provinces. Only 10,000 of these Jews would survive.

In 1938, about 135,000 Jews resided in Slovakia, of whom 40,000 lived in the territory ceded to Hungary (Ruthenia and Sub-Carpathia). About 5,000 Jews emigrated voluntarily before the war, leaving about 90,000 Jews in Slovakia itself. According to Lucy S. Dawidowicz in *The War Against the Jews: 1933-1945*, a total of 110,000 Slovak Jews were murdered.

In 1941, the Nazis occupied this walled municipality; they emptied out its inhabitants and turned a citadel into a transit camp for Jews on their way to the death camps.

A sign above the entrance of the small Fortress at Terezin declares Arbeit Macht Frei, "Work Makes You Free." That is the actual translation, but its real meaning was death. (Photo by Riva Frank)

It was as if a whole town had been cleared to become a ghost town as well as a transport center to transfer Jews to the gas chambers in Poland and beyond. Today, it still maintains a drab look, especially in the fall or winter.

Officially, Terezin was a self-governing ghetto. But in reality, it was a concentration camp, probably without the gas chambers, although bodies of people who had died of typhus there were sent to the crematorium nearby, which the visitor can still see today. About 150,000 men, women, and children passed through this ghetto for Jewish prisoners between 1941 and 1945. At least 117,000 were tortured to death and murdered elsewhere. Of 15,000 children under the age of 15 who passed through the camp, fewer than 100 survived.

Nazis Reinhard Heydrich and Adolf Eichmann met on October 4, 1941. The Germans decided on the establishment of the Theresienstadt Ghetto on October 10, 1941, in a secret meeting at the Prague Castle chaired by Reich Protector Heydrich. The Nazis planned that from Terezin (in German, Theresienstadt), the Jews were to be deported to the East. Adolf Eichmann's plan was to evacuate the Jews from Terezin and transfer them to the concentration camps in Poland and beyond and then turn the whole area into a model German settlement. But Terezin took on an atmosphere that was worse than an "animal-like holding pen." At one point, nearly 60,000 persons lived in barracks designed to house 7,000 combat troops.

As a young child, the Czech author and one of the best-known Czech writers in the West, Ivan Klima, was packed off to Terezin. He writes about seeing the constant presence of death. "People died in the room where I lived. They died by the dozens," he wrote, adding, "the constant threat of the transports hung over the inhabitants."

Terezin also served as a "showplace," a facade for the International Red Cross monitors. The Nazis spruced up the camp to make the inspectors believe the Jews were being treated well. It was trickery par excellence—even in the midst of fake cultural activities, such as an orchestra concert given by the prisoners, transports from Terezin were continuously leaving for Auschwitz and Birkenau camps.

Several hundred Danish Jews were sent to Terezin because not all the Jews of Denmark escaped to Sweden. But the Danish government never gave up on their Jewish citizens and representatives from Denmark did visit the camp. And the government in Copenhagen sent food supplies to the Jewish Terezin. On April 14, 1945, the Danish prisoners left Terezin in Swedish Red Cross buses that were bound for freedom.

Above all, it is clear from all that the visitor sees, that the Terezin inmates fought back with art and music.

The Small Fortress at Terezi

A sign above the entrance of the Small Fortress declares: *Arbeit Macht Frei*. *"Work Makes You Free,"* is the literal translation, but its real meaning was death. We know that now; the six million did not.

The first stop at Terezin might be the Small Fortress on the outskirts of town. This fort was built as part of the fortification system near the confluence of the Elbe and Ohre rivers. From the beginning, it was used as a prison. Jailed here, for example, were many nationalist leaders who wanted to overthrow Austrian rule. The 1914 assassins of Franz Ferdinand d'Este—archduke of Austria—were imprisoned here.

When Bohemia and Moravia were occupied by the Nazis in 1940, the Small Fortress became the prison of the Prague Gestapo. The first prisoners were brought there on June 14, 1940, and some 32,000 inmates, including 5,000 women, passed through the fortress during the war. The life of imprisoned Jews in this fortress was especially difficult, because it was a way station to Nazi trials, jails, prisons, and the concentration camps.

At the end of the war a typhoid epidemic killed many prisoners. On May 8, 1945, the first Soviet armored vehicles arrived in Terezin.

Between 1945 and 1948, the Small Fortress served as a detention camp for the Germans expelled from Czechoslovakia. During your visit, you will see the guards' office; the prison commander's office; the courtyards; the prison block cells, as well as 20 solitary confinement cells; the hospital block; the mortuary; places of execution; the SS barracks; and the national cemetery.

A documentary film is shown and there are special exhibits. It is also possible to purchase brochures, literature, and videotapes.

The Ghetto Museum at Terezin

After you visit the Small Fortress, turn right on the main road into the town of Terezin and you will come to the Ghetto Museum. On the front door are the Hebrew letters forming the word, Yizkor, "Remember." The museum was opened on October 17, 1991, fifty years after the beginning of the deportation of Jews from Czech lands.

Only after the 1989 Velvet Revolution could the building be handed over to serve as a memorial. Before the war, the museum building housed a school. During the ghetto period, it became, "L-417," and served as a home for boys 10 to 15 years old. Ironically, a "museum of Czechoslovakian police and revolutionary traditions of the Northern Bohemian region," was later set up in this former home of Jewish prisoners.

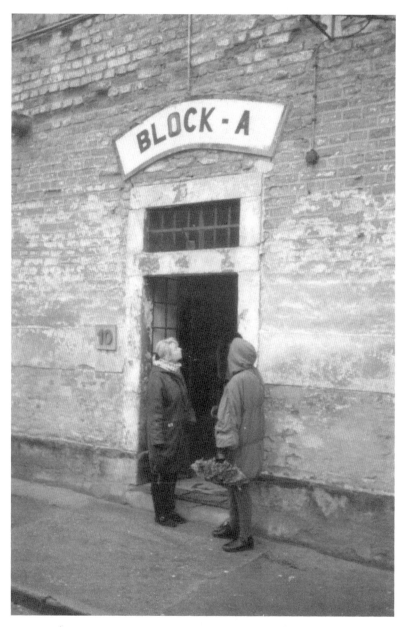

A cell block at the Small Fortress at Terezin. (Photo by Ben G. Frank)

The exhibits are in good taste, well done, and include photographs, videotapes, and newspaper clippings of other materials in several languages. The exhibition is organized chronologically and begins with the Nazi take-over in Germany and ends with the liberation of Terezin.

In the Ghetto Museum, besides a tour of the permanent exhibition, there is an art gallery where you can see works of art created at the Terezin Ghetto. Guides are available.

Operating hours of the Small Fortress and Ghetto Museum, open throughout the year: Winter: October 1 to March 31, 8:00 a.m. to 4:30 p.m. Spring: April 1 to April 30, 8:00 a.m. to 5:30 p.m. Summer: May 1 to September 30, 8:00 a.m. to 6:30 p.m. The museum is closed December 24 to 26 and January 1.

The Crematorium at Terezin

While the Communists controlled the country, local Terezin residents and guides often would not even tell you about the crematorium. While there were no gas chambers at Terezin, Jews and others were shot, tortured, or died from starvation or disease. The dead were disposed of in the crematorium, an old laundry building that usually is the third stop of a visit to Terezin. One can see the ovens.

A large Jewish cemetery is located near the crematorium. The site was visited by former Israeli President Chaim Herzog, who was on a state visit in 1991. Between November 1 and February 28, the crematorium is accessible only with an official guide from the Ghetto Museum; otherwise, it is open every day, except Sunday, from 10:00 a.m. to 5:00 p.m.

Many travel agencies have tours to Terezin. The Federation of Jewish Communities, at 18 Maislova, 110 01, Prague 1, Tel:420-224-800-824. FAX: 420-224-810-912. sekretariat@fzo.cz. www.fzo.cz, can advise you and is a good source for all of your questions.

Suggested Reading

Ash, Timothy G. *The Magic Lantern: The Revolution of '89 Witnessed in Warsaw, Budapest, Berlin & Prague.* New York: Random House, 1990.
————. *The Uses of Adversity: Essays on the Fate of Central Europe.* New York: Random House, 1989.
Brogan, Patrick. *The Captive Nations: Eastern Europe, 1945-1990.* New York: Avon, 1990.
Dawidowicz, Lucy S. *The War Against the Jews: 1933-1945.* New York: Bantam, 1986.

Hoffman, Charles. *Gray Dawn: The Jews of Eastern Europe in the Post-Communist Era.* New York: HarperCollins, 1992.

Hoffman, Eva. *Exit into History: A Journey Through the New Eastern Europe.* New York: Viking, 1993.

Korbel, Josef. Twentieth Century Czechoslovakia: The Meanings of Its History. New York: Columbia University Press, 1977.

Krinsky, Carol Herselle. *Synagogues of Europe: Architecture, History, Meaning.* Cambridge, Mass.: MIT Press, 1985.

Kurlansky, Mark. *A Chosen Few: The Resurrection of European Jewry.* Reading, Mass.: Addison-Wesley, 1995.

Lendvai, Paul. *Anti-Semitism Without Jews: Communist Eastern Europe.* Garden City, NY: Doubleday, 1971.

Meyer, Peter, Bernard D. Weinryb, Eugene Duschinsky, and Nicolas Sylvain, eds. *The Jews in the Soviet Satellites.* Syracuse, New York: Syracuse University Press, 1953.

Moorhouse, Geoffrey, and the editors of Time-Life Books. *Prague.* Amsterdam: Time-Life Books, 1980.

Vital, David. *A People Apart, The Jews in Europe, 1789-1939.* Oxford: Oxford University Press, 1999.

Wechsberg, Joseph. *Prague: The Mystical City.* New York: Macmillan, 1971.

Weinberg, Gerhard L. *A World at Arms: A Global History A of World War II.* New York: Cambridge University Press, 1994.

Weisel, Elie, ed. *The Golem: The Story of a Legend.* New York: Summit Books, 1983.

Wischnitzer, Rachel. *The Architecture of the European Synagogue.* Philadelphia: Jewish Publication Society of America, 1964.

Yahil, Leni. *The Holocaust: The Fate of European Jewry, 1932-1945.* Oxford: Oxford University Press, 1990.

Hungary

The Largest Jewish Community in Eastern Europe—Welcome to the Land of the Magyars

This is Hungary: the sixteenth largest country in Europe, roughly the size of the state of Indiana. We now call this nation, the "Republic of Hungary." But from 1949 to 1989, it was known as the Hungarian People's Republic and it was Communist.

But that was nearly three decades ago. Today Hungary is a member of NATO and the European Union.

This unique country—peopled by descendants of the Magyars—a race from Central Asia who settled here in the ninth century—has a varied landscape, with forests and mountains in the north, and a vast plain covering the rest of the country.

Looking at the map, however, one can see that the area lies in an exposed crossroad of Europe. It is easy to understand why this country has expanded and contracted over the centuries. Or as common wisdom suggests, it is not Hungary that causes the problem, it is its neighbors: Austria to the west, Slovenia, Croatia and Serbia to the south and southwest; Slovakia to the north; the Ukraine to the northeast; and Romania, including Transylvania, to the east. A number of those neighbors wanted and still desire to control the Danube, which runs right through Budapest.

Although not located in the Balkans, Hungary has historic ties to the area. As we shall see the Hungarian Kingdom at its height in the 15th century stretched from Croatia to Transylvania. Ottoman and Austrian conquests in the 16th century included most of Hungary.

Created in 1867, the Austro-Hungarian Empire lost World War I, which it and Germany initiated. In 1920, the Treaty of Trianon sliced nearly two thirds of the land off the Kingdom of Hungary and bisected out of the country 58.5 percent of its population. After being carved up, Hungary tried to regain lost lands and repeatedly failed. Encompassing 35,919 square miles, Hungary contains under 10 million people, including Gypsies, Jews, a few hundred Slovaks, Schwabians (German) and Romanians. About 75 percent of the country is Catholic, 22 percent Protestant.

The word "Hungarian" comes from the Turkik on-ogur, or ten arrows, which may refer to the region's early Magyar tribes.

The Hungarian people are known as Magyars and they make up most of the population. The language of 98.5 percent of the people is Hungarian, a language belonging to the Finno-Ugric linguistic group of the Ugric family. Among the Magyar languages of Europe, it is related to Finnish and Estonian.

A most difficult language, the Magyar language is an orphan European tongue, belonging to neither Latin, nor German, nor Slavic languages.

Be that as it may, wherever there are large communities of Hungarians in the U.S., the language is preserved and spoken. Hungarians have a love affair with their language.

Where did this language and people originate?

In 896, the Magyars, a tough, pagan, Mongol tribe from Central Russia, swept into the area we know as Hungary. This pagan band fought across the steppes from the Ural Mountains to the Carpathians. Once settled in the Great Hungarian Plains, they abandoned their nomadic life and organized themselves into a state. They stubbornly held their land against invaders from all sides.

The Magyar clan chiefs had chosen a chieftain named Arpad to lead them in their migration. Under his leadership, the Magyars went on to ravage Central Europe until they were defeated by Otto I in 955. Arpad's grandson, Geza, accepted Christianity and his son Stephen I was crowned Hungary's first King, on Christmas Day, in the year 1000. December 2000 marked the 1000th anniversary of the crowning of King Stephan I. The Danube River basin offers invaders a hallway to Europe. In 1241, the Mongols, moving through the basin, invaded Hungary. After pillaging half the population, they withdrew. The native Arpad dynasty died out in 1301. From that date until 1918, Hungary was ruled almost continuously by foreign powers.

In 1456, the Hungarian army defeated the Turks at Nandorfehervar now located in the area around Belgrade. John Hunyadi was the commander of the Hungarians. It was here that the Hungarians stopped the advance of the Ottomans for about 70 years. In 1526, the Turks attacked once more and the Turks were victorious at the Battle of Mohacs. The Turks ruled for 150 years. But in 1686, the Turks were defeated at Buda. Actually the battle was over by noon time and Pope III Calixtus ordered that all the bells should be rung at 12 o'clock noon in all Christian churches throughout Europe. Even today, in many places church bells are rung at noon.

Without fail, the Hungarian people placed their faith in the losers of every war since the 15th century, including World War II. And after that bloodbath, Joseph Stalin made sure the U.S.S.R. dominated Hungary.

All of this history tells us a great deal about the nation we shall be visiting.

In this country, Hungary, especially in the western marshes of what once was the great Pale of Jewish Settlement lived the majority of Hungarian Jews. We should say they may have existed in abject poverty, but they wrote into their history the highlights and tragedies of a wonderful Jewish community, today the second largest Jewish community on the continent, not counting Russia and the Ukraine. Hungary would become the only country in Eastern Europe in which Jews eventually achieved a modicum of security and social integration, according to historian Bernard Wasserstein. Commenting on his travels between the wars, travel writer Patrick Lehigh Fermor wrote that "in spite of endemic anti-Jewish feeling in Hungary, Jews had managed to play a considerable part in the country's life—it had been better for them there than in Russia or Rumania."

Nevertheless, here, alongside advancement was the always pervasive anti-Semitism, "endemic and occasionally violent." Pogroms were common. The pressure on the Jews of Hungary mounted and a large number of Hungarian Jews, like other Eastern Europeans, migrated to the United States at the end of the nineteenth and beginning of the twentieth centuries.

It is the history of the Jewish community in Hungary that tells us not only about Hungarian Jews but also about Hungary itself. For imbedded in Hungarian history is the fact that Jews lived in the country long before the Magyars arrived in the area.

A Brief History

Jewish historical tradition mentions Jews in Hungary from the second half of the eleventh century. From that time, the pace of Jewish immigration quickly picked up, with Jews arriving from Germany, Bohemia and Moravia. By the twelfth century, Jews had settled in Bratislava which was then ruled by Hungary.

Jews settled in Buda after the Mongol invasion in the 1250s; they had been granted that privilege by King Bela IV in 1251. This sovereign also gave Jews the "right" to maintain synagogues and he guaranteed them legal status. Jews assisted the King in managing the system and lent him money.

Jews, therefore, came to occupy important positions in the economic field, so much so that the nobles, feeling threatened, sought to curb Jewish advancement. Thus, the Golden Bull of 1222 included prohibitions directed at Jews.

In the reign of Anjou Louis the Great (1342-82) Jews were expected to convert to Christianity. When they refused, they were expelled—but as it usually turned out, not for long. The Magyars were followed by the Ottoman Turks who conquered Buda and defeated the Hungarians in 1526 at the Battle of Mohacs. The Hungarian defeat paved the way for the country's occupation by the Turks. The Jews enjoyed religious tolerance. When the Turks stabilized relations, many Jews returned to Buda. We should never forget, Hungarian Jews say, that the Turks gave absolute religious freedom to the Jews. At least two synagogues existed in Buda at this time.

In the 1600s, Buda would become one of the most important communities of the Ottoman Empire before the Ottomans were chased out of all of Hungary. The Austrians drove the Turks out of Hungary in 1686. The Turks had been defeated in Buda Castle and the victorious Christian army charged the Jews with cooperating with the Turks. Hundreds of Jews were killed in the ensuing slaughter. Others were sold into slavery. After Buda had been captured, the surviving Jews left Buda for Old Buda.

Although the Hapsburgs ruled autocratically, it was Emperor Joseph II, the son of Maria Teresa, who eased the lot of the Jews with his *Toleranzpatent* of 1782 ("patents of toleration"). By the mid-1850s, the Jews, often protected by owners of large estates and local administrators, made considerable advances in business and the professions. They enhanced their adoptive Magyar culture.

In the 1848 revolution, the Hapsburg ruler called on the Russians to help quell a rebellion. Because the revolution was in full swing, Jews were granted equal rights along with other religious denominations in Hungary. But it did not matter. The victorious Austrian government did not permit Jewish emancipation, until 1868, that is.

The Emperor Franz Joseph ruled for two decades before he changed the character of the relationship between the two countries. In the second half of the nineteenth century, Hungarian leaders realized that to build a liberal Hungarian nation under Magyar leadership they had to eliminate all religious discrimination, including that against the Jews. First, the Compromise of 1867 had created the Dual Monarchy. Under that act, the Hungarian Government would take control of its own domestic affairs while the Austrians managed foreign affairs, the military and financial matters.

The Emancipation Act of 1868 granted the Jews equality before the law. No longer were they excluded from owning property or holding public office. Some barriers still kept them out of politics and public life, but they certainly would play a large part in creating the Hungarian economy. The anti-Semitic mayor of fin de siècle Vienna, Karl Leuger, even referred to Budapest as "Judapest," suggesting that Jews dominated the city.

Because the Magyars ruled and dominated society, "considerable advantages were to be gained if one acknowledged one's Hungarianess, including the ability to speak Hungarian," writes Jorg Hoensch in his book, *A History of Modern Hungary*, 1867-1986. By 1889, 700,000 Jews who already had obtained equal rights considered themselves Hungarian.

A century later, the Jewish population numbered 932,000, representing 7.2 percent of the population. Jews made up 23 percent of Budapest's citizens, and 75 percent spoke Hungarian, their first language. Jews accounted for 54 percent of commercial business owners; they comprised 85 percent of financial institution directors and owners and 62 percent of commercial employers.

As a capitalist economy grew, so did the Jewish population in Budapest. In the half-century before World War I, Jews prospered and made significant achievements in science and in the arts. Pest itself became a center of Jewish life. The period 1867-1918 was indeed Hungarian Jewry's "Golden Age."

Large numbers of Jews entered the professions: Before World War 1, 45.3 percent of all lawyers were Jewish and 78.9 of all physicians. Jews also played prime roles in government. Between 1867 and 1918, 17 Jews were members of the Upper Chamber of the Imperial Diet, 103 Jewish deputies were in the Lower Chamber.

The Jewish economic role in Hungary was disproportionately large, represented by industrialists, bankers, and tradespersons. Jews were needed to fill a gap. Hungary was being industrialized and trade and banking flourished. The Jews helped build up Hungary's banking and industry. Jews started concerns in sugar refining, flower milling, textiles, and metallurgy, according to William McCagg in *"Jewish Nobles and Geniuses in Modern Hungary."* "Still, most of Hungary's Jews would spend their lives tediously eking out pennies to survive," adds McCagg.

More than anywhere else in Central and Eastern Europe, Hungarian Jews were not only fully assimilated, they were "the only middle class between a large landowning aristocracy and an impoverished gentry on the one hand, and millions of landless peasants on the other," writes Paul Lendvai in *Anti-Semitism Without Jews: Communist Eastern Europe.*

On June 28, 1914, a Bosnian Serb assassinated the heir to the Austrian throne. Archduke Franz Ferdinand. The world shook; the course of history changed. Within days, Austria and Hungary presented

Serbia with an ultimatum that made war inevitable. For Hungary, the war was a tragedy: about 2.5 million Hungarian soldiers became casualties. The end was near. The Hapsburg Empire collapsed.

Austria-Hungary signed an armistice with the Allies on November 3, 1918, and a few weeks later was declared a republic. The new state of Czechoslovakia also raised its flag.

In the truncated state, Hungarian Jews would suffer. All the problems of Hungary after the Great War, including an unstable economy, and the Communist dictatorship of Bela Kun, who was Jewish, were vented on the Jews. A quota system, *numerous clausus*, was introduced in Hungarian colleges and universities that limited Jews to five percent of the student body. Beyond the student population, many middle-class, assimilated Jews were targeted. Hungarian Jews would "become the victim of rampant anti-Semitism and terroristic outrages," writes Paul Lendvai. Hungarian Jews would face a worldwide depression, dictatorship, the Nazis, the Holocaust, and communism. But Communism collapsed in 1989 and a new Hungary arose. For several decades now Hungary has grappled with democracy. While it has maintained a democratic government, with a parliament mostly containing center and right-wing parties, in recent years, Hungary seems to be embracing a right-wing philosophy emanating from a very conservative government.

Notable Hungarian Jews

Hungary owes much to its Jewish scientists, musicians, writers, artists, and journalists, who have been vital to the country's intellectual and cultural development. While the list of contributors is endless, let us name some of the luminaries.

In the area of science, there are Leo Szilard and Edward Teller, who helped father the atom and hydrogen bombs. Theodore von Karman, John von Neumann, Jeno Polya, a world-famous surgeon whose surgical methods are used to this day; Georg de Hevesy, and Jeno Wigner were major figures in the history of modern mathematics, chemistry, and physics—and all were sons of Jewish nobles. Dennis Gabor, 1971, Nobel Prize for Physics (Holography); George Olah, 1994 Nobel Prize for Chemistry and John C. Harsanyi, 1994 Prize for Economics.

The most surprising aspect of this galaxy of Hungarian "geniuses" is that many were related to each other and even attended the same schools.

The noted sociologists, Karl Mannheim and Oszkar Jaszi, and Sandor Ferenczi and Franz Alexander were at the forefront of psychology. Georg Lukacs was a well-known contributor to philosophical studies.

Theodor Herzl and Max Nordau were the early leaders of modern Zionism. Herzl, the founder of modern Zionism, was born May 2, 1860, in Budapest in a house that stood on the site now occupied by the Jewish Museum on Dohany Street. His bar mitzvah was in the Liberal Synagogue in Tabakgasse and he went to school in Pest. In 1878, after the death of his only sister, Pauline, who was one year older, the family moved to Vienna. As a journalist, he watched anti-Semitic outbursts in the streets of Paris during the sentencing of Capt. Alfred Dreyfus on trumped-up charges of espionage. Moved and shocked by this miscarriage of justice, Herzl wrote *The Jewish State*. And in 1897, he organized the first World Zionist Congress, which met in Basel, Switzerland. To Jews throughout the world, he is considered the father of Zionism and founder of the World Zionist Organization. Arthur Koestler, a well-known author, was the son of an unsuccessful Jewish business person. He left Budapest in the early 1920s and lived in Vienna, Palestine, Berlin, Moscow, Paris, and London. More influenced by Weimar Germany and certain German thinkers, Koestler did not write in Hungarian or identify with Hungarian causes.

Bela Kun, part-lawyer and part-journalist, seized control of the Hungarian government; and on March 21, 1919, he established a Hungarian Soviet Republic. A number of intellectuals, including many Jews, marched under his banner. His dictatorship collapsed on August 1, 1919. After the failure of a Hungarian Army counteroffensive in a battle with Romania, Bela Kun fled first to Vienna and then to Soviet Russia. He was ultimately executed by Stalin.

Budapest

Budapest is not only considered by many to be the most beautiful city in Eastern Europe, but also a well-situated portal to Western Europe. Except for Paris, Budapest stands as one of the majestic capitals in Europe; more so this writer believes, than Prague and Vienna.

Most of the historic Budapest sights lie along the banks of the Danube, including the Neo-classical Parliament, the Neo-Gothic Matyas Church and the Hungarian National Museum. Tourists should not miss the Royal Palace and the Hungarian National Gallery. Gaze at the imposing façade of the State Opera House. If the opportunity presents itself, take advantage of the fact that Hungary, and of course Budapest, is one of Europe's great spa destinations. Frequent one of the city's outdoor pools.

Climb the steps of Buda. Sit on a wall and gaze down at the bridges described by Patrick Lehigh Fermor as being "looped across the Danube in sparkling necklaces." After this gaze, it is well to look at this city's past. Buda and Pest and the densely populated Jewish Old-Buda were once three separate cities joined together to become Budapest in 1873, even at that time, one of the world's most beautiful urban centers. Budapest's growth was phenomenal and was surpassed in Europe only by Berlin. The growth rate was two-and-a-half times that of London in the first 90 years of the last century. In 1841, the population was 107,240. By 1939, it had risen to 1,115,877.

Today, 1.7 million persons live in the capital, a capital which is in decline as far as population goes. Emil Lengyel says Budapest lies in the heart of Hungary but belongs to a different world—"a world of rich culture on the threshold of Asia." **Budapest** is often called "the meeting place of Europe and the Balkans," with incidentally three English newspapers and an English radio station in a multicultural atmosphere.

Budapest still remains "Europe's most seductive capital," according to many of its visitors. The setting of Budapest is exceptionally beautiful and it costs no money to climb the hills on a Sunday afternoon and gaze out over the city spread out on the banks of the Danube. Anyone who has lived in a city alongside a river, such as Pittsburgh, Pennsylvania, knows the feeling when seeing the city below from on high. Actually, in Budapest, the Danube runs swifter than it does in Vienna. But it is not blue. As one Hungarian guide told me, the "blue" in Johann Strauss's "Blue Danube" was a figment of his wonderful imagination.

Although 850 miles from the Black Sea, Budapest enjoys the status of a harbor, thanks to the Danube; and without the Danube, Hungary could not have existed, writes Emil Lengyel. Budapest is the only large city that the majestic Danube flows through the middle of; in fact, the river evenly divides the city. It is, John Lukacs writes in *Budapest, Nineteen Hundred: A Historical Portrait of a City and Its Culture,* "as if the Danube has been invented for the esthetic purposes of the city." And if you go to an observation post high up on the Buda side, you realize Lukacs is correct.

Moreover, it is clear that in the minds of the "ruling elite" all roads lead to Budapest. "When Budapest sneezes, Hungary catches cold," it is said.

Buda was named after Buda, brother of Attila the Hun, according to *World Book Encyclopedia.* "Pest is derived from a Slavic word meaning oven, the name was given to the town probably on account of its great lime kilns," says World Book.

Most visitors are confused as to which side is Buda and which side is

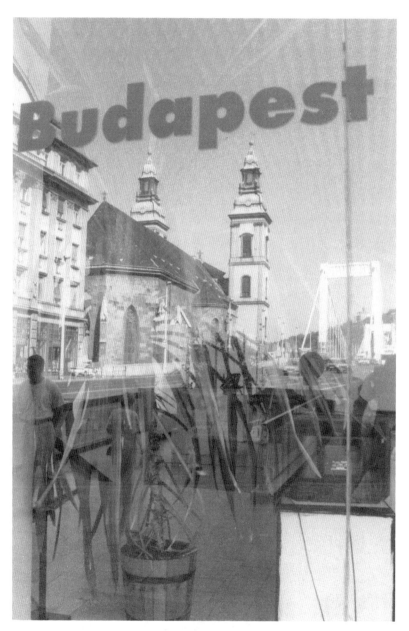

Street scene in Budapest. (Photo by Scott Michaels)

Pest. But it is really very simple. Buda rides the hills and slopes of the west bank, "garnished by gardens, crowned by castles, church spires and forts." Buda is characterized by medieval cobblestone streets and neo-Gothic buildings.

Pest, on the other hand, lies wide and flat, a tabular city, neat as a ledger, with wide massive streets, boulevards, and buildings. Crowded with shops and government buildings, Pest is the "busy corner" of Hungary.

But it does not really matter on which side of the city you stand. "Nature made Budapest one of the leading cities of the Danube," writes Emil Lengyel in *The Danube*. Budapest has become a city of museums and its architecture possesses a definite Austrian influence. One observes the embracing scene of the Buda Castle complex of buildings together with the Chain Bridge, both built in neoclassic style. Indeed, Hungarians are so proud of the Chain Bridge that to this day, they say it is a significant symbol of the beauty of Budapest. The bridge was blown up by the retreating Nazis on January 18, 1945, the same day the Budapest Ghetto was liberated by the Red Army.

Fitting in alongside the vistas are wonderful evenings at theater festivals, the opera, or ballet, and, of course, fashion and food-always part of this lovely East European metropolis.

Old and new blend well here. Visit the domed Royal Palace. It positions itself as an outstanding museum of art, sculpture, and history and it dominates Castle Hill. Today, the Royal Palace is a cultural center, including the National Szechenyi Library and the Hungarian National Gallery. And everywhere the views are magnificent.

Transportation here is good and remember, that while London was the first city to build an underground train system, Budapest boasts the oldest subway system on the European continent.

Indeed, we must mention Imre Steinde Parliament Building completed in 1902. This is the largest parliament building in the entire world. Its architecture combines Magyar medieval, French Renaissance, Westminsterian, and Gothic styles, with a neo-baroque ground plan and an interior filled with polychrome. Eighty-four pounds of 22-carat gold were used in its decoration, according to John Lukacs.

Throughout their history, each of the towns of Buda, Pest, and Obuda maintained active Jewish communities.

The **Buda-Pest Tunnel,** according to the *Encyclopaedia Judaica,* marks the area where a Jewish community was established by the end of the eleventh century. A cemetery was located near the Buda end of what is now the Pest-Buda Tunnel. We know that Jews moved here in 1250 after the Mongol invasion. In 1348 and 1360 the Jews were expelled from Buda, but they returned after a short interval.

From 1364, the Jewish quarter was located in Buda on the north and southwest side of what is today Tancsics Mihaly Street. This is where Jews lived until the Turks left Hungary in 1686. Here, they built two synagogues. The site of **Medieval Synagogue,** part of the historical section along Tancsics Mihaly Street, is located at Tancsics Mihaly 26. Open May to October, from 10:00 a.m. to 2:00 p.m., Tuesday to Friday and until 6:00 p.m. on weekends.

Whether they lived in the then-separate cities of Pest, Buda, or Old Buda, Jews built community institutions. Actually, Jews are first mentioned as being in Pest in 1406. Often these Jews welcomed merchants who between the thirteenth and fifteenth centuries brought various goods to Hungary from the Rhine district. At this time too, Polish and Lithuanian Jews participated in trade relations with Hungary and Bohemia-Moravia, according to *A History of the Jewish People,* edited by Haim H. Ben-Sasson. By 1504, Jews could own houses. In 1547 there were 75 Jewish residents in Buda and 25 newcomers. After the Austrian conquest in 1686, Jewish residence in the city was prohibited. As for Obuda, it possessed a Jewish community in the fifteenth century. An old synagogue here was demolished in 1817. An imposing new one, still in existence, was consecrated in 1820. By the mid-nineteenth century, nearly 1,500 Jewish families resided in Pest. In the 1848 revolution, a revolution that swept over much of Europe, many Jewish youths enlisted in Hungary's revolutionary cause.

The Pest Jews contributed much to the 1848 revolution, which turned into a war against Austrian oppression. But the fight for Hungarian freedom was quickly and firmly suppressed by Austria. Emancipation for Jews went out the window. After Austria granted joint rule with Hungary in 1867, the Jewish community of Hungary was emancipated in 1868. Hungarian Jewish families helped transform Budapest from a provincial bourgeois town into a large and cosmopolitan capital.

In 1869, there were 44,890 Jews living in Budapest; in 1890, 102,000; in 1920, 215,512; and by 1930, 204,371. In Hungary, as in other nations, Jews in ever-increasing numbers moved to larger towns and capital cities. After World War I, about 46 percent of all Hungarian Jews lived in Budapest, according to *A History of the Jewish People.*

JEWISH COMMUNITY

Much evidence exists that there is a revival of Jewish life in Hungary. In recent years, for instance, there was not enough matzah baked in the Budapest community's baker in what used to be an Orthodox Jewish enclave in downtown Budapest before World War II. The kosher market in Hungary is expanding. The Jews in Central Europe face a shortage of Rabbinical supervisors to certify the kosher food products for which there is a growing demand.

The Hungarian Jewish community today stands as the largest Jewish community in Central and Eastern Europe. Estimates of its numbers vary. Usually the figure given is 100,000. Some people say there are up to 150,000 Jews in Hungary if you include the many Jews who are not registered as Jews, as well as those who are considered "half-Jews" (those with one Jewish parent), according to the late Charles Hoffman in *Gray Dawn: The Jews of Eastern Europe in the Post-Communist Era*. Interestingly, many dedicated Jewish Communists were never told by their parents that they were Jewish.

Indeed, backed by very reliable population figures (DellaPergola/2016), one notes an interesting result. If one examines Hungary's Jewish population, i.e. "core Jews," the figure is 47,600. But when you use the category of "one Jewish parent," the Jewish population figure jumps to 75,000 and when you use the category of the "Law of the Return," the figure is 130,000.

Hungary and France are now the only European countries in which Jews represent as much as one percent of the population. Before World War I, Jews made up five or six percent of the population in some parts of Europe. In pre-World War II Poland and Hungary, the Jewish population was ten percent.

Today, about nine out of every ten Jews in Hungary live in Budapest. Unbelievable as it may be, anti-Semitism may be more pervasive in the provinces where there are no Jews than in cosmopolitan Budapest. Anti-Semitism is less evident now than it was in prior years, "despite the periodic charges and countercharges" in the political debate of the country. Many would like to blame the Communist fiasco on the Jews. It is true that in the beginning many totally assimilated Jews, Jews in name only—were in the top leadership of the Communist party, including Bela Kun, Matyas Rakosi, and Erno Gero. One still finds a latent anti-Semitism in Hungary. Some Hungarians see Jews, including Christians of Jewish descent, as a non-Magyar minority. But others are quick to point out that this is not so, because many Jews are from families that have lived in Hungary for more than a century.

JEWISH SITES IN BUDAPEST

Your first visit of a Jewish site can be to what one might call a complex of Jewish institutions and monuments around the Jewish Community Center and headquarters of the Federation of Jewish Communities of Hungary, at 12 Sip utca, 1075 Budapest. This complex includes the beautiful Dohany Street Synagogue, the Jewish Museum, a Holocaust memorial in a nearby courtyard, and a memorial chapel known as the Heroes Synagogue at Wesselenyi utca, 5, 7, Budapest, which was dedicated to Hungarian Jewish soldiers who were killed in World War I. Services are held every day. During World War II, most of the ghetto area was behind the Dohany Street Synagogue. **MAZSIHISZ (Magyarorszagi Zsido Hitkozsegek Szovetsege,) Federation of Jewish Communities in Hungary)** Sip utca, 12, 1075 Budapest. Tel: 36-1-413-55-00 or 36-1-413-5564. FAX: 36-1-413-5504. president@mazsihisz.hu. Facebook: www.facebook.com/mazsihisz. www.mazsihisz.hu. This is the umbrella organization for the 28 Jewish communities in Hungary. The congregations are organized around the synagogue. This is the group that makes representations on behalf of the Jewish community to the Hungarian government. Hungary for many years has had a liberal stream of Judaism called Neolog, which means "conservative." But some say that the type of Judaism that Hungarian Jews practiced in the nineteenth and twentieth centuries and known as neolog was similar to a form of Reform Judaism. Office hours are Monday through Thursday, 8:00 a.m. to 4:00 p.m.; on Friday, 8:00 a.m. to 2:00 p.m. The American Jewish Joint Distribution Committee and the World Jewish Congress also have their offices here. The Jewish Community building was built around 1860. Through its courtyard one can also reach the Dohany Street Synagogue. **BZSH (Budapesti Zsido Hitkozsegek Szovetsege) Federation of Budapest Jewish Communities,** is also located here at Sip Utca 12, 1075 Budapest.

JDC Office for Hungary. www.jdc.org. Here in Hungary, JDC partners with the community to ensure social services for poor Jewish seniors, mostly Holocaust survivors, and needy Jewish families through the Hungarian Jewish Social Support Foundation and funds from the Claims Conference for Holocaust survivors. As in other Eastern European countries, JDC's work is focused on Jewish community development and leadership training. Highlights of these programs in Hungary include the annual *Judafest* urban Jewish festival, which drew over ten thousand in the most recent celebration of Jewish culture and learning; the Balint House Jewish Community Center located in the heart of Budapest and offering Jewish programs for Jews of all ages; the JDC-Lauder International Jewish Summer Camp at Szarvas; and the Mosaic Hub, which incubates grassroots Jewish community programs and initiatives to meet the needs of a thriving Hungarian Jewish community exploring its identity in new ways. About 6,500 Hungarian Jews—all Holocaust survivors—are receiving support in their senior years through a partnership between the Hungarian Jewish Social Support Foundation, funded and supported by the

American Jewish Joint Distribution Committee and the Conference on Jewish Material Claims Against Germany, according to *The Jewish Chronicle*, London. "Although the Claims Conference funds social services for 150,000 Holocaust survivors worldwide, its work in Eastern Europe is especially necessary, where state support of the elderly can be limited."

Balint Jewish Community Center. Revay ut. 16, 1065. Budapest. Tel: 361-791-0100. info@balinhaz.hu. www.balinthuz.hu. The Bálint JCC was established in 1994 and is only a two minute walk from the Opera House and the Deak Ferenc square. A performance by a group of actors of the play, The Promised Land. A lecture on religion, tradition and culture by Rabbi Robert Frolich and Zsolt Kocsi in the Shalom Club. A piano concert, an excursion to the Jewish community of Szolnok. Hebrew language courses. These are but a few of the activities at the Balint Jewish Community Center, which includes a fitness center and sauna. In this full-service, state-of-the-art building one can immediately see a wide range of Jewish oriented educational, cultural and social activities for all ages. Many Jewish groups meet here, such as Budapest's B'nai B'rith Lodge. Also located here is a dormitory for young Jews from other towns and cities who are studying at the Rabbinical Seminary or Pedagogium Jewish Teachers Training School. A Jewish monthly magazine is produced at this address. The Balint Center was established by JDC in partnership with the World Jewish Relief (WJR) of the United Kingdom, the Doron Foundation and the Federation of Hungarian Jews. Also giving funding to the building, which is probably the first full service Jewish community center to open in Eastern and Central Europe since the Holocaust, was the Balint family, a London family of Hungarian origin for whom the center is named.

Dohany Street Synagogue, 4-6 Dohany ut., Budapest.Tel: 36-1-413-55-84. turizmus@mazsihisz.hu. www.jewishtourhungary.com. Remodeled a decade ago, it still remains one of the most beautiful synagogues in Europe, this great synagogue of Budapest, located at 4-6 Dohany ut., Budapest. The Hungarian government recently spent about $8 million in renovation and this house of worship right in the heart of the city, elicits highly complementary comments from visitors throughout the world. The largest synagogue still in use in Europe, and second largest in the world behind Temple Emanuel in Manhattan, influences people in such a way that they say, "This is the most beautiful synagogue I've ever seen in my life. It makes me so sad to know that the people who worked so hard on it, can't enjoy it," wrote one visitor. The guest probably was referring to the 600,000 Jews killed in the Holocaust. Designed by the German architect Ludwig

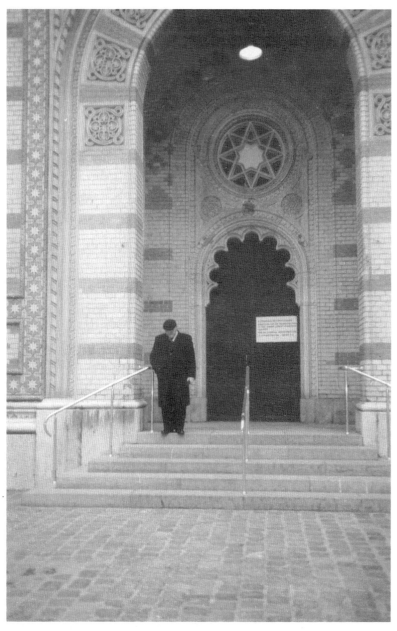

The entrance to the Dohany Street Synagogue, Budapest. (Photo by Ben G. Frank)

Forster, this impressive Moorish style building features minaret-like towers that are 43 meters high, and crowned with bulbous cupolas. The Temple is 53 meters long and 26 meters wide. When you walk into the synagogue you will notice the exquisite floor mosaics.

Established in 1859, it is probably the longest and largest synagogue in Europe and one of the largest in the world. Its length reaches 180 feet; it is 84 feet wide and 65 feet high. The synagogue was designed by the architect Ludwig Forster between 1854 and 1859. The interior was done by Frigyes Feszl. At one time it was known as Tabaktempel because the original street name was Tabak Street. It seats about 3,400 persons and has an organ of 5,000 pipes. Franz Liszt and Camille Saint-Saens played their compositions on it. Once the Nazis surrounded the synagogue with a wooden fence to create the Budapest Ghetto.

Tight security exists at the synagogue. Officials ask that visitors do not bring suitcases with them on their visit.

Heroes Synagogue, Weselenyi utca 5-7, Budapest, where there are services every day. Friday night services are at 6:00 p.m. Saturday morning services are at 9:00 a.m. Daily services include a morning service at 7:00 a.m., Sunday service at 8:00 a.m., and evening service at 6:30 p.m. Call Jewish Center headquarters at Sip utca 12, to check on the service schedule, Tel: 36-1-413-55-00.

In the courtyard of the garden of the Dohany Street Synagogue near the Heroes Synagogue is a memorial plaque to Channa Szenes (1921-44). This heroine grew up in Budapest and went to Palestine. She trained as a British commando and parachuted into Eastern Europe to locate downed Allied pilots and help the Jews. She remained with Tito's partisans in Yugoslavia. Szenes was captured shortly after she infiltrated Hungary to organize Jewish resistance in that country. After being tortured by the Hungarian fascists, she was executed on November 7, 1944 in a prison on the Buda side of the city. She was twenty-three years old. Szenes' remains were taken to Israel in 1950 and interned on Mt. Herzl. Before her death, she wrote the famous poem, *"Blessed is the Match."* In Israel and in the Zionist movement, her name became "a symbol of devotion and self-sacrifice."

According to Carol Herselle Krinsky in *"Synagogues of Europe: Architecture, History, Meaning"* the Great Synagogue was constructed in a mode that was soon to become part of the architecture of monuments in Budapest. Besides gilded cupolas, the structure contains stone and terra-cotta trim and wrought and cast iron. The two octagonal banners are more than 41 meters high.

Krinsky says the Dohany Street Synagogue shows the "greater self-confidence of Jews in the 1850's." During that period Jews were able to commission buildings with conspicuous street fronts in a supposedly Jewish style.

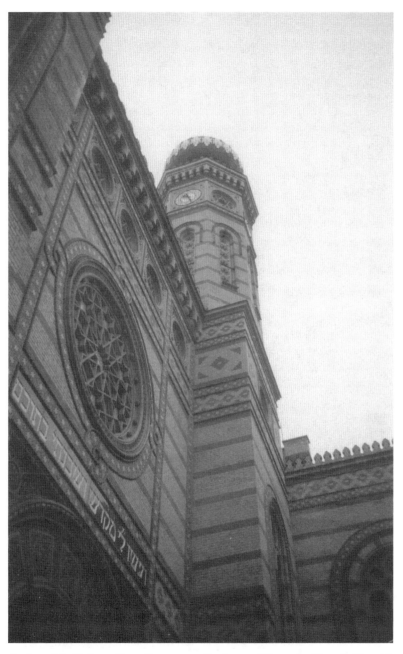

A view of the Dohany Street Synagogue, Budapest. (Photo by Ben G. Frank)

Martyrs Cemetery. Just outside the Dohany Street Synagogue and behind the Jewish Museum is a mass grave cemetery. On January 18, 1945, the Jewish ghetto was liberated thousands of Jewish bodies were buried here because they could not be taken elsewhere. The plaques do not mark individual graves; they are only markers put up by families and friends of the victims.

Weeping Willow Memorial Tree, the Memorial to the Hungarian Jewish Martyrs. This Holocaust Memorial, at the corner of Rumbach Sebestyen and Wesselenyi, Budapest, is a sculptured weeping willow tree. Cast in steel, its leaves are engraved on each side with the names of Holocaust victims as remembered by loved ones. Designed by the sculptor Imre Varga, it was first dedicated in 1988. On hand was the famous American movie star, artist, and author, Tony Curtis, whose parents came from Hungary. A plaque says the Memorial Tree was "dedicated to the nearly 600,000 Hungarian Jews who perished in the Holocaust and to the many valiant heroes of all faiths who risked their lives to save untold members of Jewish men and women from certain death." The Memorial for the Righteous Among the Nations is in the background.

Monument to the Swedish Diplomat Raoul Wallenberg. This monument is located on a grassy expanse on the Buda side on Szilagyi Erszebet Fasor, at the corner of Lupeny utca. Take metro train line two from Moszkva Terrace. Continue from there Bus 56 or Tram 56 to Szilagyi Erszebet Fasor.

The Holocaust Memorial Tree, Budapest. (Photo by Ben G. Frank)

During the war, the United States asked Sweden, who was neutral, to open a special section of its legation in Budapest to help rescue Hungarian Jewry. Raoul Wallenberg was then thirty-two years old and a distinguished Swedish diplomat who had studied architecture at the University of Michigan. Risking his life daily, he issued so-called "letters of protection" and even Swedish passports. He hoped against hope that those who possessed these documents would be spared. Wallenberg saved between 50,000 and 100,000 Hungarian Jews from the Nazis by his dedication, determination, ingenuity, and skill, according to Harvey Rosenfeld in Raoul Wallenberg, Angel of Rescue: Heroism and Torment in the Gulag. He even got hold of advance copies of the daily lists of Jews to be deported so he could provide them with protection passports. Reportedly, he was shot at and even chased by cars and trucks. He continually used his daring and resourcefulness to save Jews.

But terror reigned in Budapest. Wallenberg tried, but his protection could not reach everywhere. Bands of Arrow Cross Fascists drove Jews to the banks of the Danube, murdered them, and dumped their bodies into the river. About 130,000 Jews, mostly elderly and children, were first crammed into houses marked with yellow stars and located in the ghetto. The Gestapo under Adolf Eichmann may have directed the deportation, but it was the Hungarian fascists who beat and drove the Jews on the road to the death camps.

Many Jews starved along the way. Those who were too weak to walk were shot by Fascist guards. "The road to Vienna was lined with corpses," wrote Dr. Ilona Benoschofsky in *The History of Jews in Hungary.*

Wallenberg was arrested by the Soviets on January 17, 1945, imprisoned as a spy, and died, probably murdered by the KGB in Lubyanka Prison in Moscow in 1947. January 17, 2000, marked the fifty-fifth year of Raoul Wallenberg's disappearance. The Wallenberg committees throughout the world insist that his fate is unresolved and they continue the search. This "Swedish Angel of Rescue" will always be a hero to the Jewish people and men and women of goodwill everywhere.

Also active in Budapest during the terrible days of late 1944 was Charles Lutz of Switzerland, who helped Jews find shelter in safe homes or in neutral legations. "Wallenberg is the better known of the two because of the tragic conclusion of his mission, but Lutz was no less actively involved in the rescue operation," writes Leni Yahil in *The Holocaust: The Fate of European Jewry, 1932-1945.* In 1944, Lutz, a professional diplomat, not only represented his Swiss legation, but also other countries when he dealt with Jewish emigration from Hungary.

As noted in chapter on Sweden, in 2016, the Swedish government formally pronounced Wallenberg, dead. His family requested that he be officially declared deceased. "Let Raoul rest in peace," they said.

Memorial to Charles Lutz, Located in a small square next to 12 Dob ut., Budapest. At this site is the unique statue of figures sculptured by Tamas Szabo. Between 1942 and 1945, this Swiss diplomat saved 62,000 Jews from the death camps In December, 1944, most of the employees of foreign legations left the country, but Lutz stayed. It is said that in view of his influence and personal renown, the Germans ordered the fascist Arrow Cross Party that had been planning to blow up the ghetto, not to do so. In the 76 "protected houses" under the patronage of the Swiss Consulate, thousands were saved. Like Wallenberg, he had visited Palestine. Lutz was the consul at the Swiss consulate in Jaffa, Palestine between 1935 and 1941. He was always in touch with pioneering Zionist youth movements according to Leni Yahil. During that period, he secured the release of German prisoners, giving him leverage in his dealings with the Nazis during his later tenure in Hungary.

When standing near this Holocaust Memorial and in the cemetery area where thousands of Jewish victims were buried, it is fitting to recall the tragedy and nightmare of Hungarian Jewry at the end of World War II. If you walk through the Jewish area behind the Dohany Street. Synagogue, you undoubtedly will be in what was then the ghetto section where thousands of Jews were herded into and thousands more died a violent death at the hands of the Germans and the Arrow Cross. The Great Ghetto was the area surrounded by Dohany ut.-Nagyatadi Szabo Istvan ut., Kiraly ut., Rumbach Sebestyen ut., Madach Imre ut., Madach Imre ter, and Karoly Kiraly ut.

Holocaust Memorial Center is located in a new structure attached to the **Old Pava Synagogue,** which has been renovated. This is the home of the Holocaust Museum of Hungary, at Pava ut., 39, IX district, 1094, Budapest. Tel: 36-1-455-33-33. info@hdke.hu. www.hdke.hu.

This museum presents the tragic murder of 600,000 Hungarian Jews by the Germans. It also serves as a remembrance of the 30,000 gypsies who died in World War II. About 70,000 to 75,000 Jews survived and were saved by the Russian army which liberated the Jewish Ghetto in Budapest.

A beautiful part of the memorial is the prayer hall. Here photos of members of those who once worshipped here are on display. The glass wall around the center, designed by Laszlo Zsoter, is inscribed with the names of Hungarian Jews who perished in the Holocaust. The space allows for new names to be added. The goal is to have a complete list of all who perished in the Shoah.

Memorial to Charles Lutz, Swiss diplomat who saved Jews in Hungary during World War II. (Photo by Ben G. Frank)

Construction of the synagogue began in 1910, but was halted in World War I, and then completed in 1923 by architect Lipot Baumhorn, (1860-1932). In 2000, the Jewish community decided to build a Holocaust Memorial Center at the sight of the synagogue. The Hungarian government supported and financed the project. The Center opened in 2003. Open from Tuesday to Sunday, 10:00 a.m., to 6:00 p.m. Closed Monday.

Remember that Hungary fought alongside the Axis powers, although halfway through the conflict it tried to "disentangle" itself from Germany.

According to various Hungarian racial laws of 1938, 1939, and 1941, Jews were removed from professional and intellectual positions. Adm. Mikios Horthy was in power. Appointed originally only as a regent, he had transformed Hungary between the wars into a "Fascist dictatorship." His goal was to recapture lost lands.

In August 1941, 12,000 Jews were deported from Hungary and murdered because they were so-called "stateless Jews." Thus began the nightmare that was to last until Hungary was freed by Russian soldiers early in 1945.

Some Hungarians do not like to talk about their role in World War II. Or they answer lamely, "What could we do? We were surrounded by enemies." A Protestant cleric and historian, Jozsef Elias told the *New York Times* on April 18, 1994, "the fact is most Hungarians didn't reject Nazism, they accepted it."

When Hungary allied itself with Germany, Hungarian Jews received a reprieve from deportation. But many were pressed into labor battalions. Even in the beginning of the war, young Jewish men were sent to forced labor camps. In 1941, these boys were used as animals by Hungary's armed forces who were on the side of the Germans and who fought on the Soviet front. A lack of clothing during the Russian winter felled 50,000 out of the 70,000 Jewish youths.

Hungary participated in the German invasion of the Soviet Union in June 1941. Hungarian troops fought beside the Nazis in the Ukraine. The Hungarians suffered 200,000 casualties, including 130,000 dead, at the battle of Stalingrad in Russia during the winter of 1942-43. It is no wonder that Hungarian public opinion turned against the war.

The Nazis distrusted Horthy; they believed he might make a deal with the Allies.

Sunday, March 19—a date that will never be forgotten by Hungarian Jewry—dawned a beautiful day in the war-torn city of Budapest. Things would change very suddenly. If weather can reflect what happened that day on land itself, it was as if the sunny, bright-white day turned into a black night of plagues. The Nazi war machine moved its forces into its lackey Hungary and into the Hungarian capital. There was no resistance. Accompanying the German troops was the SS officer Adolf Eichmann, who came to "solve Hungary's Jewish problem." Hungarian Jewry was doomed, according to Charles Hoffman in *Gray Dawn: The Jews of Eastern Europe in the Post-Communist Era*. In less than 24 hours Eichmann and his agents would arrest and deport to the concentration camps the top Jewish leaders of the city, including men, women and children.

Eichmann and his staff were determined to "resettle" the approximate 800,000 Jews as quickly as possible. Immediately, Regent Admiral Horthy appointed Dome Sztolyai as Prime Minister in what was billed as a "national government under a German protectorate." The Encyclopedia Guide says Horthy told Sztolyai that the Germans firmly demanded the solution of the Hungarian Jewish question.

By April, Jews were required to wear the Yellow Star. In May, the ghetto was set up behind the Dohany Street Synagogue. Between May 15 and July 7, 1944, 437,000 Jews were rounded up in the countryside and sent to the concentration camp at Auschwitz and Birkenau. In July, there was an international outcry pointing out to Horthy that deportation meant sudden death. He had the deportations stopped on July 7, 1944, thereby saving the lives of the Jews in Budapest until the Arrow Cross fascist takeover on October 15, 1944.

From the end of July to October 12, Jews hid wherever they could to survive. Some were saved by Wallenberg, Lutz, and others. Wallenberg alone issued 13,000 passports. Interesting that before a person went into hiding he would tell everyone he was going to "Telech," which meant hiding. Also there were secret negotiations going on between various groups and the Germans, such as the Zionist Budapest Rescue Committee. According to *The Encyclopedia Guide*, "the personal message of Pope Pius XII and the firm communication from the American government also warned Horthy that he and all those who persecuted the Jews would be taken to account after the war." Papal Nuncio Angelo Rotta made frequent representations to cabinet ministers on behalf of the Jews. Rotta's demands were the first official protest against the deportation of the Jews lodged by representatives of the Pope.

Thousands of Jews were saved because of special letters of accreditation supplied by the Holy See. Horthy may have seen the handwriting on the wall; the allies had landed in Normandy. He had to know that the Russians would eventually succeed in breaking through and conquering Hungary. He tried to get an armistice with the Russians and he actually made a radio announcement that the war was over. But the Germans armed the Arrow Cross, who, along with

Ferenc Szalasi, took over the country on October 15/16 and forced Regent Horthy to resign. For the next three months they hunted down Jews with the clear intention of rounding them up and sending them to their death in Germany. In mid-November, Szalasi established a Great Ghetto in Budapest and Jews were moved into that area. About 25,000 Jews had found safety under the protection of the Swiss and Swedish embassies.

While protected zones in the Great Ghetto were set up, we should remember that the ghetto was "protected" in name only. Arrow Cross troops, Hungarian soldiers and German troops appeared every day and looted, plundered, and murdered Jews without discrimination. "The Danube became a mass grave in those days since the hiding Jews caught by the Arrow Cross were escorted in great numbers to the bank, shot, and thrown into the river from the embankment," says the *Encyclopedia Guide.*

On January 12, 1945, the Arrow Cross made plans to kill all the Jews on January 20, but the Russians had arrived two days earlier on January 18. Szalasi was captured by the American troops in 1945, was returned to Budapest and executed as a war criminal responsible for the death of about 100,000 Jews.

According to historian Jozef Elias, "whatever is said now about Horthy saving Jews is not true." Many people see Adm. Miklos Horthy as the man who presided over the deportation to Auschwitz alone of 438,000 Hungarian Jews, mostly from rural areas. Of this number, about 250,000 to 300,000 were exterminated. To others, he is seen as a leader who tried to resist German demands for the mass deportation of Budapest's middle-class Jews and who was finally pushed aside by Hitler in late 1944. After the German coup in Budapest in October 1944, Horthy was sent to Bavaria where the Americans wanted to arrest him for trial at Nuremberg. A Hungarian historian of the period, Francois Fejto, said Stalin intervened and exile in Portugal was arranged for Horthy. He died in 1957 in Portugal at the age of eighty-nine.

In 1930, 445,000 Jews resided in Hungary. After the infamous Munich Pact, Hungary added another several hundred thousand Jews to its population from Slovakia, Yugoslavia, and Transylvania for a total of about 650,000 Jews in Greater Hungary, according to Lucy S. Dawidowicz. She added in her book, *The War Against the Jews: 1933-1945,* that more than 450,000 Jews, 70 percent of the Jews of Greater Hungary, were deported or murdered under the occupation of the Nazis. Other researchers put that toll at approximately 600,000 Jews.

Dr. Ilona Benoschofsky, writing in *The History of Jewry in Hungary,* indicates that there were 700,000 Jews in Greater Hungary before the Holocaust. She says there were even 100,000 more who did not profess Judaism; still, the anti-Jewish laws applied to them.

Despite the rescue efforts of Charles Lutz and Raoul Wallenberg, by 1945, about three out of four Jews who lived in Hungary before World War II were dead. And Jews amounted to three-fourths of wartime Hungarian losses in life, according to Paul Lendvai. He added, "There is peculiar tragedy in the fate of Hungarian Jewry: it survived intact until the middle of 1944 and was then annihilated in less than eight weeks, when even the perpetrators knew that the war was lost." Almost 50 percent of Budapest's residents of Jewish origin died during the Holocaust period. Approximately 85,000 Jews remained in Budapest by the end of World War II. According to Peter Meyer, the Russian soldiers who captured the capital in January 1945 acted beastly. Cashing in on their rigged election, the Communist party followed a negative policy and the Jews who were persecuted were often shoved into camps and treated as aliens. "Eastern Europe was not livable for Jews," wrote Meyer. Jews were allowed to immigrate to Israel until 1951. "After that time, Soviet hostility toward Israel greatly increased, restrictions on Jewish life grew more severe, and harsh measures were taken to prevent contacts between Israeli diplomats and local Jews," wrote author Charles Hoffman in *Gray Dawn: The Jews of Eastern Europe* in the Post-Communist Era.

Hungarian Jewry, until the late 1980s, was on the one hand cut off from Jewry and on the other hand seemed more or less "content with their Goulash Communism and Goulash Judaism," wrote Hoffman.

Memorial to the Victims of the German Occupation. Freedom Square, Budapest. Ever since this monument—a huge bronze statue with a large German eagle with open wings that seems to be landing over innocent Hungary, symbolized by Archangel Gabriel—was erected in 2014, protests have been held daily. The date of the so-called "occupation" is given as March 19, 1944. Critics, including the entire Jewish community, stand opposed to this monument. The protesters indicate the current government is rewriting the past and manipulating its history for political purposes. There was no German occupation; Hungary was not a victim. The Nazis walked into the country in 1944 aided by the Hungarian government, which collaborated with the Germans and which acquiesced to the deportation of thousands of Hungarian Jews to the gas chambers. The statue is a pure and simple case of revisionist history. Critics declare that "Hungary has disseminated a narrative that minimizes it culpability in the extermination of a half-million Jews and at the same time rehabilitates Admiral Horthty's reputation from that of opportunistic Nazi ally to selfless defender of national independence."

In the last analysis the statue portrays the Hungarian nation as "a collective victim of Nazi predation," which it was not.

The statue was erected by the government of Viktor Orban, Hungary's prime minister. This controversial statue is a good example to observe Hungary's present government and leading party, *Fidesz,* which is Mr. Orban's party. That group pioneered Europe's "illiberal wave" when it came to power in 2010. It limited the constitutional court's powers and introduced a new constitution. *Fidesz* changed the electoral system, helping it win again in 2014, says Andras Biro-Nagy of Policy Solutions, a think tank. Orban, it was reported, has been the loudest of the anti-immigrant voices. His government now wants to introduce anti-terror laws that worry civil libertarians, though the details are vague. Like other European countries, Hungary appears to be swinging to the right. In 2017, Orban's government also pushed a bill through that critics say is aimed at shutting down Central European University, the institution founded by George Soros. This move has caused wide-spread protests. Some Hungarian Jews claim that while Orban is right-wing, the government is not following an anti-Semitic policy; others disagree. Both sides agree that the *Jobbik* extremist party, is an anti-Semitic party. The spread of *Jobbik's* ideology has alarmed anti-racism campaigners, gay rights activists, and Jewish groups.

Still there is no fear of terrorism among Jews as in France or Belgium. One Hungarian Jewish observer of the political scene told me that if *Jobbik* gained power in the 2018 election, "that would be a serious problem."

Shoes on the Danube Riverbank Statue. In 2004, a cast iron memorial about Jewish martyrs shot at the Danube during the 1944-1945 winter by the Arrow Cross militiamen was created by the late sculptor, Gyula Pauer. The monument is located near the Parliament and the Chain Bridge. Those shot, mainly Jews, were ordered to take off their shoes, and were fired at while standing on the edge of the water so that their bodies fell into the river and were carried away. The statue, displaying 60 pairs of shoes, represents their shoes left behind on the bank.

Ghetto Wall Memorial, Dohany utca, 34 Budapest, and/or 15 Kiraly utca, Budapest. Here one finds a memorial plaque placed on a wall in a courtyard. The plaque includes a map of the ghetto as it was in November 1944 with borders designated by the notorious Arrow Cross. One sees the stones that were used to separate the courtyards as barriers, topped with barbed wire. The concrete surface is delicately ornate. The inscription in the steel reminds one of the history of the city and the Holocaust. A psalm is also hidden

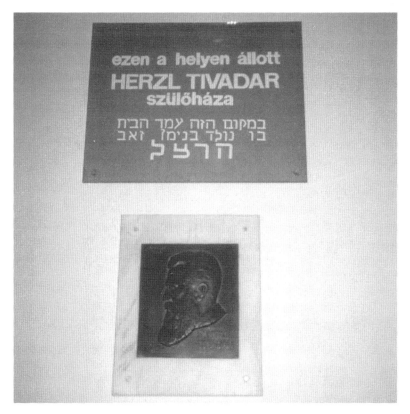

A memorial plaque in the Jewish Museum marks the birth of Theodor Herzl, the founder of modern Zionism, who was born in 1860 in a house on the site of the Jewish Museum. (Photo by Ben G. Frank)

in it. A non-governmental OVASI organization created the memorial space in the courtyard.

Jewish Museum and Archives of Hungary., Dohany ut., 2,1074 Budapest. Tel: 361-413-5550. info@milev.hu, www.milev.hu, and www. enmilev.weebly.com. (Located to the left of the synagogue as you face this house of worship). It is not difficult to locate this museum in Budapest. It is adjacent to the Dohany Street Synagogue and opened in 1932. The founders of the Jewish Museum wanted an institution that would, "awaken and maintain Jewish historical self-respect because that is tied up with the Jewish-life ambition and is more important than the collection of treasures with absolute artistic values." During the war, the museum was a hiding place for Jews and many were saved. Over the years, the collection has been as diverse as the society behind it, including objects that symbolized the extensive assimilation of

Hungarian Jews or on the contrary its dissimilation. In 2016-2017, the museum was being renovated. The building also contains the Jewish Archives. In 2017, an exhibit, "*100 Years-100 Objects*" opened.

Through original documents, manuscripts, and photographs, museum exhibits present the history of Hungarian Jews. Here are Judaic cups, rimonim, Torah crowns, candlesticks, spice boxes, and textiles along with an important collection of manuscripts. Especially meaningful are documents about Jewish participation in the Hungarian War of Independence (1848-49), as is the material introducing the Hungarian struggle for emancipation. Modern paintings, sculptures, and medals by twentieth-century Jewish artists are displayed.

As mentioned earlier, Theodor Herzl, the founder of modern Zionism, was born in 1860, in a house on this site. There is a memorial plaque marking the birthplace. The square on this site, just in front of the Jewish Museum, was recently named "Herzl Square."

Aided by the American Jewish Joint Distribution Committee, the rebuilding of the museum started in 1947. But little money was available for its upkeep during the Communist era, and for decades, only two permanent exhibits were on display: Highlights of Hungarian Jewish life during World War II and an anti-Fascist exhibit. Today, the museum presents the full Hungarian Jewish tragedy through documents, photographs, and newspaper articles.

Rabbinical Seminary, Jozsef Korut 27, Budapest. During the Iron Curtain period, it was the only rabbinical seminary in Eastern Europe. Founded in 1877, it is now old and dusty, a corner building not in very good physical shape. But its library and its history are fascinating. One can see the bullet holes in the books themselves—bullets fired during World War II. When the Russians were retaking Budapest at the end of that war, the Fascists used the roof as an army outpost against the Red Army. The building also served as a detention center during the war. The library contains 100,000 to 150,000 books. This author saw the dust on the books, dust that had accumulated during more than 40 years of Communist rule. But even in those dark days, there was hope for Jews.

Jews participated in the Hungarian Revolution in 1956 and in the events of 1989. "For 12 days in 1956, Budapest lived through one of the great dramas of the 20th century Europe," writes Patrick Brogan in his book, *The Captive Nations: Eastern Europe, 1945-1990*. It probably is hindsight, but now we know that the Revolution was in effect a rejection of Communism throughout the Eastern bloc. "Hungary cried, but no one heard," a former East European told this author. As Henry Kissinger wrote in his book. *Diplomacy*, America and its Allies, "acted as if they were bystanders with no direct stake in the outcome." Soviet tanks crushed the revolt and 2,000 persons were executed, including Imre Nagy, who had formed an obviously liberal government. About 200,000 Hungarians escaped to the West, including about 20,000 Jews, according to Mark Kurlansky in his book, *A Chosen Few: The Resurrection of European Jewry.*

A little more than thirty years later, thousands of East Germans who would flee communism, also headed westward via Hungary. Again, one sees Hungary playing a large part in the final "knockdown" of communism as it allowed the East Germans entry onto their soil and opened the floodgates to them. The Berlin Wall soon came down and East European communism crumbled because everyone knew that in 1989 the Soviets, under Mikhail Gorbachev, would not send in their tanks.

The Library in the Rabbinical School—The library has more than 90,000 volumes which makes it the third largest Jewish library in the world. Founded in 1877, this facility contains the "Hebraica-Judaica," collection based on the collection of the famous rabbi of Padova: Delio Della Torre.

In 2000, the Seminary was also given the title of "The Budapest University of Jewish Studies.".

The Old Buda Synagogue, known in Hungarian as Obudai Zsinagoga, Lajos utca, 163, 1036, Budapest. Tel: 36-1-268-01-83. posta@zsido.com. www.obudaizsinagoga.hu/eng. Founded in 1821, this house of worship served different functions for the State in the years after the Holocaust, such as a TV studio. Returned to the Jewish community in 2010, Chabad rented the building in 2010 and opened it as a synagogue. Renovation was undertaken. On April 12, 2016, the building was dedicated and stands as a marvelous neo-classical structure. Twenty-five thousand Stars of David lights are embedded in the ceiling. Rabbi Shlomo Koves is the spiritual leader of the synagogue. Services are Monday to Friday, 6:30 a.m.; Friday, during winter, 6:00 p.m., summer, 7:00 p.m.; Shabbat morning at 10:00 a.m., Sunday morning, 10:00 a.m. Friday night dinners.

Other Synagogues

Orthodox Center, Dob utca 35 and Kazinczy utca, 27, Budapest. This Orthodox complex contains a Talmud Torah, prayer centers, and offices. Services are held every day. The kosher restaurant, Hannah, which is supervised by the Orthodox rabbinate, is also situated in this center.

Main Orthodox Synagogue. The main synagogue entrance is

Kazinczy utca, 27, Budapest. The synagogue certainly is well worth a visit, although it is closed in the winter. During that season, access to a smaller synagogue as well as access to the kosher restaurant can also be from Dob utca 35. The smaller synagogue conducts services every day.

Synagogue, Dessewffy utca, 23, Budapest. Services each day.

Synagogue, Nagyfuvaros ut, 8th district, Budapest. This is one of the older synagogues in Budapest, which survived the war. Congregation is mostly senior citizens. This district was known for the many merchants and craftsmen who lived in the area.

Chabad Keren Or Center, Karoly krt 20, 1052, Budapest. Info@ zsido.com. www.zsido.com. Chabad officers are located in this main Chabad Center. www.zsido.com. In their general information program, Chabad notes that when tourists arrive in Budapest and need directions, call their office. Tel: 361-268-0183.

Shas Chevra Lubavitch Shul and the **Budapest Yeshiva** are located in VI district, Vasbari Pal utca 5. Budapest. Tel: 361-268-0183, a 15 minute walk from the Intercontinental Hotel, two blocks from the King's Hotel and a five minute walk from the Kempinski and Meridien hotels.

Lubavitch Yeshiva -The Jewish Heritage Center, Wesselenyi ut, 4 1/1 1075 Budapest, VII district. Tel: (36-1) 258-0183; FAX: (36-1) 342-7876. E-mail: oberlander@zsido.com. The boys were studying Talmud. Each with his partner. This is the yeshiva of Lubavitch of Hungary which is very active in the community. Many activities are held here, such as lectures and promotions of Jewish tradition.

Masorti Olami, Merkaz Hungary, 18 Dorzsma Doz, Budapest.

Dor Hadash, 11 Aurora utca, Budapest. Tel: 36-30-248-22-60. info@ dorhadas.org.

Rumbach Synagogue, 11-13 Rumbach Sebestyen ut, 1075, Budapest. Not far from the Dohany Street Synagogue is this beautiful synagogue designed by the famous Austrian architect, Otto Wagner. Sebestyen Rumbach (1764-1844) was the municipal health officer of Pest. Opened in 1872, the building is smaller than the Dohany Street Synagogue, but not "poorer looking." The women's gallery is separate and the bimah is in the middle of the structure. Oriental motifs are part of the atmosphere. During World War II, the synagogue was used as a detention barracks for refugees. The façade of the house of worship is accentuated by the octagonal pillars ending in two small towers.

Bet Orim Reform Jewish Congregation, Balint Community Center, Revav u., 16, 1065, Budapest. Tel: 36-70-310-2885. Betorim@gmail. com, www.betorim.hu.

Sim Shalom Congregation, Raday u., 9, floor 1, apt 2, (bell #12),

1092, Budapest. Tel: 36-1-201-7648. FAX: 36-1-201-7648. info@sim-shalom.org. www.sim-shalom.org.

Schools

The former Anna Frank High School for Boys and Girls, is now called **Scheiber, Sandor General and Secondary School,** Laky Adolf ut, 38-40, 1145, Budapest. palkocs@vipmail.hu . This institution is indeed one site that must be seen if one is to appreciate the great strides made by the Hungarian Jewish community to educate its children. A new, modern school, complete with computers, well-lit classrooms, a gym, a fitness room, and a multi-functional assembly hall, which obviously serves as an auditorium, gives meaning to the reality of the rebirth of East European Jewry. The main school auditorium hall also is used for religious services, dances, Channukah Ball, community lectures and conferences. Opened in 1998, it actually has been in existence for 81 years. Before its present name, Scheiber Sandor was known as the Anna Frank Secondary School. It was previously located in the Berkocsi ut, building of the Rabbinical Seminary. Today, about 400 students attend the school in classes which meet the needs of children between the ages of six and eighteen years of age.

The goal of the school is to give the students the means to be Jewish.

Lauder Yavneh Jewish Community Kindergarten and School. Budapest. info@lauderfoundation.com. Perched high in the hills of Buda section of the capital and in one of the city's nicest sections, is the modern, beautifully designed 21stst Century school. The attractive school is a contribution to the area's architecture. Its bright red paint on the outside give the various complex of buildings a rich, exciting look that depicts the values of the school and kindergarten which combines Jewish values with modern child-centered pedagogical approaches. Here one can see words translated into action: commitment and revival of Jewish life in Hungary.

American Endowment School, 44 Wesselenyi ut., 1075, Budapest. Tel: 36-1-322-2843. Also known as the **Reichman School**, named after the Reichman brothers now living in the United States. This Orthodox primary and partly secondary school was established in 1990 and is based on the principles of "Masoret Avot," (the traditions of the fathers").

Beit Menachem Chabad Elementary School. Dohany utca, 32, 1074, Budapest. Tel: 781-4760. www.zsidoiskola.hu.

Maimonides Jewish High School. www.zsidogimnazium.

The Lauder Foundation, which is very much involved in aiding

Jewish education in Hungary, can be contacted in its Berlin executive office at Rykesstrasse 53, 10405, Berlin. Tel: 49-30-440-13-16-10. FAX: 49-30-440-13-16-19. info@lauderfoundaton.com

KOSHER RESTAURANTS IN BUDAPEST

Hanna Kosher Restaurant, Dob utca. 35, Budapest. Tel: 342-1072.
Frohlich Cukraszda Pastry Shop, Dob utca. 22. H-1072 Budapest. Tel: 36-1-266-1733.www.frohlich.hu.
Carmel Restaurant, Kazincy ut 29,VII Budapest Tel: 36-1-322-1834. www.carmel.hu. Meat dishes.
Tel Aviv Café, Kazincy utca 28. VII. Budapest. Tel: 361-342-0231.
Kosher Market, Dohany utca 36, Budapest. Tel: 361-70-380-2776. www.koserpiac.webnode.hu.

TRAVEL CENTERS AND GUIDES

Jewish Tour Hungary. Tourism Department of MAZSIHISZ, (Federation of Jewish Communities in Hungary) Sip utca 12, 1075, Budapest. turizmus@mazsihisz.hu, www.jewishtourhungary.com. Tel: 36-1-413-55-84. FAX: 36-1-413-55-83. turizmus@mazsihisz.hu, www. Jewishtourhungary.com. Dr. Ivan Rona is managing director of the tourism department. This group can book tours for the Dohany Street Synagogue complex and other sites. A Jewish Cultural Festival is held every year during the first week of September and is sponsored by MAZSIHISZ.

Licensed tour guide, Nandor Gerei, MSc. Tel/FAX: 36-1-383-3390, 36-1-251-37-36. Cell: 36-309-217-548. tourguide@t-online.hu. www. flatrent.webs.com. Meet Nandor Gerei, an excellent licensed guide for Budapest and all of Hungary. He conducts Jewish heritage tours, general sight-seeing programs, and trips to visit Jewish landmarks in Budapest or in the countryside. He is a Holocaust survivor and historian and can organize cultural programs and conduct small or large group tours. He speaks excellent English. He and his small team conduct excursions around Budapest and metro area.

His daughter, Suzanna Gerei, is a licensed tour guide (English, Spanish). Tel: 36-30-525-39-77 as well as 36-30-397-41-81, gerei. zsuzsanna@gmail.com. Ms. Gerei can aid the traveler with transfers as well as arrange centrally-located, air-conditioned and private apartments for reasonable rates in Budapest, with Wi-Fi, with kosher appliances if needed. These apartments are located close to the synagogue, kosher shops, and restaurants. Photos on request.

Another esteemed colleague is Dr. Julia Ramotsa, a Jewish

historian, licensed freelance guide, and university lecturer In Jewish studies. Her contacts are: j.ramotsa@chello.hu, *www.julie-guide.hu* Tel: 36-1-32-05-111. Cell 36-309-215-017.

Also, a colleague is Peter Kovacsi. Tel: 36-1-26-63-327, pkovacsi18@gmail.com. Tel: 36-309-642-776.

Szarvas

The Ronald S. Lauder Foundation/JDC International Jewish Youth Camp, Szarvas. Every summer 450 children from about six countries in East Europe come to this wonderful camp in this small town 90 miles southeast of Budapest. "Paradise in Szarvas," say the brochures, and they are right. "Welcome to the summer camp that changes lives," says the sign in the main hall of the camp which opened in 1990 and draws children from six to 18. And the sign is correct, too. For if the revival of Jewish life is to continue, the existence of this camp is a must. From here will come the leaders of the future Jewish communities of Eastern Europe. The camp of course includes sports, boating, hiking and summer camp recreational activities. The camp is a truly a mirror of East European Jewry. For many campers, the Szarvas experience is their first intensive contact with Jewish tradition and the two week camp session may be their only structured Jewish educational experience

A scene from the Jewish Summer Camp at Szarvas, Hungary. (Photo courtesy of The American Jewish Joint Distribution Committee)

during the entire year. One counselor is quoted as saying, "Before they came to Szarvas, they knew that their father or their mother was Jewish. But they didn't care." Now they come to the camp, and they try to be Jewish, to learn about their Jewish identity." During each two-week camp session, counselors explain the basics of Jewish ritual. While the camp is not Orthodox, it is traditional and Shabbat and holidays are observed. Each child spends Friday mornings baking his own challah. The dining hall is strictly kosher. During each camp session, all 13-year old boys celebrate a collective Bar Mitzvah. Since its founding Szarvas has been operated by JDC, in close cooperation with the Lauder Foundation and with the assistance of the Jewish Agency.

Machol Hungaria, Szarvas.—A Dance Camp. They come from all over Hungary. They come from other countries in Eastern Europe and they learn Israeli and folk dancing. The impact of dance in the life of youth cannot be underestimated. These young people love it. To perform Israeli dancing is uplifting indeed and these Eastern and Central European young Jews enjoy every minute of it. The location is superb and provides a natural atmosphere for creative dancing, for getting to know Jewish students and for discussions on how to improve Jewish life in these newly revived Jewish communities.

Szentendre

A small town just outside of Budapest. Great for restaurants, shopping and just a nice walk along the Danube. From here you can board cruises along the Danube.

Suggested Reading

Bierman, John. *Righteous Gentile: The Story of Raoul Wallenberg, Missing Hero of the Holocaust.* New York: Viking, 1981.

Balas, Egon. *Will to Freedom: A Perilous Journey Through Fascism and Communism*, Syracuse University Press, Syracuse, N.Y. 2000.

Brogan, Patrick. *The Captive Nations: Eastern Europe, 1945-1990. New York: Avon, 1990.*

Burant, Stephen R., ed. *Hungary: A Country Study.* Washington, D.C.: Library of Congress, 1990.

Dawidowicz, Lucy S. *The War Against the Jews: 1933-1945.* New York: Bantam, 1986.

Fermor, Patrick Leigh Fermor. *Between The Woods And the Water: On Foot to Constantinople from The Hook of Holland: The Middle Danube to the Iron Gates,* New York, Elisabeth Sifton Books, 1986.

Hoensch, Jorg. *A History of Modern Hungary, 1867-1986.* Text ed. New York: Longman, 1984.

Kissinger, Henry. *Diplomacy.* New York: Simon & Schuster, 1994.

Krinsky, Carol Herselle. *Synagogues of Europe: Architecture, History, Meaning.* Cambridge, Mass.: MIT Press, 1985.

Kurlansky, Mark. *A Chosen Few: The Resurrection of European Jewry.* Reading, Mass.: Addison-Wesley, 1995.

Lendvai, Paul. *Anti-Semitism Without Jews: Communist Eastern Europe.* Garden City, N.Y.: Doubleday, 1971.

Lengyel, Emil. *1,000 Years of Hungary.* New York: John Day, 1958.

———. The *Danube.* New York: Random House, 1939.

Lukacs, John. *Budapest, Nineteen Hundred: A Historical Portrait of a City and Its Culture.* New York: Grove/Atlantic, 1990.

McCagg, William O. *Jewish Nobles and Geniuses in Modern Hungary,* text ed. Boulder, Colo.: East European Quarterly, 1972.

MacLean, Rory. *Stalin's Nose: Travels Around the Bloc.* New York: Little, Brown, 1993.

Meyer, Peter, Bernard D. Weinryb, Eugene Duschinsky, and Nicolas Sylvain, eds. *The Jews in the Soviet Satellites.* Syracuse, N.Y: Syracuse University Press, 1953.

Rosenfeld, Harvey. *Raoul Wallenberg, Angel of Rescue: Heroism and Torment in the Gulag,* rev. ed. New York: Holmes & Meier, 1995.

Sugar, Peter F, et al, eds. *A History of Hungary.* Bloomington and Indianapolis: Indiana University Press, 1990.

Yahil, Leni. *The Holocaust: The Fate of European Jewry, 1932-1945.* New York. Oxford, Oxford University Press, 1990.

Young, James E. *The Texture of Memory: Holocaust Memorials and Meaning in Europe, Israel, and America.* New Haven: Yale University Press, 1993.

Slovakia
Jews Are Here to Stay

At Chanukah in 1993, a significant event took place in the history of the Slovak Jewish community: a Chanukah torch relay lighting ceremony—the first of its kind—was held in the city of Bratislava, the capital of the new nation of Slovakia. An escort of about twenty young Jewish runners accompanied the torch from the burial place of the great Orthodox scholar, Hatam Sofer, to the old Jewish section and the site of a former synagogue that stood in the path of the newly constructed bridge now spanning the Danube. The president of Slovakia, Michal Kovach, was on hand and Chief Rabbi Baruch Myers spoke.

Ceremonies in Eastern Europe are symbolic. This **Chanukah** torch parade, similar to the carrying of the freedom torch by the Maccabees of old and run every year in Israel to the ancient town of Meron, signaled to the Slovak people that the Jews are in Slovakia to stay. This is crucial to the future of the Jews in Slovakia, for like in Russia and other countries in Eastern Europe, the Jewish community here sometimes appears to be uneasy. At the same time, there is no question that this Jewish community continues to revitalize itself.

Indeed, "anti-Semitism today is a heritage of the war-time Slovak state, a vassal republic controlled by Hitler which expelled its Jewish citizens to German extermination camps and paid the Nazis set fees for each person deported," wrote Olga S. Hruby in the *New York Times,* November 11, 1991.

If you really want to know how a small Jewish community exists in Eastern Europe, visit Slovakia. For this is one European Jewish community that is still going strong 25 years after that Chanukah torch relay in 1993. And still at the spiritual helm of this community is Rabbi Baruch Myers who today is the only community rabbi and Chabad *shaliach.* Rabbi Myers, who arrived in Bratislava in 1993, told me that the community no longer has a relay, but they do sponsor and hold a public *menorah* lighting ceremony.

Slovakia (Slovenska Republic)

Near the center of Europe, in the great Danubian valley, live the Slovaks. Today, most reside in a country called "Slovenska Republic," which covers 18,933 square miles and counts 5.4 million persons. Bordering the Czech Republic, Poland, Ukraine, Austria, and Hungary, it was once considered a "rural backwater" in the Austro-Hungarian Empire. But it is considered that no longer, because today it is strategically located between Ukraine and Hungary.

We know that Slovaks settled in Central Europe before CE 500. In the 800s, they were part of the Great Moravian Empire and around the year 900 they were conquered by the Magyars. Yet, throughout their long history, the Slovak people kept their own language, always "harboring nationalist feelings," longing for independence.

As Eva Hoffman writes in *"Exit into History: A Journey Through the New Eastern Europe,"* Slovakia's "brief moment of grandeur came in the ninth century when the Slovaks were united with the Moravians for the first time." The Great Moravian Empire was short lived and by the tenth century the Slovaks were conquered by Hungary, she adds. In fact, the Slovaks would endure Hungarian rule for most of their history. The Czechs at least enjoyed power and influence before bending to Austria Hapsburg control.

Hungarians like to call the period between 1867 and World War I (1914) a particularly creative and productive era in Hungarian history; but for the Slovaks, it brought "relentless *magyarization*," including the increasing promulgation of Hungarian as the official language. As a result, the Slovaks faced cultural extinction.

By 1918, powerful support existed among the Slovaks to unify with the Czechs, with the country to be called Czechoslovakia. So after World War I, much of the nation of Czechoslovakia was literally "cobbled together" from provinces of the defeated Austro-Hungarian Empire. Slovaks always felt the Czechs overpowered them intellectually and they resented Czech power. Constitutionally, there was no discrimination, according to author Josef Korbel. Czechs and Slovaks had common ties through ethnic identity. But over and over again the thousand-year history of separation had created two dissimilar societies and different cultural experiences. It soon became clear that the Czechs and Slovaks were "mismated," as Emil Lengyel puts it in *The Danube.*

Despite the assurances of the Czech patriot Thomas Garrigue Masaryk, who concluded what is called "the Pittsburgh Pact" in 1918 with Slovak Americans to win their support for a common state, Slovak self-rule never really occurred. During World War II Slovakia was a

Nazi puppet state. The Slovaks "never had an opportunity to establish their own identity," it was said.

With the crumbling of the Communist states, the Czechs and Slovaks parted ways on January 1, 1993, a day the Slovaks waited a thousand years for. The Slovaks once again stand on their own two feet. But the terrain of independence is rocky, especially economically. In contrast to the Czech Republic where inflation and unemployment have been kept under control, Slovakia has suffered from economic and political gyrations. It must be recalled that it was the Slovaks who pushed for separation and the Czechs went along with it; many Czechs perhaps believed they were "carrying" the Slovak sections of the country and could do better on their own.

At any rate, at that time and today, after nine centuries of rule by Hungary and nearly 70 years of Czech domination, Slovakia remains happy to be on its own after a "tumultuous past."

Vladimir Mercier and his party ran Slovakia from its independence in 1993 after the divorce from Czech Republic until September, 1998, when he was defeated by a coalition of four diverse parties. "His government was widely considered illiberal, discriminatory and corrupt, practicing crony politics," wrote Steven Erlanger in the *New York Times*, May 3, 2000. Many Slovaks thought that Merciar was "wrecking Slovakia's reputation abroad." But with Mercier out of power, Slovakia joined NATO and the European Union.

As time goes on, experts seem to agree that the Czech Republic got the better deal from the separation, certainly from an economic point of view. Some even say the Czechs all along wanted to go it alone. They probably were correct to do so. Remember as you travel through this part of Eastern Europe that a dominant sentiment is suspicion: Where once there was one country—Czechoslovakia—there now are two separate states, including separate armies, separate borders and passport control, and separate trade policies. The Czechs and Slovaks are glad they divorced. Many Slovaks do not like the Hungarians. The Hungarians say the Slovaks are causing trouble by trying to divert the Danube River. Remember the Slovaks were under the thumb of Hungary for a thousand years. Noteworthy is the fact that 600,000 Hungarians live in southern Slovakia.

But for tourists, "Slovakia is a visitor-friendly destination. Numerous historic sights, good roads, efficient internal transport . . . a wide choice of accommodation options have contributed to the steadily growing number of visitors to the country," noted one travel commentator. And today, moreover, it continues to preserve its own language and distinct cultural traditions. Above everything else, however, it rests at the very heart of Europe and its history will be intertwined with that of its neighbors, Czech Republic, Poland, Hungary, and Ukraine.

A Brief History

Who are the Jews of Slovakia? Once they were called "Highland Jews."

The history of Slovakia was often identified with Hungarian history—Slovakia was even called at various times Upper Hungary and Northern Hungary.

Slovak Jewish communities have flourished in the area since the thirteenth century.

By the fourteenth century, 800 Jews lived in Bratislava. Sometimes, they lived in an autonomous political unit headed by a communal leader. Generally, they were moneylenders engaged in commerce and finance.

After the Battle of Mohacs (1526), which began the rule of the Hapsburgs with Ferdinand I, Jews were expelled from the Slovak area towns and did not return until the beginning of the eighteenth century. From time to time, nobles granted them protection and some liberty.

The Austrian Emperor Joseph II (1780-90) granted Jews some limited civic rights, which made wider spheres of livelihood possible. This area in Northern Hungary became so popular for Jews that it was called "Magyar Israel." Many Moravian Jews arrived and created new areas of Jewish learning, especially in Bratislava itself. There, a yeshiva was established in 1700. The city became particularly prominent with the spread of the influence of Rabbi Moses Sofer, the Hatam Sofer, whose descendants for generations became rabbis of Bratislava and surrounding towns.

With the establishment of the dual monarchy of Austria and Hungary in 1867, the Hungarian Parliament passed an emancipation law the following year. The Jews of Slovakia became free men and women. The increased *"magyarization"* of the population, however, took its toll in the form of Jewish assimilation.

After the new nation of Czechoslovakia was established in 1918, Zionist activity emerged. For the first time, Jews had the right to declare themselves members of a Jewish nationality.

In the 1920s and 1930s, about 135,000 Jews, representing 4.5 percent of the Slovak population, lived in the Slovak region of Czechoslovakia. Political stability in the late 1920s brought prosperity for many Jews. Cultural and social life thrived around Zionist organizations and youth movements. The study of the Hebrew national culture and the increased focus on the Hebrew language led to close ties with the nascent Jewish community in Palestine. Jewish writers and journalists wrote in both German and Hungarian. However, in the late 1930s, as fascism spread over Europe, the position of the Jewish population deteriorated. The Munich Pact sellout resulted in the dismantlement of Czechoslovakia. Slovakia became a German satellite and agreed to set up a Nazi regime. Disaster lay ahead for the Jews. Jewish businesses became aryanized. Jews were fired from their jobs and were rounded up; they were shipped to the killing camps.

Thus began the Holocaust in Slovakia. By 1944, three-fourths of the Jewish community had been exterminated, and more than ninety percent of Jewish youth had been deported. Less zeal on the part of the Slovaks would have saved many Jewish lives. As early as 1941, Slovak leaders Tuka, Tiso, and Mach negotiated the question of deporting the Jews. Documents attest that in 1941, "Slovakia was the first state whose Jews the German Reich was prepared to take over." Adolf Eichmann gave Slovakia five hundred marks for each Jew as a guarantee that the Jews would not be returned.

The irony of it all: the first deportations from West Europe to the concentration camp Belzec took place on March 24, 1942. Two days later, the first Jews were deported to Auschwitz. They came first from Slovakia. On the following day, other Jews arrived from France. In her book, *The Holocaust: The Fate of European Jews, 1932-1945*, Leni Yahil writes that between March and November 1942, nearly 60,000 Jews were deported to Auschwitz and other concentration camps.

According to the book, *Tragedy of Slovak Jewry, prepared by the Documentation Center of CUJCR*, in Bratislava, and published in 1949, Slovak Jews "were exterminated so thoroughly and mercilessly during the years 1939-1945, that not one of the once happy and prosperous community has lived through the murderous storm without the irreplaceable loss of part or all of his family, without severe mental shock, or gravely impaired health."

Slovak Jewry lost about 110,000, including those deported in the spring of 1944 from territories that had been annexed by Hungary, according to Leni Yahil.

Bratislava

Welcome to Bratislava, the old city by the Danube—the capital of one of Europe's newest small nations, the Slovak Republic, and the country's largest city. Walk through Slovak National Uprising Square. Drive through this hilly metropolis, now trying quickly to shake off the forty-year Communist drabness, although it is succeeding somewhat.

However, it will take time to undo the poor city planning of the Communists. I think the description, *dinky city*, as described in a travel book, is not far off, that is, if you stick to the definition, meaning smallness. Even today—as in books—you cannot tell a city by its cover. There are some wonderful sites to see. Saunter through two great interlinked squares, Hlavne namestie and Frantiskanske namestie. In the first square stands the Old Town Hall; in the second stands the Marian Column, erected in 1657. Visit the gardens of Bratislava Castle. From there, you can see the splendid new bridge over the Danube. There is also the cathedral where 10 Hungarian kings and 8 Hungarian queens were crowned. Stop at the Baroque Old Town Hall courtyard and the Primatial Palace, which has its own art gallery and English tapestries based on Greek myths.

By the way, the Old Town Hall, remodeled and rebuilt many times since the 13th century, is now home to the City Museum. Worthwhile checking out the exhibits related to Slovakia's history. The city hosts a large number of festivals and special events throughout the year featuring folk and contemporary art, wine, beer, historical re-enactments, classical music, jazz and dance.

The Jewish community here is hospitable and will welcome the traveler. With a population of about 415,000 persons, Bratislava is crucial to Central Europe Jewish history. At the beginning of the nineteenth century, the noted Rabbi scholar Moses Sofer, the Hatam Sofer, made Bratislava the spiritual center of Hungarian Orthodox Judaism. The yeshiva in Bratislava once was the most important in Central Europe.

Throughout its history, the city was called, in Hungarian, "Pozsony"; in German, "Pressburg." The name Bratislava was coined by the Slovak archeologist P. G. Safarik in 1837. Some say the city was never a citadel of the Slovaks, for when it was separated from Hungary by the Versailles Treaty, its Slovak population was less than twenty percent. We must remember that Bratislava was the seat of the Hungarian Parliament for three centuries during the Turkish wars, and Hungarian kings were crowned in its cathedral. Actually, this old city on the Danube was the capital of Hungary from 1536 to 1683. It once stood as the second largest city in Czechoslovakia. Only thirty-five miles east of Vienna, it is now a center of rail and boat transport. Its factories churn out chemicals, textile machinery, and petroleum products. It is a working man's city, a factory town.

In the nineteenth and early-twentieth centuries, "a trip to Bratislava was considered a chic Sunday outing for Viennese noblemen."

Bratislava was the site in 1903 of the first Zionist convention in Hungary. Thirty-five years later, this metropolis, as capital of the

German vassal state, lives in memory for the tragedy of the Jews' mass deportation to the death camps. That forced, deadly expulsion was set in motion and organized by one man, the late dictator Monsignor Jozef Tiso. Not only was he a puppet of the Nazis, but he headed Slovak fascism and even had his troops commit anti-Semitic atrocities.

After the war, Slovak history became Czech history. Under communism, Slovak Jew and Christian would suffer alike. The postwar Jewish community was re-established on April 15, 1945, a few days after the country was liberated from the Germans.

By 1947, 7,000 Jews lived in Bratislava and a second synagogue opened. Jews had a difficult time reclaiming their property, however. Anti-Jewish riots erupted, and about 4,000 Jews immigrated to Israel just before the Communists took over. More left during "Prague Spring" in 1968, when Czechoslovakia launched fresh reforms, a new era of "socialism with a human face." This meant more civil rights, minority protection, and a possibility to emigrate.

Under the Communists, Jews could not easily or openly practice their religious or cultural customs. Jewish organizational property was turned over to government ownership and control. Any attempts to revitalize Jewish life were cut short and threats were made constantly. For example, in January 1952, the Communist newspaper, *Bratislava Pravda* warned that the country's "Jewish citizens are in the service of the American imperialists who are trying to undermine Slovak life." Only several thousand Jews resided in Slovakia during the forty years of Communist rule. They lived under the threat of dismissal from employment, compulsory manual work, evacuation from their homes, and long prison terms.

Prague Spring 1968 brought relaxation of the strictures, but the reforms did not last long. With backing from the Russians, a new Communist political leadership in the country cracked down even harder. A year later, the Jewish population of Bratislava in 1969 was estimated at about 1,500.

Today, Bratislava Jewry is participating in Jewish life.

And yet like other European countries, "negative political developments," have brought extreme right-wing nationalist and anti-Semitic parties to the fore in Slovakia, namely, *"Kotleba,"* (The People's Party Our Slovakia), which won 10 percent of the seats in Parliament in 2016.

The party takes its name from its leader, Marian Kotleba, who "previously led the banned neo-Nazi Slovak Togetherness National Party, which organized anti-Roma rallies and admired Nazi rule in Slovakia," according to Karol Janicek, writing in the *Times of Israel*. This party openly admires the Nazi puppet state that ruled the country in World War II. Unlike most of Europe's far-right groups, it's truly neo-Nazi.

In October of 2016, party members celebrated the 129th anniversary of the birth of Joseph Tiso, a Catholic priest and politician who was Slovakia's war president. During his rule, about 60,000 Slovak Jews were transported to Nazi death camps. Tiso was sentenced to death and hanged in 1947.

As other Jewish communities are rebuilding their institutions, Slovakia's Jewry is moving forward to revitalize itself and to take care of its seniors who gave so much to keep this community alive. Because of the strong tradition of Jewish scholarship in this city, it is fitting that we visit first the burial place of Hatam Sofer.

JEWISH SITES IN BRATISLAVA

Hatam Sofer Mausoleum, 811 02 Old Town, Bratislava, also known as The Hatam Sofer **Memorial** is a rarity among the sites of Slovakia. You would never know it is one of the most revered sights of Jewish Central Europe. It is located in what is called "Vajanskeho Nabrezie."

The **Hatam Sofer** Memorial is not a museum; it is a Jewish burial shrine erected over the graves of prominent rabbis and scholars who were highly esteemed by Jewish tradition. Dress appropriately.

In 2000-2002, the entire site was redeveloped and the gravestones were restored. The architect, Martin Kvasnica designed a striking new complex that adheres to the strict requirements of Jewish law, as well as to the highest standards of contemporary architecture.

But back in 1943, the sole remaining part of the centuries-old cemetery was destroyed when a nearby tunnel was constructed. Only a section of 23 graves remained. They surrounded the Hatam Sofer's tomb.

Here rests perhaps the greatest Jewish scholar of the nineteenth century. He is Rabbi Moses Sofer, known as Hatam Sofer, rabbi, halachic authority, and leader of Orthodox Jewry. He was indeed the leader of pre-modern Orthodox Jewry "in its battle against the initial manifestation of the Reform Movement of Judaism," writes Jacob Katz in *From East to West: Jews in a Changing Europe 1750-1870.* His coffin, it is said, was made from the slabs of his lecture desk.

Twenty-three graves and 41 separate tombstones are in the mausoleum today; once they were on the hillside of the cemetery behind the mausoleum. Visitors even leave notes just as they do at the Western Wall in Jerusalem. The mausoleum itself is part of the former Jewish cemetery that dates back to the years 1670 to 1847.

A "man of letters," the Hatam Sofer was the rabbi of rabbis. Rabbis came from all over Europe to Bratislava. He and his yeshiva—the largest since the Babylonian yeshivot—influenced the development of Orthodox Jews in western and central Hungary. Torah study became widespread among large sections of Orthodox Jewry. Yeshivot were established.

Hatam Sofer was born on September 24, 1762, in Frankfurt-am-Main. A brilliant scholar, he was offered many positions. But he accepted the offer of the Bratislava Jewish community and on October 13, 1806, he became Chief Rabbi. In 1809, when Bratislava was besieged by Napoleon's army, he fled and organized a charitable activity.

He was a voluminous writer. His works comprise volumes of responses, sermons, commentaries, letters, poems, and a diary-all bearing the imprint of his Orthodoxy. Hatam Sofer fought for the usage of the Hebrew language and for the idea of a return to Zion. He died on October 3, 1839. He educated many hundreds of rabbis who became spiritual leaders all over the world. He had devoted his life to religious judicial activity.

The mausoleum is visited by Jews from throughout the world who come here to say their prayers and pay tribute to Hatam Sofer. In 2016, thousands attended the *yahrzeit* (memorial service). Well worth observing this ceremony which always take place two days after *Simchat Torah*.

SYNAGOGUES, COMMUNITY CENTER
AND OTHER INSTITUTIONS

Synagogue, Heydukova St., 11-13, Bratislava. This synagogue is operated under the auspices of the Jewish Religious Community. Tel: 4212-5441-6949. znoba@znoba.sk.

During the forty years of Communism, as an act of defiance, many brave Jews, upon entering this synagogue, would wave at the hidden cameras of the secret police. Before 1989, it was difficult to be Jewish, but not any longer. Many young people are coming forward and declaring that they are Jews, even admitting that they have one Jewish parent.

Chabad Rabbi Baruch Myers leads the service on Shabbat in summer at this synagogue. This attractive synagogue schedules services on Monday and Thursday mornings, throughout the year, and Saturday mornings from Simchat Torah until after Passover. The time of services depends on the season.

Today, nearly 3,000 Jews are registered in the Slovak Republic, of whom about 1,000 live in the capital city of Bratislava. Between 500 and 1,000 Jews reside in the city of Kosice. The rest are found in small communities scattered throughout the country.

Here again, we see the phenomenon of "anti-Semitism without Jews."

Museum of the Jewish Community of Bratislava, Synagogue Slovaca, located in the lady's gallery of the main synagogue, Heydukova St., 11-13, Bratislava. The museum can be seen at specific times other than during prayer services. Welcomes tourists.

Also at the main synagogue on Heydukova stands an interesting exhibit on the community's history, including the history of this house of worship. The exhibition runs from May to October. Open Friday and Sunday from 10:00 a.m. to 4:00 p.m. No reservation necessary. Visits on other days can be arranged.

Jewish Community Center and Offices, Panenska 4, Bratislava. This building serves as the community activities center for the Jewish community. For thirty years, the community was without a spiritual leader. Rabbi Myers, who became the first post-Communist rabbi in Bratislava, studied under the Lubavitch Rebbe in Brooklyn, New York. He told this author that not too many Jews in Bratislava are totally observant, but he had managed to set up the synagogue, a kosher kitchen, and study groups. One of his first acts was to open a Jewish kindergarten with the support of the Ronald S. Lauder Foundation in 1995.

Services are held here on Saturday mornings from after Passover until Simchat Torah at the JCC. Synagogue updates, such as prayer times whether at the main synagogue or the JCC, can be seen at www.chabadslovakia.com.

The JCC is also the address for hot kosher lunches served daily from 11:30 a.m. until 2:00 p.m. under the supervision of Rabbi Myers. Lunch should be ordered in advance by email znoba@znoba.sk. All other catering requests including boxed lunches should be directed to chaniemyers@gmail.com.

Rabbi Myers was the subject of international headlines in 1993. Two teenage skinheads hurled the epithet "yuden raus"—"Jews, out"—at the rabbi. The Nazis had used that expression when rounding up Jews in the ghettos of Europe for deportation to the death camps. Myers was kicked and suffered minor injuries. He told this author he had been shaken up psychologically, but he indicated he would not be driven away. On December 6, 1996, Rabbi Baruch Meyers was again attacked again by skinheads. The attack took place at Rybne Square, where a Chanukah service was to take place the following day, and where a monument to the Holocaust victims stands today.

Chabad Center, Drevena st. 4, Bratislava. Chabad seeks to reconnect Jews with their Jewish heritage by providing them with the opportunity to learn about and live Judaism. A kosher *mikveh* is also in use at the Center, which was opened in 2016 and which had its ceremonial opening in 2017. A *mikveh* for men can be arranged.

Among the many activities at the center are Lauder Gan Menachem kindergarten, the Bratislava Hebrew School, a summer day camp, lectures and seminars, and a full range of Jewish holiday events.

The new Chabad Center also has rooms for accommodations. Contact chanimyers@gmail.com or chabad@stonline.sk. Contact Rabbi Myers at baruchmyers@gmail.com

The Headquarters of the Union of Jewish Communities in Slovakia. Kozia Street, 21, Bratislava. Although small in size, Bratislava Jewry sponsors a B'nai B'rith group with 55 members. Sixty to seventy percent of the people in the Jewish community are 80 years old or more. And many in the Jewish community help older parents.

Suggested Reading

Brogan, Patrick. *The Captive Nations: Eastern Europe 1945-1990.* New York: Avon, 1990.

Hoffman, Charles. *Gray Dawn: The Jews of Eastern Europe in the Post-Communist Era.* New York: HarperCollins, 1992.

Hoffman, Eva. *Exit into History: A Journey Through the New Eastern Europe.* New York: Viking, 1993.

Korbel, Josef. *Twentieth Century Czechoslovakia: The Meanings of Its History.* New York: Columbia University Press, 1977.

Lengyel, Emil. *The Danube.* New York: Random House, 1939.

MacLean Rory. *Stalin's Nose: Travels Around the Bloc.* Boston: Little, Brown, 1993.

Malino, Frances and David Sorkin, eds. *From East to West: Jews in a Changing Europe,* 1750-1870. Cambridge, Mass.: Basil Blackwell, 1990.

Nagorski, Andrew. *Birth of Freedom.* New York: Simon & Schuster, 1993.

Tragedy of Slovak Jewry. Bratislava Documentation Center of CUJCR, 1949.

Yahil, Leni. *The Holocaust: The Fate of European Jews, 1932-1945.* New York: Oxford University Press, 1990.

Poland

Someplace Along the Polish Road, You Will Shed a Tear

"I realized I didn't know any Jews. So, I asked myself and I asked others: Where do Jews exist? I was told: Poland. And so I went to Poland."
—Alfred Doblin

Someplace along the line, dear reader, if you travel to Poland today, you will shed a tear.

This implies, of course, that not everyone will want to visit this rapidly advancing, modern country, a nation in no way displaying the poverty one sees in Russia, a nation quickly moving along the fast track of market reform and free enterprise. Yes, it is free from forty years of the drabness and darkness of communism imposed by the former U.S.S.R. You will find no Third World country here. Actually, there are fine restaurants and extremely modern hotels, such as the Marriott in Warsaw. A high-speed train runs from Warsaw to Cracow. People are even friendly and extremely polite.

Logistics make Poland a launching pad to Eastern Europe, as well as a distribution center to Scandinavian nations and others in the European Union. Its dynamic economy exhibits "dramatic recovery with sustained growth." The country is moving fast, privatizing, and reforming. So welcome to Poland.

In the final analysis, Poland, a member of both NATO and the European Union, is developing rapidly and this can be seen in its great cities of Warsaw, Cracow, Wroclaw, and Gdansk.

In no other country since ancient Israel have Jews lived continuously for as many centuries as in as large numbers and with as much autonomy as in Poland. Eighty percent of the Jews in the world during the Middle Ages lived in Poland. In the seventeenth century, three-quarters of the world's Jews resided in this land. In 1897, despite the effects of large-scale Jewish emigration, 14 out of every 100 Polish citizens were Jews. The tourist knows from history that in the 1920s, one out of every five Jews in the world still lived in Poland, about 10 percent of that country's total population. Nowhere else in the world did Jews

519

form such a high percentage of the total population: 3,351,000 Jews made Poland the second largest Jewish community after the United States in 1939. Its capital, Warsaw, ranked as the second largest urban Jewish center with 350,000 people, or approximately 30 percent of the city's residents. By 1939, two-thirds of the world's Jews lived in Europe and three-quarters of them, half of all world Jewry, were concentrated in Eastern Europe. Remember, if you are a Jew residing in the United States or in the State of Israel, chances are your ancestors are from Poland, Czarist "Pale of Settlement," which included parts of partitioned Poland, or from Russia itself.

Jews played a key role in laying the foundations of trade and industry in Poland. They created a vast network of religious, political, and social institutions. Artistic and cultural activity reigned: Yiddish literature, Kabbala, the mysticism that lasts to this very day, and Talmudic rationality. More than three-quarters of Polish Jews settled in cities and town, constituting 27 percent of Poland's urban population. About 40 percent were engaged in industry and handicrafts, more than 33 percent in trade and commerce, and about six percent in the professions.

All came from this wonderful Jewish community.

Poland was the spiritual and religious heart of the Jewish Diaspora, which for 1,000 years followed in the footsteps of matching the achievements of the Babylonian Exile or the Golden Age of Spain and produced one of the greatest world centers of Talmudic study.

Poland's yeshivot and Talmudic libraries were the envy of world Jewry.

Poland is a country with a long and serious history of anti-Semitism that often erupted and still does, but now is labeled "anti-Semitism without Jews." Indeed, Polish "skinheads" and other extremists use the term Jew as a label for any of their targets, Jewish or not.

Poland's Jewish community in 1930 could boast 180 publications, including 20 daily newspapers, most of them in Yiddish but a few in Hebrew and Polish. By 1937, the number had grown to nearly 300. One newspaper, Haint (Today) employed 1,000 correspondents and was read by millions of Jews throughout the world. Contributors included David Ben-Gurion, the first prime minister of the State of Israel, and Sholem Asch, the noted Yiddish writer.

What hurts about visiting Poland? Three million Jews—90 percent of the Jewish community—were murdered in the killing fields of this country. This is where the Germans erected their death camps, a half-dozen in Poland alone, including Auschwitz, a name that still sends shivers down the spines of people throughout the world. The Nazis made Poland the center for the extermination of all European Jews.

With all that pain, why go? Some Jewish tourists visit Poland to seek their roots, to see the town their parents and grandparents called home, to physically observe and touch the "remnants," even a single surviving Warsaw Ghetto wall. Some place a pebble on a gravestone in the famous Jewish cemetery in Warsaw or stand in awe in front of the monument to the Warsaw Ghetto Uprising, which depicts the Jewish heroes and martyrs and marks the first armed, large-scale civilian resistance against the Nazis in occupied Europe.

Some recite psalms or a special prayer on the ground of the death camps or at the railroad platforms at Birkenau, where evil incarnate Dr. Joseph Mengele stood. Some journey here to make a statement that the Jewish people live, that "we are here." They walk with the young people who participate in the "March of the Living," where every year, about 10,000 Jewish teenagers from 40 countries march from Auschwitz to Birkenau.

Jewish tourists do go and they do meet Jews. A minimum of 5,000-8,000 Jews reside here. There are probably thousands more—some believe between 20,000 and 30,000 more. Every day more and more declare that they are Jews. A Jewish community still exists in Poland, and in the opinion of many, it should be visited and helped despite the pain of the past.

Jews don't visit Poland dispassionately. Sholem Asch once said that the broad shallow river, the Vistula, the queen of Polish rivers, spoke to him in Yiddish. No matter what language you speak, the Vistula—"on whose bank the Jews dwelt for centuries"—will speak to you about the Jewish past in Poland, a past that must be remembered. Our roots are too deep in Polish soil to die. As long as Jews live there and Jews visit there, they will not wither away.

Location

"God wanted to place Poland at the heart of Europe. But, as with man, he missed. Our heart lies off-center on the wrong side of the Germany," says the author of *Stalin's Nose: Travels Around the Bloc.* Poland should "nestle" next to France, "not lie trapped, as it is, on the open plains between two hungry autocracies, Russia and Germany." Poland lies astride the invasion corridor from Berlin to Moscow; it is too important geographically for its status to be left to chance. This frequently partitioned nation was swallowed up first by Prussia, Russia, and Austria, and later by Germany and the Soviet Union. "In the course of its history, Poland has taken a large number of different forms. Almost every century has witnessed its territory modified and the political lines that bounded it changed." But Bernard D. Weinryb, author of The Jews of Poland: A Social and Economic History of the Jewish Community in Poland from 1100 to 1800, says Poland has always remained hemmed in. For much of the past 300 years Poland did not exist as an independent state. It possessed an "unusual talent" to lose its independence for such a long time. Only after World War I, did Poland win freedom. And then after World War II, its borders were shifted from east to west by 150 to 200 miles, meaning that a big swatch of Polish territory was absorbed by the former Soviet Union.

This large Central European nation, which covers an area of 120,725 square miles, is only about 60 miles from Berlin, and from east to west, it extends about 430 miles. With a population of about thirty-nine million, Poland is named for the *Polane*, a Slavic tribe that lived more than a thousand years ago in the land we now call Poland. The name Polane comes from a Slavic word that means, "plain," or "field." Postwar Poland's population is more than 90 percent Catholic and more than 98 percent ethnically Polish.

A Brief History

And to think that it all began probably as far back as the tenth century, even though the first official documents attest to the Jews being in Poland in the twelfth century. After the Mongols overran Poland in 1240-41, many German Jews crossed the border into Poland, where they received a special invitation, also known as charters or privileges, from King Boleslav V the Pious, Duke of Kalisz, in 1264. These charters were called the "Kalisz Statutes," and they became the legal basis for the settlement of these German Jews. These privileges, too, were extended several times by King Casimir III.

To Jews, Casimir III, later known as Casimir the Great, looms large. In 1334, a year after he ascended the throne of Poland, King Casimir, who ruled from 1333 to 1370, issued a proclamation that substantially broadened those privileges originally granted to Jews. It is recorded in legend that Casimir had a Jewish mistress, Esther, and that their daughters were raised as Jews.

A crowning point, obviously affecting Jews, was the 1385 Polish Lithuanian Union. The Lithuanians wanted to rely on the Poles to stop the always present German threat. Pagan Lithuania sought a union with Christian Poland. They needed each other. In 1385, Jagiello, Grand Duke of Lithuania, "promised to convert his people to Christianity, to bind his armies to Poland's armies," writes Anne Applebaum, author of *Between East and West Across the Borderlands of Europe.* Jagiello became a Christian, married the Polish Princess Jawiga, and was named King of Poland. The Lithuanians converted to Christianity, too, and together, the Poles and Lithuanians defeated the Teutonic Guard Master at the Battle of Grunwald (Tannenberg) in 1410. This victory gave the Poles 200 years of growth and consolidation.

"The Jews are seen, accepted, and defended as a group whose main business is money lending against pledges," according to the Encyclopedia Judaica. Jews are "protected moneylenders." The pledges were protected and ratified by King Casimir IV Jagiello in 1453, and later by other Polish kings.

Certainly not lacking in the case of Poland are the facts as well as legends concerning how Jews arrived in this nation. One legend connects the Jews with the 1492 Spanish expulsion. According to this tale, when Jews were dispatched from Spain by that country's king and queen, they wandered eastward. When they finally rested, they declared, "Poh Lin," which in Hebrew means, "Here, stay overnight." Also, Rabbi Moses ben Israel Isserles coined a pun on the Hebrew form of Poland and explained that it derived from two Hebrew words: "Poh Lin": "Here he shall rest." And again we have the same Rabbi Isserles who said: "It is preferable to live on dry bread and in peace in Poland, than in other dangerous lands."

A proverb began circulating that went something like this: "Poland, the heaven of the aristocracy, the paradise of the Jews, the hell of the peasants," according to Alfred Doblin.

THE FIRST JEWISH SETTLERS

Who were these Jews, these first Jewish settlers? While there were Sephardic Jews from Iberia and the Mediterranean basin, the bulk of the first settlers were Ashkenazim and they came from the west and southwest. In the Dark Ages in Western Europe, the Jews repeatedly had been accused of causing the Black Plague, of practicing witchcraft, and of committing ritual murder. So they fled from Bohemia to the "emerging kingdom of Poland." They were welcomed, and this was the beginning, some say, of Poland itself. Many of those merchants and their co-religionists were fleeing from the Crusades. Driven from Germany, they brought with them skills in various crafts and experience in trade. Other newcomers hailed from the Ukraine and from Khazar. Early Polish rulers encouraged them to establish shops and develop industry, wrote S. L. Schneiderman in *The River Remembers*. Jews were needed in the backward economy of Poland. They became innkeepers, artisans, and traders. They plied the overland route through Poland, which linked the Ottoman Empire with Central and Western Europe. No middle class existed between the landed gentry and the peasants. So the Jews brought with them their arts, crafts, trades, professions, and ability as merchants and financial agents. International trade and banking flourished.

Moreover, during the Middle Ages, Jews were not segregated. According to the privileges granted them between the thirteenth and fifteenth centuries, they could live anywhere. By the end of the fifteenth century, 10,000 Jews resided in Poland. Already it was believed by Jews in Germany that "Poland was the safest place for Jews."

Remember that after the 1492 expulsion from Spain, the only country in which Jews were permitted to engage freely in trade and crafts was Poland. By the end of the sixteenth century, therefore, Poland still was being hailed as "the new golden land of the Jews," writes Norman F. Cantor in *The Sacred Chain: The History of the Jews.*

In the sixteenth century, a Jewish parliamentary body, the Council of Four Lands (Vaad Arba Artzot), with headquarters in Lublin, was established and became an independent representative government of Polish and Lithuanian Jewry. It distributed the tax load among the various Jewish communities. Described as the highest institution of Jewish autonomy, it also concerned itself with matters of security and morals.

Between the end of the fifteenth century and the partitions of Poland in 1772, 1793, and 1795, Poland had expanded and reached its highest peak. Territorially it was the second largest state in Europe and ranked sixth in population. By the sixteenth century, Polish rule stretched from the Baltic Sea in the north to the Black Sea in the south and eastward to the gates of Moscow. Poland then was second only to France in size and population.

Polish nobility became the dominant political force, mainly because Polish farming was "primitive and feudal." The nobles realized that greater profits could be had if the lands produced more efficiently. So they turned to the Jews, according to Abba Eban in *Heritage: Civilization and the Jews.* Jews soon became active and valued partners to the nobility in many enterprises.

Jews who leased the land from the nobles were called rendars, and they enlisted other Jews to help them administer vast domains. Thus, the interests of Jews and Polish magnates coincided and complemented each other between the huge estates of the nobles and the private towns organized by the Jews. Jews "were made estate agents sent out to the outlying properties of the nobility to govern the serfs and produce revenue for the lords," writes Norman F. Cantor. He adds that Jews obtained the monopoly of the liquor trade in the countryside in the Ukraine. Polish peasants had to buy from Jewish tavern owners, often creating friction and hatred. It was part of the age-old Jewish problem—as tax collectors, managers of estates, or distributors of wine and liquor, you don't exactly make friends. An old Polish proverb, "What the peasant earns, the noble spends, and the Jews profit by," reflects the true sentiments of the masses.

The nobles opened up huge regions of the Ukraine wilderness and brought them under Polish rule. But this also brought difficulties: the Ukrainians were Eastern Orthodox, and they hated the Roman Catholic Poles, as well as their Jewish rendars.

THE CHMIELNICKI POGROM

To Ukrainians, he is a hero. To Jews, Ukrainian officer Bogdan Chmielnicki (1595-1657) is anathema. Chmielnicki hated Poles and Jews, and after an argument with a Polish nobleman, he fled across the Dnieper River to Zaporozh'ye, a Cossack stronghold. There, he roused the Cossacks to rebellion. And in 1648, he changed the history of the Ukraine and Poland because his revolt altered the balance of power in all of Eastern and Central Europe. The Cossacks now swore allegiance to the Russian Czar and thus, the Russians would go on to become a world power.

Poles and Jews suffered horrible deaths at the hands of the Cossacks. Jews were buried alive, sold as slaves and skinned alive. They suffered through several years of massacres. Thousands were killed. Thousands were forced to convert to Christianity. Their homes were destroyed and their imposing wooden synagogues burned to the ground. From that moment on, Polish Jews began emigrating westward. The upheaval inaugurated Jewish poverty, especially in the villages of Eastern Europe.

By 1655, Poland began to decline for the Polish people and for the country's 1.5 million Jews.

By the end of the eighteenth century, Poland disappeared from the map of Europe. Major changes occurred in the Jewish community in the seventeenth century. Jews tried to move out of money lending into other occupations, even agriculture and other branches of trade. But even during this decline, Poland stood strong as a reservoir of Jewish spirit and manpower that resisted assimilation and apostasy.

In the eighteenth century, Poland was partitioned out of existence; it became the "plaything of its neighbors and its political system was the laughing stock of Europe," says Robert I. Frost in his book, *After the Deluge: Poland and the Second Northern War, 1655-1660.*

Out of the wars and the Cossack uprisings grew the great messianic movements of Eastern European Judaism. And as the eighteenth century drew near, messianic claims of Shabbetai Zevi stirred the masses.

The Shabbetai Zevi messianic movement of the seventeenth century did not originate and develop in Poland, but it had an impact upon Polish Jewry. Zevi was born in 1626 in Smyrna, also known as Izmir. Interested in Jewish mysticism, Kabbala, in 1648 he began to believe that he was destined to be the "savior of the Jews." Abba Eban says that "never before had one man united the Jewish people of all lands in a movement so inspired with enthusiasm and hope."

Zevi met and acquired a so-called "prophet," Nathan of Gaza. As the two wandered the Mediterranean area, the Turks, fearing an insurrection, arrested Shabbetai Zevi in 1666. Facing execution or conversion, he renounced Judaism and adopted Islam.

The impact of Jacob Frank was also great. Alfred Doblin says Frank was a Jewish sectarian. "He fantasized the Jews, got them to convert to Christianity." Incredibly successful, he was supported by the Polish king.

Polish-born Frank, who lived 1726-91, spent twenty-five years in Turkey before he came back to his homeland and founded the cult named after him. Like Shabbetai Zevi, whom he admired, he said people should seek the joy of life and communion with God through "ecstasy." Thousands of fanatical adherents followed him. He first became a Moslem and then a Christian. Several thousand of his followers converted to Christianity.

Jews felt they had been spiritually deserted by these false messiahs. But now a new movement came on the scene: Chassidism. Abba Eban defines Chassidism as "a special enchanting world, rich with stories, homilies, and endless wonders about the rabbinical court and dynasties that are the heart and center of the Chassidic vision."

Chassidism's founder was Israel ben Eliezer (1700-1760), who was of humble origin. We know him as the Ba'al Shem-Tov, literally, "the Master of the Good Name." After years of wandering and taking on various jobs, for example, as a beadle in a synagogue, teacher, herbal healer, and hermit in 1735, he appeared as a pious miracle worker, according to Maurycy Horn in Polish Jewry History and Culture. His main power lay in the "force of his personality" when he offered hope to the Jews of Poland. Estimates state that half of Polish Jewry flocked to Chassidism. They believed he was a prophet; they found refuge in his wishful vision. The 1648 pogroms and the closing of the Council of Four Lands in 1734 had sharply curtailed the once vibrant spirit of Polish Talmudic Judaism. The masses yearned for comfort; Chassidism filled the vacuum and became the greatest religious revival in the long history of the Jewish people.

In the nineteenth century, Poland became the seedbed for the intellectual movements that were to transform the Jewish world: Zionism, secularism, socialism, and neo-orthodoxy.

The Russians ruled Poland with an iron fist and again, after the 1863 Polish uprising, imprisoned thousands and exiled many of the Poles to Siberia. The czars, who had annexed large chunks of Polish territory, treated Poland as if it were nothing more than a "Province of Russia." They called it "Russification." These rulers of Russia kept the Jews as downtrodden as they could by confining them to a massive ghetto area of Russian Poland, called the "Pale of Settlement."

Before World War I, relations between Poles and Jews became strained. Jews were promised their own schools; that never happened. Jews were promised status as a minority with rights; that never happened. Jews were promised financial aid and support for schools; that never happened. All of these broken promises were symptomatic of Poland's difficulties, created bitterness, and even led to deaths. Gerald Stillman reports in the publication *Jewish Currents, April 1993*, that between 1935 and 1939, some 500 Jews were killed and 5,000 injured in various pogroms throughout the country.

In 1936, Ze'ev Vladimir Jabotinsky, leader of the Zionist Revisionist Party and founder of Betar, its youth movement, pleaded with Jews to leave. They did not; many could not, and often those who wanted to were barred by highly restrictive immigration policies of Western nations, including the United States. Between the wars, as we shall see, Zionism, the national rebirth of the Jewish people, was one of the most important Jewish organizations in Poland. So, too, was the BUND, the acronym for the "General Jewish Workers Union in Lithuania, Poland, and Russia."

The BUND demanded cultural and national autonomy for national minorities, especially for the Jews.

The BUND perceived the necessity of organizing Jewish workers into one national party. Generally, this group opposed political conservatives and Orthodox Jewish religion. The BUND saw that the only chance of solving the Jewish question in Poland was the building of a socialist society.

Despite the pogroms after the First World War, despite discrimination in Poland's universities, despite the increasingly hostile atmosphere, despite poverty and economic boycotts, a vast Jewish network of religious, educational, philanthropic, social, and cultural institutions flourished in Poland "without comparison elsewhere in Europe," according to Lucy S. Dawidowicz in *The War Against the Jews: 1933-1945*. Jews had political parties of all views and delegates and senators in the Polish parliament. She adds that the rise of Nazi

Germany, the death of Marshal Jozef Pilsudski in 1935, and Poland's accelerating Fascist course all brought near-disaster to the Jewish community. A torrent of anti-Semitic legislation, brutal pogroms, and an official government policy of "evacuating" the Jews from Poland overwhelmed them. By 1939, more Jews had left Poland than Germany, well over 400,000, and they went mainly to France, Belgium, and Palestine. To add insult to injury, the Polish government even studied the feasibility of settling Polish Jews on the island of Madagascar. In 1938, laws were enacted to revoke the citizenship of Polish Jews residing abroad.

The year 1938 will always be remembered as the year of Munich. On September 1, 1939, Hitler unleashed the German army and sent it into Poland. The long chapter on Polish Jewry was closed. A new disastrous chapter would begin. We know, of course, that after World War II, only about 200,000 Jews out of 3.5 million survived. Fifty years later, there would be only about 5,000 to 8,000 "registered" Jews in Poland. An even newer chapter would start.

Notable Polish Jews

Many Jews served as court physicians to Polish princes and magnates. Tobias Cohn (1652-1729) may have been the first physician to provide a detailed description of the disease known as plica polonica, a skin disease affecting the scalp.

A large number of Jewish moneylenders became involved in trade and helped establish villages on large tracts of land.

By far, some of the greatest Jewish scholars, luminaries of Talmudic scholarship, hailed from Poland. Among these rabbis were Yom Tov Lippmann Heller; Solomon Luria; Moses Isserles; Isaiah b. Abraham ha Levi Horowitz; Meir b. Gedaliah of Lublin; Mordechai b. Abraham Jaffe of Lublin; and the Chassidic masters, including Israel b. Eliezer Ba'al Shem Tov, the founder of Chassidism, to name a few.

Thirteen Jewish representatives sat in the first Polish Parliament in 1919. Noted among them was Professor Mojzesz Schorr, historian and Zionist, as well as being a member of the Polish Parliament.

Other important figures include Dr. Zygmunt Bychowski (1865-1934), prominent neurologist; Vladimir Medem (1879-1923), writer and leader of the BUND, which was founded in Vilna in 1897; Majer Balaben (1877-1942), historian, professor at Warsaw University, and once head of the Institute for Jewish Studies.

Polish Jewish musicians included Ignaz Friedman and Arthur Rubinstein, the singer Marya Freund, and harpsichordist Wanda Landowska.

Lazar Rundsztein was flyweight boxing champion of Poland in 1937.

Many of the leading Zionists and leaders of Israel came from Poland, the prime example being David Ben-Gurion, the first prime minister of Israel. Another noted Polish and later Zionist leader in Israel was Yitzhak Gruenbaum. A large part of the Israeli population had been born in Poland, and many were the organizers of the Jewish self-defense units in Palestine, known as the Haganah, which came out of Jewish defense movements in Poland, wrote Mark Kurlansky, author of *A Chosen Few: The Resurrection of European Jewry*. After the death of Theodor Herzl, the founder of modern Zionism, the leadership of the Zionism movement passed to Polish and Russian Jews, who carried on the idealistic work and vision. Poland once stood as one of the most important centers of the Zionist movement, with Polish Zionists playing an important role in World Zionist affairs. Various Zionist parties, like Hechalutz (a pioneering youth movement), were founded in Poland, as were groups such as the Revisionist Zionists. Unlike their German co-religionists, many of whom leaned toward assimilation, the Jews of Poland responded "wholeheartedly to the movement for a national revival." The first conference of the Hoveve Zion, "Lovers of Zion," movement was held in Katowice. Nahum Sokolow, who headed the Zionist movement in Poland, became a member of the World Zionist executive committee. A tremendous increase in membership in the Zionist movement occurred in Poland between the wars. According to the Encyclopedia of Zionism and Israel, "no other country with the exception of Palestine and, to a degree, Lithuania, experienced so encompassing a Zionist impact on Jewish life." The encyclopedia also notes that the Polish government in the 1930s did not place obstacles before the Zionist movement "on the assumption that this would increase the stream of emigrants from Poland to Palestine." We will see that the Zionist youth groups in particular played a crucial role during World War II in the Jewish underground and the Warsaw Ghetto Uprising. In 1965, of the 17 cabinet members of Israel, eight were of Polish extraction; of the 120 Knesset members, about 30 percent had come to Israel from Poland.

Rosa Luxemburg (1870-1919) was swept up in the radical currents of the time. Born in the area of Russian Poland, she helped found the Spartacists, the forerunner of the German Communist Party. She was murdered by German rightwing soldiers in Berlin.

Julia Tuwim (1894-1953) wrote in Polish and is considered one of Poland's greatest modern poets.Yiddish writers Solomon Rabinowitz, known as Sholem Aleichem (1859-1916); Shalom Abramovitsch, known as Mendele Mokher Soforim (1835-1917); and Isaac L. Peretz

(1851-1915) immortalized the shtetlekh (Yiddish word for those Jewish rural communities of Russia and Poland). I.J. Singer (1893-1944) and Isaac Bashevis Singer (1904-91) were Yiddish novelists and short-story writers. The Singer brothers were born in Poland. I. J. Singer achieved fame for such novels as *Yoshe Kalb, The Brothers Ashkenazim, East of Eden, and The Family Carnovsky.* Isaac Bashevis Singer won the Nobel Prize for Literature in 1979. The books he is known for include *The Family Moskat, Gimpel the Fool, The Magician of Lublin,* and *The Manor.* Simon An-sky (1863-1920), folklorist and author of the famous play The Dybbuk, and Isaac Manger (1901-69) are also noted Jewish writers. To understand the life of Jews in Poland, the works of these authors make impressionable reading.

Sholem Asch (1880-1957), Polish-born, was the foremost Yiddish novelist of the early twentieth century. Also a dramatist, short-story writer, and journalist, Asch lived in Warsaw under the influence of Isaac Leib Peretz. Asch began writing in Yiddish in order to reach a worldwide Jewish audience. He lived and worked in several European countries as well as the United States and Israel. Some charged him with "becoming an apostate" and inciting further hatred of Jews, but he denied these accusations. He wrote *The Nazarene, The Apostle, Mary, Moses, Three Cities, The Mother, and East River.*

Polish Jewry Today

A Polish woman in her late forties recalls that as far back as thirty-five years ago the Polish Jewry community had only 5,000 to 10,000 members and was dying. "Thirty-five years later, I hear the same thing," she relates.

Never write off a Jewish community. The pundits said the same thing about the Jews of Vienna in the 1970s; that it was a dying community. Today, the Austrian Jewish community is a vibrant congregation. The fact is that Polish Jewry has survived and lives. Can organized communal life continue in Poland? Polish Jewry has received strong financial and political support from the American Jewish Joint Distribution Committee, The American Jewish Committee, the World Jewish Congress, the Taube Foundation, and the Ronald S. Lauder Foundation, as well as various Jewish religious groups.

"Poland's small Jewish community is an incredible testimony to Jewish survival," says Konstanty Gebert, one of Poland's leading journalists. As a former underground journalist and one of the founders of *Gazeta Wyborcza,* Poland's biggest daily non-tabloid, newspaper, Gebert has written 11 books, covering subjects as diverse as the European 20th century, Israel, Polish Jews, and the Balkan Wars.

He is also a key figure in Poland's reconstituted Jewish community.

"Although there is quite a lot of anti-Semitism," he noted, "Jews in Poland do not feel threatened," even to the extent that those who wear a kipa (skull cap) which he does, continue to do so.

In 1939, the Jewish population of the Soviet Union numbered 2.8 million. Nearly all Soviet Jews then and until this day lived in areas that once were part of Poland. Just before World War II, therefore, nearly 40 percent of the world's Jews lived in Poland itself or in former Polish territories. At least another 20 percent were descendants of Polish Jews who had immigrated to America.

For years, the population of the Polish Jewish community has been approximated at 5,000 persons. In the 21st century, however, many Jewish leaders say the Jewish population in Poland stands at 5,000-8,000 but is probably closer to 10,000 to 15,000. The core group may number only 3,000. Rabbi Michael Schudrich, chief rabbi of Poland, notes that if the core group means, most involved; then yes, there are at least that many who are very active.

But Rabbi Schudrich believes that "at least 30,000 have Jewish roots, know it and are proud of it."

Finally, what is effecting many Jewish communities in Poland is the fact that property restitution may soon come through, which will bring financial aid and independence to Jewish communities to help in the growth of schools, education facilities, and community institutions.

After Communism fell, the Poles began the process of returning to the market economy it once maintained. Along with Hungary and the Czech Republic, it has made progress economically.

There are 39 million Poles living in an area almost as big as Germany.

As a member of the European Union and NATO, the Poles maintain a dynamic economy. "Nobody is worried yet about Russia attacking Poland, but everybody, Jews included, is worried that Russia is getting ever more aggressive and getting away with it," it is said in Polish political circles.

What worries many Poles, including Jews, is the ruling party, Liberty and Justice, abbreviated to PiS. "A right-wing nationalist and conservative party committed to upending Poland's established liberal order, it won an election in 2015, which was in Konstanty Gebert's view, "the single most important political event since the fall of Communism." With 216 seats in the Sejm and 56 in the Senate, it is currently the largest party in the Polish parliament.

Gebert adds: "The new government has proceeded to subvert and ultimately take over the Constitutional Court, undermine the independence of the judiciary, take over public media and turn it into a propaganda outlet."

"Though PiS is not anti-Semitic, and its leading figures have explicitly condemned anti-Semitism, as well as expressed deep support for Israel, much of the membership is," he declared.

"The government turns a blind eye to public demonstrations of anti-Semitism, for example, chanting, 'In the spring Zionists, instead of leaves, will hang from trees.'" That is the voice of young neo-Nazis "whose numbers are seriously on the rise," says Gebert.

According to an article in the *New York Times,* on November 2, 2016, by foreign policy expert, James Traub, PiS hopes to "deflect Poland from the orbit of Western Europe and returning it to a past defined by family, church, and home."

It should be noted that the Polish government is also dead set against any further European deals to allocate refugees among member states.

And finally, according to a report in Ynet news, Israel, Poland and the Baltic nations are among states not meeting their commitments on returning stolen Jewish property.

Much information on Poland's Jewish Community can be gleaned from the community website: www.jewish.org.pl.

Before the fall of communism, many Jewish parents masked or at least downplayed their Jewish identity because memories of the Holocaust were too painful and to be Jewish was not to their advantage. But now tens of thousands of full Jews, half-Jews, quarter-Jews, as well as non-Jewish spouses and in-laws are declaring their Judaism. In 1989, according to Rabbi Michael Schudrich, former director of the Lauder Foundation in Poland, and now chief rabbi of Poland, thousands of young Poles began seeking their Jewish roots.

Now, Jews and other minorities feel comfortable in practicing Judaism. The restrictive policy of a Communist police state toward religion, toward Zionism, toward Israel, has been lifted.

Anti-Semitic incidents may be rare, but hate speech and hate crimes have increased.

Many of the young people tell of having one Jewish parent. During the Communist regime, these youths never thought of asking their mother if she was Jewish. As the story goes, that would have been like asking one's mother if she was a virgin when she got married. These people were one step past total assimilation. One young man knew so little, he did not even recognize he was Jewish when one day his mother blurted out, "By the way, my mother's mother was Jewish." According to Jewish law, that made the young man Jewish—Orthodox Judaism states that if your mother is Jewish, you are Jewish.

"The eternal spark of the Jewish soul is never extinguished. We should not try to extinguish sparks that the Nazis and Communists failed to extinguish," declares Rabbi Schudrich.

Rabbi Schudrich urges Jewish tourists to visit Jewish institutions in Warsaw and that includes his own Nozyk Synagogue.

In the final analysis, make no mistake about it, there stands a Jewish community in Warsaw and activities are held.

In 2016, Rabbi Schudrich opined that there definitely would be a Jewish community in Poland in 15 years. "What it would look like no one can guess."

Jewish Warsaw

If Warsaw is the heart of Poland and it is, then despite all, Warsaw is still the heart of Jewish Poland. But from 1939 to the year 2000, is like the difference between night and day. The Warsaw that Jews knew and loved is gone. And indeed, "the city, its people and its life will never be the same again." Once, one out of every three Warsavians was Jewish; today nobody even knows the exact figure—more than a thousand Jews, less than a thousand Jews.

The largest city of Poland, Warsaw lies on both banks of the Vistula River. The center of Warsaw and most residential areas are on the left bank.

In the years of the 900s, a small Slavic sect lived here. From the 1200s to the 1500s, Warsaw was the home of the dukes of Mazovia, a state that entered the Polish kingdom in the 1500s. In 1596, King Sigismund III moved the capital from Cracow to Warsaw. During the partitions, Prussia controlled Warsaw in the late 1700s; then the city became the capital of the Duchy of Warsaw from 1807 to 1813. In the next phase, the Russians controlled Poland until 1914 and after the German occupation in World War I in 1918, Warsaw became the capital of an independent Poland.

Today, Warsaw is bustling. Here again, most places of interest are found in the historic center of the capital. Tourists especially flock to the Old Town and New Town sections. They have become the most popular tourist destinations.

In the Old Town square, which was reconstructed from utter ruin, we find the most elegant area in Warsaw and one of the most exciting in Poland. On an early Sunday morning, all is quiet except for the ringing of the church bells. This is what parts of Warsaw must have been like before World War II. Today Warsaw covers 170 square miles and has a population of about 2.6 million.

In 1781, 2,609 Jews lived in Warsaw, including several hundred in fashionable Praga, a suburb of the city on the east bank of the Vistula River.

In 1867, the Jewish Warsavian population reached 219,128.

Warsaw for the Jews symbolized study and cultural activities; Warsaw even had six full-time Yiddish theaters and a hundred Jewish troupes toured the country. Two major centers of Hebrew literary activity from 1880 to 1914 existed in Eastern Europe; Warsaw was one, Odessa in the Crimea, the other. Eventually, entire neighborhoods in the Warsaw suburbs were inhabited mainly by Jews, many of whom attended shtibels, Chassidic houses of prayer.

But between the world wars, the depression, the anti-Semitic policies of the Polish government, and the fall of Marshal Pilsudski, all "combined to keep the economic level of the Jewish community low," declared Lucy S. Dawidowicz. In his Journey to Poland, author Alfred Doblin was shocked by the poverty of the Jews. He described Jews in medieval garb with their own language, religion, and culture. He saw black-bearded Jews as vendors, elderly Jewish women, Jews in caftans and skull caps—they were not an "exotic tribe." They were lower middle-class workers, small businessmen, and laborers. By the 1930s, close to thirty percent of Polish Jews were receiving some form of financial assistance from Jewish communal funds.

There were renunciations of minority rights. There were pogroms. There were killings. There was anti-Semitism. There were numerous restrictive clauses. But there was not mass murder.

Warsaw remains a symbol of the tragedy of World War II. Without doubt, it had the distinction of being the "capital of the war," the first city to be bombed and the first to be turned into a battlefield.

Try to picture Stalingrad after that famous, devastating battle. Soviet officers who fought there maintain that Warsaw was the most destroyed city in Europe. Already ruined, Warsaw was burned to the ground during the German retreat. Early on, Hitler had decided to make Warsaw a "second Carthage," and in the 1944 Polish Uprising, the Germans bombarded the city, "literally to rubble," writes Eva Hoffman in Exit into History: A Journey Through the New Eastern Europe.

"Wartime in Poland lasted longer than for any other country, except Germany. In proportion to its size, Poland incurred far more damage and casualties than any other country on earth," according to Norman Davies in Heart of Europe: A Short History of Poland.

JEWISH SITES IN WARSAW

Because the Jewish community today is small, the tourist realizes that the major Jewish sites are pretty much within walking distance, so for our first visit we should head for Twarda Street and the Nozyk Synagogue.

The Nozyk Synagogue at 6 Twarda St., Warsaw. (Photo by Ben G. Frank)

Nozyk Synagogue, Twarda ul. 6, Warsaw. Tel and FAX: 22-652-28-05 or 22-620-43-24. This synagogue is open to tourists at all times, but obviously they should not come to this house of prayer during services unless they desire to pray. There is no admission for those coming to pray, though contributions to the Jewish Community of Warsaw are always welcome, according to those who regularly pray there.

Since this is an Orthodox synagogue, there is separate seating for men and women. Women may sit in a partitioned-off area of the main sanctuary or they may go upstairs to the women's balcony. Services are held twice a day. For more information contact: www.warszawa.jewish.org.pl. Tourists can visit the synagogue. Monday to Friday, 9:00 a.m. to 7:00 p.m. Sunday at 11:00 a.m. to 7:00 p.m. There is a cost of admission. The synagogue requires advance notice of organized groups. Monday to Thursday 10:00 a.m. to 4:00 p.m., Fridays 10:00 a.m. to 1:00 p.m., Przewodnik@jewish.org pl.

This stately Orthodox synagogue was founded in 1900 and named after the founders, Zalman and Rywka, who died in the early part of the last century.

The *aron ha-kodesh* (Holy Ark) is located in the main hall and covered by the curtain (parokhet) with an inscription of the prayer, "Shema Yisrael." A member of the congregation led the prayers when I attended and his stand was on the right side facing the aron ha-kodesh.

How this synagogue, with alternating square piers and columns supporting the galleries, survived the Holocaust is a miracle. The Nazis used it as a stable. The dedication of the renovated synagogue, which is mainly Romanesque, took place on April 18, 1983, a day before the fortieth anniversary of the Warsaw Ghetto Uprising.

Office of the Chief Rabbi of Poland, Rabbi Michael Schudrich, Nozyk Synagogue, ul.Twarda 6, 00-950- Warsaw. Tel: 48-22-624-14-84. naczelnyrabinpl@jewish.org.pl, to contact the guide, call: 48-502-400-849.

Union of Jewish Religious Communities in Poland, Twarda ul 6, 00-104, Warsaw. Tel: 48-22-620-06-76. sekretariat@jewish.org.pl. This organization coordinates activities for more than 15 synagogues in Poland and looks after Jewish cemeteries. It also attends to the religious needs of Polish Jewry.

Chabad, ul Slominskiego 19/508a, 00-195, Warsaw. Tel: 48-22-637-5352. office@chabad.org.pl, www.chabad.org.pl. Rabbi Szalom Stambler is rabbi at Chabad. *Minyanim* are held Sunday, scharit at 9:00 a.m. Monday through Friday, 8:00 a.m., summer kabbalat Shabbat at 7:30 p.m. And in winter, 6:45 p.m. Chabad is very active in Warsaw and sponsors a day care, kindergarten, a synagogue, a kosher soup kitchen. Mikveh.

Jewish Community of Warsaw, Twarda ul. 6, 00-104 Warsaw. Tel and FAX: 48-22-652-28-05. warszawa@jewish.org.pl., warszawa@jewish.org. pl Warsaw's Jewish community is located here. The Jewish Community of Warsaw is one of seven organizations forming the Association of Jewish Communities. A self-governing body, its members practice both traditional and liberal Judaism.

Es Chaim. www.warszawa.jewish.org.pl.

Congregation Gmina Beit Warszawa, ul Wiertnicza 113, 02-952, Warsaw. Tel: 48-22-885-26-38. Office @beit.org.pl. www.Beit.org.pl

Services are on Friday's at 7:00 p.m., and Saturday morning at 10:00 a.m.

Jewish Heritage Initiative in Poland. Founded in 2003, the JHIP nurtures the revival of Jewish life in Poland, furthers awareness of this resurgence among Jews and non-Jews, and fosters positive interest in Poland and Polish Jews among Jews worldwide. This is a peoplehood program established by the Taube Foundation for Jewish Life & Culture.

TSKZ Jewish Social-Cultural Association of Poland, Plac Grzybowski 12/16, Warsaw (Yiddish Theater Building).Tel: 22-620-05-54. Warszawa@tskz.pl. www.takz.pl. This organization deals with cultural activities in Poland and is a lay organization, active in Jewish communities. There are TSKZ branches throughout the country and it is the largest Jewish organization in Poland. Together with the Union of Religious Communities, TSKZ was the officially recognized Jewish organization under Communism. Its bilingual Polish-Yiddish biweekly publication, *Slowo Zydowskie/Dos Yiddish Vort*, can be obtained in the Yiddish Theater lobby.

Shalom Foundation, Plac Grzybowski 12/16 ul, Warsaw. This group supports cultural programs and created the Polish Jewry photo album, "I Can Still See Their Faces."

The Ronald S. Lauder Foundation, Warsaw. info@lauderfoundation. com. www.lauderfoundation. Com. Lauder Morasha Kindergarten, Warsaw. Lauder Morasha Primary and Middle School. Warsaw.

Joint Distribution Committee, JDC partners with the local Jewish community to care for the needy and continue the innovation of Jewish life for Poland's estimated 25,000 Jews. JDC supports two major JCCs in Warsaw and Cracow. They also support community-wide Sabbath dinners, camping experiences, Jewish learning conferences and education programs, Jewish music, food, as well as youth clubs, urban holiday events, and classes for those who have just discovered their Jewish roots.

E.R. Kaminska's State Jewish Theater in Warsaw Teatr Żydowski, Senatorska 35, Warsaw: http://www.teatr-zydowski.art.pl/ Named after Esther Rachel Kaminska, this 400-seat theater was opened in 1970 at a cost of more than $1 million. Its founder and star performer, Ida Kaminska, fled Poland after the anti-Semitic outburst of 1968.

It has been said that Yiddish and the Hebrew language and culture, as well as the Yiddish theater, springs from Poland and it exists because the people and the community want to keep it alive, and the government and the American Jewish Joint Distribution Committee support it. Productions are attended mainly by Poles.

In Warsaw, the first attempt to create a Jewish theater was recorded in 1837. In the 1890s, Yiddish productions were stimulated by Abraham Goldfaden, considered father of the Yiddish theater. Drama circles began to flourish in Warsaw and Cracow. The dramatists included such literary celebrities as Shalom Abramovitsch, known as Mendele Mokher Soforim, and Solomon Rabinowitz, whose pseudonym was Sholem Aleichem. The latter's plays still thrill the world, including Tevye the Dairyman, better known as *Fiddler on the Roof.*

We also recognize the Yiddish and Hebrew poet, Isaac Leib Peretz (1852-1915), and Ossip Dymov (1878-1942). Ossip Dymov, born in Bialystok, had been a publicist before he began writing for the theater. Only at the turn of the century did the Jewish theater start to actively develop.

In 1892, Esther Rachel Kaminska (1870-1925) made her appearance in Warsaw's Eldorado Theater. Kaminska, who would later found the theater in Obozna Street, won fame as an actress and performed in the first Jewish films. By her side, the great talent of her daughter, Ida Kaminska (1899-1978) grew.

The Jewish theater in Poland—chiefly in Warsaw and Vilna—gave premiers of plays, which were often dramatic adaptations by Sholem Aleichem. The audience also had the opportunity to acquaint themselves with Jacob Gordon's vast repertoire. The most creative period of the Jewish theater occurred in the 1920s and 1930s, when Yiddish theater companies were quite active in Poland, according to Lucjan Dobroszycki and Barbara Kirshenblatt-Gimblett in *Image Before My Eyes: A Photographic History of Jewish Life in Poland, 1864-1939.*

Even in the Warsaw Ghetto, the world's largest concentration camp, the Nazis permitted several theaters to operate. Between December 1940 and July 1942, five such theaters functioned. "The theatrical interlude in the Warsaw Ghetto was only one more element of the perfidious tactic of showing victims already doomed to death, a flicker of hope which would soon vanish on the way to the gas chambers," writes Zygmunt Hoffman in Polish Jewry History and Culture. After the war, Jewish theater commenced production.

It was not until 1955 that the State Theatre, named after Esther

Rachel Kaminska, found a permanent home in Warsaw. They needed something to cling to especially in the 1960s when Polish authorities forced several thousand Jews who survived the Holocaust to leave the country. Many went to Israel others to Denmark.

No wonder that 50 years later The Jewish Theater in Warsaw and the Shalom Foundation organized a ceremony commemorating the anti-Semitic campaign of the Polish government in the 1960s. Apparently, the Polish Government indicated it would restore citizenship to the expelled Polish Jews, according to *The Times of Israel.*

Kosher Food in Warsaw

Galil Kosher Café and Restaurant, 32 Zielna St., 00-108, Warsaw. Tel 48-731-492-634. Misedet.galil@gmail.com and www.galil.restaurant.pl.

Taim catering establishment. This restaurant also serves in Chabad.

Bekef, ul Hoza, 40, Warsaw 00-516. Tel: 48-22-247-84-16. (Rabbi Schudrich supervision) Open 12:00 p.m. to 8:00 p.m.

WARSAW GHETTO AREA

Those who know the tragedy that befell the Jewish people know this visit to the former Warsaw Ghetto area is not your usual simple walk-through, even though part of it is a nice, quiet area. It sports a beautiful green park and apartment buildings, children play, and shoppers hover about picking out bargains. Tourists bustle from place to place and melt into the busy scene. When the knowledgeable traveler visits the area of the former Warsaw Ghetto and its monument, he or she is reminded that between November 1940 and June/July 1943, "along this path of suffering and death," about 450,000 Jews were either driven away from the city to the gas chambers housed in the Nazi death camps, or were buried underneath these fine apartment houses.

The Jews, who accounted for thirty percent of the Warsaw population, were jammed into 2.4 percent of the city's area. We call that a ghetto—in this case, a "concentration of Jews defined by racist criteria," points out Yisrael Gutman in *The Jews of Warsaw, 1939-1943: Ghetto, Underground, Revolt.* The section that you walk in—there are memorial stones in parts of it—was known as the Central Ghetto, including the streets of Wolynska, Szczeszluva, Ostrovska, Niska, Stawki, Nalewki, Gesia, Dzika (Zamenhofa), Mila, and Maranowska. We shall visit the "Memorial Route" soon.

Actually, as best as we can tell, the Holiday Inn hotel was the southern border of the Warsaw Ghetto. Near the Holiday Inn is 60-62

Zlota (Gold) Street and in the courtyard there is a remnant of the wall of the ghetto. Also at 55 Sienna Street is another wall remnant; a plaque was placed there by the United States Historical Memorial Museum.

"The sidewalks were filled with masses of people whose threadbare clothing reeked with the smell of rotting food-stuffs, and human sweat," writes Gutman. "Dead bodies rolled in the street." People dropped like poisoned flies. The ghetto was swarming with Jews brought from outlying villages.

The smell of death was everywhere. Out of a half-million Jews, fewer than 50,000 remained by mid-1943.

The story of the Warsaw Ghetto actually begins with the victory of the Nazis over Poland. The Germans divided up Poland with the Russians, then later they established what they called the General government—an area of 39,000 square miles, composed of four districts: Cracow, Lublin, Warsaw, and Radom. This area became a dumping ground for Jews and Poles who had been expelled from Germany and parts of Poland. Now penniless and near starvation, these people were placed under German civil administration. Hans Frank served as Governor General. He was appointed on November 8, 1939, and set up his headquarters in Wawel Castle in Cracow.

With about 450,000 Jews jammed into the Warsaw Ghetto, the Nazis turned the area into a human stockyard. Isolated, they were forced into close, squalid conditions with dwindling food, fear, and intimidation. No hope for the future existed in their depressed minds.

Penned in on all sides, the sentence was death by starvation and disease. People became skeletons almost overnight. They were forbidden to teach or to learn. Escape from the ghetto was almost impossible. Marek Edelman, a survivor of the Warsaw Ghetto Uprising, said once that only one out of thousands was able to escape. You needed money to bribe the guards, including at times Polish police. Even before their scheduled final journey to the Treblinka concentration camp, many had died of disease and hunger. Others thought they could hide in the ghetto and somehow survive.

The Nazi goal was to isolate Jews, plunder their property, force them into slave labor, and actually starve them gradually to death, according to Yisrael Gutman in *Resistance: The Warsaw Ghetto Uprising.*

The Germans knew that by giving Jewish spoils to the Poles, the Nazis "gained ardent supporters. There is no doubt that Polish satisfaction with the fate of the Jews under the Nazis stemmed from economic considerations," wrote Joseph Kermisz in *The Warsaw Diary of Adam Czerniakow: Prelude to Doom.* But above all, was the dynamism shown by the Jews of Warsaw, "their tenacious resolve to hold onto life in spite of everything." With the intensification of German attempts to destroy the ghetto, resistance increased.

The Nazis concentrated Jews in cities at railway junctions and in the words of Martin Gilbert, author of *The Holocaust: A History of the Jews of Europe During the Second World War*, "into ghettos such as had not existed in Europe since the Middle Ages." The ghetto which was "shaped like a hammer head," covered 840 acres of slums and housed about 450,000, a figure that included Jews from the suburbs as well as towns, villages, and cities of Poland.

In the beginning of the Nazi occupation, Jews had no idea of the deaths that awaited them. The Germans used every possible ruse to deceive the Jews, even telling them in the extermination camps that the gas chambers were merely showers.

You could walk through the ghetto in forty minutes. Dan Kurzman, in *The Bravest Battle: The Twenty-Eight Days of the Warsaw Ghetto Uprising*, describes the ghetto as a "pressure cooker surrounded by a brick wall 10 feet high and 11 miles long." Glass splinters "embedded in plaster" were on top of the wall. The houses at that time were nineteenth-century, slope-roofed tenements, two to six stories high. The wall had twenty-two gates, reduced in the course of time to thirteen. At the final stage of the ghetto's existence, there were only four gates. At the gates stood the guards of three police forces, German, Polish, and Jewish. Every person, every wagon, and every vehicle that approached was thoroughly searched. Crowded in the narrow streets of the ghetto existed a population equal to that of a city in other parts of the world. Twenty-six thousand Jews lived in Pawia Street; 20,000 in Mila Street, and 20,000 in Gesia Street. They were for all intents and purposes at the mercy of the Nazis and the "representative of the regime," the Judenrat, which in effect was "the sole channel between hundreds of Jews and the authorities and the outside world at large," according to Yisrael Gutman. But they were handpicked by the Germans and some, like Adam Czerniakow of Warsaw, tried to mediate with the Germans, but to no avail. He later committed suicide. Others used their position to save themselves and their families. The Judenrat "was infiltrated by men who were controlled by the Germans and had been hired by express order of the authorities." A Jewish police force was established within the ghetto and "of all the frameworks and services for which the Judenrat assumed responsibility, the police force was the institution most remote from and alien to the traditions of Jewish communal life in the Diaspora."

Probably in 1940, the Germans decided to establish a ghetto to systematically segregate the Jews and by the fall of that year began to relocate them. On November 16, 1940, the Nazis sealed off the ghetto area. From that date until July 22, 1942, the isolated ghetto existed in its "normal format," according to Yisrael Gutman, but from July 22, the Germans initiated the mass deportation of Jews and in the following seven weeks of deportation of Jews, "about 75 percent of the Jews were driven out of their homes and transported to the Treblinka death camp."

WARSAW GHETTO UPRISING

The Warsaw Ghetto Uprising was the largest single act of armed civilian resistance until the outbreak of the Polish Warsaw Uprising fifteen months later, as well as the most famous armed Jewish insurrection against the Nazis. The uprising came as a result of the German cold-blooded, organized, calculated, and deliberate act to destroy Jews.

A rabble army, without a decent weapon, held at bay the mightiest military power the world had ever known for 42 days and 42 nights; all of Poland in 1939 held the Germans off for less than a month.

Furthermore, Dan Kurzman maintains that the military encounter was one of "the most stirring, impossible, and important battles in history." As for Jews, they had rebelled previously. But the uprising, "more than any other event, symbolically ended two thousand years of Jewish submission to discriminate oppression and finally genocide."

During the uprising, small episodes terrorized the Germans. Before the uprising, according to Yitzhak Zuckerman, whose code name was Antek, "all a German had to do was yell 'Raus,' and the Jews would come out. This time, no Jew came out. This time, the Germans came up to us and we killed them."

No longer did Jews feel they were going to their death, herded like cattle. Armed resistance gained mass support only when people understood that the Nazis planned to kill all Jews and that there was no way out of the ghetto, according to Yisrael Gutman. He asks why the Jews did not revolt sooner. They did not, he points out, because of extreme starvation and weakness. They were reduced to "utter impotence." They did not know death awaited them.

By January 1943, the Jews were expecting another action. Called "the second action" (aktion), it came by surprise on Monday, January 18, 1943, and lasted until January 22. Before that, Mordechai Anielewicz, who had been engaged in underground work, began to organize. He came back to the ghetto in October 1942. He was among the organizers of the Jewish Fighting Organization (Z.O.B.), whose definition was a "broad merger of political and ideological factions that bridged various and often antagonistic philosophies."

January 18, 1943 marked a turning point in the existence of the Jewish Fighting Organization. On that date, in the "second action," the Germans surrounded the ghetto. Until January 18, Jews were "passive prey." But then they fought back and those acts of resistance were very important. On January 18, with Anielewicz in command, a number of Jewish ghetto fighters attached themselves to the lines of the deportees being led to concentration camp-bound trains. Armed with pistols, and at a given signal, the freedom fighters opened fire; they shot a few German soldiers; they hurled some hand grenades and scattered the surprised Germans at the corner of Zamenhofa and Niska streets. The Jewish civilians ran and escaped.

After that day, the interval between January 22 and April 19, 1943, a space of 87 days, was used to train and prepare resistance. In April 1943, when the Germans once more moved to liquidate the Warsaw Ghetto, they again encountered armed resistance from the Jews.

The Nazis wanted the ghetto judenrein (free of Jews). And they wanted the job to be completed by April 20, Hitler's birthday. A year before, in April and May 1942, the ghetto contained about 350,000 Jews. The mass deportation of Warsaw Jews began on July 22, 1942, and continued until September 12, 1942. During those seven weeks, about 265,000 Jews were uprooted from Warsaw, transported to the Treblinka death camp, and murdered in the gas chambers.

The Germans entered the ghetto armed to the teeth on the morning of April 19, 1943; that night would be the first night of the Passover Seder. To this day, many Jewish families throughout the world pause during the Seder to recall the heroes of the Warsaw Ghetto. In that engagement thousands of German soldiers fought against a maximum of 1,200 Jewish fighters: "13 heavy machine guns against which the Jews had no equivalent armament; 69 hand-held machine guns, against which the Jews had none; a total of 135 submachine guns against which the Jews had two; several howitzers and other artillery pieces of which the Jews had none; a total of 1,358 rifles, as against only 17 rifles among the Jews," according to Martin Gilbert. The number of Jewish fighters varies. In *Admitting the Holocaust: Collected Essays,* Lawrence L. Langer says estimates of the Jewish Fighting Organization range from 250 to 800 out of 50,000 to 60,000 Jews who were still alive in the Warsaw Ghetto.

Author Ber Mark describes the Jews "as poorly equipped, inexperienced, minuscule, and starving bands of ghetto warriors, with organized forces comprised of 600 members from the Jewish Fighting Organization," and about 400 from Farband and other groups. Thousands of these survivors participated spontaneously. The Jewish fighting units greeted the Germans "with a hail of grenades, bottles, bombs, and rifle shots." The fighters trapped the invading Germans in a crossfire. The Jews fought from the rooftops and bunkers of the ruins. Their key element was surprise. They hid in cellars, bunkers, and sewers in the ghetto.

It is impossible to list all the names of the heroes of the Warsaw Ghetto Uprising. There was Yitzhak Zuckerman, Z.O.B. second in command, known as "Antek." He survived. There was Zivia Lubetkin, a Z.O.B. commander who, like others, escaped through the sewer system. She later became Zuckerman's wife. She and her husband and other ghetto fighters settled at Kibbutz Lohamei ha Gettaot in Israel. Marek Edelman, another commander, survived and still lives in Lodz, where he is a physician.

Of course, heading the list was Mordechai Anielewicz, the twenty-four-year-old commander who was born in Warsaw, attended Warsaw Hebrew High School, and was a member of Hashomer Hatzair, a pioneering socialist Zionist youth movement. At the beginning of the war, he escaped from the Nazis and helped organize Zionist activities in Russia-occupied Poland. According to Israel Gutman, writing in the Encyclopedia of Zionism and Israel, Mordechai Anielewicz was arrested by Soviet government troops as he tried to get to Palestine and was released after he volunteered to return to German-occupied Poland to help in the illegal activities of Hashomer Hatzair. He became head of Hashomer Hatzair in the ghetto and commander of the Z.O.B. and organized the remnants of the ghetto for the final battle in which he perished at MILA 18. He was "the handsome commander loved by all." In his last message sent to his deputy, Yitzhak Zuckerman, he wrote: "The dream of my life has been fulfilled. I have lived to see Jewish defense in all its greatness and glory."

Today, besides his reproduction in the statue of the Memorial to the Victims of the Warsaw Ghetto Uprising, another statue of Mordechai Anielewicz stands at Kibbutz Yad Mordechai, in Israel, in front of a bombed water tower damaged by Egyptian armed forces in the Israel War of Independence.

On May 16, 1943, Nazi commander Jurgen Stroop reported to his superiors that the Warsaw Ghetto "is no longer in existence." The action ended at 8:15 p.m. To celebrate, the Germans blew up the Great Synagogue.

But it would take months to end Jewish resistance. Jews defended building after building, bunker after bunker, and street after street. They fought. Soon, however, starvation, exhaustion, and sickness took their toll. The skirmishes lasted in the ruins of the ghetto into July 1943. According to author Ber Mark, Polish sources cited evidence of armed groups of Jews fighting on "in the razed ghetto area in

1944!" Thousands of Jews were killed, thousands were burned in their hideouts, and 56,000 who had survived the fighting were shipped off to the death camps. But the legends of the Warsaw Ghetto will grow.

Memorial to the Victims of the Warsaw Ghetto Uprising, at the corner of Anielewicza and Zamenhofa streets, Warsaw. As a journalist and editor, I had seen pictures for forty-five years of that magnificent monument of the fighters of the Warsaw Ghetto and Jewish resistance. Its dedication in Hebrew, Yiddish, and Polish moves the viewer: "To the Jewish People—its Heroes and Martyrs."

In December 1970, Willy Brandt, world Socialist leader, former mayor of West Berlin, chancellor of West Germany, was in Warsaw for negotiations for the new treaty between Poland and the Federal Republic of Germany. He visited the Memorial and he fell to his knees before it. "This gesture . . . was not planned. Oppressed by the memories of Germany's recent history, I simply did what people do when words fail them," wrote Brandt, according to The New York Review of Books, July 14, 1994. Over the years, the world's leading figures have come to the site of the memorial for the heroes of the ghetto uprising, including presidents Jimmy Carter and Bill Clinton, as well as Pope John Paul II, who in 1978, then a Polish cardinal, became pope of the Roman Catholic Church. Solidarity also held demonstrations here.

The traveler should stand at the corner of Anielewicza and Zamenhofa. Now called Anielewicza, it is the former Gesia Street where the historic Jewish community was located. It has been renamed for the heroic commander of the Warsaw Ghetto Uprising, Mordechai Anielewicz. The streetcar, with the sign Anielewicza, today motors through the new section of the city. It covers concrete streets probably laid right on top of the ruins of the Jewish ghetto and the tram ends its route at the Jewish cemetery. Also at Anielewicza Street and Zamenhofa, a stone tells us the Dr. Ludwig Zamenhof, creator of Esperanto, the International language, lived on this street at No. 5.

"Of all the thousands of memorials created after the war to commemorate aspects of the Holocaust, Nathan Rapoport's Warsaw Ghetto Monument emerges as possibly the most widely known, celebrated, and controversial," according to James E. Young in *The Texture of Memory: Holocaust Memorials and Meaning in Europe, Israel, and America*. A copy of the monument stands at the Yad Vashem Museum in Jerusalem, Israel. Interestingly, the memorial's granite blocks were originally cut and stacked for the Germans to use them in a Nazi victory monument in Berlin.

The thirty-six-foot monument was unveiled on April 19, 1948, five years after the Warsaw Ghetto Uprising, before 12,000 survivors, military personnel, and government dignitaries.

As I stood before this wall of granite, it came alive for me and I agreed with Young's description of the seven persons on the front wall that represents the burning side of the underground bunker. "A muscular prophet figure on one knee picks up a rock, a young boy at the left, clutches a dagger, a young woman at the right cradles a Kalashnikov rifle, the leader Anielewicz clenches a homemade grenade. Even the mother engulfed by flames raises her right arm defensively as does the baby in her other arm." The ghetto is being swallowed by flames, but the men, women, and children in tattered clothes are led into battle by Anielewicz.

On the back of the wall, one sees twelve stooped and huddled figures, showing fear and despair—depicting the contrasting scene of Jews hopelessly on their way to the death camps. One sees only three Nazi helmets and two bayonets barely visible in the background. There is a rabbi holding a Torah scroll in one arm. He "looks up and reaches to heaven as if to beseech God." Two huge menorahs, symbolic of Judaism and the State of Israel, flank the main part of the monument.

As you walk in the area, you will note black memorial stones. The route is called **"A Memorial Route to the Struggle and Martyrdom of the Jews 1940-1943."** Some call it Memory Lane. People come by here every day, but April 19 is special. This is the day to commemorate the Warsaw Ghetto Uprising. People march along Zamenhofa and Dubois streets to Stawki Street and then to the Umschlagplatz Wall Memorial. The groups lay flowers, light candles, and say prayers. You, the traveler, can do the same.

The memorial route begins at the Monument to the Heroes of the Ghetto; runs down Zamenhofa Street past Samuel Zygielbojm Square and the mound and stone on the corner of Mila Street (dedicated to Mordechai Anielewicz and the Jewish Fighting Organization); then goes down Stawki Street, past the S.S. Unit Command and the former school and Jewish transit hospital. It ends at the entrance to the Umschlagplatz.

Starting at the monument, we see the first monument built right after the war, in 1946, in the shape of a sewer top, to signify escape hatches—the only way out of the flaming ghetto. There are four memorial stones around the monument area. Nearby is the Tree of Shared Remembrance, an oak planted on April 19, 1988, to commemorate the murder of Polish Jews and Poles who perished saving Jewish lives.

To the left of the monument is a memorial stone dedicated to Emmanuel Ringelblum (1900-1944), historian and founder of the Underground Ghetto Archives.

At the corner of Lewartowski and Zamenhofa streets stand stones to Joseph Lewartowski and Michael Klepfisz. The former was a leader of the Communist party, and the latter was an activist in the BUND.

Then we leave Zamenhofa and come to Samuel Zygielbojm Square, where we observe a stone dedicated to Zygielbojm, the man from London who tried to alert the world to the murder of the Jews in Nazi-occupied Europe. But he felt he failed in his attempt to arouse the international community. In protest against the atmosphere of indifference to the tragedy of the Jewish people, he committed suicide on May 12, 1943.

The visitor should now head back to Zamenhofa Street toward Mila Street. There on the corner are two stones dedicated to Arie Wilner and Mordechai Anielewicz, both members of Hashomer Hatzair, the Zionist youth movement. Both died in the bunker, Mila 18.

MILA 18

Mila 18, on Mila Street, commemorates the site of the last bunker of the Warsaw Ghetto Uprising. Today a monument for all to see is mounted on top of what would have been Number 18.

Mila 18 was the central bunker of the Z.O.B., the Jewish Fighting Organization. At times, it housed about 350 persons, including 80 military personnel, according to Ber Mark. Zivia Lubetkin, a Dror activist who fought here. The Germans sought out this bunker. Probably tipped off as to its location, the German troops on May 8 surrounded the area, fired grenades, and injected gas into the bunker. The victims began choking, some committed suicide, and others were killed by German gunfire. It is clear that almost all the fighters perished.

"Thus fell Mordechai Anielewicz, one of the finest and noblest warriors, who from the beginning put his life at the service of his people," according to Emmanuel Ringelblum, the noted Jewish writer who chronicled the events in the Warsaw Ghetto. After the war, those who came to Warsaw climbed onto the heaps of ruins. Nothing was recognizable. One could not tell where a certain street had been or where a house had stood. However, they discovered the spot, the hole, where the house on Mila 18 had stood. They took a great black stone, a mass of dull rock, stone, and dirt, and placed it there. In simple lettering in three languages, the following was etched on the stone: "Here on the 8th day of May, 1943, Mordechai Anielewicz, the commander of the Warsaw Ghetto Uprising, together with the staff of the Jewish Fighting Organization and dozens of fighters fell in the campaign against the Nazi enemy."

After visiting the bunker at Mila 18, we continue our walk down Dubois Street, which is a continuation of Zamenhofa. We come across memorial stones to Pawel Frenkiel, commander of the Jewish Military Union (ZZW), and Frumka Plotnicka, liaison-officer of the Jewish Fighting Organization. Still on Dubois Street, there are memorial stones to the leader of the Religious Zionist party, Rabbi Yitzhak Nissenbaum, and a stone dedicated to Janus Korczak (Henryk Goldszmidt), educator and writer who accompanied "his" children (orphans) on their last journey from the Urnschlagplatz to Treblinka.

We then turn left on Stawki Street and observe a memorial stone dedicated to Itzhak Katznelson, a poet-author who wrote "Poem of the Murdered Jewish Nation." He fought in the ghetto, but since he had a Honduran passport, he was sent to the Vittel concentration camp in France and later to Auschwitz, where he perished. The poem is one of the greatest literary expressions on the tragedy of the Holocaust.

Another stone cites the building at 5/7 Stawki Street, the headquarters of the S.S. And another stone at 6/8 Stawki cites a building in which the Jews were held before being transported to Treblinka. A stone to the left of the Urnschlagplatz Wall Monument cites the 450,000 Jews packed into the ghetto and murdered by the Nazis.

Umschlagplatz. Today it is a busy road. The cars speed by; watch how

Memorial to the heroes of Mila 18, the central bunker of the Jewish Fighting Organization in the Warsaw Ghetto Uprising. (Photo by Ben G. Frank)

you cross the street. The wall in front of you—a fitting monument to the victims of the Holocaust—lists the first names of Jews who perished in the Holocaust and in the Warsaw Ghetto. In the early 1940s it was a large square at the northern edge of the ghetto, bordered by a railway siding, a "railhead for resettlement" to the German death camp. When the ghetto was established, food supplies were brought in to this railroad siding, which is located exactly at the foot of the ghetto. But from July 22, 1942, this loading dock became a one-way ticket to Treblinka. About 6,000 Jews were loaded into boxcars that first day the deportation began and then it was 10,000 every day after, until the ghetto was completely destroyed and no Jew could be found. In fact, whenever the Germans could not meet their daily 10,000 quota, they and their henchmen, the Ukrainians and the Latvians, even Jewish police, would guard and round up people right off the street. Chaos and hysteria ruled, thousands of men, women, and children were jammed into boxcars. Day after day, the "grisly caravans departed for the gas chambers with their loads of human flesh." Sometimes two trains would come at once. Everyone could carry only a single bundle; a three-kilogram bag. Very few escaped through the hospital, only to be picked up the next day.

As I stood on the Umschlagplatz and recalled one of the saddest events that occurred there. Janus Korczak (1878-1942), physician, children's writer, educator, and head of an orphanage, on August 5, 1942, accompanied his two hundred orphaned children to the Umschlagplatz and from there to the gas chambers at Treblinka even though he was not scheduled for deportation at that time. Korczak was a Jew who had been born Hersh Goldszmidt. However, he made Polish—not Yiddish—his mother tongue and he used his Polish name, Henryk. In other lands, he became known as Janus Korczak, which he used as a pen name. When the Germans came for his two hundred children from the orphanage, he brushed and polished the children and dressed them in their best clothes. He told them to take their schoolbooks so they could study when they weren't "working in the forest." Holding one child by the hand, he calmly signaled to the others, who were silently lined up behind him in neat rows, and they began marching toward the boxcars.

As we walk around the Umschlagplatz Wall Monument, we notice that the wall of the monument has white marble with a black band like a tallis (prayer shawl). The wall skirts a small rectangular area, one side of which is the outer wall of a school, the former Jewish hospital. The area inside the wall is symbolic. In the wall opposite the entrance from Stawki Street is a narrow opening that looks out onto a tree, a symbol of hope. Over the entrance is a black slab in the shape of a Jewish tombstone. Besides inscriptions dedicated to the Jews who were driven from the ghetto, there is a wall of four hundred first names in Hebrew, Yiddish, and Polish. Original paving stones have been preserved on the site of the former Umschlagplatz entrance, next to the former hospital and school building. On the other side wall of the school, next to the Wall Monument, is a white marble band with a verse inscribed from the book of Job (16:18): "O Earth, cover not my blood, and let my cry for justice find no rest."

Korczak Orphanage, 8 Jalikosowska St., Warsaw. This is a children's home and a statue of Janus Korczak stands tall in front of this building. He is considered a hero of Poland. A moving statue of Janus Korczak is located in the Jewish cemetery, which we shall visit next. Here, the statue shows Korczak holding a child in his arms and leading other children who are behind him.

Jewish Cemetery, ul. Okopowa 49/51, corner of Gesia Street, 01-043, Warsaw. The "Pantheon of modern Polish Jewry, a forest of the dead." Open every day except Saturday, from 10:00 a.m. to 3:00 p.m. This huge historic cemetery is not kept in the best of condition, but sincere efforts are made to keep it up. The cemetery's stone wall has gaping holes that were made by thieves who vandalized the marble tombstones and by plunderers who were still searching for gold teeth

The Umschlagplatz *wall monument, dedicated to the hundreds of thousands of Jews who were deported by train from this railroad depot in Warsaw to the death camp.* (Photo by Ben G. Frank)

as in Auschwitz, according to S. L. Schneiderman. Here, despite the weeds, broken tombstones, and blurred engravings, lie the leaders, the writers, the doctors, and the men, women, and children of the last 150 years. You can inhale Polish Jewish history from the stories recounted on the tombstones.

Dr. Zamenhof, creator of the international language, Esperanto, is buried here, as is Esther Rachel Kaminska, world-renowned Yiddish actress. Also, Rabbi Osjasz Thon, leader of Polish Jewry and noted Zionist, lies here.

In a special pantheon lie I. L. Peretz (1851-1915), Yiddish writer; Jacob Dinesohn (1858-1919), Yiddish novelist; and S. An-sky (1863-1920), author, who wrote the famous play, *The Dybbuk*.

Here is the grave of the head of the Warsaw Ghetto Judenrat, the engineer, Adam Czerniakow (1880-1942), who committed suicide on July 23, 1942, rather than living and doing the bidding of the Germans who were on a path toward total annihilation of the Jews. Born in Warsaw, Czerniakow served as the head of the Warsaw Judenrat during the "Great Action." Realizing that the Jews were being taken for extermination, he wrote many of his thoughts in the now published *The Warsaw Diary of Adam Czerniakow: Prelude to Doom*, an important source of information on the ghetto.

The Emanuel Ringelblum **Jewish Historical Institute**, ul Tlomackie 3/5, 00-090, Warsaw, Tel: 48-22-828-59-62. familyheritage@ jhi.pl, www.jhi.pl. Often, in Europe, and very often in Poland, you end up talking about a synagogue that was. In the case of the destroyed Great Synagogue in Warsaw, part of it survives in what is now the Jewish Historical Institute. The Institute was once a wing of Warsaw's Great Synagogue at Plac Tlomacki. This classical prayer building contained a large dome and on top rested the Star of David. This was the synagogue of the middle class, the enlightened, and the emancipated. The assimilated came here, wrote Alfred Doblin. The Synagogue, which recessed from Tlomacka Street, could seat 1,100 persons. The buildings boasted a porticoed central section, domed receding wings, and projecting terminal elements. "It looked remarkably secular, usually an indication that the Jews wished to avoid imitating a church or looking exotic," says Carol Herselle Krinsky in her book, *Synagogues of Europe*. It was erected in 1877, in German neo-Renaissance style. The Italian architect, Leonardo Marconi, drew the plans.

Heinrich Himmler, head of the Gestapo, ordered the synagogue destroyed at the so-called official end of the ghetto uprising. "A Wehrmacht sapper team under Stroop's supervision placed huge charges of dynamite under the building: the noise of the explosion shook all of Warsaw," wrote Ber Mark.

The Jewish Historical Institute contains one of the most outstanding collections of Judaica in the world, including manuscripts and the complete archives of Emmanuel Ringelblum, whose diary was found after the war hidden in sealed milk cans in the Warsaw Ghetto; it is one of the best records of the Warsaw Ghetto and is displayed for public viewing. Entitled *Notes from the Warsaw Ghetto*, it was not only Ringelblum's life work; it was also his death work. He did have an opportunity after the uprising in 1943 to be smuggled out of the country by the Polish underground, but he refused. He survived until March 1944, when he was discovered and shot by the Gestapo.

The JHI collection of Judaica, includes religious objects used in both the synagogue and the home. Numbering a few hundred units, it is composed of handicraft products, textiles, scrolls written on parchment and illuminated Books of Esther. The majority of these objects come from the 18th and 19th centuries.

The Institute was once the magnificent library attached to the former Great Synagogue. Today, the library contains about 50,000 to 60,000 books and periodicals gathered from all over Poland after the war. Many important manuscripts are here as well as documents from the Warsaw, Lodz, and other ghettos during the war, as well as from theological seminaries. Paintings, sculptures, Judaica art objects, and other items, many from World War II, complete the vast holdings of this building, which survived the war and the restrictions of the Communist regime.

Sculpture in the Jewish Historical Institute in Warsaw. (Photo by Ben G. Frank)

The historic collection consists of eight million pages of varied documents. The most significant part of the collection is the "*Underground Archive of the Warsaw Ghetto*," also known as "*the Ringelblum Archive*." Holocaust research began here.

The genealogy project is an official JHI department under the care of the foundation and its main sponsor, Taube Foundation for Jewish Life and Culture.

Situated here, too, is a martyrs' museum devoted to the Warsaw Ghetto Uprising.

More information can be obtained at www. jhi.pl.

The Jewish Historical Institute survived the war. East European Jewry, a reservoir of world Jewry, came to an abrupt end, and a chapter closed. After the war, the Zionist youth organization, Hashomer Hatzair, for instance, maintained that Jews should not live on the "cursed ground of Poland." "We have to leave Poland, we have to get up and go," they said. "To most Polish Jews, it was unthinkable to renew their life on the Polish soil, soaked with the blood of millions of Jews," where Nazis found "thousands of collaborators among the local population eager to cooperate in the extermination of the Jews," states the Encyclopedia Judaica. Now began a mass migration of Jews from Poland and Eastern Europe in 1945 to 1950.

The Polish attitude was disbelief that any Jew was alive. "You're still alive?" one Pole told a survivor, Harry Joskowitz, my wife's uncle. "You survived the war and you want your apartment, your houses back?" was the common attitude. The Poles indeed had expropriated businesses and real estate abandoned by the Jews.

This must be clearly stated. Many Poles experienced the annihilation of Polish Jewry as a colossal shock to their psyches. Many, however, found that "Hitler did the dirty work for us." Some did not think the work was so very dirty. The Poles considered Jews to be social outcasts and the Polish response to the Jewish plight fits in with the toothache theory of Yitzhak Zuckerman, "Antek."

Antek explains that Jews thought that once the world was aware of what was happening to them, someone would come to their rescue—certainly the Poles on the other side of the wall. "After the war, when I began reading memoirs of members of the Polish government in London, I was stunned by the extent of their alienation from and indifference to the Jewish issue, which was about as important to them as a toothache."

Jewish historians and leaders generally agree that the "Polish underground's supply of arms to the Jewish uprising leaders was scanty and inappropriate. They provided pistols when the Jews needed rifles and machine guns for the street fighting," writes Lawrence L. Langer in *Admitting the Holocaust: Collected Essays*.

And yet no matter how we view Polish anti-Semitism, we must remember the Poles did not start World War II. The Poles did not destroy Warsaw. The Poles did not order or build the death camps. The Poles did not serve as executioners; six million Poles, half of them Jews, died in the war. The Poles suffered great losses during the fighting and bombardments in 1939 and then in 1944. Approximately 2.5 million Poles were sent to Germany as forced laborers.

"Everywhere in the Nazi New Order, when faced with the plans to deport and murder local Jews, a proportion of the population attempted to aid and succor the Jews; a proportion assisted the Nazis and the majority remained inactive, somewhere in between," say the editors of *The Jews in Polish Culture.* There was no question about Polish complicity in a large segment of the population.

In discussing the Nazi policy towards Poles and Jews, a Polish underground hero who helped Jews and who tried to warn the world's leaders of the Holocaust, the late Jan Kozielewski, known as Karski during the war, told President Franklin Delano Roosevelt, "the Germans want to ruin the Polish state as a state, they want to rule over a Polish people deprived of its elites. With regard to the Jews, they want to devastate the biological substance of the Jewish nation." This underground leader went from world figure to world figure. Most of the people he appealed to did not believe him. Many did not want to believe the reports of the murder of Jews as early as the fall of 1942 or early 1943. Or, if they did believe, they did not want to do anything about it.

Elie Wiesel has written, "It is true that not all victims were Jews. But all Jews were victims." he said on the fiftieth anniversary of the liberation of Auschwitz: "The Jewish people—singled out for destruction during the Holocaust—have shouldered history's heaviest burden."

Although one-third of Jews managed to survive, says Lucy S. Dawidowicz, although the Jewish people and Judaism have outlived the Third Reich, the "Germans nevertheless succeeded in irrevocably destroying the life and culture of East European Jews." The thousand-year-old culture of Ashkenazic Jews that originated in the Rhine basin came to an end, she adds. But in *Tales of My People*, Sholem Asch maintains that "the terrible flame could destroy only the physical substance, not the spiritual essence of the Jew."

Estimates vary; however, at war's end only between 50,000 to 80,000 Polish Jews survived. An additional 180,000 were repatriated from the Soviet Union, which brought the total to somewhat over 200,000 survivors. A Jewish leader told me that every single Jew who survived had to have been saved by Poles. After the war, some Jews who remained in Poland saw communism as an answer to their problems. "For a Jew in Poland, at last, there was an answer to the Jewish question: No religion at all, for anyone," according to Mark Kurlansky. But in the 1968 anti-Semitic campaign, that belief would be meaningless.

Because this building also is a historical institute, we should recall the date of September 1, 1939, when "night" fell on Poland, the night the Nazi cancer continued its unchecked spread through the body politic of Europe. On paper, the September 1st invasion was labeled "Operation White," but we know it as Blitzkrieg.

Nearly two million German troops invaded Poland on that day. Poland was butchered; it never had a chance. The Jews of Poland were trapped. Martin Gilbert informs us that on the evening of September 1, the Great Synagogue in Tlomackie St. was "full to overflowing. Large crowds also stood outside and prayed."

On September 17, 1939, Russia—who had betrayed Poland and free men and women everywhere by signing the infamous Molotov-Ribbentrop Pact of August 23, 1939, by which Hitler and Stalin agreed to divide Poland between the two of them—invaded Polish soil. Ten days later, Poland capitulated. The partition and occupation of Poland gave Hitler the opportunity to put his racial policies into effect.

After Stalin took over, in the late 1940s, only about 70,000-80,000 Jews remained in the country. By the mid-1950s, many Poles began to express discontent with government policies and resentment of Soviet domination and its Stalinist regime. In 1956, after worker unrest, Wladyslaw Gomulka, who had been imprisoned in 1951, was freed from prison and again became head of the Communist party.

Stalin's crimes were made public. Yiddish papers blasted Soviet anti-Semitism. Approximately 2,500 repatriated Jews came back from Russia. The JDC and ORT were allowed to reopen. But many Jews moved out: 50,000 left in 1958 and 1959. At that time, approximately 30,000 Jews remained in Poland. As a result of the Six Day War and the anti-Israel stance of the former U.S.S.R., Poland, still a Communist satellite, broke relations with Israel in 1967.

Under the Communist regime, Polish media would now invent a new target for Polish hatred. The new enemy became the "Jewish conspiracy" and the State of Israel. The Polish government campaigned against Jews and intellectuals. It initiated and sponsored in 1968 a sweeping virulent anti-Semitic campaign, according to Eva Hoffman in *Exit into History: A Journey Through the New Eastern Europe.*

After the Six Day War, in 1967, Gomulka went along with Mieczyslaw Moczar, the interior minister. Student demonstrations were the pretext for the government's anti-Semitic campaign. Gomulka labeled the Jews "rootless cosmopolitans." He said the Jews were a "fifth column."

Gomulka gave the Jews permission to go; large numbers did. Jews were dismissed from jobs. Organizations such as JDC and ORT were closed down. The Polish government in effect "liquidated" all organized Jewish life. Anti-Semitism "purged" Poland of nearly all its Jewish population. In 1968, it was "a matter of mental terror, of frightening Jews out of Poland," according to the late author Kazimierz Brandys in his book, *A Warsaw Diary: 1978-1981.* Mark Kurlansky states that Jews "could forfeit their homes and whatever property they might have and immigrate to Israel." He adds, "Only Jews were allowed to emigrate and Israel was the only acceptable destination."

"Not even in the heyday of Stalinism did the world see anything like the virulent, open and institutionalized racial discrimination practiced in the spring and summer of 1968 in 'People's Poland,'" Paul Lendvai says in his *Anti-Semitism Without Jews: Communist Eastern Europe.* While no one was killed, at least forty persons from Jewish and non-Jewish families were known suicides. One thing was certain, if you wanted to be Jewish, you left Poland in 1968; or if you stayed, you opted out of Jewish life.

Polin Museum of the History of Polish Jews is located on the site of the former Warsaw Ghetto at Mordechaja Anielewicza 6, 00-157, Warsaw. Tel: 48-22-47-10-300. FAX: 48-22-47-10-398. www.polin.pl. This award-winning museum is a must visit.

Before the museum opened, I researched the Warsaw Ghetto area. When I stood on a large patch of green grass, a city park. I was told here would be the site, of a new museum that would never let the world forget the contributions of Jews to Poland.

Through much effort, the museum was constructed in front of the monument to the Warsaw Ghetto Uprising and is located in a quartet of four streets, Anielewicza, Zamenhofa, Lewartowksiego, and Karmelicka.

The Polin museum documents 1,000 years of history of Polish Jews and their contribution to Polish political economic and cultural life.

The museum stands not just as an excellent museum but a state-of-the-art cultural institution which reaches diverse publics all over the world.

The cornerstone was laid in 2007, and the museum was first opened on April 19, 2013. The museum's Core Exhibition opened in October 2014. The museum features a multimedia narrative exhibition about the vibrant Jewish community that flourished in Poland for a thousand years up to the Holocaust. The building, a postmodern structure in glass, copper, and concrete, was designed by Finnish architects Rainer Mahlamäki and Ilmari Lahdelma.

Architecturally and culturally, the Polin Museum of the History of

Polish Jews in Warsaw has received many awards, such as the European Union Prize for Cultural Heritage in 2017. In 2016, it received the European Museum of the Year Award, a distinction which has been given annually since 1977 by the European Museum Forum, which acts under the auspices of the Council of Europe.

On a clear, summer day, the green grass, the single blossoming large green tree, the blue sky with the white fluffy clouds, belie the murder that went on in this city and country, but yes, still recalls that once, this land was a spiritual and religious center of Judaism.

Note! Remember, a visit to the **Warsaw Jewish Cemetery** "alone is worth the airfare," writes Barry Lichtenberg in an article in the *Jewish Week*, September 3, 1999. "Thousands of beautifully designed and engraved tombstones huddle beneath towering oaks and fallen pines, emitting an ethereal glow."

PALACE OF CULTURE AND SCIENCE

The **Palace of Culture and Science** building is truly a bizarre sight. This monolithic building, a gift from the USSR, resembles Moscow's Socialist Realist tower blocks. It also reminds one of the Soviet oppression of Poland from 1944 to 1989.

In any book on Jewish travel and Jewish communities in Europe, certain national monuments and sites we visit invoke memory of past events. In Poland, moreover, international events—especially those between Russia and Poland—deeply affected Jews. Examples quickly come to mind: the 1939 Molotov-Ribbentrop Pact, the outbreak of World War II, and the 1989 collapse of communism. While not a monument, the Palace of Culture and Science building stands in the center of the city as a symbol. It was, after all, a Soviet gift to the Poles. Built in the early 1950s in the traditional Russian-Soviet architectural style, it was immediately labeled the "wedding cake." This massive structure contains 3,288 rooms, a Congress Hall for 3,000 people, three theaters, a swimming pool, and a museum. A view from the thirtieth floor gives the tourist a bird's-eye view of Warsaw. A Jewish leader told me he and his wife took courses there. It should have reminded them of the "looming specter of Russia."

Speaking of the Russians, some of the ire of the Poles and many other people today is the Molotov-Ribbentrop Pact, which many believe helped cause the outbreak of the war because of the secret protocol signed in Moscow by Nazi Ribbentrop and Communist Molotov on August 23, 1939. The two countries would carry out a joint attack on Poland and divvy up the area. Without the assurance of Soviet collusion, the German army could not have launched a unilateral attack on Poland. "Suddenly it became clear that if Hitler were to invade Poland, the Soviet Union would stand aside," writes Martin Gilbert in his book *The Holocaust: A History of the Jews of Europe During the Second World War*. That was "ominous news" for the Jews of Poland. Hitler indeed invaded. Two years later on June 21, 1941, he stabbed the Soviets in the back and unleashed a destructive war that would include the death of about twenty-five million Russians alone.

Survivors from Poland did fight. I heard about the Polish army unit, a certain group in Gen. Wladyslaw Anders' division, from my father-in-law, the late Rabbi Solomon Spitz. In 1941, the Soviets permitted a Polish army group to form under General Anders. Polish prisoners of war held by the Russians were allowed to join General Anders to fight with the allies. In March 1942, the new Polish unit crossed into British-controlled Iran. When the group arrived in Palestine, many Polish Jews left the unit and opted to stay in Palestine. Many, too, like my late father-in-law, joined the Jewish Brigade of the British Army in order to fight the Germans.

Warsaw Uprising Museum (Muzeum Powstania Warszawskiego). ul. Grzybowska 79, Warsaw. Tel: 48 22 539 79 05. www.1944.pl.

Hours: Monday, Wednesday, and Friday, 8:00 a.m. to 6:00 p.m., Thursday 8:00 a.m. to 8:00 p.m., Saturday and Sunday, 10:00 a.m. to 8:00 p.m. The museum is closed on Tuesdays. Admission is free on Sundays.

The heart of the museum is a steel monument passing through all the floors of the building. On its walls is engraved the Uprising's calendar of events, and the sound of a heartbeat which can be heard from inside symbolizes the life of Warsaw in 1944. A special attraction is the Museum tower, with a beautiful view of Warsaw and Freedom Park with the Memorial Wall on which are engraved the names of more than 10,000 insurgents who died during battle. In the central part of the wall, the Monter bell is hung; weighing 230 kg., and dedicated to General Antoni Chrusciel.

In 1944, the Soviet Army entered Poland and Stalin installed his Communist Poles as the new government in Lublin. On August 1, after the Red Army had reached the Vistula River, the Home Army of the London Poles launched an insurrection to liberate Warsaw before the Soviet troops arrived.

The Polish Uprising was an armed insurrection against the Germans, but, politically and more clearly, it was an uprising against the Russians. The Poles wanted to avoid a "Red Warsaw." The Soviet Army stood by and let the Germans slaughter the insurgents and utterly destroy the capital.

To this day, Poles also believe the Allies betrayed and sacrificed Poland at the February 1945 Yalta Conference held at that Crimean seaside resort. Here, the Western Allies accepted the new status quo in Poland and agreed to recognize the Stalin-backed Lublin government. Stalin would settle for nothing less than a Polish government controlled by Communists. He "scorned" his promises for a free election.

The **Ronald S. Lauder Educational Summer Camp**, Wisla. Poland. The first Ronald S. Lauder Foundation summer camp took place in Zaborow in 1988, Twenty Polish Jews came for two weeks to learn about Judaism, study Torah and meet rabbis for the very first time. Most of them had waited for decades for this moment. They come for Jewish learning and experiencing Jewish life.

The Lauder camps brings together Jews from all over Poland. The summer camp sponsors between 120 to 160 participants, rabbis and speakers from Poland, the U.S., Germany, the UK, Israel, and Australia. After more than 25 years, the camp's popularity has increased and not only serves an important educational task but also helps campers discover their Jewish roots.

The Ronald S. Lauder Foundation also sponsors an e-Learning School in Poland. The project creates a sense of belonging to Jewish children from each and every town in Poland, especially for those students who reside in places that lack Jewish communities. With the Lauder e-Learning School, every child can connect, learn about Judaism and grow individually as a Jew. Online teachers guide, teach and answer questions. Students of the Lauder-Morasha e-Learning School learn Jewish studies, Jewish history, Hebrew, English, French, and German. Students also participate in special school ceremonies, trips and *shabatons*. Top teachers with years of experience at the Lauder-Morasha School guarantee education on the highest level. Cutting technologies enable and enrich children's education.

TREBLINKA

"Before the War, on the Siedlec-Malkinia Railways, not far from the great axis running from Warsaw to Bialystok, there was a forgotten little station with the strange and beautiful name of Treblinka. It rose unexpectedly in a damp, sandy plain dotted with little pine woods and marshes," wrote Jean-François Steiner in his book, *Treblinka*. Here between 800,000 and 850,000 Jews were murdered by the Nazis, but here as in other camps, a revolt occurred on August 2, 1943; it was brutally suppressed and the camp destroyed.

This is one camp that has an unusual monument, to say the least. At least 17,000 huge stone slabs make up a symbolic cemetery. Engraved on the stones are the names of cities and villages from which the Jews were rounded up and brought here. The densely packed stones surround a huge 26-foot high obelisk-type stone sculpture shaped like a mausoleum and topped by a large menorah. It appears that the menorah is "carved into the cap" of the obelisk and is "jumbled" together. It protrudes in all directions. At the bottom of the obelisk, where there is a great crack, a stone plaque reads from top to bottom in Yiddish, Russian, English, French, German, and Polish, "Never Again."

Today, you can see that the railway, which once was abandoned, has been recreated symbolically with concrete sleepers to commemorate this railway that conveyed Jews to their deaths.

Martin Gilbert in his book, *The Holocaust: A History of the Jews of Europe During the Second World War,* says that in 1959, he ran his hand through the soil of Treblinka: "The earth beneath my feet was coarse and sharp; filled with the fragments of human bone."

At Treblinka, we again meet Janusz Korczak. In 1978, the hundredth anniversary of his birth, a stone was inscribed with his name and put with the thousands of others. It is the only stone dedicated to an individual, and Korczak is a Polish hero, too.

Treblinka itself is located in Sokolow Podlaski province near Warsaw. Jews in the Warsaw Ghetto between 1940 and 1943 who were deported to death camps probably died at Treblinka.

Nothing tangible remained at the camp as the Germans brutally destroyed it as they departed. "Yet," notes Philippe Sands in his highly recommended book, *East West Street, On the Origins of "Genocide" and "Crimes Against Humanity,"* "when the camp was discovered by the Soviets, Vasily Grossman's article, in September, 1944, "The Hell of Treblinka," offered another account, immediate and brutal. "We tread the earth of Treblinka," he wrote, "casting up fragments of bone, teeth, sheets of paper, clothes, and things of all kinds. The earth does not want to keep secrets."

The Death Camps

*Auschwitz and Birkenau—Approximately an hour's drive from Cracow.

*Majdanek—Set up in the Lublin suburb of Majdan Tartarski.

*Sobibor—The camp was located in the small village of Sobibor on the Chem-Wlodawa Railway line, almost 5 miles south of Wloadawa.

*Belzec—A small town in the southeast of the Lublin district. Located on the Lublin-Zamosc-Rava-Russkaya-Lvov railway line—The death camp was located about a third of a mile from the Belzec railway station.

*Treblinka—Located 62 miles northeast of Warsaw.

*Chelmno—Situated on the Ner River, 37 miles from Lodz.

LUBLIN

My late father-in-law, Rabbi Solomon Spitz, was born here and went to the famous Lublin Yeshiva. In 1940 the Germans took thousands of holy books out of the hallowed yeshiva library, threw them down on the ground, loaded them into vehicles and burned them in the marketplace. The fire lasted twenty hours. And the Jews of Lublin watched this nightmare. They cried so that their voices rose above those of the Nazis: the Germans had to bring in their army band to drown out the agonizing shouts of protest.

Records, incidentally, say that the Germans confiscated 22,000 volumes and about 10,000 periodicals.

The city of Lublin, wrote a Chassid, "is the land of Israel." Yes, Lublin ranks as a special metropolis in the galaxy of Jewish life in Poland. In the 1920s, Doblin described Lublin as "not sleepy" like a small town in Germany, because the poverty suffered by the Jews kept them moving. Before the war, 97 percent of all the city's tailors were Jews; it is doubtful if there is a Jewish tailor there today. Lublin in 1939 contained a population of about 40,000 Jews. It was literally "a Jewish Oxford," famous for its yeshiva throughout Europe, famous for Talmudic and Kabbalist learning. Lublin, a center of Hebrew printing, was known for its fairs and market days. Annexed by Austria in 1795, and later incorporated into Russia-Poland in 1815, Lublin served as "the spiritual heart of Polish Jewry."

Jews arrived here in 1316. At first, they were denied rights, but King Casimir III permitted them to settle nearby in 1336. In 1602, 2,000 Jews made their home in Lublin. They were expelled in 1780. By 1806, 2,973 Jews resided here and by 1897 the figure jumped to 23,586.

Synagogue, 10 Lubartowska, Lublin. This **synagogue** is not used frequently. There are no daily services scheduled and rarely a minyan. Part of the building is used as a museum.

Yeshivat Hachmei, Lublin, 85-83 Lubartowska St., Lublin, at the corner of Unicka Street. Today it is a medical college, but many Jews close their eyes and see before them youthful yeshiva students studying Torah, chanting afternoon prayers, or walking along the streets of this once great center of Judaism.

Today the medical college displays a modest plaque commemorating the yeshiva. Built with funds raised from all over the world, the yeshiva was opened in 1930. The building was designed by Agenor Senduchowski.

For centuries, the king of Poland appointed the rector of the yeshiva of Lubin. In 1935, 50,000 people, including high-ranking government officials, attended the ceremonies dedicating the new headquarters for the yeshiva. It consisted of six stories, 120 rooms, a huge auditorium, and even a scale model of the Temple of Jerusalem. In 1939, 500 students attended.

Lublin is renowned for its scholars and sages, one of them so great that he was referred to as the "Seer of Lublin." He was Rabbi Jacob Isaac ha-Hozeh. And living in Lublin were other great rabbis: Jacob b. Joseph Pollak, Jacob b. Samuel Bunim Koppelman, and Mordechai b. Abraham Jaffe.

At the densely wooded Grodzisk Hill, near the yeshiva, is the Old Cemetery. A great stone wall shields this sixteenth-century Jewish burial ground. The entrance to the cemetery is on Kalinowszcyna Street. Here rests another great Talmudic scholar, Rabbi Solomon Luria (1510-74), known by the acronym, Maharshal (Morenu ha-Rav Shelomo Luria).

Another great rabbi of Lublin buried in the cemetery is Meir b. Gedaliah (1558-1660), known as the Maharam of Lublin. The Maharam is an acronym for Moreinu-Ha-Rav Meir, "Our Teacher, the Rabbi Meir." This great halachic authority became head of the Yeshiva of Lublin at the age of twenty-four.

In Lublin, also, sat the Council of the Four Lands, which became an independent Jewish parliament and supreme court. It coordinated a system of autonomous Jewish institutions. The Council settled disputes between Jewish communities and appeals made by individuals against decisions rendered by other rabbis and courts. The Council existed from 1580 to 1764.

Majdanek

"If Auschwitz was hell on earth, then Majdanek was the morgue. Auschwitz could be smelled from afar, but Majdanek was in your living room," wrote Professor Eric Epstein in *Martyrdom and Resistance.*

The city of Lublin rises over Majdanek. The Nazis felt no need to conceal the camp from the local populace. In the summer of 1942, construction of the Majdanek concentration camp near Lublin, in the Majdan Tartarski quarter, was completed. It, too, was part of Operation Reinhard, named after S.S. General Reinhard Heydrich, who was assassinated by two Czech patriots on May 27, 1942, in the Czech town of Lidice. After his death, the Nazis began preparations for Operation

Reinhard, the deportation of Jews to Treblinka, Belzec, and Sobibor. In Majdanek, more than eighty percent of the 350,000 murdered victims were Jews. It is pretty much preserved as it was. The visitor can see guard towers, barbed wire, barracks, and crematoria. Everything is still intact. In the back of one hall, there are empty canisters of Zykon B gas. There is a prisoners' clothing display, and prisoners' shoes are piled in the barracks.

Wiktor Tolkin's monument at Majdanek conveys impending danger because the top part of it is the "great weight of memory," which stands on a proportionately undersized base that creates a sense of top heaviness, even danger, for those standing beneath it. As you walk out from the base of the monument, you can see in the distance the dome covering a mausoleum of human ash and bones and to its right, a building with a tall chimney, which was the crematorium and gas chamber complex—the whole area symbolizes a valley of death.

KIELCE

The name of this town in southeast Poland will certainly live forever in Polish-Jewish history. Just one year after the Holocaust, the Jews of Poland woke up to a good, old-fashioned pogrom. "Jews were even taken off trains and murdered," said Yitzhak Zuckerman. He believed the event may have been instigated by the police or government, a well-organized plot. Forty-two Jews were murdered. The pogrom occurred on July 4, 1946. A monument was erected in the Kielce Jewish cemetery to perpetuate the memory of the pogrom's victims. The pogrom induced a major shock for the Jews—as if they needed one. The price of remaining in Poland, legally and illegally, increased greatly. That is why a mass emigration out of the country took place. Between 100,000 to 150,000 persons departed, including the Polish Jews who had been returning from Russia.

A **synagogue** is located at Rewolucji Pazdziernikowej but is now used as a center for archives. A monument to the memory of the pogrom's victims is located at 7 Planty Street. Lodz.

Lauder Foundation. lodzlauder@idsl.pl. Tel: 48-501-271-721.

CRACOW

"And everyone crowds into the narrow little streets of the Jewish city and rushes for his place in the synagogue and Kazimierz is full of people and the old temples of Israel reflect the spell of the past."

—Majer Balaben, Polish Jewish historian

"There in Eastern Europe, the Jewish people came into its own. It did not live like a guest in somebody else's house, who must constantly keep in mind the ways and customs of the host. There, Jews lived without reservation and without disguise, outside their homes no less than within them."

—Abraham Joshua Heschel

Friday night: "*Shabbos.*" I use the Ashkenazic pronunciation because that is what was said on Friday nights by Polish Jews. They still say the Shabbos now. But now the younger ones pronounce it: "*Shabbat.*" The square is empty. I fantasize it was as if you were watching a movie: a large, oblong square, bustling with people, full of people, men in their black gabardines and round hats, milling about the marketplace. Nearby are stone houses, colored blue, white, purple, and green. Then suddenly the film script changes. The same square, but there are no people. The buildings are there, but there are no Jews. You are ready to leave. But wait, faint at first are the sounds of the song, "Peace Be With You," "*Shalom Aleichem.*"

You follow the sounds. You go in and there before you are almost fifty young people. This is the headquarters of the Ronald S. Lauder Foundation Youth Center when I visited Cracow. Every Friday night, there is a Shabbat dinner where young people are invited to attend. Sometimes, American college students come to services and then to the program dinner. Kiddush is recited. We sing Hebrew songs. We talk about Jews in nearby Ukraine. I realize a number of these young people are not Jewish, they are themselves from mixed marriages. Many will convert to Judaism. But these young adults, if they become Jews, are the future of Poland. For further information on youth groups in Poland, contact the Ronald S. Lauder Foundation at its Berlin office. info@lauderfoundation.com.

Jews once lived in the main square of the city. Today, there are very few signs of their one-time residence in the city center.

In 1335, King Casimir the Great founded this once rival city to Cracow on the southern side of town and called it Kazimierz. The Jews settled there soon after its establishment.

In 1495, King Jan Olbracht expelled the Jews from Cracow. The Jews moved to nearby Kazimierz, where they settled in a relatively small prescribed area northwest of the Christian quarter and were separated from the non-Jews by a wall. Cut off from the Poles, it would take the Jews four hundred years to get back to the environs of the Main Square in Cracow. Jews arrived in the fourteenth century.

But German and Bohemian Jews came to Cracow in the sixteenth and seventeenth centuries. Here they could live in peace. Those German Jews spoke Yiddish, similar to what the prosperous Cracovians spoke, which was mainly German. In the fifteenth century, Cracow Jews developed trade with Breslau, Danzig, Lvov, and Constantinople.

"Over the course of history," wrote the late noted writer, expert guide in the history of Cracow, Henryk Halkowski, "Jewish Kazimierz joined with Polish Cracow and together they became 'Ir-va-em be Israel,' (The Mother City of Israel)." Kazimierz was a predominantly Jewish quarter. By the end of the fifteenth century, Kazimierz consisted of a "quadrangle with a few streets enclosed on one side by the city walls and on the other by a wall with three gates leading to the non-Jewish city," says Bernard D. Weinryb.

By the 1570s, about two thousand people lived in Kazimierz, the Jewish section on the other side of town. Here in Kazimierz the famous Talmudic scholar and philosopher Rabbi Moses Isserles, known as Remuh, maintained his academy. Today his grave and synagogue remain places of pilgrimage. That sixteenth-century Cracow became the world famous center of Talmud education was due to Isserles, who is famous for his commentary to the treatise, Shulhan Arukh, the code of Jewish law. We shall learn more about him when we visit the only functioning synagogue in Cracow.

Kazimierz also was the safe haven for Jews from every corner of Europe till the 20th century, and a major center of the Diaspora. No wonder then that for more than four centuries, until emancipation in 1868, Jews of Kazimierz fought for rights to trade and work in Cracow. From the second half of the sixteenth century, a number of yeshivot were founded in Kazimierz, whose fame made Cracow a most important center of Judaism. By 1644, the community maintained seven synagogues, a main synagogue, the Old Synagogue, and Remuh Synagogue. Hebrew printing was introduced in Cracow in 1534. "This suburb was an independent town with its own municipal council until the partition of Poland in the eighteenth century," writes Rachel Wishnitzer in *The Architecture of the European Synagogue.* Until the beginning of World War II, Kazimierz remained the traditional residential quarter of Cracow's Jews. After the war, the section decayed.

A beautiful, ancient city, there is only one Cracow, the residence of the leading Polish princes and a center of Polish cultural life. Cracow is one of the most magnificent cities in all of Poland. In the sixteenth century, this Renaissance city flourished. Until 1609, this was the old capital of Poland with straight and winding narrow streets, renovated monuments, and townhouses. History has been especially kind to this city on the Vistula. Alfred Doblin described it as the cleanest and most beautiful city he found in Poland in the early 1920s. It still is proud of its university and intellectual look. Who has not heard of Jagiellonian University; Wawel Hill, the seat of Polish kings, including Casimir; or the Cracow Marketplace? Cracow is virtually the only large Polish city that has preserved its old architecture.

The Vistulans or Wislanie lived here. Cracow dates from 465 when traveler Ibrahim ibn Yaqub from Cordova visited the town and mentioned it as a trade center.

Even after World War I, Cracow still retained its cultural center status. In 1921, 45,000 Jews lived here; in 1931, 56,800. By the outbreak of World War II, the city counted 260,000 inhabitants, between 60,000 and 70,000 of whom were Jews.

After World War II, 780,000 persons resided in this third largest city after Warsaw and Lodz. Huge steel works, Howa Huta, were built a few kilometers from the historical center. An ecological disaster, the Communists had attempted to break the traditionally intellectual and religious ties of the city.

In Cracow you can still see a street called St. Anne's Lane. Documents going back to 1304 called it Jews Lane. Jewish merchants held important positions in the city's economic life. At the end of the fifteenth century, a fire destroyed Cracow's Jews Lane and the Christian citizens succeeded in having the Jews expelled from the city. The Jews settled at neighboring Kazimierz, where they were assigned a self-contained area that later was to become the ghetto.

In the early twentieth century, the Zionists and the Socialists gained influence in Cracow and the city became a major stronghold of the Labor Zionists and the Revisionist Zionists.

Before World War II, 70,000 Jews lived in Cracow, about twenty-five percent of the population. When the Nazis entered, they were moved to the ghetto in the Podgorze section. In the ghetto, the "Eagle Pharmacy" was located at 18 Bohaterow Getta and was owned by the Pole, Tadeusz Pankiewicz, one of the leaders of the Resistance who succeeded in saving the lives of several Jews. In March 1943, the Nazis liquidated the ghetto and the last residents were sent to the concentration camps, among them the Yiddish poet and singer, Mordechai Gebirdg. Today, only about 500 Jews reside in Cracow out of a population of about 750,000 residents.

Indeed, as in other parts of Europe, non-Jews are the curators and dozens of many Jewish museums and institutions. As Konstantin Gebert noted in an interview in *Moment Magazine*, September/October 2014: "The most fascinating things happening in Jewish life in Poland today are happening at the border between the Jewish community and Polish society at large. There is an epidemic of Jewish culture festivals all over Poland, and they are usually produced by non-Jews. And the audience is non-Jewish."

He noted that the performers are usually Jewish. "This is an attempt by Poles to recreate what for centuries was an important element of Polish life. That is, a Jewish presence and a Jewish culture. Jews are involved, but it's mainly a Polish initiative," he added.

Sites in Cracow

Old Synagogue-Jewish Museum, 24 Szeroka, Cracow. It was built in the late fifteenth century on what was Broad Lane in the middle of the Jewish quarter, now called 24 Szeroka. At the far end of Szeroka Street, as you come out of the Remuh Synagogue, look to your right and at the end of the square stands the Alte Synagogue, today functioning as the Jewish Museum. Displayed here are some excellent exhibits, especially on the second floor—an exhibit of photos and drawings, the faces of Kazimierz Jews. The museum is open Wednesday and Thursday 9:00 a.m. to 3:30 p.m., Friday 11:00 a.m. to 6:00 p.m., and Saturday and Sunday 9:00 a.m. to 3:00 p.m. However it is closed the first Saturday and Sunday of every month and when that occurs, the museum opens the following Monday and Tuesday. It has impressive collections of Jewish ceremonial art and works by Jewish painters. The original Gothic structure was destroyed by a fire; the Italian architect Matteo Gucci rebuilt it in Renaissance style in 1557-70. Some say the Old Synagogue housed the library of King Casimir the Great. Since 1958 the building has become a seat of the Judaic Museum, a branch of the Historical Museum of the City of Cracow.

In the room of the museum, on the second floor, such World War II photos with signs such as "Jews Are Forbidden to Enter the Park" are displayed. This room contains the history of the Jewish community of Cracow during 1939-45. The Old Synagogue is one of the most important synagogues of the medieval period in Poland. After the war the building was not used and was allowed to fall into disrepair. During the war, its massive bronze chandeliers were used to decorate the house of the Nazi governor general, Hans Frank. It is not known when the Old Synagogue, or Stara, was built in the former heart of this Jewish community, but it is believed to have been in the fourteenth or fifteenth centuries. Erected by Jewish refugees from Bohemia, it was patterned after the ***Altneuschul*** in Prague. The Old Synagogue of Kazimierz measures 17.70 by 12.40 meters, approximately 58 by 40 feet, is larger than the synagogues at Worms and Prague, and taller than the synagogue of Prague. Its two columns are slimmer than the piers of the latter synagogue, and its walls are thinner, too. "The parapet of bricks and stone, decorated with blind arcades, shows the influence of style of the medieval castles of the Cracow nobility," according to Earl Vinecour. It contains a double-nave, two-pillared edifice. The bimah (the Torah reader's platform) is not only slightly elevated between the two pillars, but is also enclosed in a canopied wrought-iron cage. From time to time, the Communists closed the building. During various insurrections against foreigners, patriotic speeches were given here urging Jews and Poles to unite in defense of their common homeland.

Popper Synagogue, 16 Szeroka St. Donated by the merchant Wolf Popper in 1620, it was rebuilt after World War II and is currently being used by the city of Cracow as a cultural center. Next door is the Ariel Café.

The High Synagogue, 38 Jozefa St., Cracow.

Kupa Synagogue, 8 Jonatan Warszauer. Erected during the building boom of the sixteenth and seventeenth centuries, restoration is now being undertaken.

Temple Synagogue, 24 Miodowa St., Cracow. It survived the war almost unscathed. It was built in 1860 to 1862, thanks to the efforts of the Association of Progressive Jews in Cracow. Magnificently restored, it is now open. There is a women's section in one of the balconies. It is only used when needed, such as on holidays.

Jewish Community Center, ul Miodowa 24, 31-055, Cracow. Tel:48-12-3705770. FAX: 48-12-3705771. office@jcckrakow.org. www.jcckrakow. org/ Opened in 2008 by the United Kingdom's Prince Charles, the JCC has quickly established itself as the focal point of Jewish life for the residents of the city, "as well as thousands of visitors from around Poland and he world every month," according to JTA. Today, it has more than 600 active members, including 75 Holocaust survivors.

In 2017, the JCC of Cracow received a half-million dollar grant from the New York City-based Erica Schwarz Family Foundation, to create an early childhood center at the JCC. According to JTA, it was the largest single grant awarded to a Polish Jewish organization in the last 20 years. The JCC is located in Kazimierz, the heart of the city's Jewish district. It was scheduled to open in 2017.

The JCC also receives support of the Ronald S. Lauder Foundation to underwrite the annual security needs of the new childhood center, to be known as *"Frajda,"* meaning "joy," in both Yiddish and Polish. The Lauder Foundation has helped rebuild Jewish life in Poland, including restoration efforts in Kazimierz district and seven historic synagogues, as well as numerous educational initiates serving the Jewish population of Cracow, according to JTA.

Community Offices, also known as TSKZ Club, is located at Estery St. 6, Cracow, Warsaw Tel: 561-758, 562-349/22-98-41.

Synagogue, also known as the Congregation of the Mosaic Faith, located at Skawinska Street. It is now empty and not used.

Eating Establishments in Cracow

Szalom Falafel, Jakuba St. 21, Warsaw, and located behind Isaac Synagogue, is a small kosher dairy place, serving up pizza, salads, shashuka, chips and snacks, such as barokas. Open every day, 10:00 a.m. to 10:00 p.m. On Fridays, Szalom Falafel closes two hours before Shabbat, and opens Saturday night after Shabbat.

Ariel Jewish Artistic Café, 18 Szeroka St., Cracow. Tel: 21-38-70. There is folk and gypsy music and concerts of Hebrew, Yiddish, and Russian. Heard above the din of the coffee shop are tapes in Hebrew. You may find that many local Polish Jews and, from time to time, many Americans stop here for coffee, cake, and sandwiches, especially on the weekend.

Hotel Eden, Cinema 15, Cracow. Tel: 430-65-55. FAX: 430-67-67. This hotel can order kosher food products for guests. Being located just behind Rabbi Isaac synagogue, guests can visit Szalom Falafel, noted above, which also serves a kosher breakfast.

Chabad Lubawitch Krakow, ul Kupa 18, 31-057, Krakow, Poland. Tel: 48-12-430-22-22. Jewish.cracow@gmail.com, www.chabadkrakow.pl Services are held here every day at 8:30 a.m. Shabbat services at candle lighting time during the winter and 7:30 p.m. during the summer.

Rabbi Eliezer Guray is head of Chabad in Cracow which started a kindergarten that expanded into a school. In 2017, the school had over 15 children. Chabad also sponsors some activities for children including a Sunday school, organized by the JCC and the organization, Czulent.

Chabad provides after-school program for Jewish children attending public schools in Cracow. A "yeshiva day" is held once a year, including kosher meals, speakers, and prayer services. Rebbetzin Guray organizes regular meetings for women and girls in the community. A feature of this Chabad center is a library whose books are in many languages. In the fall of 2016, Chabad joined the Kolel Torah program; classes are held twice a day, five days a week. There is a separate class for Polish speakers and a separate class for Hebrew speakers.

Remuh Synagogue, 40 Szeroka St., Cracow. If you are in Cracow on a Friday evening or Saturday morning, you can pray at this mid-sixteenth-century synagogue, which was built by influential members of the Jewish community. Saturday service is at 9:00 a.m. Friday evening service's time depends on sunset. This is the famous, spacious, Remuh Synagogue, whose name goes back to Israel Isserles, father of Rabbi Moses ben Israel Isserles, who is buried with his family in the cemetery, adjacent to the synagogue. In 1553, Israel Isserles, as a wealthy merchant, obtained a permit from King Sigismund August, son of Sigismund I, to build a synagogue in Kazimierz. He did not erect a new building; he merely adapted a timber structure, which he owned, for synagogue use. A 1557 fire leveled the house of worship, so he rebuilt the structure in masonry. The Remuh Synagogue and Cemetery is now open Sundays to Fridays from 9:00 a.m. to 4:00 p.m.

Remuh Synagogue is named after the founder's son, the codifier Rabbi Moses ben Israel Isserles (ca. 1525-72). He was one of Judaism's great scholars. Remuh is the acronym of Rabbi Moses Isserles, a great halachic authority. To this day, Isserles, born in Cracow, is venerated by Jews throughout the world. He is known as the "Maimonides of Polish Jewry," and the outstanding Ashkenazic codifier of religious law. Rabbi Joseph Karo codified the Shulhan Arukh, but that was intended for the Sephardim, according to writer, historian, and guide Henryk Halkowski. "Moses Isserles adapted for the use of the Ashkenazim and in this form, as a collaboration of Joseph Karo and Moses Isserles, they became the oracle of Jewish life." He adds, "Even today the Orthodox regard the codex of Joseph Karo and Moses Isserles as defining the principles of their behavior." Religious Jews undertake pilgrimages to Rabbi Moses Isserles' grave on the Lag B'Omer holiday, the anniversary of his death. He is buried in the Remuh Synagogue's cemetery. His tombstone was not damaged during the war.

The synagogue contains a nave with round-headed windows set high up in the walls, and a Roman barrel vaulted ceiling. "Tucked away" in a courtyard off the street, next to the ancient Remuh cemetery, it is a plain rectilinear building. The bimah is surrounded by a wrought-iron cage and the ark is similar to that of Old Synagogue. Before the Second World War, the synagogue was led by Rabbi Ozjasz Thon, who was also a member of Polish Parliament and a leading Zionist.

The Cemetery at Remuh Synagogue. Other graves besides that of Rabbi Moses Isserles, who is buried with his family, include Rabbi Joel Sirkes (1561-1640), head of the Cracow yeshiva and one of the greatest Talmudic scholars of Poland, and the famous Polish Kabbalist, Nathan Spira (1585-1633). Also buried here is Yom Tov Lippmann Heller (1579-1633), who also had been the rabbi of Vienna. The latter is most famous for his Tosefot Yom Tov, a commentary on the Mishnah. The Nazis razed all tombstones, but the cemetery, one of the best examples from the Renaissance, was restored in part by the American Jewish Joint Distribution Committee. A wall made out of tombstone fragments stands as a fitting symbol of the Holocaust.

The Ajzyk Synagogue, at 16 Kupa, Cracow. Also known as **The Rabbi Isaac Synagogue** founded by Isaac Jakubowicz and his wife, Brindla Jakubowicz. He was a banker and elder of the Jewish community and

The historic mid-sixteenth century Remuh Synagogue in the Kazimierz section of Cracow, Poland. (Photo by Ben G. Frank)

obtained a permit to build a synagogue from King Wladislaw IV in 1638. The opening of the building, however, was delayed by litigation brought against the Jewish community by the priests of the Corpus Christi Church, who objected to passing a synagogue when they were bearing the sacraments, according to Wischnitzer. Still, despite the objection, building commenced and the 55 x 39-feet hall was constructed, and although the exterior has weathered, the portal facing Isaac Street is still beautiful. It is now possible to visit this synagogue from Sunday to Friday, from 9:00 a.m. to 7:00 p.m.

Stowarzszenie Beit Krakow (World Union of Progressive Judaism) administrator @eupj.org.

New Jewish Cemetery. Buried in their tombs in this cemetery are the famous leaders of Cracow Chassidim, the Epstein brothers and Raphael Landau. The cemetery was laid out in the nineteenth century and contains the graves of important Jews of the nineteenth and twentieth centuries, such as the painters Mauricy Gottlieb and Arthur Markowicz; the Zionist leader and representative in the Polish Parliament, Rabbi Ozjasz Thon; the structural engineer Jozef Sare; the physicians Aaron Kirschner and Jonathan Warszauer; and many others. It is still used today for burial rites.

The Center for Jewish Culture in Kazimierz, Cracow, of the Judaica Foundation, Rabbi Meiselsa St., 17, 30-001, Cracow. Tel: 48-12-430-64-49.

The Center for Jewish Culture in Kazimierz is located at 17 Rabbi Meiselsa St., Cracow. (Photo courtesy of The Center for Jewish Culture)

www.judaica.pl/index_start.php. The Center for Jewish Culture in Kazimierz, Cracow, is one result of the revival of interest in Jewish history and culture in Poland that Joachim S. Russek, director of the Jagiellonian University Research Center on Jewish History and Culture in Poland, helped get underway in the mid-1980s. According to Professor Russek, also director of the Judaica Foundation, the goal of the center is to "help both physically preserve the Jewish heritage and to make it more accessible to all." This center provides cultural events; it runs a library; it prepares and distributes publications; it promotes research on Kazimierz; it supports restoration efforts. A recipient of a U.S. Congressional grant, the center possesses a wonderful lecture hall, a great coffee bar, and a fine place for American students to visit. Russek says the "Jewish landscape was an integral part of the Polish landscape, and he believes Poles have an obligation to take care of the entire history of Poland. Research students often come here.

The Center for Jewish Culture is housed in the former B'nai Emunah prayer house located at 17 Meiselsa, named after rabbi and Polish patriot, Dov Berush Meisels, who was in the Senate of independent Cracow and who rallied Jewish support in the 1863 rebellion against Russia. This former house of prayer was built in 1886 by a worship society, on a site where there had been a smelting facility of the Cracow goldsmith's guild until the seventeenth century. It was the work of the well-known Cracow architect and builder, Jacek Matusinski. The style of the building refers to the trends of the time,

The café at The Center for Jewish Culture in Kazimierz is a gathering place for students and visitors. (Photo courtesy of The Center for Jewish Culture)

with Oriental elements. Inside, the most interesting elements were the aron ha-kodesh, the Holy Ark, as well as an iron column in the passageway separating the men's and the women's sections. A large memorial plaque for the founders and others who were connected with the prayer house was part of the synagogue. At the end of the nineteenth century the whole interior was covered with interesting polychromy. The building consists of a library, archives, and reading and study rooms. The center opened at the end of 1993 and operates under the auspices of the Judaica Foundation.

The Jewish Culture Festival, 36, Józefa Street, 31-056 Cracow. Tel: 48-12-43-15-17 office (at)jewishfestival.pl.: jewishfestival.pl. The festival has grown to one of the most important cultural events in Cracow/ Outside of Poland, the Jewish Culture Festival is one of the best known, recognized and appreciated by both artists and audience. Every year the Festival features almost 300 events during ten days. About 30,000 participants from many countries take part in workshops, lectures, discussions, guided-tours, and of course, various musical events: from concerts to DJ-parties to jam sessions. Approximately 150 artists, instructors, and lecturers give talks and demonstrations.

The Jewish Culture Festival maintains that it is the largest presentation of contemporary culture created by the Jews in Israel and the entire Diaspora. "Israel has become our main point of reference as a place, where it naturally grows and develops," says the group.

March of the Remembrance Commemorating the Liquidation of the Cracow Ghetto. Karnet.krakow.pl. Cracow ghetto was liquidated by the Germans March 13 and 14, 1943. The march begins every year at the Ghetto Heroes' Square in Cracow's Podgorze—in the very center of the former ghetto. From there, it proceeds to a memorial in the area of the former KL Plaszow. Participants are not only from Poland, but as reported a number of former Cracovians and their descendants now living in Israel.

Schindler's List **Tour**. As I read the brochure citing the sites that would be seen on the tour of the places involved in the filming of *Schindler's List*, I could not help but recall that heart-tearing scene when the Gestapo is about to raid the Jewish Ghetto, which in the film version was right here on Szeroka Street in the Kazimierz section of Cracow. A proclamation is read which, paraphrased, said that King Casimir the Great invited the Jews to Cracow; they helped Poland prosper; they lived wonderful lives; they contributed to the community. But the Nazis made sure that that life would end. The Germans almost succeeded; they killed most of the Jews of Cracow. But as I walked along Szeroka Street, I realized Jews are still here; perhaps not in numbers, but something more spiritual. You may feel the same. As you take the tour of *Schindler's List* sites, you will recall the film and what it portrayed; and the history of the Jewish people will become more realistic for you, the traveler. Viewers of the film *Schindler's List* certainly know some of the history and sights surrounding Cracow.

The Jardan Bookstore and Jardan Company. Located right on Szeroka 2-Miodowa 41, Cracow, conducts two-hour daily tours every day to the sights from the film. Participants can travel in a car or van. It is wise to make reservations beforehand. Tel: 48-12-429-13-74. The Cracow Ghetto was located across the Vistula in Podgorze. The ghetto took up the area bounded by the Vistula, Krzemionki, and Lwowska streets, and Podgorski Square.

A Museum of the Ghetto stands at Zgoda Square, now called Pl Bohaterow Getta. From this spot, Jews were sent to the death camp. A drug store called "Pod Orlem" was here, and because it was on the edge of the ghetto, the pharmacy owners were able to save some Jews by taking them through a concealed passage, it is said. The Cracow Ghetto was "liquidated" in March 1943. A huge labor camp was set up and the tombstones of a Jewish cemetery were used in the construction of the camp buildings.

But before we see the site of the camp, the reader will note that Oscar Schindler's enamel factory building still stands, only now it is used as an electronic parts firm. The Schindler plant is located at 4F Lipowa Street, Cracow. Tel: 48-12-257-10-17.

The camp itself, now destroyed, was situated on the site of the former Jewish cemetery in Jerozolimska Street and was known as **Plaszow**. It consisted of 34 barracks and 11 watchtowers. Inmates there included about 6,000 Jews who survived the deportations from the ghetto. At certain periods, the total number of inmates exceeded 20,000. We can still see the house where the Nazi commander and chief of the camp, Amon Goeth, resided. He was hung in 1946 for war crimes. Located on Jerozolimska Street, it still contains the balcony from which he shot innocent people during his so-called target practice. On the hill site of the Plaszow camp stands a gargantuan stone sculpture of sharply etched human figures with a huge horizontal gash across their bodies.

Of course, Cracow is Poland's prime tourist attraction and a must in Central Europe. This ancient city boasts numerous world-class monuments, charming vistas, good restaurants, and a delightful atmosphere, including markets and fairs.

Wawel Castle, Cracow. Built in the eleventh century, the town grew around Wawel Hill. In 1241, Tatars set fire to the city and burned Cracow to the ground. This was the seat of Polish kings for more than five hundred years and was of symbolic importance. Buried here is Jozef Pilsudski, who in the 1930s set up a dictatorship in the country. Pilsudski (1867-1935), originally a Socialist, gained fame as a military leader and organizer of armed opposition to Russia. As chief of state at the end of War World I, he led the 1920 victory of the Poles over the Soviet army outside Warsaw. Fed up with public life and corruption, he retired from public life in 1923. Three years later, he returned to power after leading an armed coup. Sanacja (purification) was the name bestowed upon the military regime installed by Marshal Pilsudski. Most Jews felt that Pilsudski, although he remained a dictator, spoke out against violence toward the Jewish people. When he died, the constraints were lifted; a period of greater violence was ushered in. Also buried here is King Kazimierz Wiliki. He founded Cracow Academy, later renamed Jagiellonian University, "the second in Central Europe after the one in Prague." Nicolus Copernicus (1473-1543), who would later develop his heliocentric theory, studied in Cracow in 1490-91.

Guide: Mrs. Ewa Węgrzyn is a professional guide who speaks English and Hebrew. Tel: 0048-605-934-738 (also for WhatsApp). ewawegrzyn@gmail.com.

OSWIECIM

On the marshes of the River Sola, a tributary of the Vistula, lies the town of Oswiecim. Ironically, Jews settled there as early as the thirteenth century, when the town served as the capital of a Slavic duchy, all of which bore the same name.

More than a century later, in 1563, King Sigismund August II confirmed the "privilege for Jews" to live in Oswiecim. He denied them the right to own houses in the market square or to build a synagogue. He also barred a further influx of Jewish settlers. The Jews fought vigorously against such restrictions and stressed their contribution to the development of the city. The restrictions were finally lifted and in 1588 the Jews were permitted to build a synagogue and to acquire ground for a new cemetery. Thus in those days, Oswiecim became the spiritual center of the surrounding Jewish communities. In 1939, about 6,000 Jews lived in Oswiecim.

After the liberation of Poland, Oswiecim developed into an important industrial center with a population of more than 30,000.

AUSCHWITZ-BIRKENAU

This is Auschwitz-Birkenau, the "epicenter of the Holocaust."

"Please Behave Appropriately," says the sign on the entrance to Birkenau. "Respect the Memories of Those Who Suffered and Died Here."

In 2016, more than two million people from around the world visited the Auschwitz Birkenau Memorial and Museum. Nearly a half million came from Poland. The United Kingdom sent 271,000 visitors followed by the U.S. with 215,000 and Italy with 146,000.

"To understand how Auschwitz could have been the place where the extermination of millions took place you must see Birkenau, which is a short bus ride from this camp," wrote a visitor to the camp.

So, I went to the Birkenau concentration camp before I went to Auschwitz. The two camps are located next to each other, separated only by a two and a half-mile "death march road."

Birkenau is named after "birch tree woods," and was built after Auschwitz I, which was the first camp in the area. Auschwitz was originally intended as an intermittent camp for Polish political prisoners and then Russian POWs. As for Birkenau, it was built as an expansion to Auschwitz I, and was to serve as an extermination camp.

The Germans razed the Polish village of Brezezinka, three kilometers from Auschwitz. Here they built this gigantic complex of barracks, gas chambers, crematoria, and burning pits—all fed by a rail spur diverted from the main line.

"Over the next four years, some 1.6 million people, 90 percent Jews, were murdered and burned at Birkenau, their ashes plowed into the soil, dumped into small ponds and scattered into the nearby Vistula River," writes James E. Young.

The two photos shown are displays in The Jewish Museum and its core exhibit, "Oshpitzin: The Story of Jewish Oświęcim." The museum is part of the Auschwitz Jewish Center Synagogue and Museum, Oswiecim. (Photo credit: The Auschwitz Jewish Center Synagogue and Museum, Oswiecim.)

Memorial stones at the Birkenau death camp. (Photo by Riva Frank)

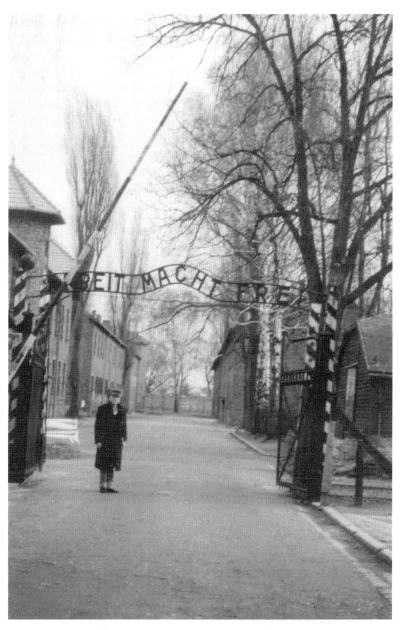

The author at the entrance to Auschwitz Concentration Camp. (Photo by Riva Frank)

This huge, flat, grassy field is still the site of the barren, desolate shacks located here; the public, inhuman "latrines" are still here; the wreckage is still here. This last-built camp had the honor of housing the largest crematorium, which could burn 3,000 bodies a day.

This is as close as you are bound to get to reality. As A James Rudin, formerly of the American Jewish Committee,, and others say that weather is playing havoc with the facility. Future generations may not be able to see the grisly horrors of Nazism firsthand.

But the consensus seems to be not to rebuild the camp, otherwise it could become a "Holocaust theme park," complete with high-tech displays. Here was the technology of genocide. It was the poison gas and the crematorium technology that combined to create mass murder. There were fifteen furnaces in every crematorium. It took only twenty minutes between the arrival of a trainload to be undressed and the arrival of the special detachment to strip the corpses of hair, gold fillings, and personal jewelry at the entrance of the crematorium, according to Norman Davies in *Heart of Europe: A Short History of Poland.*

There were four crematoria at Auschwitz: II, III, IV, and V.

A prison guard tower at Birkenau. (Photo by Ben G. Frank)

The only way out of Birkenau was through the chimney, as one Nazi said. When you see the vast piles of hair, glasses, and suitcases on display in Auschwitz, you know the people who were there were turned to ashes.

I walked from the main gate at Birkenau along the railway track that brought the prisoners into the camp. The tourist should do the same. When the boxcars opened, an unbelievable stench enveloped the area, the floors had been covered with only lime and straw, and the journey could be several days and nights. When the prisoners stood at the platform, they were groggy, to say the least. Life had oozed from them in the hours spent in unsanitary boxcars. Like cattle, they had been shipped. They were weak. Night clouded their reality. The kapos

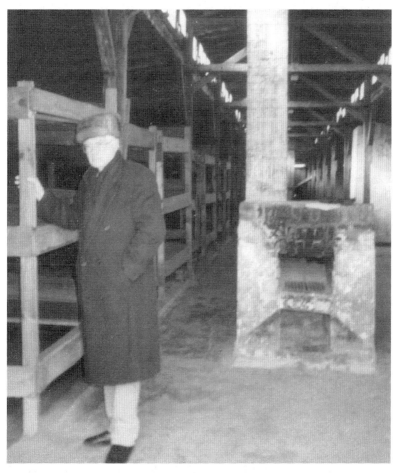

The author at one of the barracks at Birkenau. (Photo by Riva Frank)

shouted; the general selection was about to take place. New arrivals had no idea what was going on. They were confused, anxious, and frightened.

I passed the spot where Dr. Josef Mengele is supposed to have stood selecting victims as they stumbled off the transports. They were directed to the left for the gas chambers, or to the right for slave labor. The "survivors" then passed by the remains of the pylon fencing. You can still see the fences. The Jews were stopped at the gas chambers. After undressing, hundreds of Jews were shoved into the gas chambers, furnished with showers and water pipes to give a realistic impression of a bathhouse. A Zykon-B pellet was dropped from above. They died instantly.

Today the gas chambers are steel wrecks; the retreating Nazis tried to blow up the camp, to cover up their crime. You can still see the barbed wire. Many Jews committed suicide by running right smack into the barbed wire.

I then went to Auschwitz or Camp I, the main camp, and there is the cynical sign at the main gate, Arbeit Macht Frei, translated by some, "Work Brings Freedom." The prisoners passed this sign each day on their way to work. On the small square by the kitchen, the camp orchestra would play marches to muster the thousands of prisoners so that they could be counted more efficient by the S.S.

After the war, the "blocks at Auschwitz I were converted into national pavilions, each with an exposition devoted to the national memory of a different country's citizens at Auschwitz," according to James E. Young.

In Block II, you see a model of the furnace, cans of Zykon-B gas, and victims' hair.

In Block V, there are victims' glasses, prayer shawls, prostheses, canes, and crutches.

Block VII holds a swimming pool for the S.S.

Block X is where Jewish women were sterilized. There are descriptions of the sterilization process.

Each nation had its block. Block XXI tells the story of the Jews of Holland. You see a film of a train from Westerbork to Auschwitz and then back from Auschwitz to Westerbork to pick up more Jews.

What do we understand of the killers and victims through their remains? Young says that these remains "force us to recall the victims as the Germans have remembered them to us: in the collected debris of a destroyed civilization."

In Block XXVII, the Jewish prison blocks or exhibitions in Auschwitz I, you will hear on tape the chanting of "El Mole Rachamim," a Hebrew memorial prayer for the dead. I said a memorial prayer for the Joskowitz and Spitz families and as I did so, I remembered what Rabbi Besser told me. Holocaust survivors have very few relatives. How could they? For example, my wife's father lost all of his thirteen brothers and sisters and his parents somewhere in Poland, and my wife's mother lost six of her nine brothers and sisters and her parents somewhere in Poland. And to think that my wife's father did not have even one family picture or a single photo of any of his brothers and sisters to pass down to his children or grandchildren. That is what the Germans did to Jewish families—multiplied by six million dead—that is what you learn, recall, and feel at Auschwitz-Birkenau.

"The concentration camps are monuments to bestiality," writes Abba Eban in *Heritage: Civilization and the Jews*. He feels the camps are "kept as places of commemoration by governments and peoples who do not want to forget. Nothing like this violent bestial hatred had ever occurred in history," he continues. "If it had, the Jews would have known about it," he declares, adding, "had not they stood before in anguish, suffering, and martyrdom.

This is the killing grounds, the killing fields, and the cemetery of the Jewish people. This was the "Auschwitz Moloch." The greatest mass murder ever committed in human history took place in this twenty-five-square-mile area. Neal Pease, writing in Poland, A Country Study maintains that between 1939 and 1945, six million people, more than fifteen percent of Poland's population, perished in the war, including three million Jews murdered in the death camps of Poland. One out of every two Poles was either killed, wounded, or enslaved during the war. The loss of more than six million Polish citizens, half of them Jews, from a total 1939 population of 35 million "represented a casualty rate of 18 percent compared with 0.2 percent in the U.S., 0.9 percent in Great Britain, 2.5 percent in Japan, 7.4 percent in Germany, 11.1 percent in former Yugoslavia and 11.2 percent in the former U.S.S.R.," according to Norman Davies.

While estimates range as high as 4.5 million and as low as 1.1 million killed at Auschwitz, more human beings were murdered at Auschwitz than at any other place in history. Historians agree that between 1.1 million to 1.5 million were killed at Auschwitz, 90 percent of them were Jews. "When the Red Army arrived at Auschwitz," according to Rabbi A. James Rudin, "no one knew exactly how many people had been killed there and no one knows today." Auschwitz's first commandant, Rudolf Hoess, who was executed after the war for crimes against humanity, acknowledged he "personally arranged the gassing of two million persons between June and July 1941 and the end of 1943." The Russians at one time said the death toll reached four million, and Poles still view Auschwitz as a place of national martyrdom. Most of the Jews killed at Auschwitz were not from Poland. Murdered here were Jews from Hungary, Greece, France, and other nations. Only ten to fifteen percent were Polish. Both Poles and Jews are extremely vulnerable when it comes to discussing the war. Both have experienced "national suffering."

Auschwitz was liberated by Russians who arrived at the camp at 3:00 p.m. January 27, 1945. One report says the camp was liberated by one Col. Grigori Davidowich Elishavetzki, a Jew. They found 648 corpses and 7,600 survivors: 1,200 survivors in the Auschwitz main camp, and 5,800 at Birkenau, including 4,000 women. There were also 650 survivors at Monowitz, the I. G. Farber Chemical Camp, according to Martin Gilbert in *Auschwitz and the Allies*. Most were deathly sick.

Tens of thousands of others had been forced to move out westward on death marches. Elie Wiesel, the writer and Nobel Laureate, as a teenager, was one of the 58,000 inmates marched out of the camp by the fleeing Nazis. Seven thousand skeletal and sick prisoners were left behind by the retreating Nazis to wait for the advancing Soviet army.

One of the Russians, Gen. Vasili Petrenko, then a colonel of the First Ukrainian Front, tells of finding the remains of four crematoria, one still intact, which the Germans did not have time to blow up when they fled. He said that he found the gas chambers where prisoners had been killed with Zykon-B gas and twenty-nine warehouses filled with the personal belongings of the camp's prisoners. Still horrified by those images today, Petrenko recounted his discovery of thousands of suitcases arranged in rows, and shoes and clothing methodically organized according to age and size. What shocked him the most, however, was seeing the eyeglasses, the masses of false teeth, and seven tons of women's hair packed in boxes. "It is unimaginable how many women had to be destroyed to produce seven tons of hair," he says. Many have argued that Auschwitz, or at least the railroad tracks, should have been bombed; in 1944, they could have been.

The March of the Living

The March of the Living is an annual educational program which brings people—mainly students—from all over the world to Poland, to study the history of the Holocaust and examine the roots of prejudice, intolerance and hate.

During their week in Poland the students march hand in hand with Holocaust survivors from Auschwitz-Birkenau on Holocaust Remembrance Day. After visiting other places of Nazi German persecution as well as once thriving sites of Jewish life and culture, many of the participants also travel to Israel.

It must be pointed out that the March of the Living itself, a three kilometer walk from Auschwitz to Birkenau, is a silent tribute to all victims of the Holocaust. The March of the Living, which is joined each year by thousands of Jewish teens, adults and survivors from around the world—and many other people of good will of all faiths and backgrounds—serves as a hopeful counterpoint to the experience of hundreds of thousands of camp inmates forced by the Nazis to cross vast expanses of European terrain under the harshest of conditions—the infamous "death marches."

Auschwitz to Birkenau was the largest concentration camp complex built during World War II.

The numbers of attendees range year to year, from a few thousand in the earlier years, to as many 20,000 participants. In recent years, however, estimates range at around 10,000.

Since the first March of the Living was held in 1988, an estimated 250,000 people have marched down the same path leading from Auschwitz to Birkenau.

For more information, please contact: International March of the Living, I 2 West 45th Street Suite 1500, New York NY 10036. Tel: .212-869-6800. Fax: 212-869-6822. motl@motlmail.org.

Convent. In the mid-1980s, a painful controversy broke out when one of Auschwitz's original buildings, the warehouse where poison gas had been stored, was converted into a Carmelite Convent. Catholic nuns used the building to pray for those murdered at Auschwitz.

The change created an international furor that lasted almost ten years. According to Rabbi Rudin, who was "personally involved in the convent crisis," Jews felt the establishment of a convent at Auschwitz was an attempt to "Christianize" the Holocaust, to erase the particularity of Jewish suffering, and to deny that Jews were the principal target of Nazi genocide. Catholics were perplexed and often offended that anybody would object to a few nuns praying at the scene of mass murder. After all, Catholic priests died at Auschwitz.

In 1987, some European Jewish and Catholic leaders, including four cardinals, agreed the Carmelite nuns should move to a new convent to be constructed outside the camp. The nuns vacated the Auschwitz building, but only after Pope John Paul II intervened to resolve the controversy.

In 1999, hundreds of crosses that had been erected on the site by Polish Catholic extremists were removed. However, the large "papal cross" remains, demarcating where, in 1988, Pope John Paul II prayed for the 152 Polish Catholics killed at that location

Auschwitz Jewish Center: Synagogue and Jewish Museum. Pl. Ks. J. Skarbka 5, 32-600, Oświęcim. Tel: 48-33-844-7002; info@ajcf.pl, www.ajcf.pl

The Center consists of three sites: the historic Chevra Lomdei Mishnayot synagogue; the Jewish Museum and Café Bergson and is located about 3 kilometers away from the Auschwitz Memorial Museum.

The Chevra Lomdei Mishnayot synagogue was built in 1913 and is the only surviving Jewish house of prayer in Oświęcim (the town next to Auschwitz). Around twenty synagogues stood here before World War II. The Nazis devastated its interior and used the building as ammunitions warehouse.

After World War II, Jewish survivors in Oświęcim once again used it as a synagogue. In the 1950s, the last Jews of Oświęcim left, and the synagogue stood empty. In the 1970s, the Communist government nationalized the building and turned it into a carpet warehouse.

In 1998, the synagogue became the first Jewish communal property to be returned to a Jewish community in Poland. The recipients of the property, the Bielsko-Biala Jewish Community, donated the synagogue to the Auschwitz Jewish Center Foundation. The AJCF restored the building to its pre-war condition as described by survivors. It was reopened in September 2000.

As the only Jewish house of worship near Auschwitz-Birkenau, the Chevra Lomdei Mishnayot provides visitors with a sanctuary for prayer, reflection, and solace. Although it has neither a rabbi nor a local congregation today, it is under careful protection of the Auschwitz Jewish Center Foundation which is now part of the Museum of Jewish Heritage in New York.

Next door is also The Jewish Museum and its core exhibit, "Oshpitzin: The Story of Jewish Oświęcim."

The Museum through a rich collection of artifacts, pictures, documents and testimonies of survivors tells the captivating Jewish history of the town know as Auschwitz. The Museum has also an app: app.oshpitzin.pl which is a free guide to the Museum and the Jewish heritage of the town including the Jewish cemetery.

The Auschwitz Jewish Museum received nearly 2.1 million visitors in 2016. Behind the synagogue is Café Bergson. It is located in the 100-year old Kluger Family House. This is the house where the last Jewish resident of the town Szymon Kluger lived. Open daily 11:00 a.m.-7:00 p.m. and offers various drinks, cafes, teas, and homemade cakes.

Wroclaw

Now the second largest Jewish community in Poland after Warsaw, this town—with about 600 to 1000 Jews—is undergoing a Jewish revival. Once known as Breslau and located in Germany before World

War II, Wroclaw was a center of the German Reform movement. After the war, the city became part of Poland.

Synagogue, 9 Wlodkowica St., Wroclaw. Tel: 71-343-64-01.

Located here, too, is the Jewish Community of Wroclaw. **TSKZ-Club**, 28 Swidnicka St., Wroclaw.

Katowice

Synagogue and Jewish Community of Katowice, 3 Maja 16 St. Katowice. Tel: 32-253-02-09.

Jewish Heritage Europe. www.jewish-heritage-Europe.eu. or www. Jewishheritageeurope. Most Jewish travelers who explore beyond the sights and sounds of the major European cities know that many Jewish heritage sites are still empty or in ruins. Many Jewish cemeteries are neglected or abandoned. But there are lists, inventories, databases, and online resources that tell us where they are.

Jewish Heritage Europe is an expanding web portal to news, information, and resources concerning Jewish monuments and heritage sites all over Europe. A project of the Rothschild Foundation (Hanadiv) Europe, JHE fosters communication and information exchange regarding restoration, funding, best-practices, advisory services, and more.

Jewish Heritage Europe is an expanding web portal to news, information, and resources concerning Jewish monuments and heritage sites all over Europe. A project of the Rothschild Foundation, (Hanadiv) Europe, JHE fosters communication and information exchange regarding restoration, funding, best-practices, advisory services, and more.

Suggested Reading

Applebaum, Anne. *Between East and West Across the Borderlands of Europe.* New York: Pantheon, 1994.

Arad, Yitzhak, *Belzec, Sobibar, Treblinka: The Operation Reinhard Death Camps.* Bloomington: Indiana University Press, 1987.

Asch, Sholem. *Tales of My People.* New York: Putnam, 1948.

Brandys, Kazimierz. *A Warsaw Diary: 1978-1981.* New York: Random House, 1983.

Cantor, Norman F. *The Sacred Chain: The History of the Jews.* New York: HarperCollins, 1994.

Curtis, Glenn C, ed. *Poland, A Country Study.* Washington, D.C.: Federal Research Division, Library of Congress, 1994.

Davies, Norman. *Heart of Europe: A Short History of Poland.* Oxford: Oxford University Press, 1986.

Dawidowicz, Lucy S. *The War Against the Jews: 1933-1945.* New York: Bantam, 1986.

Doblin, Alfred. *Journey to Poland.* Translated by Joachim Neugroschel. New York: Paragon House, 1991.

Dubroszycki, Lucjan, and Barbara Kirshenblatt-Gimblett. *Image Before My Eyes: A Photographic History of Jewish Life in Poland, 1864-1939.* New York: Schocken Books, 1987.

Dubnow, S. M. *History of the Jews in Russia and Poland: From the Earliest Times Until the Present Day.* Philadelphia: Jewish Publication Society of America, 1918.

Eban, Abba. *Heritage: Civilization and the Jews.* New York: Summit Books, 1984.

Eliach, Yaffa, *There Once Was A World, A Nine-Hundred-Year Chronicle of the Shtetl of Eishyshock.* Boston, New York, London, London; Little, Brown and Company, 1998.

Engel, David. *In the Shadow of Auschwitz: The Polish Government in Exile and the Jews, 1939-1942.* Chapel Hill, N.C.: University of North Carolina Press, 1987.

Frost, Robert I. *After the Deluge: Poland and the Second Northern War, 1655-1660.* New York: Cambridge University Press, 1993.

Fuks, Marian, Zygmunt Hoffman, Maurycy Horn, and Jerzy Tomaszewski. *Polish Jewry History and Culture.* Warsaw: Interpress Publishers, 1982.

Gilbert, Martin. *The Holocaust: A History of the Jews of Europe During the Second World War.* New York: Henry Holt, 1987.

—. *Auschwitz and the Allies.* New York: Holt, Rinehart and Winston, 1981.

Gutman, Yisrael. *Resistance: The Warsaw Ghetto Uprising.* Boston: Houghton Mifflin, 1994.

Gutman, Yisrael. *The Jews of Warsaw, 1939-1943: Ghetto, Underground, Revolt.* Translated by Ina Friedman. Bloomington: Indiana University Press, 1989.

Halkowski, Henryk. *Cracow-City and Mother of Israel.* from Cracow: Dialogue of Traditions. Cracow: Znak Publishers, 1991.

Hart, Kitty. *Return to Auschwitz, The Remarkable Story of a Girl Who Survived the Holocaust.* New York: Athenum, 1982.

Hertz, Aleksander. *The Jews in Polish Culture.* Translated by Richard Lourie. Evanston, Ill.: Northwestern University Press, 1988.

Hilberg, Raul, ed. *The Warsaw Diary of Adam Czerniakow: Prelude to Doom.* Stanislaw Staron, and Joseph Kermisz. New York: Stein and Day, 1968.

Hoffman, Eva. *Exit into History: A Journey Through the New Eastern Europe.* New York: Viking, 1993.

Katsh, A. L., ed. *The Warsaw Diary of Chain A. Kaplan.* New York: Macmillan, 1973.

Korczak, Janusz. *Ghetto Diary.* New York: Holocaust Library, 1978.

Krinsky, Carol Herselle. *Synagogues of Europe: Architecture, History, Meaning.* Cambridge, Mass.: MIT Press, 1985.

Kurlansky, Mark. *A Chosen Few: The Resurrection of European Jewry.* Reading, Mass.: Addison-Wesley, 1995.

Kurzman, Dan. *The Bravest Battle: The Twenty-Eight Days of the Warsaw Ghetto Uprising.* New York: Da Capo Press, 1993.

Langer, Lawrence L. *Admitting the Holocaust: Collected Essays.* New York: Oxford University Press, 1995.

Lendvai, Paul. *Anti-Semitism Without Jews: Communist Eastern Europe.* Garden City, N.Y: Doubleday, 1971.

Levi, Primo. *Survival in Auschwitz.* New York: Macmillan, 1987.

MacLean, Rory. *Stalin's Nose: Travels Around the Bloc.* New York: Little, Brown, 1993.

Mark, Ber. *Uprising in the Warsaw Ghetto.* New York: Schocken Books, 1975.

Meyer, Peter, Bernard D. Weinryb, Eugene Duschinsky, and Nicolas Sylvain, eds. *The Jews in the Soviet Satellites.* Syracuse, N.Y: Syracuse University Press, 1953.

Nagorski, Andrew. *The Birth of Freedom.* New York: Simon & Schuster, 1993.

Patai, Raphael ed. *Encyclopedia of Zionism and Israel.* New York: Herzl Press/McGraw-Hill, 1971.

Polansky, Antony, Chimeri Abramsky, and Maciej Jachimezyk, eds. *The Jews in Poland.* Oxford: Basil Blackwell, 1986.

Read, Anthony. *The Deadly Embrace: Hitler, Stalin and the Nazi Soviet Pact, 1939-1941.* New York: Norton, 1989.

Ringelblum, Emmanuel. *Notes from the Warsaw Ghetto.* New York: McGraw-Hill, 1958.

Rosen, Moses, *Dangers, Tests and Miracles: The Remarkable Life Story of Chief Rabbi Rosen of Romania (as told to Joseph Finkelston).* London: Weidenfeld and Nicolson, 1990.

Rosenberg, Tina, *The Haunted Land, Facing Europe's Ghosts After Communism.* New York, Random House, 1995.

Rottenberg, Dan, *Finding Our Fathers, A Guidebook to Jewish Genealogy.* New York, Random House.1977.

Sands, Philippe, *East West Street, On the Origins of "Genocide" and "Crimes Against Humanity."* Alfred A. Knopf. New York, 2016.

Schneiderman, S. L. *The River Remembers.* New York: Horizon Press, 1978.

Singer, Isaac Bashevis. *The Magician of Lublin.* New York: Fawectt, 1985.

Steiner, Jean-Francois. *Treblinka.* New York: Simon &: Schuster, 1968.

Suhl, Yuri. *They Fought Back: The Story of the Jewish Resistance in Nazi Europe*. New York: Schocken Books, 1975.

Swiebocka, Teresa, comp. *Auschwitz: A History in Photographs.* Bloomington: Indiana University Press, 1993.

Vinecour, Earl. *Polish Jews: The Final Chapter.* New York: McGraw-Hill, 1977.

Vital, David, *A People Apart: The Jews in Europe, 1789-1939.* Oxford, Oxford University Press, 1999.

Watt, Richard M. *Bitter Glory: Poland and Its Fate, 1918 to 1939.* New York: Simon & Schuster, 1979.

Weinryb, Bernard D. *The Jews of Poland: A Social and Economic History of the Jewish Community in Poland from 1100 to 1800.* Philadelphia: Jewish Publication Society of America, 1973.

Wiesel, Elie. *Night.* New York: Bantam, 1982.

Wischnitzer, Rachel. *The Architecture of the European Synagogue.* Philadelphia: Jewish Publication Society of America, 1964.

Wood, E. Thomas and Stanislaw M. Jankowski. *Karski: How One Man Tried to Stop the Holocaust.* New York: Wiley, 1994.

Young, James E. *The Texture of Memory: Holocaust Memorials and Meaning in Europe, Israel,* and America. New Haven: Yale University Press, 1993.

Zuckerman, Vilzhak *("Antek")*. *A Surplus of Memory: Warsaw Ghetto Uprising: Memoirs of a Resistance* Trans. and ed. by Barbara and Benjamin Harshav. Leader. Berkeley: University of California Press, 1993.

Romania
Once a Large Jewish Community; Today a Small One

When the brawny arm-swinging, sword wielding, Roman legionnaires conquered Dacia, the land of the first Romanians, they chanted military songs rendered in Latin and composed in Rome. They certainly were not bellowing out the rousing Yiddish song, "*Romania, Romania, Romania,*" as sung, let us say, by the great Israeli concert folk singer, Dudu Fisher, who melodically praises *mamaliga*, translated as "corn mush." We know it as polenta.

When you hear Dudu's song, you want to jump up and dance and dance and dance. For sure, Romanians know how to dance. Was not the Israeli dance, the hora, imported from this Balkan land?

All travel writers pick up sayings and descriptions that aptly describe a municipality or country. As a reporter in New Jersey, I read that when God looked down on Jersey City, he created the beautiful beach metropolis of Rio de Janeiro.

A similar story is told about Romania. Olivia Manning, in her novel, *The Balkan Trilogy*, relates that God was so upset that he had been so generous with Romania and that he had given that country precious gifts such as "forests, rivers, mountains, minerals, oil and a fertile soil that yielded many crops," that to "strike a balance, he put here the worst people he could find." Of course, we scoff at this.

For hundreds of years, Romania has been "cursed by its geographic location" at the crossroads of Europe and Asia which has made it "a transit point of intrigue and invasion by a succession of outside powers," according to Mark Sanborne in his book, *"Romania."* These invaders plundered, raped and murdered. Plucked right smack in the middle of invasion routes, barbaric hordes were followed by the Ottoman Turks, the Hungarians, the Austrians and finally the Germans.

Under its red, blue, and yellow flag, Romania encompasses 91,699 square miles. Romania's population declined steadily in recent years, from 21.7 million in 2002 to 19.9 million in 2014 to about 19.2 million in 2017.

Its current boundaries were set after World War II. Bordering it are the Black Sea in the southeast; the Republic of Moldova to the north and northeast; Ukraine to the east; Hungary and Serbia to the west; and Bulgaria to the south.

Despite ugly urbanization, despite changes in its infrastructure, its somewhat run-down capital city of Bucharest, which counts 1.8 million inhabitants, down about 500,000 since the turn of the century. Even so, it still displays a just-below-the-surface charm.

Tourist-wise, this is a beautiful country that proudly boasts breath-taking scenery, hiking trails and resorts. It also offers a rich taste of Romanian culture. And as the largest of the Balkan countries, Romania has dramatic mountain scenery and a coastline on the Black Sea.

Like many other territories in Europe, rivers and mountains define history and character, says Robert D. Kaplan, author of *Balkan Ghosts: A Journey Through History*. Romania does not escape the impact of the Danube, which by itself touches seven countries on its 1,776 mile journey from the Black Forest in Germany to the Black Sea. The Danube flows past Budapest, past Belgrade and for 900 miles it forms Romania's southwest border with Serbia and its southern border with Bulgaria. It then flows due north through Romania before turning east again and branching into a myriad of small waterways that flow into the Black Sea, notes Kaplan.

Romania, like other countries in East Central Europe, "was less productive, less literate and less healthy than West Central and Western Europe," wrote historian Joseph Rothschild in his book, *East Central Europe Between the Two World Wars*. As recently as the end of World War II, Romania was almost totally an agricultural country; that is, until the Stalinists got their hands on the economy and forced state-controlled industrialization down the throats of the people. Result: pollution, a pollution that today chokes Bucharest.

Still, even after the fall of Communism, Romania was a slower developer than other former Communist countries of eastern Europe.

Once the food basket of Europe, Romania had been prosperous, a land of plenty, wrote Olivia Manning in her novel, *Balkan Trilogy*. Golden beaches line her Black Sea coast. But to most Americans, Romania is "remote," and a "side show." As we have seen, Americans know very little about what goes on in this end of the world, known as the Balkans. But they are missing much.

Of all the countries in the world, Romania is "trapped between great historical forces," according to author Kaplan. He must have been referring to the Balkans, where much is in dispute, even in the 21st Century.

"No country has had a more muddled past than Romania," observed

Manning. Thousands of years ago, during the Bronze Age, 2200 to 12 BCE Thraco-Getian tribes roamed the area known as Romania. Today's Romanians are in part descended from those Getai who lived north of the Danube River. Residing in the same area were the Dacians who established fortresses against the wild tribes of South Russia. Dacian civilization reached its zenith under Decebalus, who is still honored today in Romania. Decebalus fought the Romans in CE 105-106. Soon, however, Dacia was conquered and organized by Roman legions in CE 105. The Dacians, in turn, absorbed elements of Roman Culture including a Vulgar Latin that eventually evolved into today's Romanian language. Romanian is the only East European language that comes from Latin. By the 200s, the Romans completely occupied the country. When they finally departed, anarchy walked in, according to R.W. Seton Watson in his *History of the Romanians From Roman Times to the Completion of Unity*. In would come major migrations from barbarian tribes, the Visigoths, Huns, Ostrogoths, Gepides and Lombards, Avars and Slavs. All swept over these lands in the next centuries, including "a race of Turkish nomads called Bulgars." In 676, the Bulgarian Empire, for instance, absorbed a large part of Dacia. Then in the Ninth Century came the Magyars who also swept over Eastern Europe, but settled in part in the area we now know as Hungary.

Between 1250 and 1350, the provinces of Moldavia and Walachia united to form what was the nation of Romania. By 1504, however, the principalities fell under Turkish rule.

In the 16th century, a Walachian prince, Michael the Brave, won a war of liberation against the Ottomans and the three states of Walachia, Moldavia and Transylvania were united.

For its part, Transylvania, known for its mythological vampires, was independent for about 170 years, but was returned to Hungary as part of the Hapsburg Empire. In 1848, Hungary revolted and proclaimed freedom of the press and religious rights. One of the first acts of the Hungarian DIET was to attach Transylvania to Hungary. "Romania had no voice in the decision, "says author Ronald D. Backman in *Romania: A Country Study*.

Walachia and Moldavia came under Russian protection soon afterward and remained under the Czars' influence until the Crimean War (1854-56). After that conflict, the Russian protectorate was effectively ended.

While they governed Romania, the Turks had imported a group of local supervisors known as the Phanariot who hailed from Greece. The Turks allowed them to run the Romanian provinces. These Greek satraps took their name from the phanar, the lighthouse district of Constantinople. Corrupt as they were, they also made a lasting impact on the life of Romania, for they brought culture, the French language and literature, as well as a good dose of nationalism.

After the Crimean War (1854-56,) the existence of Moldavia and Walachia was guaranteed. With the help of big power intervention, Walachia and Moldavia again were united under Prince Alexandru Ion Cuza in 1861 to form the nation of Romania. He simply announced to the world that the "Romanian nation is founded." But he was forced to give up power to Prince Karl of Germany, the second son of the reigning family of Hohenzollern-Sigmaringen, and cousin to King Wilhelm I. Prince Karl was chosen King in February 1866 and ruled Romania until 1914 as King Carol I. He may have been Romania's most beloved monarch, but Radu Ioanid, author of *The Holocaust in Romania: the Destruction of Jews and Gypsies Under the Antonescu Regime, 1940 - 1944* labels him an anti-Semite.

Romania was located in the heart of the Jewish world. However, we should remember that even at this stage in Romania's history, anti-Semitism had deep roots in Romania. "The roots of anti-Semitism in Romania, as in most of Eastern Europe, stretch deeply in history," notes Ioanid.

The 1878 Congress of Berlin settled the issues resulting from the Russian-Turkish war. In the end, Romania was forced to accept Russia's annexation of southern Bessarabia from Moldavia, while in return it gained control over northern Dobruja, which included the Danube delta. Europe agreed to recognize Romania's formal and complete independence, in exchange for two main conditions: one, Romania must consent to the territorial deal with Russia, and two, that it guarantee equality of civil, political, and religious rights to all citizens, including Jews. This last condition was aimed at forcing Romania to repeal its laws discriminating against Jews. Article 44 of the Treaty of Berlin stipulated that religion must not be used to exclude anyone from "the enjoyment of civil and political rights," according to historian Radu Ionid. It never happened. In fact, on January 17, 1879, Romania's Parliament made it impossible for Jews to become Romanians unless they converted. Now an individual petition and parliamentary vote were required for naturalization, a requirement that remained on the books until 1919. Between 1866 and 1904, only 2,000 Jews would be naturalized.

In 1912 and 1913, three Balkan wars were fought between Romania and Bulgaria and Serbia and Greece and the Ottomans. In 1912, the First Balkan War broke out. A coalition of Romanians, Bulgarians, Serbs and Greeks rebelled against Turkey and the Ottoman rule and was victorious.

But in the Second Balkan War, Bulgaria, unhappy about the land reward it had obtained in the First Balkan War, flexed its muscles and attacked its allies. Romania joined the Serbs and others against the Bulgarians, who lost. No one could know that this minor fighting in a far-away region was a prelude to a bloody world war, which, in effect, was the Third Balkan War.

Meanwhile, pre-war Romania still had a well-deserved reputation of being, along with Russia, the most "anti-Semitic country in Europe," wrote Ezra Mendelsohn in *The Jews of East Central Europe Between the World Wars*. Suffering from poverty and anti-Semitism, Jews had been emigrating. By World War I, about 90,000 Jews had left Romania.

World War I

On June 18, 1914, a Bosnian Serb assassinated Archduke Franz Ferdinand. Within two months, World War I commenced.

Romania's rival, Bulgaria, joined the Central Powers of Germany, Austria-Hungary, and Turkey. Romania, however, joining the fray in 1915, fought alongside Britain, France and Russia. But Romania's armed forces were described as too late and with too little preparation, according to author Edward Behr. Romania was attacked by the Bulgarians.

After the war, the Treaty of Saint Germain with Austria and Treaty of Trianon with Hungary aided Romania. Being on the winning side, Romania more than doubled its size and population. She obtained Transylvania, which had been ruled by the Hungarians. She received Dobruja from Bulgaria; part of Bessarabia from Russia, and northern Bukovina from part of the Austrian Empire, as well as part of Banat, which was given to the Old Kingdom of Romania.

For our purposes, this meant that more than a half million Jews were absorbed into Greater Romania. Romania thus became the third largest Jewish community in Europe, according to Aron Hirt-Manheimer, who wrote the introduction and commentaries in *Jagendorf's Foundry: Memoir of the Romanian Holocaust, 1941-1944*.

According to author Aron Hirt-Manheimer, the insistence of the Allies at the Versailles peace talks that Romania honor its obligation to grant Jews full citizenship and civil rights, often unleashed a violent xenophobic backlash, particularly among Romania's anti-Semitic university students and intellectuals who rallied the nation around the slogan: "Romania for the Romanians."

Finally, in 1923, Jews were granted full citizenship. The new Citizenship Law in 1924 "extended Romanian citizenship to all inhabitants of Bessarabia, Bukovina, Transylvania, Banat, Crisana Maramures, and Satu Mare, who had been born there of resident parents," explains historian Radu Ioanid.

Anti-Semitism in Romania got a big boost with the rise of Hitler and Nazi Germany.

Octavian Goga, a nationalist anti-Semite, came to power in 1937. He accused Jews of controlling Romania's financial assets. In actual fact, the Jewish population made up only 4 percent of the population, with more than 40 percent of Jews of working age engaged in industry and commerce and three percent in the professions and civil service.

Goga enacted profound anti-Semitic legislation that actually stripped about 200,000 Jews of their citizenship. Jewish businesses were seized. The regime lasted little more than a month but set the pattern for the next five years. Romanian Jewry would suffer greatly.

In February 1938, King Carol took complete control of the government and proclaimed himself "Royal Dictator." He tried to crush the Iron Guard fascists. A court sentenced its leader, Corneliu Zelea Codreanu, to 10 years hard labor for treason. Codreanu had built the Legion of the Archangel Michael into a powerful force in Romanian politics. But on the night of November 29/30, 1938, King Carol II ordered him to be killed. We shall see when we discuss General Ion Antonescu and the Iron Guard that it was Codreanu who formed the Legion of the Archangel Michael in 1927. This was an extreme right-wing movement, of which anti-Semitism was a major component.

Edward Behr, author of *Kiss The Hand You Cannot Bite: The Rise and Fall of the Ceausescus*, says that even though Romanian public opinion was "still overwhelmingly pro-British and pro-French, many Romanians now started to believe that given Romania's geographical position and the pro-German sentiments of neighboring Hungary and Bulgaria, self-interest dictated that they should work out an accommodation with Hitler's Germany." This regime, which already hailed anti-Semitism as an "official policy," would move straight into the arms of the Nazis.

Three Dismemberments

Just about at the same time that Romania was moving into the fascist camp, large parts of Romania were soon to be divided among Russia, Hungary and Bulgaria. The whole of Moldavia would be handed to the Soviets as the price of Russia's neutrality to that point in the War; that is, 1940. Southern Dobruja, would fall to Bulgaria. The Hungarians would march into and take over Transylvania.

In less than two months, Romania would lose forty thousand square miles of territory, and with it, six million citizens and five hundred million sterling pounds.

On June 26, 1940, the Soviet Union gave Romania 24 hours to

return Bessarabia and cede it to Northern Bukovina. The Germans, who in 1939 signed a non-aggression pact with the Russians, advised King Carol to submit. He did. The Russians did not even wait; they marched right in. Romania pulled out almost without firing a shot. The humiliation and defeat was blamed on the Jews. Two months later, in August 1940, with German and Soviet backing, Bulgaria took Southern Dobruja.

In the same month, Germany and Italy persuaded Romania to accept the retrocession of Northern Transylvania to Hungary. King Carol, who had looked to Britain and France for support, gave up the territory that it had gained from Treaty of Versailles after World War I, when Romania obtained its land gains of Bessarabia, Transylvania and Bukovina.

All these boundary changes were negative and fateful for Jews. The Hungarians, without mercy, would soon deport thousands of Jews from Transylvania to the gas chambers in Poland.

Meanwhile, with the fall of France and Britain's desperate plight in 1940, the corrupt Romanian King's position became untenable, according to various historians. As we have seen, bowing to the inevitable, Romania accepted Hitler's proposal regarding the loss of its territory. It was then that King Carol called on fascist General Ion Antonescu to form a new cabinet. In September, however, General Antonescu and the Iron Guard turned around and forced King Carol to abdicate, "blaming him for the loss of Bessarabia, Bukovina and Northern Transylvania," according to Radu Ioanid in his book on the Romanian Holocaust. Antonescu took over real power and the King's 19-year-old son, Michael, took his place in the Palace. But the latter was kept in a ceremonial role, since his father, King Carol, somewhat of a playboy to say the least, had ruled Romania from 1930 to 1940 along with his mistress of Jewish origin, Elena Magda Lupescu. After obtaining Antonescu's permission to flee to Spain, the deposed king and his lady friend stocked a nine-carriage train with a fleet of bulletproof automobiles, $2,500.000 worth of Madame Lupescu's jewelry, and a cache of gold.

Despite deep anti-Semitism, widespread popular violence did not break out in Romania until after Hitler invaded the USSR in June 1941. We should not forget that "Romania contributed more combat troops to the German war effort than all of the other Nazi allies combined," according to Mark Sanborne, author of the book Romania.

Romania's army was ill equipped, ill armed, ill trained and completely unprepared for war with the USSR, which had been invaded by Germany in June 1941. In the Romanian Army, the Romanian soldier could still be flogged. That army even conscripted civilian convicts. In the battles at Stalingrad, some Romanian units fought bravely considering that they had been left alone; their officers had fled the battlefield. Romania sustained heavy losses, especially at Stalingrad. When it was all over on the Russian front, Antonescu's troops looked like "ghosts in rags," according to Antony Beevor writing in his book, *Stalingrad.*

Total Romanian World War II losses came to 110,000 killed and 180,000 missing or captured. After Romania changed sides, about 120,000 would perish helping the Red Army liberate Czechoslovakia and Hungary.

In August 1944, Romania's King Michael overthrew the country's radical right wing premier and signed an armistice with the USSR. "Moscow forced Michael to appoint a Communist sympathizer to lead the government in 1945 and three years later Romania found itself under strict Communist control," writes author Bachman.

August 23 marks the anniversary of Romania liberation by the Soviet Army. Interestingly, to this day, it is celebrated as a national independence day.

The Red Army occupied Bucharest on August 31, 1944. And on September 12, 1944, Romania and Soviet Union signed an armistice. Romania was to pay reparations, repeal anti-Jewish laws, ban fascist groups and retrocede Bessarabia and Northern Bukovina to the Soviet Union. Bessarabia would soon be called the Republic of Moldova and Northern Bukovina became part of today's Ukraine.

Actually, Romania's fate had been sealed when wartime leaders Churchill and Stalin met in Moscow on October 9, 1944. At the table, the two allied leaders drew up a list of Balkan and Central European countries. They listed the percentages and interests that each of them would obtain in the Eastern European sphere. Churchill agreed that there would be 90 percent Soviet preponderance in Romania. Romania would thus disappear into the Soviet camp. The Communists seized power, and the Iron Curtain descended with a huge bang. Moscow-trained Communist leaders took over. There is no question that the Communists were able to assume power because of the "decisive intervention of the Soviet Union," as Joseph Rothschild calls it in his book, *East Central Europe Between the Two World Wars.*

With the Soviet Army, and waiting in the wings, was Gheorghe Gheoghiu-Dej and Anna Pauker, Romanian communist leader, who organized the drive to turn Romania into a full-fledged Communist state, utterly subservient to Moscow. But as we shall see, Romania in the 1960s would pursue an independent line until Communism was overthrown in 1989.

Notable Jews

Rabbi Moses Rosen (1912-1994) Rabbi Moses Rosen was often called the "Red Rabbi," but he was not a Communist. To this very day, pictures of Rabbi Rosen adorn the walls of communal offices. A section of the Jewish Museum in Bucharest is devoted to Rosens's writings, public activities, and meetings with political and religious leaders around the world.

Rabbi Rosen was the spiritual leader of the Jewish community in Rumania during the Communist regime. Even today, years after his death, he is venerated by the community he loved and kept alive. He fought for adequate Jewish religious life in Romania. He took over from Rabbi Alexander Safran when the latter left the country, and was chairman of the Federation of Jewish Communities of the Socialist Republic of Rumania from 1964.

He was born in Moinesti, Moldavia, where his father, Rabbi Abraham Aryeh, served as rabbi. Rabbi Rosen received a secular education along with traditional Jewish learning. He was imprisoned with some of the future leaders of the Romania's Communist Party. "Rosen was not a Communist, but he developed before and during the war into an ardent 'fellow traveler,'" writes Charles Hoffman in *Gray Dawn: The Jews of Eastern Europe in the Post-Communist Era*, adding, "he stoutly asserted that he would have made a pact with the devil in order to preserve Jewish life in Romania."

The Communists expected him to go along with their wishes. Rosen turned out less pliable than they expected. "The Communists," writes author Charles Hoffman, "were extremely ruthless in purging anyone who was thought to oppose them."

From 1957, Rabbi Rosen was a member of the Great National Assembly (Parliament) of Romania; his original constituency being a quarter of Bucharest that at one time contained a large Jewish population.

"All of the things I accomplished—saving hundreds of thousands of Jews and bringing them to Israel—were possible only by working with Ceausescu. Could I do what I did by going against him?" Rabbi Rosen was reported to have remarked.

Romanian dictator Nicolae Ceausescu apparently disliked Rabbi Rosen because the rabbi fought the dictator's plans to demolish the Bucharest Great Synagogue, the Choral Temple and the Jewish Museum. "I still hold to the view that my efforts to obtain MFN (Most Favored Nation) status for Romania was in accordance with my patriotic duty. I carried out my duty both to my Jewish brethren and to the Romanian people," said Rabbi Rosen. The rabbi's "main achievement was the creation of legal conditions for adequate Jewish religious life in Rumania."

Rabbi Rosen was not the architect of the mass *aliyah*. To stand against charges that he collaborated, he "overlooked the fact that the mass *aliyah* was arranged mainly by the Israeli government, which had paid Ceausescu several thousand dollars a head or provided economic benefits to Romania in exchange for the immigrants," wrote the late Charles Hoffman in *Gray Dawn: The Jews of Eastern Europe in the Post-Communist Era.* It is a well-known fact that the Israelis paid $4,000 a person for an exit visa. Author Hoffman points out that the West Germans did the same thing to ransom tens of thousands of ethnic Germans living in Romania.

"Rabbi Rosen stands out as an exceptional figure among the tragic gallery of Jewish communal leaders who labored at the near-impossible task of maintaining Jewish life for forty years under the hostile and brutal watch of Communism," continues Hoffman in his book.

After 1947, the state controlled Jewish institutions. But Rabbi Rosen managed to keep the "Talmud Torahs" open with the support of the Minister of Cults. He always tested the limits, according to Hoffman.

With an independent policy in place after the Soviet Army pulled out in 1957, Romania, in the mid-1960s, allowed the Joint Distribution Committee (JDC) to return to its welfare and medical service work for the Jewish community. "In sum, Rosen's position in Romania and his ability to keep winning more concessions from the authorities came to be based on two external factors: his usefulness to the Romanian leadership as a 'good will ambassador' abroad, and his growing network of allies and contacts in the Jewish world and Israel, which in turn bolstered his status and influence within Romania," wrote Charles Hoffman." I continued to praise the Romanian Government for having granted us all our religious national and cultural rights. Whenever I obtained a concession, I had to pay the price by bringing it to the public's attention," said Rabbi Rosen.

Rabbi Rosen told author Charles Hoffman that when Ceausescu was deposed there were no Jews in high places in government, the dictator had long ago pushed them out.

Anna Pauker was the daughter of a Moldavian rabbi. She became a powerful figure in the Communist government, second only to Gheorghiu-Dej and was internationally known. "A good-looking Jewish woman in her early fifties, rather imposing and very bright, she became involved in the [Communist] movement as a student, and soon rose to a leading role in the party," according to Professor Egon Balas describing Pauker when she became foreign minister. Along the way to high position, she had been arrested in 1935 and served a prison term. She was almost executed in 1936.

After she was removed from power by Gheorghiu-Dej, Pauker simply became a non-person. The elimination of Anna Pauker and her group proved to be a godsend for Gheorghiu-Dej, according to author Behr. It has been said that Pauker combined atheism and an unshakable faith in Stalin with considerable sympathy for Israel and for the Romanian Chief Rabbi, Moses Rosen. Her brother Solomon, a regular visitor to Bucharest, lived in Israel. But there are those who point out that Anna Pauker was ruthless, that she had her own husband, Marcel, and other right-wing persons, shot. Marcel indeed was executed in the Soviet Union as a traitor in 1938. Marcel and Anna had a son and daughter; she also had a daughter from a love affair with a French Communist leader, according to Professor Egon Balas in his book *Will To Freedom: A Perilous Journey Through Fascism and Communism*. She was sent to Moscow in 1941 as part of an exchange with the Soviets and returned with the Russian troops in 1944. After her expulsion from the party she was too well-known to be shot. She lived in retirement until 1960, "a bitter but dignified old woman."

Elena (Magda) Lupescu. She was a Jewish stenographer, but she once was considered the power behind the throne. Born in 1895, in Iasi, the provincial capital of Moldavia, Lupescu, it is said, snared King Carol II. It was the "Purim story in reverse." Even if she tried she could not have saved the Jews as Esther had done in the Bible, according to Robert D. Kaplan in his book *Balkan Ghosts: A Journey Through History (1930 - 1940)*. Romanians felt humiliated because their king had deserted his real wife for a Jew. When King Ferdinand demanded his son break off the affair, Carol abdicated his right of succession and went into exile in Paris with Lupescu. Sources in Bucharest maintain that she really was born of a peasant family, but given over to a Jewish family, who raised her according to the Jewish religion. King Ferdinand died on July 19, 1927, and Carol's six-year-old son, Michael, was appointed king, but in reality a regency council ruled in his name. Carol came back in 1930 and he brought Lupescu with him after dissatisfaction with the regency spread throughout the country. He had agreed to rule as a co-regent, but he broke his promises and pushed Parliament to proclaim him, King Carol II. He was known as a royal dictator rather than a democratic monarch. He formed links to the fascist Iron Guard. In 1938, however, he cracked down on the Guard and had 13 of its members killed, although "they were gunned down while escaping." He also suspended the Constitution and installed his own royal dictatorship.

Forced to abdicate in 1940, he fled into exile with Lupescu, his mistress, leaving his now 19-year-old son (1940-47) to take the throne. King Carol and Lupescu left Romania in the dead of the night in late 1940, in a nine car railway train fitted with the country's gold and art treasures. He had asked for asylum in Germany, but Hitler, because of Lupescu's Jewish origins, refused to have them. Crossing the Atlantic they settled first in Mexico, then in Brazil. There they remained throughout the war, eventually marrying in 1946. King Carol bestowed upon Lupescu the title of Royal Princess. After the King died in Brazil, she lived with Carol's former Prime Minister, Erners Urdarreanu. She died in 1977.

Brief Jewish History

For most American Jews if you mention the "Old Country," three nations come to mind, Russia, Poland and Romania.

As in other states in Europe, Jewish migration to Romania did not occur at once. We do know that Jewish merchants tagged along with Roman legions to the country that was called Dacia in the first few centuries of the Common Era.

Between the 11th and 14th centuries, those Jews expelled from Hungary entered Walachia, a Romanian principality founded at the end of the fifth century. A few served as physicians and diplomats for the sovereigns of Walachia. In the 16th century, Jews from Spain set up stakes in Romania. Others, searching for a safe-haven, moved up from the Balkan Peninsula. They found it in Romania.

When the Turks took over, they also placed restrictions on the Jews who were considered a "non-Christian people with nebulous and often suspect external loyalties," according to historian Radu Ioanid, who adds that the Turks, however, actually let the Jews have a great deal of cultural autonomy as well as allowing them to pursue their livelihoods with a "minimum of official interference until the mid-nineteenth century."

When the Russians took over Bessarabia in 1812, more Jews moved into the area as well as into Moldavia which was founded in the middle of the 14th century.

What helped to bring Jewish settlers to Romania was that Walachia and Moldavia, stood on the trade route between Poland, Lithuania and the Ottoman Empire. But early in the history of Romania, commercial competition became a part of anti-Jewish hatred. In the first codes of law promulgated by the Greek Orthodox Church in Moldavia and Walachia, the Jews were seen as heretics and Christians were forbidden to have relations with them. Still by 1859, 118,000 Jews resided, in Moldavia and only 9,200 in Walachia.

The Russians peddled their anti-Semitism throughout the country. For much of the time and even until the mid-20th century, Jews were denied citizenship in Romania. Invading armies also caused difficulties for Jews. Author Sanborne says Jews came in large numbers after 1829. From 1859 to 1899, the number of Jews in Moldavia increased from about 118,000 to 200,000, while in Walachia, it grew from 9,000 to 68,000.

The winds of revolution of 1848 also spread to Romania. As in other nations, Jews fought in the 1848 Revolution alongside their fellow Romanian countrymen. S. Ettinger notes *in A History of the Jewish People*, that the Romanians were eager to win over "the few Jewish intellectuals to their cause." The major political parties, adds Jewish historian Ettinger, "outdid each other in their promises to the Jews."

But it never happened.

Anti-Jewish incitement became one of the important factors in the evolvement of the Romanian state, stresses Ettinger.

By 1859 there were about 130,000 Jews in Romania who were considered foreign subjects and who could not acquire land.

In 1866, the mob attacked Jews, destroyed the Choral Synagogue in Bucharest. The Assembly soon passed a law that only Christians could become citizens. The Government even declared that it never intended to give Jews civil rights.

The new national constitution denied Romanian Jews political emancipation, " a situation that would prevail until after World War I," declares historian Ioanid, adding "not until 1923 did Jews in Romania win legal equality."

At the Congress of Berlin in 1878, the European powers tried to persuade the Romanian Government to bestow equal rights on the Jews. Romanian leaders refused.

In the 19th century, Jewish leaders Adolphe Cremieux of France and Moses Montefiore of Great Britain visited the country and spoke to the authorities who pledged to stop the persecutions. But the promises were never kept. Indeed, after each foreign intervention, the Romanians raised the ante of hate. Over the next few years, even more pogroms occurred. While the physical attacks may have ceased, the "administrative persecution did not. Economic restrictions against the Jews were intensified," according to historian Ettinger.

By World War I, about 70,000 Jews had left Romania. The Jewish population was now 239,967.

The political unrest in the 1920s and 1930s brought the Iron Guard, a paramilitary organization with an extreme anti-Semitic program, to the fore. Indeed, King Carol II more and more was acting like a dictator and actually aided the Iron Guard. In 1933, the position of the now 750,000 Jews in Romania was different than say the Jews in France or Holland. According to the late, noted Jewish historian, Salo Baron, the Jews in Romania, more than any other group, felt a deep sense of insecurity. After Hitler came to power in Germany in 1933, even the main Romanian parties launched anti-Semitic pogroms. Jewish representation in parliament came to an end. In the mid-1930s, Jews were under attack everywhere. Jewish lawyers were disbarred.

Iron Guard students prevented Jews from not only going to university classes, but as the literature indicates these fascist university students threw Jewish students out of classroom windows. The Germans aided in this anti-Semitic tirade with hate rhetoric and money to distribute it.

In 1937, 40 synagogues, two cemeteries, 19 schools, a library, a historical museum, two hospitals, nine clinics, two senior citizens homes and two orphanages were part of the Romanian Jewish infrastructure. In short, it was an active community.

Bucharest

At first glance, Bucharest seems dark; maybe it's the city's history that clouds the reality that it is "The Paris of the Balkans." "The Paris of the East." It is still named, the "breadbasket" of the Balkans. Founded 500 years ago, Bucharest's tree-lined boulevards, *fin de siecle* architecture, its Arc de Triomphe, make it an attractive city. Its French-style architecture earned it, as we have seen, the title of "Little Paris." The History Museum and the Military Academy should be on every visitor's itinerary.

Bucharest, the country's capital, is the site of the gigantic, Communist-era *Palatul Parlamentului* government building. Ah, yes, **The Palace of Parliament.** If ever there was an example of a dictator's grim reign and megalomania, this $10 billion Parliament building built by the late President Nicolae Ceausescu, is certainly it. It stands as the second largest public building in the world, (The Pentagon is the first, the Cyclops Pyramid of Egypt is third). Inside the hideously ornate Palace lived Nicolae and Elena Ceausescu when they were in Bucharest. The palace is said to be 900 feet long, 600 feet wide; it contains 11 stories, with 1,500 rooms, 2,600 windows, 300 chandeliers and 4,200 gilded doorknobs and acres and acres of polished marble. The dictator built a Forbidden City of "fascist architecture to encircle a wedding cake structure larger than the Pentagon," wrote Robert D. Kaplan in his book *Balkan Ghosts: A Journey through History.*

While Romanians starved, this despot and his wife built this palace. About 17,000 men worked on the building, day and night. The best quality materials were used: marble from Romania itself, local wood such as walnut tree, sweet cherry tree, elm tree, and oak. Many men and women manufactured thousands of meters of carpets, silks, brocades, and gold and silver embroideries.

This palace is obviously a tourist attraction and guides told this author that visitors usually say, "this is a monstrosity, how could Ceausescu have done this to us." The other side says, "look at what we achieved; we are proud of what we have done."

Now 80 percent finished, it already has been used for concerts, forums, international meetings and conferences and the House of the Parliament. The Senate will soon move there. Hopefully, it will continue to be used even more for educational purposes.

Former Communist Party Headquarters Building. Plata Revolutiei Nr., 1, or Calea Victoriei, Bucharest. A terrible canvas has been painted about President Nicolae Ceausescu and his family. Ceausescu and his wife forced Romanians to live in anguish and poverty. He relied on a huge security apparatus to spread fear and psychological terror around them, according to author Behr who adds, Romanians suffered "malnutrition, illegal botched abortions and the death of elderly people denied operations or treatment because of their age."

"Nowhere in Europe had the failure of Communism been more stunning, the economic, social and human disaster more desperate, the anguish of the people more heartbreaking," than Romania says Nestor Ratesh in his.

Author Charles Hoffman wrote that "even in the other satellite countries, the heavy hand of Communist rule had not been this oppressive, nor had the megalomaniacal drive of the rulers gone to such pathological lengths."

"One hell bent orgy of destruction," was the way author Robert D. Kaplan describes Ceausescu's last five years in power.

Personality cults are grotesque. Most Romanians agree that Elena Ceausescu was Nicolae's "evil genie." She frequently referred to her millions of subjects as "worms," to be controlled by hard labor and food rationing. From the very beginning, she consolidated power in her own right.

Ceausescu "played an active part in arranging Egyptian President Anwar Sadat's historic visit to Jerusalem in 1977. He served as host not only to Yasir Arafat, but to every Israeli prime minister in the last 20 years, it was reported. When President Nixon visited Romania he said Ceausescu was "the good Communist." The West in effect gave him the "ok" when French President Charles DeGualle visited Romania, which received most-favored-nation status in the 1970s and 1980s.

As Nicolae Ceausescu tightened the vice on his own people, "the West was willing to overlook his dismal domestic record because he was a thorn in the side of the Soviet enemy," writes Mark Sanborne.

Ceausescu produced sprawling steel and petrochemical plants. The only trouble was the country did not have the raw materials and energy, so they had to import the precious raw materials that cost dearly in terms of hard currency, according to Ronald D. Bachman, author of *Romania: A Country Study*. As for petrochemicals, while Romania is rich in natural resources, it has few raw materials for those industries.

But tyrants eventually always are toppled.

By the end of 1989, the Berlin Wall had come down, the Poles, Hungarians, Czechs had thrown off the Communist yoke. In Prague, students and parts of the crowd were beaten up, but no one was killed. Bloodshed had to occur somewhere in the former Communist Empire and it turned out to be Romania. The best estimates are that more than 1,000 persons, including the dictator and his wife, were killed in the revolution, if "revolution" is the right word as some Romanians cynically point out. Only a spark was needed; it came from a small city called Timisoara. There, Romanian state police wanted to transfer a young Hungarian priest who they said had been preaching against the regime. Both Hungarians and Romanians who lived in the city joined the protest against removing the minister. This demonstration set off a chain of events that led ten days later to Ceausescu's execution.

The events would occur thusly:

First, there was a civilian vigil outside the priest's home on December 15. When police were sent to remove the demonstrators holding candles in the square in Timisoara, the Romanian revolution burst open with a vengeance.

At one demonstration, the Romanian flag was unfurled at Party headquarters with the Communist coat of arms cut out, leaving a hole in the middle.

The Ceausescus' had given orders to shoot to kill. So on Sunday, December 17, 1989 troops fired on the people, but it only caused the demonstrations to grow. On Tuesday, December 19th a general strike was called, only this time the army let the citizens pass the barriers and fraternized with them. Ceausescu came back from a foreign trip and on December 20, he called for a rally in Palace Square in Bucharest. That, too, was his undoing as we shall see. He realized that the army had not put down the protestors, though civilians had been killed.

On December 21, Ceausescu spoke on the balcony of the Communist Party Headquarters. It was here that the crowd turned against him, relates Scott L. Malcomson in *Borderlands—Nation and Empire*. There were shouts of "Timisoara, Timisoara," and "Down with Ceausescu." Students demanded an end to the Ceausescu dictatorship. Pandemonium broke out. Not used to the managed crowds talking back to him, Ceausescu looked confused; his wife, Elena, also looking furious and offended. She even shouted to the crowd. "Be quiet!" But they would not be silent, no matter how Ceausescu shouted. The crowd would not kowtow. From the back of the mass of people attending the rally came the boos, the catcalls and the chant of TI-MI-SOA-RA, according to author Edward Behr. Ceausescu and his wife were taken inside, where they spent the night.

The next morning, the pair tried again to speak to the audience from the balcony. When they were shouted down, when they saw that the insurgents had rushed into the building of the Communist Party Headquarters below and taken over, they realized that as the crowd surged forward, they would be lynched. The Ceausescus' fled on a helicopter that took them from Bucharest. The flight marked the climax of the Romanian revolution, according to author Nestor Ratesh. "The dictator has fled," said Ion Iliescu on television. He became Romania's president (1990-1996 and 2000-2004).

That night firing broke out, with armed cars firing on the crowds in the square. To this day, no one knows who started the shooting. Some call it an "operetta war."

Meanwhile the pilot abandoned the Ceausescus' on a highway. One of their two bodyguards commandeered two cars. The civilian drivers managed, by various ruses, to abandon the couple. One of the bodyguards then slipped away. The remaining guard then commandeered yet another car which was being washed by its owner. This man drove the Ceausescus' to an agricultural research station whose manger, by yet more ruses, succeeded in delivering the couple to the militia, who in turn handed them over to the army.

The Ceausescus' were given a very brief trial by a hastily convened military tribunal. Several people whom they knew well and whom they treated during the trial with contempt were present. However, "even by the standards of the infamous Stalinist trials of the thirties, the proceedings were farcical. As we now know, the trial's purpose was not to bring the Ceausescus' to justice but to provide a legal pretext for executing them as soon as possible," opines Edward Behr. Even today some feel that the security police would only give up if they knew the Ceausescus' were gone. That may have been the reason their dead bodies were shown time after time on television for several months.

Found guilty of "crimes against the people, and genocide"— the prosecution maintained they killed 63,000 persons; they were sentenced to death by firing squad, on Christmas Day.
Their executioners placed them against the wall and fired some two hundred rounds into their bodies. The "conspiracy theories continue to echo in Romania today." Some say it was a plot hatched by "disaffected Communists."

Ion Iliescu, a former Central Committee secretary and deputy minister of the political executive committee who had fallen into disfavor with Ceausescu took charge and organized the new ruling party, National Salvation Front. Some say the NSF "stole the Revolution." Behr argues that the revolt was "not a carefully staged event." The plotters may have been waiting for such a moment as this.

JEWISH SITES IN BUCHAREST

"Jewish people will be here in Romania as long as the earth will exist," a Jewish leader told me in an interview. But neither he nor any leader here could predict with accuracy how many Jews there would be and what kind of Jewish life they would lead? To understand the Romanian Jewish Community, one has to realize that 65 percent of the Jewish community is over the age of 65, or 9,000 persons; and that only 7 percent or 1,000 persons are between the ages of 0 to 35 years of age. With these demographics, how can there be a Jewish community in 25 years?

Where is everybody?

For the last 60 years, demographics played havoc with the Jewish community. Before World War II, Romanian Jewry contained about 800,000 persons. Nearly one half of that number were murdered by the Germans and their Axis ally, Romania. That left about 400,000 Jews, of which 350,000 went to Israel before 1948. The *aliyah* was stopped by the Government in 1954, but allowed to begin again in 1958. In the late 1960s there were 14 regular synagogues in Bucharest. Of the 44,202, 3.6 percent of the total population registered, in the city in the 1956 census, according to the Encyclopedia Judaica.

In 1969, it was estimated that 50,000 Jews lived in Bucharest. By 1977, only about 40,000 remained.

Today's Jewish population in Romania stands at about 7,000, although if you go by the "Law of the Return" for a population count, the population jumps to about 20,000, according to Della Pergola/2016. This present Jewish population is down from a prewar Jewish population of about 850,000, half of whom were killed in the Holocaust, while 95 percent of those who remained, immigrated to Israel and other countries.

The Jewish community will not roll over and play dead. Yes, answer Jewish leaders emphatically, there will be a Jewish community in 25 years. Mixed marriages will exist and people will be accepted into the community on their sincerity. Romanian Jewry has not reached the high percentage of mixed marriages such as, in Bulgaria.

Today's Romanian Jews gather at the **Jewish Community Center** at Popasoare 18, Bucharest. The problem is to bring those Jews into Jewish leadership positions. There are activities for young people, including choirs, Zionist youth movements and an active program by the Jewish Agency. If the economy does not disintegrate completely, Jews will survive.

The Federation of Jewish Communities in Romania (FEDROM). www.jewishfed.ro. is the national, community-based infrastructure representing Romanian Jewry.

A program for senior citizens sponsored by FEDROM and its Social and Medical Assistance Department is called the Dignity Program. The average age of one seventh of the Jewish population is above age 77. Assisted by FEDROM, their life expectancy is higher than that of Romanian seniors. And what is important to understand in Romania, is that over 85 percent of the senior Jewish Holocaust survivors served by FEDROM, are single.

FEDROM not only serves Jews in Bucharest, but 39 Jewish communities throughout the country. Eighty three synagogues—many of them closed—are spread out throughout the country that once counted 850,000 citizens. To make the point, I discovered that there are 830 cemeteries in Romania.

About 3,000 Jews reside in Bucharest alone. Many small country towns have only one Jew living in that municipality. However, the numbers have increased in recent years as Israelis have moved to Bucharest to work and study in the capital. Several hundred Israeli medical students are currently studying in Bucharest. But in 2016, the nation's real estate market began to crack and fewer Israeli investors arrived.

Most of the welfare assistance programs are sponsored financially in Romania by FEDROM and the Claims Conference through the close partnership and consultation of JDC, thanks to the restitution process. FEDROM remains JDC's partner in its work with the Romanian Jewish Community.

Dr. Aurel Vainer, an economist, told me the community has a strong partnership with JDC, which aids Romanian Jewry with welfare and educational needs. He also cited the Claims Conference for aid to the Jews of Romania. Dr. Vainer expressed a positive view when asked if Romanian Jewry would exist in 15 years. "I'm sure," he said, noting that educational work among the young people was very strong. Romanian Jewish youth have become involved in the community. Immigration to Israel has been down in the last decade.

Chabad maintains a center in Bucharest, office@chabadromania. com. www.chabadromania.com.

"Yeshua Tova" Synagogue and Chabad Offices. Str. Tache Ionescu Nr. 9, sector 1, Bucharest. Tel: 40-21-310-60-66. FAX: 40-21-310-60-66. "Or Avner-Green" Kindergarten and School admin@oravner.ro. www.oravner.ro is located here also. The lush interior of this house of worship features Moorish details and an elaborate *aron-ha-kodesh*.

Chabad Center in Pipera district. info@oravner.ro www.oravner.ro. Important phone numbers for Chabad. Rabbi Naftali Deutsch, Tel: 40-744.313.822. office@chabadromania.com. Risha Deutsch, Tel: 40-745-38-042. risha@chabadromania.com. Rabbi Dov Ber Orgad, Tel:

Monument to the Holocaust in front of the Choral Temple, Bucharest. (Photo by Ben G. Frank)

40-785-305-790. Fraidy Orgad, Tel: 40-785-718-770. fraidyorgad@gmail. com. Chabad Office, Tel: 40-742-148-821. office@chabadromania.com.

Choral Temple, Sfanta Vineri Str., 9-11, Bucharest, 70478. Tel: 312-25-38. For 40 years, this synagogue sheltered and kept the Jewish community alive. During the Communist era, this was the headquarters of the Jewish community. Judaism survived here, especially under the leadership of the late Rabbi Moses Rosen.

This is a synagogue that one can truly say has kept its appearance since it was opened in 1867. It actually was founded by German-Austrian members. According to Carol Herselle Krinsky, author of *Synagogues of Europe: Architecture, History, Meaning*, the architects patterned the Temple after the large Vienna-Templegasse synagogue of 1855-58.

Before the Choral Synagogue was built, 29 synagogues existed in Budapest. This house of worship was built in 1867. I found author Charles Hoffman's description of the Choral Temple, to be quite accurate: "A large, handsome Moorish-style structure whose interior walls are painted in delicate hues of blue, beige, and gold." Add to that its choir loft and organ, and it stands as the largest active synagogue in Bucharest. Throughout its history, the synagogue was plagued by vandals. The Iron Guard severely damaged the building in the 1930s. After World War II, the synagogue was repaired by various Jewish organizations. Even today at the turn of the recent century, remodeling is still going on at the site. This is a good place to discuss the deep-rooted anti-Semitism that existed in Romania.

"The roots of anti-Semitism in Romania, as in most of Eastern Europe, stretch deeply in history," notes author Radu Ioanid.

In his 1930 pamphlet, *The Jews in Roumania*, Jewish historian, Salo Baron wrote: "Anti-Semitism is in general wide-spread and deeply rooted among the Christians in Roumania." "Rumanian anti-Semitism was particularly virulent," declares Bauer, who notes that a crude anti-Semitism "affected most of Romania's working class," a safety valve used to divert discontent from the nation's real difficulties and calamities, including a succession of cruel invaders and corrupt officials.

Official anti-Semitism was widely shared at all levels of Romanian society. Indeed, Romania was "the last European nation to grant Jews citizenship, and did so only under duress," according to Hirt-Manheimer. "Thus, the Jew was the traditional scapegoat. The Romanian learned to curse the Turk, the Russian and the Hungarian. But he beat the Jew," according to author Hirt-Manheimer.

Jewish Community Offices, Sfanta Vineri Str.9-11, Bucharest. www. jewishfed.com. The president of FEDROM is Dr. Aurel Vainer. His deputy is Ovidiu Banescu. Executive Director is Eduard Kupferberg.

Monument to the Holocaust. The monument is located at the intersection of the following streets: Anghel Saligny, Mibai Voda, Brezoianu, and Lipscani. This was the location of the former Brezoianu Park.

Jewish Community and Cultural Center, Popasoare St., 18, Sector 2, 023983, Bucharest. Here one can find the kosher restaurant, the cultural center, and the community resource center. Located on the first floor, is the kosher restaurant. Served here are meat dishes. Lunch is offered every day, Monday to Sunday, from noon to 3:00 p.m. The room resembles a large dining hall, not a restaurant. On Friday nights an Oneg Shabbat is held at dinner. The restaurant is open on Saturday. Make reservations in advance.

On the second floor of this building is a large hall for meetings, concerts and performances.

A youth club meets on the third floor. Telephone: 321-3940.

In the basement of the building, a sports center/gym functions.

Social Assistance Department of the Federation of Jewish Communities, Dimytrie, Racovitza 8, Bucharest. Tel: (401) 314-86-84. FAX: (401) 322-4067. "You cannot forget so many Jews here." Jews in this country are given special food, parcels eight times a year at holidays, lunch meals on wheels, and clothes. Every Jew receives medical assistance.

Medical Center, Calea Calarasi, 57 B, Bucharest, Tel: 321-5160. This center is sponsored by the American Jewish Joint Distribution Committee.

Dr. Moses Rosen Museum of the History of the Jewish Community

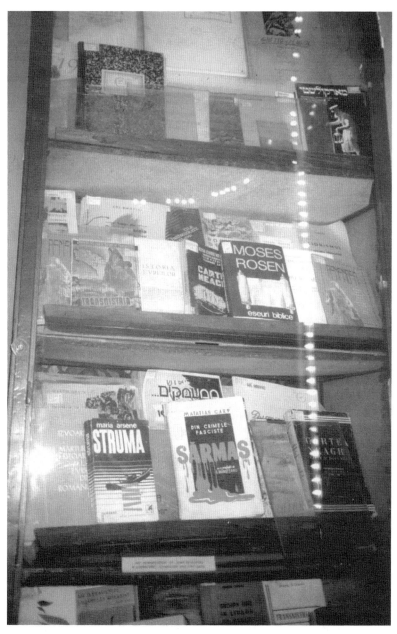

A display of books in the Jewish Museum, Bucharest. (Photo by Ben G. Frank)

in Romania–Holocaust Museum. Mamulary, 3, Bucharest. Tel: 40-21-311-0870. www.romanianjewish.org/en/fedrom_08_01.html. Once, there were eight active synagogues on Mamulary Street. Now there are none; only memories. And those memories live in the one synagogue, now the Jewish Museum. This was once called the "Tailors Synagogue." It is only five minutes from the Choral Synagogue and eight minutes from the Jewish Center. Nearby is the Great Synagogue. Ritual objects are housed in the Jewish Museum. Lazar Dubinowsky, the sculptor, designed a monument to the Holocaust, a black rug with footsteps showing an escape from Auschwitz, which obviously never occurred. The histories of Jewish communities of Bucharest, Timisoara, Iasi, Cluj, are featured as are Jews in the Romanian army, and the role of Rabbi Rosen in keeping alive the Jewish community.

The Great Synagogue, Vasile Adamache 11, Bucharest. This was one of the most beautiful synagogues in Romania. Today, it houses a Holocaust Exhibition, which tells the story of the murder of Romanian Jews in World War II. Open 10:00 a.m. to 2:00 p.m. Monday through Thursday, Friday and Sunday 10:00 a.m. to 1:00 p.m. The exhibition is closed Saturday. The building also continues to serve as an active place of worship. Morning prayers 8:00 a.m., Saturday 9:30 a.m. Evening prayers 7:00 p.m. (except Saturday).

Bucharest's Great Synagogue, often called the Great Polish Synagogue, was built from 1845-1846 by the Ashkenazi Polish-Jewish community. Rather plain on the outside, the interior is an impressive, colorful mixture of baroque and rococo styles. The Great Synagogue is perhaps today the most important Jewish building in the country. The synagogue hosts an excellent exhibition dedicated to Jewish martyrs and to Moses Rosen, who served as Romania's Chief Rabbi for 30 years until his death in 1994. Guided tours are available.

Statistics never completely tell the tale of the killing of the Jews in Europe during the war and Romania is no exception. But for the record, of the 380,000 Romanian Jews who died in the Holocaust, 260,000 were killed in Bessarabia, Bukovina and Transnistria. Between 120,000 to 150,000 Transylvanian Jews were also murdered. Most of these Jews were from Northern Transylvania which had passed to Hungarian rule in 1940. They were sent to their deaths in a sudden mass deportation in 1944.

Most Jews of Old Romania survived; a paradox in a country of such widespread anti-Semitism. Fifty seven percent of the Jewish population under Romanian rule during the war (including the Jews of Bessarabia and North Bukovina) survived the Holocaust.

Former president Emil Constantinescu publicly acknowledged Romania's responsibility in the Holocaust and the Ministry of Education has mandated the teaching of the Holocaust in the schools, says Holocaust historian Radu Ioanid.

"Romanian soldiers, police and Iron Guards initially murdered tens of thousands of Jews in vicious pogroms in Moldavia, Bukovina and Bessarabia, as well as in the Ukrainian cities they conquered with their German allies," according to Mark Sanborne in his book, Romania. The Romanians also allowed hundreds of thousands of others to perish from disease and starvation in a place called Transnistria (see below).

As Dr. Jean Ancel of Yad Vashaem has observed: The crimes were not committed by Romanian individual accomplices but by the entire state apparatus: the Romanian army, gendarmerie, police, civil authorities, prefectures, city councils and tribunals. Premeditated and uncoerced, the Romanian regime presided over the extermination of tens of thousands of Jewish civilians—old and young, women and men—in retaliation for illusory offenses. It was the recurring blood libel on a colossal scale. Instead of falsely accusing a single Jew of ritual murder, thousands of Jews were unjustly indicted for shedding the blood of Romanian soldiers."

Romanian troops and Einsatzgruppe D, "vied with each other," for the distinction of murdering Jews," according to Holocaust historian Yehuda Bauer.

Much of the killing of the Jews of Greater Romania occurred in Transnistria which comes from the Romanian, "trans-Nistru, the land across the Dniester River, according to author Aron Hirt-Manheim. Thousands of Jews from Bessarabia, Bukovina and from Dorohoi in Old Romania and other regions were shipped under conditions worse than cattle to Transnistria, a region between the Bug and the Dniester, two large rivers in the Ukraine. This area of Transnistria, twice the size of New Jersey, belonged to the Soviet Ukraine before Romania was given control of the region by Germany in August, 1941, just after the Germans and Romanians invaded the Ukraine.

Even though there were no gas chambers there, Jews perished by "terror, the threats, the nocturnal death marches, the sealed wagons, the starvation, the plagues, the humiliation, the public executions, the fires," wrote Elie Wiesel in the foreword of Rondu Ioanid's book, The Holocaust in Romania: the Destruction of Jews and Gypsies Under the Antonescu Regime. Jews would die from exposure, sickness and hunger after being housed in pigsties and village stables or slave camps on the shores of the Bug River.

In the Auschwitz gas chambers and in the shooting pits of Russia, death came quickly, notes historian Yehuda Bauer, but in Transnistria, death was slow.

But what contributed to the fact that 57 percent of the Jews under

Romanian rule survived the Holocaust. The answers appear to be: Romanian self-interest, national pride, real politik, and the fearless stand of the Jewish leaders—all helped save Jews.

Holocaust historian Leni Yahil notes that despite Romanian persecution and killing of Jews since their arrival in the country from Russia in the 19th century, "the leaders of the Jewish community succeeded in maintaining relations with the heads of state and though they could not prevent drastic measures, they did succeed in limiting and mitigating them." She claims Jewish leaders and community members used "methods of self-protection such as bribery, intercession, evasion and mutual aid to save Jews."

Jewish leaders such as Rabbi Alexandre Safran and Dr. Wilhelm Filderman continually intervened with Romanian individuals and tried to save as many Jews as possible. In addition, "those who survived could not have done so without leaders such as Siegfried Jagendorf—the man who mastered the game of survival in the wilderness of exile," says Aron Hirt-Manheimer in his comments in the book, *Jagendorf's Foundry: Memoir of the Romanian Holocaust.*

Siegfried Jagendorf, for instance, convinced the Romanian officials in Moghilev to recruit a small task force to repair the city's nonfunctioning electrical system as well as a foundry. The handful of persons grew to 15,000 who survived the war.

Jewish leader Dr. Filderman had a lifeline to General Ion Antonescu, the Romanian dictator, as they were school classmates. When Antonescu and his government first consented to the 1942 German request that the Jews of the Old Kingdom and Southern Transylvania be deported to the death camps in Poland, Dr. Filderman "framed the Jewish question in terms of national honor," according to author Aron Hirt-Manheimer. Germany had no right to ask the Romanians to turn over its Jewish population. Jews were willing to pay a "king's ransom" to redeem the Jews of Romania. "It was this intermingling of factors combined with external pressures from the Swiss, Vatican, Americans and others, that induced Bucharest to begin formulating a more independent policy in dealing with its Jewish minority," says writer Aron Hirt-Manheimer.

Of course, the man who bears the responsibility of the murder of Jews in Romania was General Ion Antonescu—who gained power near the end of the King Carol rule in 1940. At the same time, he was also responsible for saving many Jews. "But this in no way absolves him from his huge war crime against the Romanian people," wrote Rabbi Moses Rosen. His government was responsible for the murder of at least 200,000 Romanian Jews during the war, through pogroms carried out by his army and the deportations to Transnistria. Despite continual German demands for the deportation of Romanian Jews, Gen. Antonescu in 1942 finally refused transporting Jews to their death. He even brought back some veterans, seniors and widows from Transnistria. The Jews in Bucharest did not have to wear the yellow star and henceforth, Romania never sent Jews north to the German camps. In 1943, Antonescu stopped the killing of about 50,000 surviving Romanian deportees in Transnistria by the retreating German troops because these terrible murders would give him a "bad reputation," according to author Hirt-Manheimer. He may also have read the writing on the wall in that by early 1943, especially, after the battle of Stalingrad, there were signs that the Axis powers would not be victorious.

Later, Ira Hirschmann who had gone on a secret mission to Turkey for President Franklin D. Roosevelt to negotiate with Eichmann's agents for the rescue of Jewish children would save about 100,000 Romanian Jews, including thousands of children, in exchange for four visas to Alexandre Cretziannu, Romanian minister to Turkey. The visas saved the Romanian diplomat's life.

Who was General Antonescu and how did he get to rule Romania? To understand his rise to power, we have to return to Romania between the wars. This country had "the distinction of having the largest fascist movement in the Balkans," according to Charles Bachman in his book Romania: a country study. This extreme nationalist, far-right, anti-Semitic, semi-legal fascist group was known as the Iron Guard and was founded in 1930 by Corneilu Zelea Codreanu who had backing from industrialists as well as from Mussolini and Hitler. Officially, called "Archangel Michael," its fanatical members were known as Legionnaires. They wore green shirts, boots and little bags of "sacred" Romanian soil hanging from their necks. These terrorists and assassins would constantly beat up Jews and leftists.

Codreanu himself a demagogue and a shrill anti-Semite, has been described as a "murderer, a Jew baiter and a thug."

King Carol, who in August 1940 decreed his own anti-Semitic racial laws, eventually cracked down on the extreme right-wing Iron Guard. The Iron Guard had gained 66 seats at the election of 1937. The King, jealous of Codreanu's power, dissolved that party. He also ordered Codreanu shot on the night of November 29/30, 1938.The King killed 13 Iron Guard senior leaders in prison and arrested thousands of others. The King brought General Antonescu into the government. But with the fall of France and Britain's desperate plight in the latter half of 1940, the King's position became untenable. The country was beginning to display a fascination with the Nazi political model and Romanian lands had been taken away and given to Russia, Hungary and Bulgaria and the people held the King responsible for this loss of land. In September 1940, King Carol was forced to abdicate in favor of his son Michael. Not long thereafter Romania became a satellite of Nazi Germany. The government's first act was to cancel Romanian citizenship for Jews. By this time, with the King gone, Antonescu had grabbed all the power. Since young King Michael's influence was obviously reduced, the General assumed the title of Conducator (leader). His strength lay in the fact that he represented the armed forces. At first, General Antonescu cooperated with the Iron Guard, but it was only a matter of time, until it, too, clashed with Antonescu. In November 1940, the fascist Legionnaires launched a reign of terror and killed and murdered advisors to the King in revenge for Codreanu's killing. The revolt was put down by the Army, but not before the Legionnaires in January 1941 carried out a "particularly ghastly massacre and mutilation of nearly 200 Jewish civilians in a slaughterhouse." Jews were beheaded and hung on iron hooks in the slaughterhouse.

Author Robert St. John summed up his impression of the Romanians: "volatile, unpredictable, corrupt beyond imagination and cruel beyond forgiveness."

Romania, ally of Hitler, would go down to defeat in World War II. Near the end of the war, on August 23, 1944, King Michael arrested Antonescu and his ministers and declared a cease-fire. The next day, Romania, which had signed an armistice with the Allied powers, now declared war on Germany. The Russian army occupied Bucharest on August 31, 1944.

Antonescu and his henchmen as well as their families were executed by the Soviets. Romanian revisionists have attempted to rehabilitate Antonescu, saying he was only "moderately anti-Semitic." Holocaust historian Radu Ioanid notes "Romania's attempt to rehabilitate a World War II fascist leader comes as no surprise. Other countries in East Europe," he says, "attempt to rehabilitate war criminals." Yet the case of Romania is the "most egregious; nowhere else in Europe has a mass murderer, Adolf Hitler's faithful ally until the very end, a man who once declared war on the United States, been honored as a national hero, inspired the erection of public monuments and had streets named after him."

Jewish Theater, Teatrul Evreiese De State, T.E.S., Iuliu Barash Str., Bucharest.

Jewish Agency for Israel (Sochnut), Bv. Kogalniceau 57, Bucharest. Tel: 312-52-94.

Monnument to the Struma ship, Cemetery, Cimitirul Guirgiului, Soslaua Giorgiului, Bucharest. This monument, while not exactly in

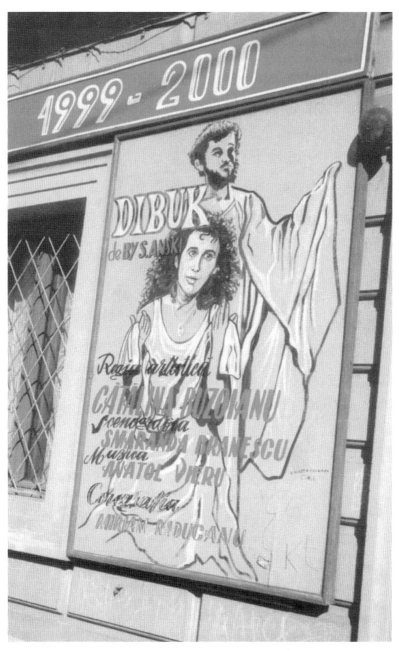

A poster at the Jewish Theater, Bucharest. (Photo by Ben G. Frank)

Monument to the Struma ship, Bucharest. (Photo by Ben G. Frank)

the center of the city, is dedicated to the cargo ship Struma and the 769 men, women and children who only wanted to reach the Jewish homeland in the then British mandate of Palestine. All they desired was to escape fascism, survive the Nazis and make a new life. They had boarded the ship in the Romanian port of Constanta. The passengers had been promised a decent ship, but not only was it technically unfit for passengers—it did not even have a kitchen—though not seaworthy it sailed on December 11, 1941, and reached Istanbul. The Turks refused to allow the passengers to depart from the ship. The British too, were extremely intransigent and refused to allow any of the passengers to move on to Palestine. To the British they were illegal immigrants. The Turks demanded that the British solve the problem and the latter again refused to become involved. "Finally on the night of February 23, 1942, the Turks towed the Struma to a point outside their territorial waters and, despite the passengers' appeals for help and even attempts at resistance, cut the ship loose and sent it floating without food, water, or fuel," writes Holocaust historian Leni Yahil. An explosion occurred shortly afterwards and the Struma sank immediately. Leni Yahil said that Turkish rescue boats did not go out to pick up survivors until the next day. They found a single person in the choppy waters. The ship was sunk by a Russian submarine for unknown reasons.

Joint Distribution Committee, www.jdc.org. Shortly after it was founded in 1914, the newly-founded American Jewish Joint

Distribution Committee responded in 1915 with financial support because of the dire conditions of the Jewish community in Romania during in the First World War. Between 1919 and 1938, JDC allocated more than $55 million to help Romanian Jews face a difficult post-war economic conditions as well as rising anti-Semitism, once the Fascist Iron Guard took power. Even when the Jews were deported to Transnistria, JDC was permitted to provide limited assistance. While the majority of the Jews in Bucharest survived, they, too, had to be aided by JDC. The Communists forced the JDC to leave the country in 1949. When Nicolae Ceausescu drew closer to the West, he allowed JDC to return to Romania in 1967, giving it the distinction of being the only volunteer relief organization invited to operate in an Eastern European country.

Iassi (Jassy)

This was the Moldavian home during World War I of the Royal family. Queen Marie and other members of the Royal family fled here after the Germans captured Bucharest.

Because it is flat, Moldavia has suffered invasion after invasion, including six invasions by the Russians in the 18th and 19th centuries. "A hotbed of Romanian nationalism," notes author Robert Kaplan, in describing this land. In 1859, Alexandru Ian Cuza proclaimed the first state of modern Romania here.

This was also the home of Elena Magda Lupescu. In Iasi, the Moldavian capital, just before World War II broke out, about 100,000 people inhabited the city, 50,000 of them were Jews. The town had a tradition of anti-Semitism. Official and local propaganda in the early 1940s made Jews out to be "enemy aliens," "Bolshevik agents," and "parasites on the Romanian nation," cites Ioanid.

Professor A. C. Cuza (no relation to Alexandru Ian Cuza, the first prince of modern Romania, who declared independence in 1859) taught at the University of Iasi. One of Professor Cuza's disciples was Cornelieu Zelea Codreanu, the founder of the fascist Legion of the Archangel Michael. Codreanu began his career in Iasi in the 1920s.

The Romanians accused the Jews of hiding so-called Romanian deserters, who were really Soviet paratroopers when the latter moved into Bessarabia in 1940.

Another horrifying incident occurred during those days in 1941. The Romanians crammed about 4,300 Jews from the Iasi region into padlocked cattle cars, which traveled around an area in the countryside for almost a week. Nearly 3,000 of these occupants died of thirst and asphyxiation aboard those death trains.

On June 28 and 29 1941, thousands of Jews were killed in one of the most savage pogroms of World War II, the Iasi pogrom, perhaps the most infamous Holocaust event in Romania during World War II. The pogrom was orchestrated by the Romanian army, police, and town citizens. The police summoned 6,000 Jews to come to their headquarters to change their identity cards. They were immediately set upon by soldiers and policemen and beaten to death in the most horrifying manner, "using the butts of their rifles to smash open the skulls of men, women and children," noted Rabbi Moses Rosen.

"Huge piles of bodies filled the large courtyard of the police station and a river of blood ran into the street, as every one of the Jews was butchered." In his book, Rosen adds, "This happened in the morning, the center of a European town, with the Christian population looking on."

To this day, it is difficult to say exactly how many Jews died in the pogroms at Iasi. Estimates range from 3,200 to about 13,000, according to Ioanid. He adds that the lower figure was that of revisionist Romanian historians. Some Communist officials had put the death toll at 10,000 and others at the 13,000 figure. Author Sanborne says 7,000 Jews were massacred on that single day in June 1941. One Nazi official commented disdainfully: "pogroms are a Slavic specialty."

The crimes committed by the Antonescu regime here at Iasi and in the transit camps in Transnistria were among the "most atrocious of the Holocaust," according to historian Ioanid.

Under the Ceausescu regime, the government diluted or denied the responsibility of Romanians in the slaughter of the Jews, placing all blame on the Germans.

Community Center and Synagogue, St. Elena Doamna, 15, Iasi. Tel: 40-32-11-44-14.

Suggested Reading

Bachman, Ronald D. *Romania: a Country Study.* Washington, D.C.: Federal Research Division, Library of Congress, 1989

Balas, Egon. *Will to Freedom: A Perilous Journey Through Fascism and Communism.* Syracuse: Syracuse University Press, 2000.

Baron, Salo. "*The Jews in Roumania*" (pamphlet). New York: American Jewish Congress, 1930.

Bauer, Yehuda. *A History of the Holocaust.* New York: Franklin Watts, 1982.

Behr, Edward. *Kiss The Hand You Cannot Bite: The Rise and Fall of the Ceausescus.* New York: Villard Books, 1991.

Ben-Sasson, H. H. *A History of the Jewish People.* Cambridge, MA: Harvard University Press, 1969.

Fermor, Patrick Leigh. *Between The Woods And the Water, On Foot to Constantinople from the Hook of Holland: The Middle Danube to the Iron Gates.* New York: Viking, 1986.

Hirschmann, Ira. *Caution to the Winds.* New York: David McKay Company, Inc., 1962.

Hoffman, Charles. *Gray Dawn: The Jews of Eastern Europe in the Post-Communist Era.* New York: Aaron Asher Books, HarperCollins Publishers, 1992.

Hoffman, Eva. *Exit Into History: A Journey Through The New Eastern Europe.* New York: Viking, 1993.

Ioanid, Radu. The Holocaust in Romania: the Destruction of Jews and Gypsies Under the Antonescu Regime, 1940-1944. Chicago: Ivan R. Dee (Published in association with the United States Holocaust Memorial Museum), 2000.

Jagendorf Siegfried. *Jagendorf's Foundry: Memoir of the Romanian Holocaust, 1941-1944.* New York: HarperCollins Publishers, 1991.

Kaplan, Robert D. *Balkan Ghosts: A Journey Through History.* New York: St. Martin's Press, 1993.

Krinsky, Carol Herselle. *Synagogues of Europe: Architecture, History, Meaning.* Cambridge, MA: MIT Press, 1985.

Lukacs, John. *The Last European War September 1939/December 1941.* Garden City, New York: Anchor Press/Doubleday, 1976.

Malcomson, Scott L. *Borderlands-Nation and Empire.* Boston and London: Faber and Faber, 1994.

Rothschild, Joseph. *East Central Europe between the Two World Wars.* Seattle and London: University of Washington Press, 1974.

Sanborne, Mark. *Romania.* New York: Facts On File, Inc., 1996.

Seton-Watson, R.W. *A History of The Roumanians: From Roman Times to the Completion of Unity.* Cambridge, MA: Cambridge University Press, 1934.

Treptow, Kurt W., ed. *A History of Romania. Iasi: The Center for Romanian Studies, The Foundation for Romanian Culture and Studies,* 1997

Vital, David. *The Future of the Jews.* Cambridge, MA, and London: Harvard University Press, 1990.

Yahil, Leni. *The Holocaust: The Fate of European Jewry, 1932-1945.* New York. And Oxford: Oxford University Press, 1990.

Bulgaria
Located in the Powder Keg of Europe

Bulgaria, is one of the least known tourist destinations in Europe. That's a shame! This is a beautiful country with enough five-star hotels, first class restaurants, and good guides to show you the sites and try to make you feel at home.

Where else but in Sofia can you travel 15 minutes to nearby Vitosha Mountain and ski on some of the best slopes in the world? As tourists, you cannot meet a friendlier and truly happy people than these eight million men, women and children of Bulgaria, who are going through difficult economic times, but still manage to wear that welcome sign on their sleeves.

History pervades the atmosphere. These Balkan lands are the sites of wars and conflicts, ethnic cleansing and mass murder. World War I started next door in Serbia. The importance of the Balkans in U.S. foreign policy was underscored by former president Bill Clinton, when he noted that he was proud to be the first American president to visit Bulgaria in 1999.

The tourist quickly recognizes that capital city Sofia pales before the shining lights of Prague and Budapest. But by traveling to Bulgaria you will see a part of Europe that is certainly worthwhile to explore for its culture, history and Jewish community.

Bulgaria Saved Jews

While the dramatic rescue of Danish Jews is well-known and has been heralded around the world, not many know that Bulgaria, a close ally of Hitler in World War II, refused to allow the Germans to send its Jewish citizens to their death.

"Not one Bulgarian Jew was sent to the death camps in Poland," according to historian Dr. Michael Bar-Zohar. Actually, Bulgarian Jewry became the only Jewish community under the Nazis "whose number increased during the Second World War," according to Bar-Zohar.

Not only did the 50,000 Jews survive, but after World War II, nearly the whole community picked itself up and immigrated to Israel. Remaining in Bulgaria were about 5,000 to 7,000 Jews.

This is not to say the Bulgarians did not commit crimes in World War II. They did. They rounded up 11,343 Jews from Thrace and Macedonia which the Bulgarians occupied on behalf of the Germans, and shipped them off to Auschwitz. "The deportation and the way it was carried out by Bulgarian officers, Bulgarian soldiers, and Bulgarian policemen, has left a dark, grim shadow over Bulgaria's past," according to Ben-Zohar.

In 1943, the Bulgarians may have robbed Jews; they may have expelled Jews to the countryside; their police may have picked up Jews and forced them to work as slave laborers, but they never carried out the orders to deport Jews from Old Bulgaria.

"The fact that not one Bulgarian Jew was transported to Auschwitz was not matched by any other country in Europe," notes Bar-Zohar.

Still, other satellites—Croatia, Slovakia, Vichy France—continued their anti-Jewish policies. "The stand taken by Bulgaria was, therefore, in that sense, extraordinary," wrote Holocaust historian Yehuda Bauer in his book, *A History of the Holocaust.*

Why did the Bulgarians desist from massacring Jews? Some say that by 1943, the news of the fate of Polish Jews had reached Bulgarian politicians. By March-April 1943, the Germans had been defeated in Stalingrad. The tide was turning in the Allies' favor. An outcry arose from a number of Bulgarian legislators, the Church, even from King Boris III himself, who halted the deportation of the Jews from within the boundaries of Old Bulgaria.

The drama of Bulgarian Jews' deliverance is indeed worth telling and we shall discuss it when we visit the Holocaust exhibit in the main synagogue in Sofia.

The Country and Its History

Former President Bill Clinton said so himself: "This is a wonderful country! Come here and help," he messaged to Americans when he spoke in Sofia on November 22, 1999.

Anyone who comes to visit, study or work here should take a real close look at this country. Plains, plateaus, hills, mountains, gorges, deep river valleys are all part of the scene. Actually, mountains cover most of Bulgaria. This pleasant, lush-green country welcomes tourists to its picturesque villages and sandy beaches along the Black Sea.

Bulgaria is a country about the size of Tennessee, with a population of 7.4 million residents in 2017. It is located in the heart of the Balkan Peninsula. Covering nearly 43,000 square miles, it borders on

Macedonia and Serbia in the west; Romania and the Danube River in the north; the Black Sea on the east and Turkey and Greece on the south. Eighty-six percent of the population is Bulgarian; 10 percent ethnic Turks and the remaining four to five percent are mostly Gypsies, Armenians, Russians, Macedonians and Greeks, according to author Steven Otfinowski. Regarding religion, 85 percent of the population are Bulgarian Orthodox, 13 percent Moslem. As in most Balkan countries, most people have left the farm and headed to the cities. Today, seventy-one percent of the population lives in urban areas.

Since the fall of Communism, Bulgaria has made a commitment to democracy and economic reform

The world's nations should pay attention to Bulgaria—and its neighbors, situated in the eastern Balkans. This is a tinder box of the world that has blown up into violence, into wars, into internecine battles, and that ugly term, "ethnic cleansing" in a land once called Yugoslavia, a neighbor of Bulgaria. Bulgaria's location at the "nexus of the European and Asian continents brought strong cultural and political influences from both the east and west," according to author Glenn E. Curtis in his book, *Bulgaria, a Country Study.*

Keep in mind, too, that this nation is located on the border of Asiatic Turkey. Just across from the Black Sea are the Russians whom the Bulgarians throughout history have embraced as brothers and liberators. The Russians actually freed Bulgaria from 500 years of Ottoman rule in 1877-1878. If any country in Europe epitomizes a Balkan past, it is Bulgaria, the last country to be freed from the Ottomans. The Turks in large part turned the Bulgarians into vassals. Much of Bulgaria's history is rooted in the past. About 3,000 years ago, a people known as the Thracians were probably the first to arrive in Bulgaria. Although the Thracians disappeared, their geographical name, Thrace, remains to this very day a geographic section of the Balkans, namely Greece. The Thracians were followed by the Romans, by the Huns under Attila who nearly destroyed the entire country; and by the Slavs who migrated to the area from southern Poland and Russia in the Sixth Century.

Less than a century later, a group of fierce warriors called Bulgars thundered across the plains of Central Asia on horseback into what we now call Bulgaria. The Bulgars, who have always been vulnerable to invasions, were warriors who had migrated from a region between the Urals and the Volga to the steppes north of the Caspian Sea. They quickly moved across the Danube into the Balkans. In 681, with 285,000 persons, the Bulgars crossed the Danube under Khan Asparukh into a land they claimed as their own and began interbreeding with the Slavs.

"The word Bulgar comes from an Old Turkic word that means one of mixed nationality." The Bulgars intermingled with the Slavs and out of this "co-mingling of the two groups, a new people were born— Bulgarians," explains author Steven Otfinoski.

According to the *Encyclopedia Judaica*, "the faith of the early Bulgarian Christians was, however, a syncretistic mixture of Christian, Jewish, and pagan beliefs." Boris I converted to Christianity in 864— probably his most important act—and the King showed no mercy to those who would not follow him, says Jewish historian Vicki Tamir in her book, *Bulgaria and Her Jews: The History of a Dubious Symbiosis.*

Twice in its history did Bulgaria reach the apex of power. First, Simeon I, known as Simon the Great, (893-927), came to power in 893 and gave himself the title of Czar—a Slavic version of "Caesar." He ushered in a golden age of art, literature, and trade. Simon conquered Albania, Macedonia, Serbia and some areas of the Byzantine Empire. He extended the boundaries of Bulgaria. After Simon died in 927, Bulgaria's power declined. In 1018 the country was swallowed up by the Byzantine Empire.

By 1186, however, Bulgarians broke free from Byzantium and established the Second Bulgarian Kingdom (1185-1393) under Ivan I, who again made the country a Balkan power.

Bulgarian power did not last long. By the end of the 13th Century, the Turks had taken over all of Bulgaria. In 1453, the Turks broke the back of Byzantium. Constantinople fell to the invaders and with them came five centuries of Turkish suppression. The Turks brought with them their government and their culture and their Moslem religion. By the end of the 16th century, two-thirds of the population of Sofia was Turkish.

This is not to say that Ottoman rule was all bad. As historian Vicki Tamir notes, when it was working efficiently, Ottoman rule "provided a more orderly system of government than the Bulgarian people had hitherto enjoyed." Still, from the 16th century to the 18th century, suffering Bulgarians unleashed a series of revolts. All were brutally put down by the Turks. To this day, Bulgarians talk of the "Turkish yoke."

By the late 19th century, Turkish oppression was heavy. The Turks cruelly put down an insurrection in 1876 and this aroused indignation in the west. In 1877 Russian forces attacked. By January 1878, the Russians stood before Constantinople. "The Ottoman era had come to an end," as historian Vicki Tamir notes. During that Russo-Turkish War (1877-78) Russian troops had marched in and enlisted Bulgarian patriots to fight with them. At the Battle of Shipka Pass, the Russians and Bulgarians, including Bulgarian Jews, were hopelessly outnumbered by Turkish troops, but they bravely resisted. Some 13,000 Turks would die in the fighting as well as 5,500 Russians.

After five centuries of Turkish rule, Bulgaria was liberated. The

Treaty of San Stefano in 1878 established Bulgaria as an autonomous republic within the Ottoman Empire. The Turks had ceded about 60 percent of the Balkan Peninsula to Bulgaria. But the West would not stand for this treaty which would have allowed "the Russian Bear" to enter the Balkans.

The Treaty of San Stefano never went into operation. The Big Powers simply revised the Treaty of San Stefano when they met at the Congress of Berlin in 1878 and reduced the area of the country by more than half. Southern Bulgaria was turned into a Turkish autonomous province. Macedonia remained part of the Ottoman Empire and it and Thrace were put beyond Bulgarian control.

"Bulgaria emerged mutilated," notes historian Tamir. Bulgarians felt "a burning sense of injustice was meted out to it by the great powers," says R. J. Crampton, author of *A Concise History of Bulgaria*.

With the signing of the Treaty of Berlin, the Bulgarian state was born. In 1879, Alexander of Battenberg, a German prince, was appointed Bulgaria's ruler. He did not last long. He was forced to abdicate. In August 1887, Prince Ferdinand of Saxe Gotham took the throne which he kept for 31 years, first as the Prince of Bulgaria, 1887-1908, and then as King of the Bulgarians, 1908-1918. In 1908, he declared Bulgaria independent and the country became a kingdom.

The Balkan Wars

During the next 60 years, Bulgaria was to go to war four times, including two Balkan wars, to redress its grievances, only to fail each time.

In 1914, when World War I broke out, Bulgaria feigned neutrality. But within a year, it sided with Germany and the Austro-Hungarian Empire. Bulgaria wanted "to back the powers more likely to satisfy her territorial ambitions," notes historian Tamir. Germany took advantage of this and actually stripped the country of its goods and services. Left to starve, Bulgaria was totally defeated. The people blamed King Ferdinand's regime for the humiliation. On October 3, 1918, Ferdinand abdicated and left the country in favor of his 24-year-old son Boris III, who was to play a major role in deciding the fate of the Jews in his kingdom.

Bulgaria was devastated by the Great War. Jews fought heroically with their Bulgarian neighbors. As historian Tamir notes: "A disproportionately large amount of Jewish blood was spilled for the Bulgarian fatherland during the two Balkan wars and World War I." Under the Treaty of Neuilly, Bulgaria was forced to pay heavy doses of reparations to Serbia and its allies. Bulgaria lost Macedonia, which it had taken during the war. It lost southern Dobruja to Romania. It lost the border town of Tzaribrod to Yugoslavia and the Aegean coastline to Greece.

The world of the 1930s brought wave after wave of economic crises, the overthrow of legitimate governments, and in their wake, authoritarianism across Eastern Europe. Boris III promised a return to constitutional government; it never happened. He took complete control of the country.

Meanwhile, the Germans had also penetrated Bulgaria economically which was very impressed with German technology and military might.

World War II

When Romania was dismembered in 1940, Bulgaria received something out of that deal with Hitler. The so-called Vienna Award restored southern Dobruja to Bulgaria. "Public jubilation in Sofia was such that Bulgarian gratitude to Berlin would henceforth know no bounds," wrote Vicki Tamir. Bulgaria tied her destiny to Germany. The age-old dream of a Greater Bulgaria, as laid out by the San Stefano Treaty, had finally, with the help of Hitler, been fulfilled.

Therefore, on March 1, 1941, in Vienna, in the presence of the Italian and Nazi leaders, Bulgaria signed the Tripartite Pact and became an official ally of Germany, Italy and Japan. German troops entered the country on their way to attack Yugoslavia and Greece. Author Bar-Zohar notes that Bulgaria was ready to do almost anything to satisfy her German ally: "Of all Germany's vassals, Bulgaria held the honor of being the most willing to cooperate with the Reich on Jewish matters." Because the Germans wanted to free its troops for the Russian front, Bulgaria got Thrace and Macedonia as an occupying power.

During World War II, the Bulgarians, even though an ally of the Germans, never declared war on the Russians. In fact, the Embassy of the USSR functioned and flew its flag, the hammer and sickle; while down the street, the Nazi swastika flew over the Embassy of Germany. In August 1943, King Boris made a visit to Hitler. It was to be his last. Historians tell us he argued furiously with the Nazi leader. The latter demanded a Bulgarian commitment to send troops to the Eastern front. Boris III declined. On August 28, at the age of 49, the king of Bulgaria suddenly died. Mystery has surrounded his death ever since. Some believe he was poisoned.

The Soviet Union invaded Bulgaria on September 8, 1944. The Fatherland Front, a group of parties led by the Communists took power in the country. The typical Communist takeover occurred. So-called non-Communist enemies of the people were shot or sent to camps. Private property was seized. The Red-dominated Fatherland

Front quickly gained control. A one-party system was imposed at the end of 1947. Communism would rule with an iron fist.

Georgi Dimitrov, the chief Communist leader, became head of the government and ruled the country from 1947 to 1949. By 1948, the Communists possessed total control of the nation. But severe shortages of goods and services would constantly wretch the nation.

Bulgaria of all the East European countries, was the most closely allied to the USSR. It also was the Warsaw Pact country "most dependent economically on Soviet aid," says Glen E. Curtis, in *Bulgaria, a country study*. Todor Zhivkov and the Communist Party maintained a solid grip on the nation. He would rule from 1956 to 1989. He was forced to resign in the 1989 repudiation of Communism. He was arrested and later charged with abuse of power and misuse of government proper and money. Despite being sentenced to seven years imprisonment for misusing state funds, Todor Zhivkov wangled a hasty release and lived comfortably in an affluent Sofia suburb until he died in August 1998.

A somewhat tarnished reputation still hovers over Bulgaria. Pope John Paul II was wounded in an assassination attempt by a Turkish nationalist who claimed the plot had been hatched by Bulgarian and Soviet intelligence agents. Bulgaria was listed by U.S. State Department as a sponsor of terrorism and a supplier of arms to terrorists. Zhivkov also initiated a drastic policy of forced assimilation. In 1984 and 1985, Bulgarian authorities forced the Turks to adopt Bulgarian names. Some of the people who refused to change their names were killed by Bulgarian troops. Others were forced to leave the country. The Turks would not give in and 300,000 fled to Turkey.

Later, the first non-Communist Bulgarian prime minister, Philip Dimitrov, in a visit to Turkey, apologized to his former Turkish citizens. The Turks were invited back; about 200,000 returned.

On November 9, 1989, the Berlin Wall was torn down boulder by boulder. In November 1989, 5,000 persons marched on the National Assembly in Sofia, the largest unofficial demonstration in over four decades. A week later, Dictator Todor Zhivkov resigned. The Communists changed their name to Bulgarian Socialist Party. In June 1990, free elections were held and the Socialists (i.e., former Communists) won a majority of seats. The new Socialists had no intention of dismantling the state they had spent the past 40 years building.

Totalitarianism may have been disbanded, but it would take time for democracy to take hold. A decade passed before the Bulgarians decided they really wanted democracy.

Under Bulgaria's former king, Simeon II, who was prime minister between 2001 and 2005, the country pressed ahead with market reforms designed to meet EU economic targets. It achieved growth, saw unemployment fall from highs of nearly 20 percent, and controlled inflation rates, but incomes and living standards remained low.

Bulgaria, a member of NATO since 2004, joined the EU in 2007 along with Romania. At the time, polling indicated that a slim majority of its population was in favor of membership, hopeful that it would strengthen the Balkan country's economy and political institutions, according to the *New York Times*.

To this day, Bulgaria is one of the EU's poorest countries, with a per capita gross domestic product about half the regional average. Organized crime and corruption have deterred investors and hindered growth with a per capita gross domestic product about half the regional average. Still, incomes have recently risen sharply; billions have been poured into infrastructure; and surveys show Bulgarians are still convinced that joining was a step in the right direction.

In the last analysis, the country is still undergoing a "slow and painful transition to a market economy since the end of Communist rule," according to the BBC. It probably will never return to the Communist system. But how it moves on the bumpy road toward a democratic system of government and a market economy depends in large part on its economic progress. The country also rid itself of old gods. In 1999, Bulgaria finally tore down of some of the Communist statues. It even dismantled the mausoleum of Georgi Dimitrov, who for 45 years had been deified by the ruling Communists.

Notable Bulgarian Jews

Sarah who became **Queen Theodora**. In 1346, King Ivan Alexander divorced his wife and married a beautiful, intelligent Jewess from Turnovo, at that time the capital of Bulgaria. But Sarah converted and became Queen Theodora. Like Queen Esther, however, she did protect her people. Author Michael Bar-Zohar notes, "while Bulgaria often followed the written politics of her neighbors, including anti-Jewish legislation and the expulsion edicts toward the Jews adopted in 1355, they were never implemented. The story does not end there. In 1356 the Turks crossed Bulgaria, and unable to check Murad's military drive, Ivan Shishman concluded a peace treaty with the sultan and in 1375 gave him his sister Maria (or Mara) daughter of the Jewish woman, in marriage. Thus a Christian Jewish princess was converted to Islam, presumably to please a Muslim sovereign who had fallen in love with her, as her Christian father had fallen in love with her Jewish mother.

"It is one of the many ironies of history that the last Bulgarian king of an indigenous Bulgarian dynasty, was, according to Jewish law, a Jew." Together with the people's eloquently attested uneasiness with

Orthodox Christianity, this attitude towards Judaism might in part account for the absence of Christian fervor and fidelity to the Cross when the Turks appeared on the scene, and conversion to Islam became the order of the day, declares historian Vicki Tamir.

Emil Shekerdjiski. He was a young Communist writer and organizer who led a partisan band against the Nazis. In World War II, he fought to the death rather than fall into the hands of the Germans. During the Communist era, the Library in the Jewish Center was named after him, according to Charles Hoffman in his book, *Gray Dawn: The Jews of Eastern Europe in the Post-Communist Era.*

A Brief History

Jews lived in Bulgaria even before Slavs and Bulgars settled the country. They probably arrived here during the time of the First Temple in 600 BCE

After Emperor Trajan's victories over the Dacians in the second century, Jews in this area moved into northern Bulgaria, including Romania.

With the destruction of the Second Temple in CE. 70, more Jews immigrated. Scholars have recorded a gravestone, discovered in Nikopol in the Second Century, which featured a drawing of a Menorah.

Even today, Bulgarian Jewish leaders are quick to point out the Bulgars came from the lands of the Khazars. The latter and the proto-Bulgarians resembled each other in looks and in customs. This is important in view of the Khazar conversion to Judaism in the Eighth Century. A strong Judaizing movement existed in that part of the Crimea during the time when the Bulgars crossed the Danube. Thus, a significant number of Bulgars already were Judaized before settling in the area.

Asparukh's army was neither ignorant of nor averse to Jewish religious practices, which were effectively established by 740. Ninth Century Bulgaria was ripe for conversion to another religion. "Had there been a concerted effort on the part of the rabbis to present Judaism as an institutionalized religion, a church of some authority, they could have transformed Bulgaria into another Khazar state, a Jewish kingdom on the Balkan Peninsula," states historian Tamir.

When King Boris I (852-89) converted to Christianity in 863, the Jews were not persecuted though they had been accused of proselytizing among the Bulgarians. His son Simeon (893-927) symbolizes a Golden Age for Bulgaria and its Jews. During this period, large numbers of Greek Jews immigrated to Bulgaria, including Nikopol, Vidin and

Sofia. Even though members of the Eastern Church, the Bulgarian church never invoked the vicious hatred of Jews of the Greek and Russian Orthodox churches. The Jewish religion was known to the population. The Bulgarians sent questions about Christianity to Pope Nicholas asking about regulations concerning such items as, when do the first fruits arrive; on which day does the Sabbath fall, Saturday or Sunday; how should animals be eaten and slaughtered?

By the 10th Century, Jewish settlements existed all along the Danube. A century later, Jewish traders and merchants came here from Italy and the area of what later would become Yugoslavia. The Bulgarian attitude toward Jews was favorable, according to the Encyclopedia Judaica. Many Jews fleeing the Crusades found safe haven here where Jewish life prospered during the Second Bulgarian Kingdom (1185-1394).

From the fourteenth through the sixteenth centuries, substantial numbers of Iberian, German, Hungarian and French Jews arrived in Bulgaria.

While the vast majority of the Jews in Bulgaria today are Sephardim, it was not always so. Actually, the Ashkenazim predate the Sephardim. By and large, until the Sephardim arrived in the 15th century, the Jews of Bulgaria and Greece as well as those in Serbia, were Romaniots. The Romaniots had their own special prayer book, which was eventually replaced by the Sephardic prayer book. Only a minority spoke Bulgarian.

The Ashkenazim may have established synagogues in Sofia, Plovdiv, Varna and Ruse, but it would fall to the Sephardim to dominate Jewish life in Bulgaria. Over the years they even maintained ties with the Spanish Embassy. Today, if you can prove you are a descendant of Sephardic Jews, you can even immigrate to Spain.

Rabbi Joseph Caro, author of the *Shulkhan Arukh*, settled in Nikopol in 1523 and set up a yeshiva there. He wrote a famous work, known as "House of Joseph."

By the 19th Century, the Ottoman Empire began to crumble and in 1878 Bulgaria shook off the "Ottoman yoke." "The Bulgarians, unlike the Romanians, accepted the Congress of Berlin's guarantee of equal rights to the Jewish community and Jews entered the new nation as full citizens, according to Steven Mark Mallinger in his booklet, *A Brief Introduction to the Jewish Community of Bulgaria.*

A cultural renaissance existed in pre-World War I years. Jewish histories were written. Sephardic rabbinic commentaries were issued. A Hebrew publishing house in Sofia produced books on mysticism. Newspapers and other publications, including Ladino tracts, were read by the community. Cultural events, specialized studies and a deep sense of learning were in the atmosphere. On the eve of the First World War, Jews numbered about 50,000, less than one percent of the Bulgarian population of about six million at the time.

Anti-Semitism increased during the 1930s, mainly because of Nazi influence imported from Germany and because of local marginal political groups.

Between 1939 and 1941, Bulgaria served as a gateway for thousands of European Jews fleeing Hitler.

But as the 1940s dawned, Jews found themselves in danger. When the war broke out, anti-Jewish legislation was introduced so that Bulgaria would conform to Nazi Germany's policies. Jews were restricted.

Bulgaria's rulers stripped its Jewish citizens of their civil rights and much of their personal and communal property. Most able-bodied men were sent to forced labor camps.

On December 24, 1940, "the Law for the Protection of the Nation," patterned after Nazi Nuremberg regulations, was passed and went into effect on January 23, 1941. But as we have noted, deportations of Bulgarian Jews within the boundaries of the nation proper were never carried out. Jews from Macedonia and Thrace, however, were sent to the gas chambers. The *Encyclopedia Judaica* states that 11,384 Jews were deported to their death.

According to Jewish community figures, 49,172 Jews lived in Bulgaria in the fall of 1944, three quarters of them residing in urban areas, including Sofia, with 27,700 and Plovdiv, with 5,800.

With war's end, what started as a trickle turned into a mass exodus to the Jewish homeland. Between 1949 and 1951, 44,267 Jews left for the State of Israel. This emigration hit the 90 percent mark of the Jewish population figure. Unlike Jews in other European countries leaving their former homes, Bulgarian Jews only moved to Israel. "No other Jewish community in the Diaspora has ever voluntarily uprooted itself in toto," points out Vicki Tamir in her book, *Bulgaria and Her Jews: The History of a Dubious Symbiosis.* No other sizeable group adjusted as fast and as well to Israel as the Jews of Bulgaria, she added.

In 1945, the ax of Communist repression come down hard on Jewish life. Jewish contact with fellow international organizations was halted. All Jewish schools, hospitals, reading rooms and even some synagogue buildings were transferred to state government. Jewish schools were closed. Zionism was suppressed. The synagogues and rabbinate were left to fend for themselves. In the 1950s, Jewish clubs were used as Communist indoctrination units.

Certain Jewish holidays were banned, such as Passover and Rosh Hashanah. Even Purim was reinterpreted as a "rebellion of the oppressed Jews against the monarch and his clique." Jewish books were removed from the libraries; summer camps were closed. Jewish communal institutions were Jewish in name only. No recognized rabbis could administer religious instruction. Communist indoctrination would take place as Jews mingled with non-Jews, according to author Charles Hoffman. All young Jews were being educated by the Communist Party.

The Bulgarians followed the Soviet line so strongly that it was hard to discern which was tougher. The world was shocked in August 1955, when a Bulgarian air force plane shot down an El Al Israeli airplane that had crossed over into Bulgarian air space by error. Bulgaria severed diplomatic relations and trade with Israel following the 1967 Six-Day War. Often attacking Israel verbally, they unleashed anti-Israel invective in the halls of the United Nations.

But hateful propaganda could not dampen Jewish hearts. They hoped for a return to Israel. It came in 1989. Communism fell. Arriving, too, were what everyone calls "the changes" of 1989, when Communism moved to a form of socialism and more freedom for the populace as well as the subsequent revival of Judaism.

The Jewish Community Today

"A small candle of Jewish life has survived here," is the best way to describe the Jewish community of Bulgaria.

"The Jewish community of Bulgaria is vibrant and strong, and has come a long way in the last two decades. There is a JCC, Jewish kindergarten, Jewish youth camps, leadership training programs and more," noted a JDC representative who covers the Balkans.

At the beginning of the current millennium, between 5,000 and 7,000 Jews called Bulgaria their home. Of these, between 3,000 and 4,000 live in Sofia, with 800 in Plovdiv, 220 in Varna, and 200 in Ruse.

Today, the Jewish population is estimated between 5,000 and 6,000, with most living in Sofia, and a few hundred in Plovdiv. Small numbers of Jews live in Varna and Ruse. The majority of Bulgarian Jews are Sephardim; less than 10 percent comprise the Ashkenazic community.

True, this community contains a high percentage of those on pension. Yet, there is a growing number of youth and young adults who are active in the community.

According to statistics, Bulgarian Jewry should have long ago ceased to exist. The demographers say that with those small numbers, of which 90 to 95 percent are mixed marriages, they cannot build a united community, let alone keep it alive. Not only that, but 50 percent of the community is above the age of 60 and 20 percent falls between the ages of 30 and 50 years old. Only 1,000 persons are between the ages of one and 18.

When discussing Eastern European Jewry, one must take into account that many Jews have kept secret the fact that they are Jewish. If you count so-called "hidden Jews," the number might reach 7.5 thousand.

Despite the high rate of intermarriage and an aging population, Bulgarian Jews have not only kept Judaism alive but also have been engaged in putting forth a serious program of Jewish education. And they did this in the short time since the fall of Communism in 1989.

Problems abound: community leaders are trying to rectify the lack of Jewish education with adult classes, lecture series, and a new Jewish school. Today, prayer books, *mezuzot, dreidels* and sabbath candle holders are handed out freely to Jews.

A publishing house known as "Shalom Publishing" produces three to four books a year. They are translated into Bulgarian, including, for example, Max Dimont's *Jews, God and History.*

One should not always believe statistics. Jews sometimes have a strange way of surviving. There is an old Jewish proverb that warns against "sounding the death knell for any Jewish community."

But even a small Jewish community fights anti-Semitism today. According to Alek Oscar, the new leader of "Shalom," the organization of Jews in Bulgaria, there has not been a rise of physical attacks against Jews in Bulgaria in recent years. "However, there is a dramatic increase of anti-Semitic posts on social media and websites. Members of the Jewish community work with a group of volunteers who monitor the situation online and prepare monthly reports," he reported.

"Unfortunately," added Oscar, "lately we hear more and more hate speech coming from members of parliament from different parties. It is very alarming," he says, adding that "United Patriots" gained in the recent election and probably will be in the government. Their election slogan was "Bulgaria above all," a common nationalist chant in other nations.

Volya, a populist, right-wing party, became the fifth party to enter Parliament with a little over four percent of the vote. The party is led by Veselin Mareshki, a wealthy businessman who combines patriotic rhetoric with promises of strict immigration controls and friendlier relations with Moscow.

Still, the center-right GERB party of former prime minister Boiko Borisov negotiated a government with the nationalist United Patriots in 2017.

Some 10 percent of Bulgarians are of Turkish origin or Muslim. More than 300,000 Bulgarians have settled permanently in Turkey, but still hold Bulgarian passports and are eligible to vote, according to the *New York Times.*

The entrance to Beit Am *in Sofia.* (Photo by Ben G. Frank)

So make no mistake about it, these Bulgarian Jews of the 21st Century are proud to be Jewish. And many will keep alive Jewish tradition, especially some of the young ones, many of whom even in their teens went through the ritual of circumcision. Jews here celebrate all the holidays and send their young children to Jewish day schools. They will belong to B'nai B'rith and other organizations and visit Israel. Like Jewish communities around the world, they, too, crowd the synagogues on high holidays. They will carry on Jewish life.

Sofia

"Sofia is so small; the overshadowing mountain, the low buildings, and the glimpses of open country at the end of long streets make the newcomer feel that he is in the middle of a country town rather than a capital city," wrote Patrick Leigh Fermor in his *The Broken Road*.

Those words were written before World War II, but they still have meaning.Although Sofia, the capital, stands taller and more attractive now, it is still small as capital cities go. That smallness brings a pleasant and relaxed quality to the city.

What impresses one about Sofia is its past. Drive a short distance on the Tzarigradsco shose, (Tsars Boulevard) and you will be moving along the same road as many Jewish traders and merchants did when they traveled to Constantinople (now Istanbul). Drive on to Plovdiv, Bulgaria's second largest city, and then onto Edirne, and finally to Istanbul.

Stop off at the city center where the Parliament now stands and recall the year 1878: The Russians are about to capture Sofia from the Turks, who prepare to torch their city. Rabbi Almoz Nino pleaded with the Pasha to spare the capital. The Turkish commander did not set fire to the city and when some Turkish soldiers started a few fires themselves, a Jewish Fire Brigade rushed to the scene and put out the flames.

Indeed, the Bulgarians called Constantinople "Tzarigrad, the City of the Emperors," though they really meant the earlier Roman-Greek-Orthodox Emperors and not the Turkish Sultans who replaced them in 1453.

Sofia gives you the impression of an unplanned town. This is not a high-rise building city; there are no real skyscrapers. About 1.5 million persons make Sofia the country's largest city. It sits in the foothills of the Vitosha Mountains in the western region of Bulgaria.

Founded nearly 2000 years ago by Roman Emperor Trojan, Sofia is the second oldest capital city in Europe, after Athens.

The Byzantines gave it the name Sofia in honor of Saint Sofia, whose cathedral was built centuries earlier in the heart of the city by the Romans. The Turks occupied the area in 1382. The Ottomans changed the skyline of the ancient city, building massive onion-domed mosques. In 1878, Sofia was named the capital of Bulgaria.

From a small town of 20,000, Sofia grew into a metropolis. "Today," says Steven Otfinoski, author of *Bulgaria*, "one in every nine Bulgarians lives in Sofia and 20 percent of Bulgarian industry is located here."

Home to 400 parks, the great National Museum and many other monuments attract and intrigue tourists.

JEWISH SITES IN SOFIA

Beit Am. 50 Stambolijski Blvd., Sofia, Tel: 359-2-4006301. FAX: 981-11-39. info@shalom.bg, www.shalom.bg. Facebook: @ ShalomBulgariaOrganization.

The first stop the visitor should make is the five-story Beit Am, known as the Jewish Community Center and community headquarters at 50 Stambolijski Blvd., Sofia. This 1927 building is the address of the Jewish community of Bulgaria. You have a chance to hear not only Hebrew, but also the medieval Spanish dialect known as Ladino or "*spanyol*," spoken by the "seniors" or "pensioners."

Cultural events and holiday programs including the four-day "Esperanza Sephardic Cultural Festival," complete with concerts, performances, discussions, and fine cooking, all eminate from this building.

A medical clinic is located in the Beit Am.

OJB "Shalom," (The umbrella organization of the Jewish Community) is located in the Beit Am, 50 Stambolijski Blvd., Sofia. Alek Oscar is president of Shalom and head of the community.

Commenting on the Bulgarian Jewish community, Alek Oscar noted: "Bulgarian Jewry very much reflects the general Bulgarian society— we have a little bit of everything, really. Naturally, intermarriage is an issue in a small community like ours. But 'Shalom' is seen as an organization, which is inclusive towards gentile spouses and partners and offers enough entry points and education programs for everyone who feels related to Judaism and the Jewish traditions."

JDC-Joint Distribution Committee. It is certainly clear that without the aid of the American Jewish Joint Distribution Committee—and here we mean economic, financial, social, and moral aid, as the Bulgarians themselves put it—the Jewish community might not have survived after the governmental changes of 1989. At least 80 percent of the social, welfare, educational costs of the Bulgarian Jewish community is borne by the American Jewish Joint Distribution Committee. For example, Jewish seniors receive health care and clothing. Here in Sofia, JDC even provides a dental clinic located in the local Jewish school.

Today, the social welfare and other aid programs are financed by

Former First Lady, Secretary of State, and US senator from New York, Hillary Rodham Clinton was greeted by Robert Djerassi, former assistant to the JDC Country Director for Bulgaria at Beit Am, the center of the Jewish community in Sofia. The photo was taken in the late 1990s.

JDC in partnership with "Shalom," the local community institution.

Because of JDC and the Lauder Foundation assistance, as well as World Jewish Relief and other sponsors, Jewish life is being maintained and expanded.

Lauder Ort Jewish Elementary & High School, Sofia. For further information contact the Ronald S. Lauder Foundation, info@lauderfoundation.com.

No kosher restaurant is located on the premises of the JCC, though kosher catering for events and tourist groups is offered.

Sofia Central Synagogue, 16 Exarch Joseph St., Sofia, 1000. Tel: 359-2-831-273. This may very well be the largest Sephardic synagogue in Europe. It is also the last remaining Jewish house of worship in the capital city. Since the fall of Communism, it has undergone much reconstruction. The synagogue remained open during the Communist era. But probably out of fear, out of believing that prayer in a synagogue was a remnant of capitalism—did not Marx say religion was "the opiate of the people"?—young people never went there.

This synagogue uses Sephardic prayer ritual. Services are at 10:00 a.m. Saturday morning. Services are often held in the small prayer hall. The synagogue displays a Sephardic style with the *bimah* in the center of the hall, Carol Herselle Krinsky, author of *Synagogues of Europe: Architecture, History, Meaning*, says that its architectural plans probably derived from Byzantine rather than indigenous European or Islamic sources. Still, it has a semblance of cupola architecture. Construction of the synagogue began in 1903 in the community which was organized like the French Consistory. Located in the center of the city and on its own block, the building is near the famous Alexander Nevsky Cathedral, which is the city's centerpiece.

Seating capacity is about 1,170 persons. Its dedication on September 23, 1909, was a gala affair. A holiday not only for Jews but for the whole Bulgarian Community was declared; King Ferdinand cut the ribbon. For 40 years, the synagogue enjoyed wonderful times, that is, until World War II. The emigration to Israel in 1948 also obviously reduced the number attending services.

Although the synagogue, now a landmark, was closed during the years 1943-44, when most of the Jews were deported to the countryside, the house of worship was not desecrated. Allied bombs hit the building several times during World War II. Later, the Communist Party's attempts to turn the synagogue into a concert hall would fail. If this was not enough, the large synagogue was damaged by an earthquake in 1977 and was repaired at government expense. After you visit the beautiful Sephardic-designed synagogue at Exarch Joseph St. 16, in Sofia, built in 1909, you might notice that the Synagogue, the Mosque, and the Church in the center of Sofia are equidistant from each other. This is called the Triangle of the Three Houses of Worship, which shows the timelessness and stability of Bulgaria's three religions.

Rohr Chabad Jewish Community Center. Stara Planina 38, Sofia, 1504. Tele: 359-2-9443380. www.ChabadBulgaria.org. This facility maintains a synagogue, a community center, a library, a mikveh, and a bar mitzvah club. Rabbi Yosef Salamon, who arrived in Bulgaria in 2001, is director of this center.

Kosher restaurant. Vkusove-tastes, Trapezitsa St., 4. Sofia. Tel: 359-884-157-377.

The Jewish Museum, Tel: 359-2-9831-440 is located on the second floor of the Synagogue. This museum is open from 9:00 a.m. to 1:00 p.m. on Tuesdays and Wednesdays, and on Thursdays and Fridays from 1:00 p.m. to 5:00 p.m. Since there is a wonderful exhibition regarding the story of the Holocaust as it pertains to Bulgaria, one should stop at the Museum to relive and learn about the Holocaust in Bulgaria.

The Holocaust Memorial Exhibit in the Synagogue. Here again, as in Romania and Hungary, sources say that Bulgaria may have wanted to remain neutral, in World War II, but Germany and Italy would not permit it. Some historians say that the country "blundered" into the Nazi camp. What is clear is that Bulgaria became increasingly dependent on Germany. And what probably clinched the deal was that Germany held out the promise of regained territory. This set off old nationalistic dreams, so much so that the government clamored for an alliance with the Germans. Although she had signed a Treaty of Friendship with Yugoslavia, Bulgaria immediately deserted Yugoslavia and joined the Axis powers. Bogdan Filov, who was pro-German, served as prime minister and Peter Gabrovski became interior minister in a new government. Both brought fascism to the country. Alexander Belev, a fervent anti-Semite was soon to become the Commissar for Jewish Affairs. These supporters of the Nazis were also going to solve the "Jewish question."

As we have seen, on March 1, 1941, Bulgaria signed the Tripartite Pact with Germany, Italy and Japan. By joining the Axis powers, King Boris III would gain the territory he coveted, according to author Bar-Zohar. He also would have to pass anti-Semitic legislation, which he eventually did, even though as Bar-Zohar tells us, he was "far from being an anti-Semite."

Interestingly, Bulgaria did not send troops to fight alongside the Germans in Russia, although the Germans used Bulgaria as a military base.

In the beginning at least, the Bulgarians also did not want to be outperformed by their Nazi partners when it came to the treatment of Jews. They, too, passed a law similar to Germany's Nuremburg Laws and in January, 1941, the King signed it.

In August 1942, the Bulgarian parliament passed a bill depriving Jews in the occupied territories of Bulgarian citizenship. That piece of legislation would cost those Jews their lives.

Bulgarian and German officials signed an agreement to deport 20,000 Jews from Macedonia and Thrace. They knew there were only about 12,000 Jews from Macedonia and Thrace, but they decided secretly to add 8,000 Jews from Old Bulgaria to make up the difference, according to author Bar-Zohar. In the spring of 1943, nearly 12,000 Jews of Thrace and Macedonia, living in terrible conditions, were deported to their deaths.

But back in Old Bulgaria, Jews who already had been rounded up and prepared for death in March 1943 were somehow saved. When it became public knowledge that these Jews from Bulgaria proper, too, would be deported, there was an outcry in the press, from the Orthodox Church, and within the parliament. "All these protests had the whole-hearted support of the king," says R.J. Crampton in his book *A Concise History of Bulgaria*. Metropolitan Cyril also helped, and sent a telegram to King Boris, asking him to show mercy toward the Jews, according to Bar-Zohar. "Once again, the Church stood firm against the government's policy. There is no doubt that in the entire history of the Holocaust, the Bulgarian church stood high above any other Pravoslav, Protestant, or Catholic Church, in her bold and unyielding struggle to rescue the Jews," writes Bar-Zohar. Historian Vicki Tamir confirms that "the most courageous stand was that of the Church."

The Jews of Bulgaria were saved. A leading member of Parliament, Dimitry Peshev, had gathered up a delegation and had protested the impending deportation. Interestingly, nearly 60 years later, a bust of Peshev was unveiled in January 2000 in a gallery at the Council of Europe's headquarters in Strasbourg that honors politicians and intellectuals who have made special contributions to European civilization. Peshev had been deputy chairman of the Bulgarian National Assembly during World War II at the time when Nazi Germany started the deportation of Jews to concentration camps.

Although a member of the fascist establishment, Peshev "undramatically, modestly, but sincerely tried to save thousands of Jewish lives." His action will remain perhaps the greatest single exploit in Bulgarian resistance, notes historian Vicki Tamir.

Jews scheduled for deportation from Bulgaria were released on March 10, 1943. That is the day of their salvation. Author Bar-Zohar argues that King Boris III had intervened and stopped the deportation, recalling that the King felt he changed his position regarding Bulgarian Jews, but did not have the power to save the Jews of Thrace and Macedonia.

"Peshev's eleventh-hour initiative, combined with the staunch struggle of the Church and the intellectual elites, had shaken the king and made him come to his senses. It had torn him from his meek obedience to the Germans. He could no longer afford the luxury of looking the other way," wrote Bar-Zohar.

But the Germans and their Bulgarian lackeys did not stop there. They would try again in May 1943. May 24, 1943, was an important day in the struggle to save Bulgarian Jewry. The Communists, too, got on the bandwagon. Later, Todor Zhivkov, the Communist leader, was to claim that he was there. Bar-Zohar says that Communist leader Zhivkov "was very sympathetic to the Jewish cause." He had written the first Communist flyer against the persecution of the Jews. But according to records, Zhivkov was nowhere to be found during that day of protest.

The dramatic protest occurred on May 24, 1943, when many Sofia Jews attempted to march to the royal palace to protest, but they were stopped by the police. Stephen Mark Mallinger, author of *A Brief Introduction to the Jewish Community of Bulgaria*, says that on that day,

Rabbi Daniel Tsion delivered an impassioned plea to the crowd urging them to action. The protestors were joined by official and unofficial protests from pro-Jewish public leaders.

Once again, the King again ruled out the plan to deport Jews from Old Bulgaria, even though he agreed to the plan to expel the Jews from Sofia to the countryside. Bar-Zohar notes that the decision to deport the Jews only to the interior of the country was officially approved by the government in a meeting on May 24, 1943.

King Boris turned the forced labor into a scheme to protect the Jews from a much worse fate. The Jews and the road construction became King Boris' biggest bluff during the war. "All Jewish males were drafted for compulsory, unpaid hard labor," notes Vicki Tamir. Jews were to be scattered throughout the country.

Not only did the church plead with the king not to deport Jews in May, but diplomats, writers, religious leaders, and labor groups, including the Communists, added their protests.

In May 1943 the Jews of Sofia were resettled in the provinces in what could have been a first step toward deportation to the death camps. But the Bulgarian Jews would survive the war. By 1944, Bulgaria wanted to extricate itself from the war. This nation also wanted to appear more reasonable in the eyes of the allies. By August 24, 1944, the Commissariat for Jewish Affairs had been abolished and all anti-Jewish legislation was officially abrogated on August 29. The Decrees of Abolition were published on September 7, 1944, an important day in Bulgarian history as that is the day the Soviet Union declared war on Bulgaria and launched the Red Army across the border. A few days later, a coalition government of the Fatherland Front took over and organized Jewish life was re-established. In September 1944, 34 Jewish communities were in existence.

"Only years later did the truth about these days come to light," says Bar-Zohar. The events of May—the protests, the letters, and the delegations—were a dramatic expression of the support many brave Bulgarians extended to the Jews. But they didn't change the fascist government's plans. Even before May 24, King Boris had decided not to send one single Jew out of Bulgarian territory, maintains author Bar-Zohar.

After King Boris died, a new government came into power.

Also, in May 1944, secret talks were held in Turkey between the Bulgarian minister and Ira Hirschmann, representative of the U.S. War Refugee Board. All anti-Jewish measures were annulled. In August, Sofia demanded the evacuation of German troops. On September 7, 1944, Bulgaria declared war on Germany. World War II ended in Europe nine months later.

Holocaust Memorial Plaque. A memorial plaque was placed on the back of the Parliament building and in front of the Academy of Art in 1993. It cites the saving of the Jews of Bulgaria. It also takes note of the 11,363 Jews killed in Thrace and Macedonia.Senior Citizens Home. High up in the hills of the city is a new white building that will serve as a home for seniors. Funding came from the World Jewish Relief, the Claims Conference as well as a per capita commitment from the municipality. The local "Shalom" organization is raising funds from various sources to support the home.

Holocaust Monument is located right behind the building of the National Assembly, Sofia. This new monument was dedicated by Israel's President Rivlin and Bulgaria's President Plevneliev, in 2016.

Summer Camp at Kovacevski. Opened in 1996, this facility hosts a winter camp and seminars year-round. But it is in the summer that much progress is made on educating Bulgarian Jewish children.

Plovdiv

Situated along the two banks of the Maritsa River, Plovdiv is Bulgaria's second largest city.

About 500 Jews live in this well-organized Jewish community where at least 10 organizations and clubs meet in a center that holds many activities and organizes events. The synagogue in Plovdiv is the only functioning synagogue in Bulgaria, other than the beautiful house of worship in Sofia. On March 10, 1943 as we have seen, the Jews in Plovdiv also were saved from deportation. In the center of the city stands a monument commemorating the Bulgarians who stood by the Jews as the latter faced deportation to Nazi concentration camps.

Holocaust Monument, Tzar Kaloyan Square, Plovdiv. Situated almost halfway between the community center and the synagogue is "the monument of gratitude." The words inscribed in Bulgarian, Hebrew, and English, declare, "With gratitude to all who contributed to our salvation on March 10, 1943—from the grateful Jews in Plovdiv." Every March 10, the entire Jewish community gathers at the monument to commemorate the day of remembrance. The community hopes that soon "Tzar Kaloyan Square" will be renamed "Spasenie na Plovdivskite evrei Sqr" ("The Saving of the Jews of Plovdiv Square").

"Shalom" Jewish Community Headquarters, 20 Hristo G, Danov st., 4000, Plovdiv.Tel: 359-32-268-023. Tel/FAX: 359-32-632-622. This is the headquarters of the Jewish community.

Synagogue "Zion," 13 Tzar Kaloyan str. Plovdiv. Considering the attachment of the community to Israel, it figures that the name of the Synagogue is "Zion." There is an entrance to the synagogue on

Tzareva Livada st. It is only a five-minute walk from the synagogue to the community center.

A Brief History

The ancestors of today's Jews in Plovdiv were part of the Sixteenth Century immigration from Spain. These were the exiled Jews who were welcomed by the Sultan of Turkey Bayazid II to help his stagnant economy. Jews had lived in the area but in small numbers.

When the Spanish Jews arrived after their expulsion from Spain, they immediately built synagogues, schools, and libraries. Historians such as Joseph Benaroiah, vice chairman of the Regional Organization of Jews, "Shalom," in Plovdiv, note today that until they learned Bulgarian, Jews spoke Ladino, which he describes as a mixture of Hebrew and Spanish.

As time went on, both Bulgarian and Ladino were spoken. Today, in fact, we still have in Plovdiv a rich treasure of Ladino songs, proverbs, and even cuisine.

In 1878, at the time of the liberation of Bulgaria from the Turks, there were 1,164 Jews out of a total town population of about 30,000. The Jews had backed the struggle of the Bulgarian people from their Turkish oppressors.

Between the liberation of Bulgaria and the Second World War, the Jews in Plovdiv immersed themselves into the economic and cultural life of the Jewish community. Many Jews served in the Bulgarian Army.

Bulgarian Jewry is well known, as we have seen, for its strong

An American Jewish Joint Distribution Committee board delegation visiting the synagogue in Plovdiv, Bulgaria.

backing of Zionism, even in its infant stages at the end of the 19th century. The first Zionist Association in the country was established in Plovdiv. The first translation of Herzl's book, *The Jewish State*, was published in Bulgaria. As historian Benaroiah notes, "Zionism was viewed by Bulgarians and Jews as a natural and logical movement connected with the 2,000 year aspiration of the Jews to regenerate their own state."

In any discussion of the history of the Jews of Plovdiv, mention of the saving of Bulgarian Jews must be made. Even before March 1943, Jewish men between the ages of 18 and 55 were called up for forced labor in work gangs. But on March 10, 1943, when the first group of Jews were waiting with their luggage in the local Jewish school, ready to be dispatched to concentration camps in Poland, the order to stop the deportation came. On that day, the local Bishop of Plovdiv, Cyril, obtained permission from authorities for the Jews to return to their homes. Later in Israel in 1962, Bishop Cyril said, "We would not have had the courage to ask for abrogation of the anti-Jewish laws if we were not supported by the whole Bulgarian people. We just expressed its will." Every March 10, the Jews of Plovdiv bring flowers to the graves of the patriarchs Stephan and Cyril in the Monastery of Bachkovo

In 1948, 5,000 out of 6,000 Jews in Plovdiv left for Israel. With the Communist takeover, the Jewish "municipality" was closed down, as was the Jewish school. The synagogue did not have a rabbi. There was very little Jewish life.

After the fall of Communism in 1989, Jewish life revived, and the "Shalom" organization was restored. The synagogue was saved and work began on its restoration.

A Sunday school exists and Hebrew is one of the languages offered in a high school. Jewish holidays are celebrated in the community center. "The Jews in Plovdiv are loyal citizens of their country and town," wrote Community historian Benaroiah. "Jews in Plovdiv have never lived in a ghetto and they do not today. Anti-Semitism has never been a government policy and it is not today," added Benaroiah.

Varna

Chabad of Varna, 5 Ticha St., Varna. Tel: 359-888-719770. Rabbi Yosef Halperin leads this congregation.

Burgas

Every summer, Sunny Beach, the resort area near Burgas and on the Black Sea attracts thousands of tourists, including European Jews as well as many Israelis who vacation here in the summer. **Chabad Bulgaria** has a welcome place in Sunny Beach, but only in the summer. Tel: 359-887-224405. www.chabad-bulgaria.org. 124193. In 2012, an explosion caused by a terrorist attack, attributed to Hezzbollah, killed a Bulgarian bus driver and five Israelis.

In the last analysis, always sympathetic to the struggles of the Bulgarian people, Jews, though small in numbers, have become part of the economic and cultural life of Bulgaria.

Suggested Reading

Bar-Zohar, Michael. *Beyond Hitler's Grasp: The Heroic Rescue of Bulgaria's Jews*. Holabook, MA: Adams Media Corporation, 1998.

Bauer, Yehuda. *A History of the Holocaust*. New York, Franklin Watts, 1982.

Crampton, R.J. *A Concise History of Bulgaria*. Cambridge, MA: Cambridge University Press, 1997.

Curtis, Glen E. *Bulgaria, a Country Study*. Washington, D.C.: Federal Research Division, Library of Congress, 1993.

Fermor, Patrick Leigh. *Between the Woods and the Water*. New York: Viking, 2005.

———. *The Broken Road*. New York, ed. Colin Thubron and Artemis Cooper: New York Review Books, 2013.

Hoffman, Charles, *Gray Dawn: The Jews of Eastern Europe in the Post-Communist Era*. New York: Aaron Asher Books, HarperCollins Publishers, 1992.

———. *Exit Into History: A Journey Through The New Eastern Europe*. New York: Viking, 1993.

Kaplan, Robert. *Balkan Ghosts: A Journey Through History*. New York: St. Martin's Press, 1993.

Krinsky, Carol Herselle. *Synagogues of Europe: Architecture, History, Meaning*. Cambridge, MA: MIT Press, 1985.Malcomson, Scott L. *Borderlands-Nation and Empire*. Boston-London: Faber and Faber, 1994.

Mallinger, Stephen Mark. *A Brief Introduction to the Jewish Community of Bulgaria*, Sofia, Bulgaria. RIVA Books, 1996.

Otfinoski, Steven. *Bulgaria*. New York: Facts On File, Inc., 1999.

Rosen, Moses. *Dangers, Tests and Miracles: The Remarkable Life Story of Chief Rabbi Rosen of Romania* (as told to Joseph Finkelstone). London: Weidenfeld and Nicolson, 1990.

Tamir, Vicki. *Bulgaria and Her Jews: The History of a Dubious Symbiosis*. New York: Sepher-Hermon Press, Inc., 1979.

Yahil, Leni. *The Holocaust: The Fate of European Jewry, 1932-1945*. New York and Oxford: Oxford University Press, 1990.

Index